The Eleanor
Roosevelt
encyclopedia

D0215780

THE
ELEANOR ROOSEVELT
ENCYCLOPEDIA

Eleanor Roosevelt looks solemnly at the camera at the age of fourteen before she goes to Allenswood, a boarding school near London. *Courtesy of Franklin D. Roosevelt Library*

THE
ELEANOR ROOSEVELT ENCYCLOPEDIA

Edited by Maurine H. Beasley,
Holly C. Shulman, and Henry R. Beasley

Foreword by Blanche Wiesen Cook
Introduction by James MacGregor Burns

GREENWOOD PRESS
Westport, Connecticut • London

Library of Congress Cataloging-in-Publication Data

The Eleanor Roosevelt encyclopedia / edited by Maurine H. Beasley, Holly C. Shulman, and Henry R. Beasley ; foreword by Blanche Wiesen Cook ; introduction by James MacGregor Burns.
    p. cm.
    Includes bibliographical references and index.
    ISBN 0-313-30181-6 (alk. paper)
    1. Roosevelt, Eleanor, 1884–1962—Encyclopedias. 2. Presidents' spouses—United States—Biography—Encyclopedias. 3. United States—Politics and government—1933–1945—Encyclopedias. 4. United States—Politics and government—1945–1989—Encyclopedias. I. Beasley, Maurine Hoffman. II. Shulman, Holly Cowan. III. Beasley, Henry R., 1929–
    E807.1.R4 2001
    973.917'092—dc00   00–023530
    [B21; aa05 02–11]

British Library Cataloguing in Publication Data is available.

Library of Congress Catalog Card Number: 00–023530
ISBN: 0-313-30181-6

First published in 2001

Greenwood Press, 88 Post Road West, Westport, CT 06881
An imprint of Greenwood Publishing Group, Inc.
www.greenwood.com

Printed in the United States of America

The paper used in this book complies with the
Permanent Paper Standard issued by the National
Information Standards Organization (Z39.48–1984).

10 9 8 7 6 5 4 3 2 1

We Dedicate This Volume to Our Mothers:
THELMA McELVEY BEASLEY
POLLY SPIEGEL COWAN
MAURINE HIERONYMUS HOFFMAN

CONTENTS

Illustrations and Charts   ix

Foreword *by Blanche Wiesen Cook*   xi

Preface   xv

Introduction: Eleanor Roosevelt: Learning, Teaching, Doing
by James MacGregor Burns   xix

Chronology of Eleanor Roosevelt's Life and Career   xxiii

Well-Known Quotations by Eleanor Roosevelt   xxvii

The Encyclopedia   1

Index   599

Editors   618

Contributors   619

ILLUSTRATIONS AND CHARTS

Eleanor Roosevelt with Elinor Morgenthau and Jane Addams	2
Eleanor Roosevelt on a World War II tour of Great Britain	27
Chart of honorary degrees conferred upon Eleanor Roosevelt	42
Eleanor Roosevelt and Mary McLeod Bethune at a residence for African American women workers	48
Eleanor Roosevelt and women reporters in the Caribbean	63
Eleanor Roosevelt as a young mother with four of her children	76
Eleanor Roosevelt and Madame Chiang Kai-shek	82
Eleanor Roosevelt with her father and brothers	84
Eleanor Roosevelt with members of the Howard University Honor Guard	90
Eleanor Roosevelt in her gown for Franklin D. Roosevelt's second inauguration	97
Eleanor Roosevelt with Nancy Cook, Caroline O'Day, and Marion Dickerman	106
Eleanor Roosevelt at the Democratic National Convention in 1940	128
Eleanor Roosevelt with two grandchildren and Fala	167
Eleanor Roosevelt with Bess Truman and Lady Bird Johnson	185
Chart of Roosevelt family lineage	207
Chart of Eleanor Roosevelt's family line	209
Eleanor Roosevelt with Mary Harriman Rumsey and Isabella Greenway	218
Eleanor Roosevelt with her first baby, Anna	223
Eleanor Roosevelt and Lorena Hickok on a vacation trip	233
Eleanor Roosevelt with journalist Ann Cottrell in Geneva	257

Eleanor Roosevelt with David Gurewitsch and Maureen Corr
    in India   270

Eleanor Roosevelt in Israel   276

Eleanor Roosevelt and Esther Lape en route to Bok Peace Prize
    hearings   302

Eleanor Roosevelt and enlisted men in Latin America   311

Eleanor Roosevelt with Earl Miller, "Missy" LeHand, and
    Franklin D. Roosevelt   317

Eleanor Roosevelt as a newlywed with Franklin D. Roosevelt
    and Sara Delano Roosevelt   324

Eleanor Roosevelt and Earl Miller in a home movie scene   340

Eleanor Roosevelt with Aubrey Williams and Mary McLeod
    Bethune at a National Youth Administration conference   368

Eleanor Roosevelt and Lorena Hickok on an inspection trip in
    Puerto Rico   376

Eleanor Roosevelt at a press conference as assistant director of
    the Office of Civilian Defense   388

Eleanor Roosevelt as chair of the President's Commission on
    the Status of Women   408

Eleanor Roosevelt behind a network radio microphone   426

Eleanor Roosevelt on horseback in Yosemite National Park   438

Eleanor Roosevelt and Franklin D. Roosevelt in the White
    House study   452

Eleanor Roosevelt and Franklin D. Roosevelt on a visit to a
    battleship with family members   464

Eleanor Roosevelt and Adlai Stevenson with Polly Cowan   503

Eleanor Roosevelt and her secretary, Malvina Thompson   513

Eleanor Roosevelt with teachers and students at Todhunter
    School   516

Eleanor Roosevelt knitting while traveling by airplane   519

Eleanor Roosevelt with John Foster Dulles and Adlai Stevenson   535

Eleanor Roosevelt with the Universal Declaration of Human
    Rights   540

Eleanor Roosevelt and a workman at the Val-Kill furniture
    factory   543

Eleanor Roosevelt and youth leaders at a conference at
    Campobello   592

FOREWORD

Blanche Wiesen Cook

This unique encyclopedia is a wonderful introduction to Eleanor Roosevelt Roosevelt's unprecedented, exhilarating, and ardent life. The power and wonder of her works and legacy, her friends, travels, and associations are generously represented by a range of scholars and activists, engaged students of ER's enduring impact.

ER was convinced that governments exist for only one purpose: to make things better for all people. But, she advised, never depend on politicians to do anything about that. You have to be part of a movement, active locally and nationally, to put pressure on politicians. Emotionally driven by her own family's torment, her childhood of tears and longing, surrounded by the bitterness and confusion of alcoholism and marital discord, ER always identified with people in want, in need, and in trouble.

Educated at Allenswood School near London, she was inspired by Marie Souvestre, the school's famous headmistress, a great teacher who recognized and promoted young Eleanor's many talents. ER wanted to go to college and return to teach at Allenswood. But her grandmother insisted that she remain home at eighteen to "come out" into society. In 1903 ER volunteered at the College Settlement founded by her girlhood friend Mary Harriman with other Barnard students. With Harriman, ER helped found the Junior League to promote social work among New York's debutantes.

While ER endured the social whirl by night, she taught calisthenics and dancing to the needy children of New York City's Lower East Side. That began her long relationship with the leaders of the social reform movement, notably, settlement house pioneers Florence Kelley, Lillian Wald, and Mary Simkhovitch; and the activists of the Women's Trade Union League (WTUL), who remained her mentors and friends. Through them she met earnest progressives dedicated to changing society, ending poverty, protecting workers, ensuring public health, building model housing, and promoting quality education and real opportunity for all people—including women and children, who suffered most because of political neglect and economic violence.

After she married Franklin Delano Roosevelt in 1905, her social work friends and their supporters, including Robert Wagner and Al Smith, played increasingly important roles in what became America's most extraordinary political partnership. Even during the years (1906–1916) ER was most with child and largely out of the political fray, her friendships and alliances influenced FDR's strategies as New York state senator and Woodrow Wilson's assistant secretary of the navy. During the war years, ER's organizational talents focused on servicemen's canteens and comforts, while her political scope widened and varied.

After the war, liberated by her own marital crises, ER's energies were increasingly devoted to the postsuffrage women's movement and the international peace movement. An advocate of the World Court and League of Nations, she forged new friendships with internationalists Esther Lape and Elizabeth Read, who ran the American Foundation, which ER supported, to promote U.S. membership in the World Court. Lape and Read also encouraged ER to become active in the new League of Women Voters and the Women's City Club. In these umbrella organizations, ER's talents as fund-raiser and publicist soared. She quickly became a leader of the national women's movement and a progressive voice for women's influence and power.

She understood the need to go door to door, block by block to educate the public about the real conditions of needy people even in periods of seeming affluence. She saw the need for newsletters and bulletins; she argued that little would be achieved without a mimeograph machine, and on 3 October 1922, persuaded New York's League of Women Voters to purchase one. During the 1920s ER helped organize the network of women activists who met, debated, initiated legislation, lobbied for causes, partied together—and transformed America at midcentury. They worked to end sweatshop conditions, promoting labels to give assurances of pure food and drugs and decent production of clothing and merchandise; they worked to end child labor and protect the environment; they sought an end to war, bigotry, and violence.

Through her work with the WTUL, the Women's Division of the New York state Democratic Committee, the League of Women voters, and various social organizations, including Heterodoxy, the City, and Colony and Cosmopolitan clubs, ER and her allies—Wald, Jane Addams, Elinor Morgenthau, Carrie Chapman Catt, Frances Perkins, Belle Moskowitz, Lape, and Read—and her Democratic activist circle, who after 1923 became her Val-Kill partners, Nancy Cook, Marion Dickerman, and Caroline O'Day, helped change the world of women in political life and the role of politics in life.

Because FDR contracted polio in 1921, part of her activism was dedicated to keeping his name and vision in the public arena. But another part was to achieve the women's agenda, which men only slowly endorsed. In 1928 ER wrote an article for *Redbook* that detailed her belief that women go into politics to improve conditions, while men go into politics to win elections. From the time she wrote "Women Must Learn to Play the Game as Men Do" to the end of her life, ER was certain that only when women were well represented in the citadels of power, with their own "bosses" providing real equity supported by strong networks of women activists, would society really improve.

Teacher, journalist, broadcaster, diplomat, political activist, human rights crusader, ER devoted her public life to expanding the meaning of the New Deal: real economic and social security for all—by which she meant housing security, job security (full employment), health security, and old age security—universal and without racial or gender discrimination. In 1935 she embarked on a yearlong lecture tour to protest the stingy discriminatory clauses of the Social Security Act. She helped pioneer a model community, Arthurdale, that remains for today a much-needed example of a sustainable community to wipe out the blight of millions of homeless Americans; and she campaigned for affordable decent housing for all Americans throughout her life. She worked with Esther Lape to guarantee health care for all until her own death and was appalled that the United States never agreed in her lifetime on this basic human right. She dedicated herself to the fight against racial discrimination and segregated education during the 1930s. Among the first white Americans to make the connection—segregation, lynching, race violence at home; hatred, race violence, fascism abroad—ER worked with black and white race radicals, Mary McLeod Bethune, Lucy Randolph Mason, Virginia Durr, Walter White, and others for dignity and equality. Later a member of the National Association for the Advancement of Colored People's advisory board, she was a lifelong crusader for prison education, prison reform, democracy, and justice.

After FDR's death on 12 April 1945, she turned her attention to the global challenge for peace and dignity for all people. As the first U.S. woman delegate to the United Nations (UN), she campaigned for the promises of the New Deal, at home and abroad. The UN Declaration of Human Rights, agreed to on 10 December 1948, was for ER a new Magna Carta—beacon and guide for a future of hope for everyone on earth. With its promise of civil and political rights and economic and social rights, ER considered FDR's Four Freedoms written for the future into international law. You cannot, she insisted, talk political rights to people who are hungry.

With an ever-growing network of activist allies, ER crusaded for housing, work, education, health, harmony, and peace for all people everywhere. From the 1920s, when she went campaigning with the women of
the New York Democratic Party, until her death on 7 November 1962,
ER never turned her back on a challenge, never stopped growing. She
listened to the people, and everywhere she went she asked: Tell me, what
do you need; what do you want?

Her example of determined activism remains an abiding challenge.
Her friend and authorized biographer, Joseph Lash, noted during ER's
centennial year that Eleanor Roosevelt is infinite! This encyclopedia is a
basic and essential guide to her multiple interests and many lives.

PREFACE

The editors of the *Eleanor Roosevelt Encyclopedia* have designed this book to be an introduction to Eleanor Roosevelt and her world; we hope that you, the reader, will find it a helpful volume. It is the first attempt to pull together in one volume the manifold material about Eleanor Roosevelt that elucidates her complex career and makes the interaction of her public/private life more accessible to scholars, students, and the general public. A total of 237 entries presented in an A to Z format provide a guide to basic biographical facts about Eleanor Roosevelt and offer insights into her multiple roles in six main areas: as wife and mother, First Lady, humanitarian, diplomat, public communicator, and, perhaps most of all, symbol of the changing position of women in the twentieth century. We chose the topics on the basis of recommendations from senior scholars and the staff of the Franklin D. Roosevelt Library at Hyde Park, New York, selecting those that related broadly to one of these six categories.

Cutting across our six areas are three main themes. One is Eleanor Roosevelt's relationship to various networks of reformers and politicians. The second is her remarkable ability to communicate with the public through her speeches, press conferences, interviews, newspaper column, magazine articles, advice columns, books, and radio and television broadcasts. The third is her performance in different roles: as the wife of a leading political figure, as a mother, as First Lady, as an independent career woman, as an activist for humanitarian causes, as a diplomat who also was the widow of one of the world's most revered figures, and as a global leader who personified the emergence of women in the twentieth century.

We hope that this book will serve two purposes: to offer a synthesis of the information now available on Eleanor Roosevelt and to suggest new avenues for scholarship. By no means does it purport to cover all areas of her activities or to include mention of all her personal friends, family members, and causes. No single volume could. It is designed primarily to permit those seeking information on Eleanor Roosevelt's connection with a specific topic, individual, or geographical locale to readily gain a general overview before going on to other sources for more intensive study. It has been our aim to make each entry stand alone, although because of the overlapping nature of many of Eleanor Roosevelt's interests, some entries may duplicate parts of other entries.

We wish to thank all those who have contributed essays to the encyclopedia. Our contributors, who number more than 150, include senior and emerging scholars, journalists, and professional writers as well as individuals who knew Eleanor Roosevelt personally. Coming from varied backgrounds and perspectives, they have presented a broad mosaic of Eleanor Roosevelt's life, work, and continuing significance. Three are Pulitzer Prize winners, several hold academic chairs, and many are distinguished for their scholarship. Among them are well-known authors of the most outstanding books that have been written about the Roosevelt era.

Other contributors, however, are just beginning their careers. We have deliberately sought them for the encyclopedia because we want to interest younger scholars in the life and work of Eleanor Roosevelt as a way of broadening Roosevelt studies. Our intent has been to make this a scholarly, factual volume, not a eulogy. Nevertheless, the esteem in which Eleanor Roosevelt is held by many of our contributors inescapably flavors the work. Taken as a whole, however, the entries present her as a representative of her times with the strengths and weaknesses common to all human beings.

We also wish to express our appreciation to the many individuals without whose support, guidance, and assistance the encyclopedia would never have been completed. We particularly want to acknowledge our deep gratitude to Ambassador William J. vanden Heuvel, Arthur Schlesinger Jr., and John Sears of the Franklin and Eleanor Roosevelt Institute, Hyde Park, New York. A grant from the institute has supported both research and expansion of the volume. Without this support the encyclopedia could not have been completed.

We also want to acknowledge the invaluable assistance of the staff at the Franklin D. Roosevelt Library, including Frances Seeber, chief archivist (now retired), and John Ferris, education specialist. Raymond Teichman, supervisory archivist, and archivists Robert Parks, Alycia Vivona, Lynn Bassanese, Nancy Snedeker, Karen Burtis, David Bassano, and Gerald Kolenda have responded patiently to our frequent inquiries and continuously aided us. Archivist Mark Renovitch has been extremely helpful in our efforts to locate pictures. In addition, Barbara Natanson of the

Prints and Photographs Division of the Library of Congress and Bo Kim, a graphic designer, aided us in securing illustrations.

We are grateful for the assistance of many others. Foremost among them is Dean Reese Cleghorn of the University of Maryland College of Journalism, who has been an enthusiastic backer of this project, which was begun with a grant from the college's L. John Martin Research Fund. Three graduate students at the college, Liubov Fortuno Russell, Etienne Karekezi, and Izabella Zandberg, worked with us at various times. We thank them as well as an undergraduate research assistant, Sinead O'Brien.

We received invaluable guidance in selecting topics for the volume from Blanche Cook and our board of advisers, including Allida Black, James MacGregor Burns, William H. Chafe, Lewis Gould, Richard Kirkendall, Richard Lowitt, Linda Read, Lois Scharf, Susan Ware, and Betty Winfield. Among others who deserve our thanks are Daniel A. Strasser, executive director of the Eleanor Roosevelt Center at Val-Kill (ERVK), and M. Glen Johnson, who has been president of the ERVK board; two granddaughters of Eleanor Roosevelt, Eleanor Seagraves and Nina Gibson; John Gable, executive director of the Theodore Roosevelt Association; and Trude Lash, Nelson Lichtenstein, Carolyn Eisenstadt, Wilson Dizard, and Carole Lindell-Ross.

Two educators in the Hyde Park area, Linda A. Bouchey and Albert F. Vinck, who are members of the board of directors of both Wilderstein Preservation and the Roosevelt-Vanderbilt Historical Association, generously gave us their time and passed on their enthusiasm for educating the public about the Roosevelt era. Patricia Baillargeon, secretary to Eleanor Roosevelt at the American Association for the United Nations from 1953 to 1960, graciously shared her personal knowledge of Eleanor Roosevelt. In addition, we want to express special appreciation to Carl Bon Tempo, who served as assistant research editor for Holly Cowan Shulman. Our thanks also go to J. C. A. Stagg for his support.

Finally, we cannot express sufficiently our appreciation to Cynthia Harris, senior reference book editor for Greenwood Press, who has been a steadfast adviser throughout this endeavor, faithfully answering our questions and leading us forward. We have found working in the field of Eleanor Roosevelt studies a worthwhile and absorbing experience, and we thank her for asking us to do this book.

NOTE ON USING THE ENCYCLOPEDIA

A chronology of Eleanor Roosevelt's life is included in the introductory material. Essays on individuals, organizations, events, issues, places, and activities with which Eleanor Roosevelt was associated are arranged alphabetically in the encyclopedia. Sources of additional information about these subjects are provided in a brief bibliographic list after each article. The entries are cross-referenced through the use of asterisks placed after terms that constitute the title of other entries in the encyclopedia. Eleanor and Franklin D. Roosevelt are referred to by their full names at the beginning of individual entries; in subsequent references ER and FDR are used. Most entries are signed by contributors; those that are not are the work of the editors. The contributors are identified in a special section at the end of the volume. An index is also provided at the end of the volume.

INTRODUCTION
Eleanor Roosevelt: Learning, Teaching, Doing

James MacGregor Burns

If any American most embodied moral leadership in all its dimensions in the twentieth century, it was Eleanor Roosevelt. Such leadership calls for definition. I see two levels of moral leadership: day-to-day "ethical values" that we learn from the great religious teachings, from our parents, from Girl Scout or Boy Scout handbooks, such as fidelity, truthfulness, kindness, decency, good sportsmanship; and the supreme "public values" of liberty, equality, justice, community, defined in the words and acts of our greatest spiritual, intellectual, and political leaders.

Some leaders—especially American presidents—exemplified ethical values, as most notably with George Washington. Others thought and acted in terms of lofty public values, as with Jefferson, Lincoln, Theodore Roosevelt,* and Franklin D. Roosevelt.* ER glows in history as an exemplar of both levels of values.

Having lost both parents by the time she was ten, ER first learned ethical values at her grandmother's knee. These were mainly Protestant ethics as applied narrowly and rigidly by Grandmother Mary Livingston Ludlow Hall. An early indication of ER's independence was her ability to adhere to this conventional religious code in the family while moving toward benevolent and compassionate Christianity.

Her crucial learning experience came in England, in the school of Madame Marie Souvestre* near London. A daughter of the French Enlightenment, Mlle. Souvestre was a true nineteenth-century liberal, pro-Dreyfus, pro-Boer, pro-equality. She helped restore the self-esteem of her young American charge. "For three years," ER wrote later, "I basked in her generous presence, and I think those three years did much to form my character" (Roosevelt, "The Seven People Who Shaped My Life," 56). This was Eleanor's higher education; she never attended college.

Her next great teacher was her husband, FDR. "It was he who taught me to observe," she wrote many years later. "Just sitting with him in the observation car at the end of a train, I learned how to watch the tracks and see their condition, how to look at the countryside and note whether there was soil erosion and what condition the forests and fields were in, and as we went through the outskirts of a town or village, I soon learned to look at the clothes on the wash line and at the cars and to notice whether houses needed painting" (Roosevelt, "The Seven People Who Shaped My Life," 58). Inevitably, she became FDR's eyes and ears when he could not travel widely.

Behind this learning lay an insatiable curiosity. When her husband campaigned for the New York state Senate in 1910, she began to understand the intricacies of local politics. Presiding over a large Washington household while FDR was assistant secretary of the navy, she saw the politics of the nation's capital firsthand. Riding with him across the country when he campaigned for the vice presidency in 1920, she gained a sense of the enormous diversity of America.

During the early 1920s, with her husband immobilized by polio, ER moved into the economic and social infrastructure of New York. Working with the Women's Trade Union League,* the National Consumers' League,* the League of Women Voters,* and myriad other organizations, she came face-to-face with the hardships confronting women in all walks of life. Helping Democratic Party* candidates, she got rid of the old aristocratic disdain for "bosses," coming to realize how vital political parties were to a working democracy. These were her classrooms for her own future leadership.

As First Lady she continued to learn, but now she undertook a historic teaching role. Amid all the talk of FDR's taking over the "bully pulpit" of the White House, she created her own pulpits inside and outside the executive mansion. She held press conferences,* policy discussions, and other sessions in the East Wing, and, even more, she moved about the country incessantly and, perhaps, almost obsessively. But her main outreach lay in her writings.

Even those of us today who recall meeting the First Lady through her daily columns and magazine articles may have forgotten the sheer number and variety of her "magazine outlets." Some were "serious" journals—the *Atlantic Monthly*, the *New Republic*, even the *Harvard Law Review*. Others were "popular": *Colliers, Cosmopolitan, Ebony, Redbook, Liberty, Woman's Home Companion,* *Good Housekeeping*, and a dozen or so others. During her husband's presidency she averaged twenty-five to thirty separate articles every year—and she kept on writing voluminously after his death. Writing for such magazines gave her a highly selective set of audiences, and collectively they provided her with a reading constituency that broadened her husband's voting ranks.

What did she write about? Everything. Politics, of course, but also civil rights,* women's rights, labor* legislation, education, subsistence farming, and, increasingly in the presidential and postpresidential years, peace and foreign policy.* But she wrote a good deal, especially for popular "ladies magazines," about women's problems as wives and parents. Their titles tell the story: "Women Must Learn to Play the Games as Men Do," "Ten Rules for Success in Marriage," "Today's Girl and Tomorrow's Job," "Should Wives Work?," "What's the Matter with Women?" As for raising children, this mother of five did not conceal some old-fashioned views about good manners and table behavior. "No child should be allowed to be too choosy about food" (Roosevelt, *Eleanor Roosevelt's Book of Common Sense Etiquette*, 40), she advised.

She knew, though, that learning, teaching, and preaching were not enough. There had to be results. Inevitably, she had to confront the most difficult questions about the uses and abuses of power. She believed in political parties but recognized their excesses and weaknesses. She sympathized with the concerns of women, trade unionists, and radicals who, impatient with the slow pace of the New Deal,* called for a third party— a strategy that she flatly opposed. She was especially responsive to the needs and claims of young people on the Left—but wary of their willingness to partner in any way with American communists.

As a "practical idealist"—a term she liked to see applied to herself— how effective was ER in the long run? In three ways, certainly. One was to establish a standard for First Lady leadership that would affect all First Ladies* to come. Another was to issue early calls for governmental reform—establishment of a Department of Education, for example, and appointing a woman to the cabinet—that later came about. A third was the most triumphant and most historic—her leadership in the drafting and acceptance of the Universal Declaration of Human Rights.* Still, today she surely would mourn the continuing weaknesses of the United Nations* and the erratic support and nonsupport it has received from the country in which it is situated.

ER had her flaws. It took her some years before she overcame the blindness of her class to the plight of blacks, poor women, and, indeed, her own servants. In 1912 she opposed granting women the right to vote, as well as for many years the Equal Rights Amendment,* until she publicly changed her position. Sometimes, she could be morally blind, most notably, when she excused the Japanese American internment* in concentration camps early in World War II* on the grounds, she said, that it was for their own safety!

Still, what stands out in the longer view of her life is her adherence to the three Cs of moral leadership—conviction, commitment, and courage, all of which turn on another C, character. She was embattled most of her life, whether with the Daughters of the American Revolution, who would not allow blacks to use their auditorium, or with racists who spread the most ugly personal rumors about her, or with Soviet diplomats who initially intended, she thought, to sabotage the Universal Declaration of Human Rights. Her ultimate commitment was to American democracy, despite its failings and disappointments. In terms of both her private and public character, while she was no saint, she probably came closer to secular sainthood than any other American political leader in the twentieth century.

By living so intensely," political psychologist James Chowning Davies has summed up,

she progressed from the elitism of high society to a humanism. Her Protestant and her social background did indeed contribute to establishing the direction in which she grew, not just negatively but also positively. She learned from her religious background to recognize right from wrong, but she redefined for herself, in real and direct contact with her life circumstances, what was right and wrong for her and for millions of others. She had the unique experience of living with one of the world-class political giants of the Twentieth Century. She discovered and at last accepted that they both were flawed. Neither individual outgrew some of their flaws but each succeeded in growing despite them. She did this by discovering, knowing, and finally believing in herself. (Davies, 21)

By strengthening herself she mightily strengthened a host of others.

In her personality, her politics, and her philosophy, ER bound her explicit and comprehensive ethical values to her—and the nation's—great public values, such as real equality of opportunity. She applied both sets of values to her leadership. If for some transactional politicians the "devils are in the details" of compromise and brokerage, for her as a transforming leader the angels were in the loftiest democratic ideals. By brilliantly and persistently fusing personal ethics and public values she set a standard for all future First Ladies—and for presidents, too.

SELECTED BIBLIOGRAPHY

Davies, James Chowning. "ER's Beliefs, Faith, and Religion." Unpublished manuscript. 1998.
Roosevelt, Eleanor. *Eleanor Roosevelt's Book of Common Sense Etiquette*. 1962.
———. "The Seven People Who Shaped My Life." *Look* 15 (19 June 1951): 54–56, 58.

CHRONOLOGY OF ELEANOR ROOSEVELT'S LIFE AND CAREER

1884—Born 11 October in New York City.

1892—Mother, Anna Hall Roosevelt, died 7 December; maternal grandmother, Mary Ludlow Hall, assumed responsibility for ER's care.

1894—Father, Elliott Roosevelt, died 14 August.

1899–1902—ER attended Allenswood School in England.

1902–1903—ER made her debut and participated in the New York fall-winter social season.

1903–1904—ER taught dancing and calisthenics at the Rivington Street Settlement House and investigated sweatshops for the National Consumers' League in New York City.

1905—ER married Franklin D. Roosevelt 17 March in New York City, where the couple established their first home.

1906—Daughter, Anna, born 3 May.

1907—Son, James, born 23 December.

1909—Son, Franklin Jr., born 18 March; died 8 November.

1910—Son, Elliott, born 23 September. FDR elected to the New York state Senate.

1913—ER and FDR moved to Washington, D.C., after his appointment as assistant secretary of the navy.

1914—Son, Franklin Jr., born 17 August.

1916—Son, John, born 17 March.

1917–1918—ER worked as volunteer during World War I with American Red Cross canteens, Navy League knitting projects, and naval hospitals.

1918—ER in September discovered FDR's affair with Lucy Mercer (Rutherfurd); FDR and ER decided not to divorce after he promised never to see Mercer again.

1920—ER and FDR returned to New York City after his defeat as the Democratic candidate for vice president of the United States. ER joined the New York League of Women Voters and later became chair of its legislative committee.

1921—FDR crippled by polio.

1922—ER joined the Women's Trade Union League; began work with the Women's Division of the New York state Democratic Committee; and became acquainted with Democratic Party activists Nancy Cook, Marion Dickerman, and Caroline O'Day.

1923—ER helped organize and publicize the Bok Peace Prize competition.

1925—ER became editor of *Women's Democratic News*, published by the Women's Division, New York state Democratic Committee. ER, Cook, and Dickerman built Stone Cottage as a retreat beside Val-Kill stream on the Roosevelt estate in Hyde Park, New York.

1927—ER, Cook, and Dickerman, with O'Day's help, opened Val-Kill furniture factory adjacent to Stone Cottage. ER began teaching history, literature, and current events at Todhunter School in New York City after purchasing the school with Dickerman and Cook.

1928—ER placed in charge of women's activities for the Democratic National Committee. FDR elected governor of New York in November, after which ER resigned political posts.

1929–1932—ER sold occasional articles to national magazines, taught part-time at Todhunter School, and carried out inspection trips of state institutions on behalf of FDR.

1932—FDR elected president of the United States in November. In December, ER began a series of twelve weekly radio commentaries with a commercial sponsor.

1933—ER started White House weekly press conferences for women reporters only on 6 March. She undertook fact-finding travels and appearances for the administration; became an advocate for the Arthurdale resettlement community in West Virginia for destitute coal-mining families; and on 2 November opened a White House Conference on the Emergency Needs of Women who were unemployed.

1934—ER was the host on 30 April for a White House Conference on Camps for Unemployed Women. She became a conduit to FDR for views of African American leaders. She also resumed commercially sponsored radio broadcasting.

1935—ER championed the National Youth Administration, which was established in June. She started her "My Day" newspaper column on 30 December.

1936—ER began making two paid lecture tours a year. The Val-Kill furniture factory closed; ER converted the building into living quarters and an office for herself and her secretary, Malvina Thompson.

1937—ER published the first volume of her autobiography, *This is My Story.*

1938—ER invited participants to a 4 April White House Conference on Participation of Negro Women and Children in Federal Welfare Programs. She attended the first meeting of the Southern Conference for Human Welfare in November in Birmingham, Alabama, defying segregation laws by sitting in the aisle between black and white participants.

1939—ER resigned from the Daughters of the American Revolution on 26 February after it denied the African American singer, Marian Anderson, a booking in Constitution Hall. In November she attended hearings of the House Committee to Investigate Un-American Activities in a show of support for young people called to testify about communist connections.

1940—ER addressed the Democratic National Convention in July, helping unite the party, which was divided over FDR's advocacy of Henry Wallace for vice president.

1941—ER appointed assistant director of the Office of Civilian Defense (OCD) on 22 September. Her brother, G. Hall Roosevelt, died on 25 September.

1942—ER resigned her OCD position in February; joined the board of the Wiltwyck School for troubled New York City youth; and made a wartime visit to England in October–November.

1943—ER visited servicemen and women in South Pacific in August–September.

1944—ER visited troops in Latin America in March. On 14 June she opened a White House Conference on How Women May Share in Post-War Policy-Making.

1945—FDR died 12 April. ER joined the board of the National Association for the Advancement of Colored People in May. She was appointed a U.S. delegate to the United Nations in December by President Harry S Truman.

1947—ER helped found the Americans for Democratic Action.

1947–1948—ER chaired and led the Human Rights Commission of the United Nations in developing the Universal Declaration of Human Rights, which was adopted by the U.N. General Assembly without dissent on 10 December 1948.

1949—ER published the second volume of her autobiography, *This I Remember.*

1953—ER resigned from her UN positions after Dwight D. Eisenhower became president but began working as a volunteer for the American Association for the United Nations. During a round-the-world trip she spent five weeks studying the progress of democracy in Japan and interviewed President Tito of Yugoslavia in July.

1956—ER supported Adlai Stevenson's unsuccessful campaign as the Democratic presidential candidate.

1957—ER traveled as a journalist to the Soviet Union and interviewed Soviet premier Nikita S. Khrushchev at Yalta in September.

1958—ER published the third volume of her autobiography, *On My Own*.

1961—ER appointed chair of the President's Commission on the Status of Women in December by President John F. Kennedy.

1962—ER died in New York City, 7 November.

SELECTED BIBLIOGRAPHY

Eleanor Roosevelt Papers, Franklin D. Roosevelt Library, Hyde Park, NY.
"Eleanor Roosevelt's Timeline." <http://www.academic.marist.edu/fdr/ertime. htm>

WELL-KNOWN QUOTATIONS BY ELEANOR ROOSEVELT

"[A]s a rule women know not only what men know, but much that men will never know. For, how many men really know the heart and soul of a woman?" ("My Day," 6 March 1937)

"[T]he most important thing in any relationship is not what you get but what you give." (*This Is My Story*, 1937, p. 361)

"People can gradually be brought to understand that an individual, even if she is a President's wife, may have independent views and must be allowed the expression of an opinion. But actual participation in the work of the government, we are not yet able to accept." ("My Day," 23 February 1942)

"A woman will always have to be better than a man in any job she undertakes." ("My Day," 29 November 1945)

"It is very difficult to have a free, fair, and honest press anywhere in the world. In the first place, as a rule, papers are largely supported by advertising, and that immediately gives the advertisers a certain hold over the medium which they use." (*If You Ask Me*, 1946, p. 51)

"For it isn't enough to talk about peace. One must believe in it. And it isn't enough to believe in it. One must work at it." (Broadcast, Voice of America, 11 November 1951)

"You gain strength, courage, and confidence by every experience in which you really stop to look fear in the face. . . . You must do the thing you think you cannot do." (*You Learn by Living*, 1960, pp. 29–30)

"Women have one advantage over men. Throughout history they have been forced to make adjustments. . . . [w]omen today appear to be able to adjust themselves to the conditions and the concepts of a changing world more easily than men." (*You Learn by Living*, 1960, pp. 77–78)

"Life was meant to be lived. Curiosity must be kept alive. The fatal thing is the rejection. One must never, for whatever reason, turn his back on life." (Quoted in the *New York Herald Tribune*, 11 October 1961)

"In the final analysis, a democratic government represents the sum total of the courage and the integrity of its individuals. It cannot be better than they are. . . . In the long run there is no more liberating, no more exhilarating experience than to determine one's position, state it bravely and then act boldly." (*Tomorrow Is Now*, 1963, pp. 119–20)

"No one can make you feel inferior without your consent." (Attributed to Eleanor Roosevelt in Alex Ayres, ed., *The Wit and Wisdom of Eleanor Roosevelt*, 1996, p. 92)

"A woman is like a teabag. You never know how strong it is until it's in hot water." (Attributed to Eleanor Roosevelt in Alex Ayres, ed., *The Wit and Wisdom of Eleanor Roosevelt*, 1996, p. 199)

A

ADDAMS, JANE (6 September 1860, Cedarville, IA–21 May 1935, Chicago).

A settlement house founder, social philosopher, and peace advocate, Addams established herself as a leading social reformer in the United States during the early twentieth century. The best-known woman of her day, she played a dominant role in a network of prominent women activists who surrounded Eleanor Roosevelt. The lives of the two women intersected in both reform and peace movements.*

An 1881 graduate of Rockford Female Seminary in Rockford, Illinois, Addams dropped out of medical school in Philadelphia the following year due to poor health. After travel in Europe, where she observed the new settlement house movement to help the poor in London, she and a Rockford classmate, Ellen Gates Starr, opened Hull House in Chicago in 1889. The center of clubs, services, and facilities in an overcrowded neighborhood, it provided the opportunity for wealthy, educated young people to live in the midst of the city's growing immigrant population, attempting to ameliorate poverty, aid in assimilation, and publicize inhuman conditions brought by industrialization.

Due to Addams' talents as a leader, Hull House, although not the first of the social settlements* in the United States, became a model for similar institutions. One was the College Settlement on Rivington Street in New York's Lower East Side, also opened in 1889, where ER taught calisthenics and dancing before her marriage.

A prolific writer and speaker, Addams played a leading role in progressive causes. In 1903 she helped found the Women's Trade Union League,* which ER joined in 1922. Addams campaigned vigorously for ER's uncle, Theodore Roosevelt,* in his unsuccessful presidential bid on

Eleanor Roosevelt and Elinor Morgenthau (left) visit with Jane Addams, settlement house founder and peace advocate, in Westport, Connecticut, in 1929. *Courtesy of Franklin D. Roosevelt Library*

the Progressive Party* ticket in 1912, backed woman suffrage, and worked for international peace.

Unlike ER, who supported the interventionist views of both Theodore Roosevelt and her husband, Franklin D. Roosevelt,* Addams opposed U.S. involvement in World War I. In 1919 Addams was elected the first president of the Women's International League for Peace and Freedom (WILPF), an outgrowth of the Woman's Peace Party that she had organized in 1915 with Lillian Wald,* another settlement house pioneer, and others. In the 1920s ER became an enthusiastic supporter of the league. Addams also backed the National Committee on the Cause and Cure of War founded by Carrie Chapman Catt* in 1925, another organization that drew ER's allegiance. In 1931 Addams was a corecipient of the Nobel Peace Prize.

ER expressed her admiration for efforts to alleviate human suffering by Addams, as well as Wald and Mary Simkhovitch, another social worker, in a 1933 *Pictorial Review* article. That same year ER and Elinor Morgenthau* spent an evening with Addams and Alice Hamilton,* an industrial medicine pioneer, at Wald's home in Connecticut. ER and Addams both were involved in the Mobilization for Human Needs campaign to increase charitable giving during the Great Depression* by consolidating local fund drives.

Shortly before Addams' death, ER, speaking at a White House dinner honoring the twentieth anniversary of the WILPF, praised Addams as a pioneer for peace. In a radio broadcast* the next day ER thanked Addams for making other women aware of their own interest in peace. After Addams died, ER became the single most visible woman in the peace movement.

SELECTED BIBLIOGRAPHY

Berger, Jason. *A New Deal for the World: Eleanor Roosevelt and American Foreign Policy.* 1981.

Cook, Blanche Wiesen. " 'Turn toward Peace': ER and Foreign Affairs." In Joan Hoff-Wilson and Marjorie Lightman, eds., *Without Precedent: The Life and Career of Eleanor Roosevelt.* 1984.

Elshtain, Jean Bethke. "Eleanor Roosevelt as Activist and Thinker: 'The Lady' and the Life of Duty." *Power Trips and Other Journeys: Essays in Feminism as Civic Discourse.* 1990.

Hareven, Tamara. *Eleanor Roosevelt: An American Conscience.* 1968.

Roosevelt, Eleanor. "Jane Addams." *Democratic Digest* 12 (June 1935): 3.

————. "What I Hope to Leave Beyond." *Pictorial Review* 34 (April 1933): 4, 45.

Jason Berger

AFRICAN AMERICANS. See ANDERSON, MARIAN; ANTILYNCHING MOVEMENT; BETHUNE, MARY MCLEOD; CIVIL RIGHTS; DU BOIS, W.E.B.; JOHNSON, JOHN HAROLD; KING, MARTIN LUTHER; MURRAY, ANNA PAULINE; NATIONAL ASSOCIATION FOR THE ADVANCEMENT OF COLORED PEOPLE; SOUTHERN CONFERENCE MOVEMENT; WHITE, WALTER F.

ALLENSWOOD SCHOOL. See SOUVESTRE, MARIE.

ALSOP, CORINNE ROBINSON (2 July 1886, Orange, NJ–24 June 1971, Avon, CT).

A first cousin of Eleanor Roosevelt, Robinson was bright, accomplished, and strong-willed and influenced by the political ideas of her uncle, Theodore Roosevelt.* Her father, Douglas Robinson, came from a wealthy family of real estate developers. A childhood companion of ER, she was a source in later years of reminiscences that pictured young Eleanor as pathetic, plain, and serious-minded. At a New Year's house party, Robinson recalled, a tall, fourteen-year-old ER appeared in an unbecoming child's short, white dress chosen by her grandmother and refused to borrow a fashionable gown from her cousin. Robinson thought ER had no sense of fun. She speculated that ER's lack of gaiety, born of the hardships she had experienced in her early years as the ward of a moody and austere grandmother, contributed to the iron will that made ER a great asset to the nation as First Lady.

Robinson followed ER to Allenswood school outside London, where she found ER had bloomed under the tutelage of Marie Souvestre,* the headmistress. After ER left Allenswood, Robinson took her place as Souvestre's favorite pupil and heard her exclaim how much she missed ER. Robinson considered it a mark of ER's character that other pupils had not resented Souvestre's favoritism and that ER had made no enemies as a result.

On Robinson's return home she was a bridesmaid at the wedding of ER and Franklin D. Roosevelt* in 1905. She herself was married in 1909 to Joseph Wright Alsop IV, a gentleman farmer from Avon, Connecticut, and had four children, including the influential journalists Joseph Alsop* and Stewart Alsop. A third son, John Alsop, made several unsuccessful bids for governor of Connecticut on the Republican ticket.

A lifelong Republican herself, Corinne Alsop organized the Connecticut League of Republican Women during World War I and, like her husband before her, was elected to the state legislature, where she served three terms. She also served twenty years as Republican Party chair in Avon. In spite of their lack of allegiance to the Democratic Party, she and her husband enjoyed easy access to the White House during the Roosevelt years, and FDR loved to exchange political gossip with her. The friendship continued even after Corinne Alsop seconded the nomination of Alf Landon, who ran for president on the Republican ticket against FDR in 1936.

Widowed in 1953, she married Francis W. Cole, former chairman of Travelers Insurance Company, in 1956. She helped narrate *The Eleanor Roosevelt Story*, a 1965 film written by Archibald MacLeish.

SELECTED BIBLIOGRAPHY

Alsop, Corinne Robinson. "Reminiscences," Robert W. Merry files, Washington, DC.
Lash, Joseph P. *Eleanor and Franklin*. 1971.
Merry, Robert W. *Taking on the World: Joseph and Stewart Alsop—Guardians of the American Century*. 1996.

Robert W. Merry

ALSOP, JOSEPH W. (11 October 1910, Avon, CT—28 August 1989, Washington, DC).

An influential journalist and political columnist for some thirty-seven years, Joseph W. Alsop V was the son of Corinne Robinson Alsop,* ER's first cousin. Like Franklin D. Roosevelt,* Alsop was a graduate of Groton School and Harvard University. As a young reporter in Washington for the *New York Herald Tribune*, he received invitations to Christmas dinners and other White House gatherings during the Roosevelt years and used his connections there to further his career. Although a Republican, Alsop treated the New Deal* favorably in a syndicated political column that he coauthored and in articles for national magazines. Following World War II,* he collaborated with his brother, Stewart, on a column that covered global events during the Cold War.*

In *FDR: A Centenary Remembrance*, Alsop offered intimate insights on the Roosevelt family, commenting on the poor quality of food served in the White House under ER's management and criticizing her wardrobe. Himself of homosexual leanings, he pointed out that ER had numerous lesbian friends during the 1920s and 1930s and enjoyed their admiration, but he declared it "unthinkable" that she herself could have had a lesbian relationship because "of the strength of her character and her training" (Alsop, 110). Giving the Roosevelt family's view of the impact of FDR's affair with Lucy Mercer (Rutherfurd*) upon ER and FDR, he contended that FDR's decision to stay with ER instead of seeking a divorce changed their marriage into a working partnership and matured FDR's personality (Alsop, 73).

SELECTED BIBLIOGRAPHY

Alsop, Joseph. *FDR: A Centenary Remembrance*. 1983.

Joseph W. Alsop and Stewart Alsop Papers, Library of Congress, Washington, DC.

Merry, Robert W. *Taking on the World: Joseph and Stewart Alsop—Guardians of the American Century*. 1996.

Robert W. Merry

AMERICAN ASSOCIATION FOR THE UNITED NATIONS. In the later years of her life, Eleanor Roosevelt devoted herself to promoting public support for the United Nations* (UN), mainly by working as a volunteer for the American Association for the United Nations (AAUN). Founded in 1943 as the United Nations Association and renamed two years later, the AAUN was a nonpartisan, private organization to encourage popular awareness and understanding of the United Nations and to support policies to make the United States an effective UN member. The organization was an outgrowth of the old League of Nations* Association, created in the 1920s, in which Carrie Chapman Catt,* ER's long-time friend in the peace movement,* had played a leading role; Catt was an honorary vice-president of the AAUN and served on its board of directors until her death.

While serving as a U.S. delegate to the United Nations, ER joined the AAUN board, made up mainly of prominent individuals, in December

1947, seven months after Catt died. When the election of President Dwight D. Eisenhower* in 1952 led to ER's resignation from the United Nations, she decided to make the AAUN her chief interest. She explained in her "My Day"* newspaper column on 5 January 1953 that when she tried to think of the most useful thing she could do, she decided it would be to help strengthen the AAUN. She worked for the AAUN as a volunteer organizer, publicist, speaker and fund-raiser from 1953 until her death in 1962.

According to Clark Eichelberger, national director of the AAUN, ER went to the New York office of the association and simply said, " 'I want to volunteer, and I want to serve. Can I be a volunteer in the American Association for the United Nations?' " (Eichelberger interview, 2). Her offer was immediately accepted, and ER, in the words of Estelle Linzer, the organization's associate director, "gave her invaluable service and indomitable courage to the AAUN as the nation's most respected and loved volunteer" (Linzer, introduction, n.p.).

In advocating support for the United Nations (UN), ER repeatedly stressed that she was carrying out the work of her husband, President Franklin D. Roosevelt,* who had sought to establish the United Nations to guarantee collective security and peaceful resolution of conflict following World War II.* ER saw the organization's goals as extremely important since the failure of the League of Nations to prevent World War II had led to great skepticism as to whether an international organization could provide for collective security and avoid future wars.

Even before she officially joined the AAUN board, she had lent her prestige to the organization's efforts. Calling the United Nations "mankind's last and best hope of peace on earth" (ER to AAUN mailing list, 24 April 1947), ER wrote on AAUN stationery in 1947 to thousands of potential supporters, encouraging political support of the United Nations and financial support of AAUN. After joining the AAUN board, she signed letters urging support of the UN's role in the creation of the state of Israel,* questioning how the North Atlantic Treaty Organization would affect the United Nations, and endorsing the UN role in the Korean conflict of the early 1950s as the first example whereby humankind, acting through an international organization, "fought aggression to a standstill" (ER and Ralph Bunche to AAUN mailing list, 31 July 1953). She cochaired AAUN dinners and national conferences and offered support in myriad ways. According to tax and personal records of her finances,* she made personal donations totaling $67,000 to the organization between 1953 and 1961.

Many influential persons were connected with the organization. ER's old friend, Sumner Welles,* former undersecretary of state, was honorary president. The presidents were William Emerson, a dean from Massachusetts Institute of Technology, Charles Mayo, founder of the Mayo

Clinic, Oscar de Lima, founder of the Roger Smith hotel chain, and Herman Steinkraus, chair of the U.S. Chamber of Commerce. Among board members were Jacob Blaustein, founder of Amoco Oil and former president of the American Jewish Committee; Ralph Bunche, former undersecretary general of the United Nations; Norman Cousins, editor of the *Saturday Review*; Senator Herbert Lehman; Myrna Loy, the actress; labor leader George Meany; Walter Reuther,* president of the United Auto Workers; pollster Elmo Roper; Adlai Stevenson*; Anna Lord Strauss, president of the League of Women Voters;* and Thomas Watson, president of International Business Machines.

The aim of the organization, however, was to mobilize support from both elite circles and the grassroots level. ER stated her initial goals were to enlarge and increase the number of chapters across the country and to make them information centers for other organizations in communities. She later noted, "We had thirty [AAUN chapters] when I took the job in late 1953 but by 1957 we had about two hundred" (Roosevelt, 17).

Those who worked most closely with ER at the AAUN commented on how clearly she understood—and acted upon—the need to transform lofty public feelings of support for the concept of the United Nations into practical action, in terms of memberships, stronger chapters, community-wide activities, and educational initiatives. Her years of political organizing and campaigning led her to focus on organizational basics.

AAUN activities and program initiatives emphasized several key issues: (1) moral support for the principles of the United Nations; (2) collective security; (3) economic advancement; (4) human rights; and (5) universal UN membership. The AAUN undertook educational programs, particularly for high school and college students, took positions on issues before the United Nations, conducted fund-raising, established collaborative activities with other nongovernmental organizations, developed contacts with other UN associations abroad, and performed some direct services for the United Nations such as arranging guided tours.

ER participated in these endeavors, signing policy statements, undertaking travel,* making speeches,* attending dinners, and appearing on radio* and television.* She also kept up a huge correspondence related to the AAUN. In her work she emphasized the difference each individual could make in public affairs through participation in voluntary organizations. According to Linzer, she "was a very good listener" (Linzer, Oral History, 34) who "never said anything in public that she didn't say privately" (Linzer, Oral History, 45). At the association she kept regular office hours and had good rapport with staff members, Linzer recalled: "She disarmed us completely because she was so natural" (Linzer, Oral History, 3).

In September 1953 ER began a series of speaking tours for the AAUN that took her to nearly every state over the next few years. While there was great support for the United Nations across America during the period of her AAUN activity, it was not universal. Republican senator John W. Bricker of Ohio proposed a constitutional amendment that would limit U.S. authority to approve UN treaties, such as those being developed to implement the Universal Declaration of Human Rights,* claiming they might threaten American sovereignty. Having played a key role in UN work on the declaration and its implementing covenants, ER bitterly opposed the Bricker proposal. In addition, in the face of op-position, she also advocated that the United Nations be made responsible for control of atomic energy for peaceful use.

ER was elected chair of the board of the AAUN in 1961 and helped oversee the initial stages of its merger with the U.S. Committee for the United Nations, which represented 138 national organizations support-ing the United Nations. Concerned about potential rivalry and compe-tition between the two groups, before her death in 1962 she arranged for Robert Benjamin, chair of the U.S. Committee for the United Nations, to succeed her as chair of the AAUN. He facilitated the conclusion of the merger in 1964, creating the United Nations Association of the United States of America. In 1999 it had 23,000 members and more than 100 major national organizations in its Council of Organizations, including such groups as the Girls Scouts of the U.S.A.

SELECTED BIBLIOGRAPHY

Baillargeon, Patricia. "Eleanor Roosevelt and the American Association for the United Nations." In Jess Flemion and Colleen M. O'Connor, eds. *Eleanor Roosevelt: An American Journey.* 1987.
Eleanor Roosevelt Oral Project, Interviews with Robert Benjamin (1977), Clark Eichelberger (1977), and Estelle Linzer (1978), Franklin D. Roosevelt Li-brary, Hyde Park, NY.
Eleanor Roosevelt Papers, Franklin D. Roosevelt Library, Hyde Park, NY.
Emblidge, David, ed. *Eleanor Roosevelt's "My Day."* Vol. 3. 1991.
Linzer, Estelle. "The Way We Were: An Informal History of the American As-sociation for the United Nations." Unpublished manuscript. United Nations Association of the United States of America. 1995.
Roosevelt, Eleanor. *On My Own.* 1958.

                                                                    Felice D. Gaer

AMERICAN NEWSPAPER GUILD. Eleanor Roosevelt became the first president's wife to join the ranks of organized labor* when, in 1936, she affiliated with the American Newspaper Guild, a union for newspaper workers. She based her eligibility on the fact that she had written a syn-dicated daily column of her activities, "My Day,"* for one year. While her membership was controversial, especially in view of accusations that the union was dominated by communists, ER continued to write her column and remained a loyal guild member until her death in 1962.

ER may have been influenced to join the guild by its president, Heywood Broun, a popular columnist with whom she was acquainted. A former socialist, Broun founded the union in 1933, when publishers attempted to classify reporters and other newspaper employees as professionals so they would be exempt from the overtime provisions of New Deal* labor codes. Under his vibrant leadership, the guild, which sought a forty-hour, five-day workweek, collective bargaining, minimum-wage scales, and paid vacations, affiliated with the American Federation of Labor (AFL) in 1936. The following year it left the AFL and joined the more militant Congress of Industrial Organizations (CIO). When Franklin D. Roosevelt* and John L. Lewis, CIO president, feuded two years later, ER continued to pay her union dues and strike assessments. By doing so, she showed support for both organized labor and her associates in journalism, who had suffered depression-era pay cuts and were subject to notoriously poor working conditions.

When she joined the guild, ER said she would not be involved in guild activities. As noted in the guild newspaper, *The Guild Reporter*, of 15 January 1937, ER announced at her press conferences* that she would not strike, picket "in the immediate future, at least," or attend guild meetings. But, on 29 December 1939, she was pulled into union politics when the Denver chapter nominated her for national president to succeed Broun, who had died earlier that month, promising her election by acclamation. Harry Wohl, president of the Chicago chapter, also urged ER to serve. He sent a telegram to her saying that "you are only figure in America able to take place of Heywood Broun" (HW to ER, 29 December 1939).

ER quickly declined, replying, "consider this a full-time job and do not feel qualified to accept" (ER telegram to HW, 29 December 1939). She was not swayed when Wohl tried one more plea in a 1 A.M. telegram: "Guild presidency not a full time job merely requires presence at four board meetings yearly" (HW to ER, 30 December 1939). The attempt to make ER president, however, gave rise to speculation that guild factions allied with communists were attempting to use her as a front for their activities. During the summer of 1940, the acerbic columnist, Westbrook Pegler,* launched an attack on ER's qualifications to belong to the guild, contending that she did not meet the requirement that members devote a majority of their time to journalism. He argued that her membership aided communists in the union and called for her to resign.

In response, ER announced that she would attend New York guild meetings to decide for herself what the guild's politics were and, if she found communists in control, to fight against them. She soon spoke out against the guild opposition to drafting young men into military service on the eve of World War II.* In the 1940 New York guild elections, she backed candidates who ran against an incumbent slate seen as communist-leaning. ER said she endorsed the challengers' assertion that the leadership's "actions over a period of years have paralleled the Communist party" (*New York Times*, 12 December 1940). Nevertheless, the incumbents won. At that time the New York guild had thousands of members and by 1948 grew to a membership of about 7,500, when national membership reached only about 23,911.

In 1941 on a write-in vote, the Washington chapter of the guild elected ER as a delegate to the city's Industrial Union Council, a group said to be communist-dominated. ER quickly declined and served informally on a committee that recommended the guild withdraw from the council. In December 1940 a United Press dispatch reported that ER had attended her first Washington Newspaper Guild meeting, her ivory knitting needles clicking away as she listened to long speeches. On that occasion she voted with the majority in support of a resolution by her press conference friend, May Craig,* that the chapter denounce communism, fascism, and Nazism.

ER's participation in the Washington guild also was ceremonial. For example, in 1943 she met with chairmen of the annual "Page One" ball to receive the first ticket for the event, although she said she could not attend.

ER remained a stanch advocate of guild objectives. To commemorate the union's twenty-fifth anniversary, she wrote in *The Guild Reporter* of 26 December 1958, "I do recognize how valuable the Guild has been in raising standards for people working on newspapers, getting better pay and better working conditions for them." Upon her death she was praised in *The Guild Reporter* of 23 November 1962 as the "First Lady of the Guild." The American Newspaper Guild became the Newspaper Guild in 1972, when Canadian news workers joined the union.

SELECTED BIBLIOGRAPHY

Black, Ruby. *Eleanor Roosevelt*. 1940.
Eleanor Roosevelt Papers, Franklin D. Roosevelt Library, Hyde Park, NY.
"Eleanor Roosevelt Remembered as 'Tough Unionist.'" *The Guild Reporter* (26 October 1984): 5.
Kramer, Dale. *Heywood Broun, a Biographical Portrait*. 1949.
Ruby Black Papers, Manuscript Division, Library of Congress, Washington, DC.

                                                                              Beth Haller

AMERICAN RED CROSS. Eleanor Roosevelt was involved in American Red Cross (ARC) activities in both world wars, with the nature of her participation changing as her own role expanded. In World War I, ER was a young matron who wished to help the war effort as did other women of her acquaintance; Daisy Harriman,* for example, formed a

motor corps auxiliary for the ARC. ER volunteered for the ARC canteen
at Union Station in Washington, D.C., where, in often steamy heat, she
served coffee, soup, and sandwiches to soldiers on as many as ten troop
trains a day. Her exemplary service led to an invitation from the ARC
to travel to England and establish a canteen there, but ER declined, saying she needed to stay close to her five children, then ranging in age
from two to twelve.

By the time of World War II,* ER had moved far beyond the confines
of traditional domesticity. Her connection with the ARC occupied a
global stage when she traveled to battle zones and witnessed firsthand
the work of the humanitarian organization. As First Lady, ER made both
public and private reports on ARC operations, pressing for improvements behind the scenes while promoting the organization in her newspaper columns and magazine articles. Although controversial, her trips
overseas as an ARC representative served to spotlight the organization's
activities.

Founded in 1881, the ARC was authorized in 1905 by the U.S. Congress* as the official agency for voluntary relief on behalf of the nation's
armed forces. According to its charter, the president serves as honorary
chairman. When Franklin D. Roosevelt* occupied this position, ER was
appointed honorary vice chairman, receiving an official ARC pin during
a White House garden ceremony in 1933. Despite her official appointment, during the early years of the New Deal,* ER chose to work with
Clarence Pickett* and the American Friends Service Committee (AFSC)
on issues of domestic and international relief and rescue, rather than
with the ARC. Perhaps this was because its major contributors, as well
as members of its advisory board, were largely wealthy and conservative
Republicans.

With the growing international crises of the late 1930s, ER began to
work more closely with the ARC, a decision made far easier by FDR's
appointment of Norman Davis to head the organization in April 1938.
A banker turned diplomat, Davis was devoted to humanitarian causes
and international peace. Working with Davis, ER endeavored to aid refugees,* assist individuals in need, help the ARC raise money, and act as
its emissary around the world. For example, in 1937 she sought a way
for America to help refugees cross into France to escape the depredations
of the Spanish civil war. She wrote Davis, "I do think that, considering
our record in the [last] world war, we might be doing something for
these poor children on a bigger scale than we are doing it at present"
(ER to ND, 1 June 1937).

In 1939 she sought to go to England as an ARC ambassador to plan a
refugee relief effort, but the trip was vetoed by both Davis and Secretary
of State Cordell Hull on grounds that the risk of her capture as a prisoner
of war would be too great. She turned to the ARC, however, for assis-

tance when letters came to her asking for help in locating refugees. She also became involved in the internal policies of the organization, recommending people for jobs. By 1943 she expressed concern over the lack of African American ARC nurses and encouraged the organization to integrate its employment policies.

As First Lady ER used her access to the media to publicize the ARC, particularly after the Japanese attacked Pearl Harbor on 7 December 1941. At Davis' request she broadcast an appeal to the American people on 12 December 1941 to donate money to the ARC. She did so again in April 1943, informing Americans about blood donor centers and programs for home service volunteers. She also made her own contributions, at first $50 a month and, after May 1940, $100 a month. Speaking across the country on behalf of the organization, she frequently visited ARC conventions and meetings.

In the fall of 1942 Queen Elizabeth invited ER to visit England to review the work British women were doing and to visit American servicemen who were stationed there. Although ER did not officially represent the ARC, from 21 October until 17 November she toured ARC canteens and recreation centers, greeting soldiers and examining the quality of facilities and services. On her return to the United States, she publicly reported that the ARC was doing an outstanding job in its recreation services. Privately, however, she told FDR and Davis that officers were receiving preferential recreation treatment—getting a greater selection of movies, for example—compared to enlisted men.

ER's travels* brought criticism as well as praise. Her critics, such as Westbrook Pegler,* accused her of wasting taxpayers' money and rationed goods. They attacked her for being photographed with African American servicemen and accused her of making pointless junkets.

Ignoring barbs from the press, in 1943 ER flew to the South Pacific as an official ARC representative. She undertook her mission with specific humanitarian, diplomatic, and personal goals. In part, the trip was to ensure that American troops serving in the Pacific were receiving treatment comparable to that given servicemen in Europe. This concern stemmed from the Europe-first policy of the administration, as well as from the impact of a tropical climate, the remoteness of island battlefields, and the brutality of the Japanese prosecution of the war. In addition, the mission was an extension of administration concerns over a growing rift between Australia and the United States. There was, also, her wish to see her close friend, Joseph P. Lash,* stationed at Guadalcanal.

Wearing an ARC uniform, ER traveled more than 25,000 miles, making seventeen stops at small Pacific islands and Australia and New Zealand. Between 17 August and 24 September she visited about 400,000 servicemen at military bases, hospitals, nursing home, and ARC recreation clubs. In New Zealand she met with representatives of several women's groups and pledged with them to work for warm postwar relations; behind the scenes she discovered a strong current of anti-Americanism expressed in the treatment of wounded American soldiers. In Australia, an ally important to the United States, she worked hard to improve relations between the two nations, drawing large crowds for her appearances and gaining extensive press coverage.

Finally, the First Lady visited Guadalcanal. No advance notice was given soldiers, who were surprised, indeed shocked, to see her. There she greeted troops, inspected recreational and medical facilities, and paid a visit to a military cemetery touchingly surrounded by a white picket fence. And she got a chance to talk with Lash.

Typing her "My Day"* columns herself and wiring them back to the United Sates, ER stressed the ARC. She wrote that it was performing excellent service in the South Pacific, although privately to FDR and Davis ER urged the establishment of more recreational facilities for the troops. When she received $500 from the Ladies' Home Journal* for an article about her South Pacific trip in its December 1943 issue, she handed the money over to the ARC; when she received $690 for a radio broadcast* in March 1944, she also sent it on to the organization.

The South Pacific trip was not an unqualified success. Both ER and the ARC received hundred of letters of protest, with critics contending she had no right to wear an ARC uniform since she had not received the required training for ARC volunteers. Others, particularly Pegler, claimed she had no right to travel so far during wartime and that the trip had wasted fuel, money, and manpower. Supporters, however, sent hundreds of letters thanking her for visiting their loved ones in the South Pacific.

Apparently in view of the criticism of her ARC role in the South Pacific, ER did not wear an ARC uniform or mention the ARC in her column when she traveled six months later, from 4 March 1944 to 28 March 1944, to visit troops stationed on remote islands in the Caribbean. Yet she remained an advocate of the ARC. In September 1951, for example, she wrote a "My Day" column urging people to donate blood during the Korean War. She herself had given blood to the ARC, she told her readers, until she had been declared too old to do so. But, she lectured, "giving one's blood was quite the easiest service that one could render" (Emblidge, 240). She had certainly done far more for the ARC with her years of commitment and service.

SELECTED BIBLIOGRAPHY

Eleanor Roosevelt Papers, Franklin D. Roosevelt Library, Hyde Park, NY.
Emblidge, David. Eleanor Roosevelt's "My Day." Vol. 2. 1990.

Hurd, Charles. *The Compact History of the American Red Cross.* 1959.
Lash, Joseph P. *Eleanor and Franklin.* 1971.
Maga, Timothy T. "Humanism and Peace: Eleanor Roosevelt's Mission to the
    Pacific, August–September, 1943." *The Maryland Historian* (Winter 1988):
    32–47.
Whiteman, Harold B. "Norman H. Davis and the Search for International Peace
    and Security, 1917–1944." Ph.D. dissertation. Yale University. 1958.

Joan London

AMERICAN STUDENT UNION. The American Student Union (ASU),
an activist organization, drew the attention of Eleanor Roosevelt and led
to her association with Joseph P. Lash,* a young man who became one
of her chief biographers and closest friends. Founded in 1935 by 450
liberal, socialist, and communist college students representing 200
schools, the ASU was committed to arousing student action on issues
ranging from the Spanish civil war to domestic reforms that would benefit youth.* The ASU was one of the most influential member organizations in the American Youth Congress* (AYC), a consortium of youth
organizations active during the Great Depression* era.

The majority of ASU members were not communists, and in its early
days, the organization focused on a combination of domestic reforms
that would benefit young people. The ASU's first platform called for
legislation to ensure low-income young people educational opportunities. In 1936 several ASU members were among a delegation of youth
leaders who met with ER seeking her support of the American Youth
Act, an ambitious proposal that would have mandated federal aid to all
needy American youth between sixteen and twenty-five. ER was patient
and tactful with the young people and acknowledged the shortcomings
of the recently established National Youth Administration* but refused
to endorse the proposed youth act because it was too expensive and had
no chance of passing in the U.S. Congress.* The First Lady was impressed
with the diligence and idealism of the young members of the ASU and
other student groups of the day, and she soon became their link to the
administration. ER believed that many of their communist tendencies
were misguided, and she hoped to persuade them that a democratic,
reform-minded government could serve the interests of America's youth.

ASU members also strongly supported the peace movement* and initially advocated an isolationist stance in American foreign policy. In
1936 and 1937 the ASU mobilized 500,000 students in nationwide peace
demonstrations. In 1937 the organization endorsed the idea of democratic and communist nations working together to pursue their collective
security in the face of fascist aggression in Europe. Because of their opposition to fascism, ASU leaders supported the Loyalist government in
Spain* in its efforts to quell a fascist rebellion led by General Francisco

Franco and called for the U.S. government to abandon its neutral stance and assist the Loyalists. A number of ASU members joined the Abraham Lincoln Brigade, made up of American volunteers who fought with the Loyalists.

ER was convinced that the ASU served as an important training ground for young leaders. In 1938 and 1939 the ASU held summer leadership institutes for student organizers. Many of its officers went on to lead other grassroots social reform efforts. For example, its first chair, George Edwards, later became a United Auto Workers organizer and then a federal judge in Detroit. Molly Yard, a Swarthmore student who was its treasurer and later chair, became an ardent feminist and was president of the National Organization for Women in the 1980s.

ER's relationship with the ASU was severely strained in the late 1930s when communists came to dominate the organization. Under communist leadership, the ASU turned against New Deal* domestic policies and criticized the administration's internationalist stance after the Soviet Union signed a nonaggression pact with Germany in August 1939. Led by Joseph Lash, a founder and executive secretary, a number of members condemned the Soviet action. Although communists were a minority of the ASU, by this time they held a majority of the leadership positions and exerted powerful control over the organization's national board. Communist ASU officers condemned Lash for his views, organized a successful campaign to vote him out of office, and adopted a communist, anti–New Deal, isolationist position.

In spite of its communist stance, ER did not immediately distance herself from the leadership of the ASU. In fact, she supported the group when, in 1939, it became the target of investigation by the House Un-American Activities Committee,* chaired by Martin Dies. Lash, as the most recent executive secretary, was summoned to appear. To show her longtime support of the organization, belief in the good intentions of the youth movement, and disapproval of what she called the Dies Committee's "Gestapo methods" (Roosevelt, 202), ER attended the hearings. Lash was evasive about the ASU's communist connections, but he defended the right of communist students to express themselves through a student organization. ER recalled that Lash "took refuge in being rather flippant" (Roosevelt, 202), provoking committee members into a new round of harsher questions.

At this point, ER took pencil and paper and went to sit at the press table, apparently prepared to write about the hearing in her "My Day"* newspaper column, and committee members moderated their tone. No action was taken against Lash or the ASU by the committee. Lash later recalled that the event marked a change in his relationship with ER from mere acquaintanceship to friendship.

Alarmed at the communist takeover of the organization, two-thirds of its members left it in late 1939 and early 1940. Many joined the International Student Service (ISS) organization, a refugee* aid group that began to assist the Allies in Europe in 1939. By the summer of 1940 ER had withdrawn support for the ASU and other leftist student groups and turned her efforts to helping the ISS promote fund-raising and public relations events for the interventionist cause. That same year Lash became general secretary of the ISS. The ASU met for the last time in 1942 before it quietly disintegrated.

SELECTED BIBLIOGRAPHY

Eagan, Eileen. *Class, Culture, and the Classroom: The Student Peace Movement of the 1930s.* 1981.
Lash, Joseph P. *Eleanor: A Friend's Memoir.* 1964.
"Pink to Red." *Time* (8 January 1940): 32.
Roosevelt, Eleanor. *This I Remember.* 1949.
Wandersee, Winifred D. "E.R. and American Youth: Politics and Personalities." In Joan Hoff-Wilson and Marjorie Lightman, eds., *Without Precedent: The Life and Career of Eleanor Roosevelt.* 1984.
"War and Peace." *Time* (10 January 1938): 42.

Melissa Walker

AMERICAN YOUTH CONGRESS. In the 1930s students and other young people in the United States became politically active on and off campus. They responded to the economic collapse of the Great Depression* and to international threats of war. Many were influenced by Marxist, pacifist, and progressive ideas of the time. Eleanor Roosevelt was closely connected to the student movements of the period. In public addresses, private letters, and in her public behavior she encouraged and supported individual students and organizations such as the American Youth Congress (AYC) and the American Student Union* (ASU). Her interest in the youth* groups was both political and personal. She saw them as important allies in pursuing the kind of society she wanted the United States to become and in supporting an expanded role for the government in promoting the causes she believed in. Although often critical of the New Deal* for not going far enough, the groups were potentially allies against the pressures from the Right on President Franklin D. Roosevelt* and the U.S. Congress.* In addition, remembering her own experiences of being criticized and controlled by older relatives, she was perhaps more tolerant of the group's and its leaders' behavior than she would have been tolerant of behavior in other organizations.

The AYC was initiated in 1934 by Viola Illma, the editor of a journal called *Modern Youth,* who wanted to provide a forum for young people to discuss current issues. However, young socialists and communists soon turned the AYC into a permanent structure to offer an alternative to the New Deal and to promote more radical social change. Unlike the

ASU, the AYC included nonstudent as well as student organizations. These included representatives of the Young Women's Christian Association, the National Intercollegiate Christian Council, the Southern Negro Youth Congress, Young Judea, and the Youth Committee against War. Notably absent were Catholic youth organizations, which, although sharing some interests with the other groups, were wary of the leftist reputation of the AYC. The ASU, the Young People's Socialist League, and the Young Communist League were particularly influential in the AYC.

For five years the organization was remarkably successful in dealing with the tension between the socialists and communists, and pacifists and supporters of resistance to fascism. This involved disputes not only on organizational issues but on such key questions as attitudes toward peace and fascist aggression and support for, or criticism of, the New Deal. Yearly meetings and national lobbying efforts reflected the shifting alliances within the coalition. They also tended to reflect the changing positions of the Communist Party. In the end the AYC, like the ASU, collapsed in the face of the difficulties of maintaining a genuinely independent youth movement and the advent of World War II.* While it lasted, however, the AYC provided a vehicle for young people's activism. It also, with ER's assistance, offered a view of students and other youth as citizens and actors on the public scene.

Confronted with economic turmoil and the examples of workers' and farmers' mobilization, many students developed an active political identity. Liberal students found in the New Deal, personified by the president and the First Lady, a positive program to support. Radicals, especially Marxists, had a mixed response. Like the liberals, they were glad to see an active role for the federal government in solving social problems. They, however, were skeptical of the possibilities of change within a capitalist economy. ER had little sympathy for such a Marxist critique, but she sympathized with the frustration that underlay the young people's radicalism.

In the AYC major issues involved the economic concerns of young people themselves and international issues. The first led to support for an American Youth Act, which called for federal financial assistance to students and for training and employment programs beyond those provided by the New Deal's National Youth Administration.* The second saw a seesaw between support for neutrality and antimilitarism and advocacy for nations joining together to pursue collective security and/or intervention to combat fascism.

ER had long been interested in issues of war and peace and international relations. She believed that it was possible to be an internationalist without being a militarist. She was, therefore, pleased to see young people's groups dealing with world issues. Two crucial events led the AYC to focus on international developments. The first was the Spanish civil war. Despite their revulsion against the memory of World War I, many young people were touched by the struggle in Spain* against forces of reaction. Some members joined the Abraham Lincoln Brigade to fight for the Spanish Republic. A second development was the Communist Party's move to seek coalitions with socialists and other left-wing groups to form a Popular Front against fascism, a move that brought them closer to the New Deal but in conflict with some young pacifists. The new alliance with liberals and rapport with ER and FDR were demonstrated at the World Youth Congress at Vassar College in August 1938.

ER addressed the group; FDR later met with representatives and sent a friendly letter. Writing to Lorena Hickok,* ER described her feelings about the young people who had assembled at Vassar: "I for one feel sad at the sight of all those young people & so earnest & full of hope"(Lash, 281). She continued to encourage the leaders of the AYC and befriend many of them, inviting them to dinner at the White House, going to their weddings, and in some cases providing financial assistance.

The Nazi–Soviet Pact of 1939, however, ended the honeymoon between the AYC and the New Deal. It also led to a break between ER and the AYC. The young communists in the group and their allies switched back in opposition to collective security; they also organized opposition to military preparation and to conscription. At the same time, many young people were torn between hostility to fascism and the fear of war, a feeling that ER understood, even while she increasingly came to favor more direct opposition to fascist expansion.

In some ways this conflict embodied ER's own divided mind on issues of war and peace. Like many of the young people, she looked at World War I as a failure and a symbol of the dangers of national rivalries and military buildups. She also saw peace as a woman's issue. On the other hand, by the end of the decade she came to support efforts to move toward a more active role for the United States in opposing expansion by Germany, Italy, and Japan. She supported FDR's call for support of the Allies and the institution of a draft in 1940.

A break came in 1940 between the administration and the AYC following a confrontation over foreign policy. Ironically, shortly before, in November 1939, ER had made her most visible show of support for leaders of the youth groups. Martin Dies, the chair of the House Un-American Activities Committee,* called leaders of the AYC and ASU, including Joseph P. Lash,* before the committee to interrogate them about their connections to the Communist Party. ER invited six of the leaders to dinner and to stay at the White House. She also attended the hearings in a sign of support and sympathy.

In February 1940 FDR gave a speech to delegates to an AYC pilgrimage to Washington. Strongly defending the New Deal, he also criticized the AYC's opposition to aid to Finland in its struggle against the Russian invasion. He was greeted with boos and hisses. ER appeared later for a question-and-answer session and defended the president's positions. She soon began to distance herself from an organization whose connections with the Communist Party were becoming more evident to her. After the German invasion of the Soviet Union in June 1941, the AYC changed its position again to support collective security and intervention. By then, however, the organization was rapidly losing credibility, and ER was no longer interested in it.

To some extent ER's experience, especially her discovery that some of her young friends in the AYC had deceived her about their connections with the Communist Party, shaped her attitudes toward the Soviet Union and the Cold War.* She later wrote that she had "felt a great sympathy for these young people, even though they often annoyed me. . . . In fact, I think my work with the American Youth Congress was of infinite value to me in understanding some of the tactics I have had to meet in the United Nations!" (Roosevelt, 205).

Although ER dissociated herself from the AYC, she continued to see youth as an important force for positive social change. After World War II, ER would seek to promote student activism under liberal auspices, in groups such as the American Youth for Democracy.

SELECTED BIBLIOGRAPHY

Cohen, Robert. *When the Old Left Was Young: Student Radicals and America's First Mass Student Movement, 1929–1941*. 1993.

Eagan, Eileen. *Class, Culture, and the Classroom: The Student Peace Movement of the 1930's*. 1981.

Lash, Joseph P. *Love, Eleanor*. 1982.

Rawick, George. "The New Deal and Youth: The Civilian Conservation Corps, the National Youth Administration, and the American Youth Congress." Ph.D. dissertation. University of Wisconsin. 1957.

Roosevelt, Eleanor. *This I Remember*. 1949.

Wandersee, Winifred. "ER and American Youth: Politics and Personality in a Bureaucratic Age." In Joan Hoff-Wilson and Marjorie Lightman, eds., *Without Precedent: The Life and Career of Eleanor Roosevelt*. 1984.

Eileen Eagan

AMERICANS FOR DEMOCRATIC ACTION. In January 1947 Eleanor Roosevelt joined other leading liberals in attending the founding convention of the Americans for Democratic Action (ADA). Later, ER served as honorary chairman of the organization. An anticommunist, independent political group dedicated to preserving the New Deal* legacy, the ADA played an active role in national politics for the next two decades.

By early 1947 two groups were battling over Franklin D. Roosevelt's legacy. Both embraced the New Deal and hoped to save it from conservative attacks and from what they saw as the ineptitude of Harry S Truman.* But they disagreed about how to respond to Soviet intransigence in Europe and about whether communists should be included in the liberal coalition. The Progressive Citizens of America (PCA), which rallied around former vice president Henry Wallace,* believed that Soviet actions in Eastern Europe at the end of the war were inspired by legitimate security needs and did not present a serious threat to American interests. They opposed what they called the "militarization" of American policy abroad and welcomed communist political support at home. The ADA, on the other hand, was convinced that it was impossible to achieve liberal goals in a political alliance with communists. They placed blame for the Cold War* squarely on the Soviet Union and supported the general outlines of Truman's "get-tough" policy.

The organizers of the ADA solicited the support of ER, who they thought was the only person who could effectively counterbalance Wallace's enormous appeal in the liberal community. The former First Lady and her son, Franklin D. Roosevelt Jr.,* both added their names and their prestige to the new organization. Although sympathetic to Wallace's criticisms of America's "get-tough" policy with the Russians, the former First Lady's personal experience with Soviet truculence at the United Nations* convinced her that more than simple misunderstanding had fostered postwar tensions. Nurturing a healthy skepticism of communist intentions, ER became disenchanted with Wallace when he accepted communist support without acknowledging Soviet responsibility for international tensions.

ER also agreed with the ADA position of excluding communists from the liberal coalition. In her "My Day"* column for 25 January 1947, she wrote: "I would like to see all progressive groups work together. But since some of us prefer to have our staffs and policy-making groups completely free of any American Communist infiltration if we can possibly prevent it, while others have not quite as strong a feeling on this subject, it is natural that there should be two set-ups." She wanted to see the two groups work together, but only if the PCA removed "from its leadership the Communist element" (Lash, 93).

On 4 January 1947 ER and 130 anticommunist liberals gathered in Washington to chart the direction of the new group. Among those attending were intellectuals such as the historian Arthur Schlesinger Jr., the economist John Kenneth Galbraith, and the Protestant theologian Reinhold Niebuhr; labor* leaders Walter Reuther* and David Dubinsky; and rising politicians such as Minneapolis mayor Hubert Humphrey. ER set the tone for the meeting. "If we fail to meet our problems here, no one else in the world will do so," she told the founding members. "If we fail, the heart goes out of progressives throughout the world" (Lash,

91). Still hoping for some accommodation with the Russians, she steered the delegates away from adopting a strident anti-Soviet platform. Despite our differences, she informed the convention, "we must make peace with the Russians" (Gillon, 20).

For many of those present, one of the most memorable moments of the convention occurred just before the group adjourned for the evening. After sitting through a full day of deliberations, ER stood to remind the assembled "best brains of liberalism" that they had said nothing about how to finance the new organization. "Now there's plenty of people with money in here who can make a substantial contribution to getting this thing going" (Gillon, 21), she told the group. She volunteered the first $100 and pledged to raise another $1,000. James Loeb, who became ADA executive secretary, recalled, "That's all she said, but there followed the most rapid and spontaneous and most successful fund raising in ADA's history" (Lash, 92). David Dubinsky pledged $5,000, and soon all participants were reaching deep into their pockets for money.

After the founding convention, ER rarely involved herself in the day-to-day affairs of the organization. Over the next few years, however, she gave advice freely to the organization's leaders, attended annual Roosevelt Day gatherings, and occasionally addressed local chapters. In 1953 she agreed to serve as honorary chairman to help the organization weather the era's "Red Scare." With Senator Joseph McCarthy and the right-wing press taking aim, ADA's leaders once again turned to the former First Lady for help. They needed someone of her stature to help bolster their public position, boost morale, and demonstrate that they would not be intimidated by McCarthy's tactics.

As honorary chairman, ER tried to steer the organization toward adopting positions that would be more acceptable to mainstream Democrats. The ADA had always been divided between visionaries who viewed the organization as a source of liberal ideas and practical politicians who saw it as a pressure group within the Democratic Party. ER wanted to temper the ADA's commitment to vision with a healthy dose of practical politics. Her efforts led to her highly publicized dissent from the organization's civil rights* policy at the 1956 Democratic convention. The question revolved around whether the Democrats should include language specifically mentioning and endorsing the Supreme Court's decision in *Brown v. Board of Education* (1954), which ruled that "separate educational facilities are inherently unequal."

ER, fearing a fight over civil rights would damage the party and diminish the chances of victory of Adlai Stevenson,* opposed a strong endorsement. The former First Lady, a lifelong supporter of civil rights, believed that the white South, which was essential for a Democratic victory, would revolt if the ADA waged a successful fight for a tough stand. "I think," she had said in a letter on 13 June 1956 to Stevenson, "understanding and sympathy for the white people in the South is as important as understanding and sympathy and support for the colored people" (Lash, 246).

Nevertheless, Joseph Rauh, the leading voice on civil rights issues in the ADA, in a letter to ER on 2 August 1956 insisted that the Democratic civil rights plank "must contain a provision endorsing the Supreme Court's desegregation decisions as ones which are morally right and deserving of implementation by all branches of Government" (Lash, 252–53). The organization supported Rauh, who testified before the platform committee. "Once and for all," he said, "the Democratic Party must set to rest the notion that the geographical division of the Party requires compromise" (Minutes of ADA Board Meeting, 11 August 1956).

At a press conference,* ER appealed for moderation. She asked liberals to drop their demand for specific language endorsing the Supreme Court's decision against racial discrimination in public schools. The word "moderate" does not mean "stand still," she claimed; "it means going ahead one step at a time in accordance with the realities, and the priority of importance" (Gillon, 101). With ER taking such a public stance, liberals accepted a compromise recognizing Supreme Court decisions as the law of the land but avoiding specific mention of the *Brown* decision.

According to Rauh, chairman of ADA in 1955–1957, ER's opposition to the ADA position on the 1956 civil rights platform plank was simply a matter of political tactics dictated by her support for Stevenson. Subsequently, she continued to make speeches for the organization.

SELECTED BIBLIOGRAPHY

Americans for Democratic Action Papers, Wisconsin State Historical Society, Madison.
Eleanor Roosevelt Oral History Project, Interview with Joseph L. Rauh Jr. (1978), Franklin D. Roosevelt Library, Hyde Park, New York.
Gillon, Steven M. *Politics and Vision: The ADA and American Liberalism.* 1987.
Hamby, Alonzo. *Beyond the New Deal.* 1978.
Lash, Joseph P. *Eleanor: The Years Alone.* 1972.

Steven M. Gillon

ANDERSON, MARIAN (27 February 1897, Philadelphia–8 April 1993, Portland, OR).

Marian Anderson and Eleanor Roosevelt are linked as much in myth as in fact. The story goes that in 1939, when the Daughters of the American Revolution (DAR), a patriotic women's organization, denied the African American contralto Marian Anderson a booking in the organization's "white only" Constitution Hall, ER saved the day by organizing an Easter Sunday recital on the steps of the Lincoln Memorial. The 9 April 1939 concert proved unforgettable because it helped establish the format of the modern civil rights* demonstration and consecrate Lincoln's shrine as moral high ground for generations of protesters. Not least among the day's legacies was the abiding linkage of two courageous women whose association brought each closer to the status of American icon. Arguably, ER is remembered for no specific act more than for her patronage of Marian Anderson, but that sponsorship was both more and less extensive than popularly believed.

ER invited Anderson to sing at the White House in February 1936, two months after the diva's triumphant American homecoming recital in New York. Anderson had spent five years studying and performing in Europe, where she had fled because of artistic disappointments and persistent discrimination during the 1920s. A native of Philadelphia, she began singing publicly at age six, in the Union Baptist Church choir. Wider acclaim came in 1925, when she won a New York Philharmonic vocal competition that resulted in a notable recital debut. But the singer found greater success and acceptance in Europe than in her own country. Racism, she later said, was like "a hair that blows across your face. Nobody sees it, but it's there and you can feel it" (Klaw, 53). When she sang at the 1935 Salzburg Festival, Maestro Arturo Toscanini gasped, "A voice like yours is heard once in a hundred years" (Sandage, 143). She soon returned to the United States under the management of impresario Sol Hurok. Throughout the late 1930s, she sang seventy concerts a year throughout the United States.

ER's role in the 1939 DAR affair lay less in tactical involvement than in provoking national publicity and outrage toward an act of unequivocal racism. In February Anderson's sponsors were swiftly rebuffed when they sought to have her concert in Constitution Hall (a large and distinguished venue in the capital and a tax-exempt public accommodation). A letter of 3 February 1939 from DAR president-general Sarah Robert stated that by contract and by custom the hall was available to white artists only. Urged by black activists to denounce the DAR in a press conference,* ER instead sent a letter of resignation to the DAR on 26 February and one day later announced her action in her column, "My Day,"* without identifying the organization by name. The controversy had not gone unnoticed before, but ER's stance conferred unprecedented attention and gave activists a chance to achieve more than a Sunday concert.

No written evidence, however, proves that ER participated in the ensuing flurry of activity that brought Anderson to the Lincoln Memorial. Historian Nancy Weiss reports that ER's travel* schedule in February and March 1939 made her involvement unlikely. Walter White* of the National Association for the Advancement of Colored People* (NAACP), Sol Hurok, and interior secretary Harold L. Ickes* worked with a local coalition, the Marian Anderson Citizens' Committee, to craft a painstakingly symbolic recital that would be subtly political yet irreproachably dignified. On Easter Sunday, Anderson sang a short program of arias, spirituals, and the national hymn "America" before an integrated crowd of 75,000. "Mrs. Franklin D. Roosevelt" was the first name among the distinguished sponsors listed in the program, but she did not attend. Three days later, however, ER directly dissuaded activists from picketing the DAR's annual convention, an action she warned would be counterproductive.

Although the two women did not meet on the steps of the Lincoln Memorial, in June 1939 Anderson was invited back to the White House to sing for the visiting king and queen of England, and on 2 July 1939 ER presented the Spingarn Medal to Anderson at the NAACP convention in Richmond. In January 1943 Anderson finally sang in Constitution Hall for a benefit that ER attended.

Anderson's subsequent career included becoming the first African American to sing a major role at the Metropolitan Opera (in 1955, thirty years after her New York debut) and to serve as an alternate representative to the Human Rights* Commission of the United Nations.* She sang again at the Lincoln Memorial for the 1963 March on Washington and gave her farewell performance in 1965. The two women remain linked as icons of racial justice. Anderson's reaction on hearing in 1939 that ER had resigned from the DAR equally described the singer herself. She told a reporter, "I am not surprised at Mrs. Roosevelt's action, because she seems to me to be one who really comprehends the true meaning of democracy" (*New York Times*, 28 February 1939).

SELECTED BIBLIOGRAPHY

Anderson, Marian. *My Lord, What a Morning: An Autobiography*. 1956.
Black, Allida M. "Championing a Champion: Eleanor Roosevelt and the Marian Anderson 'Freedom Concert.' " *Presidential Studies Quarterly* 20 (Fall 1990): 719–36.
Klaw, Barbara. " 'A Voice One Hears Once in a Hundred Years': An Interview with Marian Anderson." *American Heritage* 28 (February 1977): 51–57.
Sandage, Scott A. "A Marble House Divided: The Lincoln Memorial, the Civil Rights Movement, and the Politics of Memory, 1939–1963." *Journal of American History* 80 (June 1993): 135–67.

                                                            Scott A. Sandage

ANDERSON, MARY (27 August 1872, Lidkoping, Sweden–29 January 1964, Washington, DC).

Mary Anderson was a Swedish immigrant, factory worker, and trade union organizer who rose to become the first director of the Women's Bureau of the Department of Labor, a post she held nearly twenty-five years, under five presidents, until her retirement in 1944. While not a close associate of either Franklin D. Roosevelt* or Eleanor Roosevelt, she was acquainted with ER and noted that "during the years of the Roosevelt Administration, I felt much closer to the White House because of Mrs. Roosevelt's interest and friendship" (Anderson, 178).

When her family in Sweden lost their farm, she and a sister were sent in 1889 to Michigan, where another sister had emigrated a year before. At the age of sixteen, speaking no English, Anderson took a job washing dishes in a lumber camp. Later she worked as a domestic, then moved to Chicago, where she took a job in a shoe factory. In 1894 Anderson joined the International Boot and Shoe Workers Union and quickly became a committed union worker. In a year she was president of her local; eventually, she was named to the union's executive board.

In 1903 she joined the Women's Trade Union League (WTUL),* where she acquired a lasting friend and mentor—Margaret Dreier Robins, the sister of Mary Dreier,* who was a friend of ER. Robins was elected president of both the Chicago branch of the WTUL and the national WTUL in 1907 and hired Anderson four years later to work for the Chicago branch of the WTUL as an investigator and union organizer. In 1917 Robins sent Anderson to Washington, D.C., to participate in the subcommittee on women in industry of the Advisory Committee to the Council of National Defense. Her work on the subcommittee led to her appointment in 1918 as assistant director of the Women in Industry Service in the U.S. Department of Labor; when this became the Women's Bureau two years later, she was named director—the first woman from union ranks to head an executive department of the federal government. She had become a U.S. citizen in 1915.

Under Anderson's leadership the bureau issued more than 150 bulletins, publicizing the conditions confronting women in various industries, recommending standards of safety, and advocating better wages, hours, and working conditions for women. She was instrumental in including women under the 1938 Fair Labor Standards Act, setting minimum wages and working hours.

Anderson was pleased with FDR's election. She had met ER at WTUL meetings in New York, once attending a picnic at Hyde Park* given for the WTUL, and felt she was a kindred spirit. "I felt working women everywhere could turn to her for help and support and through her find the kind of sympathetic interest from the President that would be very helpful" (Anderson, 178), she later wrote. She was disappointed, however, that FDR's secretary of labor, Frances Perkins,* appeared to distance herself from the Woman's Bureau and failed to support increases in the bureau's budget to match its growing responsibilities. Anderson apparently never felt it appropriate to presume on her relationship with ER to make her dissatisfaction with Perkins known at the White House.

After her retirement in 1944, Anderson stayed in Washington, occasionally testifying before Congress* on women's work issues. She chaired the National Committee on Equal Pay until the Equal Pay Act was passed in 1963. In 1962, on her ninetieth birthday, she was presented with the Labor Award of Merit.

SELECTED BIBLIOGRAPHY
Anderson, Mary, as told to Mary N. Winslow. *Woman at Work: The Autobiography of Mary Anderson.* 1951.
Mary Anderson Papers, Schlesinger Library, Radcliffe College, Cambridge, MA.

Judy Oppenheimer

ANGLO-AMERICAN RELATIONS. Eleanor Roosevelt played a significant part in promoting Anglo-American understanding during World War II.* She knew Britain well, having spent three happy years at Allenswood School, in Wimbledon Park. She maintained correspondence with her friends from this time and revisited the country with her family in 1929. Her affection for Britain was not shared by many Americans. As Europe slipped toward war in the 1930s, the U.S. public saw little reason to abandon neutrality to come to Britain's aid. When King George VI and Queen Elizabeth accepted the invitation of President Franklin D. Roosevelt* to visit in 1939, the press muttered against British propaganda. In the end the visit was a triumph for both the royal couple and the Roosevelts. By inviting the king and queen to Hyde Park,* New York, for an informal weekend and serving beer and hot dogs, the Roosevelts helped to dispel Anglophobic stereotypes of stuffiness.

Once World War II had begun, ER gave vocal support for aid to Britain and opposition to fascism. In 1940 she even appeared in a special introduction to the British anti-Nazi film *Pastor Hall.* (See Motion Pictures.) In the spring of 1940 she prevailed on the president to allow British evacuees into the United States. She kept these children in the public eye by inviting them to a picnic at the White House on Easter Monday 1941.

In March and November 1941 ER used the platform of her press conferences* to present details of the privations of life in Britain. She personalized this by citing letters from her old school friends. But it was after the United States had joined the war that she made her most significant contribution.

By the autumn of 1942 significant tensions had opened in the Anglo-American alliance. Many Americans, ER included, mistrusted the evident wish of Winston Churchill* to restore the British empire at the end of the war. Others felt that the British were not pulling their weight in the conflict. In a letter to a British friend, she stressed the need for the British and American people to learn a great deal more about each other. To this end ER traveled to Britain, arriving in London on 23 October 1942, and spent three weeks touring the country. She visited American servicemen and British women defense workers; she toured bomb-scarred Buckingham Palace with the queen and met the socialist Labour Party

Eleanor Roosevelt reviews troops at a U.S. Army Air Force base in November 1942 while on a World War II goodwill tour of Great Britain in this picture taken by Toni Frissell, a photographer for the American Red Cross. *Courtesy of Library of Congress*

ministers from Britain's wartime coalition government. She also broadcast to the British people over the BBC.

Her visit was an astonishing success. Churchill wrote, saying that "you certainly have left golden footprints behind you" (Lash, *Eleanor and Franklin*, 668), while Chalmers Roberts of the U.S. government's Office of War Information* in London reported that she had "done more to bring real understanding of the spirit of the United States to the people of Britain than any other single American who has ever visited these islands" (Lash, *Eleanor and Franklin*, 669). No less significantly, she presented British experiences to the American public. Throughout her trip she filed her "My Day"* column, in which she stressed not only the rationing and other hardships of life in Britain but the promise of the new Britain that was emerging from the ashes of the old.

After FDR's death, ER returned to England in 1946 as a U.S. delegate to the first meeting of the United Nations* (UN) General Assembly in London. She remained keen to support Anglo-American cooperation, but unlike Churchill she always hoped that this would be to progressive and liberal ends and in cooperation with other democratic nations. She was in great demand while attending the UN meetings and became the first woman to address the prestigious Pilgrim Society, which was dedicated to Anglo-American friendship. She also made a point of meeting the ordinary British women preparing to leave Britain for the United States as wives of American servicemen. ER never forgot that international relations hinged on relationships between people—people of all classes. She knew that Anglo-American relations could not be left only to the era's transatlantic elite.

SELECTED BIBLIOGRAPHY

Beasley, Maurine H., ed. *The White House Press Conferences of Eleanor Roosevelt.* 1983.

Cull, Nicholas John. *Selling War: British Propaganda against American Neutrality in World War Two.* 1995.

Lash, Joseph P. *Eleanor and Franklin.* 1971.

———. *Eleanor: The Years Alone.* 1972.

Reynolds, David. *Rich Relations: The American Occupation of Britain, 1942–1945.* 1995.

Roosevelt, Eleanor. *This I Remember.* 1949.

Nicholas J. Cull

ANTILYNCHING MOVEMENT. As First Lady, ER championed the crusade of African Americans for a federal law to eradicate lynching, which was murder by mob action without due process of law. Although her efforts were not backed by President Franklin D. Roosevelt* and ultimately failed, they established ER as a key supporter of the National Association for the Advancement of Colored People* (NAACP) and a voice for racial justice. ER promoted antilynching legislation as publicly as presidential politics permitted her to do so and privately as a valuable and conscientious liaison between the NAACP and FDR. The legislative campaign floundered because FDR did not dare to oppose southerners who held key committee posts in Congress.*

Since the Civil War, lynching had been used, most notably in the segregated South, as a way of enforcing a subordinate role for African Americans. Shortly after the Roosevelts moved into the White House, legislation to use federal force against lynching became a key objective of the NAACP in the wake of an epidemic of crimes that captured public attention. In 1933, from Maryland, to Mississippi, to California, the frequency of mob murders had quadrupled over the previous year, with twenty-four African American men lynched that year compared with six in 1932.

African American newspapers detailed these barbarities with photographs and demanded federal action. An editorial in the *Pittsburgh Courier* of 4 November 1933 declared, "We have the plainest proof that action by the federal government is needed if lynching is to be stamped out." Indeed, individual states had failed to prosecute lynchers. From 1900 to 1930, more than 3,500 persons were lynched; only twelve cases resulted in convictions, involving sixty-seven offenders.

In autumn 1933, Walter White,* NAACP executive director, revived the campaign for a proposed federal antilynching bill similar to ones that had failed to pass in 1901 and 1919. White was heartened that December when FDR in a national radio broadcast condemned lynching as murder, although he did not advocate a federal remedy. In January 1934 an antilynching bill drafted by the NAACP was introduced by two Democratic senators, Edward P. Costigan of Colorado and Robert F. Wagner of New York. White believed that, with FDR's vocal support, it would pass—despite passionate opposition from southern senators. The measure proposed to penalize state officials found delinquent in protecting citizens and prosecuting violators and called for federal intervention when local authorities did not act.

ER tried hard to urge support for the bill. In 1934 she met with Jesse Daniel Ames, president of the Association of Southern Women for the Prevention of Lynching. A Texas suffragist, Ames led an antilynching movement among southern women that stressed social persuasion. ER tried to convince her that without federal intervention lives would be sacrificed to the idea of gradual, voluntary change.

When White sought ER's help in getting an appointment with FDR, after the White House staff refused his request, ER arranged a meeting on 7 May 1934. Before he saw FDR, ER briefed White on her husband's fears that support for the antilynching bill would delay passage of crucial New Deal* legislation. When FDR presented his arguments, White refuted him so readily that the president observed, "Somebody's been priming you. Was it my wife?" (Lash, 516). Confiding his dread of a filibuster, FDR told White, "If I come out for the anti-lynching bill now, they will block every bill I ask Congress to pass to keep America from collapsing. I just can't take that risk" (Lash, 516).

FDR's assessment was accurate. South Carolina's Senator "Cotton Ed" Smith, a Democrat, prepared to filibuster until Christmas. White southerners voiced fears of a return to Reconstruction with federal agents dominating southern life and politics. White journalists, among them an influential moderate, Ralph McGill of the *Atlanta Constitution*, characterized any move by the federal government to police the South as a resurgence of arbitrary federal rule. A few weeks after White's meeting with the president, Congress adjourned without voting on the bill.

ER did not abandon the struggle. In October 1934, when an Alabama man, Claude Neal, was kidnapped and lynched in Florida, White asked ER to address a protest rally in Carnegie Hall. "FDR I would like to do it," she appealed to her husband but added that she would "do whatever you say." The president's private secretary, Missy LeHand,* reported, "President says this is dynamite," and ER did not speak (Lash, 516–17). In 1935 southerners did filibuster the antilynching bill, and FDR refused White's request to condemn the filibuster. ER wrote White that "all of us are going on fighting and the only thing we can do is to hope we have better luck next time" (Lash, 518).

The bill died without a vote. Another effort in the seventy-fifth Congress (1937–1938) seemed promising. Again White hoped to meet with FDR, but other matters prevented it. ER served as a two-way conduit for information, explaining that FDR favored the bill but was preoccupied. The southern bloc threatened another filibuster, and the legislative campaign failed.

ER continued to use her position to call attention to racial injustice. In December 1939, after White reported on two lynchings in Mississippi, ER asked the president's advice. His memo referred her to Attorney General Frank Murphy, who might discover an "interstate activity or effect in the crime" that would justify Federal Bureau of Investigation (FBI) investigation (Lash, 471). Thus, the Roosevelt administration moved toward low-profile interstate inquiries and did not support legislative action.

SELECTED BIBLIOGRAPHY
Cook, Blanche Wiesen. *Eleanor Roosevelt*. Vol. 2. 1999.
Hall, Jacquelyn Dowd. *Revolt against Chivalry: Jesse Daniel Ames and the Women's Campaign against Lynching*. 1979.
Lash, Joseph P. *Eleanor and Franklin*. 1971.
Teel, Leonard Ray. "The African-American Press and the Campaign for an Anti-Lynching Law, 1933–1934: Putting Civil Rights on the National Agenda." *American Journalism* 8 (Spring/Summer 1991): 84–107.
White, Walter. *A Man Called White: The Autobiography of Walter White*. 1948.
Zangrando, Robert L. *The NAACP Crusade against Lynching, 1909–1950*. 1980.

Leonard Ray Teel

ARTHURDALE. Eleanor Roosevelt was the driving force in the planning, construction, and development of Arthurdale, West Virginia, the first of a series of New Deal* resettlement communities to aid the poverty-stricken. The project, begun in 1933 to improve the lot of destitute coal-mining families, quickly became mired in controversy over cost overruns and opposition from critics, who alleged it was socialistic. Although Arthurdale was not an economic success, ER remained its most vocal booster. She took influential friends and associates to visit both Arthurdale and other resettlement communities, making them symbols of her interest in bettering the lives of the poor.

A staunch defender of Arthurdale in the face of accusations of bureaucratic bungling, ER saw in it what its residents did—a opportunity for individuals to improve their lives through access to decent housing, education, medical care, and an improved environment. Today her memory lives on in Arthurdale, now a rural bedroom community of well-maintained homes and gardens proud of its past. In 1985 Arthurdale

Heritage, Inc., was founded to enable restoration of community buildings constructed during the New Deal period.

Arthurdale was part of the "back to the land" movement of the early twentieth century, which interested both Franklin D. Roosevelt* and ER. It sought to ameliorate the hardships of industrial capitalism by moving the poor from squalid surroundings to new rural communities. Supporters hoped that relocation would enable the jobless to combine subsistence farming with employment in handicraft-type industries like the Val-Kill* furniture factory at Hyde Park* operated by ER and two friends.

Under its subsistence homestead program set up in 1933, the New Deal created communities where families on relief could acquire homesteads consisting of housing and garden plots. The government made it possible for the homesteaders to have access to land, houses, and farm equipment, encouraged cooperative endeavors, and tried to attract small-scale industries to resettlement communities.

Although the Roosevelt administration established some fifty of these projects by 1935, critics focused their attention on West Virginia mainly because the three resettlement projects there drew ER's dedicated and uncompromising support. Her passionate commitment to Arthurdale, which started with its inception in 1933 and continued after FDR's death in 1945, as well as her interest in the homesteads of Tygart Valley, located south of Elkins, and Eleanor, a community named in her honor southwest of Charleston, made them easy targets for attack. While the communities provided residents with monetary assistance and new opportunities, they ran into management and political problems.

Bureaucratic mistakes made in establishing Arthurdale near the town of Reedsville in Preston County can be attributed to the haste of the early New Deal to help those most adversely affected by the Great Depression,* who might be influenced by Communist Party activity and resort to violence. These mistakes, ironically, led to Arthurdale's acquiring an infamous reputation as a "communistic" project (Lash, 400). The community passed through the hands of six federal agencies until 1947, when the government finally ended its ownership after administrative and financial difficulties. At the time it was sold to the public at a loss of $2 million, the settlement consisted of some 165 homes, most of which were purchased by the homesteaders, six school buildings, three factory buildings, a store, a forge, and a community center.

ER's interest in resettlement communities began when she visited Scotts Run, West Virginia, a coal-mining area northwest of Morgantown and approximately thirty miles northwest of what became the Arthurdale site. At the urging of her friend, Lorena Hickok,* an investigator for the Federal Emergency Relief Administration (FERA), and representatives of the American Friends Service Committee (AFSC), ER drove to

Scotts Run in August 1933 to see for herself the impact of the depression in West Virginia. She found working miners who did not earn enough to feed their families as well as unemployed miners living in appalling circumstances. In the face of this situation, she was impressed with the work being done by Clarence Pickett* and the AFSC to develop self-help programs for the miners and their families.

During her visit, ER learned of a plan by the Agricultural Extension Service of West Virginia University and welfare workers to move the miners to a 1,200-acre farm, formerly owned by the Arthur family, near Reedsville and fifteen miles southeast of Morgantown. The concept called for the relocated miners to combine part-time farming and co-operative industry to protect themselves against exploitation caused partly by absentee land-ownership.

After ER brought the plan to FDR's attention, it was taken over by the federal government as the initial project of the Subsistence Homestead Division under the Department of the Interior. The division had been established when supporters of the back-to-the-land movement slipped a revolving fund of $25 million for subsistence homesteads into the National Industrial Recovery Act, one of the major pieces of legislation passed in the first 100 days of FDR's administration.

Following ER's visit to Scotts Run, Louis Howe,* FDR's personal adviser, set up a committee that included the First Lady, Pickett, and others to oversee the development of a subsistence homestead project. On 13 October 1933, Secretary of the Interior Harold Ickes* announced that the federal government had purchased the Arthur farm and planned to relocate 200 miners and their families there. In November ER, Howe, and Pickett made a trip to Arthurdale, as the project became known, to check on progress there.

In a burst of enthusiasm, Howe had ordered fifty prefabricated homes from the Hodgson Company of New England in hopes that the first families would be moved in by Thanksgiving. This was the first of many mistakes that made headlines across the country. Problems began when the houses arrived and did not fit the foundations that had been prepared. Architect Eric Gugler, a friend of the Roosevelts, was hired at what critics complained was considerable expense, to adapt the houses to the foundations and strengthen the flimsy construction of the dwellings, which had been intended only for summer homes. Subsequently, 115 more substantial homes, some made of stone, were erected.

The First Lady's insistence on indoor plumbing, electricity, and refrigerators, seen as luxuries that many rural homes in the area did not have, pushed construction costs to $10,000 per family unit. A high figure for the times and far beyond the estimated expense, this led to a barrage of unfavorable publicity. Costs were increased because of the difficulty of ensuring a safe water supply due to a stratum of porous rock on the site.

Ickes complained that "we have been spending money down there like a drunken sailor" (Thomas, 169). ER, however, upheld the idea of making Arthurdale, which became known as her "baby," a model demonstration project (Lash, 398). She persuaded her friend Dorothy Elmhirst* to contribute money for a small hospital and clinic there and donated to them herself.

Sympathetic to the plight of African Americans, ER also explored the problem of discrimination in the homestead communities. Through Pickett she arranged a meeting of African American university heads and advocates of civil rights* at the White House on 26 January 1934. Bowing to community pressure against the inclusion of African Americans and immigrants, however, the Division of Subsistence Homesteads followed a policy of selecting only native-born whites as homesteaders. A few homestead projects for African Americans eventually were built, but none in West Virginia.

From the beginning Arthurdale was a partnership of West Virginia University's Agricultural Extension Service, the AFSC, which attempted to support a crafts program, and various federal agencies. The university ran an experimental farm, still in operation today, where Arthurdale residents raised cash crops, particularly potatoes. Whereas in most of West Virginia there were only two extension agents per county, the community of Arthurdale itself had two—one for agriculture and one for home economics. To preserve Appalachian folk culture as well as to provide work, ER employed her Val-Kill partner, Nancy Cook,* to help set up a handicraft center. The AFSC marketed some of the handicrafts produced there nationally but had little success.

To complete the industry-subsistence farming concept, ER and others worked diligently to bring industry to the community. Despite their efforts, enemies in Congress* blocked government contracts there. When the Public Works Administration allocated $525,000 for a factory in Arthurdale to construct post office equipment in 1934, congressional advocates of private enterprise were outraged and defeated funding for it.

To gain a business perspective, ER turned to an old acquaintance, Bernard Baruch,* a wealthy Wall Street investor, who visited Arthurdale. Baruch arranged for a General Electric subsidiary to operate a vacuum cleaner assembly plant there, but it proved unprofitable and closed. Other efforts at recruiting industry also failed in the stagnant depression economy.

Widespread employment in the community did not occur until the defense industry moved in during World War II.* At that time, Arthurdale homesites no longer were limited to the unemployed. By 1938, when the last group of homesteaders arrived, no homesteader could move in without already having a job, because of the difficulty of locating employment there.

ER believed that all aspects of the community, particularly the school, should be designed to overcome the debilitating effects of the coalfields. Under her guidance a school committee was organized that named Elsie Clapp, who had worked under the leading progressive educator, John Dewey, principal of a six-building school complex. Financed by ER's efforts, this included a model day nursery. Baruch donated $20,000 to launch a school fund drive and contributed additional sums, although he did not think the community would ever be economically viable. ER herself earmarked earnings from her sponsored radio broadcasts* for Arthurdale. During 1934 and 1935 she and Baruch together gave more than $50,000 for the school and $40,000 for the handicraft program.

School problems arose when the high school had difficulty receiving state accreditation because of the progressive curriculum. In addition, many families were uncomfortable with the methods employed and wanted a traditional education for their children. By 1936 local authorities took over primary responsibility for school operations, and the progressive experiment ended. In spite of the changeover, ER remained a staunch supporter of the Arthurdale schools. She attended every school graduation from 1935 to 1944 and even convinced FDR to join her for the one in 1938. Her last visit to Arthurdale was in 1960, when she dedicated the Community Presbyterian Church.

ER was not as involved with the other homesteads in West Virginia as with Arthurdale, but she tried to help them, too. Tygart Valley Homesteads was established because the timber, coal, railroad, and manufacturing industries in Randolph County were hard hit by the depression, which put 30 percent of the population on relief. Legislators from West Virginia, most notably Representative Jennings Randolph, a Democrat, pushed for a county project, leading the Division of Subsistence Homesteads to announce on 21 December 1933 that it would construct Tygart Valley Homesteads near Beverly. While not directly involved in Tygart Valley's development, ER made four separate trips there to meet with the residents and to promote the community as a factory site. Settlers built 198 homes, a saw mill, and a trade center for the new community. Like Arthurdale, Tygart Valley Homesteads was unsuccessful in attracting industry and went into bankruptcy in 1944.

State officials also pushed for a resettlement project to alleviate the economic plight of the southern West Virginia coalfields. In 1933 the newly created Rural Relief Division of the FERA announced that it would construct one of its first subsistence homesteads at Red House in Putnam County. As was the case at Arthurdale and Tygart Valley, the settlers performed the construction work, building 150 cinder-block homes and a factory building. To show her support, ER made five separate trips to Red House to check on progress.

The settlers were so impressed that they renamed the community

Eleanor in her honor. But the First Lady's name did not keep the project from being transferred to other agencies. In 1935 Eleanor, like Arthurdale and Tygart Valley, was placed first under the Resettlement Administration and then transferred to other agencies until eventually sold to private owners. In all three cases, lack of viable industry handicapped the efforts to make the communities self-sustaining.

While opponents argued against the effectiveness of government-sponsored resettlement communities, ER's goals of social improvement were realized in the improved lives of the homesteaders. There was no comparison between the desperation of the coal and timber camps and the green fields and tidy surroundings of the new communities. In her autobiography, ER conceded that "much money was spent, perhaps some of it unwisely." But she answered the critics, "I have always felt that many human beings who might have cost us thousands of dollars in tuberculosis sanitariums, insane asylums, and jails were restored to usefulness and given confidence in themselves" (Roosevelt, 131). No doubt, Arthurdale and other resettlement communities benefited those who lived there.

SELECTED BIBLIOGRAPHY
Cook, Blanche Wiesen. *Eleanor Roosevelt*. Vol. 2. 1999.
Haid, Stephen. "Arthurdale: An Experiment in Community Planning, 1933–1947." Ph.D. dissertation. West Virginia University. 1975.
Lash, Joseph P. *Eleanor and Franklin*. 1971.
Roosevelt, Eleanor. *This I Remember*. 1949.
Thomas, Jerry B. *An Appalachian New Deal*. 1998.
Ward, Bryan, ed. *A New Deal for America*. 1995.

Bryan Ward

ASIA. Eleanor Roosevelt's chief concerns on the three Asian trips she took in the 1950s were advancing the cause of democracy and human rights* and promoting the emancipation of women. Her keen understanding of the suspicions Asians felt toward Caucasians gave her insights into their apprehensions about American aims at a time when Asia had become a battleground in the Cold War.* While she defended the U.S. policy of containment, she believed that America's interest in thwarting communism was best served by foreign aid programs that emphasized economic and humanitarian assistance rather than military support for the world's needy nations.

ER's 1952 tour of Pakistan and India* was part of a round-the-world trip that included visits to the Middle East, Asia, and the Philippine Islands. In an echo of the Soviet criticism leveled at her throughout her years as a member of the U.S. delegation to the United Nations,* Radio Moscow denounced her as "a sworn enemy of peace and democracy" during the ten-week trip and charged that Secretary of State Dean Acheson had sent her to Pakistan and India "to promote the formation of a police force for combating the people's struggle for freedom" (Steinberg 348).

Crowds of Pakistani officials and large numbers of women greeted her arrival at Karachi Airport. Along her motorcade route into the capital city, still more throngs welcomed her with the chant, "Long live Mrs. Roosevelt" (Roosevelt, *India and the Awakening East*, 58). In her talks with officials, ER learned about their difficulties in establishing government structures and an economic system in those early days after the British partitioned the Indian subcontinent into Hindu and Muslim states. From her talks with women, ER drew the conclusion that they were slowly emerging from the servitude to which they were consigned by the strictures of tradition.

In her travels to Karachi, Peshwar, and Lahore, she visited—as was her custom—with both the nation's potentates and its poor. She lectured a group of purdah-clad women about the League of Women Voters* and gamely taught a class of Pakistani teenagers how to dance the Virginia reel. With their "courage and great vitality," ER concluded, these people would surely build a great country, despite their dire shortages of equipment and technical expertise (Roosevelt, *India and the Awakening East*, 91). In a memorandum to President Harry S Truman,* Secretary of State Dean Acheson called ER's trip—especially her stops in Pakistan and India— "a great success" and added that "although it was undertaken in a purely unofficial capacity, Mrs. Roosevelt's journey has served the public interest exceedingly well" (Lash, 204).

ER returned to Asia in 1953. She was saluted as a visiting dignitary, even though her role as a U.S. delegate to the United Nations had ended after the election of President Dwight D. Eisenhower.* She toured Japan for five weeks under the sponsorship of Columbia University and once again focused her attention on democracy and the status of women. She was distressed to learn from Prime Minister Shigeru Yoshida that Japan planned to rearm but would do so quietly due to political reasons. ER marveled at the contradictory character of the Japanese government, in which she saw reactionary political leaders upholding the liberal constitution America had imposed after World War II.*

At her insistence, a visit to Hiroshima was added to her itinerary by Japanese hosts, who had wanted to spare her the emotional pain of seeing the city where the first atomic bomb was dropped. While she believed America was justified in using the bomb, bearing witness to its consequences caused her considerable distress.

On her last day in Japan, ER had an audience with Emperor Hirohito and his wife. After listening to the emperor recount the efforts he had made to prevent the war, ER broached women's rights issues. Drawing on the information gleaned from her trips to Pakistan and India, ER told the empress that efforts to redefine the role of women were being led by those nations' most influential women. But the emperor curtly interrupted the discussion, observing that Japanese customs were different. "We have government bureaus to lead in our reforms," he declared. "We serve as an example to our people in the way we live and it is our lives that have influence over them" (Roosevelt, *On My Own*, 124).

ER returned to Asia in 1955 for a meeting of the World Federation of United Nations Associations in Bangkok. Her itinerary also included visits to Japan, Indonesia, and Hong Kong with a brief stop at Cambodia's Angkor Wat. During the week she spent in Japan, she found the "people looked happier" than they had in 1953, and, although the standard of living was still low, the nation was overcoming difficulties in establishing a democratic government (Roosevelt, *On My Own*, 178). In Hong Kong she was dismayed at the overcrowded conditions brought about by the influx of refugees* from communist China. Compared with the frightful conditions in which these Chinese exiles lived, ER wrote her daughter in August 1955, "Harlem is luxury!" (Asbell, 305).

ER's trips to Asia during the 1950s, although taken in an unofficial capacity, highlighted her position as America's most popular ambassador. Displaying a remarkable understanding of America's strategic needs while engaged in the Cold War and the Asian nations' hopes of modernizing in order to compete with the industrialized countries of Europe and the United States, ER emerged as an articulate advocate of the needs and goals of both the United States and Asia.

SELECTED BIBLIOGRAPHY

Asbell, Bernard, ed. *Mother and Daughter: The Letters of Eleanor and Anna Roosevelt.* 1982.
Berger, Jason. *A New Deal for the World: Eleanor Roosevelt and American Foreign Policy.* 1981.
Lash, Joseph. *Eleanor: The Years Alone.* 1972.
Roosevelt, Eleanor. *India and the Awakening East.* 1953.
———. *On My Own.* 1958.
Steinberg, Alfred. *Mrs. R: The Life of Eleanor Roosevelt.* 1958.

Joyce Hoffmann

AUTOBIOGRAPHY. Eleanor Roosevelt published three separate autobiographies, dealing with different portions of her life. *This Is My Story* (1937) ends with her first awareness of political activity, fostered by the involvement of her husband, Franklin D. Roosevelt* in the 1924 gubernatorial campaign of Al Smith.* *This I Remember* (1949) continues her narrative to FDR's death in 1945. In 1958 ER published *On My Own*, an account of her independent activity in her widowhood. Finally, in 1961 she collected the three books into one, making relatively minor excisions in each and adding a short, but illuminating, preface and a coda entitled

"The Search for Understanding," which articulates her political and moral philosophy. Now she used an inclusive title, *The Autobiography of Eleanor Roosevelt*.

As the dedication to the combined volume emphasizes, ER wished to employ her account of her experience to illuminate her husband's life as well as her own and to represent the times through which both lived. In other words, she understood her project primarily as producing a historical, rather than a personal, document. Emphasizing public, more than private, happenings, providing lists of activities and descriptions of persons she meets, subordinating feelings to convictions, she offers no gossip, uncovers no secrets, and resolutely eschews vanity. In many ways she preserves her privacy even while telling her life story. She writes rather flat, uninflected prose. Even her assertions of emotion—over the bombing of Pearl Harbor, for instance, or the death of an infant son— avoid intimate revelation. What ER feels, as she reports it, is what anyone would feel. Moreover, the events and attitudes she relates are by now familiar through numerous other accounts.

Nonetheless, ER's story of herself constitutes a moving narrative of personal growth, the more poignant for its reticence. Each of its sections—the original three separate volumes and the preface and coda— conveys a distinctive tone. Cumulatively, they record the development of strength, confidence, and a complicated sense of self.

In *This Is My Story*, ER often criticizes the self of her early years. Product of a strict upper-class upbringing, the young Eleanor, she claims, was excessively idealistic, rigid, and timid. She disappoints her adored father (Elliott Roosevelt*) by her unwillingness to ride a donkey down steep inclines; in retrospect, she appears to disappoint herself still more. She sees herself as essentially unattractive, both physically and psychologically. Her mother (Anna Hall Roosevelt*), herself a beauty, typically addressed her (in what tone we cannot know) as "Granny." ER took the designation as an allusion to her unfortunate ugliness. After her mother's death, her grandmother (Mary Ludlow Hall) dresses her in short skirts, despite her great height, long beyond the time when other young women lengthened their hems.

When her cousin Franklin proposed marriage, ER, aged nineteen, consented, she suggests, because of her eagerness to get on with her life and to experience whatever a woman should experience. Her grandmother inquired whether she was really in love. Although she answered yes, the autobiography emphasizes that not until years later did she have any idea what being in love meant. She does not explain how she ultimately acquired this knowledge or who was the object of her love.

The autobiography proceeds partly by a series of such conspicuous omissions. Almost never does ER directly acknowledge complex feelings, yet she conveys their importance in her life. *This Is My Story* consistently stresses her early dependence. In her girlhood, dutiful always, she did as she was told. Even after her marriage, she followed paths determined by others, her own relatives and FDR's, as well as FDR himself. She did not know how to cook, nor did she learn. She subordinated her own desires to those of nursemaids and governesses. She sent her young sons to boarding school, against her own inclinations, because such was the established ritual. Some mode of escape seems urgent, although ER does not quite say so. Even in this first volume, though, she narrates the burgeoning of independence as she discovers the possibility of doing work of her own. Characteristically, she does not directly indicate her feelings at the time about her self-subordination, although hints of rage and depression emerge.

This I Remember focuses on ER's developing sense of vocation in the context of FDR's political career, including the presidential years. Dramatic national and international events help to shape her psychological landscape: the urgency of action becomes ever more apparent to her. She begins the book by suggesting that most people will want to know mainly what she has to tell about her husband: she doubts her centrality even to her own autobiography. Nor does she claim political influence. Indeed, she strongly denies that her views had the slightest effect on her husband, although she subsequently reports the ever-increasing number of trips and investigations she pursues in order to provide information and opinion for his enlightenment.

With due decorum, the autobiographer hints at the difficulties of enforced existence in the public eye. She tells an anecdote about her husband's failure to attend to a problem experienced by one of his sons, although the boy actually makes an appointment to see his presidential father. Ostensibly, she justifies the neglect, but the paragraph after the justification offers a kind of apology for her frankness in narrating the incident. She has provided such detail, she explains, because she wants to reveal the painful lack of privacy experienced by the families of public servants, since the public encourages the press to "delve into" their private lives (Roosevelt, *Autobiography*, 140). The point may reverberate more loudly in the late twentieth century than when ER wrote the sentence, but in any case her self-justification is a non sequitur. Her account of her family life does not concern lack of privacy. It seems, rather, an overflow of personal resentment.

Clearly, ER admired her husband. *This I Remember* praises his political acumen, his concern to better the lives of people in general, his sense of public responsibility. But it appears equally clear, even from her own reticent account, that he offered little intimacy, thus indirectly encouraging her efforts to find fulfillment in public activity. She develops organizational skill, demonstrating the distance she has traveled from her early dependence. She discovers her interest in meeting people of every kind. She learns to function effectively as a public speaker, in the service of her own causes and on behalf of her husband. Once World War II* begins, she throws herself into the cause of public defense. Increasingly, she exercises her own judgment, although she reports herself as still subject to fits of social panic. When, for example, she makes her first independent visit to Buckingham Palace, she feels full of terror. In the event, though, she enjoys herself immensely, as she typically enjoys getting to know new people. Her accounts of visits from and to world dignitaries reveal both her capacity for pleasure and, at least intermittently, her sharp eye for narrative detail.

At the beginning of *On My Own*, the autobiographer reflects briefly on her husband's life and her life with him. Expressing once more her admiration for FDR as public man, she explicitly acknowledges his consequent limitations as husband, father, and friend. She speaks of the new kind of self-subordination she experienced in the White House years, her self hidden behind the facade of president's wife. After her husband's death, she discovered for the first time the possibility of knowing and being the person she wanted to be. If her account of her activities (on behalf of the United Nations,* for instance) often sounds as though it had been transcribed from a rather truncated diary, the sheer multiplicity of those activities and the energy of involvement that ER manifestly brought to them generate emotional power. In an offhand summary of her history during the years alone, the writer mentions loneliness as an experience she, like everyone else, endures on occasion. But her detailed account conveys no sense of loneliness. Rather, it communicates increasing gusto for life and its minutiae. At its best, this volume expresses its author's delight in unexpected trivia: the firehouse cat that slides down the pole after all the firemen have done the same, the yellow damask in a Moscow hotel room. It also contains statistical summary, sociological generalization, and an increasing emphasis on ER's political and social opinions, especially her anxiety about what she considers general misunderstanding of the precise nature of the communist menace. Directly and indirectly, it dramatizes how and why a woman learns really to be "on her own."

In her preface to the collected autobiography, ER observes that fiction as a literary form holds special interest because it can really tell the truth. To tell the truth in autobiography, she continues, is difficult, although autobiography's value derives from its honesty. In the concluding section, looking back on her life, she confesses her sense of the danger of introspection, which can lead, she believes, to excessive self-absorption. Even at the age of seventy-five, she would rather look forward than back. Briefly retrospective, though, she recapitulates her escape from class restrictions and her growth toward independence, declares her preference for the personal over the abstract, and formulates explicitly her goal in life: to create greater understanding between peoples. Her evolution not only toward independence but toward passionate conviction is the truth this autobiography tells: like the truth of fiction, a revelation of character.

SELECTED BIBLIOGRAPHY

Roosevelt, Eleanor. *The Autobiography of Eleanor Roosevelt*. 1961.
———. *On My Own*. 1958.
———. *This I Remember*. 1949.
———. *This Is My Story*. 1937.

Patricia Meyer Spacks

AWARDS. Numerous organizations bestowed awards upon Eleanor Roosevelt while she was First Lady, as well as during her post–White House years. She was recognized for advancing human rights* and humanitarian causes, peace, international understanding, and civil rights,* as well as for her work on behalf of education, refugees,* labor,* and those with disabilities. She received thirty-five honorary degrees, exceeding the thirty-one honorary degrees awarded her husband, Franklin D. Roosevelt.*

One of her first notable awards as First Lady was the Gimbel national award for being an outstanding American woman, with which she was honored in Philadelphia on 12 December 1934. She asked that her $1,000 prize be used to send a child with polio to Warm Springs, Georgia, for treatment. On 30 June 1938 she was given a Life Membership Key by the National Education Association of the United States. On 29 November 1939 at a dinner in New York City attended by 1,000 people, *The Churchman* publication gave ER its first award for the promotion of good will and understanding among all peoples. On 4 December 1939 the Philadelphia chapter of the Order of the Eastern Star presented its Humanitarian Award of $1,000 to ER, which she donated to the American Friends Service Committee. On 1 May 1940 the *Nation* magazine gave her its first annual award for distinguished service in the cause of American social progress.

Among the honors ER received after leaving the White House was the Democratic Legacy Award presented in 1948 by the Anti-Defamation League of B'nai B'rith. That year she also received Bryn Mawr College's M. Carey Thomas Award for her work at the United Nations.* In 1949 ER's support for the newly established nation of Israel* was recognized when she was honored with the first Henrietta Szold Award, named for the founder of Hadassah, the Women's Zionist Organization of America. On 10 February 1950 the National Society for Crippled Children and Adults gave ER its Distinguished Service Medal for her efforts on behalf of the handicapped. On 8 March 1950 Sweden presented ER with its Prince Carl Medal for humanitarianism. In 1955 ER was the first recipient of the Nansen Medal, established by the United Nations General Assem-

Honorary Degrees Conferred upon Eleanor Roosevelt

13 June 1929	Russell Sage College	Doctor of Humane Letters
1 June 1933	Washington College of Law	Doctor of Laws
11 June 1935	University of North Carolina	Doctor of Laws
16 June 1937	John Marshall College of Law	Doctor of Laws
25 May 1942	Washington College	Doctor of Laws
June 1942	Muhlenberg College	Doctor of Laws
3 Dec. 1945	Hebrew Union College	Doctor of Hebrew Letters
25 May 1947	MacMurray College for Women	Doctor of Humane Letters
5 June 1947	Hobart College	Doctor of Laws
8 Jan. 1948	Queens College (Canada)	Doctor of Laws
20 April 1948	University of Utrecht (Netherlands)	Doctor of Laws
16 May 1948	West Virginia State College	Doctor of Humanities
3 Nov. 1948	University of Lyon (France)	Doctor of Laws
13 Nov. 1948	Oxford University (England)	Doctor of Civil Law
1 March 1949	Manitoba University (Canada)	Doctor of Laws
9 Oct. 1949	Universite Libre of the International Federation of Scientific Research Societies (Calcutta, India–Teheran, Iran)	Doctor of Civil Sociology
20 Oct. 1949	Smith College	Doctor of Laws
16 Sept. 1950	Jewish Theological Seminary	Doctor of Laws
16 June 1951	Bard College	Doctor of Laws
20 Jan. 1952	Templi Academia (Italy)	Doctor of Laws
14 March 1952	Aligarh University (India)	Doctor of Literature
15 March 1952	University of Delhi (India)	Doctor of Letters
18 March 1952	University of Allahabad (India)	Doctor of Laws
22 March 1952	Santiniketan University (India)	Doctor of Literature
17 June 1952	Yeshiva University	Doctor of Humane Letters
12 Feb. 1953	University of Rhode Island	Doctor of Laws
18 March 1953	Bethune-Cookman College	Doctor of Laws
6 Nov. 1953	McGill University (Canada)	Doctor of Laws
13 June 1954	Brandeis University	Doctor of Humane Letters
25 May 1955	Roosevelt University	Doctor of Humanities
11 Dec. 1956	Philathea College	Doctor of Humanities
8 Aug. 1958	Colorado State University	Doctor of Laws
12 June 1960	Amherst College	Doctor of Laws
10 Oct. 1961	University of Newfoundland (Canada)	Doctor of Laws
4 June 1962	Atlanta University	Doctor of Laws

Source: Franklin D. Roosevelt Library, Hyde Park, NY.

bly to recognize distinguished services on behalf of refugees. That year the Congress of Industrial Organization (CIO) presented her with the $5,000 Philip Murray Award for community service. In accepting the award, she said she would donate the money to health causes.

Recognition of ER continued in her later years. On 17 January 1956—the 250th anniversary of Benjamin Franklin's birth—the mayor of Philadelphia on behalf of the city presented ER with a commemorative Franklin medal for her work in promoting world understanding. She received the Decalogue Society of Lawyers Merit Award in 1957 for her uncompromising initiative and idealism. On 12 November 1960 the National Council of Negro Women honored ER with its first Mary McLeod Bethune* Human Rights Award. On 24 February 1961 the Women's National Book Association gave ER the Constance Lindsay Skinner Award for her contributions to the world of books.*

In 1968 ER was honored posthumously with the United Nations prize for outstanding achievement in human rights. In 1973 she was inducted into the National Women's Hall of Fame for her efforts to end discrimination against minorities.

SELECTED BIBLIOGRAPHY

Eleanor Roosevelt Papers, Franklin D. Roosevelt Library, Hyde Park, NY.
Hareven, Tamara K. *Eleanor Roosevelt : An American Conscience.* 1968.
Lash, Joseph P. *Eleanor: The Years Alone.* 1972.
Walter, Claire. *Winners, the Blue Ribbon Encyclopedia of Awards.* 1978.

Marilyn Elizabeth Perry

B

BABIES-JUST BABIES. One of Eleanor Roosevelt's major nonpolitical commitments as she began her tenure as First Lady in 1933 was the editorship of a new monthly magazine, *Babies-Just Babies*, aimed at middle-class parents. While the slick-paper publication lasted only six months, it drew considerable publicity and presented ER to the U.S. public as a career-minded individual. Each issue was about sixty-five pages and featured glossy black-and-white photographs of appealing infants and toddlers, as well as fiction, true stories, health and consumer advice, and children's tales and lullabies. Although it did not last, its overriding theme, education for motherhood, fitted well with new ideas on parenting in the 1930s as middle-class couples reduced the size of their families and attached more importance to raising the children they did have. ER's motivation for taking the editorship was unclear. She said her interest stemmed from nationwide travels* that had convinced her many young mothers lacked the necessary information to care for their infants properly. But she also appeared eager to locate a job for her daughter Anna Roosevelt Dall (Halsted*), who was in the process of separating from her husband. Under the terms of ER's contract, Anna was paid for helping her.

The idea for *Babies-Just Babies* originated with Bernarr Macfadden, well-known publisher of bodybuilding, confession, and mystery magazines. Months before Franklin D. Roosevelt* was elected president in 1932, Macfadden had signed ER to a contract to edit the magazine in collaboration with her daughter. The contract gave ER complete editorial control over the magazine, including approval of its advertising. Her pay was $500 per issue, with a provision that the sum would double at the time of the contract renewal if she were living in the White House.

Macfadden's rationale for employing ER may well have included a political dimension. A Macfadden spokesperson said that ER was chosen because of her experience editing the *Women's Democratic News** and interest in child welfare work. According to Mary Macfadden, Macfadden's ex-wife, however, the publisher sought a high-level federal appointment and gave ER and her daughter top jobs on the most costly magazine he had ever produced in hopes of securing one. An article in *Time* magazine implied Macfadden's hunger for power had motivated the arrangement and that Macfadden expected to advise FDR.

As editor, ER had numerous ideas for the magazine. She generated long, typed lists of suggested topics, departments, and story ideas but avoided controversial topics such as birth control and illegitimacy. The first issue appeared in October 1932, with articles on "I Am a Real Bachelor Father," by a theatrical producer who was raising an adopted son, and "24 Hours of a Baby's Life," coauthored by Anna Roosevelt Dall and a doctor. ER's first editorial emphasized the importance of a well-adjusted marriage in which to raise a child. Her subsequent editorials emphasized the need for nurturing familial and social relationships: parents should encourage their children to trust them; society should help children and parents in need; study of the lives of great men can inspire parents and children to overcome present-day difficulties.

The magazine folded in May 1933, when ER withdrew as editor after facing disapproval and ridicule. Some came from those who did not think the First Lady should engage in commercial ventures. Others involved teasing over the title. For instance, at the annual dinner of the Women's National Press Club* members satirized ER's efforts with a song: "We're babies, just babies, just babies," and the *Harvard Lampoon* created a parody called "Tutors, Just Tutors."

More important, the magazine was not a financial success, drawing limited advertising, mainly for health foods aimed at children, in the midst of the Great Depression.* Also, ER and Macfadden had differences of opinion over its direction. Her correspondence with Macfadden indicates a curt reference to changes he had requested in her final editorial; he did not want her to make it seem that she was "giving up the magazine too emphatically" (ER to Lorena Hickok,* 11 April 1933). ER, however, was quoted as saying that the "onerous character of her duties at the White House" left no time for the magazine (*New York Times*, 5 May 1933).

Macfadden tried to continue his acquaintanceship with ER after *Babies-Just Babies* folded and asked her to write articles for his *Liberty* magazine, which she occasionally did. She also kept a promise to invite the publisher to the White House (15 May 1933). Yet, she never again edited a magazine, and Macfadden did not attempt another publication for new parents.

SELECTED BIBLIOGRAPHY
Cook, Blanche Wiesen. *Eleanor Roosevelt*. Vol. 2. 1999.
Eleanor Roosevelt Papers, Franklin D. Roosevelt Library, Hyde Park, NY.
Hickok, Lorena. *Reluctant First Lady*. 1962.
"Just Babies." *Time* (20 July 1932): 24.
Lash, Joseph P. *Eleanor and Franklin*. 1971.
Macfadden, Mary, and Emile Geauvreau. *Dumbbells and Carrot Sticks: The Story of Bernarr Macfadden*. 1953.

Beth Haller

BARUCH, BERNARD MANNES (19 August 1870, Camden, SC–20 June 1965, New York).

Eleanor Roosevelt knew Bernard Baruch for nearly half a century, from Woodrow Wilson's administration to her death. A financier, Baruch was chairman of the War Industries Board under Wilson and a major contributor to the Democratic Party.* Later, he became the classic elder statesman, an adviser to both Democratic and Republican presidents as well as numerous members of Congress.* He was also, in his era, the most prominent American Jew.*

Indeed, it was Baruch's Jewish identity, as well as his reputation as a Wall Street speculator, that initially prevented ER from considering him as a potential friend. But Baruch's kindness and ER's capacity to transcend her prejudice eventually led to a warm, mutually supportive relationship. During and after her husband's presidency, ER relied on Baruch for advice, financial support for worthy causes, even assistance in solving family problems. Baruch, who was always ambivalent toward Franklin D. Roosevelt,* found in ER an appreciative and influential proponent for some of his public policy prescriptions.

ER and Baruch's friendship was cemented early in the New Deal* through his promotion of her beloved Arthurdale* project, a subsistence homestead community near Reedsville, West Virginia. Baruch visited Arthurdale, lobbied for it in Congress, and encouraged ER to contact General Electric about establishing a factory there. Moreover, he generously backed the progressive school in Arthurdale with his own funds, paying most of its expenses. Ultimately, Baruch concluded that Arthurdale could not survive as originally conceived and so informed ER, who concurred in his decision to withdraw his sponsorship of the school. But during World War II* Baruch helped to gain an aircraft factory for Reedsville.

In 1943 ER was elated when Baruch was named head of a special Office of War Mobilization unit to plan for postwar industrial reconversion. As she wrote her son-in-law, John Boettiger: "Baruch is still the most comforting person I know" (Goodwin, 469). After the war, she lauded the Baruch Plan for international control of atomic energy and attempted to overcome the opposition of former vice president Henry

Wallace* to it. She also deeply resented Soviet foreign minister Vyacheslav Molotov's characterization of Baruch as a warmonger. In 1952 she unsuccessfully tried to keep Baruch on good terms with Democratic presidential nominee Adlai Stevenson.* Baruch endorsed Republican Dwight D. Eisenhower* but later failed to alter the new president's adamant opposition to ER's continued service at the United Nations.* In 1960 ER urged Democratic presidential candidate John F. Kennedy* to consult Baruch, who decided to remain neutral through that election.

In a sense, the enduring Roosevelt–Baruch friendship was a "Victorian affair" (Schwarz, 569). Each signed letters to one another, "Affectionately" (Schwarz, 308). Yet, meeting for lunch or dinner, they addressed one another as "Mrs. Roosevelt" and "Mr. Baruch" (Schwarz, 308). He "looks on me as a mind," ER once confided to one of Baruch's biographers, "not as a woman" (Coit, 451).

SELECTED BIBLIOGRAPHY

Coit, Margaret L. *Mr. Baruch*. 1957.

Cook, Blanche Wiesen. *Eleanor Roosevelt*. Vol. 2. 1999.

Goodwin, Doris Kearns. *No Ordinary Time: Eleanor and Franklin D. Roosevelt: The Home Front in World War II*. 1994.

Lash, Joseph P. *Eleanor and Franklin*. 1971.

———. *Eleanor: The Years Alone*. 1972.

Schwarz, Jordan A. *The Speculator: Bernard M. Baruch in Washington, 1917–1965*. 1981.

Myron I. Scholnick

BETHUNE, MARY MCLEOD (10 July 1875, Mayesville, SC–18 May 1955, Daytona, FL).

Mary McLeod Bethune, president of Bethune-Cookman College, civil rights* advocate, and New Deal* official, was a very significant African American friend and political partner in Eleanor Roosevelt's life. ER first met Bethune in 1927 at the Roosevelt home in New York at a luncheon for leaders of the National Council of Women of the U.S.A., which Bethune attended as president of the National Association of Colored Women. The two women developed a close relationship after ER arranged for Bethune's appointment in 1935 to an unpaid position on the national advisory committee of the National Youth Administration* (NYA), the New Deal agency to help young people secure education and job training. The following year Bethune accepted a full-time NYA job, overseeing activities involving African Americans. In 1939 Aubrey Williams,* NYA head, named her director of the division of Negro affairs.

Bethune was the most influential black woman in the United States through more than three decades. Her determined efforts to bring New Deal programs to depression-stricken African Americans provided the Roosevelt administration, particularly ER, with the opportunity to cul-

Eleanor Roosevelt and Mary McLeod Bethune attend the opening in May 1943
of Midway Hall, a federally built residence hall for African American women
government workers in Washington. *Courtesy of National Archives*

tivate a significant constituency within black America. Together, Bethune
and ER provided a powerful image of interracial cooperation in the 1930s
and 1940s, while also furnishing a major impetus for African Americans
to shift their party allegiance from the Republican "Party of Lincoln" to
the Democratic Party.* The picture of partnership that ER and Bethune
projected through joint appearances was revolutionary in the 1930s,
when virtually no Caucasian political leaders showed themselves as close
associates of African Americans. Bethune and ER also worked on a
shared agenda in the aftermath of the New Deal, including the advancement of domestic liberalism, the promotion of racial justice, and the creation of international understanding.

Bethune was different from other African American leaders of the day,
including those connected with the Roosevelt administration. She was a
woman, whereas the others were men. She had been born poor and was
strikingly dark, compared, for example, to the middle-class and fair-
skinned Walter White,* executive secretary of the National Association
for the Advancement of Colored People* (NAACP), or Robert Weaver,
an economist who advised Interior Secretary Harold L. Ickes.* She was
a Republican who changed her party allegiance in the 1930s only because
of the policies of Franklin D. Roosevelt.* Described as "an imperious,

matriarchal figure" in dealing with other African Americans, she was a dazzling and magnetic personality who exercised power with flourish and enjoyment (Weiss, 142). Her tools of leadership in dealing with the white power structure, however, were negotiation and conciliation, not confrontation.

Bethune and ER used and inspired each other in numerous ways. Through Bethune, ER learned about race and African American issues, gaining contacts in a world about which she previously had known little and personally surmounting the racial feeling of her class and day. According to Joseph P. Lash,* ER's authorized biographer, it was only after ER was comfortable giving Bethune a kiss on the cheek, as she did her Caucasian friends, that "she felt she had at last overcome the racial prejudice within herself" (Lash, 523). Through ER, Bethune lobbied for the right of African Americans to look to the federal government for greater economic and political opportunity. She also gained ER's help in promoting her college.

Born Mary McLeod in 1875 near Mayesville, South Carolina, the fifteenth of seventeen children of Sam and Patsy McLeod, former slaves, Bethune harbored an intense, lifelong pride in her African heritage. She began her formal education at the age of ten at the Trinity Presbyterian Mission School near Mayesville and continued it at Scotia Seminary (later Barber-Scotia College) in North Carolina until she went to Chicago to attend the Institute for Home and Foreign Missions (which became the Moody Bible Institute) to prepare for a career as a missionary to Africa. After a year's study, she applied to the Presbyterian Mission Board for an assignment, only to learn that it had no openings in Africa for black missionaries.

In 1896 McLeod thus began a career as a missionary educator in the Deep South, organizing a Sabbath school for hundreds of poor black children in Augusta, Georgia. In 1898, while teaching in Sumter, South Carolina, she married Albertus Bethune, a salesman, and moved to Savannah. Their son, Albert, was born in 1899. That same year Bethune set out for Palatka, Florida, to open a mission school. Her husband did not share her missionary interests, and the couple separated.

In 1904 she moved on to Daytona Beach, Florida, where she organized the Daytona Normal and Industrial Institute to teach young black women basic academic skills, homemaking, and agricultural arts, along with religion. Beginning with only $1.50 in cash and dry goods boxes for benches, Bethune utilized extraordinary skills as an orator, fundraiser, and administrator to expand the school. In 1923 it became coeducational after merging with the Cookman Institute of Jacksonville. Four years later it was renamed Bethune-Cookman College, which evolved into an accredited four-year institution. Bethune continued as president until 1942, even though her NYA position meant she lived in Washington. In 1935 she was awarded the Spingarn medal of the NAACP as the African American achieving the greatest distinction on behalf of the race.

While directing her school, Bethune was active in the most important national African American women's political network, the National Association of Colored Women (NACW), becoming national president in 1924. Although she established its national headquarters in Washington, its thrust remained local-level organizing. With the rise of the New Deal, however, Bethune sensed an opportunity for a new black woman's organization to project itself at the national level. In 1935 she founded the National Council of Negro Women (NCNW) by bringing together representatives of thirty organizations, including collegiate sororities, occupational societies of businesswomen and nurses, and various auxiliaries and Christian denominational groups. She established the NCNW's permanent headquarters in the nation's capital. As NCNW president, she led delegations to the White House, petitioned Congress* on behalf of antilynching* and fair housing legislation, and in 1938 convened a major conference on governmental cooperation in dealing with problems of Negro women and children.

As a New Deal employee, Bethune maximized every opportunity to make the growing federal government more responsive to African Americans. She worked to ensure that the NYA hired more black men and women and treated them fairly in an organization whose local leaders remained white. She pressed for an equitable measure of NYA programs for African American youth and achieved the adoption of nondiscriminatory policies, although the proportionate amount spent on African Americans remained less than that spent on white youth. She lobbied for similar goals in other federal programs, meeting with limited success.

Bethune carefully cultivated personal friendships with both ER and FDR. With the exception of Walter White,* Bethune was the only African American leader with access to the White House. Her NYA programs provided the opportunity for ER to visit black communities throughout the nation, personifying the New Deal. The two women visited projects together, posing for news photos that certified the First Lady's concern for African Americans—and Bethune's ability to elevate the status of African Americans to presidential attention.

Believing in the power of cooperation, Bethune revived the interdepartmental group of African Americans in 1936, forming the Federal Council on Negro Affairs, which became known as the Black Cabinet. It included about two dozen African American administrators and advisers from cabinet-level departments and special agencies such as the Works Progress Administration* (WPA). All members were male except Bethune. She used her stature as head of the Black Cabinet, which met in her home, as well as head of the NCNW, to convene two well-publicized conferences sponsored by the NYA in Washington.

The more important was the January 1937 Conference on the Problems of the Negro and Negro Youth. Bethune secured ER to give the keynote speech and, with her help, lined up the secretaries of commerce and agriculture as additional speakers. Bethune delivered the conference's final report to FDR herself, noting that ER's presence represented the first time the federal government had ever demonstrated such an interest in the plight of African American citizens. ER had the report, considered the best consensus document on African Americans produced during the 1930s, distributed within the government and to the public. Two years later Bethune held a follow-up conference.

With the advent of World War II,* Bethune sought the maximum possible access of African Americans to job training and military service. She praised FDR's 1941 executive order banning racial discrimination in government and defense industries and advised on the training of African Americans inducted into the Women's Auxiliary Army Corps (WAACS) in 1942. With the end of the NYA, she left the federal government in 1944, but her role as a leader continued. Bethune took a keen interest in the fate of colonial liberation movements throughout the world and became a close friend of the Indian leader Jawaharlal Nehru. In 1945 she was appointed as an official U.S. observer to the founding conference of the United Nations*—along with W.E.B. Du Bois* and Walter White—where the three pressed for maximum self-determination of colonial peoples in Africa, Asia,* and the Caribbean.

Bethune's health had begun to fail in 1940, after which she suffered repeated hospitalizations. When she was a patient in Baltimore, ER arranged for flowers from the White House greenhouse to be delivered to her every week. Bethune made an ill-advised return to the presidency of her college in 1946, but by 1949 she resigned from both this position and the presidency of the NCNW. She retained memberships, however, on the boards of more than thirty associations including the NAACP, the Southern Conference Educational Fund,* and the United Negro College Fund.

Of the many themes in Mary McLeod Bethune's life, one of the most fascinating is her relationship with ER. The two mirrored each other in several ways. Each had the ability to cultivate effective political networks, especially among female colleagues, using these networks to advance political objectives as well as for personal and emotional support. Each wrote newspaper columns: ER's "My Day"* column was somewhat similar to columns written by Bethune in the 1940s and 1950s for the *Pittsburgh Courier* and the *Chicago Defender*, two nationally circulated African American newspapers. During the Cold War* years, they found themselves together on the ramparts of liberalism, interracialism, and internationalism. ER and Bethune shared, as well, the experience of venomous political attacks. Each endured false accusations of being communists, and on occasion they sought counsel and sympathy from each other in the face of vilification. When a speaking engagement for Bethune in Englewood, New Jersey, was withdrawn on the grounds that she was a communist, ER came to Bethune's defense in a "My Day" column of 3 May 1952: "She has the gift of getting people to cooperate with her. She is the kindest, gentlest person I have ever met. . . . She is the last person that I can imagine any thinking person would believe to be a Communist" (Emblidge, 2: 266). Paying tribute to Bethune after her death in a "My Day" column of 20 May 1955, ER wrote, "I will cherish the spirit she lived by and try to promote the causes that she believed in, in loving memory of a very wonderful life" (Emblidge, 3: 64).

SELECTED BIBLIOGRAPHY

Emblidge, David, ed. *Eleanor Roosevelt's "My Day."* Vols. 2, 3. 1990, 1991.
Kirby, John B. *Black Americans in the Roosevelt Era.* 1980.
Lash, Joseph P. *Eleanor and Franklin.* 1971.
Mary McLeod Bethune Papers, Bethune Foundation, Bethune Cookman College, Daytona Beach, FL.
Weiss, Nancy J. *Farewell to the Party of Lincoln: Black Politics in the Age of FDR.* 1983.

Randolph Boehm and Linda Reed

BIBLIOGRAPHIES. Bibliographies of works by and about Eleanor Roosevelt have been issued as separate publications and as parts of scholarly works about her. No single source identifies and provides annotations for all works by and about ER.

The first bibliography of ER was compiled in 1940. When Pauline Edelstein, a library science student at Simmons College, prepared her "Bibliography of Eleanor Roosevelt: First Lady of the Land" as a class paper, ER had written eight books and more than 163 articles. She also had written several series of periodical columns, and her syndicated newspaper column "My Day"* was in its fifth year. Since there are no known copies of Edelstein's unpaged work, it is impossible to know how many of these writings she included. In 1948 the Library of Congress produced a four-page list of references to writings by and about ER entitled *Mrs. Eleanor (Roosevelt) Roosevelt (Mrs. Franklin D. Roosevelt): A List of References.* This brief bibliography lists books written by ER and the more significant works about her that were available at the time.

The Franklin D. Roosevelt Library has prepared "Periodical Articles by Eleanor Roosevelt, 1923–1971." This thirty-three-page finding aid, compiled in 1965 and revised in 1979, identifies articles by ER and published versions of some of her speeches, arranged according to date of publication. Articles published or reissued after her death are included. Some of the entries are for articles written about her.

Two bibliographies were issued in 1984 on the occasion of the centenary of ER's birth. *Eleanor Roosevelt Centenary Bibliography* was compiled by Barbara H. Kemp of the Smithsonian Institution. This annotated bibliography contains eighty-seven entries for books by or about ER arranged under several headings.

The second work, *First Lady: A Bibliography of Selected Material by and about Eleanor Roosevelt*, was compiled by R. David Myers, Margaret L. Morrison, and Marguerite D. Bloxom of the Library of Congress. The 235 entries in the bibliography, some of which are annotated, are presented in three categories: works by ER arranged according to types of writings or topics, works about her presented according to the decade in which the work was published, and family accounts. There is an index to authors and titles.

The most extensive bibliography of ER to date is *Eleanor Roosevelt: A Comprehensive Bibliography*, compiled by John A. Edens and issued in 1994. The bibliography identifies and annotates over 3,780 sources by or about ER. Entries for works by ER are arranged by date of publication and include all editions and reissues of her writings and 274 published versions of addresses or other public statements that she made. All periodical columns that she wrote are identified and annotated. Her newspaper column "My Day" is not included. Writings about her are arranged alphabetically under an extensive number of subjects. There are separate chapters devoted to reviews of her writings, interviews, writings for younger readers, poetry about her and works that portray her as a fictional character, and recordings and films that either feature her or are about her. It includes an index to authors and a detailed subject index.

The collection of articles selected by Allida M. Black and published as *What I Hope to Leave Behind: The Essential Essays of Eleanor Roosevelt* (1995) includes a chronological listing of published articles written by ER from 1921 to 1963. The list also includes published versions of some of ER's speeches* as well as book prefaces. There are no annotations.

Some of the bibliographies of ER included in scholarly works about her have contributed to the development of general bibliographic treatment of ER. James R. Kearney in *Anna Eleanor Roosevelt: The Evolution of a Reformer* (1968) provided what was then the most comprehensive list of articles by and about ER. Tamara K. Hareven included a lengthy discussion of sources in *Eleanor Roosevelt: An American Conscience* (1968). As part of her Ph.D. dissertation, "Eleanor Roosevelt and Federal Responsibility and Responsiveness to Youth, the Negro, and Others in Time of Depression" (1970), Mildred Abramowitz listed writings by ER as well as unpublished material, articles, books,* films, and interviews for which ER was the principal subject.

Jason Berger included a list of articles by and about ER in *A New Deal for the World: Eleanor Roosevelt and American Foreign Policy* (1981). *Eleanor Roo-*

sevelt: First Lady of American Liberalism (1987) by Lois Scharf contained a bibliographic essay and an annotated list of selected books about her. Geoffrey C. Ward's *Before the Trumpet: Young Franklin Roosevelt, 1882–1905* (1985) and *A First-Class Temperament: The Emergence of Franklin Roosevelt* (1989) are also studies of ER, and, therefore, the extensive bibliographies that accompany both of these works are of interest.

In the first volume of her *Eleanor Roosevelt* (1992), Blanche Wiesen Cook included a selective bibliography of articles by ER and books about her for the period 1884–1933. A selective bibliography of books by ER and books about her appeared in the second volume of Cook's *Eleanor Roosevelt* (1999), covering the years 1933–1938. The entry for ER prepared by Debra L Petersen in *Women Public Speakers in the United States, 1925–1993: A Biocritical Sourcebook* (1994) included a well-organized list of sources. Allida M. Black in *Casting Her Own Shadow: Eleanor Roosevelt and the Shaping of Postwar Liberalism* (1996) offered an unannotated list of articles by ER, many of which lie outside the scope of Black's work.

Lacking from the bibliographies of ER is a complete and annotated list of her newspaper column, "My Day." Future bibliographical projects also could include a continuation of Edens' effort to identify published versions of addresses and remarks by ER. Of additional use would be an annotated listing of her unpublished articles that are available as part of the Eleanor Roosevelt Papers at the Franklin D. Roosevelt Library.

John A. Edens

BILBO, THEODORE GILMORE (13 October 1877, Poplarville, MS–21 August 1947, New Orleans).

Theodore Bilbo, a U.S. Democratic senator known for racial demagoguery, was a sharp critic of Eleanor Roosevelt. He attended, but did not graduate from, Peabody College and Vanderbilt University. He taught in rural Mississippi schools and began a law practice before being elected in 1908 to the Mississippi Senate. His colorful political oratory, invective, and stance as a champion of poor white farmers and workers opposed to corporations and wealthy planters carried him to two terms as governor of Mississippi, the first of which (1916–1920) was characterized by a series of progressive reforms but the second (1928–1932) by charges of scandal and corruption. Nevertheless, he won election to the U.S. Senate in 1934.

As a senator, Bilbo was a consistent supporter of New Deal* legislative initiatives but became increasingly absorbed with racism. He fought against federal antilynching* legislation and anti–poll tax bills. He also attacked the Fair Employment Practices Commission, a wartime program to prevent hiring discrimination. These views brought Bilbo into direct confrontation with ER. In 1944 Bilbo proposed that she be sent to Liberia to rule over African Americans, whom he wished to deport with her.

When Harry S Truman* nominated ER in 1945 as a U.S. delegate to the United Nations,* Bilbo cast the only negative vote at her Senate confirmation. When reporters queried his actions, he responded that a book would be required to explain ER's unfitness for office. ER shared equally strong feelings for Bilbo. She told May Craig,* a journalist friend, that he probably would behave the same way as Germans who ran concentration camps if he had their power. Bilbo's career ended when Republicans challenged his seating in the eightieth Congress in 1947. Illness prevented him from fighting for his office.

SELECTED BIBLIOGRAPHY
Green, A. Wigfall. *The Man Bilbo*. 1963.
Lash, Joseph P. *Eleanor: The Years Alone*. 1972.
Luthin, Reinhard H. *American Demagogues: Twentieth Century*. 1954.
Morgan, Chester M. *Redneck Liberal: Theodore G. Bilbo and the New Deal*. 1985.

Nancy Beck Young

BIOGRAPHERS. Opinions about Eleanor Roosevelt varied greatly during her lifetime: she was simultaneously one of the most revered and despised women of her times. Somewhat similarly, her biographers have differed widely in their evaluations of her, although none has been as harsh as some of her contemporary critics.* Sixty years of her biographies and of New Deal* historiography reflect not only changing understandings of the woman herself but also profound changes in the practice of writing history—most notably, the major impact of women's history on the ways in which she is portrayed.

ER herself provided the first interpretation of her life in the initial volume of her autobiography,* *This Is My Story* (1937), depicting an orphaned girlhood and early marriage. It was followed by *This I Remember* (1949), which spanned the period from 1924 through the White House years, and *On My Own* (1958), which dealt with her life after the death of her husband, Franklin D. Roosevelt.* Revised and collected into one volume, *The Autobiography of Eleanor Roosevelt* (1961), these memoirs offered a self-deprecating account of her activities that shaped the work of her early biographers.

Written by journalists, rather than historians, the first book-length biographies of ER were published before her death in 1962. Ruby Black,* a reporter who covered ER at her press conferences,* published the first full-length biography, *Eleanor Roosevelt: A Biography* (1940). Black drew from her own observations, ER's public statements and writings, interviews both with ER and others, and *This Is My Story*, noting that while her biography was not an authorized volume, ER had been most generous in offering information for it. Like Black's book, Alfred Steinberg's *Mrs. R: The Life of Eleanor Roosevelt* (1958) did not include footnotes and was generally laudatory. Thus, Black concluded: "Her [ER's] hard-won courage gives courage to others—to 'the bewildered, the simple, and the voiceless.' Thousands upon thousands are not afraid because she learned not to fear" (R. Black, 315). Steinberg was somewhat more critical, writing that too often ER depended on her emotions rather than her reasoning, but nevertheless he concluded, "Despite these pinpricks, her unique position as the most renowned and admired woman in American history is assured. The like of Eleanor Roosevelt is not apt to appear again" (Steinberg, 371). Both biographers presented ER as a woman of conscience and compassion who had influenced FDR and played a central role in the development of New Deal policies.

Political historians writing in the 1950s and 1960s about FDR and the politics of the New Deal and World War II* generally attributed ER's importance to her position as FDR's wife. Biographers and historians like James MacGregor Burns in *Roosevelt: The Lion and the Fox, 1882–1940* (1956), Arthur M. Schlesinger Jr. in his three-volume *The Age of Roosevelt* (1957–1960), and William E. Leuchtenburg in *Franklin D. Roosevelt and the New Deal, 1932–1940* (1963) accepted ER's self-presentation of her role as the agitator in comparison to FDR the politician. In *This I Remember* ER had said very plainly: "He [FDR] might have been happier with a wife who was completely uncritical. That I was never able to be, and he had to find it in other people. Nevertheless, I think I sometimes acted as a spur, even though the spurring was not always wanted or welcome. I was one of those who served his purposes" (Roosevelt, *This I Remember*, 349).

This view of ER's influence has retained its potency and is reflected to some extent in Doris Kearns Goodwin's Pulitzer Prize–winning social history, *No Ordinary Time: Franklin and Eleanor Roosevelt: The Home Front in World War II* (1994). Through the use of voluminous details in her nostalgic, best-seller account, Goodwin presented ER as a key representative of humane values in FDR's administration. Other FDR biographers have subscribed to similar characterization of the Roosevelt political partnership. For example, Kenneth Davis in *FDR into the Storm: 1937–1940* (1993) referred to FDR and ER "as a team, complementary" with FDR as "team captain," while "a subordinate role was perforce accepted by her, if with considerable secret resentment" (Davis, 290).

The first full-length academic studies of ER to be published—both of which came out of doctoral dissertations that were completed before ER's papers were available to the public—developed a portrait of ER as a reformer in her own right. Tamara Hareven's *Eleanor Roosevelt: An American Conscience* and James Kearney's *Anna Eleanor Roosevelt: The Evolution of an American Reformer* were both published in 1968. These two books, while offering different interpretations of ER, marked an important turning point in the historical literature. Thereafter, the majority of academic biographers and historians discussed ER within the context of her own actions and evaluated her as a political and social reformer. Historians henceforth looked at ER as an independent force. The subsequent historiographical debates centered on what kind of reformer she was, what created her reforming zeal, and what she was like as an independent woman.

Hareven and Kearney both focused on her public life, with Hareven examining ER's social thought over her lifetime and finding in it tensions between the naive and the realistic. Hareven leaned heavily on the theoretical formulations of the social psychologist Abraham Maslow, who had constructed the concept of the self-actualizing person who could fully exploit his or her own talents, capacities, and potential. According to Maslow, ER achieved a graceful union between being a woman and a public figure. Whereas Ruby Black had described ER as a woman in whom there was from childhood "the compulsion to duty," who "steeled herself to do what she had to do" (R. Black, ix, x), Hareven, referring to Maslow, argued that ER did things because "they were natural to her" (Hareven, 278).

Kearney also painted ER as a reformer in her own right, but one with weaknesses as well as strengths. Concentrating on her career before the United States entered World War II, he concluded that ER was a warm and deeply sincere humanitarian who accomplished much that was positive, even though "she was not often responsible for cogent or workable solutions" and remained "essentially gullible and disturbingly ignorant." On the other hand, he emphasized her communication, "to an unprecedented degree," of concern for human suffering and found her at her best in calling attention to abuses (Kearney, 277, 278).

In 1971 Joseph P. Lash* published *Eleanor and Franklin: The Story of Their Relationship Based on Eleanor Roosevelt's Private Papers*. The biography was authorized by ER's literary executor and son, Franklin D. Roosevelt Jr.,* who gave Lash the first access to her extensive private papers. A close friend of ER, Lash presented a detailed and careful study of ER, covering both her personal and her public life. His book won both a Pulitzer Prize and a National Book Award and helped transform the public interpretation of ER.

Generally sympathetic toward ER as an independent woman who acted out of a politics of conscience, Lash disagreed with previous biographers in critical ways. He credited her independence not to her personality structure—as had Hareven and Black, albeit in different ways—but to her personal history. Drawing on her papers, Lash described her life as a chain of events touched with sorrow and challenge, beginning with an unhappy childhood, progressing to FDR's affair with Lucy Mercer (Rutherfurd*), and then moving through FDR's polio and her nurturing by Louis Howe* as a political figure in her own right. He detailed her development as a skilled participant in the political process from the

1920s on through the White House period to her years as a widow, as presented in his second volume, *Eleanor: The Years Alone* (1972).

Given the comprehensiveness of Lash's study, it is not surprising that for more than a decade, writers looking at ER used his work as a backdrop while concentrating on a specific topic or aspect of her life. Jason Berger, for instance, examined her thinking on foreign affairs from 1920 to her death in his *A New Deal for the World: Eleanor Roosevelt and American Foreign Policy* (1981).

By the early 1980s women's historians began to offer a broader context in which to examine ER—the women's social reform networks of the Progressive Era and beyond. Susan Ware's *Beyond Suffrage: Women in the New Deal* appeared in 1981 and Joan Hoff-Wilson and Marjorie Lightman's edited volume, *Without Precedent: The Life and Career of Eleanor Roosevelt*, in 1984. In *Without Precedent* historians like Ware, Elizabeth Israels Perry, and Lois Scharf all pointed to the importance of ER's involvement in the 1920s with the League of Women Voters,* the Women's Trade Union League,* the Women's City Club,* and the Women's Division of the New York state Democratic Committee, developing a context for ER's career apart from her husband's.

Unlike Lash, they emphasized her activities in social settlements* and with the National Consumers' League* before her marriage* in 1905 and argued that her activities during what ER had called her private interlude, the 1920s, should be seen as part of a larger political transformation, in which women altered the nature of American politics and society by networking with other women. From this perspective, politics was based to a greater degree on the interpersonal than on the ideological. Women rewarded other female political leaders, and they built a movement of political activism. This process, moreover, was part of a larger fusion of reform and party politics that served to explain the character of the Democratic Party* during the New Deal.

As women's historians called for the rethinking of political history, especially in terms of the relationship between the private or personal and the public or political, new studies of ER appeared that drew on previous work. J. William T. Youngs's *Eleanor Roosevelt: A Personal and Public Life* (1985) treated her achievement as a triumph over inner turmoil. Lois Scharf's *Eleanor Roosevelt: First Lady of American Liberalism* (1987) examined ER's private life as a "springboard" for her public career, giving voice to American liberalism (Scharf, 3). Taking a different approach, Maurine Beasley in *Eleanor Roosevelt and the Media: A Public Quest for Self-Fulfillment* (1987) argued that ER made herself the most influential woman of her times by skillfully using "the media to make her life stand out before the world" (Beasley, 2).

In *Without Precedent* William Chafe contended that "the interaction of her private and public roles" offered "testimony to one person's struggle to find individual fulfillment in the process of making the world a better place in which to live" (Hoff-Wilson and Lightman, 3). Carrying this concept considerably further in referring to ER in 1995, Chafe argued that "*not to explore* the personal is to distort and *misunderstand* the political" in "The Personal and Political: Two Case Studies," *U.S. History as Women's History*, edited by Linda K. Kerber, Alice Kessler-Harris, and Kathryn Kish Sklar (213).

Chafe's 1995 essay focused on topics that various historians discussed in the 1990s—the relationship between the personal and the political in terms of gender construction and sexuality. These topics have thrust the debate over ER's sexuality—and possible lesbianism—and the nature of her feminism into the limelight. The question of lesbianism first arose in 1980, when Doris Faber published *The Life of Lorena Hickok: E.R.'s Friend*, based on newly opened correspondence at the Roosevelt Library between ER and Lorena Hickok,* a journalist, who addressed each other in passionate terms.

In response, Joseph Lash published two collections of ER's correspondence, *Love, Eleanor: Eleanor Roosevelt and Her Friends* (1982) and *A World of Love: Eleanor Roosevelt and Her Friends, 1943–1962* (1984), arguing that there was nothing specifically sexual or unique in ER's letters to Hickok. Rodger Streitmatter countered this interpretation with *Empty without You: The Intimate Letters of Eleanor Roosevelt and Lorena Hickok* (1998), an edited collection of the correspondence. In 1998 Susan Ware in *Letter to the World: Seven Women Who Shaped the American Century* contended it may well be that ER was "bisexual" in the sense that "in her life-long quest for love and friendship, she drew no artificial boundaries between men and women" (Ware, 30).

The debate over the significance of ER as a political figure has hinged, in part, on the definition of feminism. In *Without Precedent* Lois Scharf quoted Ruby Black as saying in 1935 that ER "talks like a social worker and acts like a feminist" (Hoff-Wilson and Lightman, 226), reflecting the distinction between female social reformers identified with peace, workers' rights, and protective legislation and feminists who advocated the Equal Rights Amendment.* Scharf argued that because ER placed greater emphasis on social welfare than on the position of women, she was a reformer. Susan M. Hartmann, on the other hand, in "Eleanor Roosevelt and Women's Rights," published in *Eleanor Roosevelt: An American Journey*, edited by Jess Flemion and Colleen M. O'Connor (1987), emphasized the importance of ER's life as a role model for women and concluded that she was a feminist.

In 1992 Blanche Wiesen Cook, in the first of her multivolume biography, *Eleanor Roosevelt*, challenged prevailing interpretations of ER's career. Presenting ER as a passionate woman who insisted on "self-identity," Cook saw her as a figure whose "consummate power and courageous vision" had been brushed aside by previous biographers (Cook, 1:3). Cook argued that the roots of ER's independence lay not in an unhappy childhood and misery over her husband's unfaithfulness but in her close and supportive relationships with other women. According to Cook, the core of ER was formed during her adolescent years under her boarding school headmistress, Marie Souvestre,* who introduced her to the possibility of being "assertive, independent and bold" (Cook, 1:4). Her eventual independence thus became not an act of compensation for a failed marriage, as Lash and others had portrayed it, but the product of the women's world in which she had thrived in her youth. Another biographer, Betty Boyd Caroli, in *The Roosevelt Women* (1998) set ER in the context of strong women within her own family.

By the end of the 1990s ER had emerged in the historiography as a visionary and self-propelled leader. In Cook's second volume (1999), which carried ER's life through 1938, ER was pictured as a tireless advocate for New Deal liberalism, a skilled and shrewd fighter in Washington's political battles, and a woman who insisted on the right to private relationships, even though they were circumscribed by her official role as First Lady. Although Cook continued to show ER's association with women's networks, she delineated a shift on her part away from them to alliances with two other groups, African Americans and youth.* In both volumes Cook portrayed ER not simply as an influential voice for reform but as a powerful politician in her own right, not merely as a junior partner but as a full partner with FDR in political life.

In *Casting Her Own Shadow: Eleanor Roosevelt and the Shaping of Postwar Liberalism* (1996) Allida Black presented ER as "the consummate liberal power broker" and an "accomplished political insider" (A. Black, 3). Widowhood, for Allida Black's ER, was a period when she was "freed from the constraints of the White House" (A. Black, 2). While the book focused on ER's efforts to advance a liberal agenda in domestic politics, in her introduction, Black encouraged "scholars to follow Cook's lead and reconstruct the influence that ER had as a feminist within public and private associations and use ER as a prism through which to examine the issues of human rights,* containment, and nuclear disarmament" (A. Black, 3).

Over the past sixty years ER has come to be seen as an important American leader in her own right. But debates over the wellspring of her independence, the extent of her political power and impact, and the nature of her private life remain.

SELECTED BIBLIOGRAPHY
Edens, John A. *Eleanor Roosevelt: A Comprehensive Bibliography.* 1994.

Nancy Marie Robertson

BIRTH CONTROL. Eleanor Roosevelt became involved in the birth control movement in the 1920s at a time when other women of her social class found this a worthy cause. As chair of the legislative committee of the Women's City Club,* a New York organization that encouraged women to exercise political influence, she gained national publicity in 1928, when the club backed a proposal to permit physicians to distribute birth control information. Her picture appeared in newspapers in connection with a club debate and referendum on the issue, but the measure did not pass in the New York legislature. That same year she joined the board of directors of the American Birth Control League, although her involvement was minimal. In 1931, when she spoke at a testimonial dinner for Margaret Sanger, the nation's best-known birth control advocate, ER received unfavorable press attention from Sanger's opponents.

When Franklin D. Roosevelt* was elected president in 1932, ER was constrained from taking an active role in the birth control movement. Ambivalent about birth control personally and as a politician with a large urban Catholic and rural southern constituency, FDR avoided putting the issue on the political agenda. Birth control had no place on the New Deal* social agenda as part of either public health or welfare programs. FDR's advisers—like Harry Hopkins*—who previously had supported the movement severed their connections and refused to comment.

Not surprisingly, as editor in 1933 of a magazine called *Babies-Just Babies*,* ER made no mention of the subject. In 1935 she wrote George T. Bye, her new literary agent, "I am very sorry that I cannot write on birth control as long as my husband is President because I feel that as long as it offends the religious belief of a large group of citizens, I have no right to express my own opinion publicly" (Beasley, 78). When Ruby Black,* a reporter friend of ER, transmitted a letter from Sanger to the First Lady in 1934, stressing the need to provide birth control information in Puerto Rico, there was no official response. ER, however, sent money anonymously to a birth control clinic there (ER to Clarence Pickett,* 28 May 1937).

In 1940 ER took some tentative steps toward speaking out on birth control, telling reporters she did not oppose "planning of children" but would never impose her views on others (*New York Times*, 17 January 1940). In 1941 ER, acting at the request of Mary Lasker, a philanthropist funding a birth control project aimed at southern blacks, helped arrange White House meetings that brought about U.S. Public Health Service approval of some family-planning programs. She and Sanger met privately at both the White House and Hyde Park,* and ER sent a ten-dollar contribution to Planned Parenthood in November 1941 in response to a Sanger appeal. A few months later ER declined to accept an award for her birth control efforts, telling Lasker, "There is no use antagonizing people at this time" (Chesler, 390).

ER spoke favorably of family-planning methods (as long as they were not used to avoid having children) in her *Ladies' Home Journal** column in July 1944. For the most part, however, she took little notice of the birth control movement while she remained in the White House. Subsequently, she lent her name to international family-planning endeavors. In 1946 Sanger, who admired ER's personality and accepted the constraints under which she operated, hosted a reception in her honor when she spoke at the University of Arizona in Tucson.

SELECTED BIBLIOGRAPHY

Beasley, Maurine H. *Eleanor Roosevelt and the Media: A Public Quest for Self-Fulfillment.* 1987.

Chesler, Ellen. *Woman of Valor: Margaret Sanger and the Birth Control Movement in America.* 1992.

Eleanor Roosevelt Papers, Franklin D. Roosevelt Library, Hyde Park, NY.

Gordon, Linda. *Woman's Body, Woman's Right: A Social History of Birth Control in America.* 1976.

"Margaret Sanger and Eleanor Roosevelt—The Burden of Public Life." *Margaret Sanger Papers Project Newsletter* (Winter 1995, no. 11): 5–6.

McCann, Carole R. *Birth Control Politics in the United States 1916–1954.* 1994.

                                                                    Ann Mauger Colbert

BLACK, RUBY AURORA (14 September 1896, Thornton, TX–15 December 1957, Washington, DC).

Ruby Black, a feminist who was one of the most prominent women journalists of the 1930s, was devoted to Eleanor Roosevelt and wrote her first biography. Black's notable career, which showed her spunk and determination in spite of prejudice against women, received its greatest boost when the United Press (UP), which traditionally had refused to employ women, hired her in 1933 to cover ER as its first woman Washington correspondent. Not receiving the pay she thought she deserved, she left the UP in 1942, and her career began to drift, leading to hard times in later life.

Black spent her first ten years on an East Texas cotton farm and ranch, the youngest of eight children. Her father, George Washington Black, who was elected to one term in the state legislature and served as longtime mayor of Thornton, stimulated her early interest in politics. Working her way through the University of Texas by teaching in public schools, she graduated in 1921 with a Phi Beta Kappa key and the distinction of having been the first woman to serve as editor in chief of the *Daily Texan*. She also worked on her hometown newspaper, the *Thornton Hustler*.

Having been initiated into Theta Sigma Phi, an honorary journalism sorority, in 1921, she became editor of its magazine, *The Matrix*, and moved to Chicago as director of its employment agency. She kept *The Matrix* editorship until 1929, when she was elected national president of the sorority. While doing graduate work and teaching journalism at the University of Wisconsin in 1922, Black married Herbert Little, a reporter

Women reporters who covered Eleanor Roosevelt's trip to the Caribbean gather around her in Puerto Rico on 5 March 1934 (l. to r. Emma Bugbee, *New York Herald Tribune*, Dorothy Ducas, International News Service, Ruby Black, United Press, and Bess Furman, Associated Press). *Courtesy of Franklin D. Roosevelt Library*

for the United Press, but she refused to take his name. The couple moved to Missouri, where she was labor editor of the *St. Louis Times*. In the 1920s Black won a fight with the U.S. Department of State to have a passport issued in her maiden name.

A slight woman with the fashionable boyish bobbed hair of the 1920s, Black went to Washington in 1924, when the UP assigned Little to the capital. Encountering the newspaper employment bias against women in that era, she started her own news bureau in 1928. During the next twelve years her bureau, which had a staff of two to four reporters, provided political and governmental news to twenty daily newspapers in Wisconsin, Maine, Massachusetts, Iowa, Nebraska, Texas, New York, and Puerto Rico. Black also acted as managing editor of *Equal Rights*, the newspaper of the National Woman's Party, to which she belonged.

Employed part-time by the UP when it became known that ER intended to hold women-only press conferences,* Black first met ER just prior to the inauguration of Franklin D. Roosevelt* as president in 1933. Immediately drawn to the First Lady, Black took pride in covering her press conferences, trips, and other activities. The two established a personal relationship, with Black and Little visiting ER and FDR at Hyde Park,* New York, and ER going to Black's home in Alexandria, Virginia. ER invited Black's small daughter, Cornelia Jane, to a White House birthday party for her own granddaughter, Eleanor "Sisty" Dall, and honored Black's father at a luncheon there.

Accustomed to investigating congressional issues for her newspaper clients, Black did not hesitate to make occasional suggestions to ER regarding political matters and to pass on information she thought would be of value. A correspondent for *La Democracia*, Black, who was fluent in Spanish and an ally of Luis Muñoz-Marin, later elected governor, interested ER in attempting to improve conditions in Puerto Rico. Black helped arrange for, and accompanied ER on, a 1934 inspection trip there and to the Virgin Islands with Lorena Hickok* and three other reporters, Bess Furman,* Associated Press; Emma Bugbee,* *New York Herald Tribune*; and Dorothy Ducas, International News Service.

Black took issue with critics who had not covered ER's press conferences but who, nevertheless, charged that Black had lost her objectivity. Black was thought to be the main target of Dorothy Dunbar Bromley, a New York newspaperwoman who wrote in a magazine article that ER's press conference reporters were her "willing slaves" (Bromley, 134).

Instrumental in securing membership for ER in the Women's National Press Club,* Black was elected president of that group in 1939, but by that time Black was running into major financial difficulties. Finding it hard to collect from some of her newspaper clients, Black coedited a book, *Washington, Nerve-Center* (1939), for which ER wrote a foreword. Faced with a deteriorating marriage and the onset of epilepsy, believed to stem from a fall from a horse in 1938, Black staked her monetary hopes for the future on writing the first full-length biography of ER. Although this was not an authorized biography, Black was careful to check her material with ER and her secretary, Malvina Thompson* (Scheider), who exercised some oversight over the contents. Black also obtained an interview with FDR, who sidestepped her questions.

Black herself thought the strongest part of the book, *Eleanor Roosevelt: A Biography*, which appeared on ER's birthday, 11 October 1940, was the portion dealing with ER's role in the New Deal.* She credited the First Lady with numerous government initiatives, including programs to give surplus farm products to the jobless and to provide employment for women, white-collar workers, and youth.* The book, however, was not footnoted, and relatively few sources were cited. While the book brought her a national award from Theta Sigma Phi, it received mixed reviews and sold poorly, much to Black's disappointment.

ER mentioned the volume in her "My Day"* column of 24 October 1940, although she gave it faint praise: "I began to feel I was being introduced to someone I really did not know." But ER wrote Black that "you give me a feeling that as long as there is much that ought to be done, any of us who had any kind of capacity to be of use should keep our shoulder to the wheel. . . . If anything particularly useful is chalked up to me in the next few years, I think you should rightly feel that you had a part in urging me on. Of course, I do not object to any part of the book" (ER to RB, 13 November 1940). One knowledgeable reader, Joseph P. Lash,* ER's friend and later biographer, found the book shallow because Black did not understand the complexities of the Roosevelt family relationships, but both FDR and Hickok liked it. It pictured ER favorably as her husband's political partner.

Over the years Black sought ER's help in obtaining employment for herself and her husband. In 1938 Little left the Scripps-Howard Newspaper Alliance, where he had been employed for six years, to become a regional director for the New Deal's National Youth Administration.* Black withdrew from her faltering bureau operation in 1940, although she continued covering ER for the UP for two more years. In 1941 she began part-time work as an editor-writer for the federal Office of the Coordinator of Inter-American Affairs, headed by Nelson Rockefeller, taking a full-time public information job there the following year. In that role she attended ER's press conferences, although she could not ask questions as a government employee, and wrote about ER for a Latin American audience.

Black's devotion to ER never abated, even though their relationship became increasingly distant after ER left the White House. Suffering from alcoholism as well as epilepsy, Black left her job in 1947, two years after separating from Little, from whom she was divorced in 1955. That same year *The Matrix* paid homage to her career. In a four-paragraph tribute, ER wrote that Black was "one of the best of the American women journalists," had been instrumental in creating "better understanding" between the United States and Latin America,* and "will always be remembered as one of the women who helped gain recognition for women in the field of journalism" ("The Thornton Hustler," 12).

Black died as the result of a fire at her apartment believed to have been started by a burning cigarette. In her obituary on 16 December 1957, the *Washington Post* called her "a bright star of Washington journalism for many years." At Black's request her ashes were scattered in Puerto Rico.

SELECTED BIBLIOGRAPHY

Beasley, Maurine. *Eleanor Roosevelt and the Media: A Public Quest for Self-Fulfillment.* 1987.

Black, Ruby. *Eleanor Roosevelt.* 1940.

Bromley, Dorothy Dunbar. "The Future of Eleanor Roosevelt." *Harper's Magazine* 180 (January 1940): 129–39.

Kelly, Eugene A. "Distorting the News." *American Mercury* (March 1935): 307–18.

Ruby Black Papers, Manuscript Division, Library of Congress, Washington, DC.

"The Thornton Hustler." *The Matrix* (March 1955): 11–16, 25–26.

Ann Cottrell Free

BOK PEACE PRIZE. In 1923 and 1924 Eleanor Roosevelt helped organize and promote the Bok Peace Prize competition. The prize, named after its founder, Edward Bok, was designed to energize what its namesake saw as a flagging and unsuccessful peace movement.* That ER participated in this project underscored her commitment to world peace, a commitment that remained with her for the rest of her life. ER's involvement with the Bok prize, in addition, represented her earliest encounters with the harsh and critical attention of the national political spotlight.

Edward Bok, a Philadelphia publicist who previously edited the *Ladies' Home Journal,** proposed a competition for "the best practicable plan by which the United States may cooperate with other nations to achieve and preserve the peace of the world" (Lash, 282). The winner could receive $100,000, half to go to the winner on selection of the plan and the other half to be given if the plan was accepted by the U.S. Senate or endorsed by a large percentage of the U.S. population. With its large monetary award and timely acknowledgment of a leading issue of the day (the hope for world peace), the competition earned front-page coverage in major newspapers and was the lead story in the *New York Times* on 2 July 1923. Bok asked Esther Lape,* a college professor and publicist with an interest in international affairs, to direct the contest. Lape agreed, but only when assured that she could invite her close friends, ER and Narcissa Vanderlip,* to work with her. The three had worked together in the League of Women Voters* in New York since 1920.

The women became the leading members of the Bok prize policy committee and were influential in naming a bipartisan Jury of Award consisting of prominent Americans to select the winner. While her duties were largely organizational, ER also promoted the prize by writing an article on it for the October 1923 *Ladies' Home Journal.* Over 22,000 entries, including one from Franklin D. Roosevelt,* poured in to the policy committee. After considerable winnowing by ER and Lape, on 7 January 1924, the jury selected a proposal by Charles Levermore, a former president of Adelphi College, which called for the United States to join the

World Court* and cooperate with, but not hold membership in, the League of Nations.*

The announcement of the winning entry produced a storm of criticism, much of it from isolationists, who feared that the Levermore plan would lead to American membership in the league. Senator James Reed (D-MO) launched an investigation by a Senate Special Committee on Propaganda, charging that the competition had attempted improperly to influence congressional action. Bok and Lape (the latter accompanied by ER) defended themselves so effectively at the Senate hearings that Reed quietly dropped his inquiry.

The excitement produced by the Bok prize soon dissipated because of a lack of public interest in both the peace movement and Levermore's winning entry, the refusal of the Senate to consider the winning plan, the opposition of policymakers to "democratic diplomacy," and the burgeoning Teapot Dome scandal of the Coolidge administration (De Benedetti, 246). ER's participation, although largely limited to administrative duties, illustrated her belief in the peace movement. Her appearance with Lape at the Senate committee hearings, more importantly, provided her with a preview of the turbulent political world she would fully enter in the 1930s.

SELECTED BIBLIOGRAPHY
Cook, Blanche Wiesen. *Eleanor Roosevelt*. Vol. 1. 1992.
De Benedetti, Charles. "American Peace Award of 1924." *The Pennsylvania Magazine of History and Biography* 98 (April 1974):224–49.
Lash, Joseph. *Eleanor and Franklin*. 1971.
Roosevelt, Eleanor. "The American Peace Award." *The Ladies' Home Journal* 40 (October 1923): 54.
Scharf, Lois. *Eleanor Roosevelt: First Lady of American Liberalism*. 1987.
Steinberg, Salme. *Reformer in the Marketplace: Edward W. Bok and The Ladies Home Journal*. 1979.

                                                             Caryn Neumann

BOOKS. Eleanor Roosevelt was an accomplished communicator, and books were one of her foremost methods of reaching an audience. Well known to her contemporaries through her newspaper columns, magazine articles, broadcasts, and speeches,* ER also wrote two dozen books that gained widespread attention, ranging from her autobiography,* to political commentary, women's advice, and children's fiction. These books stand today as an important source for those interested in understanding ER and the world in which she lived.

ER grew up when the book publishing world was rapidly expanding and, with it, the range of books available to the ordinary reader. As a young girl she relished reading. At Allenswood, her English boarding school, ER enjoyed the evenings when Mlle. Marie Souvestre,* the headmistress, invited a select few of her students for an evening of literature. "She had a great gift for reading aloud," ER recalled, "and she read to us, always in French, poems, plays and stories" (Roosevelt, 23). As an adult, ER loved to share her world of books with others by reading aloud, a widespread nineteenth-century practice that she continued throughout her life,

In her later years, for example, at Christmastime ER read aloud to her family and friends from Charles Dickens' *A Christmas Carol*. In the 1950s she read this same story, seated in the center of the Trusteeship Council chamber, to the Secretariat staff at the United Nations.* During summer picnics at her Val-Kill* cottage, troubled boys from the nearby Wiltwyck School* heard her read Rudyard Kipling's "How the Elephant Got His Trunk." She also made monthly visits to the women's detention center in New York City to read to the inmates.

It seems reasonable, therefore, to assume that ER's love for books motivated her to write them as part of her career and that her enjoyment of reading lay behind her belief in the importance of the written word. Her books presented what she was willing to share of her life, offered counsel to others, and gave her views on democracy and global affairs based on her extensive travels* and her experiences at the United Nations. They show the way she wanted others to see her—how she fashioned herself in the public imagination—and her relationship to the momentous events of her time. Their hallmark is a personal quality that enabled individuals to identify with her (or with the ER she created in her books), despite the differences in her experience and theirs.

ER's interest in writing for youth began with fiction. One of her early books, *A Trip to Washington with Bobby and Betty* (1935), told the imaginary story of a visit to the nation's capital—highlighted by lunch with the president. Five years later she published *Christmas: A Story* (1940). Written when Europe was plunged into the darkness of World War II,* the story took place in the Netherlands* during the Nazi occupation and told of a young girl's faith and refusal to allow evil to influence her. Along with ER's accounts of Christmas at Hyde Park* and Christmas at the White House, it was reissued posthumously in *Eleanor Roosevelt's Christmas Book* (1963). The story was republished in 1986 in a format designed to appeal to adults as well as children.

For many years ER served on the editorial board of the Junior Literary Guild, a book club for young readers, helping choose monthly selections for teenage girls and reviewing manuscripts, often during airplane travel. In 1950 she and Helen Ferris, former editor in chief of the book club, coauthored *Partners: The United Nations and Youth* for the guild. A decade later they collaborated again on *Your Teens and Mine* (1961), in which ER described her own difficulties growing up in response to letters from club members seeking her advice. *Your Teens and Mine* dealt with themes repeated throughout her work: developing self-confidence, taking an active role in citizenship, understanding the importance of family life, pursuing learning as a lifelong objective, and valuing books for both education and entertainment.

ER's most lasting books, however, were nonfiction works for adults, dominated by autobiography and written in a conversational style. Her first book was an edited volume of the correspondence of her father, Elliott Roosevelt,* *Hunting Big Game in the Eighties: The Letters of Elliott Roosevelt, Sportsman* (1932). It included his letters to her as a small child and expressed her love for him. Her most enduring work was her three-volume autobiography: *This Is My Story* (1937), *This I Remember* (1949), and *On My Own* (1958), all of which were condensed into the single-volume *Autobiography of Eleanor Roosevelt* (1961).

This Is My Story guided the reader through ER's growing-up years, her 1905 marriage to Franklin D. Roosevelt,* his suffering from polio, and her political activities on his behalf. This section of the trilogy, which ended in 1924, provided insight into her personal life, but it also was a detailed documentary of privileged New York society in the late 1800s and first part of the twentieth century. *This I Remember* spanned the years from the 1920s to FDR's death in 1945. Much of it was an account of political life: FDR's governorship and four presidential terms spanning the Great Depression* and World War II, as seen from ER's unique vantage point.

On My Own showed a change in approach as well as subject matter. After 1945, ER wrote about her own life as an individual, her United Nations service, her worldwide travels, and what she thought should be done about major issues of the day. The final section of the *Autobiography* brought the reader through 1960 and the election of President John F. Kennedy.* It ended with ER's emphasizing the need for humanitarian work throughout the world.

ER also wrote books of political commentary and personal advice. While in the White House, she published *It's Up to the Women* (1933), *This Troubled World* (1938), and *The Moral Basis of Democracy* (1940). These addressed the concerns of citizens, particularly women, as they struggled, first, to survive the Great Depression and, second, to comprehend the threat of the global war exploding in Asia* and Europe. Presenting involved issues in terms that could be easily understood, they discussed the relationship between individual actions and moral values in times of crisis.

In the 1950s she shared insights from her extensive travel. In 1952 she visited India* at the invitation of Prime Minister Jawaharlal Nehru, but her itinerary also included Lebanon, Syria, Jordan, Israel,* Pakistan, and the Philippines. In *India and the Awakening East* (1953), she informed readers about the poverty, politics, economies, and cultures of parts of the world with which many Americans were not familiar at that time.

The next year ER coauthored *Ladies of Courage* (1954) with her friend, Lorena A. Hickok.* The book profiled women in public life who stood up for what they believed—from Elizabeth Cady Stanton, who advocated women's voting rights in 1848, to Mary Lord, the Republican who was appointed to take ER's place on the United Nations* Human Rights Commission in 1953. It was aimed at inspiring other women to follow their examples.

Another collaborative effort was a booklet, simply titled *The United Nations* (1955), written by Jean S. Picker and edited by ER. An illustrated primer on how the United Nations worked, it was updated several times, with the last revision in 1971. She also coauthored *UN: Today and Tomorrow* (1953) with William DeWitt.

You Learn by Living (1960) presented everyday wisdom accrued during her eventful life. It covered various aspects of living, but one theme predominated: be useful to others. In two previous books, *If You Ask Me* (1946) and *It Seems to Me* (1954), she had collected her answers to a wide range of questions on both her private life and public issues. These originally had appeared in her monthly columns that ran, first, in the *Ladies' Home Journal** and then in *McCall's** magazine. A third book, *The Wisdom of Eleanor Roosevelt* (1962), contained selections from her *McCall's* columns. Her advice on handling social situations was featured in *Eleanor Roosevelt's Book of Common Sense Etiquette* (1962), written with Robert Ballou.

Her last book, *Tomorrow Is Now* (1963), published posthumously, addressed the dangers and challenges of world conditions during the Cold War.* In particular, she wanted young people to understand U.S. history and use it as a foundation for overcoming obstacles facing democracies. In this book ER reaffirmed her faith in America and urged long-range planning and foresight in preparing for the future.

In her early books (other than children's fiction) ER focused on reporting and recording the events of her lifetime as she saw them, but in later volumes she became teacher, adviser, and advocate. Although most critics* looked kindly on her work, some accused her of being naive and platitudinous. Books, nevertheless, were a significant medium through which she made her own life experiences accessible and meaningful to others.

SELECTED BIBLIOGRAPHY

Edens, John A. *Eleanor Roosevelt: A Comprehensive Bibliography*. 1994.
Roosevelt, Eleanor. *The Autobiography of Eleanor Roosevelt*. 1961.
Tebbel, John. *Between Covers: The Rise and Transformation of Book Publishing in America*. 1987.

BOWLES, CHESTER (5 April 1901, Springfield, MA–25 May 1986, Essex, CT).

After a successful career in advertising, Bowles served as director of the Office of Price Administration (1943–1946), governor of Connecticut (1949–1951), ambassador to India* (1951–1953, 1963–1969), and under secretary of state (1961). From his first political moves in the 1930s until her death, he collaborated with Eleanor Roosevelt on political and diplomatic issues. As World War II* drew to a close, she supported his efforts to persuade Presidents Franklin D. Roosevelt* and Harry S Truman* to continue price and wage controls and to promote full employment. With other New Dealers, she and Bowles searched in vain for viable alternatives to Truman in 1948 and helped found Americans for Democratic Action.*

After Truman appointed him ambassador to India, Bowles championed the use of economic aid in lieu of military aid to cement Cold War* alliances in the Third World. In 1952 he orchestrated a month-long tour of India for ER. Though both Bowles and ER nurtured goodwill among the peoples of the developing world, neither could elicit much support in Washington for capitalizing on that goodwill. Bowles' opportunity to advocate for their vision seemed to come when President John F. Kennedy* appointed him undersecretary of state in 1961. But Kennedy rarely followed Bowles' advice to eschew covert actions, like the disastrous Bay of Pigs invasion of Cuba, which ER criticized, and military interventions in Vietnam.

SELECTED BIBLIOGRAPHY

Bowles, Chester. *Promises to Keep: My Years in Public Life 1941–1969*. 1971.
Schaffer, Howard B. *Chester Bowles: New Dealer in the Cold War*. 1993.

Robert W. Morrow

BUGBEE, EMMA (13 May 1888, Shippensburg, PA–6 October 1981, Warwick, RI).

Emma Bugbee, one of the relatively few women to make a name for herself in New York City journalism in the early twentieth century, frequently covered Eleanor Roosevelt and became a close friend. The daughter of high school teachers, Bugbee was drawn to journalism as campus correspondent for the *New York Tribune* while attending Barnard College in New York City. After graduation in 1909, she taught Greek for a year at the high school she had attended in Methuen, Massachusetts. Unhappy as a teacher, she eagerly accepted employment as a summer replacement on the *Tribune* in 1910.

The temporary job turned into a reporting career that continued for a record fifty-five years on the *Tribune*, which became the *Herald Tribune* after a 1924 merger. For decades Bugbee, a warm, motherly individual, was the token woman on the newspaper's general assignment staff, generally given stories on women's activities. One of her first major assignments was marching through snow for three weeks in 1911 with a group of suffragists who were hiking from New York to Albany.

From the 1930s on, Bugbee's career became identified with her coverage of ER. Assigned to go to Washington for a few days to help with inaugural coverage of Franklin D. Roosevelt* in 1933, Bugbee was present for the first of ER's press conferences* for women only. She ended up remaining in Washington for four months to write additional stories on ER after the First Lady invited her to lunch at the White House. She went along, for example, when Amelia Earhart* gave ER a night ride in an airplane. In 1934 Bugbee was one of the small group of women reporters who accompanied ER and Lorena Hickok* on an inspection trip of conditions in Puerto Rico and the Virgin Islands. In following years she covered ER on numerous occasions in Washington and New York.

An admirer of ER who occasionally was invited to stay overnight at the White House, Bugbee pictured her as committed to worthy causes. Since the *Herald Tribune* was staunchly Republican, this gave the Roosevelt administration a positive image in a newspaper that opposed it politically. Along with Bess Furman,* Ruby Black,* and May Craig,* Bugbee was among the handful of reporters who formed an inner circle in ER's press corps and socialized with her at small gatherings.

A feminist who worked to open journalism to other women, Bugbee was a founder in 1922 of the Newspaper Women's Club of New York.* She served three terms as its president and involved ER in its activities. She also wrote a series of five books for girls revolving around the career of a fictional heroine, Peggy, who achieved success as a newspaper reporter. One book, *Peggy Covers Washington* (1937), featured ER as a gracious First Lady.

Bugbee's last story for the *Herald Tribune* ran on 24 April 1966, the last day the newspaper was published before merging into a joint operation that lasted only eight months. The story described dedication of a memorial bench to ER at the United Nations.* Showing the way the careers of the two women had been linked together, the newspaper ran a picture of Bugbee seated on the bench along with a story on her retirement the previous day. The headline was "A Parting Salute to a Great Lady."

SELECTED BIBLIOGRAPHY
Beasley, Maurine H. *Eleanor Roosevelt and the Media.* 1987.
Collins, Jean. *She Was There: Stories of Pioneering Women Journalists.* 1980.
Furman, Bess. *Washington By-line.* 1949.
Kluger, Richard. *The Paper: The Life and Death of the New York Herald Tribune.* 1986.
Ross, Ishbel. *Ladies of the Press.* 1936.

BUNDLES FOR BRITAIN. By 1940 Eleanor Roosevelt had begun indirectly to support the badly struggling British war effort. One means she employed to effect this end was to assist a private, largely female war relief group, Bundles for Britain. She did this while also bolstering the work of Bundles' main rival, the British War Relief Society, as well as supporting the American Red Cross.*

Bundles for Britain was started in January 1940 by a New York society matron, Natalie Wales Latham. Born in Massachusetts in 1909, Latham was young and energetic and determined to make her organization a national success. She began with a single storefront in New York City where knitted goods—socks, gloves, hats, sweaters, and scarves—were made and shipped to Britain. Within sixteen months Latham expanded Bundles into an organization with 975 branches and almost a million contributors, and by the spring of 1941 it had delivered 40,000 sleeveless sweaters, 10,000 sweaters with sleeves, 30,000 scarves, 18,000 pairs of seaboot stockings, 50,000 pairs of socks, and 8,000 caps. By 1941, moreover, Bundles had also shipped ambulances, surgical instruments, medicines, cots, blankets, field-kitchen units, and operating tables, along with used clothing of all sorts. The total value of the goods shipped reached $1,500,000; another $1 million was raised in cash.

Bundles was part of a larger impulse on the part of Americans to send aid to war-torn nations abroad, much of which was dictated by ties of kinship or sentiment. Latham herself had first visited England in 1927 and traced her family tree back to seventeenth-century Britain. As a child she lived in Bermuda for a year, where she attended an English school and developed what she described as a passion for England. "I felt that England was utterly familiar," she recounted, describing her first visit there in 1927. "I didn't have this feeling about the other countries [of Western Europe]" (Hellman, 22).

Latham's decision, however, was not simply a personal one. During the years of American neutrality, 1939–1941, the chief focus of American overseas philanthropy was Great Britain. In part, this was dictated by economic, diplomatic, and cultural ties between the two nations, reinforced by a widely shared admiration for British bravery during these years; but the Roosevelt administration's Lend-Lease program also gave British war relief an official imprimatur. Donations to Britain generally and to Bundles specifically provided an easy way for Americans to express sympathy for Britain, without the United States entering World War II.*

For ER, there were advantages and disadvantages to working with Bundles. It was a way for her to express her concern for Britain both indirectly and within the limits of U.S. foreign policy. But it was also an arena in which she felt she had to guard against the overuse of her name. She was so urgently wooed by so many wartime relief organizations that she constantly walked a thin line between lending support and not appearing overcommitted to any single group. After her resignation from the Office of Civilian Defense,* she noted in her "My Day"* column on

23 February 1942 that both the *New York Times* and the *New York Herald Tribune* had pointed out "that the wife of any president cannot be looked upon as an individual." Rather, she "must always carry the reflection of influence or power." Sadly, she wrote, she had found that this was true (Chadakoff, 241).

While conceding this publicly in 1942, ER had long been sensitive to the use of her name. She lent her support—but only within limits. She wrote about Bundles in "My Day." She sponsored benefits, contributed money, and donated clothes. In 1940 she did a broadcast on WMCA, a New York radio station, in which she asked Americans to contribute to Bundles. But her support had its boundaries. She agreed to be a patron of a benefit but refused to attend. She would not pose for a publicity photo for the Washington, D.C., Bundles chapter. She refused to become a national sponsor for the Bundles anniversary celebration in January 1941. She made sure that she also worked with Bundles' main rival, the British War Relief Society, so that she would not appear to favor one relief organization over the other.

After the United States entered the war, the First Lady's support for Bundles came to a logical end. In 1942 she donated clothes but did not publicly endorse the organization. It was no longer important to help England through voluntary, nongovernmental organizations, and ER turned her attention to the home front and winning the war.

SELECTED BIBLIOGRAPHY

Chadakoff, Rochelle, ed. *Eleanor Roosevelt's My Day*. Vol. 1. 1989.

Cull, Nicholas John. *Selling War*. 1995.

Curti, Merle. *American Philanthropy Abroad*. 1963.

Dimitrova, Anelia K. "Constructing the Image: Gender in Bundles for Britain's Public Relations Campaign, 1940–1942." Ph.D. dissertation. University of Missouri, Columbia. 1996.

Hellman, Geoffrey. "Profiles: Active Sparkler." *New Yorker* (19 April 1941): 21–26.

Anelia K. Dimitrova

C

CAMPOBELLO. Campobello, the remote Canadian island in New Brunswick off the Maine coast, was a second home to Franklin D. Roosevelt* during the first part of his life, a place where he spent leisurely summers with his parents and, after marriage to Eleanor Roosevelt, many summer vacations with his own young family. It eventually came to occupy a special place in ER's heart.

Campobello also was indelibly associated with FDR as the place where he came down with polio in 1921. FDR's crippling illness, which so tested and tempered his character, became a turning point for ER, forcing her to develop latent strengths as she ministered to his needs. Admiring his courage, she nurtured his stubborn determination not to become an invalid as she did her best to provide nursing care.

FDR first introduced the island's charms to ER during their courtship, when she visited briefly in the summer of 1903 and went for a longer stay in August 1904—all under the watchful gaze of Sara Delano Roosevelt,* her future mother-in-law.

For the first four summers after her marriage in 1905, ER's visits to Campobello meant living under the same roof with her mother-in-law, who took complete charge of family affairs. Then, in 1909 a neighbor, Mrs. Hartman Kuhn, who had grown fond of the young couple, left a will stating that Sara could buy her thirty-four-room cottage for $5,000, if she would give it to FDR and ER. The house, now the centerpiece of the Roosevelt Campobello International Park, was the answer to ER's prayers for a home of her own, and she quickly and joyously rearranged all the furniture in every room.

FDR returned to Campobello only three times after the polio attack, but ER went there much more often. She returned to Campobello four summers later in 1925, having taught herself to drive the old family

Eleanor Roosevelt gets ready to stargaze at Campobello in 1920 with four of her five children—l. to r. Elliott, John, Franklin D. Roosevelt Jr., and Anna, accompanied by the family dog, Chief. *Courtesy of Franklin D. Roosevelt Library*

Buick. Her entourage included her sons, Franklin Jr.* and John,* two other youngsters, and her friends, Nancy Cook* and Marion Dickerman.*

In later years her visitors ranged from leaders in trade union and social causes to reporters and notables like Justice Felix Frankfurter and poet Archibald MacLeish. In 1941 and 1942 she hosted International Student Service gatherings for youth* leaders at the Roosevelt cottage. She last visited the island just a few weeks before she died in 1962 when the FDR Memorial Bridge linking the island with Lubec, Maine, was dedicated. A bronze plaque, unveiled at a centennial program at the park in her honor in 1984, is a paean to her love of the island, its scents, sunsets, and silent ambience.

SELECTED BIBLIOGRAPHY

Lash, Joseph P. *Eleanor and Franklin.* 1971.
Muskie, Stephen O. *Campobello: Roosevelt's Beloved Island.* 1982.
Nowlan, Alden. *Campobello: The Outer Island.* 1975.

Donald R. Larrabee

CARTOONS. Eleanor Roosevelt's large frame and prominent teeth, combined with her precedent-breaking activity as First Lady, presented an irresistible target to the nation's cartoonists. Although some were hostile, others celebrated ER's legendary stamina and efforts to do good. After her death in 1962, Bill Maudlin drew a cartoon showing three awed cherubs looking down from their clouds at an approaching angel. "It's her," one said, and viewers had no doubt who was meant—Eleanor Roosevelt (*St. Louis Post-Dispatch*, 13 November 1962). Cartoonists had helped make her the best-known woman of her age.

The cartoons in which ER appeared as First Lady from 1933 until 1945 generally fell into three categories—those dealing with her peripatetic involvement in social issues, her journalistic writings and meetings with the Washington women's press corps, and her liberated views of the role of women. While examples of outright male bias can be found, her portrayals generally depended more on the political ideology of the publications in which they appeared than on sexism per se.

Examples of cartoons that focused good-humoredly on her extensive travels* included Paul Carroth's drawing of a repeatedly forwarded letter addressed to "Mrs. Franklin D. Roosevelt" (Flemion and O'Connor, 186) and a Lariar drawing of a man studying a globe with the caption, "The way I figure it, Eleanor still has F.D.R. beat by some 14,716 miles" (*Philadelphia Evening Post*, 1 April 1943). One of the best known, by John Knott, showed ER offering a lift to "the Forgotten Woman" while driving down a road in the midst of the Great Depression* (*Dallas Morning News*, 22 November 1933).

Other cartoons displayed the hostility of many newspapers toward the Roosevelt administration. Her traveling in spite of gas rationing for civilians during World War II* was targeted by Joseph Parrish, a cartoonist for the arch Republican *Chicago Tribune*, whose work also appeared in the *Washington Times-Herald*. Parrish showed ER waving cheerfully from a gas-guzzling plane flying above a motorist being ordered home by an authority figure yelling, "Now where does Hitler's little helper think he's goin'? Git that junk heap back where it belongs. Dontcha know there's no tellin' when or where she's liable to light?!!" (*Washington Times-Herald*, 15 September 1943). Another cartoon took a crack at ineffective military planning. It pictured ER suddenly appearing in Australia before astounded troops who had been waiting for long-promised military reinforcements (*Chattanooga News-Free Press*, 19 September 1943).

More frequently, the travel cartoons depicted her gumption or registered the surprise of various groups of Americans as she appeared in their locales. Karl Kneght showed her visiting an ordinary Indiana home (*Evansville Courier*, 13 November 1937). Robert Day drew two men deep in a coal mine above the often-quoted caption, "For gosh sakes, here comes Mrs. Roosevelt" (*New Yorker*, 3 June 1933).

Mrs. Roosevelt's syndicated newspaper column, "My Day,"* was a frequent subject for cartoonists who ridiculed it as being filled with trivia or domestic duties not worth reporting. Richard Decker showed a United Features Syndicate staffer reporting to his editor, "It's Mrs. Roosevelt calling from Washington. She says nothing happened yesterday" (Flemion and O'Connor, 192). Women reporters who covered her press conferences* were pictured as silly or bored children by Clifford Berryman (*Washington Evening Star*, 19 March 1934).

On the other hand, Jacob Burck portrayed ER as a true journalist, typing "My Day" in bed while wishing she could wheedle information from her husband, Franklin D. Roosevelt,* on whether he intended to seek a third term as president (*Chicago Times*, 12 May 1940). This cartoon was ER's personal favorite. Answering a reader's question in her *Ladies' Home Journal* column, "If You Ask Me," she wrote: "The humorous drawing which amused me most is the cartoon of me sitting up in bed with a typewriter on my knees, a picture of my husband hanging on the wall above. I am looking very thoughtful and saying, 'But it would make such a nice scoop if you'd only tell me, Franklin' " (Roosevelt, 106).

In contrast, her opinions that women should be included in universal military training and that housewives should have regular hours and regular pay like other workers elicited traditional sexist imagery. For example, John Morris drew a comic strip showing an apron-clad husband with a dish towel saying, "I'm sure I never said anything about a pension" as his wife sits with her feet on a footstool and her hands folded (*Jersey City Journal*, 15 May 1937). Two days later, under the title "Mrs. Roosevelt Says Wives Should Be Paid for Housework," he pictured a stereotypical wife threatening her husband with a rolling pin as she demands her wages (*Newark News*, 17 May 1937). On the universal military training issue, ER was shown in a cartoon as a befuddled schoolteacher reading from a book, "And we shall let the little girls play too" (*New York Daily News*, 1 September 1944).

After leaving the White House, ER appeared less frequently in cartoons, although her activities still were celebrated in political drawings. As a U.S. delegate to the United Nations* (UN) and then as a private citizen working to advance the UN, she was sometimes pictured as the embodiment of the American spirit. With the United Nations in the background, she was depicted by Alexander as watering a sapling labeled Human Rights Commission (Flemion and O'Connor, 206). A well-known cartoon by Herbert Block ("Herblock") of the *Washington Post* celebrated ER's seventieth birthday in 1954 by showing a little immigrant girl and her mother looking at the Statue of Liberty and the girl commenting, "I know. It's Mrs. Roosevelt" (Lash, 173).

Even her death did not mean escape from the cartoonist's pen. A 1964 Gladys Parker cartoon showed two country bumpkins sitting on a stoop sharing the opinion, "We've Had a Long Hard Row . . . from Eleanor to Lady-Bird" (*Washington Post*, 23 May 1964). In 1996 ER again appeared in political cartoons after news accounts related that First Lady Hillary Rodham Clinton used imaginary conversations with ER as a psychological exercise to deal with the pressures of her White House role. That year she also appeared in a cartoon calmly stirring her tea as "the Spirit of '96" (*New Yorker*, 21 October 1996). It is unlikely the cartoonists of the future will let her spirit rest, as they find ER an instantly recognizable image for both humanitarian service and other First Ladies* who defy stereotypes.

SELECTED BIBLIOGRAPHY

Basil O'Conner Papers, Franklin D. Roosevelt Library, Hyde Park, NY.
Flemion, Jess, and Colleen O'Connor. "The Unorthodox First Lady Meets the Political Cartoonists." In Jess Flemion and Colleen O'Connor, eds., *Eleanor Roosevelt: An American Journey*. 1987.
Hess, Stephen, and Milton Kaplan. *The Ungentlemanly Art: A History of American Political Cartoons*. 1968.
Lash, Joseph P. *"Life Was Meant to Be Lived."* 1984.
Roosevelt, Eleanor. *If You Ask Me*. 1946.

Anna R. Paddon

CATHOLIC CHURCH. See SPELLMAN, FRANCIS JOSEPH.

CATT, CARRIE CHAPMAN (9 January 1859, Ripon, WI–9 March 1947, New Rochelle, NY).

Carrie Chapman Catt and Eleanor Roosevelt maintained a long-term friendship built on mutual admiration and respect for each other's tireless efforts for humanitarian causes. An activist, organizer, administrator, lobbyist, and speaker for woman suffrage and pacifism, Catt help inspire ER's work for peace. Catt was graduated first in her class from Iowa State University in 1880 and worked as an educator and journalist before joining the Iowa Woman Suffrage Association in 1885. Her skills and dedication were key factors in the success of the woman suffrage movement.

Succeeding Susan B. Anthony in 1900 as president of the National American Woman Suffrage Association (NAWSA), she shifted the focus of the organization to political action. Although the ill health of her husband, George Catt, a well-to-do structural engineer, led to her resignation in 1904, that same year she was elected president of the International Woman Suffrage Alliance. She presided over its conferences in various European capitals until stepping down in 1923. Resuming the presidency of NAWSA in 1915, Catt led the successful campaign that culminated with the proclamation on 26 August 1920 of the woman suffrage amendment as part of the U.S. Constitution.

To help prepare women to take advantage of their new rights, she called in 1919 for the establishment of the League of Women Voters*

(LWV). She looked to younger women to lead the new organization when it was organized a year later and shifted her focus increasingly to international and peace issues. In 1915 Catt and Jane Addams* had organized the Woman's Peace Party in hopes of working with European women to find a way to end World War I.

In 1921 ER attended the national convention of the LWV in Cleveland and was impressed by Catt's dramatic appeal for a women's crusade to put an end to war. In 1925 ER was present in Washington, D.C., at the first conference on the Cause and Cure of War, a coalition of women's organizations including the LWV, the General Federation of Women's Clubs, and the Women's Trade Union League.* At the convention ER spoke from the floor on the necessity to outlaw war and the need for a World Court.* Showing her recognition of ER's potential for leadership, Catt added her in 1926 to the board of the Leslie Suffrage Commission, the group that oversaw use of a substantial bequest from Mrs. Frank Leslie (Miriam Squires) to advance the cause of woman's rights.

Supporting Catt, in turn, ER in the July 1927 issue of the *Women's Democratic News** urged readers to circulate and discuss Catt's article, "An Open Letter to the D.A.R." Published in the *Woman Citizen*, a magazine that Catt had set up with Leslie funds, Catt's article criticized the Daughters of the American Revolution for applying a communist label to women's organizations that had a pacifist stance. Catt was the keynote speaker when ER hosted a meeting at Hyde Park* in 1927 to support a women's peace movement* and promote the Kellogg-Briand Pact to outlaw war. For the next ten years, Catt was associated in the antiwar movement with ER, who was one of its most prominent members. When Catt, acting as chair of the book committee of the Cause and Cure of War organization, published a book, *Why Wars Must Cease* (1935), she included chapters by Addams, Alice Hamilton,* and ER, who referred to war as obsolete.

As the threat of war again hung over Europe in the 1930s, ER praised Catt's work with Jewish refugees.* She presented the American Hebrew Medal to Catt in 1933 for her work in the Protest Committee of Non-Jewish Women against the Persecution of Jews in Germany. ER invited Catt to the White House and in 1938 dedicated her book, *This Troubled World*, to Catt as a tribute to her continuous crusade for peace. Although Catt had supported Herbert Hoover* instead of Franklin D. Roosevelt* for president in 1932 and opposed FDR's bid for a third term in 1940, she praised ER's performance as First Lady and placed her at the top of lists of outstanding American women that she selected in 1933, 1934, and 1935.

In 1941 ER presided at a White House dinner at which Catt received the Chi Omega Achievement Award for her work on behalf of women. A supporter of the Allied cause in World War II,* Catt took part along with ER in a radio broadcast* on 9 January 1944 that celebrated Catt's eighty-fifth birthday. The same day they also appeared together at a luncheon sponsored by the Women's Action Committee for Victory and Lasting Peace, successor organization to the Cause and Cure of War.

SELECTED BIBLIOGRAPHY
Carrie Chapman Catt Papers, Library of Congress, Washington, DC.
Catt, Carrie Chapman. "An Open Letter to the D.A.R." *Woman Citizen* (July 1927): 11.
———. *Why Wars Must Cease*. 1935.
Fowler, Robert Booth. *Carrie Catt: Feminist Politician*. 1986.
Peck, Mary Gray. *Carrie Chapman Catt*. 1944.
Van Voris, Jacqueline. *Carrie Chapman Catt*. 1987.

Julieanne Phillips

CHIANG KAI-SHEK, MADAME (5 March 1897, Shanghai, China–   ).
In the early 1940s Eleanor Roosevelt was an admirer of Madame Chiang, the second wife of the head of the Chinese Nationalist government, Chiang Kai-shek. Born Mei-ling Soong, she was one of three sisters who were active in the movements leading to the rise to power of the Chinese Nationalist Party. One sister, Ch'ing-ling, was married to Sun Yat-sen, the party's founder. In the aftermath of World War II,* ER's enthusiasm for Madame Chiang faded when she recognized that Chiang Kai-shek's authoritarian government was thwarting, rather than nurturing, hopes for a democracy in China.

Madame Chiang made an extended visit to the White House in 1943 after she had been hospitalized in New York for several weeks and had convalesced in the Roosevelt's Hyde Park* home. A day following her arrival in Washington, Madame Chiang—who was educated at Wellesley—made a much-publicized plea to Congress* on 18 February 1943 for increased aid to China in its struggle with Japan. ER, who heard the speech, applauded her performance and declared in her "My Day"* column on 19 February 1943 that China's First Lady, "through her own personality and her own service, has achieved a place in the world not merely as the wife of Generalissimo Chiang Kai-shek but as a representative of her people" (Chadakoff, 283).

ER was pleased and amused by Madame Chiang's ability to hold her own with President Franklin D. Roosevelt* and congressional leaders, noting that she disguised a steely determination with a velvet hand and a gentle voice. "Pa is a little afraid of Madame Chiang & yet he likes her I think," ER wrote to her daughter Anna (Asbell, 155).

Although White House staffers and ER's associates were offended by Madame Chiang's imported silk sheets and her custom of summoning servants with a hand clap, the First Lady's esteem for her guest initially was firm. That admiration, however, began to wane even before China's

Eleanor Roosevelt and Madame Chiang Kai-shek are
wrapped in their furs in February 1943 as they sit on the
south lawn of the White House during Madame Chiang's
visit there in this Office of War Information photograph.
Courtesy of Library of Congress

First Lady concluded her White House visit. ER was chagrined by Madame Chiang's disinterest in an invitation to address a mass meeting
sponsored by the National Association for the Advancement of Colored
People* (NAACP). Madame Chiang was even unwilling to meet Walter
White,* executive director of the NAACP. Her appearances, she insisted,
would be limited to venues sponsored by her "Chinese and American
friends" (Lash, *Eleanor and Franklin*, 679).

Madame Chiang invited ER to visit China and proposed that the two
First Ladies journey back to Chungking together—a prospect that enthralled ER. Although FDR initially approved of the idea, he later
changed his mind. Much to ER's disappointment, the president decided

that a trip to China—which out of political necessity demanded a stop in Moscow—was ill advised at the time.

Madame Chiang called on ER at Hyde Park soon after FDR's death. During a long luncheon, they spoke of the news media's occasional hostility toward the Roosevelts. China's leaders, Madame Chiang declared, would never tolerate such press criticism. Elliott Roosevelt* recalled that as his mother watched Madame Chiang's limousine depart, she said with a sigh, "Her looks don't change and neither do her autocratic ways, I'm afraid" (Roosevelt and Brough, 89).

During ER's 1952 tour of Asia, Madame Chiang invited her to visit Formosa, where the generalissimo had established his government following the communist takeover of mainland China in 1949. ER declined and explained in her book *On My Own* that if she had gone to Taipei, she would have been compelled to speak out and tell Madame Chiang that her husband had missed his chance to unify China and that their dreams of returning to the mainland were futile.

ER's relationship with Madame Chiang mirrored the changing relations between their two nations. The friendship that developed between Chiang and the Roosevelts, both FDR and ER, during the war years helped seal the Chinese–American alliance against Japan. But with the conclusion of World War II, the commencement of the Cold War,* and the communist takeover of China—along with ER's disillusionment with Madame Chiang's displays of elitism and racism during her visit to Washington—their relationship took on a decidedly cooler tone.

SELECTED BIBLIOGRAPHY
Asbell, Bernard, ed. *Mother & Daughter: The Letters of Eleanor and Anna Roosevelt.* 1982.
Chadakoff, Rochelle, ed. *Eleanor Roosevelt's My Day.* Vol. 1. 1989.
Lash, Joseph P. *Eleanor and Franklin.* 1971.
————. *A World of Love: Eleanor Roosevelt and Her Friends, 1943–1962.* 1984.
Roosevelt, Eleanor. *On My Own.* 1958.
Roosevelt, Elliott, and James Brough. *Mother R.* 1977.

Joyce Hoffmann

CHILDHOOD. Eleanor Roosevelt once wrote of her parents' marriage, "Tragedy and happiness came walking on each other's heels" (Roosevelt, *Autobiography*, 5). The same could be said of her own childhood. She was born to a life of privilege as the daughter of aristocratic parents—Anna Hall Roosevelt* and Elliott Roosevelt*—and yet she was fated to a premature taste of tragedy as their lives ended in disaster.

ER was born in New York City on 11 October 1884. A schooner coming into New York that day would have found a harbor full of sails. On the waterfront a latticework of timber, the spars of ships, framed row upon

Eleanor poses with her adored father, Elliott Roosevelt, and her two brothers, Hall (on his father's lap) and Elliott, in this portrait made about 1892. *Courtesy of Franklin D. Roosevelt Library*

row of warehouses, stores, and office buildings. Flat facades of wood and brick rose to five stories above the water as far as the eye could see. No skyscrapers broke the horizon; the skyline belonged to church steeples and to the Brooklyn Bridge, completed a year before her birth.

New York would change rapidly in the early years of Eleanor's life. During the 1880s and 1890s millions of immigrants would come to the United States from Southern and Eastern Europe. Often poor, they crowded into places like New York's Lower East Side, where each acre of dingy tenements housed more than 700 people. Eleanor's life would someday involve her in the broad currents of history and bring her into contact with immigrants and the poor. But she lived her childhood in the narrow world of New York's aristocracy. Her life was shaped by that world and by the peculiar tragedy of her own family.

Anna and Elliott Roosevelt were among the leading socialites of New York, constantly engaged in entertainments with their friends. The child Eleanor spent much of her time with servants: her first language was ch, which she learned from her nurse. But she did spend many moments with her parents. On winter days they sometimes took leigh rides. On Fifth Avenue Elliott would coax his horse into a d join other sleighs speeding along in stately haste. On such mornings the air danced with the music of hundreds of harness bells, and horsemen sought good-naturedly to outpace one another. Then the family would drive home, and a chilly Eleanor would stamp snow from her boots, brush her coat, and rush to the sitting-room fire. When Eleanor was four, her parents built a country house in Hempstead, Long Island, on ten acres of land. There Eleanor could play with cats, dogs, and chickens, and she had her own kitten, an angora—which she called an "angostura."

Yet, not all of Eleanor's childhood consisted of innocent pleasures. When she was two and one-half, she embarked with her parents on a voyage to Europe. Another ship hit their vessel, and the passengers had to abandon ship. A screaming Eleanor was dropped from the deck to her father in a lifeboat below. The incident left her afraid of water and heights and led soon afterward to separation from her parents. When she was three, they embarked again for Europe, but this time they left her with relatives on the grounds she was too afraid of the ocean to accompany them.

During her early years Eleanor was apparently confident of her parents' love. In the mornings she liked to visit her father in his dressing room and chatter to him and dance in circles. He might complain that she made him dizzy and then toss her in the air. She called herself "father's little golden hair" (Roosevelt, *Hunting Big Game*, 168). As Elliott tucked her into bed on the night of her fourth birthday, she told him, "I love everybody, and everybody loves me" (Elliott Roosevelt to his sister, Anna Roosevelt [Cowles*], 13 October 1888, Family Papers). "With my father I was perfectly happy," she would later declare (Roosevelt, *Autobiography*, 5). But as she grew older, she was less confident of her mother's love. She was hurt to realize that her "lack of beauty" troubled her mother. "I knew it as a child senses these things" (Roosevelt, *Autobiography*, 6).

In 1889 Anna gave birth to a second child, Elliott Jr.—known as "Ellie"—and two years later she bore a second son, G. Hall Roosevelt.* But just as the family was growing, the life of the parents began to unravel. Elliott fell victim to a sequence of maladies brought on by alcohol, drugs, and misplaced sexual ardor. He had an affair with one of the household servants, Katy Mann, and fathered her child. Unable to settle down, he took the whole family to Europe to escape his problems in 1890, but he sank deeper into despair and dissipation.

Not yet eight, Eleanor could only sense that something was wrong with her family without understanding the cause. For her, the most apparent symptom was that suddenly her father was no longer there when she came back to the United States with her mother and brothers. After unsuccessful treatment in Europe, Elliott returned home but was not allowed to rejoin his family. At the urging of his brother, Theodore Roosevelt,* Elliott was sent into a kind of exile in Virginia, where he was expected to overcome his alcohol problem and establish himself in business. Then he might be permitted to return to New York and Anna. The possibility of reconciliation came to an end on 7 December 1892, when Anna died of diphtheria following an operation. A few months later, Ellie and Hall contracted scarlet fever. Hall recovered, but Ellie died.

Schooled in the acceptance of death by her family, Eleanor wrote her father, "We must remember Ellie is going to be safe in heaven and to be with mother. She is waiting there, and our Lord wants Ellie boy with him now" (ER to Elliott Roosevelt, [May 1893], Family Papers). The loss of his wife and eldest son increased Elliott's solicitude for his daughter. From Virginia he wrote that she was his love and joy. In his letters he counseled her on a multitude of affairs ranging from the care of her hands, to the building of her character. In one letter he urged her to attend to the "big" virtues: "unselfishness, generosity, loving tenderness, and cheerfulness" (Roosevelt, *Hunting Big Game*, 171–75).

Occasionally, Elliott visited his daughter in New York. The moments when he appeared at the house where she lived with her maternal grandmother, Mary Ludlow Hall, were the most joyous in Eleanor's life. But such visits were infrequent and sometimes ended badly: he once left her with the doorman at his club, went in for a drink, and was later carried out unconscious. During the summer of 1894 Elliott fell into a coma, induced by his heavy drinking, and died. On learning of her father's demise, Eleanor pressed her regret into one pathetic sentence. "I did want," she said, "to see my father once more" (Mary Hall to Corinne Robinson,* 25 August 1894, ER Papers).

Thus, Eleanor was orphaned shortly before her tenth birthday. During the next few years she lived with her grandmother and an assortment of aunts and uncles in a house on New York's 37th Street. They spent their summers at Oak Terrace, the Hall family estate on the Hudson River at Tivoli. ER later remembered the tranquillity of those times. It was most apparent on Sundays, when she could not play games and had to read the books that her grandmother considered appropriate. In the morning she recited biblical passages and hymns in French that she had memorized during the previous week. On Sunday evenings the family sang hymns around the fire.

Yet, there were many discordant notes in family life among the Halls. One of Eleanor's uncles had a severe drinking problem and enjoyed shooting his rifle from a window in Oak Terrace. Grandmother Hall's attention was intermittent and sometimes wrong-headed, as in her requirement that her granddaughter continue to wear children's dresses when she became an adolescent. Without a mother and father to call her own, Eleanor built her early adolescent life around rather casual associations with her relatives and household servants. She chatted by the hour with the laundress, Mrs. Oberhalse, who taught her to iron. Quite possibly, the ease with which the mature ER was able to associate with men and women in all walks of life resulted from her childhood experiences.

In 1899 Eleanor, almost fifteen, boarded a ship for England and a new life as a pupil in Allenswood School. She took with her then, and would carry with her for years to come, the letters that her father had written her from Virginia. To all appearances she was a confident young woman on the brink of an exciting adventure. Still, she had already experienced more personal tragedy than many people endure in a lifetime. Years later she would write, "You gain strength, courage and confidence by every experience in which you really stop to look fear in the face. . . . You must do the thing you cannot do" (Roosevelt, *You Learn by Living*, 29–30). The combination of vulnerability and courage underlying that statement came into play often in ER's adult life as First Lady and as a delegate to the United Nations.* But the deepest roots of her personal strength—of her character which would inspire millions throughout the world—lay in a child's triumph over bereavement and loneliness.

SELECTED BIBLIOGRAPHY

Cook, Blanche. *Eleanor Roosevelt*. Vol. 1. 1992.

Eleanor Roosevelt Papers and Roosevelt Family Papers, Franklin D. Roosevelt Library, Hyde Park, NY.

Roosevelt, Eleanor. *The Autobiography of Eleanor Roosevelt*. 1961.

———. *You Learn by Living*. 1960.

———, ed. *Hunting Big Game in the Eighties: The Letters of Elliott Roosevelt, Sportsman*. 1933.

Youngs, J. William T. *Eleanor Roosevelt: A Personal and Public Life*. 1985.

J. William T. Youngs

CHURCHILL, WINSTON LEONARD SPENCER (30 November 1874, Oxfordshire, England–24 January 1965, London, England).

The friendship between Britain's wartime prime minister Winston Churchill and Franklin D. Roosevelt* was referred to by Joseph Lash* in the subtitle of his 1976 book on the two leaders as "the Partnership That Saved the West." In contrast, despite her affection for Britain, relations between Eleanor Roosevelt and Churchill were strained. At one level the problem was personal. She disliked Churchill's keeping her husband awake deep into the night, recalling, "It always took him several days to catch up on sleep after Mr. Churchill left" (Roosevelt, 243). Churchill also had his reservations, especially after one of ER's dinner guests, Louis Adamic, breached etiquette by writing an indiscreet book about meeting Churchill at the White House in December 1941. The prime minister sued for libel. But more than this, ER was consistently suspicious of Churchill's support for imperialistic policies. She worried that Churchill's vision of balance of power politics might divert FDR away from her vision of a world founded on a new international organization.

These differences never prevented the two families from enjoying one another's hospitality during wartime visits; however, ER did not allow herself to be browbeaten by Churchill. During her visit to London in 1942 they clashed during a dinner party while discussing the Spanish civil war.

ER was unimpressed when, in a speech to Harvard University in October 1943, Churchill proposed joint Anglo-American citizenship. It seemed an obvious bid to revive his dream of an English-speaking postwar order. In deference to her husband's wishes, she kept her concerns private. Both FDR and ER, however, reacted negatively to favorable comments about the Spanish dictator Francisco Franco that Churchill made in a foreign policy speech on 24 May 1944 before the British House of Commons, in which he also said that the Atlantic Charter setting forth shared U.S. and British aims for the postwar world was not binding with regard to the future of Germany. FDR at his press conference on 30 May 1944 said, "Spain* has been less than satisfactory in her operations as a neutral power." At ER's press conference a few hours earlier a reporter had asked if Churchill's speech* was a whitewash of Franco, and ER had answered cryptically, "Mr. Churchill has thought a certain way for sixty years and doesn't want to change." But when a reporter also asked if Churchill's speech had shelved the Atlantic Charter, ER replied in his defense, "I think he'd be quite shocked if you were to say that" (*New York Times*, 31 May 1944, 1, 4).

Her concerns about Churchill increased as the war drew to a close. When President Harry S Truman* confided his frustration with the prime minister to ER, she reminded him of Churchill's suspicions of the Russians and failure to appreciate the Russian sense of humor. She recommended that Truman try to "get on a personal basis" with the prime minister (Lash, *Eleanor: The Years Alone*, p. 29). By 1946 she feared that Churchill's view of the Russians was prevailing in Truman's mind. Her assessment neglected the degree to which Truman was influenced by warning voices nearer to home.

ER did not allow her vision of the postwar world to wither without a fight. She worked to ensure that the world knew that Churchill and her husband had not always seen eye-to-eye during the war years. She encouraged her son Elliott Roosevelt* to proceed with his plans to expose these differences in his book, *As He Saw It*. When Churchill warned against Soviet aggression in his Iron Curtain speech of March 1946, Roosevelt used her "My Day"* column of 16 March 1946 to argue for a strong United Nations* as an alternative to balance-of-power politics, though she did concede, "No matter how much any of us may differ at times with the ideas which Mr. Churchill may hold, none of us will ever cease to be grateful to him for the leadership which he gave during the war" (Lash, *Eleanor: The Years Alone*, 84).

In *This I Remember*, ER made no secret of her opinions of the prime minister. She reported conversations with her husband in which she warned that Churchill would have difficulty in the postwar world, as "the world that had existed before the war had been a pleasant world as far as he was concerned" (Roosevelt, 253). It was hardly surprising that, contrary to Elliott Roosevelt's assurance to NBC, Churchill declined to appear on ER's television* show in 1950.

SELECTED BIBLIOGRAPHY

Lash, Joseph P. *Eleanor: The Years Alone*. 1973.
———. *Franklin and Eleanor*. 1971.
———. *Roosevelt and Churchill, 1939–1941: The Partnership That Saved the West*. 1976.
Nicholas, Herbert G., ed. *Washington Despatches 1941–1945, Weekly Political Reports from the British Embassy*. 1981: 363.
Roosevelt, Eleanor. *This I Remember*. 1949.
Scharf, Louis. *Eleanor Roosevelt: First Lady of American Liberalism*. 1987.

Nicholas J. Cull

CIVIL RIGHTS. Racial justice did not always concern Eleanor Roosevelt. Although she began her social activism in 1903 working with the immigrant communities of the Rivington Street Settlement House in New York City, ER began to recognize racial discrimination only after she moved to the White House in 1933.

As she traveled the nation, ER witnessed the seemingly intractable hardships wrought by the Great Depression.* Field reports from Lorena Hickok* detailed the inadequacies of Federal Emergency Relief Administration programs and brought individual stories of personal hardship to ER's attention. Although ER had visited African Americans when she toured poverty-stricken areas the summer after she became First Lady, she did not recognize the depth of institutional racism until she pressured the Subsistence Homestead Administration to admit African Americans to Arthurdale.* Her intervention failed, and she invited Walter White,* executive secretary of the National Association for the Advancement of Colored People* (NAACP), and the presidents of African American universities to the White House to discuss the situation. This unprecedented meeting, which took place on 26 January 1934, quickly became a tutorial on racial discrimination and lasted until midnight. ER then pressured National Recovery administrator Donald Richberg to investigate the race-based wage differentials implemented by southern industries and asked navy secretary Claude Swanson why blacks were confined to mess hall assignments.

Members of the honor guard of Washington's Howard University escort Eleanor Roosevelt to the university's faculty club in 1936, causing an outcry from segregationists who used this picture to attack the racial policies of the Roosevelt administration. *Courtesy of Library of Congress*

ER had embraced a civil rights agenda that accepted segregation but championed equal opportunity. Quality education became her top public priority. As she told the National Conference on Fundamental Problems in the Education of Negroes on 11 May 1934, "[W]herever the standard of education is low, the standard of living is low" and urged the nation to address the inequities in public school funding (Roosevelt, "Address," 574). Her symbolic outreach generated a strong response from African Americans. The African American press and a strong communication network among blacks extolled her efforts. By January 1934 she received thousands of letters describing racial violence, poverty, and homelessness exacerbated by racial discrimination and pleading for some type of assistance. She frequently forwarded some of these letters to Harry Hopkins* and Aubrey Williams,* to whom she had already sent a list of suggestions on ways to include African Americans more fully within Federal Emergency Relief Administration programs.

Aides of Franklin D. Roosevelt* tolerated ER's intercessions, but became incensed when she supported Walter White's relentless efforts to secure administration support for the Costigan–Wagner antilynching* bill. The bill had been introduced in early 1934, and while FDR agreed with its sentiments, he did nothing to urge its passage. White turned to ER for advice and additional pressure. Her support not only frustrated FDR but enraged press secretary Steve Early,* a southerner from Virginia who sent ER a strong memo condemning White's single-mindedness. The tension within the White House increased when Claude Neal in October 1934 was abducted from an Alabama jail and lynched in Florida. Despite her best efforts, ER could not convince FDR either to lend public support to the bill for fear of alienating the senior southern senators or to argue that lynching was covered under the federal Lindbergh kidnapping statute.

Southern critics, in turn, led by Georgia governor Eugene Talmadge, attacked FDR through ER's support of the NAACP and throughout 1935 published photos of ER with blacks in *The Georgia Woman's World*. Rumors circulated throughout the South of Eleanor Clubs,* mythical organizations that purported to urge African American domestics to refuse to work for white women. Federal Bureau of Investigation* (FBI) director J. Edgar Hoover was so offended by her actions that he became convinced that she had black blood. Other Americans did as well and wrote to ask if this were true, only to receive a reply from ER that said that her family had lived so long in the nation that she could not answer the question with certainty.

Mary McLeod Bethune,* whom ER had first met in 1927 at a women's conference and who ER had urged be appointed to the National Youth Administration* (NYA) in 1935, also helped shape the First Lady's understanding of the problems facing black Americans. Bethune brought lists of requests for ER's intervention when the two met and often sent the First Lady reports, novels, and other reading material. A close relationship developed between the two women. ER's decision to challenge the local ordinance requiring segregation at the 20–23 November 1938 convening of the Southern Conference for Human Welfare* (SCHW) in Birmingham, Alabama, was based partly on her wish to sit with Bethune. Writing in 1953, ER credited her deep affection for Bethune for helping her move beyond her racial awkwardness; the former First Lady called Bethune her "closest friend in her own age group" (Roosevelt, "Some of My Best Friends," 17).

Young, outspoken blacks also shaped ER's perspectives. Richard Wright's collection of short stories depicting mob violence, *Uncle Tom's Children*, so moved ER that she agreed both to help publicize the book and to endorse Wright's Guggenheim application for a fellowship to complete *Native Son*. She developed a lifelong association with activist

Pauli Murray*—creating what Murray later called a friendship grounded in "confrontation by typewriter" (Murray interview, 8). By 1940 the two women had worked together to promote National Sharecroppers Week, to organize the National Committee to Abolish the Poll Tax, and in the Odell Waller case* to defend a sharecropper against charges of premeditated murder. Many years later they continued their collaboration, with Murray reporting on civil and political rights to the President's Commission on the Status of Women,* set up by John F. Kennedy* in December 1961 with ER as chair.

Ironically, the event for which ER received the most press was the issue upon which she took the least public action. ER had first invited the contralto Marian Anderson* to perform in the White House in 1936, after which she wrote in her 21 February 1936 newspaper column, "My Day,"* that she had "rarely heard a more beautiful and moving voice or a more finished artist." After the Daughters of the American Revolution (DAR) refused to allow Anderson to perform in Constitution Hall in the spring of 1939, ER resigned from the DAR, commenting in her 27 February 1939 "My Day" column that she believed that if you differed with the policy of an organization to which you belonged, you should work from within to alter that policy. "But in this case," she explained, "I belong to an organization in which I can do no active work. They have taken an action which has been widely talked of in the press. To remain as a member implies approval of that action, and therefore I am resigning." Although ER refrained from naming the organization or the issue involved in her column, her statement made the front pages of more than 400 newspapers. ER's resignation from the DAR put the organization on the defensive and transformed the incident from a local slight to a consequential issue.

By 1939 ER began to attack the way in which the nation dealt with racial injustice. She wanted her fellow citizens to understand how their guilt in "writing and speaking about democracy and the American way without consideration of the imperfections within our system with regard to its treatment . . . of the Negro" encouraged racism (Black, 89). Americans, she told Ralph Bunche in an interview for Gunnar Myrdal's *American Dilemma*, wanted to talk "only about the good features of American life and to hide our problems like skeletons in the closet" (Black, 89). Such withdrawal only fueled violent responses; Americans must therefore recognize "the real intensity of feeling" and "the amount of intimidation and terrorization" racism promotes and act against such "ridiculous" behavior (Black, 89).

By the early 1940s ER firmly believed civil rights to be the real litmus test for American democracy. She declared over and over again throughout World War II* that there could be no democracy in the United States that did not include democracy for blacks. In *The Moral Basis of Democracy* she asserted that people of all races have inviolate rights to "some property" (Roosevelt, *Moral Basis*, 42). Repeatedly, ER insisted that education, housing, and employment were basic human rights* that society had both a moral and political obligation to provide its citizens. The government must not only provide protection against discrimination but develop policies that create a level economic playing field. In making clear exactly what she meant, ER explained: "This means achieving an economic level below which no one is permitted to fall, and keeping a fairly stable balance between that level and the standard of living" (Roosevelt, *Moral Basis*, 50).

When white America refused to see how segregation mocked American values, ER addressed this issue sternly and directly: "We have never been willing to face this problem, to line it up with the basic, underlying beliefs in Democracy" (Roosevelt, *Moral Basis*, 43). Racial prejudice enslaved; consequently, "no one can honestly claim that the Indians or the Negroes of this country are free" (Roosevelt, *Moral Basis*, 48). "Perhaps one of the things we cannot have any longer is what [Rudyard] Kipling called 'The White Man's Burden,' " she wrote in an article titled "What Are We Fighting For?" in *The American Magazine*. She continued this theme in a 3 August 1942 article in the *New Republic*, contending that both the private and the public sector must acknowledge that "one of the main destroyers of freedom is our attitude toward the colored race." Furthermore, she told those listening to the radio broadcast* of the 24 February 1945 National Democratic forum that "democracy may grow or fade as we face [this] problem" (all quoted by Black, 89).

This outspokenness exacerbated the tensions within the wartime White House. ER had championed the creation of the Fair Employment Practices Committee. Her behind-the-scenes efforts to push FDR to defend the integration of Detroit's Sojourner Truth housing development for defense workers in 1943 angered Early and other key aides. When Detroit erupted in flames after African American families moved in, many in the White House blamed ER for the riot. FDR then reversed himself and allowed his wife to visit troops overseas because, as Henry Wallace* later recalled, "the Negro situation was too hot" (Black, 92). While touring the South Pacific, ER was photographed visiting wounded black soldiers and when she returned home, she helped open an integrated Congress of Industrial Organizations canteen. Criticism of her civil rights activities increased.

FDR's death freed ER from the constraints the White House had imposed on her activities. She joined the NAACP board of directors in May 1945 and the Congress of Racial Equality (CORE) board that fall. When a white-induced race riot nearly destroyed Columbia, Tennessee, in 1946, she responded to White and Bethune's request to chair the investigative committee and worked with Thurgood Marshall to force the Justice Department to look beyond the scenario painted by town officials. The NAACP then appointed her to its legal affairs committee. She pressured the administration of President Harry S Truman* to recommend a permanent Fair Employment Practices Commission (FEPC), to lobby against the poll tax, and to propose low-income, federally financed housing. She urged Truman to address the 1948 NAACP annual convention and joined him on the steps of the Lincoln Memorial as he became the first president to address the organization's national convention. Although Truman had appointed her to the American delegation to the United Nations,* their early relationship was rocky. His NAACP speech and his decision to integrate the military encouraged her to reassess his leadership and played a strong role in her endorsement of his reelection.

ER used her "My Day" column, her monthly question and answer column, "If You Ask Me," and her lecture tours as a public tutorial on race relations. She assumed the responsibility of explaining NAACP legal strategy in terms that the majority of her readers could understand. She criticized restrictive housing covenants, segregated schools, employment discrimination, literacy tests, and voting procedures with increasing impatience. She often responded with single-spaced, typed letters to those who wrote questioning the legality of her stances and urging patience. In the throes of Cold War* politics, she argued against groups that used Red-baiting tactics to attack civil rights organizations and declared that the best defense against communism was making democracy work.

The Supreme Court's *Brown v. Board of Education* decision to desegregate schools in 1954 pleased her, but she knew that integration would not be a swift or temperate exercise. The Montgomery bus boycott by African Americans to protest segregated public transportation reinforced her fears and her determination. She worked with Martin Luther King Jr.* and Rosa Parks to raise money for the boycott and introduced Autherine Lucy, an African American student who had tried to integrate the University of Alabama, at a Madison Square Garden fund-raiser. She supported the Southern Conference Education Fund's (SCEF) efforts to desegregate hospitals and protect voting rights.

Knowing that her credibility with the civil rights community was beyond reproach and worried that *Brown* might divide the 1956 convention, Democratic National Committee chair Paul Butler asked her to chair the platform hearings on civil rights. She agreed and, after moderating a heated debate between those opposed to the decision and civil rights activists who favored it, drafted a plank that condemned the use of force and declared the Supreme Court as the nation's legal arbiter. Although the plank did not mention *Brown* by name, it passed the committee by only one vote. ER proceeded to mention the decision in every speech she gave for presidential candidate Adlai Stevenson,* endorsed the Powell amendment to bar federal funds for construction of segregated schools, and chided those Americans who did not see the inherent hypocrisy of criticizing communism and supporting Jim Crow.

By 1957 ER had become impatient with the Democratic Party's commitment to civil rights and began identifying more strongly with activists who wanted to change the system rather than with cautious politicians. She wrote an article for *Ebony Magazine* titled "Some of My Best Friends Are Negro." The struggle to integrate Little Rock's Central High School made her question the courage of President Dwight D. Eisenhower* in upholding the Supreme Court decision, declaring that he was absent without leave from the major domestic crisis of his presidency.

As Congress* began to debate the Civil Rights Acts of 1957 and 1960, ER criticized those Democrats who evaded the issue. She bitterly condemned the decision to include a jury trial amendment, which placed voting rights obstructionists in front of an all-white jury instead of a federal judge. She wrote to activists that she understood their frustration and struggle against despair. She opposed John F. Kennedy's* nomination for president as much for his tepid support of civil rights as for his silence in the face of the communist witch-hunting activities of Senator Joseph McCarthy. She chaired a Highlander Folk School* workshop on nonviolent civil disobedience for civil rights activists. In her introduction for a pamphlet *Cracking the Color Line*, published by CORE, she wrote that "advocating civil rights does not constitute anarchy" (Black, 127).

The violent treatment received by the Freedom Riders, an interracial group protesting segregation in railway and bus terminal accommodations in 1961, provoked ER's harshest comments. Asked by CORE and the NAACP to chair a hearing in 1962 investigating the conduct of federal judges before whom assailants of Freedom Riders were tried, ER lost her temper with administration supporters who urged the committee go into executive session to hear testimony. She brusquely responded that she did not come to the hearing to equivocate. She "found it terribly painful," she wrote in her last book, "to accept the fact that things [such as the attacks on peaceful protesters like the Freedom Riders] could happen here. . . . This was the kind of thing that Nazis had done to the Jews* in Germany" (Roosevelt, *Tomorrow Is Now*, 51).

By 1962 ER was dying. Praising the courage of King and other civil rights advocates, her columns and interviews became increasingly pessimistic. She criticized Kennedy for showing more profile than courage on civil rights issues. When she learned of the Birmingham church bombing that killed four African American girls, she phoned King to ask him to appear on her television* show to discuss racial violence. He agreed, but the show was never taped. Two days later, ER entered the hospital for treatment of her fatal illness.

When she died on 7 November, King summarized her commitment to racial justice. "The impact of her personality and its unwavering dedication to high principle and purpose cannot be contained in a single day or era" (Black, 203). Three months later, her final book was published. In it, ER had issued her own call for civil rights activism: "[S]taying aloof is not a solution; it is a cowardly evasion" (Roosevelt, *Tomorrow Is Now*, 19).

SELECTED BIBLIOGRAPHY
Black, Allida M. *Casting Her Own Shadow: Eleanor Roosevelt and the Shaping of Postwar Liberalism*. 1996.
Eleanor Roosevelt Oral History Project, Interview with Pauli Murray (1978), Franklin D. Roosevelt Library, Hyde Park, NY.
Roosevelt, Eleanor. "Address to the National Conference on the Education of Negroes." *The Journal of Negro Education* 3 (October 1934): 573–75.
———. *The Moral Basis of Democracy*. 1940.
———. "Some of My Best Friends Are Negro." *Ebony* (February, 1953): 16–20, 22, 24–26.
———. *Tomorrow Is Now*. 1963.

Allida M. Black

CLOTHING. The prevailing public perception today regarding Eleanor Roosevelt and fashion is that she lacked interest in her appearance and projected the image of a rather dowdy matron. While fashion critics often complained that her clothes left much to be desired, the remaining items of her wardrobe, housed at the Roosevelt Library* at Hyde Park,* New York, and in the First Ladies Collection of the National Museum of American History at the Smithsonian Institution in Washington, D.C., as well as the photographic record show this perception to be incorrect. Throughout her life, ER selected exquisite fabrics and had them designed and made into well-tailored clothing, although she sometimes purchased inexpensive items. While never on the cutting edge of fashion, her clothes while she was in the public eye were well within the stylish guidelines of the period.

As a small child, ER was dressed by her mother, Anna Hall Roosevelt,* even though she was convinced that Eleanor was unattractive, in the fashionable clothing that befitted the daughter of an affluent family. Later, under the watchful eye of her grandmother, Mary Ludlow Hall, Eleanor was dressed in garments made from fine fabrics, although, as biographer Blanche Cook has noted, some of Eleanor's clothes were hand-me-downs that were unflattering and made her look somber and older than her years.

During her teens, under the wise and loving guidance of Marie Souvestre,* head of the Allenswood boarding school in England, who encouraged her to spend her allowance on a stylish wardrobe, Eleanor's fashion sense blossomed. With her tall, lithe figure and long, flowing, light hair, her appearance was often stunning. "On a daily basis she looked very smart in the school's dapper uniform of long dark skirts,

Eleanor Roosevelt wears a gown from Arnold Constable & Co., a New York store, intended for the formal White House reception on 20 January 1937, the day of Franklin D. Roosevelt's inauguration for his second term as president. *Courtesy of Library of Congress*

high-collared and occasionally ruffled shirts, striped ties, blazers, and boaters" (Cook, 107).

After her schooling abroad, ER returned to New York to make her debut in society. After being encouraged by Souvestre, she enjoyed dressing stylishly, especially for formal occasions. Her Aunt Tissie, her mother's sister, Elizabeth Hall Mortimer, sent her Paris designs from the finest fashion couturiers. She shopped for her wedding trousseau with one of her cousins and, on her three-month European honeymoon with Franklin D. Roosevelt* in 1905, they "shopped and shopped, for clothes," and, she wrote, her young husband insisted on buying her "such lovely furs . . . of course I am delighted with them" (Cook, 170–71).

Throughout her life, ER loved to wear fashionable hats. Although her often-attention-getting selections were not always flattering, they became one of her trademarks. Photographs show her wearing furs, both as coats and as trim for her stylish outfits, all her life, in an era before the use of furs became a politically charged issue. During the 1920s, she came under the fashion influence of her close friends Esther Lape* and Elizabeth Read.* With their own wardrobes "custom-made of the finest imported fabrics," they persuaded her to use their designer and often "gave her gifts of unique and dazzling fabrics" (Cook, 297).

After FDR's election, as First Lady ER was expected to sit for formal portraits and to model her clothes for the new season and for special occasions. While never a trendsetter, during the first two Roosevelt terms, she posed for extensive photographs and fashion layouts for the women's and society pages of national newspapers. Many photographs record her modeling her wardrobe selections for inaugurations, Easter, or the visit of the king and queen of England in 1939.

For FDR's first inauguration in 1933, ER sat for fashion photographs wearing the smart daytime dress, now on display at the Smithsonian's National Museum of American History, that she had selected for the swearing-in ceremony. According to a clipping from an unidentified newspaper in the scrapbook collection of the Roosevelt Library, extensive details of the dress accompanied the photographs:

Mrs. Roosevelt shows in these especially posed photographs how she will be attired at the Inaugural ceremonies when she becomes First Lady of the Land. Her costume will be in the blue shades that have been named for her. The gown . . . is of Eleanor blue [lavender] crystelle velvet with long sleeves tapering to tight cuffs. The skirt, 10 inches from the floor, flares slightly at the bottom. The coat . . . is of a darker shade of crystelle velvet, called Anna blue, after her daughter. It is three/fourth length, with shirred scarf collar and epaulet shoulders. The hat is of Anna blue Milan straw, and the purse and pumps are of matching blue kid. The gown, coat, and matching accessories were made by Arnold Constable, New York, and these photos are copyrighted by the firm.

Indeed, ER had arranged with Arnold Constable & Co. to obtain fashionable clothing at reduced rates in return for being photographed in outfits from the store. Yet, she did not relish the role of model. According to Anne Wassell Arnall, who photographed ER for Arnold Constable, ER hurried through the photographic sessions and "never bothered to look at herself before her picture was taken" (Beasley, *Eleanor Roosevelt and the Media*, 56). The sessions, however, turned into news articles for women's pages, which depended heavily on advertising from department stores, and served to promote the nation's fashion industry.

Not limiting purchases to one firm, during her White House years, ER ordered her clothes by correspondence from a variety of fashionable

New York and Washington clothiers, a pattern probably established earlier because of her demanding public schedule. Her secretary, Malvina Thompson* (Scheider), wrote to the stores stating ER's clothing needs, often including swatches of the type of fabric desired along with lengthy descriptions of the color preferences, sizes, and styles of clothing, undergarments, and hats being sought. Schedules for fittings also were arranged through correspondence, and the finished clothing was sent to her by mail. In addition to Arnold Constable & Co., ER patronized such notable stores as Lord & Taylor, B. Altman, Milgrim, Lilly Dache (for her hats), Mary Hayden (for undergarments), Nudelman & Conti, Inc. Sportswear in New York, and Kaplowitz Bros. and Julius Garfinckel & Co. in Washington.

Yet, ER, who stood 5 feet 11 inches tall and weighed 160 pounds in 1940 and was said to make a marvelous appearance in a full-length gown, did not make a point of dwelling on her attire. In 1934, when she was selected to head the list of the "ten best-dressed women of the year" by the U.S. fashion industry, she did not discuss the subject at her press conferences,* leaving Martha Strayer, one of the reporters present, to write in her notes that ER usually cut discussion of fashion "off with a vague single sentence, or, at the most, two" (Beasley, *White House Press Conferences*, 27).

Perhaps this was partly because it seemed inappropriate to ER to emphasize fashion when the nation was in the grip of the Great Depression.* Strayer, a reporter for the *Washington Daily News*, who was a personal friend of the First Lady, also noted that ER was "as nearly oblivious of her personal appearance as any woman in public life could be" (Beasley, *White House Press Conferences*, 27). Yet, without doubt ER wanted to wear suitable clothing to fulfill her role. Twenty years later, in her "My Day"* column of 3 December 1954, she wrote that to have had "that title" of best-dressed woman was one of the "grandest" things that had ever happened to her. During FDR's last two administrations, ER greatly cut back on fashion photographs as World War II* intervened, and she increased her traveling abroad and visited men in the military.

In the years after World War II, style changed radically. The 1950s style that prevailed in postwar fashion was delineated by a defined waist and narrow, fitted bodice—styles unbecoming to a large woman like ER in her sixties. She also was captive to the cultural convention of her time that decreed that older women should dress in matronly attire. Sometimes ER opted for becoming outfits—plain suits and dresses with jackets made of fine fabrics, which she wore on public occasions when meeting with important personages and during her frequent speeches* and radio* and television* broadcasts. Frequently, however, she appeared in photographs garbed in the large, belted, floral print dresses that today are associated with older women; these became one source of the modern perception of her as dowdy. From the 1940s throughout her later years, her photographs show that the camera was often unkind; frequently, she did not photograph well.

In her seventies, she summed up the fashion philosophy of her later years. Writing in her "My Day" column of 3 December 1954, she reflected,

The woman who dresses to suit her particular type, with only a moderate bowing acquaintance with fashion, comes out better than the woman who is a slave to the designer of the moment.

When one is very young, very slim, and very pretty, one can afford to go from one extreme to the other. . . . But later on, it seems to me, though one must keep a nodding acquaintance with the fashions so as not to be too conspicuous, it is not such a bad idea to find a style that suits and stick to it.

According to reminiscences of her neighbors as written by Nancy Alden in the *Hyde Park Townsman* of 3 March 1994, ER frequently was seen in her hometown of Hyde Park,* New York, wearing cotton dresses from W. T. Grant's (a chain selling inexpensive items). "She liked their dresses because they buttoned up the front and that was very handy for her," Alden wrote. ER told readers of her column in *McCall's** in March 1959 that she spent as much as $1,500 annually on clothes, although "very often it is less than $1,000." By this time comfort had become her main concern in selecting clothing when she was not in the public eye.

SELECTED BIBLIOGRAPHY

Beasley, Maurine. *Eleanor Roosevelt and the Media: A Public Quest for Self-Fulfillment.* 1987.
———. *The White House Press Conferences of Eleanor Roosevelt.* 1987.
Cook, Blanche Wiesen. *Eleanor Roosevelt.* Vol. 1. 1992.
Eleanor Roosevelt Papers, Franklin D. Roosevelt Library, Hyde Park, NY.
Mayo, Edith P., and Denise D. Meringolo. *First Ladies: Political Role and Public Image.* 1994.

Edith P. Mayo

COLD WAR. Among the sculptures in the vast expanse of the President Franklin Delano Roosevelt* memorial in Washington, D.C., is one of Eleanor Roosevelt. It is significant that she stands in front of the seal of the United Nations* (UN), for the memorial recognizes her unique contribution to the world after the president's death. It also illustrates the assumption that most of that contribution rested on her years at the United Nations, perhaps because they were the most visible. Whether focusing on her achievements at the United Nations or elsewhere, the memorial aptly demonstrates that it was ER, not her husband, who had to face the Cold War.

As the wife of the commander in chief, ER played an important, but supporting, role in the wartime years of 1941–1945. With the death of

FDR and the onset of the Cold War, however, ER moved to the front lines. A member of the UN delegation from 1945 to 1952, she often was compelled to confront the Soviets and forced to do rhetorical battle with them. These experiences shaped her view of the communist threat, but ER never became the stereotypical "cold warrior." While her opposition to the spread of communism never wavered, ER brought her own approach to the escalating Cold War. In her unique position, she attempted to persuade her fellow Americans that the Cold War was the result of both the expansionist ideology of the Soviets and the wrong-headed American response to them.

ER was not an eager Cold War recruit. Witnessing her husband's dealings with Stalin during World War II* made her wary of the Soviets, yet she steadfastly held onto FDR's belief that peace could be maintained in the postwar era. The agency of that peace, she believed, would be the emerging United Nations organization. But when President Harry S Truman* recruited ER to serve on the first American delegation to the United Nations, she hesitated at such a public role. Only at the urging of her friends and family did ER step into the role that would showcase her talent for negotiation and her commitment to maintaining the hard-won peace.

During her early years at the United Nations, ER became increasingly convinced that the relationship between the United States and the Soviet Union was to be one of confrontation and even hostility. Events in the world, especially the Korean War, compelled this belief, and her personal experiences dealing with the Soviet delegates confirmed this view. Yet ER never subscribed to the hard-line opinion that nothing useful could come of discussion or negotiation with the Soviets. Throughout her political life ER was committed to the principles of face-to-face contact and the maintenance of personal connections. She continued to pursue this personal approach, insisting that Americans should respond with strength, but also with friendliness, despite the fact that the Soviets could be "irritating" (Black, 418).

Throughout the Cold War, ER continued to write, travel,* and make speeches* in support of these views. She sought to convince the American people that although she disapproved of communism, there was much to be gained by continued contact with the Soviets. She argued that as much as one abhorred the Soviets' goals, one had to admire their commitment to their ideology. In fact, when she compared the way each side promoted its ideologies, she found Americans lacking. In a 1959 article entitled "What Are We For?" (Black, 121–129), ER argued that while the United States was on the side of right, its message was not getting across to the world as effectively as the communist message because Americans were reactive, while the Soviets were proactive. Soviet efforts to achieve support in the emerging Third World had begun in earnest in the mid-1950s; their apparent success there struck ER not as proof of the content of their message but rather of its dynamism.

She again held to her belief in the principle of continued personal contact in 1960, when she invited Soviet premier Nikita Khrushchev to join her for tea at her Val-Kill* home in Hyde Park,* New York. A hail of criticism rained down on her for this invitation, because it came after Khrushchev's angry and violent display of anti-Americanism at the United Nations. Responding to this criticism, ER wrote, "We have to face the fact that either all of us are going to die together or we are going to learn to live together and if we are to live together we will have to talk" (Lash, 273).

Although she never doubted the pernicious nature of the Soviets' goal for worldwide expansion of communism, her commitment to the anti-communist crusade was constantly called into question. In part, this was due to her refusal to demonize the Soviets, demonstrated by her willingness to drink tea with Khrushchev and to compliment the Soviets on positive attributes of their commitment to their own ideology. But her commitment to anticommunism was also challenged because she refused to accept the conventional view that the best way to protect against communist aggression was to create a climate of suspicion and fear. She made her opposition to the scare tactics of such prominent cold warriors as Joseph McCarthy and Richard Nixon publicly known. The Federal Bureau of Investigation* kept a file of her "My Day"* newspaper columns, which, to it, demonstrated a willingness to be duped by communists.

From 1952, when she resigned her post at the United Nations upon the election of President Dwight D. Eisenhower,* until her death ten years later, ER continued to exercise her unique style to persuade others of the virtuousness of the American way. It little mattered that she no longer had an official government role, because her prestige and popularity had always sprung from other sources. Instead of negotiating directly with Soviet agents, she turned her attention to her writings, her public speeches, and her travels. She spoke personally or by radio* to people in many countries around the world who seemed vulnerable to the communist message. Through her columns, she tried to warn Americans of the dangers of loyalty oaths and secrecy.

Her active political support of Adlai Stevenson,* the Democratic candidate for president in 1952 and 1956, reflected her belief that he would respond to the Soviet threat in a less confrontational manner than his opponent. All these activities were carried out in her singular style and served to remind the American people that one could be opposed to communism without resorting to demonization of the enemy or undermining the American system through violations of civil liberties. Given the rarity of this combination of beliefs in American politics during the first decades of the Cold War, ER's stance on this issue was an important counterbalance to the prevailing attitudes of the day.

SELECTED BIBLIOGRAPHY

Black, Allida M., ed. *What I Hope to Leave Behind: The Essential Essays of Eleanor Roosevelt*. 1995.

Lash, Joseph P. *Eleanor: The Years Alone*. 1972.

Anna Kasten Nelson and Sara E. Wilson

CONGRESS. Eleanor Roosevelt charmed and exasperated members of Congress by her unconventional behavior as a president's wife and widow. Northern liberals applauded her as an ally, while southern conservatives objected to her civil rights* advocacy. Republicans often suspected her motives, and Democrats sometimes regarded her as a cross to bear. She raised issues that many in Congress preferred to avoid, agitated their constituents, and challenged their assumptions about "a woman's place."

Previous First Ladies* had provoked sporadic congressional criticism and scrutiny, but none had engendered so much controversy. ER was the first wife of a president to testify before a congressional committee; first to hold a government office (as the assistant director of the Office of Civilian Defense*); first nominated to a post requiring Senate confirmation (as a U.S. representative to the General Assembly of the United Nations*); and first to promote or oppose legislation through newspaper columns and radio* addresses. Her travels* also took her into almost every state and congressional district.

At the White House, ER observed how President Franklin D. Roosevelt* always counted potential votes in Congress before determining his "must" legislation, which did not necessarily include the bills that she wanted. Blaming his hesitation on a general lack of votes for civil rights, stemming in particular from opposition by southerners who chaired key committees, FDR was unwilling to endorse the civil rights measures that his wife championed. She accepted the need for caution but worked behind the scenes to assure Senate sponsors of antilynching* legislation that her husband wanted it enacted. Such indirect presidential support failed to impress Senate leaders, and a federal antilynching law never was passed.

ER's sponsorship of a community-run factory in Arthurdale,* West Virginia, where workers would make equipment for post offices, aroused the first criticism of her in Congress. In 1934 Senator Thomas Schall (R-MN) accused ER of spending taxpayer money on a "West Virginia commune" (Lash, *Eleanor and Franklin*, 400). Although she refuted the charges, Congress rejected government financing for the factory. She reluctantly abandoned the project to avoid more criticism on Capitol Hill.

When the House Un-American Activities Committee* called leaders of the American Youth Congress* to testify before it in 1939, ER urged the young people to act with restraint, even if the committee appeared unfair. She personally attended the hearings, saying, "I just came to listen" (Lash, *Eleanor and Franklin*, 599). When the committee began to grill Joseph P. Lash,* ER moved to the press table as if to report on the hearing, "and the tone of the questions changed immediately," she observed (Roosevelt, 202). On the House floor, Representative Clare Hoffman (R-MI) accused the American Youth Congress of having communist connections. ER should realize, said Hoffman, that she was not simply an individual who could associate with anyone she chose but was someone who spoke with authority because she lived in the White House.

ER herself testified before congressional committees in 1940 and 1942. Called as the nation's "Migrant No. 1" because of her travels, she was invited to address select committees on migration (National Defense Migration, 9766). Whenever these committees went into the field to investigate migrant conditions, they found that she had been there before them. "Well, Mrs. Roosevelt, you speak my language," Chairman John Tolan (D-CA) commented after she called for improving the living and working conditions of migrant labor (*National Defense Migration*, 9767).

With World War II* approaching, ER accepted an unsalaried post as assistant director of the Office of Civilian Defense (OCD) in September 1941. She supervised volunteer programs, hoping to channel wartime patriotism into social reforms. By accepting this appointment, however, she offered political opponents of the New Deal* a means of indirectly attacking the commander in chief. Congressional critics railed against ER's appointments, especially the designation of Mayris Chaney, a dancer and friend, as a recreation director. Even some of her supporters voted to prohibit spending on "aesthetic diversions" in order to preserve the OCD's air-raid functions. Realizing that she was hurting the agency, ER resigned in February 1942. In her "My Day"* column of 23 February 1942, she acknowledged that "the wife of any president cannot be looked upon as an individual by other people in the government. She must always carry the reflection of influence or power beyond that of the usual government public servant. I hoped that this was not true, but I have found out that it was."

ER made a special effort to aid women members of Congress, inviting Republicans and Democrats alike to the White House. Representative (later Senator) Margaret Chase Smith (R-ME) "respected and admired Mrs. Roosevelt for her intelligence and active leadership and also because, in whatever circumstances, she was a lady" (Smith, 203). ER encouraged Helen Gahagan Douglas* (D-CA) to run for office and bolstered other women's congressional careers.

During her last years in the White House, her support for civil rights triggered vitriolic attacks from Senator Theodore Bilbo* (D-MS). He concluded one Senate speech by asserting: "If I can succeed eventually in resettling the great majority of the Negroes in West Africa—and I propose to do it—I might entertain the proposition of crowning Eleanor queen of Greater Liberia" (*Congressional Record*, 78th Cong., 2d sess., 6253). The galleries hissed these remarks. In 1945, when President Harry S Truman* appointed ER as a delegate to the United Nations* (UN) General Assembly, only Senator Bilbo opposed the nomination.

ER's post–White House newspaper columns urged Congress to take a liberal stand in the areas of domestic legislation, foreign policy, and civil liberties. She urged passage of the Employment Act of 1946 (which recognized the responsibility of the federal government to prevent mass unemployment), opposed the Taft–Hartley Labor Act of 1947 (which abolished or restricted certain labor union tactics and permitted the government to invoke "cooling off" periods in national strikes), and condemned the Mundt–Nixon bill of 1948 (which required all communist organizations and their officers and members to register with the government and eventually became the Internal Security Act of 1950).

Her columns vexed some members, but others rose in her defense and had the most invective condemnations of her views stricken from the *Congressional Record*. Further restraining her congressional critics was the service of two of her sons in the House of Representatives, Franklin Roosevelt Jr.* from 1949 to 1955 and James Roosevelt* from 1955 to 1965.

In the 1950s ER scorned the anticommunist investigations of Senator Joseph R. McCarthy (R-WI). Although McCarthy's supporters urged him to call her as a witness and "tear her to tatters" (Lash, *Eleanor: The Years Alone*, 235), the senator never dared to interrogate her. ER testified before other, more congenial committees, lending her stature to House and Senate hearings on strengthening the United Nations (1955), raising the minimum wage (1959), improving conditions for migrant labor (1959), regulating the price of hearing aids (1962), and ensuring equal pay for equal work (1962). Following her death, Congress chartered the Eleanor Roosevelt Memorial Foundation (see Memorials*) to carry on her ideals.

SELECTED BIBLIOGRAPHY

Lash, Joseph P. *Eleanor and Franklin*. 1971.

———. *Eleanor: The Years Alone*. 1972.

Roosevelt, Eleanor. *This I Remember*. 1949.

Smith, Margaret Chase. *Declaration of Conscience*. 1972.

U.S. House of Representatives. *Memorial Addresses in the House of Representatives Together with Tributes on the Life and Ideals of Anna Eleanor Roosevelt*, 88th Cong., 1st Session. House Document 152. 1963.

———. Select Committee Investigating National Defense Migration. *National Defense Migration*. 77th Cong., 2d sess., 14 January 1942.

Donald A. Ritchie

COOK, NANCY (26 August 1884, Massena, NY–16 August 1962, Trumbull, CT).

Eleanor Roosevelt hones her political skills with her three close friends (l. to r.) Nancy Cook (seated), Caroline O'Day, and Marion Dickerman at the New York headquarters of the state Democratic Committee in the late 1920s. *Courtesy of Franklin D. Roosevelt Library*

Nancy Cook was born and grew up in Massena, New York, and attended Syracuse University, from which she graduated in 1912. It was there that she met Marion Dickerman.* They became almost at once fast friends, and this friendship was cemented into an intimate, lifelong relationship when the two were fellow teachers in the Fulton, New York, High School in 1913–1918. They were both ardently liberal in their political views, committed to the battles then being waged for woman suffrage, clean government, the abolition of child labor, and world peace. In the 1920s they became close friends and associates of Eleanor Roosevelt as she was moving to take on new and broader responsibilities.

Cook had remarkable manual dexterity. During World War I when she and Dickerman served on the staff of the Endell Street Military Hospital in London, she required but a dozen lessons to became expert in the making of artificial legs and thereafter made every one of them fitted to an amputee before his hospital discharge. She became expert also in woodworking, in photography, as a cook, and in both landscape and interior design. Equally notable was her talent for organizing and managing human activities—a talent she exercised as campaign manager in Dickerman's race for the New York State Assembly in 1919. Although Dickerman lost, she ran a surprisingly strong campaign, thanks in good part to Cook.

For Cook, this 1919 campaign experience was career-decisive: she found political activity much more to her liking than teaching and therefore eagerly accepted in early 1920 an offer to organize a Women's Division of the New York state Democratic Committee. She did so with dispatch, becoming then the new division's executive secretary and holding that position for nineteen years, during which she was active in the gubernatorial and presidential campaigns of both Alfred E. Smith* and Franklin D. Roosevelt.* As executive secretary in quest of a "name" speaker for a large fund-raising luncheon in New York City, in the spring of 1922, she introduced herself over the phone to ER and persuaded her as the wife of the 1920 Democratic vice presidential candidate to make the first public speech* she ever made before a large audience. Thus, Cook introduced Dickerman to ER in the early summer of 1922.

In the extraordinarily close triple friendship that then thrived all through the 1920s and well into the Great Depression* years, Cook played an entrepreneurial and managerial role. In the New York Democratic Committee Women's Division activities in which they all engaged, in the long camping trips they took with the two youngest Roosevelt sons (Franklin Roosevelt Jr.* and John Roosevelt*), in the design of the grounds of the Val-Kill* cottage at Hyde Park,* which the three women had built in 1925 as a home for Cook and Dickerman and vacation retreat for ER, in the furnishing of that house—in all these, Cook's was the practical directing hand. She did the planning and organizing of the frequent large picnics in the following years, which FDR hosted at Val-Kill and in 1933 on Campobello* Island, New Brunswick. The only photographs of these picnics, of which a notable one (in June 1939) had the king and queen of England as honored guests, were taken by Cook with her still and movie cameras. Cook launched and managed Val-Kill Industries, jointly owned by the three women, which from 1927 to 1936 handcrafted exact replicas of colonial furniture for sale in New York City stores and also made two four-poster beds, one for the president and one for the First Lady, when FDR moved into the White House in 1933—beds used by the Roosevelts for the dozen years of FDR's presidency. Cook, though also co-owner with Dickerman and ER of the Todhunter School,* played no very active role in that enterprise, but at ER's request she became intensely active as creator and director of a handicraft center in Arthurdale,* a community-development project of the New Deal* in West Virginia—a project in which ER was deeply involved.

During these years, Caroline O'Day,* who became New York's congress-woman at large in 1935, was only slightly less close to ER, Dickerman, and Cook than the three were to each other.

The pressures and new activities that enveloped ER during the White House years led to some loosening of her ties with Cook and Dickerman, although she involved them in as many of her White House activities as she could. With the closure of Val-Kill Industries in 1936, ER remodeled its shop building into a country home for herself and began using it in 1937.

It was evidently by Cook's agency that the strong ties between ER and her two heretofore close friends were finally broken in the late summer of 1938. During a long night conversation between ER and Cook (Dickerman was then abroad), both became emotional and said "things that should not have been said," as Dickerman later put it (Davis, 150). Cook's words so disillusioned and hurt ER that she never again communicated intimately with either Cook or Dickerman, although the three continued to exchange gifts on Christmas and birthdays. Cook and Dickerman continued to live in Val-Kill cottage until 1947, when they moved to New Canaan, Connecticut, after ER bought out their interest in the cottage for $17,500.

SELECTED BIBLIOGRAPHY
Cook, Blanche Wiesen. *Eleanor Roosevelt*. Vols. 1, 2. 1992, 1999.
Davis, Kenneth S. *Invincible Summer: An Intimate Portrait of the Roosevelts*. 1974.
                                                                    Kenneth S. Davis

CORR, MAUREEN (26 April 1917, Armagh, Northern Ireland–   ).

Maureen Corr was Eleanor Roosevelt's personal secretary from 1953 until ER's death nine years later. Corr undertook extensive travels* with ER and described herself as "especially blessed to have had the association with Mrs. Roosevelt" (Corr, Oral History, 37).

Born in a small, rural town to the southwest of Belfast, Northern Ireland, Maureen Corr did not enjoy a pleasant childhood. She became extremely ill at age nine and was largely bedridden for several years, but she battled her way back to health by the age of seventeen. In 1943 she moved to New York City and lived with her sister and brother-in-law while she sought an education, although she had to start at the elementary level since her illness had minimized her formal childhood schooling. She persevered, finally earning a bachelor's degree in English from Hunter College in New York City.

After working as a physician's assistant, Corr obtained a job with ER in 1950 through an employment agency that had been contacted by Malvina "Tommy" Thompson* (Scheider), ER's personal secretary, who needed an assistant. Thompson interviewed and hired Corr, who accepted the job, even though she took a twenty-five-dollar-a-week cut in pay. At first, Corr served as ER's assistant secretary, becoming her personal secretary in 1953 after Thompson died. A year before her death, however, Thompson's health had deteriorated to the point where Corr took her place as ER's secretary at the United Nations* in Paris and then accompanied the former First Lady on a round-the-world trip. After Thompson died, Corr immediately went with ER on a second round-the-world trip, for which arrangements had been made long in advance. "In a way I didn't ever feel I was filling Miss Thompson's shoes," Corr recalled. "Nobody ever could" (Corr, Oral History, 2).

ER cultivated an office atmosphere that was professional, yet warm and informal. She "had total confidence in the people around her," Corr remembered (Corr interview by Webster). Corr's duties included making phone calls, scheduling appointments, and answering letters on ER's behalf. Tasks that ER insisted on performing herself, though, included writing checks and balancing her checkbook.

Life with ER was frenzied but immensely interesting: taking trips abroad, greeting famous visitors, and witnessing firsthand the lifestyle of a woman who was respected worldwide and whose opinion frequently was sought on some of the day's most important issues. Yet, the paycheck never was large, the hours were long, and the office equipment was not new. Gabriele Gutkind, another secretary who joined ER's staff in 1957, recalled that ER "was oblivious to set hours . . . [and] was also a little unaware of—let's say—current salaries" (Gutkind, Oral History, 16).

These considerations were less important to Corr than a work environment where employee contributions were recognized and valued. In this respect ER satisfied Corr's needs, and Corr labored hard in return. Corr also was influenced by the example of Thompson, who had devoted herself selflessly to keeping ER's office running smoothly. Unlike Thompson, however, Corr did not share living quarters with ER and did not let her job dominate her life. Corr said ER had told her: " 'I do not want to swallow you up. I want you to have your own life. . . . ' I think she had the feeling that Miss Thompson really had no life outside hers, and that was true" (Corr, Oral History, 3).

In Corr's view she "worked with Mrs. Roosevelt as a friend" (Corr interview by Webster) and did not conceive of herself as having a particularly exalted professional status simply because the former First Lady employed her. This was a concept that ER imparted by example: never consider anyone inferior.

Familiar with ER's way of responding, Corr took care of much of ER's correspondence. Due to her busy schedule, ER did not read all incoming letters, but she did read and sign Corr's answers. During most of her post–White House years, ER received approximately 100 letters per day—some from friends and relatives but most from strangers. Letters queried her on everything from the merits of studying Latin and Greek, to her favorite recipes. Corr's undergraduate degree in English prepared her well to answer letters, and she was not intimidated by the responsibility. When it came to personal correspondence, however, ER composed her own replies, which Corr then typed.

Corr also typed many of ER's "My Day"* newspaper columns. As she dictated the columns, which generally took her less than one half-hour to compose, ER often watched Corr's expressions closely in an effort to gauge how a particular viewpoint might be received by the public. One evening, while traveling with ER, Corr memorably typed one column's final version with the typewriter perched on the toilet seat in a hotel bathroom, so as not to disturb ER's rest.

Corr often accompanied ER on lecture tours and journeys to many places such as Syria, Lebanon, Jordan, Israel,* Pakistan, India,* Japan, Hong Kong, Greece, Yugoslavia, Brussels, England, France, and Switzerland. She also joined her employer on a notable trip to the Soviet Union in 1957, when ER interviewed Soviet premier Nikita Khrushchev. Corr was by ER's side on her final visit in August 1962 to Campobello* Island, New Brunswick, where the Roosevelt family formerly had a summer home.

After ER's death on 7 November 1962, Corr helped family members send out funeral announcements and close ER's office. She later said the most meaningful thing she learned from her contact with ER was "not to be afraid to live" (Corr, Oral History, 37). From 1963 to 1965 she worked for the Eleanor Roosevelt Memorial Foundation, from 1966 to 1969 for the Asia Society, and subsequently for the U.S. mission to the United Nations. She now is retired and lives in New York.

SELECTED BIBLIOGRAPHY

Corr, Maureen. "The Eleanor Roosevelt I Knew." In Jess Flemion and Colleen M. O'Connor, eds., Eleanor Roosevelt: An American Journey. 1987.
Eleanor Roosevelt Oral History Project, Interviews with Maureen Corr (1978) and Gabriele Gutkind (1979), Franklin D. Roosevelt Library, Hyde Park, NY.
Gurewitsch, A. David. Eleanor Roosevelt: Her Day, a Personal Album. 1974.
Lash, Joseph P. Eleanor: The Years Alone. 1972.
Maureen Corr telephone interview by Scott W. Webster, 18 June 1998.
Roosevelt, Eleanor. The Autobiography of Eleanor Roosevelt. 1961.

Scott W. Webster

CORRESPONDENCE. Eleanor Roosevelt once quoted the following statistics about the volume of mail she received in the White House: "300,000 pieces in 1933, 90,000 in 1937, and about 150,000 in 1940" (Roosevelt, "Mail of a President's Wife," 1). She was quick to point out that this correspondence did not include the president's mail; frequently, however, people did write the First Lady and asked her to give their messages to the president. One correspondent wrote: "I know you can buttonhole him at breakfast and make him listen." ER responded with good humor: "He would be at breakfast all day and far into the night if he even scanned my mail!" ("Mrs. Eleanor Roosevelt's Own Radio Program," 4). But many citizens felt that she could make the president listen, and in some instances, if he would not do something, she would. A case in point was a letter written to Franklin D. Roosevelt* in 1941 by a black mother who complained about racial discrimination against her son. She concluded with a P.S.: "I expect to hear from you right away because if I don't, I'll write to Mrs. Roosevelt!" (cited in Dorothy I. Height speech, ER Centennial Conference, Vassar College, 14 October 1984).

Because of the huge quantities of mail ER received in the early days of the administration, her staff consulted the records of the previous administrations for guidance. To their astonishment they found there was little comparison between the vast number of letters she received and the smaller number sent to her predecessors. When ER attempted to determine what had been the previous custom for answering mail addressed to her predecessors, a pile of form letters was brought to her that was intended to cover every contingency. Some of these letters dated as far back as the Cleveland administration. So, for example, if a woman wrote and said her child pined for an elephant and would Mrs. (president's wife) provide one, the standard reply under the "form" system would automatically be: "Mrs. [president's wife] has had so many similar requests she deeply regrets she cannot comply with yours!" (Roosevelt, "My Mail"). Believing the form system was not adequate to reply to the grave questions being asked in the midst of the Great Depression* of the 1930s, ER quickly discarded most of the old forms and immediately began to set a new system into motion.

ER's correspondence files at the Franklin D. Roosevelt Library in Hyde Park* number roughly 2 million pages and consist largely of correspondence from the general public. Over the years, tens of thousands of citizens wrote to her for assistance, intercession, or advice. The letters of the 1930s reflect the plight of the many desperate persons hit by the depression: farmers whose properties were foreclosed; World War I veterans seeking bonuses, medical help, or hospitalization; unemployed persons appealing for jobs or funds; families in legal, social, or financial difficulties of every description. Correspondence of this type led ER to write, "I think I have been asked to do something about everything in the world except change the weather!" (Roosevelt, "Mail of a President's Wife," 2). She elaborated with the following story: "A woman wrote and asked me to find a baby for her to adopt. Her second letter explained that if I found the baby, she would need a cow, and if she had the cow, she would need an electric icebox in which to keep the milk for the baby!" (Roosevelt, "Mail of a President's Wife," 2).

Until the appropriate government agencies to address depression-era needs were established, ER sent many of the heartrending letters she received to various friends who were in a position to be of assistance; later, she was able to send these letters on to federal agencies. Many of the letters asking for material assistance were referred to government officials for action. ER replied to relatively few letters in this category, but she did carry on an extensive correspondence with department heads and federal officials, including cabinet members, about the concerns brought to her attention by the citizenry. Losing one's home was one of the great worries for the middle class in the 1930s. Incoming letters to ER concerning this fear were turned over to the newly formed Home Owner's Loan Corporation (HOLC). For many, this agency was their last resort, as the following letter demonstrates so poignantly: "Dear Mrs. Roosevelt: Thank you very much for helping me to keep my house. If it wasn't for you I know I would have lost it. . . . I would have killed myself if I would have lost my house. I will never forget you. . . . Forgive me if I caused you any trouble" (J. Graziano to ER, 28 August 1934).

Many proud, but frightened, people were embarrassed by their situation and the fact that they needed help. They, too, wrote to ER but asked that their pleas be kept confidential, and they were. One such letter read in part: "It is very humiliating for me to have to write you" and "*Please* Mrs. Roosevelt, I do not want charity, only a chance . . . somehow we will manage—but without charity" (R. Trickel to ER, 3 April 1935).

Correspondence to ER after 1940 reflected the general improvement of business conditions. Letters at this point began to deal with aspects of Selective Service, conditions in military camps, and complaints about treatment of draftees. As World War II* advanced, her correspondence reflected the pressures of wartime, including appeals from parents for release of their sons from the armed forces and complaints about gas rationing, price controls, race riots, and the shortages of goods and services.

The letters from service personnel in World War II (1942–1945) to ER provide an excellent social and historical commentary on the lives of men and women in the armed services, describing the effect of war not only on those serving but on their families and their needs. Racial discrimination was one of the many problems faced by servicemen that disturbed and frustrated ER. She wrote to her friend Joseph P. Lash* in 1942, "Young Neil Vanderbilt came to see me this P.M. and told me some shocking things about the attitude of officers towards the Negro troops. I don't wonder they are resentful & will of course tell FDR but I wonder if he can do anything" (ER to JPL, 1 May 1942).

Letters in ER's so-called personal file were handled quite differently than those in the general public category. Ninety percent of the letters in the "personal file" category were drafted and signed by her. This part of her correspondence reflected and documented her interest and service in the fields of labor,* youth,* civil liberties, public welfare, education, refugees,* woman's rights, and national defense. A statement in ER's autobiography shed light on the relationship her correspondence had with the choice of the causes and concerns she made her own. She wrote that "my interest or sympathy or indignation is not aroused by an abstract cause but by the plight of a single person" (Roosevelt, *Autobiography*, 413).

It was to this type of personal correspondent that ER gave of herself. People who wrote to her felt that she cared about them personally and individually. Often ER would answer petitions for help with a sympathetic letter, an admonition to a federal department to take some action, or even a personal check. Her correspondents ran a wide gambit and included black educator Mary McLeod Bethune,* novelist Pearl Buck, Madame Chiang Kai-shek,* Prime Minister Winston Churchill,* California congresswoman and friend Helen Gahagan Douglas,* philanthropist Mary Lasker, secretary of the treasury Henry Morgenthau Jr., Congresswoman Caroline O'Day,* Secretary of Labor Frances Perkins,* Walter Reuther* of the United Auto Workers, social welfare expert Lillian Wald,* and Walter White* of the National Association for the Advancement of Colored People.*

One of ER's enduring legacies to her successors in the White House was the life she built for herself after FDR's death, when she was on her own. Instead of retreating into private life, she became a public figure in her own right and went on to become the acknowledged "First Lady of the World," a title bestowed on her by President Harry S Truman.*

A large portion of ER's post–White House correspondence, 1945–1962, consists of letters from the general public, although she continued numerous exchanges with personal friends, acquaintances, relatives, and associates. Correspondence from her later years reflected her myriad activities of that period. For each year, a considerable amount of correspondence consisted of tributes to, and criticisms of, FDR; requests for photographs, autographs, stamps, franked envelopes, material assistance, employment, interviews and advice, statements, endorsements, and contributions; invitations to speak and to attend dinners and meetings; and requests to write books* and articles as well as prefaces and introductions for other authors. An extensive portion of ER's daily mail gave reactions from the public to her activities and comments, especially her "My Day"* columns. In 1949 she received almost 6,000 public reaction letters about her controversy with Cardinal Francis Joseph Spellman* of New York over public aid to parochial schools and again in 1957 thousands of letters on her trip to the Soviet Union.

Much of the correspondence in these years was fairly routine, but it is interesting to find that at times ER would write significant responses to ordinary citizens on any number of domestic and international issues. For example, in December 1950, when she was a U.S. delegate to the United Nations,* she replied in a two-page letter to questions raised by Mrs. Hugh Marshall of Dayton, Oregon. In the letter ER defended FDR's Russian policy; denied being a communist; denied FDR was a protégé of Gerhart Eisler (alleged communist spy); denied Joseph P. Lash* was a protégé of hers; declared her support for Helen Gahagan Douglas;* denied that Douglas' husband, actor Melvyn Douglas,* was a communist; defended Dean Acheson; said Alger Hiss was convicted of perjury on circumstantial evidence, not of being a communist; and implied that Fulton Lewis, Westbrook Pegler,* and John O'Donnell (three journalists hostile to the Roosevelts) were not "decent" people! (ER to Mrs. Hugh N. Marshall, 11 December 1950).

Most topics addressed by ER during the post–White House years were those of public concern. In the years immediately after World War II, there was much correspondence relating to the problems of refugees and displaced persons, American relief efforts, the United Nations, and American foreign policy. There also was correspondence concerning domestic politics, communism, the McCarthy hearings, presidential campaigns, racial integration, and school desegregation. Minority rights were a recurring theme, and every year there were letters concerning the plight of blacks, American Indians, and women.

The voluminous amount of correspondence received by ER during her time as First Lady and in the seventeen years after the White House perhaps was directly attributable to a short article titled, "I Want You to Write to Me," which she had written in 1933 for her page in the *Woman's Home Companion.** ER explained why she issued such an invitation this way: "whatever happens to us in our lives, we find questions constantly recurring that we would gladly discuss with some friend. . . . Often it is easier to write to someone whom we do not expect ever to see" (Roosevelt, "I Want You to Write Me," 4). Little did she realize at the time that her invitation would trigger an avalanche.

SELECTED BIBLIOGRAPHY
Eleanor Roosevelt Papers, Franklin D. Roosevelt Library, Hyde Park, NY.
Roosevelt, Eleanor. *The Autobiography of Eleanor Roosevelt*. 1961.
———. "Mail of a President's Wife," unpublished article; "My Mail," unpublished article; and "Mrs. Eleanor Roosevelt's Own Radio Program," Speech and Article File, 1939, 1940, Eleanor Roosevelt Papers, Franklin D. Roosevelt Library, Hyde Park, NY.
Roosevelt, Mrs. Franklin D. "I Want You to Write Me." *Woman's Home Companion* 60 (August 1933): 4.
Seeber, Frances M. " 'I Want You to Write to Me': The Papers of Anna Eleanor

Roosevelt." In Nancy Kegan Smith and Mary C. Ryan, eds., *Modern First Ladies: Their Documentary Legacy*. 1989.

Frances M. Seeber

COWLES, ANNA ROOSEVELT (18 January 1855, New York–25 August 1931, Farmington, CT).

Anna Roosevelt Cowles was Eleanor Roosevelt's aunt, the eldest sister of ER's father, Elliott Roosevelt.* Anna, called Bye or Bamie, suffered from curvature of the spine as a girl and debilitating arthritis and hearing loss as a woman. These painful health problems never interfered with her joy in living, passion for politics, or willingness to help out during times of crisis. Bye occupied a central place in the Roosevelt family, attempting to look after Elliott during his bouts with alcoholism and extending a sympathetic hand to the orphaned ER.

Anna played an integral role in the rise of her brother, Theodore Roosevelt,* to political prominence and cared for his infant daughter, Alice Roosevelt (Longworth),* after the death of Theodore's first wife. As president, Theodore used her Washington home as a salon where he conferred with an eclectic assortment of intellectuals, politicians, artists, and journalists that she convened. Bye was an assertive, self-sufficient, opinionated, and charismatic woman who cared deeply about domestic and international affairs. ER observed her aunt's wisdom firsthand, for she often stayed at her Auntie Bye's home when Theodore was in the White House.

At age fifteen Bye had attended Les Ruches, a school in Fontainebleau, France, run by Mlle. Marie Souvestre,* a freethinking agnostic, under whom ER later was educated at Allenswood School in England. As a young woman Bye had caught the eye of the recently widowed James Roosevelt of Hyde Park,* a distant cousin, but she had no romantic interest in him. Her mother, Mittie Roosevelt, then introduced him to Bye's friend, Sara Delano (Roosevelt*), and the two soon were married, becoming the parents of Franklin D. Roosevelt.*

A close friend of James' son by his first marriage, James "Rosy" Roosevelt, Bye traveled to London when "Rosy" was serving in the U.S. embassy there and cared for his children after his wife died. There, in 1895 at the age of forty, Bye married William Cowles, a U.S. naval officer, who subsequently became a rear admiral. Three years later she gave birth to a son, William Cowles Jr., called Shef. His godfather was Robert Munro Ferguson, with whom Bye had an intense friendship before going to England. Ferguson later married Isabella Greenway,* one of ER's bridesmaids at her wedding to FDR.

When FDR became assistant secretary of the navy, Bye schooled ER in the niceties of naval etiquette and Washington protocol, especially the art of social calling, considered a necessity for political wives at the time. After her husband's retirement from the navy, Bye lived in Oldgate, the Cowles' ancestral home in Connecticut. Worsening health restricted her civic activities, but she applauded ER's dedication to political and social causes.

ER admired her aunt. Like her Uncle Theodore, Bye was a role model for her. Bye provided solace for ER in her difficult childhood, a social and political primer for ER as she became more active, and an example of a strong, thoughtful, independent woman throughout her life.

SELECTED BIBLIOGRAPHY

Caroli, Betty Boyd. *The Roosevelt Women*. 1998.
McCullough, David. *Mornings on Horseback*. 1981.
Morris, Sylvia Jukes. *Edith Kermit Roosevelt: Portrait of a First Lady*. 1980.
Rixey, Lilian. *Bamie: Theodore Roosevelt's Remarkable Sister*. 1963.

Stacy A. Cordery

CRAIG, ELISABETH MAY (19 December 1888, Coosaw Mines, SC–15 July 1975, Silver Spring, MD).

May Craig, diminutive correspondent for a group of Maine newspapers, was a leader among the group of struggling Washington women journalists during the Roosevelt era whose efforts to compete in a male-dominated profession were enhanced by friendship with Eleanor Roosevelt. Craig, however, believed that journalists should be nonpartisan and was not afraid to speak her mind to ER.

Born Elisabeth May Adams, after the death of her mother, she was raised by foster parents, Frances and William Weymouth, who owned the phosphate mines where her father worked. She moved with the Weymouths to Washington when she was twelve, and eight years later, over their objections, married Donald A. Craig, a newspaperman. When he was injured in an automobile accident in 1923, she helped him write political columns, becoming his successor as Washington correspondent for the Gannett newspaper chain after his death in 1936. The couple had two children, a son and a daughter.

During a forty-year career, Craig wrote seven chatty columns a week for her Maine newspapers, sometimes drawing on information gained from ER, and went to Europe as a World War II* correspondent. Wearing the flowered hats that became her trademark, she drew national attention for frequent appearances on broadcasts of *Meet the Press* and tart questioning of presidents at press conferences.* She scored several "firsts"— such as being the first woman correspondent on a battleship, the first woman to cover the Korean truce talks, and the first woman to fly over the North Pole. She also served as president of the Women's National Press Club* in 1943.

A feminist and one of the few journalists admitted to the press conferences of both Franklin D. Roosevelt* and the First Lady, Craig objected to the ban on male reporters at ER's White House press conferences. Opposed to rules that barred women from covering news events at the National Press Club and elsewhere, Craig contended it was only fair to open ER's conferences to all journalists, although ER refused to do so. Craig annually attempted unsuccessfully to attend the all-male dinner of the White House Correspondents' Association.

Formal contacts between ER and Craig at ER's press conferences, which Craig attended from their inception in 1933, soon nurtured frequent correspondence between the two, trips to Hyde Park* and Campobello Island* for Craig, exclusive parties, and special visits by ER to the modest Craig home on Capitol Hill. Craig's views, on matters both public and private, got a sympathetic ear at the White House.

For instance, as a member of the American Newspaper Guild,* Craig advised ER not to leave the union at a time when it was said to be infiltrated by communists: "That would ruin us and do no good. It would please the publishers who don't want a Guild anyway" (MC to ER, 29 July 1940). ER, who claimed membership because of her "My Day"* column, answered that she would remain in, "though I feel very useless, because I cannot attend meetings or really speak out" (ER to MC, 31 July 1940). Subsequently, ER decided to become more active in spite of being First Lady.

Following the exchange of letters on the guild, Craig reported to ER that other journalists had interpreted a "My Day" column to mean that she was "bucking the old man" (FDR) on a conscription bill (MC to ER, 6 August 1940). ER replied that she was not "bucking the President" but that she wanted an expansion of national service for both men and women (ER to MC, 8 August 1940). In the same letter ER invited Craig to join her at the World's Fair in New York and then come to Hyde Park for a visit.

Craig readily reported on her contacts with both Roosevelts and lobbied them on such issues as support for a power project in Maine. Her access advanced her professional status with her employer, Guy Gannett, who was proud of her relationship with the president and First Lady. As a result he allowed her to undertake travel and assignments all over the globe. In the 1950s and 1960s Craig visited defense facilities and toured the Soviet Union and Latin America. She retired in 1965 and lived with her daughter in Maryland before entering a nursing home.

SELECTED BIBLIOGRAPHY
Eleanor Roosevelt Papers, Franklin D. Roosevelt Library, Hyde Park, NY.
Elisabeth May Craig Papers, Manuscript Division, Library of Congress, Washington, DC.
Lash, Joseph P. *Eleanor and Franklin.* 1971.

Donald R. Larrabee

CRITICS. Eleanor Roosevelt became one of the most admired women of her time, but as the outspoken First Lady of the New Deal,* she was also a lightning rod for political rancor. In the 1940 presidential election campaign, the Republicans distributed "We Don't Want Eleanor Either" buttons (Lash, 630). Such criticism not only was a spillover from that directed toward Franklin D. Roosevelt* but also was associated with her unprecedented activities as the wife of the president. She was frequently chastised for not knowing her place as a woman or how to dignify the role of the First Lady. She was castigated for making money through writing, lecturing, and broadcasting, having Jewish and African American friends, traveling extensively, and constantly being in the public eye.

With her frequent, but often measured, advocacy of reform initiatives, ER also found critics on both sides of a number of issues. Traditionalists intent on maintaining the status quo criticized her for focusing attention on causes that showed defects in American society. Activists agitating for woman's and minority rights criticized her for accepting limitations on progress toward full equality.

Many were taken aback as she moved beyond the ceremonial confines of the White House. She was everywhere Americans were, and she voiced her thoughts about the situations in which she found herself. Depicting her as a gadabout globetrotter, political pundits and editorial cartoonists regularly lampooned her travels.* Cartoonist Herbert Block captured both her travels and her willingness to share her experiences in a cartoon distributed by a newspaper syndicate in October 1942 that depicted ER dictating her "My Day"* newspaper column while riding in a boat filled with armed Allied commandos guarding Nazi prisoners.

In Congress,* the First Lady was never more hotly debated than when her independent earnings were at issue. When hotels bought furniture from her Val-Kill* factory in Hyde Park,* New York, Senator Thomas Schall (R-MN) accused her of profiteering from her position as First Lady. When newspapers purchased her syndicated column, "My Day," she was called greedy. Her unpaid five-month stint as assistant director of the Office of Civilian Defense* also drew fire, particularly when she hired her friend, dancer Mayris Chaney, to run a physical fitness program.

While she was widely criticized for supporting more active roles for women, she was reproached by some feminists for not using her position to push for passage of an Equal Rights Amendment* (ERA). During her White House years, ER supported ERA opponents, who argued that the amendment would undermine protective labor* legislation for women.

Conservatives accused her of moving too fast on race relations, while activists sometimes urged her to press for quicker reform. Segregationists objected to her appearances with African Americans, whom she made highly visible on occasion by allowing herself to be photographed with them. Some southern defenders of segregation beseeched ER not to endorse integrated gatherings on the grounds that inclusion sullied the purity of (white) American womanhood. Bigots fabricated rumors of "Eleanor Clubs,"* mythical groups to divert African American domestic workers into other employment, and told "Eleanor stories," which alleged that ER's interest in race had its basis in promiscuity and miscegenation. On the other hand, when she discouraged a proposed march on Washington in 1941 to protest the lack of integration in defense industries and the armed forces, some militants discounted her sincerity in racial equality. Inside the White House, some of FDR's advisers, particularly Stephen Early,* tried to temper her interest in minority affairs on grounds she was hurting the president politically.

ER's public career did not end when she left the White House, and neither did the criticism she encountered. The polemical columnist Westbrook Pegler* continued his attacks. Senator Theodore Bilbo* from Mississippi, a longtime critic of ER's advocacy of civil rights,* voted against her confirmation as a delegate to the United Nations* (UN) in 1945. During her work on the UN Commission on Human Rights, W.E.B. Du Bois* criticized her for not accepting a draft petition prepared by the National Association for the Advancement of Colored People* that pointed out America's poor record on race relations.

Yet, there was a positive shift in public comment on ER's activities during the post–White House years. Speaking of this period in an editorial after her death, the *New York Times* on 8 November 1962, said that "many of her erstwhile critics . . . now fell silent or joined in acclaim for this amazing woman." Nevertheless, even among the worldwide outpouring of eulogies for ER, a discordant note could be found. William F. Buckley Jr. said her "principal bequest . . . was the capacity . . . to oversimplify problems" and claimed she had "deeply wounded the processes of purposive political thought" (Buckley, 58).

SELECTED BIBLIOGRAPHY

Beasley, Maurine. *Eleanor Roosevelt and the Media: A Public Quest for Self-Fulfillment.* 1987.

Blum, John Morton. *V Was for Victory: Politics and American Culture during World War II.* 1976.

Buckley, William F., Jr. "Mrs. Roosevelt, RIP." *National Review* 14 (29 January 1963): 58.

Hoff-Wilson, Joan, and Marjorie Lightman, eds. *Without Precedent: The Life and Career of Eleanor Roosevelt.* 1984.

Lash, Joseph P. *Eleanor and Franklin.* 1971.

Wolfskill, George, and John A. Hudson. *All but the People: Franklin D. Roosevelt and His Critics, 1933–39.* 1969.

Therese L. Lueck

CUNNINGHAM, MINNIE FISHER (19 March 1882, New Waverly, TX– 9 December 1964, Conroe, TX).

Minnie Fisher Cunningham, a Texan who chose politics and social reform as her lifework, was one of the women who inspired Eleanor Roosevelt to enter the public arena. The two women first met at the 1921 convention of the League of Women Voters* (LWV) in Cleveland, where Cunningham's passionate speech on the need for child welfare legislation stimulated ER's interest in political activity. One of the first women to earn a degree in pharmacy from the University of Texas Medical Branch (in 1901), Cunningham was drawn into public life through the woman suffrage movement, serving as president of the Texas Equal Suffrage Association from 1915 to 1919 and as secretary of the National American Woman Suffrage Association's Congressional Committee in the winter of 1918–19. After the passage of the Nineteenth Amendment, she helped organize the LWV and served as its executive secretary from 1921 to 1923.

When ER initially encountered Cunningham, the latter was lobbying for the Sheppard–Towner Maternity and Infancy Act, the country's first federal social welfare program. Speaking years later on 1 May 1940 to another LWV convention, ER recalled Cunningham's 1921 oratory and said it was Cunningham "who first made me feel that you had no right to be a slacker as a citizen, you had no right not to take an active part in what was happening to your country as a whole." When ER was named chair of the Democratic Woman's Advisory Committee, formed to offer input on women's issues to the platform committee at the 1924 Democratic National Convention, she chose Cunningham as one of the members.

Living in Washington from 1925 to 1928, Cunningham served as executive secretary of the Woman's National Democratic Club* and as acting head of the Democratic National Committee's Women's Division in 1927. After an unsuccessful attempt to gain election as U.S. senator from Texas in 1928, Cunningham became associate editor and then editor in 1935 for the Texas Extension Service. She corresponded with ER during the 1930s, becoming part of the network that informed the First Lady on New Deal* programs and their effect on women. Cunningham wrote the script for a 1934 documentary film, *The Rural Community Work Center*, which ER and Franklin D. Roosevelt* showed one evening to White House dinner guests.

Cunningham continued to be active in women's voluntary organizations during the 1930s, and in 1938 the General Federation of Women's Clubs appointed her chair of its national committee on urban–rural cooperation. The following year the Department of Agriculture brought her back to Washington as a senior information specialist. Cunningham organized the department's national urban–rural conference in April 1939, which was attended by representatives from major women's organizations. At its conclusion ER invited Cunningham and the participants to the White House.

Shortly after FDR established the National Defense Advisory Commission in 1940, Cunningham was appointed chief of its civic contacts unit to coordinate the efforts of civic groups, including women's voluntary organizations. This was a temporary position; Cunningham returned to the Department of Agriculture in 1941.

ER depended on Cunningham and women in similar positions to keep her informed about women's activities during World War II* so she could publicize them. ER used material from Cunningham in her "My Day"* columns and radio broadcasts.* In her column for 15 September 1942, for example, ER wrote approvingly of efforts by the Department of Agriculture to arrange for women as well as men to serve on local committees that administered farm programs. Cunningham shared ER's concern over women's inequitable treatment during the war and on at least three occasions between March 1942 and March 1943 met with ER in the White House to discuss the situation.

When anti–New Deal forces gained control of the Department of Agriculture in 1943, Cunningham resigned and returned to Texas. She ran unsuccessfully as a Roosevelt Democrat in the 1944 Texas Democratic gubernatorial primary. In the postwar period Cunningham was a central figure in the struggle between New Deal and conservative Democrats for control of the Texas Democratic Party.* The bond between ER and Cunningham strengthened Cunningham's commitment to New Deal liberalism as a vehicle for creating more opportunity for women in American political life.

SELECTED BIBLIOGRAPHY

League of Women Voters Papers, Library of Congress, Washington, DC.
Minnie Fisher Cunningham Papers, Houston Metropolitan Research Center, Houston Public Library, Houston, TX.
Minnie Fisher Cunningham Papers, University of Houston, Houston, Texas.
McArthur, Judith N. *Creating the New Woman: The Rise of Southern Women's Progressive Culture in Texas, 1893–1918*. 1998.
———. "Minnie Fisher Cunningham's Back Door Lobby in Texas: Political Maneuvering in a One-Party State." In Marjorie Spruill Wheeler, ed., *One Woman, One Vote: Rediscovering the Woman Suffrage Movement*. 1995.
McArthur, Judith N., and Harold L. Smith. *Minnie Fisher Cunningham: Constructing a New World for Women*. 2000.

Judith N. McArthur and Harold L. Smith

D

DEATH OF ELEANOR ROOSEVELT. Tributes to Eleanor Roosevelt came from around the world after her death from anemia and tuberculosis at the age of seventy-eight on 7 November 1962 in New York City. President John F. Kennedy* called her "one of the great ladies in the history of this country" (*New York Times*, 8 November 1962). Acting secretary-general U Thant of the United Nations* said, "She was truly the first lady of the world." In a message to her family, Indian prime minister Jawaharlal Nehru* wrote, "No woman of this generation and few in the annals of history have so well understood and articulated the yearnings of men and women for social justice." A message from Soviet premier Nikita Khrushchev said, "After the death of President Franklin D. Roosevelt,* Eleanor Roosevelt remained true to his convictions about the necessity for good relations between the Soviet Union and the United States in the necessity of strengthening peace in the world." Queen Elizabeth of England noted, "The British people held her in deep respect and affection and mourn her passing" (*New York Times*, 9 November 1962).

At a special memorial service on 9 November 1962 at the United Nations, where ER had served as a U.S. delegate from 1946 to 1953, diplomats from 110 countries stood for a one-minute silent tribute. Then they heard a eulogy given by U.S. ambassador Adlai E. Stevenson,* who said, "She would rather light candles than curse the darkness, and her glow [has] warmed the world" (Associated Press and United Press International dispatches, New York, 9 November 1962).

President Kennedy, Vice President Lyndon B. Johnson, and former presidents Harry S Truman* and Dwight D. Eisenhower* attended her funeral service on 10 November 1962 in St. James Episcopal Church in Hyde Park,* New York. First Lady Jackie Kennedy, former First Lady Bess Truman, and Lady Bird Johnson also were present. ER was buried next to FDR in the rose garden of the Roosevelts' Hyde Park estate, which had been designated a national historic site in 1944. On 17 November 1962 an estimated 10,000 people attended a memorial service for her at the Cathedral Church of St. John the Divine in New York City, where Adlai Stevenson again delivered a eulogy praising ER for her efforts for the downtrodden and world peace.

ER's death was front-page news in newspapers all over the world. The major American news services—the Associated Press (AP) and United Press International (UPI)—dispatched numerous stories and wire photos on her memorial services and funeral and provided feature articles on her life and accomplishments. Her portrayal in obituaries was not entirely reverential. Note was taken of her unhappy childhood, her perception of herself as plain, her protruding teeth, and her long-lasting difficulties with her mother-in-law, Sara Delano Roosevelt.* Associated Press feature writer Cynthia Lowry, who knew ER personally, said, "She was a curious mixture of kindly, deep concern for people and impersonality" and "Mrs. Roosevelt really became interested in individuals only when they had problems" (*Los Angeles Herald-Examiner*, 9 November 1962). The traditionally anti-Roosevelt *Chicago Tribune* on 9 November 1962 headlined a Reuters dispatch on tributes to ER from world leaders: "Red Bloc Joins in Tribute to F.D.R. Widow." An Associated Press dispatch from New York that appeared 8 November 1962 in numerous newspapers said, "Mrs. Roosevelt was as controversial as she was prominent. . . . But loved or despised, she was a woman too vital ever to be ignored."

Editorial comment and appreciations, however, most often pictured her as a gracious lady of courage and devotion to her country, "a good and great individual of our time" (*Chicago Sun-Times*, 9 November 1962). Journalist May Craig,* a personal friend of ER, praised her for supporting her husband's return to politics after his polio attack. Craig wrote that ER became "his 'legs' and his eyes and ears, painfully overcoming her natural shyness, as a political campaigner and public speaker" in her efforts to keep him from becoming "a crippled invalid, pampered in the Hyde Park mansion by his mother" (*Kennebec (Maine) Journal*, 10 November 1962).

ER also was lauded for her own activities and achievements—her work at the United Nations, her world travels,* public appearances, lectures, books,* and newspaper column, "My Day."* An uncompromising sense of duty and "thirst for life and insatiable curiosity" were identified as qualities that "gave her a stature that went far beyond her position as a President's wife and widow" (*New York Times*, 11 November 1962).

Peace,* race relations, and the role of women were prominently featured as issues that interested ER. Her work on the UN Universal Declaration of Human Rights* was stressed by commentators, as was her determination to help those who needed help in her own country. Carl T. Rowan, an African American journalist, wrote, "Whether in praise or criticism, millions view Eleanor Roosevelt as one of the major reasons for the change in status of colored people, particularly American Negroes, during the last quarter century" (*Boston Globe*, 14 November 1962). There also was comment that she had been "an emancipator of American womanhood" (*Miami Herald*, 9 November 1962), "the New Woman in the White House . . . , provocative, controversial, but determined to live by her convictions" (*New York Times*, 8 November 1962), and a figure of empowerment who, "serene and undaunted, . . . went about the business of demonstrating that woman's place need not be exclusively in the home—even when that home was the White House" (*New York Herald Tribune*, 8 November 1962).

Similar themes appeared in overseas newspapers, many of which also recounted the details of her life. The *Daily Telegraph* of London noted her admiration and friendship for Britain and praised her for her strong involvement in causes "of peace and of the welfare of humanity" and for her personal quality of selflessness (8 November 1962). *De Haagse Courant*, a Netherlands* newspaper, called her one of the most influential women of the century. The *Times of India* on 9 November 1962 described her as "a Friend of the Common People" and stressed her influence "on the thought and manners of the women of her country for more than a quarter of century," as well as her international activities that "prompted writers to call her the 'First Lady of the World' and the 'Number One World Citizen.' " On 9 November 1962 *Le Monde* of France observed that ER's activities greatly increased in importance after her husband's death. On the same day, the *Japan Times* noted that following FDR's death, she "continued to retain her international fame as a traveler, writer and broadcaster, and active promoter of her political and social ideals."

The tributes of President Kennedy and Ambassador Stevenson to ER often were quoted, as were those of other world leaders and prominent figures. The *Morning News* of Sudan on 9 November 1962 ran a Reuters dispatch from New York pointing out that Stevenson found time to go to ER's bedside at the height of the crises between the United States and the Soviet Union over missiles in Cuba. In the Soviet Union *Pravda* quoted Foreign Minister Andrei Gromyko's telegram to ER's family: "Those who were personally acquainted with Eleanor Roosevelt . . . will always have the best memories of her" (9 November 1962). The *China News* of Taipei on 9 November 1962 reported President Kennedy's executive order of 8 November 1962 that flags be flown at half-mast at all U.S. government buildings until the burial of ER.

Some newspapers devoted attention to her "My Day" column, acknowledging that ER had reached millions of readers in and outside the United States and had used her columns to influence public opinion.

They also noted that her autobiographical writings, which had been translated into several languages, had contributed to her significance. The Polish newspaper *Trybuna Ludu* on 9 November 1962 mentioned not only ER's rigid work discipline and her involvement in helping the unemployed during the Great Depression* but also that she was the first President's wife to hold regular press conferences.*

In assessing her stature, the European edition of the *New York Herald Tribune* on 8 November 1962 said, "Mrs. Roosevelt first became known to the world as the wife of President Franklin Delano Roosevelt. But in her own right she grew to be one of the notable personalities of her time, standing with the handful of towering figures who molded opinion and influenced the course of events through the fateful years of the Depression, World War II* and the Cold War."*

SELECTED BIBLIOGRAPHY

McHugh, John F. "The Death of Eleanor Roosevelt." Scrapbook of newspaper clippings, Eleanor Roosevelt Papers, Franklin D. Roosevelt Library, Hyde Park, NY.

Mieke van Thoor

DEMOCRATIC DIGEST. The *Democratic Digest*, a monthly magazine published by Democratic women from 1933 until 1953, endeavored to draw women into political activity. Eleanor Roosevelt was a strong supporter of this effort. She wrote a monthly "Dear Mrs. Roosevelt" column for the magazine from August 1937 to January 1941, answering readers' questions about political and social issues. In addition, between 1933 and 1948 she contributed at least ten other articles or comments. Topics included the Mobilization for Human Needs campaign to raise funds for Community Chests (November 1933), homestead projects (March 1936), women working after marriage (May 1938), Democratic Party* organization (February 1941), home gardens to aid defense efforts (October 1941), and an international bill of rights (July 1946). The editors also frequently included excerpts from her speeches* and newspaper columns as well as features about her activities.

The *Democratic Digest* was the outgrowth of a pamphlet, the *Fortnightly Bulletin*, which Emily Newell Blair, Democratic National Committeewoman, began mailing in 1922 on behalf of the committee to Democratic women's clubs around the country to promote the organization of women voters. It was discontinued in November 1924, following the Republican presidential election victory.

The concept of the publication was revived when the Woman's National Democratic Club* (WNDC) in Washington began monthly publication of *The Bulletin* in February 1926. *The Bulletin* began to write about ER as she became active politically, and the political fortunes of Franklin D. Roosevelt* rose. In December 1928, for example, it ran a lengthy report of ER's work as head of the national women's advisory committee for the presidential campaign of Alfred E. Smith.* For the January 1932 issue, ER wrote an article urging participation by women in the Democratic Party. Shortly after she became First Lady, the magazine published a glowing description of her women-only press conferences* (May 1933).

The Bulletin evolved into the sixteen-page Democratic Digest in October 1933. Marion Glass Banister, a sister of Democratic senator Carter Glass of Virginia, was the initial editor of the Fortnightly Bulletin. A cofounder of the WNDC, she was a guiding spirit in publishing The Bulletin. In 1933 she was appointed assistant treasurer of the United States, continuing in that position until 1951.

The first editor of the Democratic Digest was Helen Essary, who wrote a political column for the Washington Times-Herald. She resigned in 1941, the year she became president of the Women's National Press Club.* Essary was followed by Virginia Rishel, who served as editor until 1945. Under Essary and Rishel, a graduate of the Columbia University School of Journalism, the magazine achieved a lively tone in content and appearance and highlighted articles by professional feature writers like Bess Furman,* a close friend of ER in the Washington press corps.

In March 1935 responsibility for the publication, which had 1,600 paid subscribers, moved from the WNDC to the Women's Division of the Democratic National Committee (DNC). Announcing the transfer, which the club initially resented, Molly Dewson,* chair of the division's advisory committee, said that the division had been "handicapped without a party organ furnishing a continuous contact with . . . women Democrats throughout the country" and expressed gratitude to the club for agreeing "to the transfer of its child and pride to the National Committee" (Democratic Digest, March 1935, 3). The Democratic Digest became the first magazine published by a major political party for its women members and the only official publication of the DNC.

Dewson soon launched a sustained circulation campaign with the motto of a Democratic Digest in every precinct. By 1938 paid circulation had increased to over 20,000, and most issues contained forty to forty-four pages. Subscriptions to the slick-paper magazine cost one dollar per year, but it was never self-supporting, although it carried paid advertising (mainly for hotels and services in Washington), and the Women's Division had to look to the DNC for financial help.

Dewson, in close consultation with ER, worked to integrate the Democratic Digest into the division outreach program that called for local Democratic women to study, analyze, and publicize governmental and political activities. Starting in 1935, each issue carried a center spread explaining a New Deal* program or the work of a federal agency. Other coverage included discussions of foreign policy, social issues, and political activities at the local and national level. Politics was linked to fashion and femininity in the magazine's frequent photographic displays of stylishly dressed Democratic women leaders.

Several state Democratic organizations paid for local sections that were included in the copies of the *Democratic Digest* sent to their particular areas. In addition to her other contributions, from 1936 to 1938 ER provided intermittent material for the New York edition on topics such as life at Val-Kill.*

Beginning in 1940, preparations for war became a recurring theme in the *Democratic Digest*. Emphasis shifted to local surveys of what the administration had done to lay a foundation for national defense. During World War II* Democratic women were pictured mainly in connection with the war effort.

The division kept control of the publication until 1953, when DNC chairman Stephen Mitchell announced "that the separate budget, magazine and staff of the Women's Division were being 'integrated' into the existing party structure" (Ware, 134). Thus ended more than three decades of a Democratic publication by and for women, which served as an influential organ for women in politics and stimulated their work within the party. The DNC continued the *Democratic Digest* as its official general publication for eight more years until shutting it down in February 1961.

SELECTED BIBLIOGRAPHY

Democratic Digest (1933–1961).

Democratic National Committee, Women's Division, Papers, Franklin D. Roosevelt Library, Hyde Park, NY.

Eleanor Roosevelt Oral History Project, Interviews with May Thompson Evans (1978) and Virginia Rishel (1978), Franklin D. Roosevelt Library, Hyde Park, NY.

Ware, Susan. *Beyond Suffrage: Women in the New Deal.* 1981.

Jewell Fenzi

DEMOCRATIC PARTY. Eleanor Roosevelt was born in 1884, a daughter of one of the oldest and most distinguished Republican families in the United States. Her branch of the family—the Oyster Bay, New York, Roosevelts, descendants of Johannes Roosevelt, born 1689—as well as the Dutchess County, New York, Roosevelts, descendants of Johannes' brother Jacobus or James, born 1692, were Democrats before the Civil War. As abolitionists, both became firm Lincoln Republicans during the war. Afterward, the Oyster Bay Roosevelts stayed Republican, but the Dutchess County Roosevelts reverted to the Democratic Party. ER's cousin and husband, Franklin Delano Roosevelt,* belonged to that branch.

It has been generally assumed that ER left the party of her forebears and became a Democrat when her husband first ventured into politics

Eleanor Roosevelt makes an address at the Democratic National Convention in Chicago on 18 July 1940 that rallies delegates behind the party ticket as Franklin D. Roosevelt launches his third-term campaign for president. *Courtesy of Franklin D. Roosevelt Library*

and was nominated and elected in 1910 as a Democratic member of the New York state Senate. Before her marriage in 1905, however, she had become aware of progressive reform politics through her volunteer work in New York City with social settlements* and the National Consumers' League.* When FDR went to the legislature in 1910, ER became an active political wife, supportive of her husband in every way.

After he was nominated as the Democratic candidate for vice president in 1920, she told the *Poughkeepsie Eagle News* that despite her personal family history, she favored Democrats, "for I believe they are the most progressive" (Lash, *Eleanor and Franklin*, 252). In her article "Why I Am a Democrat" in the Junior League *Bulletin*, November 1923, she wrote, "On the whole the Democratic Party seems to have been more concerned with the welfare and interests of the people at large, and less with the growth of big business interests" (Lash, *Eleanor and Franklin*, 280). A few years later, she explained the difference between the parties as part of the long-standing conflict between Jeffersonians, who believed in ordinary people, and Federalists, who represented the monied classes.

When FDR was paralyzed by polio in 1921, ER turned her energies toward keeping him from invalidism by involving herself in Democratic politics as his representative so that he could remain in touch with what was going on. Her presence in the party made sure that the name of Roosevelt stayed in front of political leaders. Her activity was acceptable to a male-dominated political world because it was placed in the context of a wife helping her husband.

By 1928 ER was a political leader in her own right. She had labored for six years for the Women's Division of the New York state Democratic Committee. She raised funds that gave Democratic women freedom to pursue their own goals and worked at organizing women in every county of New York, in this way becoming known to politicians through- out the state. She lobbied in Albany for legislation of interest to Demo- cratic women and attended state and national political conventions. She helped create the strong grassroots organization of New York women. Its goals and techniques were to shape women's politics for years to come. Through her work in New York, ER become so well known in the field of practical politics that she was asked to head women's work in the 1928 national Democratic presidential campaign of Alfred E. Smith.*

While Smith was defeated, FDR's narrow victory in the New York gubernatorial race changed her political life. She always had insisted that her political work was for her husband's sake and that when he returned to public life, she would withdraw. Consequently, she resigned from the board of the women's division; she no longer gave political speeches or lobbied. Nevertheless, politics was in her blood and had become a source of personal accomplishment and satisfaction, so she found less public ways of being active. "Working behind the scenes and through trusted lieutenants, as the governor's wife ER developed the political style she would raise to an art form during the opportunities presented by the New Deal*" (Ware, 51).

During those years she perfected the technique of the fact-finding tour, which was to stand her in good stead later as First Lady. She stayed in touch with other women in politics and furthered their interests and appointments to state posts, a pattern she was to continue in the New Deal. Having helped convince her husband and Democratic chairman James Farley* that the Women's Division of the Democratic National Committee (DNC) should be full-time and adequately funded, she per- suaded an ally, Molly Dewson,* to accept the directorship. Through Dewson she saw to it that there was increased patronage for women.

It is important to realize, however, that although ER's training in pol- itics had come through women's organizations, and she worked for the rights of women and sought to improve the conditions under which they lived and worked, the advancement of women was not her primary goal. Rather, she believed that women's entry into the political process would further humanitarian progress for everyone. As she wrote in *Good House- keeping* in March 1940, she believed that since women attained the vote in 1920, government had turned toward the improvement of human life in general: "[O]n the whole, during the last twenty years, government has been taking increasing cognizance of humanitarian questions, things that deal with the happiness of human beings, such as health, education, security. There is nothing, of course, to prove this is entirely because of the women's interest, and yet I think it is significant that this change has come about during the period when women have been exercising their franchise" (Ware, 45).

In the New Deal the government took drastic steps and inaugurated strong programs to cope with the Great Depression,* which gripped the country. Many of these programs were ones that reform-minded women like ER had been advocating for years. These women, largely through ER's influence, became agents of the implementation of government intervention. They shared with her a broader view of social change and economic redistribution than her husband's.

At the same time that she was cooperating with women to make the New Deal a reality, ER moved toward participation in Democratic politics as a whole, not just in Women's Division activities. She used her position to become a behind-the-scenes influence to aid causes important to her. The roles of ER and FDR grew less complementary, however, during the 1940s, as FDR shifted attention from New Deal initiatives to war issues. By 1940 ER entered the final stage of her political career, in which she began to function independently in the Democratic Party itself. By the time J. B. West became chief White House usher in 1941, there were, he said, two kinds of guests—FDR's people and ER's people.

After the United States entered World War II,* ER took an unpaid government appointment in her own right as assistant director of the Office of Civilian Defense* (OCD). She hoped that the volunteer participation program set up under it could be used to enhance the quality of life for all Americans through projects to encourage physical fitness, improve nutrition, and reduce illiteracy. But her broad concept of OCD and the people she appointed to staff positions evoked so much congressional hostility that she had to withdraw from the position.

Despite the fact that ER's influence with FDR lessened as the nation turned its attention to war, she remained a force in the Democratic Party, although there were limits to her power. It was ER who had assured the selection of Henry Wallace* for vice president in 1940, when she appeared before a deeply divided Democratic convention and spoke for him. By 1944, however, she was unable to help Wallace attain renomination. More conservative delegates at that year's Democratic convention whose support FDR needed to carry on in World War II had become mistrustful of Wallace, and their opposition was too strong for her to overcome. At this point her influence in the national party was clearly waning.

The choice of Harry S Truman* as the vice presidential candidate was a disappointment to her, but after FDR's death she became his strong adviser, whose words Truman valued. When he asked her to serve as a U.S. delegate to the United Nations,* her energies and attention turned toward world issues and forging the means to ensure a peaceful world.

Nevertheless, in the succeeding years she played a part in shaping the Democratic Party in two very significant ways. One was her cooperation in the founding of a noncommunist Left progressive organization—the Americans for Democratic Action*—to work for liberal programs purged of a communist element. She slowly had come to believe that the Russians were primarily to blame for the postwar breakup of Allied unity and that members of the American Communist Party were more faithful to Russia than to the United States. Her acknowledgment of this reality and her willingness to do something about it gave heart to those who became leaders of the liberal wing of the Democratic Party in the next political era. These individuals included Hubert Humphrey, Orville Freeman, and Eugene McCarthy of Minnesota, who led a successful struggle to rid their Democratic-Farmer-Labor party of a powerful communist element, as well as Edmund S. Muskie of Maine, A. S. Mike Monroney of Oklahoma, Wayne Morse of Oregon, and Chester Bowles* of Connecticut.

The second way of shaping the party was her unwavering support for Adlai Stevenson* after his first campaign for the presidency in 1952. Her appearance at the 1956 Democratic Party convention was credited with stopping Truman's effort to end Stevenson's candidacy with support for Averell Harriman.* She made a forceful speech to the convention, sounding the theme that it was a time for new beginnings and that Stevenson was the man to launch them, while holding on to what was valuable in the New Deal and the Fair Deal. Despite his defeat, Stevenson was to prove, as she prophesied, a bridge between the old and the new in the party.

ER's last appearance before a Democratic convention occurred in 1960 in Los Angeles, where she supported Stevenson. When she entered the convention hall, there was a standing ovation. Although the nomination of John F. Kennedy* could not be stopped, as she had hoped, her prestige and the reverence in which she was held by many party members remained.

In the two years that followed, she took on various chores for the Kennedy administration—as a member of the U.S. delegation to the Special Session of the General Assembly in 1961 and as chairman of the President's Commission on the Status of Women.* In her last months she followed the news from Washington and, at Kennedy's request, wrote him letters of advice. To the very end of her life in 1962, ER personified the liberal voice of the Democratic Party.

SELECTED BIBLIOGRAPHY
Goodwin, Doris Kearns. *No Ordinary Time: Franklin and Eleanor Roosevelt: The Home Front in World War II*. 1994.
Lash, Joseph P. *Eleanor and Franklin*. 1971.
———. *Eleanor: The Years Alone*. 1972.
Scharf, Lois. *First Lady of American Liberalism*. 1987.
Ware, Susan. "ER and Democratic Politics: Women in the Postsuffrage Era." In Joan Hoff-Wilson and Marjorie Lightman, eds., *Without Precedent: The Life and Career of Eleanor Roosevelt*. 1984.
West, J. B. *Upstairs at the White House: My Life with the First Ladies*. 1973.

Abigail McCarthy

DEWSON, MARY WILLIAMS (MOLLY) (18 February 1874, Quincy, MA—21 October 1962, Castine, ME).

From the time they met in New York City reform circles in 1925 until their deaths just weeks apart in the fall of 1962, Molly Dewson and Eleanor Roosevelt enjoyed a remarkable friendship. The height of their collaboration occurred in 1932 and 1933, when Dewson and ER worked together after the successful presidential campaign of Franklin D. Roosevelt* to win record recognition for women in the early New Deal.* ER appreciated Dewson's sense of humor and no-nonsense approach to getting things done; Dewson, like so many others, became ER's devoted follower practically from the moment they met.

Molly Dewson's upbringing and early professional undertakings hardly pointed her toward a career in partisan politics. An 1897 graduate of Wellesley College, she worked for twelve years as the superintendent of parole at the Massachusetts State Industrial School for Girls, helped draft that state's minimum wage law in 1912, became an active suffragist, and operated a dairy farm with her partner of fifty-two years, Mary (Polly) Porter. After serving with the American Red Cross* as social workers in France during World War I, they moved to New York City, settling in the same apartment building where Nancy Cook* and Marion Dickerman* lived. From 1919 to 1924 Dewson worked for Florence Kelley at the National Consumers' League,* mainly on issues surrounding the minimum wage.

The year 1925 found Molly Dewson working as the civic secretary of the Women's City Club,* a prominent New York City reform organization of which ER was a vice president. Drawn together by their shared reform agenda, the two women quickly became close friends and colleagues, part of the stimulating female reform world of New York City in the 1920s. The two women worked so well together that all it took was one phone call from ER to launch Dewson on her career as a Democratic politician. ER was in charge of the women's end of the presidential campaign of Alfred E. Smith* in 1928, and she needed help with a problem in the midwestern headquarters. Even though Dewson had never participated in partisan politics before, it never occurred to her to say no, and she proved a superb addition to the team.

Besides the opportunity to advocate larger roles for women in public life, one of the attractions of Democratic politics for Dewson was the chance to work so closely with ER. (Unlike many colleagues who called the future First Lady "Mrs. Roosevelt," Dewson always called her Eleanor.) The two collaborated on FDR's reelection campaign in 1930 for the New York governorship, and then as his presidential ambitions jelled, Dewson headed women's activities in the 1932 campaign. Even though ER was not listed on the masthead of the Women's Division, she and Dewson had back-to-back desks at Democratic Party* headquarters.

FDR's election in 1932 signaled a new phase in their friendship, bringing the two women into practically daily communication. Convinced that women had played a significant part in getting FDR elected in the first place, Dewson was determined that women get their fair share of patronage and recognition. One of her most visible successes was her role in convincing the president-elect to nominate Frances Perkins* as secretary of labor, the first woman to serve in the cabinet. On this and many other matters, having a direct line to the president through ER was an enormous help in winning support for her political and social reform agendas.

Both FDR and ER depended on Molly Dewson's astute political judgment, and she quickly emerged as the undisputed leader of Democratic Party women. From 1933 to 1934 Dewson served as the head of the Women's Division of the Democratic National Committee and then headed its advisory committee through 1937. Under Dewson's leadership, the Women's Division grew to a force of 60,000 grassroots workers. In the 1936 election, "Rainbow Fliers" (political messages on colored paper) prepared by the Women's Division constituted 90 percent of the Democratic National Committee's campaign material.

As the second term opened, Dewson yearned to get back into her old field of labor standards. In 1937 she accepted President Roosevelt's offer of a position on the newly created Social Security Board, although she served for only one year before retiring from government service because of ill health at age sixty-four. Dewson came back from retirement to play a brief role in the 1940 presidential campaign, but her days of active politicking were over. She and Polly Porter divided their time between New York City and their summer home in Castine, Maine, where they moved permanently in 1952.

After the intensity of the early years of the New Deal, Molly Dewson's and ER's paths crossed less often, to Dewson's profound regret. (This pattern characterized many of ER's friendships.) They remained friends and colleagues for the rest of their lives, exchanging warm letters on birthdays and holidays and treasuring the times that they could meet in person, but the old intimacy was gone. In 1954 ER and Lorena Hickok* dedicated their survey of women in politics, *Ladies of Courage*, to Molly Dewson; this public recognition of her role in expanding opportunities for women in politics and government brought her great satisfaction.

The lives of Dewson and ER remained intertwined until the very end. The two women met for the last time in the summer of 1962, when ER passed through Castine on her way home from her farewell trip to Campobello* Island, New Brunswick. Within several months, both these great politicians would be dead. ER was mourned worldwide, but Molly Dewson's death was greeted with far less fanfare. All her life, in the words she chose to title her autobiography, she had been "an aid to the end," shunning personal power and glory to work for the goals she believed in. Nothing in her life gave her as much satisfaction as the chance to be part of ER and FDR's New Deal.

SELECTED BIBLIOGRAPHY

Molly Dewson Papers, Franklin D. Roosevelt Library, Hyde Park, NY, and the Schlesinger Library, Radcliffe College, Cambridge, MA.
Dewson, Mary Williams. "An Aid to the End." Unpublished autobiography. 1949.
Ware, Susan. *Beyond Suffrage: Women in the New Deal.* 1981.
———. *Partner and I: Molly Dewson, Feminism, and New Deal Politics.* 1987.

Susan Ware

DICKERMAN, MARION (11 April 1890, Westfield, NY–16 May 1983, Kennett Square, PA).

Marion Dickerman, with her lifelong companion Nancy Cook,* exerted an important shaping influence on Eleanor Roosevelt during fifteen crucial years of ER's growth into the historic personage she ultimately became. For two years, 1907–1909, Dickerman was a student at Wellesley, then enrolled at Syracuse University, where she took an A.B. degree in 1911 and an advanced degree in education in 1912. She taught at Canisteo, New York, High School for one term (1912–1913), going from there to Fulton, New York, High School, where she taught American history and social studies for four school years (1913–1918). In Fulton she cemented her relationship with Cook, who taught art and handicrafts in the same school. The two had first met when they were residents of a student boardinghouse at Syracuse.

By the end of her Fulton years, Dickerman had become the person whom ER would know four years later—a woman of immense dignity and serious purpose, intensely idealistic, and actively committed to social reform, with a special interest in labor relations.

Though both Dickerman and Cook had become ardent pacifists as well as suffragists by the time they left Syracuse, in 1918 during World War

I they obtained through friends appointments to the almost exclusively female staff of the Endell Street Military Hospital in London. The two remained on the hospital staff until August 1919.

By then women had won the right to vote in New York, and Dickerman was astonished to learn, when she and Cook landed in New York City, that she had been chosen to be the Democratic candidate from Oswego County, where Fulton is located, for the state Assembly. She accepted the nomination with reluctance, knowing she had no chance to win. With Cook as her campaign manager, however, she gained enough votes to prevent her reactionary opponent, Thaddeus Sweet, speaker of the state Assembly who opposed woman suffrage, from achieving his ambition to become the Republican nominee for governor in 1920. There followed for her an unhappy year as dean in the New Jersey Normal School in Trenton and a happier time as an instructor in the Bryn Mawr College Summer School before, in the spring of 1922, she accepted an appointment as instructor in a small, expensive, and exclusive school for girls in New York City called Todhunter.*

In the summer of 1922, with her Todhunter instructorship to begin in the fall, Dickerman met ER, who was just beginning her determined effort to make a life and career truly her own and not merely functions of her husband's. The introduction was made by Cook, who in the course of her work as executive secretary of a newly organized Women's Division of the New York state Democratic Committee, had met and become friends with ER.

Abruptly, what had been a twosome (Dickerman and Cook) became a threesome (ER, Dickerman, and Cook)—an intensely active friendship. They worked hard together on New York City projects of the Women's Trade Union League* and even harder in the Women's Division, for which they helped edit and publish its official organ, the monthly *Women's Democratic News.** Through their Women's Division activities, under the guidance of Louis Howe*—the assistant and close friend of Franklin D. Roosevelt*—they played an important role in the process by which FDR, returned to active politics, worked his way toward the Executive Mansion in Albany and thence to the White House in Washington. Largely through Dickerman and Cook, ER also formed a warm friendship with Caroline O'Day,* who in 1923 became chair of the Women's Division.

Dickerman and Cook became virtually members of the Roosevelt family in the mid-1920s. In 1925 the three friends built Val-Kill* cottage as a home for Dickerman and Cook and vacation retreat for ER. It was named after the placid stream beside which it stood on land two miles from the Roosevelt mansion at Hyde Park,* New York—land owned by FDR but leased to them for life. The three women took the two youngest Roosevelt boys on a long camping trip into Canada in 1925 and on a tour of Europe in 1929 and made extended visits to the Roosevelt summer home on Campobello* Island, New Brunswick, where FDR had suffered his devastating polio attack and to which, during those years, he never returned.

Simultaneous with the move into Val-Kill cottage was the initiation of Val-Kill Industries, owned by the three women with O'Day as an honorary partner, which under Cook's management in a workshop built behind the cottage made exact replicas of early American furniture to be sold through established retail outlets. The three also jointly purchased the Todhunter School when, in 1927, Winifred Todhunter, the owner, sold it to them and returned to her native England. Dickerman became the school's principal, and ER a member of the teaching staff and a very successful one, teaching drama, American history, and current events—an activity she continued after her husband became governor, commuting from Albany for part of each week.

After ER moved, with initial reluctance, into the White House in March 1933, the number and range of her active interests increased while those of her friends remained nearly the same—her active part in their ventures necessarily waned. When Val-Kill Industries failed under depression pressures in 1936, ER took over its shop building and remodeled it into her country home. Val-Kill cottage continued to be Dickerman's and Cook's home. In the summer of 1938, Dickerman went abroad as one of a nine-member President's Commission to Study Industrial Relations in Great Britain and Sweden. She returned to find Cook and ER estranged by a recent long conversation between them in which each had said things profoundly hurtful of the other. This effectively ended the close friendship of the threesome, for Dickerman and Cook were inseparable. The friendly relationship between the twosome and FDR remained unaffected, however, and they continued to be included in otherwise exclusive Rooseveltian activities in Washington and Hyde Park.

Todhunter, from which ER had completely dissociated herself by 1939, was compelled by financial need to merge in that year with the Dalton School, which had a different educational philosophy and from which, in consequence, Dickerman resigned in 1942. Three years later, after the death of FDR, she and Cook moved from Val-Kill cottage to New Canaan, Connecticut.

Dickerman was an alternate at the Democratic National Conventions of 1928, 1932, and 1940, serving in that last year on the resolutions committee and playing an important role in modifying, along lines drawn by FDR, an originally unambiguously isolationist foreign policy plank. From 1945 to 1962 she was educational director of the Marine Museum, Mystic, Connecticut.

SELECTED BIBLIOGRAPHY
Cook, Blanche Wiesen. *Eleanor Roosevelt*. Vols. 1, 2. 1992, 1999.
Davis, Kenneth S. *Invincible Summer: An Intimate Portrait of the Roosevelts*. 1974.
                                                                    Kenneth S. Davis

DISTRICT OF COLUMBIA. Eleanor Roosevelt regarded Washington, D.C., as a place for living, not just for governing. She saw it as a local community as well as the national capital. In many ways she was in the city but also of the city. She walked to her Dupont Circle Civilian Defense office, she rode the Capital Transit streetcars, she knew firsthand the neighborhoods and the multilayered society of the District. This intimacy was not part of her first stint in Washington, between 1913 and 1920, when Franklin D. Roosevelt* served as assistant secretary of the navy in the Wilson administration. (See also Wilson Era, Sunday Evening Suppers.) From the spring of 1933 through April 1945, however, as she redefined the role of First Lady, her impact on Washington as advocate of the urban population was far-reaching.

Upon her return, ER immediately threw herself into Washington's housing crisis. The major issue concerned the deplorable living conditions of alley dwellers. Since the mid-nineteenth century, poor people had crowded into makeshift structures located at the backs of street-front houses, in the interiors of densely populated city blocks. White and black unskilled laborers, slaves, then freed persons occupied these buildings and, later, two-story frame units that tended to be hidden from the more prosperous and powerful and where rents were cheap. By 1897, 93 percent of alley dwellers were African American, and these persons constituted almost one-quarter of Washington's nonwhite population.

Nearly 70 percent of the city's alleys were segregated. Running water and electric lighting were practically nonexistent; health problems and social decay seemed rampant. Progressive reformers, principally Theodore Roosevelt* and Ellen Axon Wilson, first wife of President Woodrow Wilson, sought to end alley housing construction and eliminate alley dwelling altogether. Their early twentieth-century efforts were blunted by World War I housing demands. A combination of changing business priorities, coupled with new residential developments, however, contributed to an almost 40 percent decline of alley houses during the 1920s. Still, over 1,300 hovels remained in what threatened to degenerate into enduring slums. Enter, ER.

She not merely addressed a worsening situation but envisioned better alternatives for those displaced from squalid surroundings. An organizational and personal foundation for her energies already existed: the District chapter of the American Institute of Architects, the Washington Council of Social Agencies, the National Capital Park and Planning Commission (chaired by Frederic A. Delano, the president's uncle), and Charlotte Hopkins, an important figure in Washington society, whose crusading against alley dwellings went back to the Wilson administration. Less than a week after becoming First Lady, ER accompanied Mrs. Hopkins on an alley tour and declared her support for legislation to study the city's slum conditions.

In October 1933 ER joined an advisory committee to the Housing Division of the Public Works Administration, which led to the Alley Dwelling Authority, established by Congress* in 1934. The Alley Dwelling Act stipulated that within ten years such housing was to be abolished. Once again, wartime exigencies intervened, and alleys continued to be inhabited after 1944. Nevertheless, ER, as honorary president of the Washington Housing Association and in her press conferences* and public pronouncements, continued to hammer away at the unacceptable housing of marginal Washingtonians.

Her commitment to Washington's black community was equally important and reflected an increasing personal sensitivity toward African Americans. During the Roosevelts' initial stay in the capital city, she appeared to share stereotypical views that characterized early twentieth-century white racism. Doubtless, she was untroubled by the Jim Crow protocols of a southern city in which black residents were denied access to public accommodations, educational and employment opportunities, and entertainment and recreational facilities on the basis of race. As First Lady, however, she supported activists—notably, women of color—in pursuit of racial justice.

Generally, the issues involved were national ones to which Washington's black community related symbolically. They included urging an end to discrimination in New Deal* recovery and training programs; welcoming Mary McLeod Bethune* as the president's special adviser on minority affairs and head of the Negro Division of the National Youth Administration*; resigning from the Daughters of the American Revolution when it refused Marian Anderson* use of Constitution Hall for a 1939 concert; voicing approval of antilynching* legislation; working, albeit cautiously, for civil rights* with the Brotherhood of Sleeping Car Porters, which had a base of operations in Washington directed by Rosina Tucker; and opposing segregation in the armed forces.

Closer to home, in 1935 she invited Lillian Evans Tibbs, Washington's lyric soprano known professionally as Madame Evanti, to sing La Traviata at the Executive Mansion. She advocated integration in District public housing and recreation centers; spoke at Howard University's Rankin Chapel and the Metropolitan African Methodist Episcopal Church near Scott Circle; participated in a March of Dimes rally at the Lincoln Theater in the heart of Washington's "Black Broadway"; and served on the National Committee on Segregation in the Nation's Capital, whose 1948 report ignited D.C.'s modern Civil Rights movement.

Thus, ER was at the core of sweeping changes in race relations not only nationally and politically but at basic levels in the capital city. Appropriately, the *Washington Afro-American* commented on 17 October 1959, in an appreciation, "Until she threw open the doors of the White House to Mrs. Mary McLeod Bethune and her followers, it was an accepted belief that the White House was off limits to colored womanhood."

While Washingtonians of African descent were more attracted to the Executive Mansion than before, ER reached out to engage the entire city. Her range of involvement extended from addressing the local League of Women Voters,* to attending annual Christmas basket parties of the Salvation Army, to speaking at the 1943 Uptown Theater ceremony recognizing Connecticut Avenue junior salvage collectors and their parents. She hosted a White House garden party for delinquent girls and urged better conditions for D.C. jail inmates. Community visits took her to public welfare institutions such as the Home for the Aged and Infirm and the Industrial Home for Colored Children at Blue Plains, the Industrial Home (for white children) in Georgetown, the Gallinger Municipal Hospital at 19th and E Streets, Southeast, and St. Elizabeths, the federal mental hospital, in Anacostia.

Often these contacts reinforced her commitment to young people, and frequently they were followed by a "My Day"* column or press conference statement regarding shameful conditions: "Washington is such a beautiful city, that's why it is so pathetic that things which deal with human beings are so deplorable" (*Washington Star*, 6 May 1940). "We can be proud of our buildings, since they make our city one of the most beautiful in the world, but we cannot be proud of many of the things which do not make it a good place to live in" ("My Day," 20 February 1945). "I might have expected such negligence in rural areas, but not in a city this size" (*Washington Post*, 5 March 1940).

Disgraceful consequences of neglect called for drastic measures of reform; thus, ER espoused local self-government. Since 1874 the District of Columbia had been under the control of three presidentially appointed commissioners. Residents paid taxes and were responsible for service duties of citizenship, but they did not vote, sent no representatives to Congress,* and were powerless to determine their own priorities and policies. Ironically, those who lived in the home of democratic government were denied the most basic rights of political democracy. From a practical standpoint, local administration became snared in masses of red tape. During the hard times of the 1930s, as D.C. was excluded from some of the relief programs that benefited states, cries of inequity and ineffectiveness grew louder.

In 1940 the Democratic Party* platform demanded, "Democratic processes should operate in the District of Columbia as well as in other parts of the country" (*Washington Times Herald*, 1 August 1940). The president, typically indifferent to local problems in the city, opposed self-government, and the issue ultimately died in Congress. Those who controlled the District but whose constituencies were elsewhere simply felt no abiding concern for Washington. ER, in a manner typical of her, responded by taking up the cause with the House District Committee—the first time a First Lady testified before a congressional committee. Suffrage was essential, she said, and national representation and home rule were vital to bringing the city's "long-neglected institutions up-to-date" (*Washington Star*, 6 May 1940).

Although she looked forward to a better future for the city, ER did not show particular interest in programs established to preserve Washington's past. The New Deal marked a watershed in historic preservation as the national government moved as never before to save and study historically important structures and sites. Although ER toured Mount Vernon and Monticello and certainly supported White House restorations, she did not enter into preservation activities until planning for the tours given to visitors at the Roosevelt mansion in Hyde Park,* New York, after FDR's death.

By then it was abundantly clear that the people of Washington and the quality of their lives mattered to ER. They, in turn, seemed to appreciate both the sincerity and the substance of her efforts. As the *Washington Daily News* put it on 21 April 1945, "Washington lost one of its greatest friends. Last night she quietly left the city which has known her for so long. . . . She has fought to clear our slums, to improve our hospitals, to feed our poor, to nourish our underprivileged school children, to protect our penniless aged and infirm. . . . She has been a good citizen of our town, and we're grateful."

SELECTED BIBLIOGRAPHY

Borchert, James. *Alley Life in Washington: Family, Community, Religion, and Folklife in the City, 1850–1970*. 1980.
Diner, Steven J., ed. *Housing Washington's People: Public Policy in Retrospect*. 1983.
Gillette, Howard, Jr. *Between Justice and Beauty: Race, Planning, and the Failure of Urban Policy in Washington, D.C.* 1995.
Green, Constance McLaughlin. *The Secret City: A History of Race Relations in the Nation's Capital*. 1967.
Kemp, Barbara H., and Shirley Cherkasky. *Eleanor Roosevelt's Washington: A Place of Personal Growth and Public Service*. 1984.
Washington: City and Capital. Federal Writers' Project, Works Progress Administration, American Guide Series. 1937.

J. Kirkpatrick Flack

DOUGLAS, HELEN GAHAGAN (25 November 1900, Boonton, NJ–28 June 1990, New York). **DOUGLAS, MELVYN** (5 April 1901, Macon, GA–4 August 1981, New York).

The friendship of Helen Gahagan Douglas and Melvyn Douglas with Eleanor and Franklin D. Roosevelt* led to the first strong connections between presidential campaign strategies and Hollywood stars. It also contributed to Helen Douglas' rapid rise in Democratic politics. The two couples first met when ER invited the Douglases for a dinner and over-night stay at the White House on 30 November 1939. Aubrey Williams,* head of the National Youth Administration,* had brought the Douglases to ER's attention. Helen Douglas had recently gained considerable polit-ical recognition visiting migrant labor camps and speaking widely about the need for proper shelter, food, and health care there. Melvyn Douglas had demonstrated his organizational talent within the Democratic Party* in 1938, when he headed the southern California campaign for Culbert L. Olsen's successful bid for governor. He also had become involved in Popular Front groups opposed to fascism, such as the Motion Picture Democratic Committee, an organization from which he resigned after difficulties with its communist members. Williams envisioned the Doug-lases as a key to mobilizing Hollywood support for the 1940 Democratic presidential campaign.

Helen Douglas grew up in the well-to-do Gahagan family in Brooklyn, but she dismayed her parents with her complete lack of interest in aca-demics, offset by a passion and talent for acting. When offered a five-year contract for starring Broadway roles, she left Barnard College, which she had attended from 1920 to 1922, and launched a high-profile career. By the end of the 1920s, numerous critics placed her on lists of the top five New York actresses.

In 1931 she married Melvyn Douglas, her costar in the Broadway play *Tonight or Never*. Born Melvyn Hesselberg, he took the name of Douglas while launching his stage career. The son of a concert pianist, he had enlisted at seventeen in the U.S. Army during World War I and even-tually made his way into acting. Unlike his wife, who initially showed no interest in contemporary affairs, he sought out friends who enjoyed stimulating political discussions. After *Tonight or Never* closed, the new-lyweds moved to Hollywood, California, where he launched an ex-tremely successful, highly paid movie career. Helen Douglas found the 1930s disjointed and frustrating, as she combined a mix of New York plays, singing engagements, a failed radio program, an appearance in a vaudeville show, and the birth of two children in 1934 and 1938. Her dismay in being asked to sympathize with Nazi fascism while singing in the 1937 Salzburg Festival, however, stimulated an interest in politics when she returned to the United States.

On that November 1939 evening, the Roosevelts and the Douglases formed an immediate bond, leading quickly to meetings for the Holly-wood couple with Democratic Party leaders. At the urging of Dorothy McAllister, head of the Women's Division of the Democratic National Committee, Helen Douglas wrote a well-received article about migrant workers for the *Democratic Digest*,* which enjoyed a wide audience. In early April, the Douglases made arrangements at FDR's request to take ER to California migrant camps, and ER in her "My Day"* columns of 4–6 April 1940 wrote about the difficult living conditions she saw in many of the camps. In a thank-you note, ER invited Helen Douglas to stay at the White House in May for the Women's Division's National Institute of Government to prepare women for the campaign. Only one other woman received a similar invitation—ER's longtime friend and influential Democrat Molly Dewson.* In June ER wrote Helen Douglas to compliment her on testimony before a Senate subcommittee on migrants and one of many talks to social workers resulting from her recent appointment to the White House Advisory Committee on Community Services: "You can feel you are doing very good work," ER said, and she went on to say, that the president sent his "kindest regards" (Scobie, 115). When both Douglases found themselves the center of accusations that they were communists, ER, long the target of such comments, reassured them that they should not worry since the ruckus would not harm them in the long run.

By the end of the July 1940 Democratic National Convention, Helen Douglas had landed two top party positions for women, that of California's national committeewoman and vice-chair of the state party. After the convention, the Douglases became immersed in the campaign. Melvyn Douglas successfully brought Hollywood luminaries into the political scene, using them to assemble huge audiences for campaign rallies, including one that drew over 18,000 to hear the vice presidential candidate Henry Wallace.* Helen Douglas talked ER into a speaking engagement in California. During the fall, Helen made over 250 speeches,* as her acting skill translated well to the political stage.

The Douglases attended the 1941 inaugural events, and over the next two years ER and Helen exchanged frequent letters and occasional gifts, with Helen Douglas staying in the White House whenever she was in Washington. ER often stayed with the Douglases when she traveled west. Helen Douglas' amazing fast track in politics, made possible by ER, generated some resentment in the California Democratic Women's Division. One observer commented that Helen Douglas might know about migrants, but she did not know "what a precinct looks like" (Scobie, 119). Yet she appeared to rise above the squabbles, motivated by her growing popularity as a speaker.

Both Douglases took on political responsibilities beyond party positions. In the summer of 1941, FDR created the Office of Civilian Defense* (OCD) and appointed his wife assistant director. He then named forty-five nationally prominent appointees, including Helen Douglas, to an OCD Volunteer Committee. In early 1942, ER appointed Melvyn Douglas as a full-time OCD volunteer to mobilize writers, actors, and artists to help communicate OCD's goals. The appointment caused an uproar in Congress* on grounds of his alleged past involvement in communist-front organizations. In December 1942 he enlisted in the U.S. Army as a private, but his rapid promotion to captain caused another outcry that he had profited from his association with ER. In response ER wrote to Melvyn Douglas: "I do not mind any kind of nastiness and I hope you and Helen do not mind it either. Evidently any friend of mine has to go through [such criticism], and I hope the effect will be the strengthening of our friendship" (Scobie, 136). He later served overseas as entertainment coordinator in the Burma-China-India* theater.

By late 1943 Helen Douglas began exploring the idea of running for Congress from the Fourteenth Congressional District. In February 1944 she turned, as usual, to ER for advice. The First Lady wrote that both she and the president felt the time and conditions were right for her to run. Helen Douglas was the most prominent woman speaker at the 1944 Democratic Convention and then won a close election to Congress. The Roosevelt relationship, not surprisingly, influenced her as a new congressional member. FDR opened doors for her, urging her appointment to the Foreign Affairs Committee, for example. With his death in April 1945, Douglas lost a key intellectual mentor. Eventually, however, she became a well-respected liberal member of Congress, drawing both on FDR's legacy and on new inner strength as she shaped her own philosophy and rationale for political action. President Harry S Truman* appointed her an alternate delegate to the 1946 United Nations* Assembly. During that period, she spent more continuous time with ER, a U.S. delegate, than ever before.

In 1950 Helen Douglas ran for the U.S. Senate in a contest marked by the communist smear tactics of her opponent, Richard M. Nixon. ER helped raise funds for the campaign, used her "My Day" column to urge people nationally to support Douglas, and supplied quotes for campaign advertising. When she went to California to campaign, she gave major speeches for both her son, James Roosevelt,* the Democratic candidate for governor, and Helen Douglas.

Although she lost the race, which she had little chance of winning due to a Republican tide sweeping the country in the face of the Korean War, Helen Douglas continued her friendship with ER. Melvyn Douglas, however, became less involved, primarily because he was away from the couple's new base in New York until the mid-1960s. The two women always celebrated the birthday of Lorena Hickok,* an intimate of ER who had become very close to Helen during the early 1940s. When ER died, Helen Douglas wrote the text to accompany a collection of photographs in *The Eleanor Roosevelt We Remember*. The book provided a permanent testimony to the relationship between the two women, which Helen Douglas said "took me out of the theatre and into politics. . . . Politics for

Mrs. Roosevelt meant getting things done. . . . Her example made women believe that individual effort could mean something" (Scobie, 297).

SELECTED BIBLIOGRAPHY

Douglas, Helen Gahagan. *The Eleanor Roosevelt We Remember*. 1963.
————. "FSA Aids Migratory Worker." *The Democratic Digest* 17 (February 1940): 11–13, 37.
————. *A Full Life*. 1982.
Eleanor Roosevelt Papers, Franklin D. Roosevelt Library, Hyde Park, NY.
Scobie, Ingrid Winther. *Center Stage: Helen Gahagan Douglas, a Life*. 1992.

Ingrid Winther Scobie

DREIER, MARY ELIZABETH (26 September 1875, Brooklyn, NY–15 August 1963, Bar Harbor, ME).

A progressive reformer and philanthropist, Mary E. Dreier gained national prominence and Eleanor Roosevelt's friendship as a tireless advocate for better conditions for women in industry. In 1904 Dreier and her sister, Margaret Dreier Robins, began a long affiliation with the national Women's Trade Union League* (WTUL), an association of upper-class and trade union women founded the previous year to organize working women into trade unions and educate the public about labor* conditions. Robins became active in the Chicago league and was WTUL national president from 1907 to 1922, while Mary Dreier served as president of the New York branch of the WTUL from 1906 to 1914 and remained an active member until it disbanded in 1955. They were the privately educated daughters of wealthy German immigrants who provided them with independent means while also instilling a sense of discipline, self-development, and civic responsibility.

Dreier's arrest in 1909 for participating in a picket line of striking shirtwaist makers drew extensive press coverage, heightening public awareness of the problems of women workers. She was adept at forming cross-class friendships with working women such as Rose Schneiderman,* Pauline Newman, and Maud Swartz, who had become the leaders of the WTUL in 1922, when ER joined the organization.

While remaining a committed WTUL supporter, Dreier also undertook a broad range of reform activities. After the Triangle Shirtwaist Company fire that took 146 lives of workers in an unsafe factory in 1911, she was the only woman appointed to the New York State Factory Investigative Commission. Over the next four years it gathered evidence to support labor legislation to regulate hours and wages and to improve factory conditions. She became an advocate for woman suffrage and in 1918 formed the Women's Joint Legislative Conference (WJLC) to coordinate lobbying by women's organizations such as the National Consumers' League,* the League of Women Voters,* and the Young Women's Christian Association. In the early 1920s when ER became involved with Democratic Party* and women's reform politics, she began to participate in the WJLC as well as the WTUL.

ER and Dreier had frequent contact in these and other organizations, such as the Women's City Club of New York,* exchanging ideas and visits at each other's residence. Although Dreier was not among ER's circle of closest personal friends, the two women respected each other and worked closely for their common causes. A feature at the WTUL twenty-fifth anniversary celebration on 8 June 1929, hosted by ER's mother-in-law, Sara Delano Roosevelt,* at her Hyde Park,* New York, home was a pageant written and produced by Dreier.

Dreier actively supported the New Deal* and the presidential campaigns of Franklin D. Roosevelt.* After ER's move to Washington as First Lady in 1933, Dreier and ER kept in touch through correspondence and occasional meetings. Dreier wrote to ER about the activities of the organizations in which they had participated, sent her articles, books, and holiday greetings, and occasionally sought her support on a particular issue, such as a proposed constitutional amendment to ban child labor. ER responded to that request with an endorsement in her "My Day"* column on 15 February 1937 of efforts to achieve ratification of the amendment, which was never approved. When Rose Schneiderman arranged a dinner honoring Dreier in 1941, ER wrote Dreier, "I want to express to you my love and admiration and continuing loyalty. You have done so much for working women and you have done even more by educating women like myself who had your inspiration and leadership and who learned much that has helped us to be better citizens" (ER to MD, 8 April 1941).

SELECTED BIBLIOGRAPHY

Dye, Nancy Schrom. "The Women's Trade Union League of New York, 1903–1920." Ph.D. dissertation. University of Wisconsin at Madison. 1974.

Eleanor Roosevelt Papers, Franklin D. Roosevelt Library, Hyde Park, NY.

Mary E. Dreier Papers, Schlesinger Library, Radcliffe College, Cambridge, MA.

Orleck, Annelise. *Common Sense and a Little Fire: Women and Working Class Politics in the United States, 1900–1965.* 1995.

Payne, Elizabeth Anne. *Reform, Labor, and Feminism: Margaret Dreier Robins and the Women's Trade Union League.* 1988.

Women's Trade Union League Papers, New York State Labor Library, Cornell University, Ithaca, NY, and Library of Congress, Washington, DC.

Leonard Schlup

DU BOIS, W[ILLIAM] E[DWARD] B[URGHARDT] (23 February 1868, Great Barrington, MA–27 August 1963, Accra, Ghana).

The first African American to earn a Harvard Ph.D., a founder of the National Association for the Advancement of Colored People* (NAACP), the editor of its *Crisis* journal, a historian, sociologist, author, and activist,

W.E.B. Du Bois was arguably the most influential African American leader of the first half of the twentieth century. Eleanor Roosevelt and Du Bois shared a wide concern for international human rights,* including an interest in equality for African Americans. From the time they met in 1946, however, they frequently clashed, a consequence of their increasingly divergent political views. Du Bois' socialism put him in conflict with ER, who was an NAACP board member and a U.S. delegate to the United Nations* during the start of the Cold War.*

ER and Du Bois can be seen as representative of the growing chasm between liberals and socialists, with the latter finding the former too accommodating to the white power structure and the former frustrated with the latter's radicalism and stridency. This split became more pronounced during the postwar period, with the Cold War and relations with the Soviet Union influencing civil rights* issues. ER served on the board of the NAACP during most of the time that Du Bois served as the director of special research there (1944–1948). She also was a delegate to the United Nations Commission on Human Rights, in which Du Bois tried to introduce a petition critical of U.S. racial practices.

ER, while advocating human rights in general, was reluctant to invite criticism of the United States before its Cold War opponents. This put her in the awkward position of defending the United States' racial practices; she refused to introduce the petition and rejected the Soviet delegate's proposal to do so. ER played a major role in drafting the Universal Declaration of Human Rights* in 1948. To the irritation of the NAACP's Board of Trustees, Du Bois supported the Progressive Party* candidate for president, Henry Wallace,* that year, when ER and the NAACP leadership supported Harry S Truman.* During the campaign, Du Bois, whose growing Pan-Africanism and embrace of the Soviet Union made him politically at odds with the NAACP board, was dismissed from the organization.

In 1951 Du Bois joined Paul Robeson and others in organizing another petition to the United Nations, "We Charge Genocide," to publicize lynching and other racist practices in the United States. The growing radicalism and interest in Africa of Du Bois led him to emigrate to Ghana in 1961, where he died two years later.

SELECTED BIBLIOGRAPHY

Aptheker, Herbert. *The Correspondence of W.E.B. Du Bois*. 1978.
Du Bois, W.E.B. *The Autobiography of W.E.B. Du Bois: A Soliloquy of Viewing My Life from the Last Decade of Its First Century*. 1968.
Duberman, Martin B. *Paul Robeson*. 1988.
Horne, Gerald. *Black and Red: W.E.B. Du Bois and the Afro-American Response to the Cold War, 1944–1963*. 1986.
Lewis, David L. *W.E.B. Du Bois: Biography of a Race, 1868–1919*. 1993.

David T. Z. Mindich

DULLES, JOHN FOSTER (25 February 1888, Washington, DC–24 May 1959, Washington, DC).

Secretary of state from 1953 to 1959, John Foster Dulles, a Princeton graduate and corporate lawyer, became associated with the internationalist faction of the Republican Party after the Japanese attack on Pearl Harbor. During the post–World War II* period, he was a prominent Republican spokesman on foreign affairs. In 1946 he began working closely with Eleanor Roosevelt in the U.S. delegation to the United Nations,* to which both had been named by President Harry S Truman,* who was pursuing a bipartisan foreign policy. Although at first Dulles had not wanted ER on the delegation, he changed his mind and came to appreciate her abilities and talents. On one particular occasion he asked her to speak for the United States on the rights of refugees* in response to Andrei Vishinsky, the head of the Soviet Union's delegation and a skilled debater. ER ensured an outcome favorable to the United States by appealing to Latin American delegates with a talk on Simón Bolívar.

ER was delighted when the General Assembly adopted the Universal Declaration of Human Rights* in 1948. She and Dulles agreed that the declaration was only a preliminary step. Because this was a statement of principle having only a moral force, the Human Rights Commission also worked on two covenants—one addressing civil and political rights and the other economic and social rights—that could be legally binding treaties. Caught in the isolationist sentiment of the times, the human rights* covenants encountered stiff opposition from Republican senator John W. Bricker of Ohio and others who criticized the United Nations as a potential usurper of American sovereignty. ER defended the covenants from Bricker's attack, claiming that his attitude was more dangerous to the United States than the covenants, but at this time Dulles reversed his earlier support of the covenants.

When Dulles became secretary of state under President Dwight D. Eisenhower,* he instructed Mary Pillsbury Lord, the American delegate to the Human Rights Commission who replaced ER, to state officially that the covenants would not be submitted to the U.S. Senate for ratification. Instead, other efforts, such as education, would be used to promote human rights. ER interpreted the Republican retreat as being inconsistent with American ideals, stressing that the nation possessed a moral responsibility to raise the standards of human existence. (The United States did not ratify the Covenant on Civil and Political Rights until 1992, and U.S. ratification of the Covenant on Economic and Social and Cultural Rights was still pending in 2000.)

Dulles' appointment as secretary of state and the dismissal of the Democratic ER from the UN delegation occurred within the larger context of the Republican Party's regaining control of the White House in 1952 for the first time since Franklin D. Roosevelt* had defeated Herbert Hoover* in 1932. With ER still a leading Democratic spokesperson and Dulles assuming a highly visible role in the Republican administration, partisan politics and political competition, rather than the cooperation and congeniality of the Truman years, informed their relationship during the Eisenhower years.

ER was sharply critical of many of Dulles' actions as head of the department of state. She chastised him for reacting to the mushrooming fear of communists by failing to defend loyal civil servants in his domain who were under attack, an attitude that she believed contributed to low morale in the department of state. ER also thought that Dulles did not understand the feelings or discern the attitudes of many foreign peoples, that he erred in dealing with India* and the Middle East in the 1950s, and that he failed to recognize the powerful nationalistic forces in Third World countries. In discussing Dulles' ability to oversee American foreign policy, ER stated, "I don't believe that because a man is a successful corporation lawyer he will necessarily be the best person to direct the Department of State" (Roosevelt, 166).

SELECTED BIBLIOGRAPHY
Cook, Blanche Wiesen. "Eleanor Roosevelt and Human Rights: The Battle for Peace and Planetary Decency." In Edward Crapol, ed., *Women and American Foreign Policy*. 1987.
John Foster Dulles Papers, Princeton University Library, Princeton, NJ.
Marks, Frederick W. *Power and Peace: The Diplomacy of John Foster Dulles*. 1993.
Mowrer, Glenn A. *The United States. The United Nations and Human Rights: The Eleanor Roosevelt and Jimmy Carter Eras*. 1979.
Pruessen, Ronald W. *John Foster Dulles: The Road to Power*. 1982.
Roosevelt, Eleanor. *On My Own*. 1958.

Leonard Schlup

DURR, VIRGINIA FOSTER (6 August 1903, Birmingham, AL–24 February 1999, Carlisle, PA).

Virginia Foster Durr was a civil rights* activist whose early efforts to advance racial justice and political equality were greatly influenced by her association with Eleanor Roosevelt. Durr was born to privilege in Birmingham, Alabama. Like many of her generation, her experience of the Great Depression,* during which she was a relief worker, caused her to question the values and assumptions of the society in which she was raised. A superficial understanding of economics and politics thwarted her efforts to explore alternatives, but the New Deal* changed all of that. When she arrived in Washington from Birmingham in the spring of 1933, she recalled, that it "was just like light after darkness" (Sullivan, 11). In 1926 she had married Birmingham lawyer Clifford Durr. An Alabama native who had received a law degree at Oxford University, he joined the legal staff of the Reconstruction Finance Corporation, and both he and his wife became caught up in the energy and optimism generated by Franklin D. Roosevelt* and his New Deal initiatives. At the time, the Durrs held views common to "moderate" white southerners regarding matters of race; they were segregationists. Yet, these attitudes yielded to the democratic vision shared by young New Dealers. Both Virginia Durr and her husband, who held various positions in Washington, including federal communications commissioner, became strong supporters of the idea that government was responsible for securing the civil rights and social welfare of all citizens—black and white.

ER and Virginia Durr met at a garden party hosted by Durr's sister, Josephine Black, the wife of Supreme Court justice Hugo Black. Largely due to her admiration for the First Lady, Durr joined the Women's Division of the Democratic National Committee and sought to enfranchise more white women by working to eliminate the southern poll tax, which kept poor people from voting. Mary McLeod Bethune,* the African American adviser who often accompanied ER to meetings at the Women's Division, advised women concerned with the poll tax to join forces with black civil rights activists, who had long been working toward the elimination of discriminatory voting requirements in the South. Durr pursued the idea with Bethune, who, in turn, introduced her to William Hastie, professor of law at Howard University. Through Hastie, Durr met Charles Houston and the group of lawyers and National Association for the Advancement of Colored People* (NAACP) activists working on voting rights.

By the late 1930s, Durr had become part of a group of southerners committed to the expansion of New Deal reforms in the South and the enfranchisement of all southerners barred by legal restrictions from participation in the political process. Their concerns led to the founding of the Southern Conference for Human Welfare* (SCHW) in 1938 in Birmingham, Alabama. More than 1,200 southerners, black and white, attended the conference meeting, which had the support of FDR and ER. There Durr witnessed ER's symbolic challenge to the segregated seating enforced by police commissioner Eugene "Bull" Connor, when she placed her chair in the aisle separating blacks and whites.

Virginia Durr and labor activist Joseph Gelders organized SCHW's first major initiative—a national campaign for legislation banning the poll tax in federal elections. In 1941 the National Committee to Abolish the Poll Tax was established, with Virginia Durr as its sole staff member. ER offered immeasurable support to Durr. Durr and ER were in frequent contact and met several times in the White House to discuss the legislative effort. ER served as an intermediary with key political figures in Washington, including Ben Cohen and Tom Corcoran, who helped draft the legislation against the poll tax, and Senator Claude Pepper of Florida and Representative Lee Geyer of California, both Democrats, who cosponsored it. Through ER, Durr obtained letters of introductions to labor* leaders Sidney Hillman, David Dubinsky, and Daniel Tobin. Organized labor became a major source of financial support for the anti–poll tax campaign.

The Geyer–Pepper bill reached the floor of the House in 1942, where it sparked the first full-scale congressional debate over federal protection of voting rights since the 1890s. Southern Democrats led the opposition, arguing, in effect, that any federal regulation of voting in the states would threaten the segregation system. The bill passed the House but was tabled by a filibuster in the Senate, a pattern that was repeated several times throughout the 1940s.

Durr and other southern progressives depended on ER's support of these early organized efforts to advance political and civil rights in the South. SCHW leader James Dombrowski observed that "support for any kind of interracial activity was very scarce . . . Mrs. Roosevelt's stand strengthened the backbone of Southerners who wanted to take a decent stand. Her moral stature was very meaningful" (Dombrowski interview). Noting the contribution of both FDR and ER, Virginia Durr explained that the First Lady plowed the ground while the president tried to placate the southern wing of the Democratic Party.*

Durr's association with ER cooled during the early years of the Cold War,* when liberals divided over the issue of anticommunism. ER supported the approach of the Americans for Democratic Action* in excluding and isolating communists, while Durr and her associates in the SCHW argued that such a policy was unnecessary and that a campaign to purge communists would undermine the integrity and purpose of democratic movements and organizations.

In 1951 Virginia and Clifford Durr and their daughters returned to Alabama and settled in Montgomery. The Durrs were among the few whites who publicly supported the 1955–1956 Montgomery bus boycott by African Americans struggling to overturn legal segregation and, consequently, endured social ostracism and constant harassment. Virginia Durr occasionally wrote to ER, suggesting ways that she might help secure national support for the southern Civil Rights movement. For her part, ER followed the efforts of the Durrs with admiration and empathy. After a trip south in 1956, during the height of the region's "massive resistance" to the end of segregation, ER commented in a letter to Pauli Murray*: "I think the courage being shown by the Williams* [Aubrey and Anita] and the Durrs . . . at the present time is really something quite extraordinary and I hope it will get recognition and praise . . . though I would not like the praise to be voiced just now because it would make life harder for these courageous Southerners" (ER to PM, 22 February 1956).

SELECTED BIBLIOGRAPHY

Hollinger, Barnard, ed. *Outside the Magic Circle: The Autobiography of Virginia Foster Durr*. 1985.

James Dombrowski interview by Patricia Sullivan. 8 November 1981.

Pauli Murray Papers, Schlesinger Library, Radcliffe College, Cambridge, MA.

Sullivan, Patricia. *Days of Hope: Race and Democracy in the New Deal Era*. 1996.

Patricia Sullivan

E

EARHART, AMELIA (24 July 1897, Atchison, KS–c. 2 July 1937, near Howland Island in the Pacific).

Amelia Earhart and Eleanor Roosevelt were kindred spirits, and they developed a special, if brief, friendship that lasted until Earhart disappeared on her round-the-world flight in 1937. The pioneering female aviator had been the first woman to fly the Atlantic Ocean in 1928, although only as a passenger; in 1932 she soloed the route, the second person after Charles Lindbergh and the first woman to make the dangerous flight. Her exploits were widely covered in newspapers, journals, and the newsreels, making her one of the most widely known women of the 1930s, a trait she shared with ER.

In 1931 Earhart had married her publisher and manager, George Palmer Putnam, and shortly after the inauguration of President Franklin D. Roosevelt,* they went on 20 April 1933 to a dinner at the White House. Afterward, the First Lady, her brother, Hall Roosevelt,* Earhart, George Putnam, and a group of women reporters flew from Washington to Baltimore and back—the First Lady's first night flight. This generated an Associated Press story beginning, "The first lady of the land and the first woman to fly the ocean went skylarking together tonight in a big Condor plane" (*New York Times*, 21 April 1933). ER considered getting a pilot's license herself, but FDR vetoed the idea. That did not stop her from becoming a vocal and enthusiastic supporter of the infant airline industry. As early as 1933, *Good Housekeeping* called her "our flying First Lady" (Juno, 26).

Earhart stayed at the White House several times when business or lecturing took her to Washington. On one such occasion the aviator was immensely embarrassed when a wire-service story mistakenly quoted her as saying she had not had enough to eat while a guest there. ER just

laughed it off, saying she would teach Earhart how to raid the refriger-
ator next time she came. In the 1936 campaign, Earhart publicly supported the Roosevelt ticket and appeared with ER at the New York state
Democratic Convention. Right after the election, Earhart and Putnam
enlisted the support of the Roosevelts for her plans to fly around the
globe at the equator, receiving State Department help with some of the
complicated logistics. When word came of Earhart's disappearance on
the difficult leg from New Guinea to Howland Island, a saddened ER
told reporters at her press conference* that she was sure Earhart's last
words were, "I have no regrets" (*New York Times*, 20 July 1937).

SELECTED BIBLIOGRAPHY
Earhart, Amelia. *The Fun of It: Random Records of My Own Flying and of Women
    in Aviation*. 1932.
———. *Last Flight*. 1937.
Juno, Irene. "In the Air with Our Flying First Lady." *Good Housekeeping 96* (June
    1933): 26–27, 162.
Rich, Doris L. *Amelia Earhart: A Biography*. 1989.
Ware, Susan. *Still Missing: Amelia Earhart and the Search for Modern Feminism*. 1993.

Susan Ware

EARLY, STEPHEN "STEVE" TYREE (27 August 1889, Crozet, VA–11
August 1951, Washington, DC).
    Early, secretary to Franklin D. Roosevelt* for press relations, 1933–
1945, and the administration's number one press agent, also oversaw
Eleanor Roosevelt's press relations. Early had a broad-ranging press
background as an Associated Press reporter, FDR advance man in the
1920 campaign, and Washington editor for Paramount Newsreel Company before he became the first designated press secretary to a president
in U.S. history.
    ER posed a unique situation for Steve Early and the administration
because of her breaks, all newsworthy, with precedents set by other First
Ladies.* Her wide-ranging activities included a social reform agenda,
press conferences* for women only, magazine articles, syndicated columns, radio* series, speeches,* and much public travel.* Because what
the First Lady did reflected upon the president, by necessity Steve Early
also became a media adviser to ER, especially after Louis McHenry
Howe* grew increasingly ill before his death in 1936.
    ER worked in concert with the press secretary as an administration
spokesperson and advocate. Early counseled her about her own press
relations and writings. He controlled the admission to her press conferences; prior to World War II* his office handled actual admissions requests. Initially, only one female representative of each American daily
was admitted; by 1939 radio correspondents attended, too.
    ER referred to "Mr. Early's" rules in the press conferences. He enforced

the stipulations, such as "off the record," by taking away eligibility (Winfield, 1981, 63). ER told journalists during the meetings to check with Early's office for clarification or the details about White House scheduling, entertaining, and dinners.

Many times, journalists sought responses from him about ER's newsworthy activities and controversial remarks. For example, in 1933 the Associated Press called to verify that she had fallen off her horse in Rock Creek. As an administration spokesperson, Early tried to lessen embarrassing stories about ER's radio and lecture fees in 1937 and 1940. He also placated those news reporters who were worried about ER's scooping them in her columns on the Roosevelt children's weddings or other noteworthy events.

As the liaison between the White House and the press and radio, Early carefully monitored news coverage and suggested ways to give both Roosevelts a positive image. He gave ER story ideas or particular emphases. She helped by letting her newspaper column "sometimes serve as a trial balloon" (Roosevelt, 164). Early encouraged the correspondents to use her expertise. In 1938 he wired another presidential secretary traveling with the Roosevelts through West Virginia that "she is an expert authority on Arthurdale* and I am sure her comments would be of great value to the newspaper members of the party" (Winfield, 1990, 82).

Early also taught Eleanor Roosevelt how to respond to public criticism. Instead of angrily answering a harsh local newspaper editorial, she was convinced by Early that it was better to have the writer challenged by a reader, "a man of reputation for honesty and fair play, a Republican rather than a Democrat," as Early explained to her secretary, Malvina Thompson* (Scheider) (SE to MTS, 24 June 1937). This indirect tactic could be used without her public involvement and served to apply pressure to stop the criticism.

ER's beliefs in racial equality and actions gave Early grave concern. As she explained, he was afraid that she "would hurt my husband politically and socially" (Roosevelt, 164). When a black woman reporter from a weekly black newspaper sought admission to her press conferences, Early said no, just as he had to black reporters in the case of the president's press conferences. He wrote her secretary, "I have taken care of the Negro requests for the President's press conferences and if Mrs. Roosevelt opens hers it just makes the President more vulnerable" (SE to MTS, 11 September 1935). The reason ostensibly given was that black reporters represented weekly, not daily, newspapers. Although ER was willing to make an exception because there were so few black dailies, she complied with Early's wishes.

In general, Early was admired for his unflagging loyalty to the president, so much so that there was often conflict between the president's staff and ER's staff. Yet, much of the media access to both FDR and ER during the New Deal* period has been credited to Early. After the United States entered World War II, the White House became more closed to reporters, and Early's overall duties increased. Early then helped organize Mrs. Roosevelt's Press Conference Association to handle admissions and enforce the rules for her press conferences.

SELECTED BIBLIOGRAPHY
President's Personal File, Franklin D. Roosevelt Library, Hyde Park, NY.
Roosevelt, Eleanor. *This I Remember*. 1949.
Schoenherr, Steven E. "Selling the New Deal: Stephen T. Early's Role as Press Secretary to Franklin Roosevelt." Ph.D. Dissertation. University of Delaware, 1975.
Stephen T. Early Papers, Franklin D. Roosevelt Library, Hyde Park, NY.
Winfield, Betty Houchin. *FDR and the News Media*. 1990.
———. "Mrs. Roosevelt's Press Conference Association, the First Lady Shines a Light." *Journalism History* 8:2 (Summer 1981): 54–58, 63–67.

Betty Houchin Winfield

EISENHOWER, DWIGHT DAVID (14 October 1890, Denison, TX–28 March 1969, Washington, DC).

Raised in Abilene, Kansas, before graduating from the U.S. Military Academy at West Point in 1915, General Dwight D. Eisenhower was supreme commander in Europe during World War II* and president of the United States from 1953 to 1961. During the war Eleanor Roosevelt and "Ike," as Eisenhower was popularly called, enjoyed cordial, if formal and distant, relations. In 1948 two of the Roosevelt sons, Franklin D. Roosevelt Jr.* and Elliott Roosevelt,* flirted with the idea of getting Eisenhower to run for president on the Democratic ticket, although their mother did not endorse the idea.

Not until the 1950s, however, when both Eisenhower and ER emerged as political actors with their own and their respective parties' positions, did they engage each other on substantive issues. Once this battle was joined, the rancor between the two sometimes reached testy levels. With ER one of the most recognizable members of the Democratic Party* during this period, while Eisenhower headed the Republican Party, it was not surprising that the two differed, but their disagreements were personal as well as political.

The 1952 presidential election, in which Eisenhower ran as a Republican against the ER-supported, Democratic candidate Adlai Stevenson,* found ER publicly criticizing Eisenhower for not speaking out against Senator Joseph R. McCarthy of Wisconsin, a Republican who achieved national attention by unsubstantiated charges that government agencies were harboring communists. McCarthy's charges became a polarizing issue between the parties.

At a Stevenson campaign rally in Harlem in 1952, ER berated Eisenhower for his failure to defend General George C. Marshall,* army chief of staff during World War II, secretary of state from 1947 to 1949, and secretary of defense in 1950–1951, against the attack of Republican Senator William E. Jenner of Indiana, a follower of McCarthy. Eisenhower, whose military career had been backed by Marshall, privately opposed McCarthy's excesses but publicly supported his goal of hunting down communists and did not come to Marshall's defense. ER, abhorring vacillation on this issue, wanted public officials to take a forthright stand against what has become known as McCarthyism.* Her comments angered Eisenhower and contributed to the deterioration of their public relationship.

Despite ER's support, Stevenson lost the election. Ike's Republican victory ended ER's appointment as a U.S. representative to the United Nations,* a position to which she had been named by Democratic president Harry S Truman.* Eisenhower quickly accepted the resignation that ER, like other Democratic appointees, had submitted as a matter of courtesy to the Republican winner. Speculation ensued that political differences were not the only reason for his action; rather, Eisenhower allegedly was angered by a mistaken report that ER had said Eisenhower's wife, Mamie, was an alcoholic.

ER remained a persistent critic of Eisenhower and his administration during the eight years of his presidency, attacking both the style and substance of his leadership. Claiming that Eisenhower had established an administration patterned after big business, she observed that a team of business cohorts would not automatically produce good government. In addition, she contended that he had neglected the important presidential role of educating the public on national problems. Her critique of Eisenhower encompassed both domestic and foreign policy issues. ER argued that what Ike called "modern Republicanism," in fact, kept the party a bastion of conservatism tied to business interests. She criticized the president for not taking firmer steps in civil rights.* In addition, she attacked the policies of Eisenhower and Secretary of State John Foster Dulles* toward the Middle East.

Although she doubted that Adlai Stevenson could defeat Eisenhower in their 1956 rematch, ER assumed an active role in that campaign, emphasizing that Stevenson would make a better president than Eisenhower. Stevenson's crushing defeat, losing by over 9 million votes, discouraged her but did not soften her criticism during the Eisenhower administration's second term.

Eisenhower attended ER's funeral in 1962, where David Gurewitsch,* ER's confidant, asked him why he never found a place for her in his administration; the ex-president only shrugged and walked away. As skilled and powerful members of opposing political parties, each with his or her own faithfully held opinions, cooperation between ER the

Democrat and Ike the Republican would have been surprising in its presence but was not so in its absence.

SELECTED BIBLIOGRAPHY

Ambrose, Stephen E. *Eisenhower*. Vols. 1, 2. 1983, 1984.
Dwight D. Eisenhower Papers, Eisenhower Presidential Library, Abilene, KS.
Lash, Joseph P. *Eleanor: The Years Alone*. 1972.
Pach, Chester J., Jr., and Elmo R. Richardson. *The Presidency of Dwight D. Eisenhower*. 1991.

Leonard Schlup

"ELEANOR CLUBS." In the early 1940s a rumor spread throughout the South that Eleanor Roosevelt was actively encouraging African American domestics to unionize in what were said to be "Eleanor Clubs." The goal of these purported organizations was to challenge the inequities of domestic employment and racial relations in the South. Their slogan was "nearly always a variation of 'a white woman in every kitchen by 1943' " (Odum, 72). ER herself received letters and even phone calls about the "Eleanor Clubs."

These rumors were widespread enough to cause official alarm. In 1942 the Federal Bureau of Investigation* (FBI) investigated the matter and concluded the rumors had no basis in fact, a finding ER herself announced to the press, according to an Associated Press report in the *New York Times* on 23 September 1942. The news account quoted ER as saying that she had received letters and telephone calls about the clubs but that no one had been able to give the name of a club member or a place where such a group met. The Office of War Information* (OWI) included the "Eleanor Clubs" in its own investigation of wartime rumors, worried that rumors of this nature might impair civilian wartime morale.

Reports and denials could not counter the force of the rumors. The war produced profound social and economic changes in the South, shifts that implicitly and explicitly threatened to disrupt the existing system of racial segregation. ER was known for her outspoken support of civil rights* and for her friendship with prominent African Americans. She had chosen a role as an independent woman, moreover, that potentially undermined traditional gender relations. In the climate of anxiety produced by the disruptions of war, ER became a scapegoat—a way for southerners to displace anxiety, fear, and even hostility. The rumors of "Eleanor Clubs" were an expression of these anxieties, a way for white southerners to assure each other that their African American domestic help had joined an "Eleanor Club" and thus protested against white supremacy, not because they hated their employers or discrimination— but because ER had made them do it.

SELECTED BIBLIOGRAPHY

Allport, Gordon W., and Leo Postman. *The Psychology of Rumor*. 1965.
Eleanor Roosevelt FBI File, Department of Justice, Washington, D.C.

Eleanor Roosevelt Papers, Franklin D. Roosevelt Library, Hyde Park, NY.
Garson, Robert A. *The Democratic Party and the Politics of Sectionalism, 1941–1948.*
    1974.
Odum, Howard W. *Race and Rumors of Race: Challenge to American Crisis.* 1969.

Caryn Neumann

ELEANOR ROOSEVELT CENTER AT VAL-KILL. The Eleanor Roosevelt Center at Val-Kill (ERVK) is a nongovernmental, not-for-profit, and nonpartisan organization that operates at the site of Eleanor Roosevelt's home at Val-Kill* in Hyde Park,* New York. It began in the mid-1970s with efforts by citizens in Hyde Park (organized as the Eleanor Roosevelt Cottage Committee of the Hyde Park Visual Environment Committee) to save ER's home at Val-Kill from commercial development and to preserve it for future generations. Actress Jean Stapleton played an important role in this effort. In 1977 federal legislation creating the Eleanor Roosevelt National Historic Site at Val-Kill authorized the National Park Service to enter into a cooperative agreement with ERVK to conduct studies, lectures, seminars, and other endeavors relating to the issues to which ER dedicated her considerable intellect and humanitarian concerns.

Since 1984, ERVK has been located in Stone Cottage, the original structure ER and her friends, Nancy Cook* and Marion Dickerman,* had built in 1925 at Val-Kill on land leased to them by Franklin D. Roosevelt* about two miles from Springwood, the Roosevelt family estate. The cottage is adjacent to the building, used originally by the three women for their Val-Kill Industries furniture factory, which ER later converted into a home for herself, making it her principal residence after she left the White House in 1945.

ERVK seeks to preserve Val-Kill as a vibrant living memorial, a center for the exchange of significant ideas, and a catalyst for change and for the betterment of the human condition. Since 1987, ERVK has awarded the Eleanor Roosevelt Val-Kill Medal to individuals who have made significant contributions to society in the arts, education, citizenship, community service, and other humanitarian concerns. Recipients have included Harry Belafonte, Barbara Jordan, Hamilton Fish, Jean Stapleton, Robert F. Kennedy Jr., John Chancellor, Marian Wright Edelman, Hillary Rodham Clinton, Lea Rabin, Queen Noor, and Rachel Robinson as well as community figures.

ERVK conducts programs that promote racial harmony, youth development, and women at the local, national, and international levels. Early programs focused on studies of Val-Kill Industries and crafts, women and work, and the local environment. In the late 1980s, ERVK organized a community-based program in the Mid-Hudson Valley region to promote interracial dialogue in areas of education, housing, law enforcement, media, and employment. ERVK carries out Elderhostel programs in the fall and spring. It also works collaboratively with other organizations and colleges. In 1997 ERVK launched the Girl Leadership Workshop, bringing girls from several northeast states to Val-Kill to learn about ER and develop self-awareness, confidence, and a devotion to community service and citizenship. In 1998 ERVK emphasized programs to celebrate the fiftieth anniversary of the Universal Declaration of Human Rights,* one of ER's greatest legacies.

Daniel A. Strasser

ELEANOR ROOSEVELT WINGS OF THE FRANKLIN D. ROOSEVELT LIBRARY. Among the memorials* to Eleanor Roosevelt are two wings of the Franklin D. Roosevelt Library in Hyde Park,* New York. They contain the first collection of materials that are devoted to a First Lady and housed within a presidential library. Artifacts and documentary materials cover the broad spectrum of ER's public and private life and work.

Construction of the wings, which were dedicated in ER's honor on 3 May 1972, cost a total of $1.5 million. The U.S. Congress* appropriated $767,000 for the project, and the remainder of the funds came from the Eleanor Roosevelt Memorial Foundation, which solicited private contributions.

The wings include the ER Gallery, an auditorium, museum and archival storage areas, an education center, and conference and research rooms where scholars study the Roosevelt era. Exhibits in the gallery comprise an introductory film, displays of her jewelry and personal objects, an interactive audiovisual exhibit, and other exhibits built around the following themes: ER as a self-determined activist, her White House years, her knitting, her apartment in New York City, Val-Kill,* the United Nations,* and her death* and funeral.

The Franklin D. Roosevelt Library, first and smallest of the presidential libraries, was conceptualized by President Roosevelt D. Roosevelt* himself and built on the Roosevelt estate near the family mansion, Springwood, now a national historic site. Approved by Congress* in 1939 and opened to the public in 1941, the library was envisioned by FDR as a public repository for his official papers and documents relating to the Roosevelt family, to be administered under the supervision of the National Archives. In 1942 he provided his own rough sketches for the structure, modeling it on the lines of colonial Dutch residential buildings in the Hudson River Valley. The initial phase of the project, constructed by the government from private donations, included only the central portion of the building as planned by the president. The Eleanor Roosevelt wings completed FDR's early vision of the structure.

SELECTED BIBLIOGRAPHY
Eleanor Roosevelt Papers and Franklin D. Roosevelt Papers, Franklin D. Roose-
    velt Library, Hyde Park, NY.

Joyce C. Ghee and Joan Spence

ELMHIRST, DOROTHY WHITNEY STRAIGHT (23 January 1887,
Washington, DC—13 December 1968, Devon, England).

Born into the social circle that included the Vanderbilts, Astors, and
Roosevelts, Elmhirst believed that wealth entailed civic responsibility.
Her father, William C. Whitney, was secretary of the navy under Grover
Cleveland, and her mother, Flora Payne Whitney, had family money
from Standard Oil. Like Eleanor Roosevelt, Dorothy was educated by
Frederic Roser, who tutored the daughters of the wealthy, but the two
did not attend his private classes at the same time.

On her twenty-first birthday she came into control of a fortune she
had inherited earlier and became a major financial backer of the New
York state Woman's Suffrage Party. As a young woman she moved in
the same world as ER, taking part in the Junior League and becoming a
close friend of Mary Harriman (Rumsey*), its cofounder, and helping
Lillian Wald* at the Henry Street Settlement. Dorothy was also friendly
with Daisy Harriman* and a member of her Colony Club. As a 1906
debutante, Dorothy dated Howard Cary, who had been a suitor of ER
before her engagement to Franklin D. Roosevelt.* Dorothy was shocked
over Cary's sudden death, an apparent suicide, attributed by gossip to
her rejection of his marriage proposal.

On a round-the-world tour in 1909, she enjoyed the attentions in China
of Willard D. Straight, a graduate of Cornell University. He represented
a banking coalition allied with J. P. Morgan and led by Frank Vanderlip,
husband of Narcissa Vanderlip,* who later helped draw ER into politics.
Straight, who came from a poor family, previously had held U.S. diplomatic posts abroad and looked after the financial interests of E. W.
Harriman, Mary Harriman's father. A friend of Theodore Roosevelt,*
Straight enlisted TR's sister and ER's aunt, Corrine Robinson,* to help
him convince Dorothy to marry him. Wed in Switzerland in 1911, the
couple returned to China and then came back to the United States. Seeking to promote progressive ideas and social reforms, they founded the
New Republic magazine in 1914, which Dorothy supported until 1953. She
also was a founder of the New School for Social Research in New York.

During World War I, Dorothy involved herself in war work, raising
funds for the American Red Cross* and the defense effort and contributing $1 million to the Liberty Loan drive. After her husband, who
served as a major with the U.S. Army, died of pneumonia in France
in 1918, she continued her philanthropic activities and served in 1921–

1922 as first president of the National Association of Junior Leagues of America.

In the early 1920s she and ER worked together in both the Women's Trade Union League* (WTUL) and the League of Women Voters* (LWV). At Straight's home ER met Rose Schneiderman,* the WTUL president who helped connect her to the labor* movement. In 1922 Straight made the down payment for a building for the WTUL, and ER chaired the committee to pay off the mortgage. In 1923 both ER and Straight were elected vice-chair of the New York LWV. Each also was a member of the Women's City Club.*

In 1924 Straight, fulfilling a provision of her husband's will to make Cornell a more "human" place, oversaw completion of a student union there, assisted by Leonard Elmhirst, an Englishman who had done rural reconstruction work in India.* In 1925 they were married and moved to England, where they bought a crumbling manor and set up Darlington Hall, a progressive school and community center aimed at rehabilitation of a blighted rural area.

When ER became interested in Arthurdale,* the New Deal* project to resettle unemployed West Virginia miners, she sought advice from the Elmhirsts. Dorothy Elmhirst gave funds for a health clinic there. Just before World War II* broke out, ER made time in her schedule to host the Elmhirsts at a White House breakfast, maintaining ties with an old friend who, like herself, had moved far behind the narrow society in which she had grown up.

SELECTED BIBLIOGRAPHY

Dorothy Whitney Straight Elmhirst Papers, Cornell University, Ithaca, NY.
Frank Vanderlip Papers, Columbia University, New York.
Hareven, Tamara K. *Eleanor Roosevelt: An American Conscience.* 1968.
Lash, Joseph P. *Love, Eleanor: Eleanor Roosevelt and Her Friends.* 1982.
Swanberg, W. A. *Whitney Father, Whitney Heiress.* 1980.
Young, Michael. *The Elmhirsts of Dartington: The Creation of an Utopian Community.* 1982.

Hilda R. Watrous

EQUAL RIGHTS AMENDMENT. In 1923 the National Woman's Party (NWP) proposed an Equal Rights Amendment (ERA) to the Constitution. Members who had constituted the radical branch of the woman suffrage movement realized that female enfranchisement, granted three years earlier, had not addressed inequalities in political citizenship, economic opportunity, or social status. A broad spectrum of female activists examined with interest the concept when it was first presented to Congress.*

Within one year and after several conferences, women in social reform organizations like the League of Women Voters* and National Consumers' League* and in government agencies like the Women's Bureau concluded that the amendment jeopardized legislation that protected women in the workforce. Equality before the law would invalidate maximum-hour laws, bans on presumably dangerous jobs, and pending legislation that would guarantee minimum wages for women workers. By the mid-1920s, battle lines were drawn. The gulf between the NWP and the vast majority of women's groups sundered any semblance of unity among those who envisioned themselves as advocates for female advancement. Eleanor Roosevelt, who rose to prominence as a social and political activist during the 1920s, identified with the anti-ERA social reformers.

Political conflict and ideological positions hardened. Amendment supporters stressed the negative impact of restrictive laws on individual potential: hampering women who wished to earn more by working longer hours or in a better-paying occupation. Opponents stressed the exploitation of women collectively, the necessity of protecting against the physical harm of long hours in factories, or the moral degradation of employment in jobs like bartending or assumed dangers of working after midnight. Pro-ERA positions often reflected situations that favored white-collar career women rather than working-class women in industry.

This apparent occupational, class divide rested on a fundamental disparity in attitudes toward the nature and roles of women. Like many female reformers over the previous century, ERA opponents clung to notions of the special and different qualities of women—their moral sensibilities, their social roles as wives and mothers, their physical weaknesses. NWP members rejected the notion of female difference as a rationale for the perpetuation of any practices or policies that mitigated blanket equality before the law.

Conflicting rationales and remedies masked the similar social profiles of ERA proponents and opponents. NWP members and social reformers alike were primarily middle-class, highly educated, professional women. ER was a notable exception. In her elitist social circle, college education and a professional career were discouraged. She was, however, a foremost worker on behalf of the Women's Division of the New York state Democratic Committee, and a partisan divide did distinguish women battling over the ERA. Many early twentieth-century reformers and suffragists had roots in the Whig reform wing of the Republican Party and maintained allegiance to their party's Progressives. By the 1920s, however, a new generation of female activists gravitated to the Democrats and supported policies that would lay the foundation for the New Deal.*

The Roosevelt administration's response to the Great Depression* affected the women involved in the conflict over the amendment. Discriminatory features in National Recovery Administration (NRA) industrial codes and later in Social Security provisions provided the NWP and female reformers, including ER, the opportunity to work together in protest. Reformers invariably opted for politically expedient compromises, but common action proved possible. More problematic was the Fair Labor Standards Act (FLSA) of 1938. The law set minimum wages and maximum hour standards for men and women alike. When validated by the Supreme Court, ERA backers could claim, as they had from the start, that working conditions should be regulated on the basis of class or occupation and not according to gender.

During the 1930s, support for the ERA grew. First, small professional associations like those comprising female doctors and lawyers backed the blanket amendment. Then the National Federation of Business and Professional Women (BPW), a large combination of groups of women ranging from secretaries and nurses to executives and managers, endorsed the constitutional change. The NWP was no longer isolated from all women's organizations.

For ER, these developments presented a conundrum. On one hand, she had been concerned with woman's rights from her early membership in the League of Women Voters and introduction to Democratic Party* politics. In the early 1920s she was already lobbying for greater representation of women as convention delegates and as appointed and elected officials. Her connections to the Women's Trade Union League* and National Consumers' League underscored her concern for working women. In general terms, her stature as a feminist seemed secure. But in spite of commitment and action on a broad spectrum of issues to address female inequality and discrimination, the NWP made support of the ERA the litmus test for feminism. "They are reformers—we are feminists" (Becker, 171), proclaimed one member, and that distinction included the First Lady.

Several of the female reporters who attended ER's press conferences* belonged to the NWP. Gratitude and respect for ER vied with their support for the amendment. The result was confusion and regret. Ruby Black* of the United Press wire service admired ER's activities and independence and wrote the first published biography of the First Lady. Black tried to reconcile the disparity between ER's broad-based actions on behalf of women and her attacks on the ERA. "She talks like a social worker and acts like a feminist" (Scharf, 226), Black wrote in a 1935 issue of the NWP periodical *Equal Rights*.

ER did mute her rhetorical opposition to the amendment as the 1930s wore on. Still, she worked behind the scenes to blunt the efforts of NWP delegates at international conferences where the feminists worked on behalf of equal rights provisions in international treaties. She supported the efforts of her friends and colleagues when they successfully blocked an ERA endorsement in the 1940 Democratic Party platform. Republicans backed the amendment for the first time during that campaign.

The World War II* years added to pro-ERA momentum. Women workers responded to labor shortages and the need to produce weapons; protective regulations were modified or ignored completely. In 1944, an NWP leader who was active in the General Federation of Women's Clubs maneuvered an ERA endorsement from the large women's group. During the election campaign that year Democrats as well as Republicans included pro-ERA planks in their respective party platforms. As the war drew to an end and the United Nations* charter was written, the document contained an equal rights resolution. ERA backers were buoyed by the hope that gratitude for women's war efforts would be rewarded with a constitutional amendment, as had occurred with the suffrage amendment after World War I.

But just as success seemed possible, internal schism stilled the voices of the NWP's seasoned proponents. Amendment opponents rallied with revived rhetoric stressing women's special needs for special privileges and protections. Prominent reformers and government officials organized the Committee to Defeat the Unequal Rights Amendment, to which ER lent her name. Stalemate in Congress mirrored the continuing, unresolved conflict among women. While the Senate Judiciary Committee reported on the ERA—albeit with limiting riders—Congressman Emanuel Celler of New York, a Democrat and chair of the House Judiciary Committee, refused to even hold hearings after 1948. For twenty-three years he stood firm.

During this period, newly widowed ER accepted appointment by President Harry S Truman* as delegate to the United Nations. There she headed the commission to draft a Universal Declaration on Human Rights* and covenants to implement the document. The Covenant on Civil and Political Rights addressed political rights for women, and ER welcomed this attention to women's status around the world. In May 1951 she stated her modifying views in a published article in which she also addressed women's needs on the domestic scene. Now that working women had access to membership in flourishing trade unions, she wrote, special laws might no longer be necessary for their protection. Hesitantly, she concluded that perhaps women would benefit if they were "declared equal before the law and equal politically and in whatever work" (Scharf, 245) they did. Then the president of the NWP wrote her for explicit support of the ERA. She responded in curt, noncommitted fashion. "While I am not going to fight the Equal Rights Amendment, I really do not feel enthusiastic enough about it to write you a letter in its favor" (Scharf, 246).

For the remaining decade of her life, her ambivalence persisted. She shared the nation's awareness and anxiety over the stunning increase of women in the workforce; she believed in the potential value of American women as a positive resource in the world of Cold War* competition; and she castigated the administration of President John F. Kennedy* for its paucity of women appointees. Kennedy's undersecretary of labor, Esther Peterson,* who was a former union official and an adamant foe of the ERA, suggested the creation of the President's Commission on the Status of Women* to study these issues. Kennedy asked ER to chair the commission.

ER died before the commission issued its final report. It was a massive study that, in summary, restated the decades-old stance that female equality was best achieved by recognition of gender differences and need. ER would undoubtedly have agreed with these findings, made public in 1963 on the eve of the resurgence of a strong feminist movement in the United States.

Passage of the ERA was prominent on the long, varied list of second-wave feminists' goals. By 1971 Congress passed the amendment, and all but three required states ratified it one year later. Then the process stalled and failed by 1977, buffeted by ideological backlash over gender issues. At one point during the extended time limit granted to seek the necessary ratifications, four former and present First Ladies* appeared at a massive convention to demonstrate bipartisan support. Some delegates may have wondered if the most influential First Lady in American history could have brought about an earlier victory. It is possible that in the aftermath of World War II a grateful nation might have rewarded its women and their contributions with blanket constitutional equality. Forceful feminist rhetoric and demands had not yet engendered an equally strident response.

ER took firm, outspoken positions on numerous controversial issues involving race and class, which lent them credibility. A constitutional amendment addressing gender was not among them. It would be unfair, however, to overlook ER's concern for difficulties and discrimination faced by American women because of her inaction on behalf of the ERA. Unlike egalitarian feminists, her concept of woman's rights did not include the blanket amendment. One must look in other directions to discover her contributions to the advancement of American women.

SELECTED BIBLIOGRAPHY

Becker, Susan. *The Origins of the Equal Rights Amendment: American Feminism between the Wars.* 1981.

Berry, Mary Francis. *Why ERA Failed.* 1986.

Hoff-Wilson, Joan, ed. *Rights of Passage: The Past and Future of the ERA.* 1986.

Scharf, Lois. "ER and Feminism." In Joan Hoff-Wilson and Marjorie Lightman, eds., *Without Precedent: The Life and Career of Eleanor Roosevelt.* 1984.

Lois Scharf

F

FALA (7 April 1940, Westport, CT–5 April 1952, Hyde Park, NY).

Fala, the Roosevelt family's best-known dog, was loved by both Franklin D. Roosevelt* and Eleanor Roosevelt. A Scottish terrier, Fala was a gift to FDR from his cousin Margaret Suckley* and arrived at the White House on 10 November 1940.

FDR named the terrier "Murray of Fala Hill" in honor of an outlaw Roosevelt ancestor whose home was Fala Hill in Scotland. The president and the dog were inseparable, and Fala accompanied FDR on trips both in the United States and abroad. When a false story was spread in the 1944 presidential campaign that a destroyer had been sent at great expense to bring Fala back from an Aleutian Island where he had been left by mistake, FDR responded with a speech that became famous. He declared that the dog's Scottish soul had been outraged, making Fala a symbol of the Roosevelt administration's ability to deflect criticism and speak personally to voters.

After FDR's death, ER and Fala became close companions. Although FDR had bequeathed Fala to Suckley, she agreed to give the dog to ER after she asked to keep him. ER bathed Fala, had him do tricks, wrote about him in her newspaper and magazine columns, walked with him in the woods around Val-Kill,* and had photographs taken with him. On a trip to Campobello* Island, New Brunswick, in 1946, ER was refused a hotel room because Fala was with her, so she stayed in a cabin that welcomed pets.

Fala died just before he was twelve years old and, as FDR had requested, was buried in the rose garden at Hyde Park* near his master's grave. Although she had not shed tears in public at FDR's funeral, ER cried openly when Fala was interred.

Eleanor Roosevelt strolls on the Val-Kill grounds in November 1951 accompanied by two of her grandchildren, Nina (left) and Sally, the children of John and Anne Roosevelt, and Fala. *Courtesy of Franklin D. Roosevelt Library*

SELECTED BIBLIOGRAPHY
Lash, Joseph P. *Eleanor: The Years Alone*. 1972.
Roosevelt, Eleanor. *The Autobiography of Eleanor Roosevelt*. 1961.
Ward, Geoffrey. *Closest Companion*. 1995.

Leonard Schlup

FAMILY INFLUENCES. Although Eleanor Roosevelt and her biographers tend to ignore the positive influences that her relatives had on her, substantial evidence points to their examples as helping to shape her career. This is particularly true in the case of the Roosevelts, her father's family, who provided examples of individuals who achieved in ways that her mother's family did not.

ER's maternal grandmother, Mary Ludlow Hall, with whom she lived from the time of her father's death (1894) until she entered boarding school in England (1899), was too busy with her own large family to give

much attention to her grandchildren. ER speculated that her Grandmother Hall, who showed artistic talent in her youth but failed to develop it, would have been a happier woman had she done more on her
own. Similarly, ER's Aunt Pussie (Edith Hall Morgan), her mother's sister, was a society belle who, in ER's opinion, could have developed her
talent "into something useful professionally," but she did not because
she "did not have to" (Eleanor Roosevelt, 56).

On the Roosevelt side, the story is different. Certainly, the charitable
work of Theodore Roosevelt Sr., ER's grandfather, influenced ER, as did
the public service and fights for reform of his son and ER's uncle, Theodore Roosevelt.* Although Theodore Sr.'s wife and ER's paternal grandmother, Martha "Mittie" Bulloch Roosevelt, died a few months before
ER was born, her Georgia upbringing also left its mark on her granddaughter. Mittie and her sister Anna (who tutored Mittie's children in
their youth) regaled ER's father, Elliott,* and his siblings with stories
about life in the antebellum South. Mittie's brothers, staunch Confeder-
ates in the Civil War, led such colorful, eventful lives, especially during
their long exile in England because they did not receive post–Civil War
amnesty, that they provided ER's generation with vivid examples of risk-
takers. Although ER rarely referred to the fact that the Bullochs owned
slaves and defended slavery, she sometimes mentioned her Uncle Irvine
Bulloch with admiration.

ER's two Roosevelt aunts (the sisters of Elliott Roosevelt* and Theodore Roosevelt) both took active roles in the political as well as social
life of New York City and the nation, although they did not favor the
vote for women. Anna Roosevelt Cowles* (called Bamie or Bye) and
Corinne Roosevelt Robinson* supported Theodore in his early forays into
politics in the 1880s; they entertained his political friends, joined in discussion of policy, and offered their opinions on policy and personnel.
During Theodore's presidency, Bye lived in Washington, D.C., in a house
at 1733 N Street, sometimes dubbed the "little White House." ER commented that her Uncle Theodore rarely made an important decision
without discussing it first with his sister, Bye.

Bye played a key role in sending ER to Allenswood, the boarding
school outside London that she often credited with changing her thinking about the world and her place in it. After ER's father died, Theodore's wife, Edith, and his sisters began to emphasize the importance of
finding a good school for her. Bye, who had attended the school run by
Mlle. Marie Souvestre* while it was located in France, arranged for ER
to enter Souvestre's school, now relocated near London. ER later singled
out the years that she attended Allenswood (1899 to 1902) as immensely
valuable in her development: "Mlle. Souvestre [unlike her Hall relatives]
laid a great deal of stress on intellectual achievements and there I felt I
could hold my own" (Eleanor Roosevelt, 56).

When ER moved to Washington in 1913, she turned to her Aunt Bye for advice on how to manage social duties in the capital. By that time Bye had moved to Connecticut, and Franklin D. Roosevelt* and ER rented Bye's house on N Street, where they lived while FDR served as assistant secretary of the navy.

Corinne Roosevelt Robinson, Elliott Roosevelt's younger sister, set important examples for her niece in the areas of both political involvement and writing. After 1912, Robinson acquired a national reputation as a public speaker on Republican causes, and in 1920 she became the first woman to give a nominating speech at a major party convention.

While still a child, Corinne started to write poems, and in her forties she submitted some of them for publication, using a pseudonym, but when the poems were accepted, she used her own name for publication. Those poems and others were gathered into five volumes published between 1912 and 1930. Her articles on a variety of subjects, ranging from her brother's work to women in politics and from the reasons for divorce, to art and travel, appeared in several magazines after 1919.

Other Roosevelt women beat Corinne Robinson into print. Eleanor Butler Alexander Roosevelt, sometimes called the "other Eleanor," married ER's cousin, Theodore Roosevelt Jr., the eldest son of Theodore Roosevelt, in 1910. When he went to France in 1917 as part of the American forces, she left her three young children with her mother and signed up with the Young Men's Christian Association (YMCA) so she could follow him, becoming one of the first women that organization accepted to work abroad in the war effort. In France she helped organize vacation camps where American soldiers could spend their short furloughs. After she returned to the United States, she described that work in an article, "The AEF at Play," in the *Woman's Home Companion** in June 1919. ER sometimes cited the example of "the other Eleanor" as helping convince her that women needed interests outside their homes. Belle Willard Roosevelt, wife of another of Theodore's sons, Kermit, had published even earlier. In 1916 her article "Two Book Hunters in South America" appeared in the *Bookman*.

Another cousin of ER, Corinne Robinson Alsop,* the only daughter of Corinne Roosevelt Robinson, was two years younger than ER but preceded her as the wife of a state legislator and then became a legislator herself. Joseph Alsop, Corinne's husband, served in the Connecticut legislature and later on that state's Public Utilities Commission. Corinne Alsop represented her town, Avon, in the Connecticut legislature for two terms, 1925–1927 and 1931–1933. Although she was a Republican, she and ER remained friendly. Corinne Alsop sometimes pointed out to ER that she had actually been in politics because she had won elective office. According to her family, Corinne Alsop was a shrewd political observer and could predict the vote in her district with remarkable accuracy. Two of her sons, Joseph Alsop* and Stewart Alsop, began their journalistic careers during ER's lifetime.

ER visited the White House during the administration of her uncle, Theodore (1901–1909), and was familiar with the activities of his wife, Edith Carow Roosevelt, as First Lady. Often credited with helping to institutionalize the position of First Lady, Edith Roosevelt was the first to hire a social secretary, and she carefully rationed the press' access to her young children. It was sometimes said that she spent "seven years in the White House without making a mistake" (Jensen, 191). Although she and ER were separated by a wide political gulf by the time ER moved into the White House in 1933 (Edith had spoken at a rally for Herbert Hoover* at Madison Square Garden in the election of 1932), ER is one of the very few First Ladies* who had a close relative precede them in that role.

ER thus had many examples within the Roosevelt family of women, as well as men, who pursued life in the public arena by writing, giving speeches to large audiences, and involving themselves in politics and government.

SELECTED BIBLIOGRAPHY

Caroli, Betty Boyd. *The Roosevelt Women*. 1998.
Jensen, Amy La Follette. *The White House and Its Thirty-Three Families*. 1962.
Rixy, Lilian. *Bamie*. 1963.
Robinson, Corinne Roosevelt. *My Brother Theodore Roosevelt*. 1921.
Roosevelt, Eleanor. "The Seven People Who Shaped My Life." *Look* (19 June 1951): 54–58.
Roosevelt, Mrs. Theodore, Jr. *Day before Yesterday*. 1959.

Betty Boyd Caroli

FARLEY, JAMES ALOYSIUS (30 May 1888, Grassy Point, NY–9 June 1976, New York).

Chairman of the Democratic National Committee and postmaster general from 1933 to 1940, James A. Farley was a skillful and prominent New York politician who helped engineer the presidential landslides of Franklin D. Roosevelt* in 1932 and 1936. A former bookkeeper, salesman, and Stony Point town clerk, his acquaintance with the Roosevelts began in the early 1920s, when he chaired the Rockland County Democratic Committee. In 1928 he became secretary and in 1930 chairman of the New York state Democratic Committee while retaining the presidency of the General Building Supply Corporation, a business he organized to supply lime and cement to contractors.

Farley and Eleanor Roosevelt enjoyed a genial and constructive relationship. Each recognized and respected the other's abilities. At the Democratic National Convention in New York in 1924, when ER waited all night to go before the platform committee to advocate planks desired by women but was never allowed to appear, Farley agreed to present her proposals to the committee, although it did not accept them.

Farley praised her successful political efforts to cultivate the feminine vote, saluting her as a pioneer in helping to give women a positive and enlarged role in Democratic Party* affairs. In FDR's 1928 and 1930 gubernatorial campaigns, Farley observed a 10 to 20 percent increase in the Democratic vote in upstate counties where local women's organizations had been set up by ER and her associates in the Women's Division of the state Democratic Committee. Farley saw ER as a strong and influential figure in her own right. He thought she had "a genuine gift for organizational work, a tactful understanding manner in handling people, and above all a real sense of politics" (Farley, *Behind the Ballots*, 354).

As postmaster general, Farley had oversight of patronage appointments after FDR was elected president. ER worked closely with Molly Dewson* in the Women's Division of the Democratic National Committee to encourage Farley to recommend appointments for women. An article in the February 1938 issue of the *Democratic Digest** noted that 7,560 women were among the 28,092 postmasters commissioned between 4 March 1933 and 1 October 1938.

Farley's own political aspirations for high office and opposition to a third term strained his relationship with FDR by 1940, but Farley and ER retained their friendship. On 18 July 1940, after ER had been asked by Frances Perkins* and Farley to appear at the rebellious Democratic National Convention in Chicago, Farley met her at the Chicago airport and discussed the delegates' resistance to Henry Wallace* as FDR's choice for vice president. That evening in an address to the unruly convention, ER began with a tribute to Farley for what he had done for the party, urged the delegates to put aside partisanship, and respect the president's judgment regarding who he thought could be of most help in what ER emphasized was "no ordinary time" (Goodwin, 133). Farley later said that ER's "appearance and speech about the burdens of the Presidency in critical times saved the day for the President" (Farley, *Jim Farley's Story*, 302).

Both FDR and ER urged Farley, who had received seventy-two votes himself for the presidential nomination on the first ballot, to remain at least as nominal chairman of the Democratic National Committee during FDR's third presidential campaign. Nevertheless, he resigned both the chairmanship and his cabinet post to accept the position of chairman of the board of Coca-Cola Export Corporation. For the rest of his life, he remained active in Democratic Party activities, but he took little part in national campaigns.

SELECTED BIBLIOGRAPHY
Farley, James A. *Behind the Ballots*. 1938.
————. *Jim Farley's Story: The Roosevelt Years*. 1948.

Goodwin, Doris Kearns. *No Ordinary Time: Franklin and Eleanor Roosevelt: The Home Front in World War II.* 1994.

Newquist, Gloria A. "James A. Farley and the Politics of Victory, 1928–1936." Ph.D. dissertation. University of Southern California. 1966.

Syrett, John. "Jim Farley and Carter Glass: Allies against a Third Term." *Prologues* 15 (Summer 1983): 89–102.

Leonard Schlup

FEDERAL BUREAU OF INVESTIGATION. Eleanor Roosevelt was part of the world of American reform that J. Edgar Hoover, longtime director of the Federal Bureau of Investigation (FBI), spent his life studying for evidence of communist influence. Given Hoover's ill-concealed suspicions of ER's associates, of her friends, and, indeed, of her, it would have been other than natural if ER had not reciprocated in kind. If Hoover's contempt for ER was expressed only on the margins of FBI memorandums and in conversations with his friends, hers surfaced at times in ugly name-calling. In correspondence with Hoover she referred to the "Gestapo methods" (ER to JEH, 26 January 1941, FBI file) of the FBI at a time when Hoover's men were engaged in surveillance of the real Gestapo.

The Bureau of Investigation, as it was known until the mid-1930s, was founded in 1908 to give President Theodore Roosevelt* and the Justice Department the ability to investigate political scandals and antitrust violations. With U.S. entry into World War I in April 1917, the bureau was given the responsibility of enforcing the wartime espionage and sedition laws that made the antiwar Left, particularly the Socialist Party and peace organizations, liable to prosecution. J. Edgar Hoover, who would lead the bureau from 1924 until his death in 1972, was at this time a young attorney who spent the war years processing the cases of thousands of German and Austrian nationals made subject to internment under the president's "alien enemy" proclamation. The bureau's files on the Left grew mightily after August 1919, when Attorney General A. Mitchell Palmer placed Hoover in charge of a new Radical Division in the Justice Department to plan the government's response to a wave of political bombings that spring. One of these bombs destroyed the front of Palmer's Washington home, which was across the street from the home of Eleanor and Franklin D. Roosevelt,* who returned home on the night of 2 June 1919 to find their son, James Roosevelt,* awakened by the commotion. The Roosevelts were on friendly terms with the Palmers and at the time did not criticize the anti-Red campaign that ensued.

Although it was soon learned that all the bombings were the work of a few minuscule Italian anarchist organizations, Hoover and the Justice Department launched a drive against what Hoover termed the radical movement. He threw himself into the task of collecting data on the world of American radicalism and reform. The best-known results of his research were the notorious Red Scare raids of November 1919 and January 1920, in which several thousand alleged anarchists, communists, and radicals were arrested with little regard for their constitutional rights. Most were later released, but a few hundred aliens were deported.

Probably just as important a consequence of these raids, in the long run, was the stereotype of a "Red network" as a fixture in the imagination of the countersubversive Right in America. The "Red network" mirage was treated in the literary efforts of Elizabeth Dilling, in whose books, *The Red Network* and *The Roosevelt Red Record*, ER cavorted at the center of expansive Red webs. Network conspiracy theorists were convinced that there were hidden connections linking all of American reform with the Moscow-based Communist International. That meant Hoover's bureau would be the constant recipient of tips from right-wingers on the activities of such mainstays of American reform as ER, tips that became lodged in ER's voluminous file, which eventually bloated to 3,271 pages. (An FBI file is the repository of any information that comes to the bureau by way of unsolicited communication or during the course of an unrelated investigation, as well as during an investigation of the subject.) ER was never the subject of an FBI investigation, although there is evidence that the bureau on at least several occasions followed up on information about her that came its way from unrelated sources. While Hoover was too canny to commit himself fully to the "Red network" delusion—since the theory was demonstrably false—he did socialize and politicize in circles where the "Red network" was accorded credibility.

To understand the relationship between ER and Hoover's FBI, it is important to remember that both were, in large measure, products of the early ideological clashes between the American Left and Right during the early 1920s, when Hoover absorbed not only concerns about "Red networks" but dark imaginings about the activities of the "parlor pinks," wealthy socialites, preeminent society ladies, and clergymen who allegedly bankrolled the "Red networks." ER stood high in any countersubversive's roll call of "parlor pinks." For her part, ER seems to have absorbed an idea that became a conviction on the American Left almost as strong as that of a "Red network" on the Right: that there existed an organized conspiracy by conservatives to repress American reform and that Hoover's bureau was at the center of it.

There is no doubt that Hoover's relationship with FDR was as cordial as he had with any president, with the possible exception of Lyndon Johnson, and it was certainly the most productive. Hoover was an enthusiastic supporter of FDR as long as the president lived, although in later years Hoover moved in Roosevelt-hating circles. FDR and his first attorney general, Homer S. Cummings, launched the war on crime that made Hoover and the FBI (as it was renamed in 1935) into national heroes. Similarly, FDR ordered Hoover to revive the bureau surveillance of political dissidents that had been ordered suspended in 1924 by the Coolidge administration: investigations of Nazi-linked groups began in 1934, of communists in 1936. That put Hoover (and the Red-hunting House Un-American Activities Committee* [HUAC] of Martin Dies) on a collision course with the post-1935 Popular Front (an alliance of communists and liberals to fight fascism), which actually put many American reformers into contact with the Communist Party. ER put herself in the public spotlight defending such Popular Front–affiliated groups as the American Student Union* (ASU). She attended HUAC's hearing on the ASU in 1939 in a sign of support for the students. The countersubversive Right took this as an endorsement of the Popular Front by the First Lady, and they were not mollified when ER denounced the front after the Hitler–Stalin Pact.

The FBI's file on ER grew throughout the 1930s, fed largely by information that came the bureau's way during investigations of Left-leaning or communist-affiliated reform organizations. There is no evidence, however, that Hoover developed an active interest in (or dislike for) the First Lady until 1941, when Eleanor objected to what evidently was a routine FBI investigation of Edith Helm, White House social secretary, when Helm was named to the Advisory Commission to the Council of National Defense. ER sharply rebuked Hoover in a letter that referred to the bureau's "Gestapo methods," and although Hoover apologized profusely, he never forgot or forgave any attack on the bureau.

Hoover's opinions of ER's continued contacts with Left-leaning organizations during the war were recorded in his own handwriting. After a December 1942 FBI break-in of the headquarters of the International Student Service, Hoover was informed that ER was active in trying to dissuade the Lithuanian delegation to the organization's convention from protesting Stalin's annexation of their country and that she was supporting, in general, all the demands of the Russian delegation. Hoover wrote in the margins of the report of the information that he found this nauseating. Another file records the FBI's efforts to verify the existence of the mythical "Eleanor Clubs,"* supposedly organized by black maids to make trouble for their white employers. Hoover's agents dutifully reported to the director that they could discover no evidence that the clubs existed but that they would keep trying.

By far the most explosive FBI documents on ER in the FBI files were not FBI documents at all but photostatic copies of the records of a 1943 Army Counter-Intelligence Corps (CIC) investigation of ER's friend, Joseph Lash,* at that time an enlisted man in the army air force. These records were discovered in Hoover's Official and Confidential file after his death in 1972. Lash was of interest to the CIC because of his prewar membership in groups generally regarded as communist-front organizations. CIC agents shadowed Lash when he went on leave to Urbana, Illinois, and were fascinated to discover that he met ER there and that they checked into adjoining hotel rooms. The next weekend Lash again visited the Hotel Lincoln in Urbana, this time meeting Trude Pratt, who was planning to leave her husband to marry Lash, an affair being carried on with ER's knowledge. Electronic listening devices were planted in Mrs. Pratt's room, and the surveillance report stated that "Subject and Mrs. Pratt appeared to be greatly endeared to each other and engaged in sexual intercourse a number of times during the course of their stay" (Morgan, 670). The head of CIC, Colonel John Bissell, was convinced he was on the verge of discovering a fantastic conspiracy linking members of the president's personal and official family with radicals like Lash. When Lash journeyed to Chicago for another meeting with ER, the CIC also installed bugs in her room. The next day a hotel employee tipped off the First Lady about the CIC surveillance. She complained to Harry Hopkins,* who told General George Marshall,* and so word reached FDR, who ordered the CIC disbanded for having conducted an investigation of his wife.

Bissell perceived that his career was ruined. Embittered, he peddled salacious stories around the Washington cocktail party circuit. At one of these affairs an FBI agent overheard Bissell's vituperations and contacted him for a follow-up interview. Bissell claimed that his recordings had captured sexual encounters between the fifty-eight-year-old ER and the thirty-three-year-old Lash and that the upshot had been a battle royal in the White House between the president and his wife, resulting in a presidential order for the entire CIC to be sent to the Pacific and ordered into combat "until they were killed" (Morgan, 672).

This explosive material, largely a mendacious embroidery woven by the disappointed Bissell, was housed in Hoover's confidential files until his death, and it was used to blacken ER's reputation in 1953, when the administration of President Dwight D. Eisenhower* was looking for persuasive reasons not to reappoint her as a delegate to the United Nations.* Evidently, Hoover's assistant director Louis B. Nichols briefed two Eisenhower aides on the supposed "affair" as something likely to come out in a confirmation hearings. Paradoxically, the surveillance of Lash and ER had almost nothing to do with the FBI, although it is invariably discussed in the context of a Hoover–ER relationship.

Another staple in the conspiratorial Right's secret history of the Roosevelt administration, Communist Party boss Earl Browder's supposed conduit to the White House through ER, may have had far more serious impact on Hoover's sentiments toward the First Lady. Among ER's friends was a communist named Josephine Truslow Adams, regarded by the party as something of a trophy because of her descent from President John Adams. Josephine Adams convinced Browder that she could provide, via ER, a way for the party to get its ideas on the president's desk, a notion Browder was more than happy to believe and to brag about to his American and Russian colleagues. Adams invented conversations between herself and the First Lady that were uncomplimentary toward Hoover: "Now you see what a bastard Hoover is . . . That's how he covers up his fascist attitude. Pretty smug, isn't he? . . . You should have seen Franklin. He hit the ceiling. He said this was just another proof of the duplicity of that smug would-be Himmler" (Morgan, 674). This was duly reported verbatim to Hoover by an FBI informant in the party. One can assume he was not pleased.

There is no doubt that a cordial dislike developed between Hoover and ER, and over the years they revealed their sentiments to friends who shared their sensibilities. From that evidence, political partisans of the two have concocted a conflict of quasi-epic proportions, but it is unlikely the antagonism had any important consequences for American history or, indeed, for the careers of either individual.

SELECTED BIBLIOGRAPHY
Eleanor Roosevelt FBI File, Department of Justice, Washington, D.C.
Morgan, Ted. *FDR: A Biography*. 1985.
Powers, Richard Gid. *Not without Honor: The History of American Anticommunism*.
     1995.
———. *Secrecy and Power: The Life of J. Edgar Hoover*. 1987.
Theoharis, Athan. *From the Secret Files of J. Edgar Hoover*. 1993.

Richard Gid Powers

FICTION. Since fiction about Eleanor Roosevelt began appearing in the 1950s, ER has been used by writers as a prism through which to view their times as well as hers. While there has been only one major historical novel to date, ER has appeared as the central character in a series of popular detective stories and made brief appearances as the president's wife in a number of other books. Whether she has been pictured as the long-suffering wife of Franklin D. Roosevelt* or as an independent woman is related to changing perceptions of the role of women in American society as reflected by individual authors.

Novels about First Ladies are part of the tradition of historical fiction, with several of ER's predecessors—most notably, Abigail Adams, Dolley Madison, and Mary Todd Lincoln—being used as the subject matter for writers to explore such themes as the relationships of famous couples who play leading roles in tumultuous times. The only serious novel about ER takes a different tack. Published after women's liberation took root in the United States, Rhoda Lerman's *Eleanor: A Novel* (1979) was limited to three years in ER's life: the period between the summer of 1918, when ER discovered FDR's affair with Lucy Mercer (Rutherfurd*), and the summer of 1921, when FDR contracted polio. Lerman did meticulous research in primary documents and interviews and used the fictional form of the novel to attempt to imagine the inner reality of her subject's mind and emotions. Writing in a time of consciousness-raising for women, Lerman presented the period of personal consciousness-raising for ER. This novel of human potential and transformation began with ER as a bored and unhappy society matron, narrow, snobbish, and bigoted. Over the course of three years, it showed her poised for greatness of accomplishment and spirit, able to employ the tragedy of her marriage and FDR's polio to reconstruct herself into a remarkable woman. This was, in Lerman's imagery, the alchemy of making lead into silver.

Lerman's novel received critical acclaim and sold some 50,000 copies. It has continued to have devoted readers and was reprinted in 1998 to accompany a one-woman play based on the novel. The show starred Jean Stapleton, who portrayed ER in an ideological and spiritual journey of liberation.

ER's best-known literary role to date, however, is as the crime-solving heroine of a series of mystery stories written under the name of her son, Elliott Roosevelt.* These stories began appearing in 1984 and have been published on a nearly yearly basis since then, despite Elliott's death in 1990. ER is their central figure, the problem-solving sleuth who unravels the puzzle at the end of each book. The stories, the most popular of which are set in the White House, conform to a set of literary conventions wherein the detective is a private citizen—an older woman—who is smarter and shrewder than the police but also gracious and unfailingly polite. The prototype seems to be Miss Marple in Agatha Christie's detective novels.

The Elliott Roosevelt stories have the added attraction of being a kind of memoir mystery, wherein the reader is invited into the world of ER and introduced to notable men and women, told bits and pieces of Roosevelt administration history, and given an intimate detail or two that presumably only a family member would know. Various celebrities are presented (Greta Garbo, Charles Lindbergh, and others). The ER pictured here is not only a woman of class and intelligence but a person with a keen sense of social justice and a commitment to better the world. According to the publisher, St. Martin's Press, the books have sold well, showing there was a market in the late twentieth century for a favorable portrayal of ER as a supersmart sleuth who can outthink males. Individual titles, such as *Murder in the Oval Office* (1989), and *Murder in the Red Room* (1992), had sales of more than 20,000 each in hardcover and more than 55,000 in paperback.

Lerman and Elliott Roosevelt have been the main authors to use fiction to attempt either to deepen the reader's understanding of ER or to amuse and give the reader an insider's view of her. Elliott's brother, James Roosevelt,* however, with Sam Toperoff, wrote one novel in which his parents prominently appeared, *A Family Matter* (1980). In this spy story, James portrayed ER as a tertiary character whose inclusion seemed to be more for the purpose of criticism than plot. It pictured ER as a dysfunctional mother who submitted weakly to being reprimanded by the not-very-fictionalized James himself for having failed to leave her dinner party when he arrived home from prep school with a severe case of flu that led to his later hair loss. In a critique of this behind-the-scenes tale of intrigue set in World War II* amid the building of the atomic bomb, a reviewer commented, "I cannot think of another writer [besides James Roosevelt] who has built such an elaborate pedestal for himself to climb upon and be identified by name" (*New York Times*, 20 July 1980).

In other novels, mysteries, and thrillers ER has played a small role. Most of these have focused on FDR, with ER given somewhat mixed treatment as a wife. Jerome Charyn wrote *The Franklin Scare* (1977), a thriller with FDR's personal barber, an innocent who lives in the attic of the White House, as the protagonist. Charyn showed ER as kind and wise, genuinely committed to civil rights, if at times a bit naive. Similarly, Kurt Vonnegut in *Deadeye Dick* (1982), depicted ER, visiting a war plant in Ohio and staying to have lunch with some of the major characters for a few pages, as insightful, kindly, and concerned with the plight of the poor. Paul Spike in *The Night Letter* (1979), constructed a thriller about an attempted assassination of FDR, with assumptions about ER as an understanding wife and political partner par excellence as part of the story line.

Stefan Kanfer, however, published *Fear Itself* (1981), another World War II thriller about FDR in which the First Lady appeared as a prudish and repressed Victorian woman who instructed her daughter in the burdens of sex. By contrast, in 1984 Stuart Kaminsky wrote *The Fala Factor*, featuring a Hollywood private eye asked by ER to find the presidential dog, Fala, whom she is convinced has been kidnapped. ER was presented as homely but a sympathetic and thoughtful wife, albeit content to sit on the sidelines throughout this investigation. Quite a different image appeared in David Williams' *Eleanor Roosevelt's Niggers* (1976), a fictionalized account of the humiliations and exploits of the African American 761st tank battalion. Although references to ER were brief, a notable feature of the book was its assumption that she held sufficient power to influence military policy.

In addition, ER has been depicted in a number of dramas written for theater, motion pictures,* and television.* The most famous, *Sunrise at Campobello*, was also the first, written by Dore Schary for the Broadway stage in 1958. It became a film and was widely acclaimed in both versions, offering a view of a woman's role accepted in that time period. ER is a secondary character compared to FDR. As Schary wrote to ER in 1957, he wanted to write a play about FDR that would "tell the story of a man and the people around him, who after an ordeal emerged strong and triumphant" (*New York Times*, 26 January 1958). In this story about FDR's battle with polio—a drama of illness, determination, and victory—ER was the supporting wife who found herself thrust into politics only in the wake of a major illness affecting her husband. She was pictured in the subordinate position of women during the 1950s—overseeing her family at play, picking up their things, getting them to the dinner table with a minimum of complaining.

Two decades later, as an outgrowth of the feminist movement, came dramatizations that focused on ER herself. In 1974 Zelda E. Kessner and Winnie Newman wrote *Eleanor: A Musical Biography Based on the Life of Eleanor Roosevelt*. Two years later Gloria Goldsmith wrote *Womanspeak*, in which notable American women talked about themselves and, in the case of ER, their youth. Neither play received professional staging.

In 1976, however, *Eleanor*, a play by Arlene Stadd, toured the nation, a one-woman show filled with ER's speeches,* press conference* remarks, and letters and portions of her autobiography* dictated to an invisible secretary. Stadd's ER, played by Eileen Heckart, was smart and courageous, although shy and self-conscious about her looks. A very public, busy, and successful woman with her own priorities, her source of strength did not come from her husband, as a result of either his polio or his affair with Mercer.

In 1984 came *First Lady* by Jonathan Bolt, a one-act musical that celebrated ER as the more sensitive partner in the Roosevelt marriage. Bolt's play, first performed in schools, was produced in New York and presented at the White House on the centenary of ER's birth. Two years later came two more plays. *Eleanor (Don't Frighten the Horses!)*, a musical written by Gretchen Cryer in collaboration with Rhoda Lerman, was based on the idea of a birthday party thrown for ER by her gossipy cousin Alice Roosevelt Longworth.* *Triangles* by June Bingham, produced on Broadway, focused on a group of women in FDR's life with ER as the major character. It highlighted the Mercer affair as the seminal point in ER's evolution into a world figure. In 1999 a full-length musical by Jonathan Bolt, *Eleanor: An American Love Story*, based on his earlier *First Lady*, played around the nation, including performances at Ford's Theater, Washington, D.C., a monument to the fact that audiences have not tired of the ER saga.

There have, as well, been numerous television programs about ER, ranging from her appearance in narratives of American First Ladies* to made-for-television dramas such as *Eleanor, First Lady of the World*, a CBS-TV movie that first aired in 1982 with Jean Stapleton playing ER. A 1979 dramatization, *Backstairs at the White House*, showed ER from the perspective of White House servants and was based on a novel by Gwen

Bagni and Paul Dubov that itself was made from a memoir, *My Thirty Years Backstairs at the White House* by Lillian Rogers Parks, a retired maid. In the work ER appeared as a warm, unpretentious First Lady.

As the century ended, ER had emerged in the majority of her fictional portrayals as a beloved figure, admired for her strength and wisdom, although her presentation had changed over time. As befitted the way society looked at women in the 1950s, Schary dramatized her in an idealized role as wife and mother. Many of the men writing about ER continued in this vein, giving her cameo roles as a great president's admirable wife. Perhaps, more important, ER also became an icon through which feminist writers could examine the way in which women can face adversity and become independent and powerful.

SELECTED BIBLIOGRAPHY
Edens, John A. *Eleanor Roosevelt: A Comprehensive Bibliography.* 1994.

Susan Ikenberry

FINANCES, PERSONAL. Eleanor Roosevelt, accustomed by birth and marriage* to a world of wealth and privilege, nevertheless, in midlife began working diligently to earn her own money for the fulfillment of personal goals. She eventually attained a high level of income, but she either paid in taxes or gave away a large portion of her earnings in later life.

At the beginning of her married life with Franklin D. Roosevelt,* ER had income from family trusts that "varied from $5,000 to $8,000 a year" (Roosevelt, 14). Her husband had inherited about $200,000 from his father and also enjoyed the security provided by the fortune of his mother, Sara Delano Roosevelt.* When ER moved into her first home with FDR at 125 East Thirty-Sixth Street in New York City, she found that her mother-in-law had furnished and staffed the rented house with three servants. Later, Sara Roosevelt had duplex town houses built at 47–49 East Sixty-Fifth Street, into which she and the young couple moved in 1908. She also maintained the family estate at Hyde Park,* New York, and a vacation retreat at Campobello* Island, New Brunswick, Canada.

After passing the bar exam in 1907, FDR began supplementing his investment income with a small remuneration from the law firm of Carter, Ledyard, and Milburn. In 1910 he began earning $1,500 a year as a state senator from Dutchess County, and during 1913–1920 he earned $5,000 a year as assistant secretary of the navy in the Wilson administration.

During 1917–1920 FDR's investments and rental income from the New York house raised his average annual income to over $22,000 a year, and ER's independent income added another $8,000 a year. By this time, however, their income was strained by the expense of maintaining a household of five children and up to ten servants, while meeting the demands of official entertaining in Washington society. Thus, FDR was effusive in his thanks to his mother for her generous check on his thirty-eighth birthday in 1920.

The defeat of the Democratic Party* in the 1920 presidential elections, when FDR ran for vice president, brought the family back to New York and the private sector for the next eight years. During this period, ER began writing articles for publications of the League of Women Voters,* the Democratic Party,* and, eventually, national magazines—activities that would in time give her independent income as a journalist. Meanwhile, in spite of an extended period of convalescence and recovery from infantile paralysis, which he contracted in 1921, FDR was earning $25,000 a year as vice president of the Fidelity and Deposit Company of Maryland, a company with a large bonding and insurance business.

With his election as governor of New York in 1928, FDR returned to public life with a salary of $25,000 a year. During the four years he was governor, ER wrote more than twenty articles for mass periodicals. During the same period she commuted from Albany to New York City for three days a week to teach at the Todhunter School* for girls, in which she had purchased an interest in 1927. Her 1932 tax return reported her income as $25,000 from teaching, writing, editing, speaking, and broadcasting work. Trust and investment income added $8,000 for a total taxable income of $33,000. Her charitable contributions amounted to $5,000.

In adapting to her new role as First Lady in 1933, ER gave up teaching but continued writing. From August 1933 to July 1935, she wrote a monthly column for *Woman's Home Companion*,* for which she received $1,000 a month. In the first seven years in the White House, she sold at least fifty-one articles, primarily to women's magazines. Her tax returns for 1933–1935 reported net earnings averaging about $26,750 a year, investment income of about $8,700 a year, and annual charitable contributions ranging between $2,000 and $6,100.

ER's tax returns, however, do not reflect her substantial radio broadcast* earnings of $36,000 in 1934, $29,832 in 1935, and $32,535 in 1937, which she had the sponsors pay directly to a special ER Transit Fund set up by the American Friends Service Committee. The fund helped start a school and handicraft program at the Arthurdale* resettlement project in West Virginia and in later years assisted various schools, organizations, and individuals. The U.S. Treasury Department advised ER on 4 July 1934 that she would not owe taxes on such assigned earnings, but in 1937 the arrangement drew congressional criticism. This led ER to pay taxes on further periodic donations to the fund, which included over $9,000 in 1940 and lesser amounts annually through 1944.

On 30 December 1935 ER began her daily "My Day"* newspaper column, which was to go on until her death in 1962. In the spring of 1936, ER also contracted with the W. Colston Leigh agency for two lecture tours a year at $1,000 a lecture. In 1937 her agent, George Bye, sold serialization rights for the autobiography* of her early life, *This Is My Story*, to the *Ladies' Home Journal** for $75,000 (which matched FDR's salary as president). The book, published by Harper and Brothers, sold well.

In 1937–1939 her earnings averaged about $68,000 a year, $62,000 after expenses. Taxable income from investments and trusts of about $8,000 a year brought her average income to about $70,000 annually, with 27 percent going for taxes and about 5 percent for charitable contributions.

During World War II* she frequently wrote articles for the *Ladies' Home Journal*, in which appeared her monthly question-and-answer column "If You Ask Me," which she began in 1941. During 1941–1944 her average annual earnings increased to $76,900, or about $65,800 after expenses, but taxes absorbed almost 49 percent of her taxable income, and charitable contributions absorbed 17 percent. Some of her larger donations went to the American Friends Service Committee, the American Red Cross,* and the International Student Service.

ER said that she left the White House in 1945 with less capital than when she had come to Washington. After her husband's death on 12 April 1945, ER announced her intention to pursue a career as a journalist, although FDR had provided for her financially. He had left the income from his estate, valued at about $1.4 million after taxes, in trust for her. She relinquished a $5,000-a-year pension given other widows of presidents but accepted franking privileges for her mail.

ER served as a U.S. delegate to the United Nations* from 1946 to 1953, for which she was paid at the rate of $12,000 a year, but only for days actually worked, so her salary averaged no more than $4,900 a year during 1946–1951. Earnings from her "My Day" remained rather stable until she lost a number of subscribing newspapers as a result of her partisanship in the 1956 presidential campaign. This cut her "My Day" income from $28,000 in 1956, to $9,600 in 1957. Income from her other writing also remained steady in the initial post–White House years and then jumped dramatically in 1949 and 1950 with the publication of the second volume of her autobiography, *This I Remember*. In 1949 her total earned income was $198,865 ($175,957 after expenses), and her total taxable income was $206,542, of which 66 percent went for taxes.

While such a peak was not sustained, her earnings continued at a high level for the rest of her life. In 1949 she increased her earnings from her question-and-answer page from $2,500 to $3,000 a month when she moved it from the *Ladies' Home Journal* to *McCall's*.* She also continued writing for other magazines. The third volume of her autobiography, *On My Own*, was published in 1958 after portions had appeared in the *Saturday Evening Post*.

After leaving the United Nations, she increased her paid speaking engagements, averaging about $31,000 a year in payments from the Colston Leigh agency in 1954–1961. She also undertook various broadcasting activities during 1948–1951, in collaboration with her daughter, Anna Roosevelt Halsted,* and son Elliott Roosevelt.*

In 1961, the last full year of her life, when she was seventy-seven years old, she reported earnings of $135,552 ($75,874 after expenses). Included were $7,794 from "My Day" (now a three-day-a-week feature), $59,000 from other writing, $6,500 from Brandeis University, where she was a visiting lecturer, $33,477 from lectures, $8,430 from her appearances on radio and television, and $20,000 from American Broadcasting–Paramount Theaters, which were preparing a documentary series on FDR.

Set against this income were high taxes and her substantial costs for travel* and maintaining a residence in New York City as well as her Val-Kill* cottage at Hyde Park. Her staff submitted detailed records of expenses to her tax accountant so she could take all allowable deductions. From 1953 through 1961, her yearly taxable income averaged slightly over $97,000, of which 47 percent went for taxes and about 25 percent for charitable contributions. (During this period, distributions to ER from FDR's estate included both taxable and nontaxable income, with the amount not subject to federal taxes averaging about $20,000 a year.) Some of her larger charitable donations from 1953 through 1961 included $67,000 to the American Association for the United Nations, a total of $37,000 to various schools and colleges, $23,000 to the Franklin D. Roosevelt Library, $9,900 to St. James Church in Hyde Park, and $9,000 to the United Jewish Appeal. In addition, she contributed annually to well over 100 other organizations and causes, although some of her donations were for token amounts of $5 to $10.

She also tried to help her children. In 1947 she paid FDR's estate $85,000 for 842 acres of land at Hyde Park to establish a farming venture in partnership with her son, Elliott, to whom she deeded the property. She took out a $37,000 mortgage to complete the purchase. Unfortunately, the venture was not profitable, and the partnership ended in 1951. She also loaned $100,000 to her son James Roosevelt.*

When she died on 7 November 1962, her estate was valued at about $340,000 before taxes. Most of her estate was left in trust for the benefit of her daughter, Anna, during her lifetime. Her will, dated 31 May 1961 and admitted to probate in Dutchess County, New York, on 15 November 1962, also left $10,000 to David Gurewitsch,* who had been responsible for her medical care since 1945. Varying amounts, not exceeding $2,000 per person, were left to her personal employees. In addition, she gave $1,000 to both her niece, Eleanor Roosevelt Elliott, and her friend, Lorena Hickok,* and a $100 U.S. savings bond to each of nine godchildren. She also left to Joseph Lash* and his son, Jonathan Lash, twenty-seven and nine shares of stock, respectively, in Liberian Enterprises. Her silver, jewelry, and other personal items were distributed among her family and friends, and her personal papers were bequeathed to the Franklin D. Roosevelt Library.

Her financial records show how hard she worked pursuing her career as a writer, speaker, and media personality. They also show how relatively little she herself profited from her earnings, which were large for a woman of her day.

SELECTED BIBLIOGRAPHY

Anna Roosevelt Halsted Papers, Franklin D. Roosevelt Library, Hyde Park, NY.
Beasley, Maurine H. *Eleanor Roosevelt and the Media: A Public Quest for Self-Fulfillment.* 1987.
Eleanor Roosevelt and Franklin D. Roosevelt Papers, Franklin D. Roosevelt Library, Hyde Park, NY.
Henry T. and John Hackett Papers, Franklin D. Roosevelt Library, Hyde Park, NY.
Lash Joseph P. *Eleanor and Franklin.* 1971.
Roosevelt, Eleanor. *This I Remember.* 1949.

FIRST LADIES, CONNECTIONS WITH. Eleanor Roosevelt's relationships with her predecessors and successors stretched the full length of the twentieth century but began with a familial one, that between her and Edith Roosevelt, the wife of her paternal uncle, Theodore Roosevelt.* In observing her shy and withdrawn young niece, Edith Roosevelt nevertheless declared that the "ugly duckling" might very well develop into a beautiful "swan" (Anthony, 1:280). When Edith Roosevelt was First Lady (1901–1909), young ER visited her relatives in the White House and, in observing the public role assumed by Mrs. Roosevelt, felt that such a life of public expectations was stifling and limiting. Edith Roosevelt was an outspoken critic of Franklin D. Roosevelt* as president, but she wrote an encouraging and supportive letter to her niece, Eleanor, when she assumed her First Lady role.

As the wife of the assistant secretary of the U.S. Navy, ER came to know Ellen Wilson, the first wife of Woodrow Wilson, who led a public campaign to demolish the alley dwellings of Washington's African Americans. Mrs. Wilson helped pass federal legislation to this effect, and ER was among those young cabinet wives who followed Ellen Wilson into the slums; it can be speculated that Ellen Wilson influenced ER as First Lady, for when the latter assumed the role, she took an interest in the deplorable housing conditions of African Americans in the District of Columbia* as well.

The second wife of Woodrow Wilson, Edith Wilson, had a more complicated relationship with ER. They first came to know each other when

Eleanor Roosevelt wears a button backing Adlai Stevenson as she sits with another former First Lady, Bess Truman (on her left), and a future First Lady, Lady Bird Johnson (fourth from her left) on 13 August 1956 at the Democratic National Convention in Chicago. *Courtesy of Library of Congress*

both women accompanied their husbands to Europe for the post–World War I Conference at Versailles, frequently visiting American soldiers in hospitals together. After the Wilson administration (1913–1921), ER, in her work with the National Democratic Committee, frequently, but vainly, implored Mrs. Wilson to take part in party activities. Edith Wilson would not even lend her name and photo to largely apolitical activities. Only later, when ER was First Lady, and it served Edith Wilson's purpose of perpetuating the memory of her late husband, did the former First Lady cooperate with her successor, accepting nearly every invitation offered her by the Roosevelts, including the honor of sitting beside ER in Congress* on 8 December 1941, when FDR announced the attack on Pearl Harbor by Japan.

In Washington during World War I, ER also first came in contact with Lou Henry Hoover,* the wife of Herbert Hoover,* then the food administrator, and Florence Harding, the wife of Warren G. Harding, then an Ohio senator. In both cases there was every indication of an amicable acquaintanceship. When President Warren Harding died in 1923, ER wired her condolences to Florence Harding. While the Roosevelts lived on R Street, the Hoovers lived on S Street, one block north, and both couples even picnicked together on at least one occasion. Consequently, despite the political acrimony that existed between FDR and Hoover during their race against each other for the presidency in 1932, neither Lou Hoover nor ER crossed each other, publicly or privately.

During ER's tenure as First Lady (1933–1945), she maintained cere-monious relations with several of her predecessors. She corresponded briefly with Frances Cleveland and met the former First Lady in her hometown of Princeton, New Jersey, after giving a speech* there. When ER hosted a Blue Room reception in 1941 for the wives of members of the Supreme Court, she welcomed Helen Taft there, not only a prede-cessor but widow of a chief justice. The two had met once before, only briefly, at the Taft summer home at Murray Bay, Canada. An isolationist, Helen Taft strongly disagreed with ER's war-preparedness efforts at the time. During World War II,* Grace Coolidge corresponded with ER and hosted a reception for her when she came to an event in Northhampton, Massachusetts, the hometown of the former First Lady, for women serv-ing in the navy auxiliary.

As a former First Lady (1945–1962), ER had varying degrees of contact with her successors. She had hoped that, as First Lady, Bess Truman would continue holding press conferences,* and ER had even offered to help her, but Bess Truman refused. Nor would Bess Truman accept an ill-advised invitation sent by Elliott Roosevelt* to appear on ER's tele-vision* interview program. Indeed, Bess Truman make a conscious effort to avoid any kind of public remark or activity in the pattern of ER's activist interpretation of the First Lady role. "The country was used to ER. I couldn't possibly be anything like her. I wasn't going down in any coal mines," she later quipped (Anthony, 1:517).

A statement of concern by ER for the health of Mamie Eisenhower was unfortunately misinterpreted as spreading gossip about rumors that Mrs. Eisenhower had an alcohol dependence problem and may have influ-enced the decision not to invite the former First Lady to any White House events during the Eisenhower administration. As the wife of the World War II general, Dwight D. Eisenhower,* Mamie Eisenhower had personal admiration for ER and had eagerly met her at several White House events during the Roosevelt administration. During the Eisen-hower years, ER wrote a flattering account about her in a "My Day"* column. That column, ironically, symbolized how differently Mamie Ei-senhower saw her role as First Lady from that played by ER. To Mamie Eisenhower, the open discussion of not only controversial public issues but personal reflections was not for her. When it was suggested to Mamie Eisenhower that she follow in ER's tradition and write a column, too, the former wrote in a note to her secretary, preserved at the Eisenhower presidential library, "It sounds like a terrible chore, and smacks of [the] 'My Day' column, of which I have a perfect horror!" (Anthony, 1:569).

Jacqueline Kennedy first met ER during the primaries for the 1960 Democratic presidential nomination but personally resented the political criticism of her husband, John F. Kennedy,* made by the former First Lady. During the 1960–1961 transition, however, the two women carried on a brief correspondence about raising children in the White House. Like Bess Truman and Mamie Eisenhower before her, Jacqueline Kennedy had a self-definition of her role as the wife of a man who happened to be president that was much more traditional than ER's. Although evidence shows that Jacqueline Kennedy privately held many of the same liberal political views that ER did, she assiduously avoided public discussion of them. In his oral history for the Kennedy Library, August Hecksher, the first adviser on the arts appointed by a president, recalled a meeting with Jacqueline Kennedy about her willingness to quietly lobby on behalf of government support for the arts. She would not, however, testify before Congress. "After all," she said, "I'm not Mrs. Roosevelt!" (Anthony, 2:39).

Other women who would become First Lady met ER. As a congressional wife, Senate wife, and vice president's wife, Lady Bird Johnson was often in the presence of her predecessor. ER invited Lady Bird Johnson to her first White House dinner, and the latter even took color motion pictures of ER as she was leaving the mansion one day to attend an event. As a young woman, Pat Ryan Nixon greatly admired ER and met her at a hospital workers' conference in New York. Betty Ford was among the congressional spouses attending the 1961 Kennedy inaugural, at which ER was also present, but they did not see or speak with each other. As a teenager, Nancy Davis Reagan heard ER speak at the 1940 National Democratic Convention in Chicago. In the 1950s Barbara Bush met ER in the Texas home of her granddaughter, a friend of the Bush family.

First Ladies after Jacqueline Kennedy emulated ER more directly than did their predecessors. Lady Bird Johnson not only shared the same political views as ER, but her sense of social responsibility in projects affecting disadvantaged children, equal rights for women, and civil rights* for minorities. As the files of Liz Carpenter, press secretary to Lady Bird Johnson, in the Lyndon Johnson Library prove, the Johnson administration made a concerted effort to directly link Lady Bird Johnson's activism with ER's.

To a lesser degree, Pat Nixon also followed this approach. With the publication of the book *Eleanor and Franklin* by Joseph P. Lash* during the Nixon administration, Pat Nixon told a *Ladies' Home Journal** reporter that she had read it with great interest and admiration for ER, remarking that although the Roosevelt marriage* was now revealed to be less of a romance than people had assumed during the Roosevelt administration, that fact did nothing to diminish ER's contributions. Pat Nixon's effort to highlight and encourage people to volunteer their time and skills to remedy social problems was certainly something no First Lady had done since ER.

Betty Ford, in a 1983 interview with this author, remarked that ER had been one of her women role models during Mrs. Ford's own youth in the 1930s and 1940s. Mrs. Ford's willingness to speak out on controversial social issues of the 1970s, such as abortion, breast cancer, mental health, and the Equal Rights Amendment*—and even to sometimes disagree with the president—prompted public reaction and media attention at a level not seen since ER's tenure and evoked the same debate about what the "proper" public role was for a First Lady.

Although Eleanor Rosalynn Carter was not named for ER, as has been mistakenly reported at times, Mrs. Carter, too, recalled the strong impressions left by her predecessor when she herself was young. In a 1984 interview with this author, Rosalynn Carter recalled that her notion of a First Lady was changed by ER from the more placid images of Martha Washington and Dolley Madison that were taught to her in school in the 1930s. Rosalynn Carter's overt political activism on behalf of federal legislation followed ER's pattern directly. Rosalynn Carter made frequent fact-finding missions around the nation on behalf of health, energy, and welfare projects, then reported back on them in writing and in meetings with the president in exactly the same fashion that ER had. Rosalynn Carter became only the second First Lady to testify before Congress— on behalf of mental health legislation, which she had lobbied for—thus following, again, directly in ER's footsteps.

Rosalynn Carter's two immediate successors, Nancy Reagan and Barbara Bush, chose to follow the more conservative public role of First Lady. Nancy Reagan did host a White House lecture and luncheon in October 1984 to commemorate the centennial of ER's birth. She also frequently quoted a line of ER's in her own speeches: "A woman is like a teabag. You never know how strong it is until it's in hot water" (Ayres, 199). In correspondence with this author in 1989, Barbara Bush recalled her own parents' meeting ER in the White House and how her mother— who had previously disapproved of the First Lady's activism—became a great supporter of ER after a personal conversation.

No successor of ER, however, more directly studied, appreciated, and emulated her than Hillary Rodham Clinton. Beginning in the 1992 presidential campaign and continuing through her own tenure as First Lady, Hillary Clinton read numerous books and articles on ER's life. She supported the effort to have a statue of ER erected in a New York City park and presided over its unveiling. Her own brand of political activism on a full range of issues (equal rights for women, education, welfare reform, health care, democracy across the globe, adoption, historic preservation) was clearly the most public and controversial since ER's own tenure. With ER as her personal heroine and role model, Hillary Clinton even had what she called "conversations" with her predecessor, thinking about how ER would handle difficult situations and problems facing her as First Lady and then attempting to emulate what she believed would be ER's reaction. In a December 1998 speech at Georgetown University, Hillary Clinton spoke at length about ER's vision for human rights* around the globe and how she, Mrs. Clinton, was attempting to continue this work at the turn of the twenty-first century.

SELECTED BIBLIOGRAPHY

Anthony, Carl Sferrazza. "First Ladies on Parade." *Vanity Fair* (January 1989): 94–101, 111–118.

———. *First Ladies: The Saga of the Presidents' Wives and Their Power.* Vols. 1, 2. 1990, 1991.

Ayres, Alex, ed. *The Wit and Wisdom of Eleanor Roosevelt.* 1996.

Daniels, Jonathan. *Washington Quadrille.* 1968.

Lash, Joseph P. *Eleanor and Franklin.* 1971.

Smith, Richard Norton. *An Uncommon Man: The Triumph of Herbert Hoover.* 1984.

Carl Sferrazza Anthony

FIRST LADIES, RANKINGS OF. During the past half century, many empirical efforts have been undertaken to evaluate the performances of America's political leaders. A spin-off of these "rating games" has been the ranking of First Ladies. In contrast to the findings on American presidents, where most research has been concentrated, First Lady polls were not undertaken until at least a quarter century later, and research remains limited.

Ratings by scholars have established the five highest-ranking presidents (Abraham Lincoln, Franklin D. Roosevelt,* George Washington, Thomas Jefferson, and Theodore Roosevelt*) as well as the lowest-ranking presidents. In addition, the general tier (great, near-great, above average, average, below average, and failure) to which each president belongs has been determined. The only consensus about First Ladies, however, is that Eleanor Roosevelt nearly always is ranked first and is regarded as the highest-ranked American woman in general by historians.

In 1982 two scholars at Siena College, Thomas O. Kelly II and Douglas A. Lonnstrom, conducted a survey of historians at 102 randomly selected four-year colleges and universities, fifty-seven in the North and forty-five in the South. Respondents rated the First Ladies on a scale of one to five in ten categories: background, value to country, integrity, leadership, intelligence, own person, accomplishments, courage, public image, and value to president. Overall rankings for the top five were (1) Eleanor Roosevelt, (2) Abigail Adams, (3) Lady Bird Johnson, (4) Dolley Madison, and (5) Rosalyn Carter. Mary Todd Lincoln ranked last. No effort was made to subdivide the First Ladies into tiers or groups.

In 1993 the Siena Institute replicated the 1982 study with slight revisions. The results were (1) Eleanor Roosevelt, (2) Hillary Rodham Clinton, (3) Abigail Adams, (4) Dolley Madison, and (5) Rosalyn Carter. Though First Lady only a short time, already Clinton was rated among the top First Ladies, while Johnson fell from third to sixth place. Mary Todd Lincoln remained last.

That same year, the *Journal of American History* conducted a survey of its readers. The 1,047 respondents ranked Eleanor Roosevelt above all other females in the "most admired person in American history" category. Overall, she ranked sixth in the group. For a special April 1997 issue of *Life*, its editors conducted a survey of historians, politicians, and writers. Eleanor Roosevelt was the only First Lady and the highest-ranking female selected among America's twenty-five greatest heroes/heroines in that survey.

In contrast to scholarly evaluations, public opinion polls* have tended to rank contemporary individuals much higher than historical figures, although ER stands well with the public over the long run. For example, a 1976 Gallup poll found Betty Ford as the most admired woman, while *Good Housekeeping* readers selected Pat Nixon. The *National Enquirer* also reported in 1976 that its readers had picked Pat Nixon as their favorite among the most recent seven First Ladies; Eleanor Roosevelt ranked a distant second, despite serving the longest as First Lady. On the other hand, in July 1980, when *Good Housekeeping* editors ranked twentieth-century First Ladies, Eleanor Roosevelt placed second behind Lady Bird Johnson out of fifteen First Ladies.

Eleanor Roosevelt's place among the public is likely to be enhanced in the future. With the unveiling of a memorial* located in New York City's Riverside Park in 1996, she became the first presidential spouse commemorated with a public statue in the nation. Of even greater significance is that the Franklin D. Roosevelt Memorial in Washington, D.C., which opened in 1997, is the first presidential memorial with a section depicting a First Lady. That memorial is likely to engrave in the public psyche recognition of Eleanor Roosevelt as the greatest First Lady.

SELECTED BIBLIOGRAPHY

Caroli, Betty Boyd. *First Ladies*. 1987.
Gould, Lewis L., ed. *America's First Ladies*. 1996.
Pederson, William D., and Ann McLaurin, eds. *The Rating Game in American Politics*. 1987.
Troy, Gil. *Affairs of State*. 1997.

William D. Pederson

FIRST LADY, CEREMONIAL ROLE. Eleanor Roosevelt did not look forward to the ceremonial duties of being First Lady at the White House. Yet, the traditional expectations of the wife of the president of the United

States to manage the household, serve as hostess at a multitude of social and cultural events, and be involved in the preservation and care of the historic house received her attention and energy, and she dealt with each of these areas in her own thoughtful, well-organized way.

In her first weeks in the White House, she organized the household staff as well as her own small staff, inspected the entire house, and moved furnishings in the private apartments to suit the Roosevelt family. She made the house comfortable for the family and guests, and, as time went by, her interest in the history of the house grew, as did her affection for the mansion.

Before the inauguration in 1933 ER had hired as housekeeper a woman she had known in Hyde Park,* New York, Henrietta Nesbitt,* who, working directly with her, supervised the domestic staff and assumed the duties of planning menus and managing the food budget. Even during the height of the World War II* years, when ER was traveling a great deal, she always stayed in touch with the housekeeper regarding the running of the household through notes, memos, and letters. To please her guests, ER put menus together and thought up dishes for them, often sending overnight notes to the housekeeper regarding guests' breakfast preferences. ER suggested that a new, modern kitchen with electrical appliances be installed in the White House in 1935, bringing the first changes to the cooking area since the Taft administration. Proud of the result, she conducted a tour of the remodeled area for reporters attending one of her press conferences.*

She also devised an economy program to save money on food, which resulted in many negative comments about the food by the president and White House guests. J. D. West, former chief usher, noted that she did not have much time for housekeeping problems and that the house suffered because of it. As her interests and schedule increased, she delegated more and more of the traditional responsibilities to her staff, although she continued daily meetings with her social secretary, Edith Helm, with whom she reviewed guest lists and table seatings and went over any question relating to entertaining.

Her concern for guests extended also to those invited to White House social functions. Helm recalled that she was hard put to think of any area in which ER did not offer special hospitality. Initially, ER felt that certain duties such as standing in receiving lines were unimportant, useless burdens. But, in her autobiography* she reflected that she grew to realize they had real meaning and value, and she discovered that the White House as a symbol of the U.S. government had deep significance, especially to those people visiting from out of town. At these receptions she met people from throughout the country and noted, "[T]hat in itself seems to me one of the worthwhile experiences to be gained from living in the White House" (Roosevelt, 91).

Although ER continued many traditional social customs such as formal teas and state dinners, she introduced innovations. She changed the pattern of White House entertaining by bringing to the house more varied groups of people than had ever been there before, and she began having teas for people known to her or the White House staff instead of only those on Washington social lists. She originated garden parties for women who held executive and administrative jobs in government departments and the White House and suggested an annual spring dance for accredited newspaper correspondents in the city. She used the house to draw attention to subjects of interest to her. Meetings such as the Conference on the Cause and Cure of War and another dealing with the National Youth Administration* were held in the East Room.

The social schedule was daunting. During each social season, which began in December and continued until June, there were five state dinners and five state receptions at which the president and First Lady received guests, and many nonofficial luncheons and dinners often were followed by musicales. After Lent began, what was called the "little season" took place with musicales, teas, and large garden parties. Members of the White House staff observed that ER never sat down to a meal alone. She had guests for lunch nearly every day, using these occasions to elicit new ideas from an assortment of people. During a typical week in the social season, there were as many as eight teas, four luncheons, and two dinners in addition to many private functions. In 1939 alone, 4,729 people were served meals, 323 were houseguests, 9,211 attended teas, and 14,056 were received at receptions. Anywhere from 15 to 1,000 people attended these teas and receptions. So many people were invited to teas that on some days, ER scheduled two of them, one right after another.

ER took the initiative in planning social events for her family and friends. Every year when her grandchildren were young, she arranged a children's party with a program for them. She also organized White House dances for her sons, relatives, and close friends and debutante dances for her niece, Eleanor Roosevelt, and Joan Morgenthau, the daughter of the secretary of the treasury. Her thoughtfulness extended to other young people; she held an annual party for congressional pages.

During the Roosevelt years there were a wide variety of musical performances and styles in the Executive Mansion and increased opportunities for artists to perform. ER was actively involved in making suggestions, approving artists, and indicating the types of music that she and the president enjoyed. She encouraged American folk singers and musicians and invited them to perform for the official visit of the king and queen of England in 1939. Many concert and operatic artists performed, as did professional dancers such as Martha Graham and a large number of African American artists and choirs, Works Progress Administration* choruses, and musicians from a variety of ethnic groups. Dance bands were brought to the White House for the first time, and the first staged opera was performed there. Her involvement extended to working with folklorist Alan Lomax to design the program for a 1941 concert for soldiers. The social season was canceled after war was declared in 1941, but ER continued to hold afternoon teas for wounded servicemen and provided for the increased number of houseguests, including royal refugees from Europe, for whom small state luncheons and dinners were planned.

ER felt a special responsibility for the historic public spaces in the Executive Mansion. She wrote that "a house that is always on exhibition should look its best at all times" (Roosevelt, 87). She consulted with the Commission of Fine Arts and members of an advisory group on changes in the rooms and on new objects to be acquired by purchase or donation. In 1934–1935 she conferred with Eric Gugler, the architect who expanded the West Wing for President Franklin D. Roosevelt,* about wallcoverings, upholstery, and lighting fixtures for the Red Room and was involved in selecting fabrics and colors. Two years later, she again worked with Gugler and the advisory committee on issues relating to refurbishing the Blue Room.

In 1941 ER established a permanent Subcommittee on Furnishings and Gifts for State Rooms of the White House to advise the Commission of Fine Arts and make recommendations on the acceptance of gifts offered to the White House and the arrangements of furnishings in the state rooms. She served as an ex officio member of this committee, under which the museum function of the White House was established. The committee remained active until the Kennedy administration and was the predecessor of the Committee for the Preservation of the White House, established by President Lyndon B. Johnson in 1964. ER supported New Deal* artists by installing many works done under the Public Works of Art Project in the family quarters and office spaces in the White House after seeing them at an exhibition at the Corcoran Gallery of Art in 1934.

Her initial dread of performing the ceremonial duties of the First Lady changed as she assumed the responsibilities of the role. Although she delegated many of the social and house duties to her staff, she maintained an active interest in them and participated with her full energy in the numerous events in the White House. She brought to these functions her interest in, and concern for, people, her advocacy for American cultural life, and her extensive organizational skills and attention to detail.

SELECTED BIBLIOGRAPHY
Eric Gugler Papers, Office of the Curator, the White House.
Helm, Edith Benham. *The Captains and the Kings*. 1954.

Kirk, Elise K. *Music at the White House: A History of the American Spirit.* 1986.
Roosevelt, Eleanor. *This I Remember.* 1949.
Van Deman, Ruth. "U.S. Kitchen No. 1." *Journal of Home Economics* 28 (February 1936): 93–94.
West, James B. *Upstairs at the White House.* 1973.

Betty C. Monkman

FLANAGAN, HALLIE (27 August 1890, Redfield, SD–23 July 1969, Old Tappan, NJ).

Hallie Ferguson Flanagan headed the Federal Theatre Project (FTP) in the Works Progress Administration* (WPA) from its inception in May 1935 until its termination in June 1939. Over 25 million people attended performances of the FTP as it put unemployed theater people to work across the country. Prior to accepting the request of WPA administrator Harry Hopkins* that she become FTP national director, Flanagan met with Eleanor Roosevelt, who asked, "Would a federal theater project be accepted if in the process of entertaining people it also taught them . . . something about the world they lived in?" (Bentley, 188). Flanagan was receptive to ER's approach and took the job.

She had become interested in dramatics at Grinnell College in Iowa and studied the theater in Europe on a Guggenheim Fellowship in 1926. Founding the Experimental Theatre at Vassar College, between 1925 and 1942 she staged 100 plays there, ranging from new interpretations of Shakespeare and Chekhov, to modern works by T. S. Eliot and W. H. Auden. With the onset of the Great Depression,* she turned to plays demonstrating the plight of unemployed workers and idle farmers.

Under her direction the FTP offered musicals and vaudeville as well as plays by classical and modern dramatists, including Eugene O'Neill, George Bernard Shaw, Elmer Rice, and Sinclair Lewis. Flanagan supported almost every kind of creative entertainment and was particularly interested in works of social consciousness, such as the project's Living Newspaper presentations documenting housing problems, poverty, and disease. She carried the FTP far beyond the confines of a relief program, always balancing the needs of actors on relief with artistic achievement. She enjoyed the continuous support of ER, who brought Flanagan to one of her press conferences,* attended a number of FTP plays, and in her 20 June, 1939 "My Day"* column expressed concern over the proposed ending of the FTP. Nevertheless, the House Un-American Activities Committee* in its 1938 investigation of the FTP accused the program of being tainted with communism, and Congress* ended all appropriations for the FTP on 30 June 1939.

Flanagan returned to Vassar briefly before becoming dean of Smith College in 1942. She was professor of drama at Smith from 1946 until her retirement in 1955.

SELECTED BIBLIOGRAPHY
Bentley, Joanne. *Hallie Flanagan: A Life in the American Theatre*. 1988.
Flanagan, Hallie. *A History of the Federal Theatre*. 1940.

June Hopkins

FOREIGN POLICY. Eleanor Roosevelt's thinking about foreign policy underwent four distinct phases: a period before and during World War I noteworthy for her support of American intervention and internationalism; the interwar years, a phase marked by ER's growing involvement in the peace movement*; World War II* and the Truman* presidency, which witnessed a distinct advocacy of American internationalism and intervention in world affairs; and the Eisenhower and Kennedy years, characterized by a growing mistrust of the means and objectives guiding American foreign policy. Throughout these phases, ER consistently strove to balance two sometimes-contradictory concerns: a hope for world peace and stability and the realization that the use of military force was at times necessary. This apparent incongruity symbolized a larger tension present in her foreign policy views, a balance between idealism and pragmatism. Each period contained a competition between the idealistic and pragmatic sides of her foreign policy views. The degree to which she sided with one or the other depended on a number of factors, most importantly her occupation, her husband's political situation, her education, and the state of global affairs.

Before World War I, ER did not identify with any of the peace movements led by women or any of the advocates of American neutrality, although many of her colleagues from the social justice wing of the Progressive movement and the female suffrage drive advocated such a foreign policy. Instead, in keeping with her husband, Franklin D. Roosevelt,* and her uncle, Theodore Roosevelt,* ER supported American intervention in World War I on the side of the Allies. During the conflict she volunteered for the American Red Cross* and the Navy Relief Society, yet she later regretted that she could not do active war work overseas on account of her young children. This is not to describe her as a militarist. She wrote a German friend in May 1915, "This war seems to me too terrible . . . and I wish it could be wiped from the face of the earth" (Cook, "Turn toward Peace," 110). During this period the pragmatic side of ER's thinking, however, recognized that Germany had to be stopped. Thus, she supported American intervention, despite her horror of war. Moreover, it seems reasonable to assume that with FDR serving as a high-ranking member of Woodrow Wilson's Department of the Navy and emerging as a leading advocate of military preparedness, ER's pragmatic understanding of her husband's political situation most likely kept her from publicly expressing antiwar sentiments.

After witnessing firsthand the destruction unleashed upon Europe during a visit overseas in 1919, ER's support for world peace began to grow, thus marking the second stage in her thinking about foreign affairs. She enthusiastically endorsed U.S. entry into the League of Nations* and the World Court* and began associating with the women peace activists whom she had ignored in the years before World War I, including Jane Addams,* Elizabeth Read,* Lillian Wald,* and Esther Lape.* She worked with Lape on the controversial Bok Peace Prize* competition, a contest designed to facilitate and publicize world peace plans. As First Lady, she lent her name to such pro-peace organizations as the American Friends Service Committee, the Fellowship of Reconciliation, and the War Resister's League, and she supported the Nye Committee hearings (1934–1936) investigating war profiteering before and during World War I. Although she publicly displayed a belief in world peace during the interwar years, ER cannot be classified as a pacifist or an isolationist. She described herself in 1934 as a "very realistic pacifist," saying, "We can only disarm with other nations; we cannot disarm alone" (Black, 138). In 1938 she supported the war against the dictator Francisco Franco in Spain* over the objections of some pacifists. "I have never believed that war settled anything satisfactorily," she said in response to their complaints. "[B]ut I am not entirely sure that some times there are certain situations in the world such as we have in actuality when a country is worse off when it does not go to war for its principles than if it went to war" (Black, 138). Moreover, ER clearly rejected the currents of isolationism popular in America during the 1930s. During this period, the balance between peace and force shifted toward the former, but her outlook remained tempered with the pragmatic understanding that force was sometimes necessary in foreign affairs. Once again, her husband's political position, this time as president, dictated that her public comments remain judicious and guarded, so as not to overtly offend any of FDR's many enemies.

World War II changed ER's views on foreign policy for a third time. As early as 1939, with the German invasion of Poland, ER recognized that America would eventually become entangled in the European conflict. With the bombing of Pearl Harbor, the United States entered the war in December 1941, and ER steadfastly supported the war effort, forsaking her public posture as a peace advocate. She traveled throughout the nation and overseas, greeting American servicemen and encouraging factory workers (many of whom were women) engaged in military production. Her "My Day"* newspaper columns provided an inspiring mix of anecdotes and encouragement designed to promote the war effort. At the White House, she was a valuable unofficial diplomat, entertaining foreign heads of state such as Winston Churchill* and Madame Chiang Kai-shek,* helping cement their alliances with America. While thoroughly committed to defeating Germany and Japan, ER also understood the domestic political scene and, for FDR's benefit, refused to vigorously push divisive issues, such as her objection to FDR's Japanese American internment* policy and her belief in civil rights,* lest she upset the unified home front needed for the successful prosecution of the war. For ER, war, especially World War II, was an instrument of foreign policy she could accept as a route to world peace.

ER's commitment to internationalism continued in the wake of FDR's death, the end of World War II, and the beginning of the Cold War.* Consistent with her thought process during World War II, the early years of the Cold War found her an advocate for world peace and stability, this time through American strength and leadership. She became an archetypal liberal cold warrior, supporting the Truman Doctrine and the Marshall Plan while joining the anticommunist Americans for Democratic Action.* Appointed by President Harry S Truman as a member of the American delegation to the United Nations* (UN) (an organization whose existence she heartily endorsed), she relentlessly battled with the Soviets on questions of refugees* and human rights.* ER continued to understand the domestic political implications of her actions and refused to undercut the Truman administration by deviating from administration policy, most famously on the question of a petition that the National Association for the Advancement of Colored People* wanted her to present to the UN in an effort to shame America into a more activist civil rights policy. ER, however, certainly was not a blind supporter of America's early Cold War policies; she disagreed with the Anglo-American decision to reindustrialize and rearm Germany, questioned American involvement in Greece in the late 1940s, and took a courageous stand against McCarthyism* at home.

With the defeat of Adlai Stevenson* by Republican Dwight D. Eisenhower* in the 1952 presidential election, ER submitted her resignation from the UN to the new president, who accepted it. Freed for the first time since 1932 from having to guard her statements and actions because of her relationship to the White House, ER became more critical of American foreign policy, marking the last of the four phases of her thinking. Still an internationalist, she displayed a growing disillusionment with the Cold War policies of both Presidents Eisenhower and John F. Kennedy.* ER criticized Eisenhower and his secretary of state, John Foster Dulles,* for not halting the virulent anticommunist attacks of McCarthy and the extreme right wing of the Republican Party and for the administration's handling of the events associated with Egypt's seizure of the Suez Canal in 1956. She saw President Kennedy, whom she reluctantly supported in the 1960 election, as too militant and inexperienced in foreign affairs, chastising him for the Bay of Pigs fiasco in Cuba and his commitment of troops to Vietnam. Instead, ER again gravitated toward her desire for world peace and stability. She visited several foreign nations, notably, India* and Pakistan, and argued that American policy must take into account the needs of these nations and their struggles to escape the damage of colonialism. She visited the Union of Soviet Socialist Republics* twice and came away impressed by the strides made in Soviet industry, health care, and education, although she refused to soften her critique of the Soviet government. Perhaps because she feared the increasing militarism of the Cold War, this last phase represented a return to the more idealistic concepts always present in her beliefs but often subordinated to other pragmatic concerns.

With her passing in 1962, ER capped a remarkable, nearly fifty-year career as an observer, shaper, and instrument of U.S. foreign policy. Along with other Americans of the twentieth century, she wrestled with the key issues concerning American conduct in foreign affairs: the use of military force, the pursuit of world peace and stability, the impact of America's foreign policy on its domestic policy, and the place and role of the United States in the world. While her pronouncements on these vital topics waxed and waned in accordance with her circumstances, her commitment to American engagement in the world never ceased, and she believed that the nation could, under the right guidance and precepts, become a constructive and beneficent actor in world affairs.

SELECTED BIBLIOGRAPHY

Berger, Jason. *A New Deal for the World: Eleanor Roosevelt and American Foreign Policy*. 1981.

Black, Allida. *Casting Her Own Shadow: Eleanor Roosevelt and the Shaping of Post War Liberalism*. 1996.

Cook, Blanche Wiesen. *Eleanor Roosevelt*. Vol. 1. 1992.

————. "Turn toward Peace." In Joan Hoff-Wilson and Marjorie Lightman, eds. *Without Precedent: The Life and Career of Eleanor Roosevelt*. 1984.

Hoff-Wilson, Joan, and Marjorie Lightman, eds. *Without Precedent: The Life and Career of Eleanor Roosevelt*. 1984.

Scharf, Lois. *Eleanor Roosevelt: First Lady of American Liberalism*. 1987.

Joan Hoff

FRANKLIN D. ROOSEVELT LIBRARY. See ELEANOR ROOSEVELT WINGS OF THE FRANKLIN D. ROOSEVELT LIBRARY.

FRY, VARIAN (15 October 1907, New York–13 September 1967, Easton, CT).

A Harvard-trained classicist who was an editor at the Foreign Policy Association, Varian Fry volunteered in June 1940 to go to France to rescue the cultural elite of Western Europe for the newly formed Emergency Rescue Committee (ERC). His qualifications were enthusiasm, command of French and German, and youth; the ERC had been inaugurated on 25

June 1940 for the express purpose of rescuing writers, artists, musicians, and academics from the Germans. The organization hoped to obtain support from Eleanor Roosevelt, who had expressed interest in the project. On 27 June Fry met with ER and Clarence Pickett* to explain the ERC's mission and to ask ER to forward a message to President Franklin D. Roosevelt* asking him to appeal to the governments of Latin America* for asylum for European refugees.* This she promptly did, writing Fry that "the President has seen your letter of June 27. He will try to get the cooperation of the South American countries in giving asylum to the political refugees" (ER to VF, 8 July 1940).

The circumstances of Central European refugees in France had plunged after the German armies swept through France in June 1940. Central European political refugees and cultural elites who had sought haven in Paris from the Nazis since 1933 now fled south to Vichy, where they found themselves trapped. Almost instantly some Americans began voicing concern and organizing groups to save them. Dr. Frank Kingdon, president of the University of Newark, organized the Emergency Rescue Committee that June to coordinate the disparate rescue efforts. The U.S. State Department initially reacted to these efforts by declaring that it would issue emergency visas, especially to those French and Central European elites whom the Germans and their French allies would target for imprisonment and perhaps death.

As Fry began his preparations to go to France to rescue as many elites as possible—a mission he initially thought would take about one month—he sought support from the Roosevelt administration. Toward that end he attempted to see a variety of U.S. leaders including Undersecretary of State Sumner Welles,* Norman Davis, head of the American Red Cross,* and ER. She was too busy at the time to see him. Her secretary, Malvina Thompson* (Scheider), wrote Fry that she had received his wire, "but ER was away and already had all the appointments she could keep over the weekend" (MT to VF, 21 July 1940).

Fry left for Marseilles on 5 August, 1940 with a list of 200 endangered refugees and $3,000 strapped to his body. He quickly established a rescue operation, working with the émigré community and French nationals. Cooperation with the State Department broke down almost immediately, however. In August the ERC turned to ER for help, and she, in turn, appealed to Sumner Welles. For a month all went smoothly. But by late September the conflict between ERC and the State Department over the emergency visa policy had reached a crisis point. Thus, almost without exception, Fry found himself working outside formal American and French channels and often, despite State Department protests, establishing a clandestine means of escape from France by ship, by train, and even by foot over the Pyrenees into Spain. He used extralegal means, including forgery, bribery, and the black market to finance his operation.

Subject to arrest and facing constant danger, in his thirteen months in France Fry saved more than 2,000 men and women, including such artists as Marc Chagall and Max Ernst; writers like Hannah Arendt and Andre Breton; scientists like Nobel Prize–winning biochemist Otto Meyerhof and physicist Jacques Hadamard; and musicians like Wanda Landowska. He added to his list men and women of talent and distinction but remained faithful to his mission of saving Europe's cultural elite.

By the summer of 1941 the State Department had eliminated its emergency visa program. As Fry wrote to Frank Kingdon, president of the ERC, "[I]n a very modest way I have been one of the many pawns in the great diplomatic game which Germany, France and the United States have been playing" (VF to FK, 24 June 1941). In this contest, the State Department's goals were quite different from those of Fry, Kingdon, or the ERC. Fry sought to save refugees; the State Department strove to minimize Vichy support for Germany. ER ultimately would not cross State Department—and Roosevelt administration—policy.

This became clear when she was contacted by Fry's wife, Eileen Hughes Fry, in an attempt to aid her husband. Through Clarence Pickett, ER first responded to her in March 1941. "ER spoke to me the other day about your husband's situation in France," Pickett wrote. "Of course, my information about his situation in France is inadequate, but I do know . . . he would be disappointed in what he could accomplish by staying on. It seems to me that, disappointing as it will be for him to return, that's probably the best thing to do" (CP to EF, 4 March 1941). Two months later ER wrote to Eileen Fry directly: "Miss Thompson gave me your message and I am sorry to say that there is nothing I can do for your husband." ER continued: "I think he will have to come home because he has done things which the government does not feel it can stand behind" (ER to EF, 13 May 1941).

In September 1941 Fry was forced to flee France for the United States, where he continued as a writer and public speaker to press for rescue attempts. On 28 April 1945 Fry sent ER a copy of the book he had just completed on his experiences in France, *Surrender on Demand*. "I have sent you a copy of it," Fry wrote, "because I feel pretty sure you will want to read it and learn what was really going on in France that caused you so much trouble over here. And I also want to thank you once again for all the help you gave me and the Committee during those trying months" (VF to ER, 28 April 1945). Unheralded at home for his efforts, Fry died in 1967.

SELECTED BIBLIOGRAPHY
Feingold, Henry L. *The Politics of Rescue*. 1970.
Fry, Varian. *Assignment Rescue*. 1968.
———. *Surrender on Demand*. 1945.
Gold, Mary Jane. *Crossroads Marseilles 1940*. 1980.

Ryan, Donna F. *The Holocaust and the Jews of Marseilles: The Enforcement of Anti-Semitic Policies in Vichy France.* 1996.
Varian Fry Papers, Columbia University, New York.

Michael Berenbaum

FURMAN, BESS (2 December 1984, Danbury, NE–12 May 1969, Bethesda, MD).

Bess Furman, a journalist, achieved recognition partly on the strength of her coverage of Eleanor Roosevelt. As a reporter for the Associated Press (AP), Furman attended the first of ER's press conferences* on 6 March 1933. She also was present for the last conference on 12 April 1945 representing the *New York Times*. Although Furman maintained she never compromised her objectivity, she gave the First Lady extensive and favorable news coverage.

Prior to the inauguration of President Franklin D. Roosevelt* in 1933, Furman, along with Lorena Hickok,* ER's intimate friend, advised ER to hold press conferences. Meeting with ER at her request, Furman quickly voiced approval when ER suggested dispensing with Secret Service protection and meeting the press regularly. Furman wrote, "Instantly I saw vast news possibilities opening before me—what you could do with a President's wife if she didn't have the Secret Service tagging along to fend you off—what you could do if you could ask questions and get answers" (Furman, 139).

An award-winning journalist by the time she met ER, Furman moved to Washington in 1929 to work for the AP. She became the first woman reporter regularly assigned to the House of Representatives by a press association. In 1932 she married Robert B. Armstrong Jr., a reporter for the *Los Angeles Times*, but she continued to use Furman as her professional name.

A native of Nebraska, Furman learned to set type when she learned to read since the family home doubled as the office of the Danbury newspaper published by her father. She taught in rural schools to gain money for college and graduated from Kearney (Nebraska) State Teachers College in 1918. Soon thereafter she left teaching for journalism, first at the *Kearney Daily Hub* and then at the *Omaha Daily News* (which became the *Bee-News*). Her sprightly feature stories, illustrated with her own photograph, appeared under the name "Bobbie O'Dare" and portrayed her as a bobbed-hair flapper who drove a Model T Ford. Furman also wrote poetry and opened many stories with rhyme.

Red-haired and assertive, Furman showed her skill at covering political figures when she won a prize for a story on Alfred E. Smith* during his unsuccessful presidential campaign in 1928. Her style impressed the AP at a time when it was just beginning to hire women, and she landed the top job for a woman in AP's Washington bureau. One of her assign-

ments was to cover First Lady Lou Henry Hoover,* who distanced herself from reporters. Desperate to get a story for Christmas, Furman posed
as a Girl Scout singing carols so she could attend a White House party.

ER's willingness to hold press conferences delighted Furman and other
women of the Washington press corps, like Ruby Black,* Emma Bugbee,*
and May Craig,* who soon established an amiable relationship with the
president's wife. "To my continuous astonishment, I found myself riding
in the White House car, lunching at the White House table, receiving
Easter lilies from the White House green houses, carrying the cards of
the President and Mrs. Roosevelt," Furman noted (Furman, 153).

When the Great Depression* took its toll on Furman's family, ER tried
to help out. Knowing that both Furman's husband and his father had
lost their newspaper jobs and that family investments had disappeared,
ER attempted to arrange a part-time government publicity job for Furman. Although she could not accept it because of AP rules, ER's offer
tightened the bonds between the two women.

Furman faced perils on several occasions when she covered the First
Lady. When she accompanied ER to a mountain music festival in Virginia, Furman missed the messenger assigned to take reporters' copy
down the mountain, so she enlisted two policemen who drove her at
breakneck speed to the Western Union office. In 1934 when Furman and
three other reporters went with ER and Hickok to Puerto Rico and the
Virgin Islands, the group's airplane got lost in fog between Santo Do-
mingo and Port-au-Prince. Furman made furious notes in case the plane
crashed, so someone might find them and file the story. The previous
year ER's dog, Meggie, had bitten Furman on the lip when ER gave
Furman a ride in her car after a hospital tour. ER personally took Furman
to get emergency treatment and called the AP, volunteering to write
Furman's story for her. An astonished deskman turned down the offer,
saying the AP did not want to trouble the First Lady.

Furman continued to cover ER until December 1936, when she resigned due to pregnancy, after being the only journalist assigned full-
time to ER during the 1936 presidential campaign. Furman found the
assignment disappointing because ER had been relegated to a minor role
and told to say little. On 4 April 1937 Furman gave birth to twins, a boy
and a girl, in McCook, Nebraska, where she had gone for the delivery.
ER, who had knitted a baby blanket as a gift, made the twins the subject
of her news conference and sent a telegram that she would have to knit
another blanket. AP carried the story. ER became the godmother of the
girl, Ruth Eleanor, named for her and another close friend of Furman,
Ruth Bryan Owen Rohde, FDR's minister to Denmark.

After giving birth, Furman, joined by her sister, Lucille, started a freelance writing business called Furman Features. Furman continued to attend ER's press conferences and participate in her Gridiron widows'

parties for women excluded from Washington's exclusive, male-only Gridiron Club for journalists. ER helped Furman Features obtain assignments to write features for the *Democratic Digest** and to prepare "Rainbow Fliers," commentary on colored paper that gave the Roosevelt administration's position on various issues, for the 1940 Democratic presidential campaign.

During World War II* Furman sought employment in government information offices. In May 1942 she found a job in the Office of Facts and Figures and then moved to the magazine division of the Office of War Information. There she worked under Dorothy Ducas, another journalist friend of ER who had accompanied her to Puerto Rico as the representative of International News Service. Furman did not hesitate to ask ER to use her "My Day"* column to promote Furman's pamphlet, *War Jobs for Women* (BF to ER, 17 November 1942).

In 1943 Furman joined the Washington bureau of the *New York Times*. Again a full-privileged member of ER's press conference group, she showed herself one of ER's most loyal friends at a time when a few women journalists began to question the news value of the conferences. Many of Furman's stories pictured ER's concern for postwar social improvements and publicized her humanitarian efforts. Recognized for her abilities by her peers, Furman was elected president of the Women's National Press Club* in 1946.

Furman remained with the *Times* until 1961, when she joined the Department of Health, Education, and Welfare. Subsequently head of its Press Information section, she was assigned to do a history of the U.S. Public Health Service. Furman published two books, *Washington Byline* (1949), her autobiography; and *White House Profile* (1951), a history of the White House. In her autobiography, she paid tribute to ER: "The particular shooting star I followed through the newest New Deal years was Eleanor Roosevelt. No newspaperwoman could have asked for better luck" (Furman, 153).

SELECTED BIBLIOGRAPHY

Beasley, Maurine H. *Eleanor Roosevelt and the Media: A Public Quest for Self-Fulfillment*. 1987.

Beasley, Maurine H., ed. *The White House Press Conferences of Eleanor Roosevelt*. 1983.

Bess Furman Papers, Manuscript Division, Library of Congress, Washington, DC.

Furman, Bess. *Washington Byline*. 1949.

Ross, Ishbel. *The Ladies of the Press*. 1974.

Liz Watts

G

GELLHORN, MARTHA (8 November 1908, St. Louis, MO–16 February 1998, London).

As a journalist, war correspondent, novelist, and the third wife of Ernest Hemingway, Martha Gellhorn traveled the world and recounted major twentieth-century events to a rapt audience, including her friend Eleanor Roosevelt, with whom she engaged in a lively correspondence. According to Gellhorn, she first met ER at the White House in November 1934, although ER had long been acquainted with Gellhorn's mother, Edna Gellhorn, who was active in the League of Women Voters* and the Women's Division of the Democratic Party.* Despite an almost twenty-five-year age difference, ER and Gellhorn developed a friendship buttressed by their similar political and social views.

Gellhorn was the only daughter of an outstanding physician and his suffragist and social reformer wife, who were prominent figures in St. Louis. Dropping out of Bryn Mawr College to pursue a career as a journalist, Gellhorn showed a lifelong concern for those attempting to live decently in the face of adversity. At the time she became acquainted with ER, Gellhorn was one of a group of field investigators for Harry L. Hopkins,* head of the Federal Emergency Relief Administration.

Lorena Hickok,* Hopkins' chief investigator and ER's intimate friend, arranged the meeting with the First Lady in response to Gellhorn's outrage over what she had seen, including inadequate New Deal* relief efforts, while investigating conditions faced by millworkers in the South and East. ER, in turn, introduced the attractive and sophisticated Gellhorn to Franklin D. Roosevelt* so that she could give the president her vivid, firsthand observations, and Gellhorn thereafter was a welcome White House guest. After Gellhorn left the job with Hopkins in the summer of 1935, her field reports became the basis of a book of short stories,

The Trouble I've Seen (1936), which ER praised in her "My Day"* column (Chadakoff, 29).

Gellhorn's various writing assignments and unbridled sense of adventure took her all over the world from the 1930s through the 1990s. A chance meeting with Ernest Hemingway while vacationing in Key West in 1936 led to her covering the Spanish civil war and having a romance with Hemingway, which ER encouraged, offering the couple the use of her Hyde Park* cottage on a visit there. As a correspondent for *Collier's* magazine, Gellhorn enthusiastically supported the Loyalist (republican) cause in Spain,* sending ER personal letters that enlarged her understanding of the conflict. When Hemingway and Gellhorn collaborated in the production of a movie that showed the dangers of Franco's fascism, ER had it screened at the White House so FDR could see it, but it had no impact on his policy of strict neutrality toward Spain. Hemingway and Gellhorn, who was a war correspondent in World War II,* were married in 1940 and divorced five years later.

For the duration of her career, Gellhorn, who moved to London following the divorce, maintained a compassionate and liberal vision that decried human misery and senseless violence—sentiments that ER embraced as well. Gellhorn reported on wars all over the world, borrowing from her journalism and autobiographical experiences to gain material for her fiction. She published some 150 articles and short stories and more than a dozen novels and collected works.

In 1951 the association between Gellhorn and ER, which previously had something of a mother–daughter quality, became strained when ER's close friend, Dr. David Gurewitsch*, began to court Gellhorn, and it appeared that the two might have a long-lasting relationship. This did not occur, but the prospect was upsetting to ER, who feared that Gurewitsch might move to Mexico to be with Gellhorn. Yet, until her death, ER remained a loyal, if somewhat more distant, friend to Gellhorn. Returning the warmth, Gellhorn wrote in an introduction to the first of the three-volume collection of "My Day" columns: "No one seeing her could fail to be moved; she gave off light, I cannot explain it better" (Chadakoff, ix).

SELECTED BIBLIOGRAPHY

Chadakoff, Rochelle, ed. *Eleanor Roosevelt's My Day*. Vol. 1. 1989.
Kert, Bernice. *The Hemingway Women*. 1983.
Lash, Joseph P. *A World of Love*. 1984.
Rollyson, Carl. *Nothing Ever Happens to the Brave: The Story of Martha Gellhorn*. 1990.

Randolph Lewis

GENEALOGY. Anna Eleanor Roosevelt's family background offers a short course in the history of the United States. Of her four grandparents, three were from families that had come to America before the Revolution.

The Roosevelts. Her father, Elliott Roosevelt* (1860–1894), was the younger brother of President Theodore Roosevelt* (1858–1919). Theodore and Elliott were descended from Claes Martenszen van Rosenvelt (whose name in Dutch means Nicholas, son of Marten of the rose field) and his wife, Jannetje, who went to New Amsterdam, probably from the Island of Tholen in the Netherlands,* before 1650. (It is near the present-day Roosevelt Study Center, founded by the Dutch government for the study of American history in Europe and named in honor of Theodore, Eleanor, and Franklin D. Roosevelt.*)

Claes' son, Nicholas (1658–1742) was the last ancestor ER and her husband, Franklin D. Roosevelt, had in common. Both ER and FDR were descended from sons of Nicholas—Franklin from Jacobus (1692–1776) and Eleanor from Johannes (1689–1750). Jacobus and Johannes were New York City (New Amsterdam) businessmen who also were concerned with community affairs. They had another brother, Nicholas, whose son, Nicholas "the Goldsmith" Roosevelt, created some of the finest examples of colonial gold and silver work. ER's great-great-granduncle, also named Nicholas Roosevelt, designed a steamboat that traveled down the Mississippi River in 1798 before Robert Fulton invented his steamboat. Interestingly, another of ER's ancestors, Robert R. Livingston, was first a partner of "Steamboat" Nicholas but switched his backing to Fulton. Consequently, Fulton named his steamboat, *Clermont*, for Livingston's family home on the Hudson River in upstate New York.

ER's paternal grandfather, Theodore Roosevelt Sr. (1831–1878), was known as "Greatheart." He was instrumental in the founding of such New York City institutions as the American Museum of Natural History (whose charter stipulates the museum be open seven days a week so that working-class families, who in his era worked six days a week, could visit), the Metropolitan Museum of Art, and the New York Orthopedic Hospital. He was on the committee that raised the funds for the brick pedestal that the Statue of Liberty rests upon. During the Civil War, he helped establish the Allotment Commission, whereby Union soldiers set aside a part of their salaries to be sent home for their families (before this, many families were left virtually destitute when the main wage earner of the family went off to war). It was Theodore Sr.'s mother, the former Margaret Barnhill of Philadelphia (1799–1861), who brought humanitarian ideals to this branch of the Roosevelt family. She taught her sons that wealth brought with it responsibility and encouraged Theodore's charity work.

The Bullochs. ER's paternal grandmother, Martha ("Mittie") Bulloch Roosevelt (1835–1884), was descended from a Revolutionary War general, Daniel Stewart (1761–1829), on her mother's side and Archibald

Roosevelt Family Lineage

Eleanor Roosevelt was a niece of President Theodore Roosevelt and a fifth cousin, once removed, to her husband, Franklin D. Roosevelt. Shown below is a direct line of the Roosevelt family which explains this relationship. Note that their common ancestor was born in 1658.

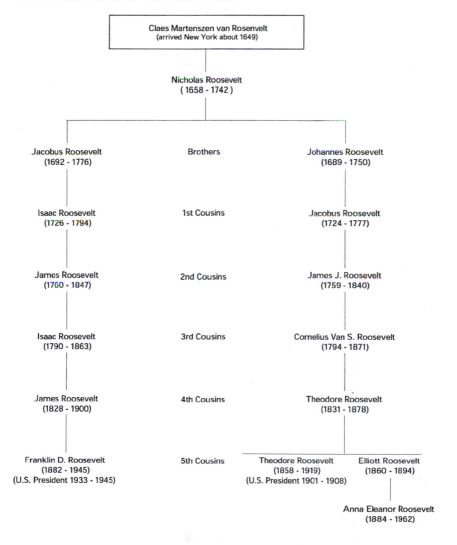

Stobo Bulloch (1730–1777), the first Revolutionary president (governor) of Georgia, on her father's side. As a youth Stewart had been promoted to brigadier general after leading a campaign against marauding Indians on the Georgia frontier during the American Revolution. Archibald Bulloch's son, James Bulloch, became a captain in the Continental army at age seventeen. James married Anne Irvine (1770–1810), the daughter of John Irvine, head of the Georgia medical society. Their son, James Stephens Bulloch (1793–1849) married Martha Stewart Elliott (1799–1864), the daughter of General Daniel and Susannah Oswald Stewart and widow of U.S. senator John Elliott, in 1832. Their daughter, Martha "Mittie," became ER's grandmother.

James Stephens and Martha Bulloch, who were slave owners, built Bulloch Hall in Roswell, Georgia, moving there from Savannah in 1840 when "Mittie" was about five years old. After James Bulloch died, Martha, a staunch Confederate sympathizer, and her daughter, Anna, went to live in New York City in 1857 with "Mittie," who had married Theodore Roosevelt Sr. four years earlier. Aunt Anna Bulloch taught her Roosevelt nieces and nephews to read and write and later married James King Gracie, the son of Archibald Gracie, who built Gracie Mansion (current home of the mayors of New York City).

The Livingstons. ER's mother, Anna Rebecca Hall (1863–1892), was, on the side of her mother, Mary Livingston Ludlow (1843–1919), descended from two branches of the Livingston family. Mary Livingston Ludlow was the daughter of Elizabeth Livingston (1813–1896), who was the granddaughter of Robert R. Livingston (1746–1813), the New York chancellor who administered the oath of office to George Washington. Livingston was also a member of the committee of five, along with Thomas Jefferson and Benjamin Franklin, that drew up the Declaration of Independence, but he did not sign it himself because of business in New York. The chancellor's cousin, Philip Livingston (1716–1778), however, was a signer. He was Elizabeth Livingston's great-grandfather. Other Livingston family members raised the funds to establish the first circulating library in New York City in 1754. The Livingstons were an old Hudson River family, and Elizabeth Livingston married Edward Hunter Ludlow (1810–1884), a doctor who was a scion of another Hudson River family.

The Halls. ER's maternal grandfather, Valentine Gill Hall Jr. (1834–1880), married Mary "Molly" Livingston Ludlow. He brought his family to live at Tivoli on the Hudson, the home where ER lived with his widow, her Grandmother Hall, after her own parents' deaths. Valentine and Mary Hall had six surviving children: four daughters, Anna (ER's mother), Elizabeth ("Tissie"), Edith ("Pussie"), and Maud, and two sons, Valentine ("Vallie") and Edward ("Eddie"). Valentine was the son of Valentine Gill Hall Sr. (1797–1880?), an Irish immigrant who lived in Brooklyn, and Susan Tonnele (1813?–1880?), the daughter of the senior Hall's business partner in the firm of Tonnele & Hall, a New York City

Eleanor Roosevelt's Family Line

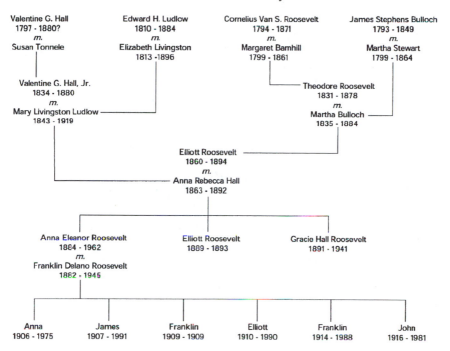

commercial house. The senior Hall managed to amass a large fortune, including considerable holdings in New York City real estate.

Descendants of Eleanor Roosevelt. The marriage of ER and FDR produced six children, five of whom survived to maturity—Anna Eleanor Roosevelt Dall Boettiger Halsted* (1906–1975), James Roosevelt* (1907–1991), Elliott Roosevelt* (1910–1990), Franklin D. Roosevelt Jr.* (1914–1988), and John Aspinwall Roosevelt* (1916–1981). The five children were married a total of nineteen times. Their marriages resulted in twenty-two biological grandchildren for ER and FDR and five adopted grandchildren. Two other biological grandchildren died in infancy.

SELECTED BIBLIOGRAPHY

Brandt, Clare. *An American Aristocracy: The Livingstons.* 1986.

Caroli, Betty Boyd. *The Roosevelt Women.* 1998.

Cook, Blanche Wiesen. *Eleanor Roosevelt.* Vol. 1. 1992.

Genealogical Archives, Theodore Roosevelt Association, Oyster Bay, NY.

Martin, Clarece. *A Glimpse of the Past: The History of Bulloch Hall and Roswell, Georgia.* 1973.

"The Roosevelt Family in America." Parts I, II, III. *Theodore Roosevelt Association Journal* 16 (Winter, Spring, Summer 1990): 1–155.

Linda E. Milano

GRAHAM, FRANK PORTER (14 October 1886, Fayetteville, NC–16 February 1972, Chapel Hill, NC).

A prominent educator, government official, and civil rights* leader, Frank P. Graham won national recognition and Eleanor Roosevelt's admiration for his advocacy of social justice, academic freedom, and world peace. The paths of Graham and ER crossed often in the course of their pursuit of social justice and world peace. Starting in the late 1930s, they both worked to advance the cause of civil rights through such organizations as the Southern Conference on Human Welfare* (SCHW) and the National Association for the Advancement of Colored People.*

Graham was president of the University of North Carolina, Chapel Hill, from 1930 until 1949. In June 1935 he invited ER to speak to the campus, after which he wrote her that she talked "the language of the new America" (Lash, 421). In 1938 they both addressed the first meeting of the SCHW. Ironically, in the same year Graham's university denied graduate school admission on the basis of race to the young civil rights activist Pauli Murray,* who sent such a strong critique of this discrimination to ER that they began a correspondence and friendship. At the time of Murray's application, Graham favored improving educational opportunities for African Americans but within the segregated university system that marked North Carolina education until 1955. President Harry S Truman* appointed Graham to the first President's Committee on Civil Rights, which in 1947 issued a report calling for substantial changes in U.S. racial relations, including desegregation of the armed forces. In 1949 North Carolina governor William Kerr Scott appointed Graham to the U.S. Senate—a position he lost in a hotly contested race the following year due to his liberal stand on civil rights.

Both Graham and ER were advocates for the New Deal* who shared similar views and respected each other. An excellent raconteur and loyal companion, Graham earned ER's confidence. She admired his courage, intellectual curiosity, and diplomatic skills when they worked together at the United Nations* (UN). In 1961 Graham, who served as a UN mediator in the dispute between India* and Pakistan over Kashmir, received the World Peace Award from the Freedom Association for his efforts.

SELECTED BIBLIOGRAPHY

Frank P. Graham Papers, Southern Historical Collection, University of North Carolina, Chapel Hill.

Lash, Joseph P. *Eleanor and Franklin*. 1971.

Pleasants, Julian M., and Augustus M. Burns. *Frank Porter Graham and the 1950 Senate Race in North Carolina*. 1990.

Leonard Schlup

GREAT DEPRESSION. Eleanor Roosevelt was possibly the most visible figure of the New Deal* during the years of the Great Depression. Certainly, she was seen by more people than her husband, the president. She chose to be in locales that manifested her genuine compassion for the underprivileged, underrepresented, and dispossessed. Her empathy with ordinary citizens developed at least as early as her school years at Allenswood when she had gone into London areas where the working class lived. Before she was out of her teens, she plunged into settlement house work in New York City and joined the National Consumers' League,* an organization that advocated improved conditions for women workers and opposed child labor.* At age forty-five, in 1930, she wrote for *Vogue* magazine of her readiness to "strike deep roots in some community where her presence [would] make a difference to the lives of others" (Chafe, 13). In 1933 the nation would become for her that community.

ER took extraordinary steps to learn how the Great Depression affected people's lives. She learned to use the media effectively. In the first of a two-year series of monthly columns she began for the *Woman's Home Companion** in August 1933, she invited readers to write to her about their problems. By the end of the year, more than 300,000 letters had arrived, enormously informative about how the depression affected the everyday life of women and their families. Long after that series ended, she continued to write in a vein that reflected her understanding of social and economic conditions, most notably, in her long-lived syndicated newspaper column, "My Day."* Numerous magazines, particularly those that reached women readers, published her articles expressing her concern and creed. Furthermore, the give-and-take openness of ER's relationship with the Washington women journalists who covered her press conferences* expanded her knowledge. Her close association with outspoken Lorena Hickok,* on official assignment from 1933 to 1935 to report on relief conditions to Harry L. Hopkins,* assured ER an honest account of public want.

The First Lady maintained correspondence and frequent consultations with administration officials whose work was of vital interest to her. Ellen S. Woodward* and Florence Kerr* of the New Deal women's work programs drew upon her in their battles with federal budget managers, but, in turn, she forwarded to them most of the personal requests for assistance that flooded her mail. Lucy Randolph Mason* of the Congress of Industrial Organizations (CIO) kept her abreast of southern labor conditions that cried for attention. Mary Simkhovitch, founder of the Greenwich House settlement, wrote her about the need for slum clearance and public housing. In addition, ER invited Anna Strong,* a radical journalist, to write of her impressions as she traveled around the country. ER encouraged them all and used her strong contacts with Democratic national committeewomen to ascertain the extent and authenticity of need by individuals and institutions in their home states. No presidential wife in history has written public officials and private citizens on the scale of ER.

ER did far more than simply depend on others for information on social and economic needs. During her husband's tenure as New York governor she had been his "eyes and ears." She learned from his instructions how to become an astute observer, going into the kitchens of state institutions, visiting farm women in upstate New York, even looking at people's clotheslines to assess their economic conditions. Soon after becoming First Lady, she went with presidential aide Louis Howe* to meet a contingent of bonus marchers who had gone to Washington in 1933 seeking veterans' benefits. She visited the offices of countless public relief agencies and counted the needs of private charitable institutions. She inspected factories, not a new venture since she had joined the Women's Trade Union League* in 1922.

ER's appearance in the least expected places was the subject of much comment and of the famous *New Yorker* cartoon of the astonished coal miner deep in the shaft who exclaimed, "For gosh sakes, here comes Mrs. Roosevelt" (see Cartoons). She often traveled unobtrusively with women friends, always taking notes. New friendships formed in the 1930s led her to explore conditions previously unknown to her. For instance, Helen Gahagan Douglas* developed ER's support for itinerant laborers after the two spent time in California migrant worker camps. She visited a Shawnee Indian reservation sanitorium in Oklahoma in 1937 and went to see Dust Bowl victims that same year. In 1940 she gave a simple explanation to a woman writer friend for her travels*: "Somebody had asked me to 'come and let us show you what is happening here,' and being interested I went" (Hareven, 42). Her unflagging efforts resulted in gains, in particular, for women, youth,* minorities, and displaced workers.

A cartoonist in the *Dallas Morning News* on 22 November 1933 captured ER's spirit when he drew her at the wheel of an automobile stopped to give "a lift to town" to a "forgotten woman." The plight of unemployed women led ER to urge their inclusion in new federal jobs programs. Single women, widows, and married women whose families depended on their income all found some measure of assistance after Ellen Woodward, head of women's work relief, and ER became close collaborators in creating and maintaining a number of projects that could provide income to needy women. Most were successful and became the basis for continued community and institutional service long after the depression ended. Some proved unpopular with workers and never measured up to expectations. A case in point was training for domestic workers, a beleaguered group whose work conditions had prompted ER to accept the honorary chairmanship in 1928 of the National Committee on Household Employment. Despite the project's failure to substantially im-

prove conditions for household workers, ER's interest in a field employing a large proportion of black and immigrant workers never waned.
She returned to the subject often in her writings. In addition, ER worked
assiduously with Hilda Worthington Smith* in the Federal Emergency
Relief Administration to see that young women were given an opportunity, along with men, for training in resident camps, and she adopted
Camp Tera in New York's Bear Mountain area as her favorite. As was
the case with many endeavors dear to her, she donated funds and materials to help equip the camp.

Unlike the Civilian Conservation Corps camps for young men, Camp
Tera and other "she-she-she" camps, as the women's units were known,
did not offer significant employment opportunities and brought only
temporary respite to unemployed girls. This served to channel ER's compassion for youth into other programs. She was one of the architects of
the National Youth Administration* (NYA), established in 1935. She kept
in close contact with state NYA leaders, as well as with regional directors
of the women's work program. She knew that youth were victimized by
high unemployment, disrupted family life, and unremitting poverty. She
feared what the future held for young people if government failed at
rescue measures, and she was apprehensive about the future of a democracy that neglected its youth.

Concern for women and children likewise led to ER's cooperation with
Mary (Molly) Dewson* and Ellen Woodward in their capacities as successive members of the Social Security Board from 1937 to 1946. She
joined the women board members and Jane Hoey, an old New York
friend who became the director of public assistance under the Social
Security Act, in enlightening the public about benefits available to mothers, widows, and children. ER called for improvements to increase family
security. She was anxious to see that Social Security options were open
to servicemen's wives and children. She wanted health care included in
Social Security amendments deliberated by successive Congresses. She
also used her radio* talks, newspaper columns, and speeches* to promote
the extension of Social Security benefits to working women in uncovered
professions. Regional and state Social Security offices were subject to her
promotional visits and encouragement.

ER believed in the power of organized attack on inequities and injustices. From 1933 on, she chaired the National Woman's Committee of
the Mobilization of Human Needs, set up to coordinate women's efforts
to confront deprivation and suffering by consolidating charitable fund-
raising on the local level. She lent her prestige to the Southern Conference on Human Welfare*, the Southern Tenant Farmers Union, and even
the League of Women Shoppers, fearless of critics who impugned them
all with charges of radicalism and even communism.

ER's interventions included abiding interests in the welfare of blacks.

She was determined that New Deal programs reach them, whether in the area of work and general relief, the NYA, public housing, rural re-settlement, or public health care. She pressed for the appointment of black officials, most notably, Mary McLeod Bethune,* to the Negro Affairs office within the NYA. In one of several White House conferences* she promoted, ER provided a forum for leaders of black women's organizations to explore the limited impact of federal programs on Negro women and children. That assembly occurred in 1938 at the suggestion of Bethune. ER, more than any other individual, was responsible for whatever attention Franklin D. Roosevelt* gave to a New Deal for blacks. Through her intercession leaders of the National Association for the Advancement of Colored People* had an entrée to the president.

No single New Deal venture was known as "Mrs. Roosevelt's project" as much as Arthurdale,* a resettlement community created in whole in 1933 and 1934 in a depressed area of West Virginia. Down-and-out tenant farmers and displaced coal miners were the beneficiaries of an idealistic plan to offer them housing, employment, a model school, and recreational facilities, in short, a new lease on life for a poverty-ridden group that had won ER's full sympathy. On behalf of Arthurdale, she invested great emotion, as well as generous sums of her own money, and held serious discussions with federal officials and philanthropists. Arthurdale afforded her a hands-on approach to age-old problems of economic depression and social deprivations that had long troubled her. Long-range success as a planned community with financial stability eluded Arthurdale and its inhabitants, but the experiment reflected ER's personal dedication to alleviating the distress of the Great Depression.

When the United States entered World War II* in 1941, ER did not forget the groups she had championed for ten years: women, children, minorities, the disadvantaged. She remained their advocate and a supporter of New Deal social programs, even though the administration's focus shifted to war.

SELECTED BIBLIOGRAPHY

Beasley, Maurine H. *Eleanor Roosevelt and the Media: A Public Quest for Self-Fulfillment.* 1987.

Chafe, William H. "Biographical Sketch." In Joan Hoff-Wilson and Marjorie Lightman, eds., *Without Precedent: The Life and Career of Eleanor Roosevelt.* 1984.

Eleanor Roosevelt Papers, Franklin D. Roosevelt Library, Hyde Park, NY.

Hareven, Tamara. *Eleanor Roosevelt: An American Conscience.* 1968.

Roosevelt, Eleanor. *This I Remember.* 1949.

Scharf, Lois. *Eleanor Roosevelt: First Lady of American Liberalism.* 1987.

Martha H. Swain

GREENBELT TOWNS. Eleanor Roosevelt took a personal interest in the creation of controversial planned communities known as greenbelt towns. Although they were surrounded by unoccupied land, they were built near major cities to provide employment for residents. While twenty-five were planned, only three, built by the Resettlement Administration between 1935 and 1938, actually were constructed.

Both ER and President Franklin D. Roosevelt* reviewed plans for Greenbelt, Maryland, outside Washington, D.C., the first of the three towns. ER made repeated trips to Greenbelt and also visited Greendale, near Milwaukee, a similar community. Although she never went to the third project, Green Hills, Ohio, near Cincinnati, she retained a lifelong commitment to the greenbelt concept. She was, said historian Joseph L. Arnold, "one of the most valuable defenders of the greenbelt town programs" (Arnold, 28).

In America in the 1930s the idea of planned cities was new, although an English reformer, Ebenezer Howard, had earlier developed the concept of garden, or greenbelt, towns. These featured a belt of grass and trees as a buffer encircling the site, with smaller belts of green within, separating residential clusters of attached dwellings on culs-de-sac. Highways remained on the outskirts. Services, stores, and offices were built in a central place, predating the development of commercial malls. No industry was located in the towns, which meant residents had to commute to work.

The greenbelt idea excited Rexford G. Tugwell,* who, as assistant secretary of agriculture, persuaded FDR that building such towns would help in providing work for the unemployed and, at the same time, supplying much-needed housing for families of modest means. Eventually, more than $36 million was spent on the three towns, a high cost for the times, partly because they were used as work relief projects for the unskilled. Overlooking expenditures for community facilities, critics* contended the greenbelt dwellings themselves cost an average of $15,968, a sum said to defeat the goal of constructing low-cost housing. Private development interests also attacked the towns as being socialistic, since residents were encouraged to organize consumer cooperatives. The federal government, however, continued to act as the landlord for the towns until the 1950s, when they were broken up into tracts and sold.

Because Greenbelt was located only twelve miles northeast of Washington, next to the federal agricultural research center that lay between Washington and Baltimore, ER took special notice of its construction. It started on 10 October 1935, when a few men began clearing the site. On the following two days some 1,500 unemployed and mostly untrained men were sent out from Washington to work on the project, clearing trees from a swampy area and building a dam to create a lake. By the time actual roads were laid out, the whole area was a sea of mud.

ER visited the site a number of times, often accompanied by her friend Elinor Morgenthau,* wife of Henry Morgenthau, secretary of the treasury, who ER hoped would support the project. For her first trip logs were laid across the mud, forming a corduroy road that led to the spot where the first homes were being built. To enable her to view the scene, workmen constructed a platform for her in the limbs of a tree near the roadway. Similarly, she visited Greendale on 11 November 1936, while it was under construction. In touring a home there, she commented that the coal bin had been placed next to the basement laundry tubs, persuading architects to change the plan.

At one of her press conferences* she showed her continuing interest in the new towns by introducing a New York designer of inexpensive furniture for smaller homes. According to the *Washington Daily News* on 20 April 1937, ER said, "I think it is very significant that an expert of this type would be willing to come to Washington and devote her skill toward developing better standards for low-income families." Some of the furniture served more than one function: a sofa, for example, could double as a single bed.

After the first residents, many of whom were federal government workers, moved into Greenbelt in 1937, ER went there often, usually visiting the school. "It was a shock," one teacher remembered, "when the door would open and she would appear with her secret service escorts" (Williamson, 73). In a letter to Greenbelt residents on 5 January 1938, she congratulated them on their newly formed community newspaper. After World War II* began, she returned to Greenbelt for a rally to raise money for war bonds.

Yet, ER never spoke out against the racial segregation that marked Greenbelt, to which some 900 white families had moved by 1939. In her "My Day"* column of 1 August 1947, one day before the town celebrated its tenth anniversary, she commended to the nation the greenbelt experiment: "Anyone who is able to visit these towns should do so, and should carefully consider their planning and the consumer activities. . . . by and large, I think they have been very successful."

Her legacy lives on in both Greenbelt and Greendale. In Greendale a restaurant, Eleanor's, was named for her, and her visit is commemorated on plaques placed on a fountain. One reads: "First Lady Eleanor Roosevelt, who had a high regard for the welfare of children and a great concern for impoverished people, visited Greendale in 1936. . . . After clambering through one of the two-story homes, she stated Greendale was 'absolutely wonderful' and 'laid out beautifully.' "

In Greenbelt on 2 November 1968, the tree in which she stood on her first visit was dedicated in her name with a memorial plaque. In the 1970s when a new high school, under construction, was to be named for FDR, citizens petitioned to have it named instead for her. Today Eleanor Roosevelt High School, which emphasizes science and technology, is the largest in Maryland.

SELECTED BIBLIOGRAPHY
Arnold, Joseph L. *The New Deal in the Suburbs: A History of the Greenbelt Town Program, 1935–1954*. 1971.
Williamson, Mary Lou, ed. *Greenbelt: History of a New Town, 1937–1987*. 1987.

Virginia W. Beauchamp

GREENWAY, ISABELLA SELMES FERGUSON (KING) (22 March 1886, Boone County, KY–18 December 1953, Tucson, AZ).

Isabella Selmes Ferguson Greenway King was Eleanor Roosevelt's friend for half a century. Their lives were oddly parallel: both lost their fathers at the age of nine, both coped with invalid husbands, both were active politically. They admired each other's courage and ability.

Their families were intertwined. Isabella's father, a lawyer, ranched near Manden, North Dakota, where he and his wife were friends of Theodore Roosevelt.* After his death, Isabella and her mother moved to New York, where Isabella attended private schools. They met ER in 1903. At ER's wedding to Franklin D. Roosevelt* two years later, Isabella was a bridesmaid. While the Roosevelts were on their European honeymoon, Isabella married Robert Munro Ferguson, one of Theodore Roosevelt's Rough Riders and a longtime friend of ER's. Isabella was godmother to ER and FDR's first child, Anna.

Bob Ferguson was diagnosed with tuberculosis, and in 1910, he, Isabella, and their two children moved for his health to New Mexico, where they lived for three years in tents. The two women kept in touch by letter for the next four decades, producing what Isabella called "a volume of friendship" (Ward, 33).

Bob Ferguson died in 1922. The following year Isabella married his friend and fellow Rough Rider, Colonel John Campbell Greenway. After his death in 1926, she increased her political activity, as ER was increasing hers. Isabella became Democratic national committeewoman for Arizona in 1928, while ER headed women's activities for the Democratic National Committee. In 1932 Isabella persuaded her state convention to support FDR for the presidential nomination; she made a seconding speech* for FDR at the Democratic National Convention.

In 1933 President Roosevelt appointed Arizona's lone congressman, Lewis W. Douglas, director of the budget, and Isabella Greenway successfully campaigned to succeed him, becoming Arizona's first congresswoman. She moved to Washington, where she visited the White House often. She supported ER's controversial Arthurdale* project to settle unemployed West Virginia miners into a planned community, but she was sometimes at odds with FDR's legislative programs.

Isabella Greenway was reelected in 1934 but retired after 1936, citing personal reasons. In 1939 she married Harry O. King, a New York industrialist who had been an official in the National Recovery Adminis-

Mary Harriman Rumsey, Eleanor Roosevelt, and Isabella Greenway meet at the White House on 5 February 1934 to discuss plans for the Washington Junior League ball. *Courtesy of Mary Marvin Breckinridge Patterson, photographer*

tration. In 1940 she supported Wendell Wilkie for president, explaining in a letter to ER her opposition to a president's serving more than two terms, interest in Wilkie's proposed reemployment program, and confidence "that my participation (in the campaign) will be kept to impersonal issues and that our lifelong family relations will be safeguarded to the best of my ability" (IG to ER, 19 August 1940). In her reply, ER noted strong reservations about Wilkie and attributed FDR's third-term nomination to world conditions but concluded that "as far as I am concerned political differences never make any difference in one's own personal feelings" (ER to IG, 22 August 1940).

Although FDR was bitter over the defection, the friendship between the two women survived. They continued to visit on occasion and to exchange Christmas gifts and notes.

SELECTED BIBLIOGRAPHY

Chamberlin, Hope. *A Minority of Members: Women in the U.S. Congress.* 1973.
Cook, Blanche Wiesen. *Eleanor Roosevelt.* Vol. 1. 1992.
Eleanor Roosevelt Papers, Franklin D. Roosevelt Library, Hyde Park, NY.
Lash, Joseph P. *Eleanor and Franklin.* 1971.
———. *A World of Love: Eleanor Roosevelt and Her Friends, 1943–1962.* 1984.

Ward, Geoffrey. *A First Class Temperament: The Emergence of Franklin Roosevelt.*
  1989.

Kristie Miller

GUREWITSCH, ARNO DAVID (31 October 1902, Zurich, Switzerland–
30 January 1974, New York).

Dr. David Gurewitsch was close friend, companion, and personal physician to Eleanor Roosevelt from the late 1940s until her death in 1962.
He frequently accompanied ER on her overseas travels* and played an
extremely important role in her life in her later years.

Born to Russian Jewish parents, Gurewitsch graduated from medical
school in Basel, Switzerland, and then went to Palestine as a doctor in
the new Hadassah Hospital in Jerusalem. He came to the United States
in the mid-1930s on a fellowship to do research at Mt. Sinai Hospital in
New York City. Deciding to remain in the United States, he joined the
staff of Columbia-Presbyterian Medical Center in New York City in 1939,
where he rose to become clinical professor of rehabilitation medicine. In
1952 he was named medical director of the Blythedale Children's Hospital in Valhalla, New York. He was also the first medical director of the
United Nations* and during the administration of President John F. Kennedy* served on a panel of advisers to the secretary of health, education,
and welfare.

Gurewitsch first met ER in 1939 at a reception she hosted at the White
House. The encounter was brief, but ER saw him again in 1945 while
visiting her friend, Trude Lash,* who was a patient of his. ER asked
Gurewitsch to be her personal physician when she established a residence in New York City, as well as Hyde Park,* New York, following
the death of Franklin D. Roosevelt* on 12 April 1945.

Late in 1947, the relationship between Gurewitsch and ER grew beyond the usual bounds of doctor and patient. After Trude Lash told her
that Gurewitsch, who had been diagnosed with tuberculosis, was seeking
medical treatment in Davos, Switzerland, ER helped arrange passage for
him on the same plane she was taking to Geneva for a meeting of the
United Nations Commission on Human Rights.* At this time ER was
sixty-three, and Gurewitsch was forty-five. When their flight encountered extended delays due to weather and mechanical problems, first in
Newfoundland and then in Shannon, Ireland, they had abundant opportunity for conversation. Recalling the experience later, Gurewitsch
said,

We discovered that although we had each come from different parts of the world,
from different backgrounds, and were of different ages, we had much in common. We had both grown up fatherless and during our impressionable years had
been raised by grandparents. We each had experienced feelings of deprivation.
A sense of "service" had been instilled in each of us. . . . After these unusual four

and a half days and by the time our plane finally landed in Geneva, what had been essentially a professional relationship changed into a friendship that grew with the years and lasted until the end of Mrs. Roosevelt's life. (Gurewitsch, *Eleanor Roosevelt*, 30–31)

During her brief stay in Switzerland ER began a correspondence with Gurewitsch that would grow over the years to hundreds of letters. Her letters reveal a burgeoning affection for him and an openness about her life and concerns. Before he left the sanitarium in Davos in July 1948, she sent him a copy of the first volume of her autobiography, *This Is My Story*, as well some draft chapters of the second volume, *This I Remember*, on which she was working. In early 1948 Gurewitsch's wife, Nemone, and their young daughter, Grania, visited ER at her home in Hyde Park. Relations between David and Nemone were strained, however, and they were often apart before their divorce in the mid-1950s. ER at times became a counselor to Gurewitsch about his involvements with women, which included a short-lived romance with ER's old friend, the journalist and novelist Martha Gellhorn.*

In the 1950s and early 1960s Gurewitsch frequently spent his vacation time traveling abroad with ER. Often accompanied by ER's personal secretary, Maureen Corr,* they visited Israel,* Pakistan, India,* Greece, Yugoslavia, Japan, Indonesia, Morocco, the Soviet Union, Belgium, England, France, and Switzerland. He spoke Russian and was with her when she interviewed Soviet premier Nikita S. Khrushchev in 1957. An excellent photographer, Gurewitsch took hundreds of photographs of ER on these trips, providing invaluable historical documentation of her travels. Some of these photographs appeared in his book, *Eleanor Roosevelt: Her Day*, published after her death.

Gurewitsch married Edna Perkel on 23 February 1958, and she frequently joined her husband and ER on overseas trips. Perkel first met ER in 1956, when the former First Lady and Gurewitsch attended an art preview that Perkel helped to arrange. By that time, Perkel, an art historian and art dealer, already had become acquainted with Gurewitsch, and they soon fell in love. ER's feelings of loneliness, combined with her fond regard for Gurewitsch, led her to despair when he and Perkel announced their marriage date. But ER remained generous and desirous of nurturing her relationship with Gurewitsch, even persuading the couple to hold their nuptials in her New York City apartment.

ER remained closer to David Gurewitsch than to Edna, but the interaction between ER and Edna was warm, for, as Edna later noted, "Mrs. Roosevelt was prepared to love whom David loved." Edna had long admired ER from afar and, after years of close interaction, continued to call ER "wise, a fascinating companion, and an adorable person." Edna said she tried to absorb from ER the lesson of "selfless, unpossessive love; [that] it is better to give than to receive" and also learned much from the former First Lady "about how to organize one's time and try to make time count for something" (EG to SW, 13 July 1998).

Not long after the marriage, the Gurewitschs bought a town house with ER at 55 East Seventy-Fourth Street. There the three lived together but maintained separate quarters. Nonetheless, they saw each other frequently, often eating dinner in ER's apartment and then going together to the theater or to concerts. The Gurewitschs also occasionally stayed in a guest room at Val-Kill,* ER's cottage in Hyde Park.

ER's relationship with Gurewitsch fulfilled an emotional need for her, but she paid a price, for she endured the suspicions of some that she and the doctor were secretly involved romantically. Commenting on this closeness, Edna explained

It is not unusual for a vigorous older woman to be attracted to a younger, handsome man. Their relationship made her feel alive, womanly. She could love this man because he could be trusted to keep within the bounds of an idealized love. It was idealistic on both sides, although David's idealism did not include romantic fantasy. (Mrs. Roosevelt inscribed a photograph of herself as a young woman "To David, From a Girl He Never Knew.") She could express such feelings freely because she knew the setting was safe. She said in a letter that although she could never forget the difference in their ages, she would like David to call her by her first name. He could not and always referred to her as "Mrs. Roosevelt." (Gurewitsch, "Mrs. Roosevelt," 346)

ER's interaction with David was mutually enriching. With Gurewitsch, ER would discuss the most personal of concerns such as her fear of being buried alive and issues relating to her possible future mental or physical incapacitation. Gurewitsch continued, at ER's insistence, to be her principal physician during her final illness, although some family members questioned this arrangement. Gurewitsch valued ER's advice on a wide range of private and professional matters, and ER enjoyed the devotion of a younger man with whom she felt comfortable being herself.

In 1971 Gurewitsch asked ER's old friend, Esther Lape,* about the propriety of possibly publishing ER's letters to him. Lape replied that "this is a story of a great love that confers nothing but honor upon you and her," but she counseled against publication at that time (Lash, 441).

SELECTED BIBLIOGRAPHY

Edna Gurewitsch letter to Scott W. Webster, 13 July 1998.

Eleanor Roosevelt Oral History Project, Interviews with Martha Gellhorn (1980) and Nina Roosevelt Gibson (1979), Franklin D. Roosevelt Library, Hyde Park, NY.

Gurewitsch, David A. *Eleanor Roosevelt: Her Day.* 1973.

Gurewitsch, Edna P. "Mrs. Roosevelt: An Intimate Memoir." In Jess Flemion and Colleen M. O'Connor, eds., *Eleanor Roosevelt: An American Journey.* 1987.

Lash, Joseph P. *A World of Love: Eleanor Roosevelt and Her Friends, 1943–1962.* 1984.

Roosevelt, Eleanor. *The Autobiography of Eleanor Roosevelt.* 1961.

Scott W. Webster

H

HALSTED, ANNA ELEANOR ROOSEVELT (3 May 1906, New York–
1 December 1975, New York).

Anna Eleanor Roosevelt Halsted, the first child and only daughter of
Eleanor Roosevelt and Franklin D. Roosevelt,* sought a livelihood in
newspaper publishing, broadcasting, and other communications-related
occupations, while retaining ties to both of her parents. Closer to her
father than her mother as a child, she experienced an upper-class upbringing with strict nannies and attendance at Miss Chapin's finishing
school in New York City. In later life, ER said that her children would
have had happier childhoods if she had not relied on servants for child
care, while Anna said that her mother was inconsistent and unpredictable in raising her children. As an adult, however, Anna reached an
understanding of her parents' complex marriage* and more fully com-
prehended ER's alternating moods. Of all her children, ER considered
Anna the strongest in terms of character.

A tense relationship between daughter and mother escalated after FDR
was stricken with infantile paralysis in 1921, when Anna was fifteen.
Anna, with the encouragement of her paternal grandmother, Sara Delano
Roosevelt,* resented ER's insistence that she give up her bedroom to
FDR's chief political associate, Louis Howe,* who had moved into the
Roosevelts' New York City home to assist FDR during his illness. Out
of that family crisis, intimacy between Anna and her mother began to
emerge after ER took Anna into her confidence and made her realize that
it was important for her father to keep involved in politics in spite of
the objections of her grandmother. When Anna was eighteen, ER told
her about the event that had nearly destroyed the Roosevelt marriage—
her discovery in 1918 in FDR's luggage of letters from Lucy Mercer
(Rutherfurd*) that revealed a love affair between her and FDR.

Eleanor Roosevelt holds her first baby, Anna, at Hyde Park, New York, in 1906. *Courtesy of Franklin D. Roosevelt Library*

Nevertheless, the bond between mother and daughter grew slowly and suffered setbacks. Anna protested going to Newport, Rhode Island, in 1924 for her debut in society, but ER and Sara Delano Roosevelt both insisted that she undergo this formal ritual. An outraged Anna resented their intrusion, and ER did not accompany Anna when she went to Newport for the occasion, staying with ER's cousin, Susan Parish, who, in turn, had taken ER to the first ball of her debutante season in 1902.

Another disagreement occurred over college. ER, who had not gone to college, supported higher education for women. Anna's grandmother, however, argued that attending college would threaten her chances for marriage. After prolonged family discussions, ER and FDR decided on a compromise: they persuaded Anna to enroll in Cornell University in 1925 for at least a year to study agriculture, assuming that she might want to help manage the family estate at Hyde Park.* An irate Anna refused to speak to her mother when she drove her to Geneva, New York, for a summer course to prepare for her studies.

Within a year, Anna quit academic life to marry Curtis B. Dall, a New York stockbroker, in 1926. Later she wrote that the marriage was prompted by a desire to get away from family conflict between her mother and grandmother. The Dalls had two children, Anna Eleanor, known as "Sistie," and Curtis Roosevelt, known as "Buzzie." The youngsters were frequently photographed with ER at the White House, where Anna lived in 1933–1934 while separated from Dall before their divorce in 1934.

During this period ER encouraged Anna to become financially independent and arranged for her to be the associate editor of *Babies-Just Babies** during the six months in 1932–1933 that ER was the editor of the monthly magazine. Anna also started writing for magazines, broadcast on the radio, and published two children's books, *Scamper* and *Scamper's Christmas*, about a bunny that moved into the White House.

In 1935 Anna married John Boettiger, a newspaper correspondent, with whom ER developed a warm relationship. They had one son, John Roosevelt Boettiger. In 1936 Boettiger became publisher and Anna associate editor of the women's section of the *Seattle Post-Intelligencer*, a newspaper owned by William R. Hearst, who originally had backed FDR for the presidency but had opposed his reelection in 1936. Hearst may have employed the Boettigers to ensure that he had a link with the Roosevelt administration.

In 1943, when her husband was on military duty, Anna resigned from the newspaper and returned to live in the White House as her father's confidential assistant. Her presence gave FDR a confidante to replace Marguerite "Missy" LeHand,* his private secretary and intimate friend, who had suffered a stroke in 1941. As FDR's aide, Anna played an active role during the last year of his administration. She accompanied him to the Yalta conference in 1945, where FDR met with Winston Churchill* and Joseph Stalin to discuss arrangements for the post–World War II* world.

During ER's frequent absences, Anna functioned as the official White House hostess, a role that revived tensions with her mother. Although FDR had promised ER never to see Lucy Mercer Rutherfurd again after discovery of their affair, he occasionally asked Anna to invite Rutherfurd, now a widow, to dine at the White House when ER was away. Rutherfurd was also present when FDR died unexpectedly at the Little White House in Warm Springs, Georgia, on 12 April 1945. When ER learned of Rutherfurd's presence in Georgia and at the White House, she concluded that Anna had connived with FDR behind her back at her expense.

Following her return to Washington on the train bearing FDR's casket, ER immediately summoned Anna and asked why she had not been informed of Rutherfurd's clandestine return to FDR's life. Anna responded that she thought FDR had the right to visit with an old friend in view of his burdens of office and declining health. After a brief period of hostility toward Anna, ER resumed her normal relationship with her daughter and never mentioned the matter again.

After FDR's death, ER helped Anna and John Boettiger raise money to buy a weekly free-circulation newspaper in Phoenix, Arizona, which they attempted to transform into a profitable daily newspaper. The venture failed, and Boettiger eventually separated from Anna in late 1947. After their divorce in 1949, Boettiger committed suicide the following year. ER was greatly disturbed by his act, which compelled her again to think of her children's difficulties and problems.

In an effort to assist her daughter in paying debts from the newspaper venture, ER agreed in 1948 to join Anna on an American Broadcasting Company afternoon radio* discussion program five days a week. ER was able to record her part of the program even when her responsibilities at the United Nations* took her to Europe. After thirty-nine weeks the *Eleanor and Anna Roosevelt Program* was dropped in September 1949 for lack of commercial sponsorship. Although the enterprise was disappointing, ER remained closely connected with her daughter's life.

In 1952 Anna married Dr. James A. Halsted, a physician with the Veterans Administration. As his career took them to different cities, including Syracuse, New York, and Detroit, Michigan, Anna pursued job opportunities in medical public relations. From 1958 until 1960 they lived in Iran, where Halstead was a Fulbright visiting professor. There they assisted in establishing a medical school in Shiraz. From 1964 to 1971 they lived in Washington, D.C., where Dr. Halsted was assistant medical director of the Veterans Administration. They then retired in Hillsdale, New York.

After ER's death in 1962, Anna was active in organizations that had been important to her mother, including Americans for Democratic Action* and the United Nations Association of the United States. In 1963 she was appointed by President John F. Kennedy* to the Citizen's Advisory Council on the Status of Women, established according to recommendations from the President's Commission on the Status of Women,* which ER had headed shortly before her death. Anna also helped carry on a fund-raising campaign ER had chaired to construct a new campus for the interracial Wiltwyck School* for emotionally disturbed boys. She joined the Wiltwyck board in 1964.

Anna also was involved in activities honoring ER. She became a board member of the Eleanor Roosevelt Memorial Foundation, which helped raise funds for memorials* to ER, including a monument at the United Nations in New York City and the Eleanor Roosevelt Wings of the Franklin D. Roosevelt Library* in Hyde Park. In speeches to many groups she expressed admiration for her mother's achievements, especially in foreign affairs.

SELECTED BIBLIOGRAPHY

Anna Roosevelt Halsted Papers, Franklin D. Roosevelt Library, Hyde Park, NY.
Asbell, Bernard, ed. *Mother and Daughter: The Letters of Eleanor and Anna Roosevelt*.
    1982.
Boettiger, John R. *Love in Shadow*. 1978.
Cook, Blanche Wiesen. *Eleanor Roosevelt*. Vols. 1, 2. 1992, 1999.
Lash, Joseph P. *Eleanor and Franklin*. 1971.
Roosevelt, Eleanor. *This Is My Story*. 1937.

Leonard Schlup

HAMILTON, ALICE (27 February 1869, New York–22 September 1970, Hadlyme, CT).

Alice Hamilton, a physician who pioneered in industrial health research, was one of the women reformers who influenced Eleanor Roosevelt. Hamilton, who received her medical degree in 1893 from the University of Michigan, began her reform work in 1897, when she went to live at Hull House, the famous Chicago settlement founded by Jane Addams.* While there, Hamilton began her studies of work-caused illnesses, which by the close of World War I had gained her a national reputation as an industrial health crusader. In 1919 she left Hull House for a half-time appointment at the Harvard Medical School, making her the university's first woman professor; she remained there until retirement in 1935. During the 1920s Hamilton worked politically through the National Consumers' League* and other organizations to win recognition of illnesses caused by benzene, a paint and varnish solvent; tetraethyl lead, a gasoline additive; and radium, a watch dial illuminator.

The National Consumers' League may first have brought Hamilton and ER together. In 1928 ER hosted a league-sponsored dinner in New York City to publicize the plight of women workers who suffered from radium poisoning. Hamilton almost certainly was in attendance. Hamilton was by the 1920s a vice president of the National Consumers' League, which ER first had joined in 1903.

Hamilton and ER also shared an interest in foreign affairs and a commitment to work for peace.* Hamilton had accompanied Addams to Europe in 1915 in an attempt to mediate the war through an organization that became the Women's International League for Peace and Freedom. At the end of the war, Hamilton and Addams traveled through Europe to publicize the suffering of its people, including the defeated Germans.

Hamilton returned to Germany in 1933 and brought back personal reports on the cruelties of the Nazi regime, becoming the first person to alert ER to the menace posed by Hitler's Germany. She shared her observations with ER during an intimate supper party on 7 August 1933 at the home of reformer Lillian Wald* near Westport, Connecticut. Others present were Addams and ER's friend Elinor Morgenthau.* Afterward, ER invited Hamilton to Hyde Park* to dine with her and Franklin D. Roosevelt* on 25 August because she thought the president should hear firsthand the horrifying news from Hitler's Germany.

Striving for peace, in 1935 ER joined Hamilton and Addams to speak at the twentieth-anniversary celebration of the Women's International League for Peace and Freedom. That year both Hamilton and ER contributed articles to a volume, *Why Wars Must Cease*, published by the National Committee on the Cause and Cure of War headed by Carrie Chapman Catt.*

On 22 June 1936 ER traveled to White Sulphur Spring, West Virginia, to present the Chi Omega sorority achievement award to Hamilton in honor of Hamilton's work on industrial disease. In her "My Day"* column for 24 June 1936, ER praised Hamilton as "a woman who has proved her ability to be of use to mankind." She wrote her intimate friend, Lorena Hickok,* that Hamilton "is such a dear. So gentle and unassuming and yet look what she's done! A lesson to most of us who think we have to assert ourselves to be useful and particularly good for me as I was feeling rather annoyed with FDR. . . . [who had not taken a political suggestion of ER's seriously] until I realized how small it all was sitting by the sweet-faced woman who has probably given the impetus to workman's compensation and research into industrial disease and saved countless lives and heartbreaks!" (Cook, 366).

After retiring from Harvard, Hamilton became a consultant to the U.S. Department of Labor and conducted an investigation into the rayon industry. She served as president of the National Consumers' League from 1944 to 1949.

SELECTED BIBLIOGRAPHY

Clark, Claudia. *Radium Girls: Women and Industrial Health Reform, 1910–1935*. 1997.
Cook, Blanche Wiesen. *Eleanor Roosevelt*. Vol. 2. 1999.
Hamilton, Alice. *Exploring the Dangerous Trades: The Autobiography of Alice Hamilton*. 1943.
Sicherman, Barbara. *Alice Hamilton: A Life in Letters*. 1984.
Slaight, Wilma Ruth. "Alice Hamilton: First Lady of Industrial Medicine." Ph.D. dissertation. Case Western Reserve University. 1974.

Claudia Clark

HARRIMAN, FLORENCE JAFFRAY HURST ("DAISY") (21 July 1870, New York–31 August 1967, Washington, DC).

Florence Hurst Harriman, known throughout her life as "Daisy," moved from the wealthy New York society of her childhood to found social and political clubs for women. Eleanor Roosevelt was part of the network of political women with whom Harriman was involved.

Educated privately and married in November 1889 to the New York banker J. Borden Harriman, a cousin of Averell Harriman,* she became restless as a young society matron. In 1902 she began organizing the exclusive Colony Club for women, which opened a clubhouse offering hotel accommodations for members in New York City in 1907. Although ER joined the club before becoming First Lady, she resigned in the 1930s when her friend, Elinor Morgenthau,* was not accepted for membership because she was Jewish.

In 1912 Harriman organized women's efforts to support Woodrow Wilson in his successful campaign for president. As a reward, Wilson appointed her in 1913 to a four-year term on the Federal Industrial Relations Commission, which investigated strikes and industrial unrest. She and her husband moved to Washington, where he died in 1914. After the United States entered World War I, Harriman chaired the Committee of Women in Industry for the Council of National Defense and formed the American Red Cross* Motor Corps. ER attended an organizational meeting for the motor corps but, since she could not drive at the time, joined a Red Cross canteen instead. Following the war, both women worked on the board of the National Consumers' League.*

During the 1920s Harriman turned her social and organizing skills to sustaining the out-of-power Democrats. Her "Sunday Night Suppers," a gathering place for progressive Democrats, became a Washington institution. In 1922 she cofounded the Woman's National Democratic Club* in Washington, D.C., to facilitate meetings of Democratic women. ER, a charter nonresident member, used the club as a forum and attended its events while living in the White House. Harriman was Democratic national committeewoman from Washington, D.C., from 1924 to 1936.

In 1937 FDR named Harriman U.S. minister to Norway. She was the first diplomat to report on the German invasion there in 1940. In spite of being in personal danger, she arranged for the evacuation of refugees,* including Crown Princess Martha and her family, who returned with Harriman to the United States. In the 1950s Harriman worked for home rule for the District of Columbia. President John F. Kennedy* awarded her a citation of merit for distinguished service in 1963.

SELECTED BIBLIOGRAPHY
Harriman, Mrs. J. Borden (Florence Jaffray). *From Pinafores to Politics*. 1923.
———. *Mission to the North*. 1941.
Lash, Joseph P. *Eleanor and Franklin*. 1971.
Roosevelt, Eleanor. *This Is My Story*. 1937.
Ware, Susan. *Beyond Suffrage: Women in the New Deal*. 1981.

                                                                Kristie Miller

HARRIMAN, WILLIAM AVERELL (15 November 1891, New York–26 July 1986, Yorktown Heights, NY).

Averell Harriman, a wealthy industrialist, served Franklin D. Roosevelt* and three succeeding Democratic presidents in important assignments. He was also governor of New York from 1954 to 1958, but he lacked Eleanor Roosevelt's support when he sought the presidency in 1952 and 1956 despite the fact that they had old family ties.

ER and FDR first met Harriman as a child when he was a classmate of ER's brother, Hall Roosevelt,* at Groton School. In 1928 Harriman, a graduate of Yale University, together with his sister, Mary Harriman Rumsey,* left the Republican Party to join the Democrats. Both moved to Washington after FDR became president in 1933 to take positions in the National Recovery Administration, a key New Deal* agency. Harriman's friendship with Harry Hopkins* facilitated Harriman's entry into FDR'S inner circle. He became FDR'S special representative in London for Lend-Lease assistance in 1941–1942 and U.S. ambassador to the Soviet Union in 1943–1946. Under President Harry S Truman,* Harriman served as U.S. ambassador to Great Britain in 1946, U.S. secretary of commerce in 1947–1948, U.S. coordinator of the European Recovery Program (Marshall* Plan) in 1948–1950, and director of the U.S. Mutual Security Agency in 1951–1952.

Harriman's standing with ER was not enhanced by his ties with Hopkins, whom she perceived as allowing World War II* issues to crowd out social welfare concerns. For example, ER ignored Hopkins' request that she consult with Harriman rather than U.S. ambassador John G. Winant during her wartime visit to England in 1942.

In 1947, when she was a U.S. delegate to the United Nations,* Harriman was one of several U.S. officials who met with her to defend unilateral U.S. aid to Greece and Turkey. She questioned this action because she thought it bypassed the United Nations. In contrast, she was pleased with the Marshall Plan's broader approach and found informative the occasional discussions she had in 1950–1951 with Harriman about European economy issues.

In 1952 ER's son, Franklin D. Roosevelt Jr.,* managed Harriman's campaign for the Democratic nomination for president, and Harriman spoke that year at the Memorial Day service for FDR in Hyde Park.* Preoccupied with her work at the United Nations during the months leading up to the Democratic Convention, ER did not express a preference among the Democratic contenders. Nevertheless, she was pleased with the campaign waged by Adlai Stevenson* as the Democratic nominee, even though he was defeated by Republican Dwight D. Eisenhower.* In 1956 ER's strong support for Stevenson was a factor in his defeat of Harriman for the Democratic presidential nomination.

Harriman went on to help negotiate the 1963 U.S.–Soviet treaty limiting nuclear weapons tests during the administration of John F. Kennedy.* On behalf of President Lyndon Johnson, Harriman led the U.S. delegation at the Paris peace talks with North Vietnam in 1968.

SELECTED BIBLIOGRAPHY

Burke, Lee H. "The Ambassador at Large: A Study in Diplomatic Method." Ph.D. dissertation. University of Maryland. 1971.

Eleanor Roosevelt Oral History Project, Interview with W. Averell Harriman
    (1978), Franklin D. Roosevelt Library, Hyde Park, NY.
Harriman, W. Averell, and Elie Abel. *Special Envoy to Churchill and Stalin, 1941–
    1946.* 1975.
Lash, Joseph P. *Eleanor: The Years Alone.* 1972.
————. *A World of Love: Eleanor Roosevelt and Her Friends, 1943–1962.* 1984.
Roosevelt, Eleanor. *This I Remember.* 1949.

Kristie Miller

HEALTH. To all appearances, Eleanor Roosevelt was a remarkably healthy, energetic person. Biographers have speculated that her legendary energy had its roots in an unspoken sense of inadequacy, a result of her lonely childhood* and later her husband's romance with Lucy Mercer (Rutherfurd*).

In "Geriatric Profile of Eleanor Roosevelt," which appeared in the January 1983 *Journal of the American Geriatrics Society*, Dr. E. David Sherman noted that ER used common sense to care for herself and inherited a vigorous constitution from her ancestors. She used change—whether in seasonal activities, companionship, or environment—and relaxation techniques, such as brief naps, to maximize her energy. As she aged, she coped with partial deafness by using a hearing aid attached to her eyeglasses.

ER contended that she never expended energy on regret or indecision. Although she never commented publicly on the affair between Franklin D. Roosevelt* and Mercer, after ER discovered it in 1918, she became consumed with work for various causes that gave her an independent identity. She was convinced that being useful was the best way to overcome self-pity, a philosophy that bore witness to her own struggle with periods of despair.

Throughout her life ER experienced what she called her "Griselda moods," named for a self-sacrificing princess in a medieval legend, during which she would withdraw into silence (Lash, *Love, Eleanor*, 56). As a young woman she was subject to migraine headaches. In 1919 she wrote in her diary that her self-confidence was gone. Biographer Blanche Cook has pointed out that ER also was underweight during this period and probably had anorexia.

From time to time ER apparently suffered from what today might be termed depression. In 1933, during the months surrounding her husband's first inauguration, observers said she showed signs of melancholy. In 1940 she had difficulty getting up in the morning, a stark change for a woman who usually got by on four or five hours of sleep per night. In 1943, after a trip to the South Pacific, where she saw firsthand the horrors of war, a friend reported that ER would stare vacantly into space and not hear what was said to her. Nevertheless, she carried out an extraordinarily busy schedule and believed that individuals could overcome their own problems by self-discipline.

ER had little tolerance for those who gave in to injury or disease. Her grandson, John R. Boettiger, recalled that she believed "iron will and courage could conquer any illness" (Goodwin, 492). She saw her husband through his life-altering battle with polio in 1921 and, in opposition to her mother-in-law, Sara Delano Roosevelt,* encouraged him to continue his involvement in politics. She refused to treat him as a invalid.

When she suffered a bout of pleurisy while accompanying FDR on a tour of World War I battlefields in France in early 1919, she discounted the advice of an English doctor "to be examined for tuberculosis as soon as I reached home," quite "sure . . . that I was recovering," she wrote in her autobiography (Roosevelt, 284). The pleurisy, however, may have been an indication of an illness that contributed to her death more than forty years later. Her son-in-law, Dr. James Halsted, noted in a 24 June 1964 letter to her son, James Roosevelt,* that pleurisy often is caused by tuberculosis. Chest X-rays taken shortly before she died showed old tuberculosis lesions, and the reactivation of tuberculosis figured in her fatal illness.

From 1945 until her death in 1962 ER's primary physician was Dr. David Gurewitsch,* a clinical professor of rehabilitation medicine at the Columbia-Presbyterian Medical Center, who became a close personal friend and companion. ER shared a town house in New York City with Gurewitsch and his wife, Edna, from 1960 to 1962.

Her final illness began in April 1960, when ER was diagnosed with anemia due to bone marrow failure. Two years later her blood platelet count was so low that she was given steroids to stimulate the marrow and prevent bleeding, since platelets are necessary for clotting.

Steroid treatment sometimes reactivates tuberculous infections, which is what ER's physicians concluded happened in her case. The reignited tuberculosis infection was not confirmed until 26 October 1962, less than two weeks before ER's death. Antituberculosis treatment with streptomycin and other drugs had begun a month earlier, however, because her physicians suspected the disease. Even so, it overtook her body's defenses, and she died on 7 November 1962. In the last stages of her illness, she resisted continued medical treatment.

In an appendix to his book on ER's correspondence, *A World of Love*, Joseph Lash* noted an opinion by Dr. Moses M. Suzman, an internist who was not involved in ER's treatment, that ER's tuberculosis was the underlying cause of her anemia. Her physicians, however, maintained that the tuberculosis infection was superimposed on her primary blood disorder. A summary of ER's medical history, treatment, and autopsy, presented on 12 December 1962 at the Columbia-Presbyterian Medical Center, described extensive consultations and tests, as well as the difficulty of treating ER while she continued a rigorous schedule and allowed only irregular follow-ups of her condition.

Despite declining health in her last two years, ER remained vigorous until a few months before her death at age seventy-eight. The final diagnosis of her death was cardiac failure due to aplastic anemia and pulmonary infection, due to tuberculosis, also involving bone marrow.

SELECTED BIBLIOGRAPHY

Cook, Blanche Wiesen. *Eleanor Roosevelt*. Vol. 1. 1992.
Eleanor Roosevelt Medical Records, Anna Roosevelt Halsted Papers, Franklin D. Roosevelt Library, Hyde Park, NY.
Goodwin, Doris Kearns. *No Ordinary Time: Franklin and Eleanor Roosevelt: The Home Front in World War II.* 1994.
Lash, Joseph P. *Love, Eleanor: Eleanor Roosevelt and Her Friends.* 1982.
————. *A World of Love: Eleanor Roosevelt and Her Friends, 1943–1962.* 1984.
Roosevelt, Eleanor. *This Is My Story.* 1937.

                                                                    Jane Brissett

HICKOK, LORENA A. (7 March 1894, East Tory, WI–1 May 1968, Rhinebeck, NY).

Lorena A. Hickok, one of the top newspaperwomen in the United States in the early 1930s, entered Eleanor Roosevelt's life at a pivotal moment and became her greatest source of emotional sustenance as she began to redefine the role of First Lady.

Hickok, who was called "Hick," became an intimate friend of ER while covering her for the New York bureau of the Associated Press (AP) in 1932 during the first presidential campaign of Franklin D. Roosevelt.* One of the first women reporters to be allowed to write front-page stories, Hickok did not know ER well before the campaign but sensed that she might be an interesting news source and persuaded the AP to report on her activities. Hickok did not want the job herself because she was assigned to FDR, but when the bureau's only other woman reporter quit, Hickok was reassigned to ER. At first ER was not eager to speak with her, but Hickok gained her confidence by making friends with Malvina Thompson* (Scheider), ER's secretary.

As a trained observer, Hickok recognized that ER was apprehensive about moving into the White House (ambivalence that Hickok later wrote about in *Reluctant First Lady*). As she and ER conversed on long railroad trips, Hickok realized that ER hated to give up teaching at Todhunter School,* did not want to devote all her time to teas and social engagements in Washington, and needed to find personal fulfillment in an active career that complemented her complex relationship with her husband. As the two women got to know each other, they exchanged the stories of their lives and found increasing pleasure in each other's company in spite of vast differences in background.

Eleanor Roosevelt and Lorena Hickok stop at Lowell, Massachusetts, in July 1933 as they drive alone on a vacation trip through New England to the Gaspé Peninsula. *Courtesy of Franklin D. Roosevelt Library*

The product of an unhappy childhood* in South Dakota, Hickok had been mistreated by a sadistic father, who was a traveling butter maker, and forced to work as a hired girl at the age of fourteen after the death of her mother. Going to live with a cousin in Battle Creek, Michigan, she completed high school there and spent an unhappy period at Lawrence College, Appleton, Wisconsin, where she was teased about being overweight. She began her journalistic career in 1913, earning seven dollars a week collecting personal items about visitors for the *Battle Creek Journal*.

By 1915 Hickok had advanced to being society editor and feature writer at the *Milwaukee Sentinel*, a job that brought her into contact with the celebrated singer, Ernestine Schumann-Heink, who gave her a sapphire and diamond ring to mark what became a long friendship. Hickok treasured the ring as she rose in journalism. Eventually, she passed the ring on to ER, who wore it until her death.

A lively writer and interviewer, in 1917 the youthful Hickok made her way to New York, where she landed a job on the *Tribune*, but she left after only six weeks because she felt overwhelmed by the city. Back in the midwest, she tried college again, this time at the University of Minnesota, but she dropped out to distinguish herself as Sunday editor and then star reporter on the *Minneapolis Tribune*. In 1927 she was ready for New York, joining the AP there after a brief stint on the tabloid *Mirror*.

After being assigned to ER, Hickok quickly developed a passionate attachment that eventually overshadowed her reportorial objectivity and caused her to give up her hard-won position with the AP. ER found Hickok a stimulating companion who afforded a model of success in a man's world. She brought ER warmth and understanding at a time when she was separated from Earl Miller,* her earlier confidant, and experiencing a waning in her friendship with Nancy Cook* and Marion Dickerman,* with whom she had built her Val-Kill* cottage. After FDR was inaugurated in 1933, ER and Hickok exchanged letters daily and looked forward to opportunities when they could meet by themselves.

In recent years the exact nature of their relationship has been the object of considerable speculation. The Hickok–ER correspondence at the Franklin D. Roosevelt Library, Hyde Park, New York, which was opened to the public in 1978, contained gushingly affectionate, occasionally erotic passages. For instance, ER's declaration, "I wish I could lie down beside you and take you in my arms" (Faber, 176) was as suggestive as Hickok's comment, "I remember your eyes, with a kind of teasing smile in them, and the feeling of that soft spot just northeast of the corner of your mouth against my lips" (Faber, 152).

After the correspondence was unsealed, Franklin D. Roosevelt Jr.* emphatically denied that the women had a lesbian affair, emphasizing that his mother had used endearing terms in writing to many persons. Blanche Wiesen Cook, ER's most recent biographer, however, challenged what she considered a historical whitewash of the romance between ER and Hickok, contending that Hickok's picture had been cropped out of photographs of family dinners as part of efforts to expunge the relationship from history. (Edited excerpts of the correspondence have been published in Streitmatter's book, *Empty without You*).

Regardless of the private intimacies between the two women, Hickok's position was an important factor in introducing ER to the public in glowing terms in the crucial months just before and after FDR's election as president. Since other news organizations had not assigned reporters to ER, in keeping with the tradition that candidates' wives were not newsworthy, Hickok's dispatches about ER were run in hundreds of newspapers. They presented ER as a commendably independent woman, combining feminine virtues of modesty and service to others with modern career interests. Explaining that ER would continue her paid activities (as editor of *Babies-Just Babies**) while in the White House, Hickok translated ER's personal aspirations into an acceptable public image as a new and different kind of First Lady.

By the time of the election, Hickok had become part of the Roosevelt publicity apparatus, with ER trusting Hickok with great latitude in choosing what to quote her as saying. In clear violation of professional journalistic standards, Hickok cleared stories in advance with either ER or Louis Howe,* FDR's chief political strategist. When she withheld a story because ER asked her to (concerning a remark ER had made on one of her radio broadcasts* allegedly encouraging girls to drink), the AP reprimanded her and cut her salary. On the night before the inauguration, 4 March 1933, ER read FDR's address to Hickok. "Here I was, a newspaper reporter, right in the middle of what, that night, was the biggest story in the world. And I did nothing about it," Hickok wrote years later, musing that any other journalist would have called in the story but she did not; "that night Lorena Hickok ceased to be a newspaper reporter" (Hickok, 96).

Hickok also made suggestions for ER's long-term press relations, giving her insight into the working press that enabled her to deal more effectively with journalists. She gave ER pointers on writing magazine articles and, possibly, the idea for her "My Day"* column, which may have been an outgrowth of ER's daily letters to Hickok. These recounted ER's activities in accordance with a plan that someday Hickok could write her biography.

Hickok proposed that ER hold White House press conferences* for women reporters only, but she herself did not take part in them. Her coverage of ER ended with an exclusive interview with the new First Lady on inauguration day. The interview, which the AP copyrighted, marked the first time a First Lady had been interviewed in the White House. It announced that ER would serve as FDR's "eyes and ears," seeing as many Americans as possible and reporting to him about their concerns (Beasley, 35). The interview took place the day after ER had taken Hickok to Rock Creek Cemetery in Washington to view the famous Saint-Gaudens' statue of "Grief," which ER had found comforting during her troubled World War I days in Washington after she had learned of FDR's affair with Lucy Mercer (Rutherfurd*).

Although Hickok returned to the New York AP bureau after the inauguration, leaving Bess Furman* to cover ER in Washington, Hickok resigned in June. She went to work directly for the administration as the chief investigator of relief programs for Harry Hopkins,* head of the Federal Emergency Relief Administration. In that capacity she traveled around the country writing confidential reports on conditions during the Great Depression* (published as *One Third of a Nation*, 1981). Her memorable reports, candid and vividly written observations on the success and failures of New Deal* programs, went not only to Hopkins but to

ER, who passed Hickok's information along to FDR. They showed her own outrage over the deprivation faced by millions of Americans and gave Hopkins valuable information he would not otherwise have had, stimulating action to improve relief efforts. Hickok's gripping account of appalling poverty in West Virginia, for example, prompted ER's interest in the Arthurdale* resettlement project for miners. In her investigative role, Hickok went with ER and a group of newspaperwomen to inspect conditions in Puerto Rico and the Virgin Islands in March 1934.

During this period the personal relationship between the two women was at its height. That summer Hickok accompanied ER on a camping trip to Yosemite National Park. The previous summer ER and Hickok had vacationed together, driving by themselves through New England and the Gaspé Peninsula in Canada. Yet, as FDR's first term ended, the intensity of their attachment faded somewhat, as they expressed feelings of depression and occasional disillusionment to each other. In part, this was because Hickok sought an exclusive relationship with ER, which conflicted with ER's wide-ranging interests and enthusiasm for others.

In 1936 Hickok left federal employment but turned to ER to help her find other jobs. In the late 1930s she was a publicist for the New York World's Fair. In 1940 she returned to Washington and worked for the Democratic National Committee, serving four years as executive secretary of the women's division. ER invited her to live in the White House so she could afford to keep a weekend home on Long Island. She developed a close relationship with Judge Marion Harron of the U.S. Tax Court and was a political friend of Helen Gahagan Douglas.*

Leaving her Washington job in 1945 due to ill health, Hickok returned to New York, where she worked as a researcher for Representative Mary Norton of New Jersey and intermittently for the state Democratic Committee. In the 1950s Hickok's health failed. She went to live in Hyde Park,* New York, to be near ER. In an effort to aid Hickok financially, ER collaborated with her on a book about women in politics (*Ladies of Courage*). Hickok lived first with ER in her Val-Kill home and then in various rental units, attempting with relatively little success to earn money by writing biographies of FDR, ER, and Helen Keller and her teacher, Anne Sullivan Macy, for juveniles as well as *Reluctant First Lady*.

Her relationship with ER aside, Hickok ranks among the most important woman journalists of the twentieth century. When she was hired by the AP, she was already a veteran reporter at a time when women were still oddities in the business. In Minneapolis she had established a name for herself by reporting on murder trials and traveling with Minnesota football teams as the first woman sports reporter. At the AP she was given opportunities that no other woman on the staff had seen. She covered the kidnapping of the Lindbergh baby and tackled major political stories that ultimately led to her relationship with the Roosevelts. At the end of her life, she lamented the loss of her journalistic career.

Following ER's death in 1962, Hickok and ER's friend, Esther Lape,* burned some of the ER–Hickok correspondence. Hickok retyped other letters, deleting personal references. These edited letters plus the remaining unedited correspondence were among Hickok's personal papers that she deposited in the Roosevelt Library with the stipulation they not be opened until ten years after her death. Among the papers are records of her journalistic achievements.

SELECTED BIBLIOGRAPHY

Beasley, Maurine H. *Eleanor Roosevelt and the Media: A Public Quest for Self-Fulfillment*. 1987.
Cook, Blanche Wiesen. *Eleanor Roosevelt*. Vols. 1, 2. 1992, 1999.
Faber, Doris. *The Life of Lorena Hickok: ER's Friend*. 1980.
Hickok, Lorena A. *Reluctant First Lady*. 1962.
Lorena A. Hickok Papers, Franklin D. Roosevelt Library, Hyde Park, NY.
Streitmatter, Rodger. *Empty without You*. 1998.

Agnes Hooper Gottlieb

HIGHLANDER FOLK SCHOOL. The Highlander Folk School, established in 1932 near Monteagle, Tennessee, brought blacks and whites together in its leadership classes for years in defiance of segregation laws. The school attracted the attention and financial support of Eleanor Roosevelt during the first decade of its existence. She continued her interest in its activities for the rest of her life, even though her association with the school brought her attacks from Red-baiters and from the political Right.

Myles Horton, who had taught vacation Bible school classes in Tennessee while an undergraduate at Columbia University, founded Highlander after studying under Reinhold Niebuhr at Union Theological Seminary in New York. Horton and his supporters saw Highlander, which was modeled after Danish community folk schools, as an adult education center to "prepare rural and industrial leaders for a new social order" (Kearney, 193). A 27 May 1932 fund-raising letter written by Niebuhr to help launch the school said, "We believe that neither the American Federation of Labor nor Communist leadership is adequate to their (southern mountain people's) needs. Our hope is to train radical leaders who will understand the need of both political and union strategy" (Dunbar, 43). Highlander's activities included social evenings, informal classes, and a cooperative cannery. In the 1930s, however, the most controversial workshops taught workers in the lumber, mining, and textile industries how to organize and bargain collectively.

Among political conservatives and coal company owners, unionism, communism, and Highlander were synonymous hatreds. The *Chatta-*

nooga News and the *Nashville Tennessean* published exposés of "radical" activities at the school. When this negative public opinion began to affect contributions to Highlander, a Washington fund-raiser was held in December 1940. ER was listed among the sponsors, which included other New Deal* notables.

Since 1937 she had donated $100 dollars annually to a Highlander scholarship fund. These checks became a focus for those critical of her involvement in leftist causes. A 1940 propaganda booklet titled *The Fifth Column in the South* reproduced one of her checks to Highlander, an accompanying letter on White House stationery, and a photograph of ER with Horton, and included an entire chapter outlining ER's association with Highlander—a school that the booklet claimed produced a film with "a Communist movie outfit," "uses the drama to get its Red Message across," and "advocate[s] strikes and the overthrow of the capitalist (American) system" (Kamp, 22).

After World War II,* public animosity grew. Although the charges of socialism and communism continued, community and regional outrage against Highlander during the 1950s focused on its racially integrated programs and the training of demonstrators to press for civil rights.* (In its 20 January 1990, obituary of Horton, the *New York Times* said, "He . . . is often credited with being one of the sparks that ignited the civil rights movement in the United States. Rosa Parks, the Rev. Dr. Martin Luther King, Jr.,* former Mayor Andrew Young of Atlanta, Fanny Lou Hamer, and Stokeley Carmichael were among those who attended classes or taught at the school.") In March 1954, Horton was called to testify at a congressional hearing in New Orleans on alleged subversive influences in the South. He denied he was a member of the Communist Party, but he was ejected from the hearing while trying to read a statement explaining his refusal to answer questions about political affiliations of other people.

In making trips to Highlander, ER showed her personal courage. The FBI warned ER that the local Ku Klux Klan planned to raid the school during her appearance there at an integration workshop on 16 June 1958, but she refused to cancel her plans even though the local sheriff sympathized with the Klan and authorities could not guarantee her safety. Without any police escort ER drove over country roads to reach the school. The Klan did not act, and her visit at the workshop took place uneventfully.

It was through their Highlander connection that Rosa Parks took tea with ER in New York in 1955. In his autobiography, Horton describes introducing ER to Parks as "the first lady of the land to the first lady of the South" (Horton, 190). ER asked Mrs. Parks about her instruction in civil disobedience at Highlander, and they shared experiences about being called communists for their civil rights activities.

Although her involvement with Highlander was labeled impetuous and impolitic by many, ER continued to support its programs of community betterment, labor organization, and civil rights.

SELECTED BIBLIOGRAPHY

Black, Allida M. *Casting Her Own Shadow: Eleanor Roosevelt and the Shaping of Postwar Liberalism.* 1996.

Dunbar, Anthony P. *Against the Grain: Southern Radicals and Prophets, 1929–1959.* 1981.

Horton, Myles. *The Long Haul: An Autobiography.* 1990.

Kamp, Joseph P. *The Fifth Column in the South.* 1940.

Kearney, James R. *Anna Eleanor Roosevelt: The Evolution of a Reformer.* 1968.

Thomas, H. Glyn. "The Highlander Folk School: The Depression Years." *Tennessee Historical Quarterly* 23 (December 1964): 358–371.

Anna R. Paddon

HOLOCAUST. Eleanor Roosevelt has been termed by one historian critical of her husband's record relating to the Holocaust as "the mother hen of rescue efforts" (Feingold, 160). While officials in the administration of Franklin D. Roosevelt* were often hostile and resistant, the president's wife was a champion of the efforts to save refugees,* most especially the children. Throughout the prewar years, she joined those pro-immigration forces. She was honorary chair for several such groups and accessible to many others. She lent her name and prestige to the U.S. Committee for the Care of European Children, which moved to bring British children to the United States during the battle over Britain and later sought to bring French children, mostly Jews,* from Vichy France. She personally intervened to get the approved number raised to 5,000. The rescue effort was ultimately unsuccessful because of stalling by the Vichy government.

She supported the Wagner–Rogers* bill in 1939, which would have admitted 10,000 refugee children into the United States—primarily Jews—even while her husband remained indifferent to these efforts and refused to take any action on their behalf. The bill ultimately died in committee and was not brought for a vote.

While often unsuccessful in her chosen role as intermediary, ER did succeed from time to time. For example, in 1941 she intervened with the president when assistant secretary of state Breckinridge Long, a fierce opponent of immigration, had quietly cut the operating funds of the President's Advisory Committee on Political Refugees, forcing Long to apologize for the oversight. She intervened with her husband to obtain visas for French Jews aboard the ship *Quanza* and thus avoid a repeat of the incident in which Jewish refugees on the transport vessel *St. Louis* were denied entry and returned to Europe.

ER generally escapes the harsh criticism that has been leveled by some historians regarding FDR and the Jews. If anything, those who criticize the president wish only that he had been more responsive to the concerns of his wife, who often served as a conduit for humanitarian concerns within the Roosevelt administration and was a strong advocate for American refugee efforts. But her influence went only so far, and her failures at intervention far outnumbered her successes.

Like her husband, ER was raised in an upper-class culture when anti-Semitism was part of the milieu. It was accepted uncritically, and her youthful attitudes toward the Jews, as reflected in early correspondence, if objectionable by contemporary standards, were unexceptionable by the standards of the time. Later she overcame the prejudices of her class and had deep and personal involvements with Jews, resigning from New York's Colony Club, which refused to accept her Jewish friend Elinor Morgenthau* as a member.

In a critical showdown with the State Department in January 1944, ER supported efforts by Elinor's husband, secretary of the treasury Henry Morgenthau, to change American policy toward the refugees, following his receipt of the report, "On the Acquiescence of This Government to the Murder of the Jews." The report charged the State Department with going so far as to use "government machinery to prevent the rescue of the Jews" and "to surreptitiously attempt to stop the obtaining of information concerning the murder of the Jewish population of Europe" (Morgenthau, 693, 212–29). The memo further accused the State Department of covering up its guilt by "concealment and misrepresentation." Morgenthau condensed the report and submitted it privately to the president on 16 January 1944. Within a week, the War Refugee Board was created, and after eleven long years, the American government was on the side of rescue. These efforts were described by John Pehle, director of the War Refugee Board, as too little and too late. Still, they were instrumental in saving tens of thousands of Jewish lives.

ER was perhaps the person in the Roosevelt administration, most especially its inner circle, most available to protest groups seeking to influence the president's policy. Unlike her husband, she attended the 1943 Constitution Hall performance of Ben Hecht's cantata *We Will Never Die*. She was stirred by the performance and wrote movingly of it in her syndicated column, "My Day"* for 14 April 1943, calling it "one of the most impressive and moving pageants I have ever seen. No one who heard each group come forward and give the story of what had happened to it at the hand of the ruthless German military will ever forget those haunting words: 'Remember us.' "

ER shared the Roosevelt administration's perception that was so central to its policy that nothing could be done for the Jews until the war was won. Thus, she was unwilling to advocate special activities of rescue, such as the bombing of Auschwitz, that were directed at the victims and not just at war victory. Historians know that the decision regarding rescue through victory was made in 1941 and never reevaluated, as information regarding the full scope of the Nazis' "Final Solution to the Jewish Problem" made it seem ever more unlikely that Jewish refugees would survive the war. In her statement sent on 29 October 1943 to the Emergency Committee to Save the Jewish People of Europe, she reiterated: "The best way (to save as many individuals as possible) is to win the war as rapidly as possible and that the allied armies throughout the world are achieving."

She was, however, willing to protest loudly, clearly, and consistently what was happening and maintained an independent voice, far more forceful than her husband's. In "My Day," 13 August 1943, she wrote, "I do not know what we can do to save the Jews in Europe and to find them homes, but I know that we will be the sufferers if we let great wrongs occur without exerting ourselves to correct them."

ER's attitude toward Zionism* underwent some change during and immediately after the war. She did not see Jews as making up a separate nation but as nationals of the country in which they lived. Shortly after the war, ER visited a Jewish displaced-persons' camp in Zilcheim. She wrote:

Most of all . . . I remember an old woman whose family had been driven from home by the war madness and brutality. I had no idea who she was and we could not speak each other's language, but she knelt in the muddy road and simply threw her arms around my knees. "Israel," she murmured over and over. "Israel! Israel!" (Roosevelt, 56)

In the immediate postwar era, she was a strong supporter of a recommendation that 100,000 Jews be admitted to Palestine and ultimately came to support the recommendation for partition to set up both Jewish and Arab states in Palestine.

SELECTED BIBLIOGRAPHY

Dinnerstein, Leonard. America and the Survivors of the Holocaust. 1982.
Feingold, Henry L. The Politics of Rescue: The Roosevelt Administration and the Holocaust: 1938–1945. 1970.
Morgenthau, Henry, Jr. Morgenthau Diaries. Franklin D. Roosevelt Library, Hyde Park, NY.
Penkower, Monty Noam. The Holocaust and Israel Reborn: From Catastrophe to Sovereignty. 1994.
Roosevelt, Eleanor. On My Own. 1958.
Wyman, David S. The Abandonment of the Jews: America and the Holocaust 1941–1945. 1984.

Michael Berenbaum

HOOVER, HERBERT (10 August 1874, West Branch, IA–20 October 1964, New York).

The relationship between Herbert and Lou Henry Hoover* and Eleanor and Franklin D. Roosevelt* began as a cordial, if somewhat distant,
friendship between the two couples during World War I. Both men
played major roles in the Wilson administration, and both women acted
out the supportive parts of wives socializing to help their husbands'
careers. Over the course of the following four decades, however, ER developed her own personal and bitter conflicts with Herbert Hoover.
While the issues that separated the two hinged on the politics and diplomacy of the FDR administration, they were based on matters that had
increasingly become central to ER in her own right, rather than as FDR's
wife. The growing and increasingly personal conflict between ER and
Hoover thus reflects the trajectory of ER's adult life, as she moved from
matron to public leader.

A Quaker from West Branch, Iowa, who was orphaned at the age of
eight, Herbert Hoover graduated from Stanford University in 1895. He
spent the next twenty years as a mining engineer in Asia, Africa, and
Europe, during which time he amassed a considerable fortune and substantial organizational skills. Finding himself in London when war broke
out in 1914, he volunteered to direct the exodus home of Americans
caught in Europe. From that experience he went on to head the Commission for Relief in Belgium, a position that earned him the reputation
of a great humanitarian—a distinction he lost only after he served as
president during the Great Depression* and found himself unable to lead
the nation through that crisis.

After the United States entered World War I in April 1917, President
Woodrow Wilson called upon Hoover to serve as the national food administrator, where his tasks included encouraging production and conservation and arranging for the distribution of food. In 1918 Wilson
enlisted Hoover to direct the American Relief Administration in war-
ravaged Europe. After the war he joined the cabinets of Harding and
Coolidge as secretary of commerce until 1928, when he defeated Alfred
E. Smith* to become the thirty-first president of the United States. Four
years later FDR easily defeated him. After World War II,* Hoover went
on to serve President Harry S Truman* as coordinator of the European
Food Program (1946–1947) and then headed two commissions, one under
Truman and the other under President Dwight D. Eisenhower,* on the
organization of the executive branch of government.

Hoover and FDR began drifting apart during the early 1920s. ER, however, continued to feel that she could call on the secretary of commerce
to support issues in which she was becoming involved. When ER helped
organize the Bok Peace Prize* competition, sponsored by Edward Bok,
she asked Herbert Hoover to support the award. His response was agreeable, but it was also noncommittal. In 1924 she urged Hoover to support
the regulation of child labor.* By this time relations between FDR and

Hoover had begun seriously to deteriorate. Hoover did not respond to ER's request, but ER seemed merely to take this rebuff in stride and not view it as a reflection of a deep ideological divide.

The hostility between FDR and Hoover was deepened during the campaign of 1932. After Hoover left the White House on 4 March 1933, he refused to step foot inside the Executive Mansion until after FDR had died. There the matter stood, with an occasional letter between ER and Lou Hoover over the Girl Scouts of America—an organization both women strongly supported—until the eve of World War II in Europe, by which time ER had become personally identified with a number of administration policies.

Before Pearl Harbor, Hoover strenuously opposed U.S. involvement in the coming war in Europe. He openly criticized FDR's internationalism, and ER, in turn, publicly rebuked the former president in her "My Day"* column of 3 February 1939. But the real rift between ER and Hoover came soon after Germany attacked Poland on 1 September 1939. The Roosevelts agreed that they wanted Hoover to take over the federal government's relief enterprises, as he had done so ably in World War II. As ER wrote to the novelist Dorothy Canfield Fisher in October 1939, "It seemed to me almost imperative that where the question of relief came up it should be done by one large organization which would take in all the others working in the country." She went on, "I besought them to get Mr. Herbert Hoover to organize civilian relief in all the countries at war today" (ER to DCF, 10 October 1939).

This was a practical issue, and ER saw federal oversight of relief work, at least in part, as a pragmatic administrative matter. She understood that the proliferating number of relief organizations created problems. It prevented effective fund-raising and caused endless duplication of administrative duties. By the end of 1939 there were already 137 organizations, big and small, local and national, well-run and chaotic, registered with the Department of State to solicit funds for medical assistance and food and clothing supplies for Poland alone, all requiring federal supervision in the form of overseeing their registration and observation of State Department rules.

Hoover, however, refused to take on the task. He believed that FDR was using the issue as a means to sidetrack him from politics to relief. He publicly argued that this was the job of the American Red Cross,* although as ER explained to Fisher in her letter of 10 October 1939, it was a task apart "because the Red Cross is an emergency organization and in this country does not accept government money." In the end, ER observed, the assignment of international relief work "would need money from our government."

Hoover instead threw his energies into the Finnish Relief Fund, perhaps because Finland had paid back its debts from World War I on time

244   HOOVER, HERBERT

and had been the only nation to do so. Newspapers across the nation ran headline after headline praising Hoover's work for the Finns—thus angering the administration. He also offered his services for the relief of Poland and described the goal as "the supply of food and clothing to the underfed children in the congested districts and ghettos in Poland, and the care of Polish refugees, now scattered over Europe" (Lerski, 42). In the early months of 1940 Hoover's involvement in Polish affairs increased; but by this time the Roosevelts—as well as the British government—thought this was tantamount to aiding Hitler, who controlled the areas where the Polish aid would go. Britain threatened to block any such effort. Hoover backed down. Finally the Japanese attacked Pearl Harbor, the United States officially went to war, and Hoover, as a loyal U.S. citizen, backed the president.

During the war years, the enmity between Hoover and ER seemed to diminish. When Lou Hoover suddenly died in January 1944, the Roosevelts sent Hoover a telegram expressing their condolences, to which Hoover replied with a handwritten note exclusively addressed to ER. On 14 April 1945, after FDR's death, Hoover wrote to ER, "I need not tell you of the millions whose hearts are going out to you in sympathy. I want you to know that I join with them" (Walch and Miller, 206). But by the late 1940s their old animosity had been revived. The deep ideological differences between the two made public conflict almost inevitable.

In 1949 ER published the second volume of her autobiography, *This I Remember*, which was first serialized in *McCall's*.* She included a description of Hoover's handling in 1932 of the Bonus March of World War I veterans seeking a promised bonus ahead of schedule, and expressed shock over the use of the army to drive the marchers out of their camp. Angered by her comments, Hoover threatened a libel suit against *McCall's*. In its November 1949 issue, the magazine provided space for a rebuttal by a Hoover supporter as well as an apology by ER for any offense or misstatement she had made, but the feud had been rekindled.

ER continued to espouse the New Deal* in ways that included criticism of Hoover. In her "My Day" column of 5 October 1951, for example, she defended the Roosevelt administration against accusations that its New Deal programs included "dangerous and socialist" schemes, explaining to her readers that "occasionally I get a letter from someone who feels that in this country we have lost the old virtues of standing on our own." To maintain this position, she argued, was to forget the conditions that prevailed when FDR took office. Parts of the nation were ready for revolution, she wrote, "and that condition was brought about by the conservative, orthodox business methods that prevailed under the experienced men of business under President Herbert Hoover and his very able Cabinet" (Emblidge, 241–42). She continued in her columns to de-fend the New Deal—and in the process to attack Hoover—well into the 1950s.

ER and Hoover did not alter their basic political positions. Their early years of collegial friendship had been based on FDR and Hoover's alle-giance to the wartime goals of Woodrow Wilson and ER's supportive role as Mrs. Roosevelt. As First Lady and journalist, she defended her husband's policies against conservatives. As a widow with a political stature of her own, she asserted her basic political ideals. In so doing she denounced her erstwhile friend turned bitter enemy.

SELECTED BIBLIOGRAPHY

Eleanor Roosevelt Papers, Franklin D. Roosevelt Library, Hyde Park, NY.

Emblidge, David, ed. *Eleanor Roosevelt's "My Day."* Vol. 2. 1990.

Lerski, George J., ed. *Herbert Hoover and Poland.* 1977.

Lisio, Donald. *The President and Protest: Hoover, Conspiracy, and the Bonus Riot.* 1994.

Roosevelt, Eleanor. *This I Remember.* 1949.

Walch, Timothy, and Dwight M. Miller, eds. *Herbert Hoover and Franklin D. Roosevelt: A Documentary History.* 1998.

HOOVER, LOU HENRY (29 March 1874, Waterloo, IA–7 January 1944, New York).

Eleanor Roosevelt's relationship with the Hoover presidency was more a matter of image than substance. The comparison rather than the inter-relationship helped define the changing role of the twentieth-century First Lady.

Lou Henry Hoover, a graduate of Stanford University, was an active woman who helped to found the Girl Scouts and who traveled the world her entire adult life. Her vigorous spirit, however, did not lead to either press influence or personal political achievement. Unlike ER, she lived comfortably in the shadow of her husband.

President Herbert Hoover* was so protective of his family that he voiced loud complaints whenever reporters chose to write about his wife or family. He believed that a woman, even a First Lady, should remain in the background and never be subjected to intense reporting. During both the 1932 and 1928 elections, Hoover ordered his election staffs not to refer to the wives of his opponents in any way. When one campaign adviser suggested that the relationship of Franklin D. Roosevelt* with other women should be exploited as an election issue in 1932, the idea was soundly rejected.

Lou Henry Hoover and ER visited at the White House on 28 January 1933, five weeks before Franklin Roosevelt took office. According to the notes of Mildred Hall, a Hoover aide, ER toured the White House with

Mrs. Hoover for about an hour. The First Lady–elect and the resident First Lady chatted about curtains, decorating, furniture, pictures, and the history of the White House. The uneventful visit ended with the pair politely exchanging pleasantries at the door.

While Lou Henry Hoover had been far more active in civic affairs than either Florence Harding or Grace Coolidge, and though she had helped to write books and articles with her husband before they entered the White House, her traditional lifestyle presents a striking comparison with that of her successor. ER's travels* on behalf of her husband during his administration, her newspaper column, and her public visibility represented what would increasingly be the First Ladyship of the future. Lou Henry Hoover's stewardship in the White House represented the matronly First Ladyship of the past.

In addition to her genuine compassion and her determination, perhaps what made ER a memorable historical figure was her pride in being a successful, independent woman who was ahead of her time. Mrs. Hoover was also intelligent and individualistic but was careful never to call attention to herself. Just as FDR helped to invent big government, ER redefined the role of the First Lady. The comparison to the Hoover era particularly helps to place this activity into focus.

SELECTED BIBLIOGRAPHY

Mildred Hall notes, Eleanor Roosevelt file, Herbert Hoover Presidential Library, West Branch, IA.

Louis Liebovich

HOPKINS, HARRY LLOYD (17 August 1890, Sioux City, IA–29 January 1946, New York).

Harry Hopkins became one of the closest advisers of President Franklin D. Roosevelt,* directing relief programs to combat massive unemployment during the Great Depression,* and functioning, in effect, as the nation's first security adviser during World War II.* Early in the New Deal,* Eleanor Roosevelt worked closely with Hopkins on relief issues. She introduced him to the White House inner circle, arranging opportunities for the president to get to know him better. She took an active interest in furthering his career and was solicitous of him and his five-year-old daughter, Diane, after his wife, Barbara, died in 1937. Soon thereafter Hopkins moved into the White House, and his allegiance and friendship gradually shifted from ER to FDR. During the war years ER was unhappy with Hopkins' total commitment to winning the war without regard for the social issues that had previously commanded his interest. She was, as Harold Ickes* noted, "off of Harry" (Lash, 505).

Hopkins graduated from Grinnell College in 1912. A star basketball player, an average student, and a natural leader during his college years, Hopkins had no particular goal in mind when he took a job as a social worker on the Lower East Side in New York City. Here he encountered wrenching poverty amid vast wealth. During the ensuing two decades, Hopkins gained recognition as a tough and tireless problem solver and administrator possessed with an evocative and often profane manner of speech, suggesting that his idealism was mixed with cynicism.

In 1931 FDR, as governor of New York, recruited Hopkins as director of the nation's first executive agency to combat unemployment during the depression. As the New Deal got under way, the president brought Hopkins to Washington to direct federal relief programs. In May 1933 Hopkins became administrator of the Federal Emergency Relief Administration (FERA), created primarily to give grants to states for relief programs. In November 1933 he was also named administrator of the short-lived federal Civil Works Administration, which employed over 4 million needy individuals in the winter of 1933–1934. From May 1935 until December 1938 he directed the Works Progress Administration* (WPA), which provided federally funded jobs instead of relief payments to the able-bodied unemployed. These positions led Hopkins to employ more people and spend more money than any previous individual in U.S. history.

They also led to frequent contact with ER. She was soon on a first-name basis with Hopkins as she referred to him many of the appeals for assistance she received from persons hurt by the depression and often followed up her referrals with inquiries and suggestions. Hopkins' receptivity to ER's special interest in the needs of women and young people further expanded consultations between the two, as Hopkins established in both the FERA and WPA a division of women's programs and devised proposals for the National Youth Administration,* which was created in 1935.

As "minister of relief," billions of dollars passed through Hopkins' hands without a hint of scandal. Critics, however, considered him a squanderer of the taxpayers' money and coined the term "boondoggle" to describe his projects. Since Hopkins never recognized party as a criterion for holding a job, he aroused the ire of many Democrats clamoring for the spoils of victory.

FDR, recognizing his ability and the scandal-free nature of his massive spending programs, stood by Hopkins and soon placed more trust in him. The president bestowed more responsibilities upon him, such as a survey in 1938 of how the U.S. aircraft manufacturing industry might be expanded in the event of war. In December 1938 FDR appointed Hopkins secretary of commerce, giving him a base to launch a possible political career.

The following year was a traumatic one for the world, with war breaking out in Europe, and for Hopkins, whose health collapsed. Although he remained secretary of commerce until resigning in August 1940, serious illness limited his work. He had recovered from an operation for stomach cancer in 1937, but he became ill again early in 1939, was hospitalized in August, and spent the remainder of the year convalescing from a digestive deficiency disease. It became a recurring and debilitating ailment.

In December 1938 ER suggested to Hopkins that she act as guardian for his daughter, Diana, then six years old, in the event of his death or incapacity. He accepted her suggestion, and ER oversaw the care of Diana for extended periods until Hopkins' marriage to Louise Macy in July 1942. Remembering ER's role years later, Diana Hopkins commented that ER "found it difficult to relate easily to children" (Halsted, 3). She said ER "did everything that you would normally do with a child as a mother except [offer] warm affection" (28).

On 10 May 1940 Hopkins remained overnight at the White House after becoming ill. He stayed there, accompanied by Diana, for most of the next three and a half years. His resignation from the Department of Commerce temporarily left him without official standing in the government, but he was soon drawn into assisting in FDR's 1940 campaign for reelection. In January 1941 FDR sent Hopkins to London during the German air raids to see Winston Churchill.* The prime minister's bulldog defiance convinced Hopkins that with American assistance Britain would survive, and he so cabled the president. In March 1941 FDR returned Hopkins to the federal payroll as a presidential assistant and placed him in charge of the Lend-Lease program to provide supplies and military equipment to countries fighting the Axis powers.

In June 1941 Hopkins went to Moscow for talks with Joseph Stalin and concluded that Russia, with American planes, aluminum, and other critical war materials, could hold off the Nazis. Hopkins accompanied FDR to wartime conferences of Allied leaders at Cairo, Casablanca, Quebec, and Tehran in 1943 and at Yalta in 1945.

By 1945 the health of both FDR and Hopkins was failing. On the way back from Yalta, Hopkins left the battleship carrying the president and flew for treatment to the Mayo Clinic in Rochester, Minnesota. They never saw one another again. Weeks later FDR was dead. Though Hopkins seemed near death, at the request of President Harry S Truman,* Hopkins went again to Moscow in May 1945, where he managed to break a deadlock over the organization of the United Nations.*

Hopkins left public service in July 1945, was awarded the Distinguished Service Medal by President Truman in September 1945, and died in January 1946.

SELECTED BIBLIOGRAPHY

Eleanor Roosevelt Oral History Project, Interview with Diana Hopkins Halsted (1979), Franklin D. Roosevelt Library, Hyde Park, NY.
Lash, Joseph P. *Eleanor and Franklin.* 1971.

McJimsey, George. *Harry Hopkins*. 1987.
Roosevelt, Eleanor. *This I Remember*. 1949.
Searle, Charles F. *Minister of Relief: Harry Hopkins and the Depression*. 1963.
Sherwood, Robert E. *Roosevelt and Hopkins*. 1948.

Richard Lowitt

HORNADAY, MARY (5 April 1906, Washington, DC–20 April 1982, Riverdale, NY).

Mary Hornaday was a Washington, foreign, and United Nations* correspondent for the *Christian Science Monitor* for forty-one years. For twenty-nine years, her professional life was entwined with Eleanor Roosevelt's career, beginning in 1933, when she attended the first of ER's White House press conferences* and continuing through ER's years at the United Nations.

Hornaday's unbiased reporting and interpretive columns on national and international subjects were well regarded by colleagues of both sexes. Peer respect was manifested by her election in 1942 as the first chair of Mrs. Roosevelt's Press Conference Association. Later she became the first woman to serve as acting president of the Overseas Press Club in New York.

Hornaday scrupulously avoided becoming part of the inner circle of women journalists who covered ER's press conferences. She believed that personal closeness could be perceived as affecting her professional objectivity—a quality extolled by her journalist father, who was Washington correspondent for the *Indianapolis News*, as well as two brothers and an uncle, who also were journalists.

Her career with the *Christian Science Monitor* started in its Washington bureau in 1927, when she was twenty-one years old, after her graduation with honors from Swarthmore College. Her early mentor was the bureau chief, Cora Rigby, a founder and seven-term president of the Women's National Press Club.* Hornaday was elected club president in 1936.

Hornaday was one of the few reporters to cover all twelve years of ER's White House press conferences, from 1933 to 1945. In an unpublished memoir, she recalled one conference attended by ER's mother-in-law, Sara Delano Roosevelt,* "who wore an expression of incredulity, if not disgust, throughout" (Hornaday, 3). Hornaday remarked years later that ER appeared insecure at the early conferences, as shown by "that nervous little laugh" (Beasley, 109). Yet, Hornaday also saw the conferences as "a school to elevate women's consciousness" and not just a platform for ER (Beasley, 119).

A rare exception to Hornaday's relatively impersonal relationship with ER was a warm reunion in London on 28 January 1946. Hornaday, who had been sent overseas to cover relief efforts in Europe, gave a tea to introduce ER, recently named a U.S. delegate to the United Nations, to

British newswomen. Writing her mother afterward, Hornaday said that she thought ER "was a great woman," adding, "She's nobody's fool either, the way she sees through things that are going on. I guess she didn't live twelve years in the White House for nothing" (MH to her mother, 28 January 1946).

The postwar years for both ER and Hornaday were devoted to working for a lasting world peace. Hornaday's dispatches from war-torn Europe brought her the Order of Beneficence from Greece's King Paul. Subsequently assigned to the United Nations, she followed ER's activities there. Recalling one interview, Hornaday wrote: "Eleanor Roosevelt had a certain regalness about her, though we have no royalty in this country. Once while interviewing her I broke my pencil. Do you think she got up to get me another? . . . I struggled" (Hornaday, 3). During this interview ER expressed hope that her work on the Universal Declaration of Human Rights* would be considered her highest achievement.

With her white hair, sturdy build, and down-to-earth manner, Hornaday became a familiar figure in the hallways of the United Nations (UN), which she continued to cover until her retirement in 1968. As a volunteer she then served as the official UN observer for the Women's International League for Peace and Freedom.

In her memoir she said, "I never believed in letting my personal and professional life mix and it seldom did. . . . relations [with ER] were on a purely professional basis. She was the source of many good humanitarian stories for me" (Hornaday, 4).

SELECTED BIBLIOGRAPHY
Ann Cottrell Free Papers, Personal Collection, Bethesda, MD.
Beasley, Maurine H. *Eleanor Roosevelt and the Media: A Public Quest for Self-Fulfillment.* 1987.
Canham, Erwin D. *Commitment to Freedom, the Story of the Christian Science Monitor.* 1958.
Mary Hornaday Papers, Archive of Contemporary History, University of Wyoming, Laramie, WY.
Ross, Ishbel. *Ladies of the Press.* 1936.

Ann Cottrell Free

HOUSE COMMITTEE TO INVESTIGATE UN-AMERICAN ACTIVITIES. The House Special Committee to Investigate Un-American Activities (known as the House Un-American Activities Committee, or HUAC) was the most significant of three special House committees formed in the 1930s to examine domestic subversion. Eleanor Roosevelt was an early and frequent opponent of HUAC, writing in her "My Day"* column on 29 October 1947, "I have never liked the idea of an Un-American Activities Committee. I have always thought that a strong democracy should stand by its fundamental beliefs and that a citizen of the United

States should be considered innocent until he is proven guilty" (Emblidge, 115).

Created in 1938, the committee functioned until Congress* disbanded it in 1975. Its members and its witnesses often equated liberalism with communism and blamed the New Deal* for supposed communist advances in the public and private sector. The committee purposefully overestimated the threat that domestic communism posed, while it usually ignored right-wing radical organizations.

Martin Dies, a Texas Democrat and HUAC's first chair, often targeted for investigation organizations in which ER held memberships or with which she shared sympathy. The First Lady tried unsuccessfully to dissuade Dies from attacking people and organizations without factual evidence. In 1938 Dies attacked the Federal Theater Project (FTP), a New Deal relief program headed by Hallie Flanagan* under the aegis of the Works Progress Administration,* for presenting plays that he believed advanced communism. ER showed her solidarity with the FTP by attending its performances.

In November 1939 ER attended HUAC hearings at which leaders of the American Student Union* (ASU) and the American Youth Congress* (AYC) were called to testify about communist connections. When she moved to the press table at a tense moment in the questioning, committee members moderated their tone. Her action caused mixed reactions among liberals. Some praised her for championing free speech, while others expressed concern about her choice of causes.

During World War II* Dies renewed his committee's powers in each session of Congress, even if he no longer gained headlines. There were a few noteworthy attacks on ER and her friends. In February 1942 Dies and the committee suggested that the Office of Civilian Defense* (OCD) suffered from communist infiltration and noted that ER worked as the unpaid assistant director for the OCD. In 1944 HUAC investigated the Political Action Committee (PAC) of the Congress of Industrial Organizations (CIO), claiming it had made illegal political contributions. Dies examined the communications between the PAC and the administration, including ER, and arranged for Westbrook Pegler,* a right-wing journalist, to receive a copy of the report. Without proof, Dies publicly charged Vice President Henry Wallace* in March 1942 with harboring members of communist-front organizations in the Board of Economic Warfare. Wallace's rebuttal brought praise from ER.

Dies retired from Congress at the end of 1944. Moderates and liberals hoped that HUAC would disappear with Dies. Conservatives ensured its longevity by turning HUAC into the standing Committee on Un-American Activities. In 1947, after the Republicans gained control of Congress, J. Parnell Thomas, a New Jersey Republican who had served on the committee since its inception, began to investigate communist influence in the movie industry. One of the first hearings in May 1947 involved Hanns Eisler, a German composer who had immigrated to the United States during World War II.* Eisler was a vehicle for the committee to attack ER. In 1939 she had written letters to the secretary of state on behalf of Eisler, as she had for other Jews* seeking asylum, but HUAC suggested this had been part of a plot against national security.

Ten motion picture writers and directors defied the committee and refused to discuss their political views or activities. The "Hollywood Ten," as they were known, received contempt of Congress citations, for which they were later convicted. An industry blacklist prevented individuals known or rumored to hold communist views from working in film, television,* and radio.* In response, ER in her "My Day" column, 29 October 1947, said, "I was surprised to find that, at the start of the inquiry, some of the big producers were so chicken-hearted about speaking up for the freedom of their industry." She did not doubt the presence of some with communist leanings within Hollywood, but neither did she endorse government censorship. Saying that the committee "is growing more ludicrous daily," ER argued that "the judge who decides whether what [the film industry] does is good or bad is the man or woman who attends the movies" (Emblidge, 114–115). She compared the tactics of HUAC with those of a police state.

HUAC's attack on popular culture was just one problem ER identified. She worried more about the exacerbation of the Red Scare mentality in Washington by Richard Nixon, who had been elected to Congress in 1946 and gained a seat on HUAC in 1947. She feared that his skill as a legislator would increase the dangers HUAC posed. He coauthored legislation requiring the registration of all communist organizations with the Justice Department and generally curtailing civil liberties. The proposal was folded into the Internal Security Act of 1950.

In the summer of 1948, Nixon and the committee began hearings on alleged Soviet spy operations in the United States during and before World War II. Two self-confessed former communists, Elizabeth Bentley and Whittaker Chambers, named as communists various individuals who had held government positions in the 1930s and 1940s. Most of those named refused comment, but Alger Hiss, the head of the Carnegie Endowment for International Peace and a former State Department official, proclaimed his innocence. Hiss maintained close friendships with Washington's liberal intellectuals. The latter contacts provided him with a chorus of defenders, including ER. After a series of convoluted revelations, Hiss lost many of his friends and was convicted of perjury. ER, like some other liberals, remained a Hiss defender because she believed he was a victim of a HUAC witch-hunt.

ER also defended others attacked by the committee. In March 1948, when HUAC released a specious report that Dr. Edward Condon, a scientist who was director of the National Bureau of Standards, was "one of the weakest links in our atomic security" (Goodman, 231), ER joined scientists throughout the country in rallying behind him. As a result, Representative John Rankin, a Mississippi Democrat who was incensed over her criticism of HUAC, told Congress that "Mrs. Roosevelt has done more harm than any other woman since Cleopatra" (Black, 151). Unfazed, she argued that Rankin and the committee by their actions discouraged independent thought.

When HUAC in the mid-1950s began investigating the links between the Civil Rights* movement and communism, ER remained steadfast in her defense of free political speech and association. Her anti-HUAC statements ebbed and flowed in direct proportion to the committee's public activities. HUAC's interaction with the former First Lady and her friends, however, diminished in the 1950s, when public attention turned to Senator Joseph McCarthy and his anticommunist crusade, which became known as McCarthyism.* By the time ER died in 1962, HUAC had lost much of its public support. It changed its name in 1969 to the House Committee on Internal Security and was eliminated in 1975.

SELECTED BIBLIOGRAPHY

Bentley, Eric, ed. *Thirty Years of Treason: Excerpts from Hearings before the House Committee on Un-American Activities, 1938–1968.* 1971.

Black, Allida. *Casting Her Own Shadow: Eleanor Roosevelt and the Shaping of Postwar Liberalism.* 1996.

Emblidge, David, ed. *Eleanor Roosevelt's "My Day."* Vol. 2. 1990.

Goodman, Walter. *The Committee: The Extraordinary Career of the House Committee on Un-American Activities.* 1968.

Ogden, August Raymond. *The Dies Committee: A Study of the Special House Committee for the Investigation of Un-American Activities, 1938–1944.* 1945.

Nancy Beck Young

HOWE, LOUIS MCHENRY (14 January 1871, Indianapolis–18 April 1936, Washington, DC).

Howe, devoted friend, adviser, and associate to both Roosevelts, was Eleanor Roosevelt's political mentor.

Howe's greatest influence happened before the White House years. Initially, Eleanor Roosevelt saw Howe as an odd, disheveled, chain-smoking gnome who was impressed with leadership by Franklin D. Roosevelt* of an insurgency movement in the New York legislature against the senatorial candidate of the Tammany political machine. Howe, an Albany correspondent for the *New York Herald* and the *New York Telegram*, acted as an informal adviser of the Insurgents, offered them suggestions for publicity, and wrote favorable columns about the group, especially FDR, whom he said was the man to watch. While Howe's constant presence near FDR bothered ER, she later wrote, that "though it took me a long while to appreciate him, I came to admire his loyalty and great ability to manipulate people and events to achieve his ends" (Roosevelt, *This I Remember*, 65).

When FDR went to Washington as assistant secretary of the navy, Howe served as his doorkeeper, as well as planner and political conspirator. When FDR ran for vice president in 1920, Howe helped with his speeches and press releases and carefully cultivated the Associated Press men on long campaign train tours. He also began a conscious program of educating ER in the wiles of politics. ER developed a warm friendship with Howe's wife, Grace, with whom she exchanged small gifts and favors.

After FDR's poliomyelitis, Howe became ER's partner in keeping FDR's career alive. Howe handled business and political correspondence, which FDR initially could not even sign after his illness. Howe also became ER's most trusted adviser and behind-the-scenes public relations manager. During the 1920s he encouraged her to join the League of Women Voters* and other organizations and to become more politically active. Howe convinced her to write and edit political tracts, such as the monthly *Women's Democratic News*,* and to use her organizing skills for the Democratic Party.* Under his direction ER became a leader of the Dutchess County delegation to the 1922 state Democratic Convention. Moreover, she brought home people who kept FDR interested in state politics. Later, ER wrote that "this political work was done largely at the instigation of Louis Howe" (Roosevelt, *This I Remember*, 29).

Howe helped ER develop her communication skills in a number of ways. In the early 1920s a then-shy Eleanor Roosevelt would struggle with speeches,* while Howe sat listening in the back row and pointing out her mistakes afterward. He helped her gain confidence in her ideas, her advocacy for social reform, and her ability to respond to reporters. He also acted as her literary agent. When FDR became governor of New York in 1929, Howe directed her visits to institutions on behalf of her husband as governor and, after 1932, to various social assistance programs on his behalf as president.

When the Roosevelts moved to the White House, Howe's official title was secretary to the president. Frail by this time, Howe lived in the Lincoln bedroom and had an inside office where he did not have to meet the public but was immediately available to FDR and ER at all times. There, he encouraged ER's unprecedented public role as First Lady. He often wrote ER when she was away and once joked grimly with reporters that he and Mrs. Roosevelt were running a contest to see which one had the ugliest news photo. Howe continued to be both Roosevelts' troubleshooter until his illness worsened by 1935.

Howe's publicity tactics helped the administration, picturing ER as her husband's partner. After the 1933 inauguration, he took ER to a camp near Washington where a contentious group of bonus marchers (World War I veterans seeking a pension) had gathered, staying in the car while ER went in alone. Although ER did not offer the former soldiers the pension checks they wanted, she brought a spirit of friendship and empathy. The meeting was friendly and nostalgic as she sang old war songs with the men. The often-quoted response to this method of quieting a potential storm was that "Hoover sent the Army, Roosevelt sent his wife" (Rollins, 389). (This was a reference to the fact that President Herbert Hoover* had directed the army to clear away an earlier encampment.)

Howe advised ER about her own press meetings. He not only encouraged her to hold press conferences* on a regular basis but helped her prepare for her first press meeting and any possible "loaded questions" (Stiles, 264). When ER decided to have Gridiron widows' parties for women excluded from the annual dinners of the then all-male Gridiron club, an organization of elite Washington correspondents, Howe made suggestions for a variety of skits.

Howe enthusiastically worked for three New Deal* programs: the Civilian Conservation Corps, the anticrime crusade, and the subsistence homestead experiment to relocate the unemployed. Howe's endless publicity efforts through radio speeches and major news articles in the country's large circulation magazines, such as the *Saturday Evening Post*, helped push these pet projects. ER, particularly interested in housing, gave boundless energy to one of these: the Arthurdale* resettlement community for miners in West Virginia. Despite Howe's radio addresses on construction progress there, however, cost overruns and mismanagement became a scandal, and he withdrew from the program in 1934.

Howe's physical condition so deteriorated by 1935 that he could no longer live in the White House and was moved to the Navy Hospital in Washington. On the day of his death there in April 1936, his publicity legacy was being played out with FDR sitting with the male correspondents at the Gridiron dinner, while ER entertained the "widows." By then, both Roosevelts had turned to others for press conference advice, literary agentry, and public relations.

Unlike so many Roosevelt associates, Louis Howe had a remarkable partnership with both Roosevelts. Howe had not been a Machiavellian figure nor a hearth dog but rather held a reciprocal relationship, as a close family friend. Years later, ER wrote in a *Look* magazine article that Howe was one of seven individuals who had most influenced her life.

SELECTED BIBLIOGRAPHY

Louis McHenry Howe Papers, Franklin D. Roosevelt Library, Hyde Park, NY.
Rollins, Alfred B., Jr. *Roosevelt and Howe*. 1962.

Roosevelt, Eleanor. "The Seven People Who Shaped My Life." *Look* 15 (19 June 1951): 56.

———. *This I Remember*. 1949.

Stiles, Lila. *The Man behind Roosevelt: The Story of Louis McHenry Howe*. 1954.

Winfield, Betty Houchin. *FDR and the News Media*. 1990.

Betty Houchin Winfield

HUMAN RIGHTS, INTERNATIONALIZATION OF. World War II* and the Holocaust* internationalized human rights, with the work of Eleanor Roosevelt playing a pivotal role. Until the United Nations* (UN) was born, the treatment of people by their own governments, however arbitrary and brutal, was considered beyond the realm of legitimate intergovernmental discourse. There had been only sporadic attempts earlier to subject certain aspects of human rights to international scrutiny. Woodrow Wilson, for example, had made a world safe for democracy foremost among America's war aims in World War I, but the League of Nations* Covenant that he championed explicitly rejected consideration of what we now call human rights violations. Some brief, largely ineffectual efforts were made during the league period to introduce international protections for national minorities. The UN Charter, however, changed all that. Initially, at the insistence of the United States and even more under the pressure of some small Latin American states and influential nongovernmental organizations (NGOs), the charter broke all precedents for international agreements by mandating that this new international organization promote human rights. Yet, it also included the ritual bow to national sovereignty in Article 2(7), prohibiting the United Nations from interfering in matters essentially within the domestic jurisdiction of states.

Although the UN Charter, responding to World War II and the Holocaust, internationalized human rights, there remained the enormous tasks of defining those rights, determining how they should be protected, and reconciling the apparent conflicts between human rights protections and national sovereignty. These daunting tasks fell initially on the shoulders of ER, who, as the first chairperson of the UN Human Rights Commission, had to put flesh on the bare-bones references to human rights in the charter. ER faced a formidable set of difficulties—a U.S. State Department and Congress* doubtful about the wisdom and efficacy of genuine multilateral protections for human rights, an influential Soviet Union ideologically committed to priority for economic rights and more interested in the rights of states than in human rights, a United Kingdom hesitant to endorse any approach that might increase pressures on the British imperial system, and peoples from around the world whose traditions did not fit neatly in the evolution of Western ideas about human rights. But she also had some powerful allies in a number of deeply

Ann Cottrell, a reporter for the *New York Herald Tribune* and former chair of Mrs. Roosevelt's Press Conference Association, interviews Eleanor Roosevelt on 4 December 1947, in Geneva on the work of the UN Human Rights Commission. *Courtesy of Ann Cottrell Free*

committed representatives of NGOs, some highly skilled fellow members of the commission, including Rene Cassin of France and Charles Malik of Lebanon, and a capable and committed Secretariat staff led by the Canadian lawyer John P. Humphrey. She confronted widespread popular expectations that here at last was an organization, an institution, an agent that could and would do something to stop the abuses of human rights that had filled the international community with such a profound sense of revulsion.

Although there was a great deal of sentiment for moving directly to formal legal protections for human rights at the international level—an international bill of rights, as it was called in specific reference to the American Bill of Rights, added to the U.S. Constitution shortly after its ratification—ER was convinced that such an exercise would almost certainly be drawn out by legal squabbles and evolving political disputes. She believed that the establishment of the Human Rights Commission mandated by the charter created an unusual opportunity to respond promptly to the insistent expectations of peoples around the world. She believed the moment should be seized to create a document spelling out the content of the human rights now enshrined in the charter, a document expressing for the first time a global standard of human rights, a document that, while not binding in a formal, legal sense, would provide an international tool people could use in their varied struggles for human rights all around the globe—a Universal Declaration of Human Rights.*

From her long experience with American labor,* woman's rights, and civil rights,* however, ER also had a deep appreciation of the importance of legally binding protections as well as declarative standards of rights. She supported—indeed, she managed—the development of binding treaties by the United Nations. When it became clear that international human rights instruments would have to include notions of economic and social rights growing out of the European socialist tradition as well as the individual civil and political rights more familiar in the American tradition, ER urged that the two concepts be embodied in separate binding treaties. She knew that the United States would find it difficult to embrace binding concepts of economic and social rights, and she did not want her country to find itself unable to adhere to international protective instruments because they incorporated unfamiliar rights. Although the UN majority initially favored a single "Bill of Rights," the American position ultimately prevailed, and the International Bill of Rights came to be thought of as including the Universal Declaration of Human Rights, the International Covenant on Civil and Political Rights, and the International Covenant on Economic, Social, and Cultural Rights.

Under ER's leadership, the Human Rights Commission gave priority to a nonbinding declaration, though it continued to work on legally binding treaties at the same time. The Universal Declaration of Human Rights was adopted without dissent by the UN General Assembly on 10 December 1948, barely two and one-half years after the first meeting of the Commission on Human Rights. Although the bulk of the work on the two main binding covenants or treaties was complete before ER left the commission in 1953, the General Assembly did not finally approve them until 1966, and they entered into force only in 1976. The United States waited until 1976 to sign the binding covenants and ratified the Covenant on Civil and Political Rights only in 1992. U.S. ratification of the Covenant on Economic, Social, and Cultural Rights is still pending.

The United States did not participate in the final stages of drafting the two covenants. Abandoning the approach pioneered by ER, the administration of President Dwight D. Eisenhower* asked for her resignation and denounced the Human Rights Commission's efforts to develop binding human rights treaties. ER's human rights work—coupled with her continued prominence in the domestic American civil rights struggle— generated fear in certain quarters in Washington that the power given treaties under the U.S. Constitution might be used to alter patterns of racial segregation in the American South. Building on that fear, Republican senator John W. Bricker of Ohio proposed to amend the Constitution by limiting the president's authority with respect to treaties. President Eisenhower and his secretary of state, John Foster Dulles,* who had worked with ER earlier at the United Nations, decided that the most effective way of undercutting support for the Bricker amendment was by withdrawing U.S. participation from the effort to write binding human rights treaties.

Never again was the United States to provide the kind of leadership and support for the multilateral human rights effort that it did during ER's tenure on the UN Human Rights Commission. When the Congress and President Jimmy Carter rediscovered the relevance of the American experience to the global human rights situation in the 1970s, they chose a more unilateral approach, using American foreign assistance policies and unilateral sanctions in an attempt to enforce American concepts of human rights abroad rather than to participate in the kind of global effort at standard-setting and institution-building that the United States led in the 1940s. Although American statutory law is well sprinkled with references to "internationally recognized human rights," in fact, U.S. human rights policies at the turn of this century are characterized by unilateral assertiveness and multilateral timidity.

Meanwhile, though human rights abuses continued at an alarming and probably growing rate, peoples throughout the world struggled to build institutions and processes that protect human rights more effectively. In most cases they drew their inspiration and their sense of direction from the Universal Declaration of Human Rights. The Europeans, with specific reference to the Universal Declaration, created an elaborate regional system of legal and judicial protections for human rights. The Latin Americans, also with specific reference to the Universal Declaration, established a more limited variant but one that nonetheless offers some regional protection against human rights abuses. An African Human Rights Convention and Commission were created, based in part on the specific guarantees from the Universal Declaration, which were incorporated into many African constitutions when those countries achieved independence in the 1960s and beyond. A multiplicity of NGOs drew inspiration and sustenance from the Universal Declaration of Human Rights as they refused to accept claims of national sovereignty as legitimate limitations on their work. Many international lawyers came to view the Universal Declaration of Human Rights as a document of binding legal force in the international community both as customary international law and as the most widely accepted specification of the meaning of the human rights protected by the UN Charter, a binding international treaty.

The internationalization of human rights since World War II has been dramatic, and it has been profound, but it has been largely confined to the setting of standards. Enforcement has lagged seriously behind. Although the Human Rights Commission was charged early on with exploring implementation mechanisms, it never really made much progress in this area. It quickly decided that the consideration of specific complaints of human rights violations was beyond its competence, indeed, that it could not even take cognizance of complaints sent to it. Much of its work since then, especially since it completed the drafting process for the two major covenants in 1966, has involved a cautious expansion of its own limited powers of investigation and enforcement. There are those who argue that the commission should have boldly seized the implementation initiative as it did in standard-setting. But most of the members, including ER, believed member states would consider implementation an even greater intrusion into domestic jurisdiction than standard-setting, one they would probably regard as intolerable. Thus, enforcement has been largely left to the judicial and political pressures of regional organizations and the procedures of publicity and public pressure developed by NGOs.

SELECTED BIBLIOGRAPHY

Donnelly, Jack. *International Human Rights*. 1998.
Johnson, M. Glen. "The Contributions of Eleanor and Franklin Roosevelt to the Development of International Protection for Human Rights." *Human Rights Quarterly* 9 (February 1987): 19–48.
Johnson, M. Glen, and Janusz Symonides. *The Universal Declaration of Human Rights, 1948–1998*. 1998.

M. Glen Johnson

HURST, FANNIE (19 October 1885, Hamilton, OH–23 February 1968, New York).

An exchange of short notes brought Fannie Hurst to Eleanor Roosevelt's attention in the spring of 1931. A brilliantly successful career as a short story writer and novelist with a weekly syndicated column had given Hurst one of America's most recognized names. She was a national opinion-maker who regularly publicized worthy causes, the kind of presence the Roosevelts were glad to welcome into their camp.

A friendship was carefully cultivated. A September 1931 lunch with ER in her New York home led to Hurst's "unforgettable" overnight visit at the governor's mansion in Albany in November (Hurst to ER, 9 November 1931). It brought the opportunity for Marguerite "Missy" LeHand* to drive Hurst around in the company of Franklin D. Roosevelt* himself as he helped her look for farms to buy in Dutchess County, where the Roosevelt estate was located. This was followed by lunch at the Roosevelt home at Hyde Park* and a tour of Val-Kill.* Hurst gave a small, select lunch for ER that December, sealing their personal bond.

As soon as FDR was nominated for president, Hurst offered to "raise my pen" in his campaign (FH to FDR, 1 July 1932). Separate notes of acknowledgment came from both FDR and ER, and Hurst, who had never before allied with a major political party, made a well-received broadcast in support of FDR shortly before the November election. Over the years, Hurst often spoke unofficially in behalf of the administration in general and ER in particular, continuing the praise she first had given in a short address at a New York dinner of tribute to ER in February 1932. Subsequently, Hurst incorporated support for the New Deal* into her radio addresses, lectures, and articles.

Hurst served on ER's committee to foster the establishment of recreational centers—called "rest rooms"—for unemployed young women. She spoke on behalf of the cause whenever called upon and recruited both Millicent Hearst, wife of William Randolph Hearst, and Helen (Mrs. Vincent) Astor, to be its cochairs. Once FDR was in the White House, Hurst renewed her offer to ER directly "to perform any services in your behalf for which you think I may be especially fitted" (FH to ER, 8 March 1933). At ER's request, she helped with a tribute dinner in honor of secretary of labor Frances Perkins,* even though Hurst, who had campaigned vigorously to get a woman into the president's cabinet, had hoped her friend, Ruth Bryan Owen, would be the first woman to receive such an offer. Through ER, Perkins, Molly Dewson,* Nancy Cook,* Mary Dreier,* and other women active in the Democratic Party* became Hurst's warm acquaintances.

The "grandeur" of the Roosevelts dazzled Hurst, and her devotion to ER was unfailing (Hurst to Rosamond Pinchot Gaston, 7 December 1933). She saw it as her personal task to interpret the First Lady to a sometimes unreceptive public. In an address at Rollins College, 25 February 1934, Hurst declared that ER was "the first-lady-of-the-land-without-precedent . . . the living, animated and animating symbol" of the potential of American women. "By admitting her transcendency," Hurst continued, "we admit our own."

Hurst was a favored and repeated overnight guest in the Roosevelt White House. She was among the select women invitees to the private dinner and White House overnight that came before and after ER's larger "Gridiron widow's" party, staged as a counterfoil to the annual all-male Gridiron dinner of the Washington press corps. Hurst also stayed at the White House on less formal occasions, tightening her ties to the Roosevelts and forging her own close friendship with Louis M. Howe.*

Among the committees on which ER asked Hurst to serve was the National Advisory Committee for Community Service Projects of the

Works Progress Administration.* Such requests for involvement came repeatedly and in full knowledge that Hurst would always put her own professional and social commitments ahead of regular attendance at meetings or any real committee work. Nonetheless, the name of Fannie Hurst on a letterhead, her face in a group publicity photograph, or her distinctive voice over the radio seemed to serve sufficiently. This much, Hurst freely gave.

In 1941 Hurst offered to go on a national speaking campaign to help women understand their new role in national defense, an idea ER heartily endorsed. Hurst also made war bond tours and offered several of her then-valuable manuscripts at auction to boost sales.

Though Hurst was a fervent New Dealer, her political activity took place, as did her civic and social activism, only as a brightly illuminated sidebar to her life as a writer, which remained her primary focus. Raised in St. Louis by middle-class German Jewish parents, Hurst graduated in 1909 from Washington University, which granted her an honorary doctorate in 1953. Her career as a New York short story writer for such magazines as *The Saturday Evening Post*, *Metropolitan*, and the early-day version of *Cosmopolitan* took off in 1912. At her death, seventeen of her novels had been published, along with some 150 stories in major publications and scores of magazine and newspaper articles on a wide range of subjects. From her works of fiction, some thirty silent and sound films were made, most notably, *Humoresque*, *Back Street*, and *Imitation of Life*, from her titles by the same name, and *Four Daughters*, from her story "Sister Act."

SELECTED BIBLIOGRAPHY

Fannie Hurst Collection: Ledgers, Appointment Books, Diaries, Brandeis University Library, Waltham, MA.
———. Personal Correspondence, Harry Ransom Humanities Research Center, University of Texas, Austin.

Brooke Kroeger

HYDE PARK. Eleanor Roosevelt had a long and varied association with the village of Hyde Park in New York's Hudson River Valley. She first was taken there when she was two years old by her parents to see her cousin, Franklin D. Roosevelt,* and his family at their estate on the Albany Post Road (Route 9), two miles south of the center of the village. In a reminiscence published after her death, she recalled her honeymoon with FDR at Hyde Park and how she had gone back to his family home, called Springwood, as a young wife with a growing family for vacations every spring and autumn for years. Later, she continued, she had returned when "the old mansion was known as the Summer White House" and then on 15 April 1945 for FDR's funeral, when he "was laid to rest in the rose garden, close to the house in which he had been born and which he had loved so well for all of his sixty-three years" (Roosevelt, 72). ER, however, also remembered the Hyde Park estate as the domain of her mother-in-law, Sara Delano Roosevelt,* who, until her death in 1941, "made every decision concerning it," leading ER to conclude that "for over 40 years, I was only a visitor there" (Roosevelt, 72). The Roosevelt family deeded Springwood, known as the "Big House," to the federal government following FDR's death. After that, ER called home her cottage at Val-Kill* on the Roosevelt grounds two miles east of Springwood, even though she also maintained a residence in New York City.

The unincorporated village of Hyde Park five miles north of Poughkeepsie was initially a residential center of the thirty-seven square-mile-area established as the town (township) of Hyde Park in 1821, taking its name from a local estate named in honor of Edward Hyde, a colonial governor of New York. The town sits on the eastern banks of the Hudson River in Dutchess County, midway between Albany and New York City. It was a farming and shipbuilding area until the mid-nineteenth century, when railroad connections to New York City made it an attractive place for wealthy families like the Vanderbilts and the Roosevelts to acquire estates along the river's shoreline. Local residents, many of whom worked as servants for the newcomers, referred to them as the "River" families. When ER first visited Hyde Park in the 1880s, the population of the village was only a few hundred and that of the town about 2,800. Growth was limited until the end of World War II,* when the village numbered about 1,000 individuals. The town, which had increased to 4,000 persons by 1940, expanded to 13,000 by 1960, reflecting suburban growth fueled by the expansion of the International Business Machines Corporation in Poughkeepsie. ER indirectly facilitated change in Hyde Park when in 1947 she purchased over 800 acres of land from FDR's estate to establish a farming venture in partnership with her son, Elliott Roosevelt,* to whom she deeded the property. When the enterprise proved unprofitable, Elliott sold part of the property for commercial development, including a movie theater on the Albany Post Road near the Springwood entrance.

Although for many years ER may have seen herself as a visitor in Hyde Park, she, like FDR, took part in the life of the community. In the early 1920s ER, accompanied by her friend Elinor Morgenthau,* went from house to house in Hyde Park to persuade women to form a local chapter of the League of Women Voters.* In the mid-1920s she and her friends Nancy Cook* and Marion Dickerman* started Val-Kill Industries, which made reproductions of early American furniture and articles of pewter. On land leased to them by FDR along Val-Kill stream, they built both a cottage retreat for themselves and a small furniture factory, which they operated from 1927 to 1936. ER and FDR hoped the factory would offer off-season employment to farm youth* so they would remain in the Hyde Park area rather than seek work in cities. This plan did not prove successful, and skilled craftsmen had to be brought in, but the enterprise was a significant source of local employment during the depression. At times as many as twenty people worked at Val-Kill Industries, with ER showing particular interest in a related project to teach weaving to local women. After the factory closed, she converted the building to living quarters, which she used when FDR was not at Springwood, and made the renovated building her principal home after his death.

While she was First Lady, ER remained involved with the Hyde Park community. She hired a neighbor, Henrietta Nesbitt,* and her husband, Henry D., for the White House staff. On visits to Hyde Park, she met with local groups, including the Grange, which she had joined in 1931. Years later, Agnes Bahret, the master of Chapel Corners Grange, recalled that ER, like FDR, had attended meetings on special occasions and helped with activities. A Hyde Park resident, Ned Leadbitter, remembered in 1994 how ER had invited him and his teenage friends in the 1930s to swim in the pool at Val-Kill and talk about current events. During her Val-Kill years, she was known for remembering those in Hyde Park who had worked for her with turkeys and other gifts at Thanksgiving and Christmas.

After World War II ER was interested in a plan to make Hyde Park the headquarters of the United Nations* as a tribute to FDR. Nevertheless, she doubted this would occur because, as she wrote her maternal aunt, Maude Gray, she did not think Republicans would want to perpetuate FDR's name. A committee of local citizens put together a brochure highlighting the desirability of Hyde Park as a site and sent a delegate to London to promote the plan. There was bipartisan support initially, but Hyde Park was ultimately not selected.

After FDR's death, ER increased her role as a hostess at Val-Kill cottage, entertaining her neighbors as well as royalty and heads of state. She spoke to groups like the Roosevelt Home Club, an organization of FDR supporters, on world issues and the United Nations. When she left the United Nations in 1953, ER spent more time at Hyde Park, particularly in summer. Her son, John Roosevelt,* and his family had moved into the stone college at Val-Kill, built initially as her retreat, and ER enjoyed her role as a grandmother to his four children. A familiar sight in the village, ER sometimes did her own shopping for fresh produce at local groceries and vegetable stands. She maintained her mother-in-law's interest in the Hyde Park public library and attended board meetings there.

ER also gave her support and prestige to educational programs in the area. She was on the board of the Wiltwyck School,* a school for delinquent boys across the Hudson River in Esopus, and took great pleasure in hosting a picnic for these youngsters at Val-Kill every year. She paid visits to Dutchess Community College in Poughkeepsie, driving her Fiat car there on several occasions in the late 1950s. She backed community causes, agreeing as late as 1960 to be "Queen of the Ball" for a high school fund-raising affair on behalf of the American Field Service Exchange Program.

Years later, Hyde Park residents recalled ER as an unpretentious person who chatted pleasantly, dressed casually, and was unconcerned by her fame. Her chauffeur, Archie Curnan, recalled her speaking to the archery club he and his friends had organized. Marguerite Entrup ("Marge"), the housekeeper who worked for ER the last six years of her life, remembered how ER responded to a call for assistance from a woman in Poughkeepsie who was wheelchair-bound. ER sent Entrup and her husband, Lester, to the Salvation Army to get a kitchen set, paint it, and deliver it to the woman, whom ER continued to assist by sending money every month. Mrs. Entrup noted that people who worked for ER were introduced to others as her friends, not her help, because she said they were the people who made her "life worth living" (Entrup, Oral History Interview, 12–13). Relationships with her Hyde Park neighbors reflected ER's strengths as an advocate for human values throughout the world. They also showed her faith in religion.*

ER was a loyal member of St. James Episcopal Church in Hyde Park, which she attended whenever she was in the community, sitting in the Roosevelt family's pew and sending in an offering when she could not be present. She and her children contributed to the remodeling of the basement of the church's chapel building into a reading room for the community, and she annually gave flowers to the church in her husband's and mother-in-law's memory. She kept in close touch with the rector, the Reverend Gordon Kidd, exchanging books with him, inviting him to dinners at Val-Kill, and giving him tickets to concerts she was unable to attend. In 1956 she paid for Kidd and his wife to take part in a tour of Arab countries and Israel for clergymen and educators sponsored by the American Christian Palestine Committee.

ER was resolute in honoring all commitments she made to her community. Kidd recalled in an oral history interview how ER arrived on one occasion at the Hyde Park church ten minutes before she was scheduled to talk to twenty Episcopal clergymen. To keep the appointment she had sat up all night on a train from Pittsburgh to New York because bad weather had closed airports.

ER's funeral services were held at St. James Church on 10 November 1962 with president John F. Kennedy* and former presidents Harry S Truman* and Dwight D. Eisenhower* in attendance. ER is buried beside FDR in the rose garden of Springwood, now a national historic site along with ER's Val-Kill cottage. The Roosevelt site also includes the FDR Library and Museum. Another national historic site, the Vanderbilt mansion, is located two miles north of Springwood. Although no Roosevelts have lived in Hyde Park for a quarter of a century, the community has become synonymous with the family name.

SELECTED BIBLIOGRAPHY

Alden, Nancy. "I Remember Mrs. Roosevelt." *The Hyde Park Townsman*, 3 March 1994; 24 March, 1994; 21 April 1994; 12 May 1994; 8 September 1994.

Eleanor Roosevelt Oral History Project, Interviews with Archie Curnan (1978), Marguerite Entrup (1979), Harold Farley (1979), the Reverend Gordon Kidd (1978), Henry Morgenthau III (1978), and Eleanor Wotkyns (1978), Franklin D. Roosevelt Library, Hyde Park, NY.

Eleanor Roosevelt Papers, Franklin D. Roosevelt Library, Hyde Park, NY.

Fredriksen, Beatrice. *Our Local Heritage: A Short History of the Town of Hyde Park*. 1978.

Lash, Joseph. *Eleanor: The Years Alone*. 1972.

Roosevelt, Eleanor. "I Remember Hyde Park." *McCall's* (February 1963): 72–73, 162–63.

Margot Hardenbergh

I

ICKES, HAROLD LECLAIR (15 March 1874, Frankstown Township, Blair County, PA–3 February 1952, Washington, DC).

Secretary of the interior from 1933 to 1946, Harold L. Ickes oversaw a department with diverse responsibilities for the nation's natural resources, as well as the Bureau of Indian Affairs, and the administration of Alaska, Hawaii, and the Virgin Islands. He was also head of the Public Works Administration from 1933 until its termination in 1941, overseeing the spending of over $6 billion on a great array of public projects, including schools, hospitals, roads, bridges, dams, and housing. He earned a reputation as a diligent, outspoken, honest, and efficient administrator.

Ickes was one of the officials to whom Eleanor Roosevelt referred part of the huge volume of correspondence* she received about depression-era needs for assistance. She also corresponded with him about government programs in which she was particularly interested. He and ER were both strong supporters of liberal causes. Ickes had earned a law degree from the University of Chicago in 1907 and been active in progressive reform politics in Illinois. In 1932 he headed an independent Republican committee supporting Franklin D. Roosevelt* for president. He brought to his positions in the New Deal* a long-standing interest in improving conditions for Native Americans* and protecting the rights of minorities.

Shortly after his appointment, Ickes desegregated public facilities in his department and hired an African American, Robert Weaver, as one of his official advisers on the economic status of African Americans. When, in 1939, the Daughters of the American Revolution refused to permit Marian Anderson,* an inspiring black contralto, to perform in Constitution Hall, Ickes offered the Lincoln Memorial as a substitute place for her concert. During World War II* he campaigned for the release of interned Japanese Americans.* Nevertheless, Ickes and ER had a rather formal relationship. In their correspondence, ER never addressed Ickes by his first name, and Ickes' resented at times what he perceived as her interference, noting in his diary on 6 February 1937, "I wish that Mrs. Roosevelt would stick to her knitting and keep her hands out of the affairs connected with my Department" (Ickes, *Secret Diary*, 2:64).

Some of ER's questions and requests to Ickes were prefaced with a note that she was acting at the request of her husband, such as when she asked on 13 December 1933 if the position of assistant commissioner of education could be retained by a woman, and if women could receive half of the jobs under a plan for hiring unemployed teachers, or when she asked on 27 February 1934 that Ickes talk to Frederic Delano, who was FDR's uncle, about slum clearance in the alleys of the District of Columbia.*

The broad range of questions and issues on which she sought clarification or assistance from Ickes included resettlement communities in West Virginia (1933–1934); slum clearance and low-cost housing projects in Detroit (1936 and 1937); occupational therapy for Indians at the tuberculosis sanitarium in Shawnee, Oklahoma (1937); conditions at a hospital for blacks (1937); funding for a maternal and infant health association in Puerto Rico that offered birth control information (1939); economic assistance for the Navajo Indians (1941); and hospital facilities for native people in Alaska with tuberculosis (1944).

Ickes provided detailed responses to most of her requests for information and was in accord with, and responsive to, many of her suggestions; however, ER's strong commitment to the Arthurdale* resettlement homestead project, near Reedsville, West Virginia, became a serious irritant in her relations with Ickes. Cost overruns and bureaucratic mistakes attributed to haste in efforts to aid destitute coal miners in West Virginia were disturbing to Ickes. In his diary entry for 20 October 1934, he noted, "Of course, the Reedsville project is just one big headache and has been since the beginning . . . and then Mrs. Roosevelt took the Reedsville project under her protective wing with the result that we have been spending money there like drunken sailors" (Ickes, *Secret Diaries*, 1:207). Responsibility for the homestead projects was transferred in 1935 to the Resettlement Administration under Rexford G. Tugwell.*

Ickes also harbored a recurring, but unfounded, concern that the First Lady might be part of a group he feared was plotting to remove him from the cabinet. His misgivings surfaced by the mid-1930s, when he came to believe that he did not stand well with her. In his diary, he grew more critical of ER, even complaining about the domestic wine served at official dinners. On the other hand, he was pleased when during a tour of the new Interior Building, "she . . . cast an approving eye on the private kitchen and dining room about which the newspapers have been making such a fuss" (Ickes, *Secret Diaries*, 2:114). He also spoke very favorably about her support for the young people called to appear in late 1939 before the House Un-American Activities Committee.*

After President Roosevelt's death, Ickes pressed ER to run for the U.S. Senate in 1946, noting she "would be unbeatable" (HI to ER, 21 May 1945). In 1949 he wrote to her applauding her replies to Cardinal Spellman* on the issue of federal aid to parochial schools. After Ickes' death, ER in a note to his widow, Jane, said "it would mean a great deal to me to have . . . [Ickes' papers] in the FDR Library" (ER to JI, 29 April 1952), but she expressed understanding when Jane Ickes replied that Ickes had wanted his papers to remain in Washington, D.C.

SELECTED BIBLIOGRAPHY

Clarke, Jeanne N. *Roosevelt's Warrior: Harold L. Ickes and the New Deal.* 1996.
Eleanor Roosevelt Papers, Franklin D. Roosevelt Library, Hyde Park, NY.
Ickes, Harold L. *The Autobiography of a Curmudgeon.* 1943.
———. *The Secret Diary of Harold L. Ickes.* Vols. 1, 2, 3. 1953–1954.
Watkins, Thomas H. *Righteous Pilgrim: The Life and Times of Harold L. Ickes.* 1990.
White, Graham, and John Maze. *Harold L. Ickes of the New Deal: His Private Life and Public Career.* 1985.

Leonard Schlup

INDIA AND JAWAHARLAL NEHRU. In 1952 Eleanor Roosevelt, already one of the most widely traveled public figures in America, made a particularly significant visit to Asia.* Although her itinerary included a number of countries (Lebanon, Syria, Jordan, Israel,* Pakistan, Nepal, Indonesia, the Philippines), she spent about half of the time, a month, in India. The United States and even ER herself were sometimes accused of knowing and understanding little of the East and therefore the complexity of the world situation. It was a judgment she could not completely dismiss. Therefore, responding to an invitation from Indian prime minister Jawaharlal Nehru, she welcomed an opportunity for a study trip. In her book *India and the Awakening East*, as well as in her "My Day"* columns, she chronicled the trip and her growing sensitivity to the major issues and problems of India and the rest of Asia. Through her writings and speeches* during and after the visit to India, she made as much effort to educate Americans about this little-known, yet populous and democratic, country, pivotal in the Cold War* period and thereafter, as she did to explain America and American policy to Indians.

Chester Bowles,* the immensely popular and respected American ambassador in India who was also an old friend and collaborator of ER in American liberal democratic politics, provided a thorough briefing. Their correspondence and other sources make clear ER's expectations. She wanted plenty of time with Nehru. She also wanted to meet religious leaders and to go to smaller places as well as to urban centers. Taking the idea of a study trip seriously, she asked only one self-indulgence—

Eleanor Roosevelt visits the city palace in Agra, India, with David Gurewitsch and Maureen Corr on 12 March 1952, as a guest of the Indian government. *Courtesy of Press Information Office, Government of India/Franklin D. Roosevelt Library*

to visit the Taj Mahal at full moon and at sunrise. She remembered her father's descriptions of the Taj in letters written during his own extended visit to India in 1880–1881.

As usual, ER traveled at an indefatigable pace. She explored and admired the Etwah project, a pilot project for rural development. She visited hospitals, schools, universities, and women's and social work organizations, specifically encountering Indians of diverse caste, class, and religious backgrounds. Several major universities conferred honorary degrees upon her, and she spoke to university audiences explaining American positions on the issues of the day. In her site visits and in her speeches and interviews, ER stressed the importance of an American commitment to the development aspirations of the Indian people and demonstrated her own support for what some were calling a New Deal* for the world.

These were not always easy visits. Indian intellectuals were attracted by Marxist ideals, and there was a good deal of sympathy for the Union of Soviet Socialist Republics* in the Cold War. For many Indians, the United States seemed more and more to have inherited the mantle of imperialism from the British. Nehru himself, although firmly committed to political democracy and determined to plant its roots deep in Indian soil, had also imbibed Fabian socialism as a student in Britain and championed centralized economic planning. More problematic for Americans, he conceived and promoted for India and other newly independent countries a foreign policy of "nonalignment," a refusal to adhere to either of the rival alliance structures that were making the Cold War increasingly rigid. For many Americans this constituted an immoral neutrality between an America championing freedom and democracy and a Soviet Union epitomizing autocracy and aggression. Without approving India's policy, ER came to understand it not as moral neutrality between dictatorship and democracy but as a policy choice dictated more by political considerations, comparing it to American neutrality in the 1930s. She also advised President Harry S Truman* that, while India's problems were similar to China's, Nehru was a leader of "infinitely higher quality" than Chiang Kai-shek (ER to HST, 7 March 1952).

Both pitfalls and successes were demonstrated during her visit to Allahabad, Nehru's hometown. She had agreed to speak to a student assembly at the university, but a number of student organizations issued a particularly critical open letter to her early on the appointed day. Fearing discourtesy to ER, Nehru and his sister, Madame Vijaylakshmi Pandit, who was also head of the Indian delegation to the United Nations* and with whom ER was staying, advised university officials to cancel the appearance. After a sharp encounter between Madame Pandit and one of the student leaders, a large group of students assembled in front of her house to protest. An agitated Madame Pandit was convinced by ER herself to allow ER to receive the leaders of the students and later speak to the whole group. She was received courteously and, after speaking briefly, was given a warm ovation. Nehru wrote the students, paternally chastising them for their behavior, but much of the Indian press praised ER, contrasting her openness and candor to Madame Pandit's heavy-handedness and Nehru's criticism of the students.

Like most Western visitors, ER was impressed by the seeming chaos of the varied transport system, noting the hazards of travel on the Indian roads, heavy with bullock carts and herds of goats, donkeys, and camels as well as motorized vehicles. She experienced cultural confusions and shared them with her readers in both the United States and India, where the English-language press widely published her regular columns during her visit. At one point, for example, she described Gandhi's cremation site, or *samadhi*, as a tomb. In her "My Day" column of 26 March 1952, she publicly berated herself for her ignorance of the Hindu custom of cremation and her "stupid acceptance" of Western assumptions, affirming both the importance and difficulty of really knowing another culture.

Wherever she went, she was greeted by large, enthusiastic crowds seeking almost what the Indians call *darshan*, the blessings of an auspicious sight of a great moral leader. Newspaper reports of her visit were, with few exceptions, extremely positive. She was praised for her thoughts and conduct and for her openness and understanding. She also was compared to Chester Bowles in terms of having an instinctive understanding of India as well as to the admired and popular Lord Louis Mountbatten, the last viceroy of British India and the first governor-general of independent India, and even to Gandhi. One editorial writer observed, "Those who have seen Mrs. Roosevelt speak will testify that she has an extraordinary moral atmosphere about her and her speeches and utterances are on the highest plane, ranking in some cases with some of Gandhiji's own speeches" (*The Hitavada*, Nagpur, 21 March 1952).

Although she never developed for India the kind of deep engagement she had for Israel, in her relations with India, in general, and Nehru, in particular, ER continued to demonstrate that it was at least possible to rise above what Selig Harrison called the "dialogue of the deaf" so often characteristic of the political and cultural discourse between Indians and Americans (Harrison, 45). Moreover, she continued to champion American assistance to economic development projects in India and other newly independent countries through Point IV and other programs.

SELECTED BIBLIOGRAPHY

Berger, Jason. *A New Deal for the World: Eleanor Roosevelt and American Foreign Policy*. 1981.
Eleanor Roosevelt Papers, Franklin D. Roosevelt Library, Hyde Park, NY.
Harrison, Selig S. "Dialogue of the Deaf: Mutual Perceptions and Indo-American Relations." In Sulochana Rahgavan Glazer and Nathan Glazer, eds., *Conflicting Images: India and the United States*. 1990.
Roosevelt, Eleanor. *India and the Awakening East*. 1953.

Sipra B. Johnson and M. Glen Johnson

INTERNET RESOURCES. Developed and introduced more than thirty years after the death of Eleanor Roosevelt, the World Wide Web offers students, teachers, and researchers an interesting array of materials and resources related to the First Lady. These resources may be grouped into three main categories—brief biographies, on-line reference sites, and virtual exhibitions.

The most common ER resource found on the World Wide Web is the brief biography. Usually composed of two to three screens of text, a number of images, and a set of hyperlinks to other related sites, these biographies serve both students and teachers as convenient and instructive resources. While some of these sites are sponsored by commercial enterprises such as Grolier Online, the majority are put together and maintained by governmental and nonprofit organizations.

One such site is part of the official Web site for the White House. Entitled "Anna Eleanor Roosevelt Roosevelt 1884–1962," it briefly sketches her early upbringing, her personal and professional relationship with her husband, and her dramatic transformation of the role of First Lady. Biographical information is taken directly from Frank Freidel and Hugh S. Sidey's *The Presidents of the United States* and Margaret Brown Klapthor's *The First Ladies*.

As part of the on-line site provided by Marist College, Poughkeepsie, New York, in association with the Franklin D. Roosevelt Library and Museum, "Eleanor Roosevelt 1884–1962" provides similar information to that found in the White House site. The difference, however, is that the library site contains a number of hyperlinks to additional sites on the Web. For example, for further information regarding ER's later years, users can click on the hyperlink labeled "Val-Kill."* Similarly, readers can click on the hyperlinks labeled "Theodore Roosevelt,"* "Franklin Delano Roosevelt,"* and "World War II."*

In addition to the brief biographies put together by the White House and the Roosevelt Library and Museum, there are others, including the Women's International Center's "Eleanor Roosevelt: Tribute to Greatness" and Grolier Online's "Encyclopedia Americana: Eleanor Roosevelt." Although limited in content and scope, these brief biographies serve as useful introductions to the life and accomplishments of ER.

Students, instructors, and researchers who wish to explore the life of ER in more depth should visit on-line reference sites such as "Eleanor Roosevelt's Timeline" and "Eleanor Roosevelt Motion Pictures in the Public Domain." The time line posted by Marist College from material provided by the Roosevelt Library spans seventy-eight years and includes many personal, professional, and political milestones in ER's life. With over seventy entries in all, the time line serves as a useful resource for teachers and students alike.

A second on-line reference site is the "Eleanor Roosevelt Motion Pictures in the Public Domain" page. Another dimension of the Marist College operation that features material from the Roosevelt Library, this on-line archive lists thirty-two films featuring ER. Among the films are home movies shot by John Boettiger, a son-in-law, short films made by the National Youth Administration,* and various newsreels.

In addition to brief titles (such as "ER's South Pacific Tour, Aug.–Sept. 1943"), the motion pictures* are described in terms of sources, running times, sound or silence, color or black and white, and form (16mm, 35mm, or videotape). Most of the descriptions include brief summaries of the contents of the films. A few of the listings, however, provide detailed information, including references to the events and participants shown and the importance of the motion pictures.

The third type of ER resource found on the Web is the virtual exhibition. The richest on-line exhibition is "Dear Mrs. Roosevelt," a site featured within the New Deal Network, a project of the Franklin and Eleanor Roosevelt Institute, Hyde Park,* New York. "Dear Mrs. Roosevelt" explores the thousands of letters written by young Americans to ER to request assistance during the Great Depression.* While certainly of interest to the general public, the material is especially designed to be used in social studies classrooms. Prepared by Robert Cohen, formerly of the University of Georgia and now of New York University, the site is divided into five chapters or sections: How the Depression Affected Children, The Letters, Mrs. Roosevelt's Response, Digging Deeper, and Lesson Plans.

While the first two sections serve to contextualize the material and exhibit some of the letters, the third section examines the First Lady's response to the pleas of young people, including her role in the formation of the National Youth Administration and the youth programs of the Works Progress Administration.* The last two sections—Digging Deeper and Lesson Plans—provide a reading list and lesson plans that incorporate the Web site.

Finally, an excellent last-stop resource is the National First Ladies' Library home page, an on-line archive backed by a number of corporate sponsors. The section for ER contains a rich array of resources, including listings of articles by and about her, references to related archives, and bibliographies of relevant monographs, theses, and dissertations.

It is important to note that sites on the World Wide Web are extremely transitory. Web sites appear today and disappear tomorrow. With this in mind, the author has chosen the Web sites described earlier and listed in the following because they are maintained by relatively stable institutions and organizations, thereby increasing the chances that they will exist over time.

SELECTED WORLD WIDE WEB SITES

Anna Eleanor Roosevelt Roosevelt 1884–1962
<http://www.whitehouse.gov/WH/glimpse/firstladies/html/ar32.html>
Dear Mrs. Roosevelt
<http://www.newdeal.feri.org/eleanor/index.htm>
Eleanor Roosevelt 1884–1962
<http://www.academic.marist.edu/fdr/eleanor.htm>
Eleanor Roosevelt Motion Pictures in the Public Domain
<http://www.academic.marist.edu/fdr/video.htm>
Eleanor Roosevelt: Tribute to Greatness
<http://www.wic.org/bio/roosevel.htm>

Eleanor Roosevelt's Timeline
<http://www.academic.marist.edu/fdr/ertime.htm>

Encyclopedia Americana: Eleanor Roosevelt
<http://www.grolier.com/presidents/ea/first/32pw.html>

Franklin D. Roosevelt Library and Museum
<http://www.academic.marist.edu/fdr/>

National First Ladies' Library—Eleanor Roosevelt
<http://www.firstladies.org/ANNA_ROOSEVELT/FL.HTML>

David Silver

ISRAEL. Eleanor Roosevelt became a strong supporter of Israel from that nation's founding in 1948 until her death in 1962. Yet, ER's call in 1947 for the creation of a Jewish state could hardly have been predicted from a study of her attitudes toward Jews.*

ER came of age in a privileged world of late nineteenth-century, white, Protestant America where anti-Semitism was widespread; for example, she voiced the common stereotype that Jews were obsessed with money. Although her attitudes changed over time, as late as 1939, ER had not shed all of her past anti-Semitism. She wrote to an old German friend that "there may be a need for curtailing the ascendancy of the Jewish people" (Cook, *Without Precedent*, 115), but she commented that this should be carried out in a more humane and decent way than Hitler was doing it. After the United States entered World War II,* and news of the Holocaust* reached Washington, ER's sincere compassion for the Jews erased any lingering prejudices. Not only was she moved by the horrific news from Europe, but she also awoke to the destructiveness of American anti-Semitism when—despite her best efforts to lobby State Department officials—she was unable to pry open American doors to Jewish refugees.*

Following the war, ER's concern for the survivors of the Holocaust grew. She was particularly swayed by what she saw when she visited the European refugee camps in 1946, writing of the plight of Jewish displaced persons in her "My Day"* column on 26 February 1946. Nevertheless, although she expressed great frustration with Britain's refusal to let Jewish refugees into Palestine, initially she was opposed to Zionism* (the movement for a Jewish state). When the United Nations* voted for the partition of Palestine into Jewish and Arab states in 1947, however, ER changed her position. As a U.S. delegate to the United Nations, she viewed the move for partition as a test of the strength of the international organization. Over the next six months, ER argued in correspondence with President Harry S Truman* and Secretary of State George Marshall* that the United States had to work to implement partition or risk damaging the United Nations, even threatening to resign

Eleanor Roosevelt views the Jordan River project during a five-day tour of
Israel in February 1952 and is impressed by the reclamation efforts under-
way. *Courtesy of Maureen Corr/Franklin D. Roosevelt Library*

her position over the issue. This overarching concern for the United
Nations was even reflected in her reaction to American recognition of
the Jewish state in May 1948. Although ER had argued strenuously that
the United States should recognize the new state as soon as it was announced, she protested to both Truman and Marshall that the White
House had not informed the American delegation to the United Nations
of its intention to recognize ahead of time and, therefore, had weakened
the organization.

Once Israel was an established state, ER became an ardent admirer.
She used her political influence on Israel's behalf many times. For example, in late 1948 she lobbied Washington officials not to support a
proposed peace plan that would have given the Negev Desert to the
Arabs instead of the Jews. In this case as in others in subsequent years,
she based her argument on what she believed to be the great drive and
initiative of the Israelis, for development of the area. In 1952 she visited
the Middle East and drew a sharp contrast between the accomplishments
of the Arabs and those of the Israelis, identifying strongly with the Israelis. Traveling from the Arab nations to Israel was, she wrote, "like
breathing the air of the United States again . . . once I was through the

barrier I felt that I was among people . . . dedicated to fulfilling a purpose" (Roosevelt, 102).

While ER celebrated Israeli efforts at modernization, she focused on the Arab lack of economic development and Westernization and concluded that the Arabs were wholly inflexible when it came to Israel. She blamed Arab leaders and communists for the plight of Arab refugees, arguing that they wanted to keep the refugees "stirred up" as a weapon against Israel instead of resettling them in Arab countries (Lash, 137). While she pitied the Arab refugees, she believed that Israel was not to blame for their situation. ER looked forward to the day when the refugee problem would be solved and Israel would work together with its neighbors to encourage economic development.

Throughout the 1950s her support of the Jewish state grew stronger, and she increasingly viewed the Arab–Israeli conflict as a reflection of the Cold War* tensions in the world. In a 1953 letter to President Dwight D. Eisenhower,* for example, she argued that aid to Israel should not be lessened, because Israel espoused the cause of the free world, while the Arab states did not. ER was never reluctant to make her views of the conflict public. Following a dispute among Saudi Arabia, Israel, and the United States in 1957 over access to the Gulf of Aqaba, ER wrote in her "My Day" column, 16 April 1957, "I hope this incident with Saudi Arabia will teach us that we have no friends in countries like this" (Emblidge, 3:127). As a reflection of her support for Israel, ER repeatedly called for economic and military aid for the Jewish state. She used her influence to lobby officials in Washington and to sway public opinion through her column and articles. In addition, she frequently spoke for the United Jewish Appeal and Hadassah, lending her name and reputation to these pro-Israeli organizations.

ER's enthusiasm for the Jewish state increased as she made trips there in 1952, 1959, and 1962. She saw in Israel what she believed to be an activism and hopefulness that were similar to the American spirit and missing from the social climate in other Middle Eastern states.

SELECTED BIBLIOGRAPHY

Cook, Blanche Wiesen. "Eleanor Roosevelt and Human Rights: The Battle for Peace and Planetary Decency." In Edward Crapol, ed., *Women and American Foreign Policy: Lobbyists, Critics, and Insiders.* 1987.

———. " 'Turn toward Peace': Eleanor Roosevelt and World Affairs." In Joan Hoff-Wilson and Marjorie Lightman, eds., *Without Precedent: The Life and Career of Eleanor Roosevelt.* 1984.

Emblidge, David, ed. *Eleanor Roosevelt's "My Day."* Vols. 2, 3. 1990, 1991.

Lash, Joseph P. *Eleanor: The Years Alone.* 1972.

Roosevelt, Eleanor. *On My Own.* 1958.

                                                        Michelle A. Mart

J

JAPANESE AMERICAN INTERNMENT. After Pearl Harbor, the Roosevelt administration ordered General John L. DeWitt, commander of the Western Defense Command, to carry out an investigation of the many reports of Japanese spy activity on the West Coast. DeWitt concluded in his 14 February 1942 report to President Franklin D. Roosevelt* that although no sabotage had taken place to date, he had discovered "a disturbing and confirming indication that such action will be taken" (Smith, 124) by the Japanese American population. As a result, FDR approved an internment program, giving military commanders on the West Coast the power to evacuate persons they felt constituted a threat to the war effort and national defense. Eleanor Roosevelt initially vigorously and publicly opposed the arguments to intern Japanese Americans, but she ceased her public criticism once internment became administration policy, accepting it as a military necessity.

DeWitt responded, in part, to public opinion. The press, patriotic organizations, western farming interests, and a growing number of public and political figures called for evacuation. ER, however, emphatically opposed internment in the aftermath of Pearl Harbor. A week after the attack on Hawaii, she toured the West Coast, posing with Japanese Americans for photographs distributed by the Associated Press wire service, one of which was published in the *New York Times* on 15 December 1941. In her "My Day"* column of 16 December 1941, she issued a challenge to her readers: "This is, perhaps, the greatest test this country has ever met," she wrote. If the country could not make fairness a practical reality, "then we shall have removed from the world, the one real hope for the future on which all humanity must now rely." These people "are good Americans," she told FDR, "and have the right to live as anyone else" (Black, 143). She worked with Attorney General Francis Biddle to ensure that the Justice Department presented a strong case against the policy to the president. She hoped to convince FDR that he had the moral authority to call the country to tolerance.

Yet ER fought a losing battle, as Japanese military successes mounted in the Pacific, producing a near crisis in the United States. Between 7 December 1941 and 19 February 1942, Hong Kong surrendered, Manila was captured, and Singapore fell to the Japanese. Reports from California of vigilante actions taken against Japanese Americans presented an additional argument in favor of internment. On 19 February 1942 FDR signed Executive Order (EO) 9066, conferring on secretary of war Henry L. Stimson the authority to designate military zones "from which any or all persons may be excluded" (Daniels, 113). Under the order, all people of Japanese extraction in the Western Defense Command were required to report to evacuation areas and be registered. First taken to crude temporary shelters—stockyards, fairgrounds, and racetracks—by the end of 1942, all but a few Japanese Americans on the West Coast had been moved to ten relocation centers in Utah, Arizona, Colorado, Arkansas, Idaho, California, and Wyoming.

ER ceased her direct public statements opposing internment and recast her rhetoric immediately following the announcement of EO 9066. In one of her radio broadcasts* she stated, "It is obvious that many people who are friendly aliens have to suffer temporarily in order to insure the safety of the vital interests of this country while at war." Further, the removal of the Japanese population was "going to be done so that they will not waste their skills" (Pan-American Coffee Bureau Broadcast, 15 February 1942).

ER turned her energies to the relocation process itself. She monitored evacuation procedures, making sure families remained together. She helped to secure early releases and intervened with the War Relocation Authority (WRA) when noninterned Japanese protested the treatment that their family members were receiving in the camps. She had the bank accounts of the Issei (citizens of Japan barred by the Supreme Court from becoming citizens of the United States), which had been frozen after Pearl Harbor, made accessible once again in cases where no disloyalty had been found. She asked the Justice Department to oppose the disfranchisement of Japanese Americans still living in California and to investigate claims of employment discrimination and violence there. She made occasional references to the internees in "My Day," carefully balancing her comments by presenting both the WRA and the Japanese Americans in a positive light.

In 1943 FDR became concerned about several demonstrations that had occurred in the camps and asked ER to visit the Gila River Camp in Arizona. Her public report of this visit on 23 April revealed the difficulty of her position. Rather than discussing the political climate of the camps, she wrote about the internees' contributions to the war effort and their attempts to organize schools and beautify their environment. She noted, however, that family structures were disintegrating under the stresses of internment, and she joined Dillon Meyer, director of the WRA, in advocating to FDR a relaxation of the exclusionary ban that kept Japanese Americans out of the Western Defense Command areas. In response, FDR upheld the segregation of a small number of pro-Japan internees in the Tule Lake Camp in California, where a mutiny was staged in November 1943, but he also backed efforts to allow individual Japanese to obtain exit permits from the camps. The ban itself, however, stayed in place until after the 1944 election. On 17 December 1944 FDR lifted the ban, and the WRA began closing the internment centers. The last residents of the camps were finally released in the middle of 1946.

Privately, ER wrote of her sense of guilt about the internees. To her friend and head of Cornell University's Home Economics Department, Flora Rose, she wrote, "This is just one more reason for hating war—innocent people suffer for a few guilty ones" (ER to FR, 10 June 1942). She was well aware of the racism underlying the West Coast's insistence that the Japanese be removed, and she did not entirely accept the administration's contention that they had been relocated for their own protection; on the West Coast, she noted, they were also "feared as competitors" (Black, 145).

After FDR's death, ER reiterated her profound disagreement with his position, aligning herself with the critics* of internment. Yet, during the war itself, her position on internment showed particular attention to the nation's military demands and FDR's sensitive political position. She believed that the American people needed a unified White House around which to rally after the Pearl Harbor attack. The larger issues of war and—perhaps most significantly—the limitations of her position dictated that she confine her protests to practical, individual interventions. As Peter Irons has suggested, the White House discussions concerning internment policy and the court challenges it engendered "were as much political as legal in substance" (Irons, xi). ER, as a highly visible symbol of the White House, understood the political implications of her comments and desisted from publicly criticizing a policy she disliked out of concern for both the war effort and the Roosevelt administration.

SELECTED BIBLIOGRAPHY

Black, Allida M. *Casting Her Own Shadow: Eleanor Roosevelt and the Shaping of Postwar Liberalism*. 1996.

Daniels, Roger. *The Decision to Relocate the Japanese Americans*. 1990.

Eleanor Roosevelt Papers, Franklin D. Roosevelt Library, Hyde Park, NY.

Goodwin, Doris Kearns. *No Ordinary Time: Franklin and Eleanor Roosevelt: The Home Front in World War II*. 1994.

Irons, Peter. *Justice Delayed: The Record of the Japanese Internment Cases*. 1989.

Smith, Page. *Democracy on Trial: The Japanese-American Evacuation and Relocation in World War II.* 1995.

Sharon L. Smith

JEWS. By the time of her death in 1962, Eleanor Roosevelt had become a beloved figure among American Jews. Partly due to the political reverence that most Jews felt for her husband, President Franklin D. Roosevelt,* and partly because of the overwhelmingly liberal orientation of American Jews, in the post–World War II* world ER had become a sought-after speaker at Jewish communal events and was lionized with awards and citations by all of the major Jewish organizations. She had been named, for example, as one of the founding trustees of Brandeis University, which opened its doors in 1948. In 1957 she dedicated the Four Freedoms Library of the B'nai B'rith Women in Washington, D.C. Such Jewish activities were common for her, particularly after the White House. Her death brought forth a flurry of tribute and recollection of her special status in the American Jewish consciousness.

While the fondness Jews expressed for ER, in part, derived from the special status that FDR had enjoyed in American Jewish political consciousness, on her own she forged special and close connections with organized Jewry. Indeed, on the level of real relationships and actual political cooperation, she, much more than he, operated comfortably in Jewish institutions and with Jews as individuals.

Her close association with Jewish causes and institutions evolved slowly. In her youth and early adulthood she seems to have felt and expressed the generalized anti-Semitism prevalent in American society, particularly among the native-born elite class from which she came. All of her biographers have quoted several comments from letters she wrote early in her marriage to FDR that bore witness to the social anti-Semitism that she imbibed freely from the world around her. When in 1920 she attended a party for financier Bernard Baruch,* a Jew who would later become a close friend, she wrote, first, on her reluctance to attend the event: "I'd rather be hung than seen at" a gathering that was "mostly Jews." Afterward she asserted, "The Jew party [was] appalling. I never wish to hear money, jewels and . . . sables mentioned again." Likewise, when first introduced to Felix Frankfurter, she wrote that he was "an interesting little man but very Jew" (Lash, *Eleanor and Franklin*, 214). She certainly never foresaw that during World War II she would work closely with Frankfurter to try to bring information about the systematic murder of millions of European Jews to FDR's attention.

ER and FDR did socialize before World War I with Elinor Morgenthau* and her husband, Henry Morgenthau Jr., who were active Democrats in Dutchess County. Even ER's mother-in-law, Sarah Delano Roosevelt, approved of them, writing ER that Mrs. Morgenthau was "very Jewish but appeared very well" (Lash, *Eleanor and Franklin*, 215). As she began to move away from her early attitudes and work with Jews in a variety of liberal causes, ER still was conscious of the social gap between herself and them. She, for example, became close friends and a major ally of Rose Schneiderman* of the International Ladies Garment Workers' Union and the Women's Trade Union League.* It was some time, however, before she invited Schneiderman to the Roosevelt family home at Hyde Park* because of concerns about the generally anti-Semitic attitude of her mother-in-law.

Given the milieu from which she came, ER's later close relations and perhaps, more important, her political activities with Jews become that much more notable. The genesis of this development lay partly in her early involvement with progressive, social settlement–oriented activities in New York. She volunteered at the Rivington Street Settlement House on New York's Lower East Side before her marriage. As she became involved in Democratic Party* politics in the 1920s, she came into contact with Jews like Lillian Wald,* founder of the Henry Street Settlement, and Belle Moskowitz,* a key adviser of Alfred E. Smith* when he was governor of New York in the 1920s. ER's exposure to the world of social settlements* led her to a belief that the problems of poverty grew out of systemic inequalities. To help ameliorate these, she turned to the trade union movement, particularly the Women's Trade Union League. Here she met and came to respect Schneiderman, Fannia Cohn, and others who would be allies and friends for decades to come. She would serve as a bridge between them and their causes with FDR when he was governor and president.

ER's initiation into the world of the Jewish community began in the mid-1930s as the crisis of European Jewry became acute with Hitler's rise to power and the aggressive persecution of Jews in Germany and the rest of Europe. She seems to have been considered a key player in international efforts to rescue refugees* as early as 1935, when telegrams and other communiqués about Jewish persecution began to come to her personally as a matter of course. Despite her earlier commitment to pacifism, in light of German aggression on the European continent, she came to view Germany's defeat as crucial. Despite the primacy of winning World War II, however, ER cajoled FDR repeatedly to do more to rescue Jews from almost inevitable death.

Her pressure on FDR was not solely personal but took place in a political context. Working with individual Jews like Rabbi Stephen Wise, his daughter Justine Wise Polier,* and others, ER intervened in debates over particular pieces of legislation and proposed recommendations for specific policies. Thus, in 1939 she actively lobbied FDR to support the Wagner–Rogers Bill,* designed to allow Jewish refugee children to come to the United States, and prodded members of Congress* to back the measure. According to several historians of the Holocaust* and the U.S. government's action—or inaction—during it, this unsuccessful effort represented the first time that ER publicly supported a specific bill.

Throughout the years of World War II, ER played a pivotal role in trying to take action to rescue the Jews of Europe. She consistently took information to FDR about the crisis and implored him to do more to save the Jews of Europe. She confronted FDR about the anti-Semitism that pervaded the Department of State and particularly criticized assistant secretary of state Breckenridge Long, whom she told FDR was a "fascist" (Goodwin, 175).

She seemed ever mindful of the conflicted position she occupied. On one hand, her profound and deep humanitarian feelings put her on the side of action on behalf of the refugees, a move that the United States consistently refused to make. She was willing to speak publicly of the slaughter of Europe's Jews and the fact that the United States should undertake some efforts at rescue. She met with individual Jews like Peter Bergson (Hillel Kook), who organized in 1943 the militant Emergency Committee to Save the Jewish People of Europe. Rabbi Wise, who shared many speakers' platforms with ER, had total and direct access to her. She devoted several of her "My Day"* columns to the plight of Europe's Jews and delivered radio broadcasts* on the subject. She attended the March 1943 pageant at Madison Square Garden of *They Shall Not Die*, a vain effort to use public drama to stimulate American sympathies.

On the other hand, ER had no power independently of her husband. She could only go so far in pushing him or in openly criticizing his policies. How much cooperation existed between the two is a matter of speculation. Did she engage in her very public and emotional activities on behalf of European Jews with FDR's private blessings so that he could pursue a more cautious policy and yet appear in the eyes of American Jews as deeply concerned? Certainly, Jewish leaders saw her as their special friend, and FDR did not mind that connection.

ER's relationship with organized Jewry and the deep affection that the Jewish masses had for her grew greatly after the death of FDR and her entry into the political arena as a private individual. Jews knew and revered her through her work on behalf of the state of Israel,* which declared its existence on 14 May 1948. Originally, ER did not support Zionism.* Perhaps because of her long friendship with the Morgenthaus, who were non-Zionist, ER did not support the idea of a Jewish state in Palestine. During the war years she did not identify with those Jews who believed that the only solution for the crisis of world Jewry lay in an independent Jewish homeland.

When the issue become a matter of public discussion, she took an anti-Zionist stance. In 1943, for example, 796 Jews from Romania set sail for Palestine on the *Struna*. Since they had no British entrance papers, they were turned back, and Jewish public opinion around the world focused on the fate of these whom the British were returning to Europe and certain death. ER described British policy as "cruel beyond words" (Wyman, 159) yet suggested that the British send the refugees to East Africa for the duration of the war. She did not make the connection between their homelessness and the absence of a Jewish homeland. In the mid-1940s she wrote, "I do not happen to be a Zionist and I know what a difference there is among such Jews as consider themselves nationals of other countries and not a separate nationality" (Lash, *The Years Alone*, 115).

By 1946, however, she had begun to shift her position. In her autobiographical work *On My Own*, ER related an encounter in 1946 at a refugee camp in Zilcheim, Germany, with an old woman who approached her and repeatedly called out, "Israel! Israel!" ER wrote, "I knew for the first time what that small land meant to so many, many people" (Roosevelt, 56). In March 1948, when the State Department and President Harry S Truman* wavered in their support of the United Nations* plan to partition Palestine into Jewish and Arab states (as approved by the General Assembly in November 1947), ER threatened to resign as a U.S. representative to the United Nations.

Over the years her identification with, and support for, Israel grew. She visited Israel three times and established warm relations with David Ben-Gurion, Golda Meir, and other Israeli political figures. She served as a patron for Youth Aliyah, an international organization dedicated to resettling young Jews in Israel. In 1956 she personally intervened with the sultan of Morocco to allow the Jews of his realm to emigrate to the Jewish state.

Such behavior on specifically Jewish issues and her consistently liberal positions on civil rights* in America and trade unionism made her a hero to American Jews. She not only championed their cause but stood for universal concerns. They had no idea how far she had come from her early years, steeped as she had been in genteel anti-Semitism. What they saw was the wife and widow of a beloved president speaking out for Jews in distress and for the liberalism many of them cherished, too.

SELECTED BIBLIOGRAPHY

Feingold, Henry. *Bearing Witness: How America and Its Jews Responded to the Holocaust*. 1995.
Goodwin, Doris Kearns. *No Ordinary Time: Franklin and Eleanor Roosevelt: The Home Front in World War II*. 1994.
Lash, Joseph P. *Eleanor and Franklin*. 1971.
———. *The Years Alone*. 1972.
Roosevelt, Eleanor. *On My Own*. 1958.
Wyman, David S. *The Abandonment of the Jews: America and the Holocaust, 1941–1945*. 1984.

Hasia R. Diner

JOHNSON, JOHN HAROLD (19 January 1918, Arkansas City, AR–   ).
John Harold Johnson credited Eleanor Roosevelt with helping ensure
the success of *Negro Digest*, the monthly he founded in Chicago in 1942.
The magazine was to become the foundation of Johnson Publishing Company, America's largest black-owned publishing firm.

Johnson grew up in Arkansas City near the Mississippi River and
moved with his family to Chicago in 1933 so he would have the opportunity—not available to blacks in rural Arkansas—to attend high school.
Because of the Great Depression,* the family had to go on relief, as welfare was then known, from late 1934 until 1936. They were found eligible
for relief after Johnson's mother, Gertrude Johnson Williams, wrote a
personal appeal to President Franklin D. Roosevelt,* an approach Johnson would later emulate in approaching ER for help.

After graduating from high school in 1936, Johnson worked for Liberty
Life Insurance Company, the biggest black-owned business in Chicago,
and became involved with the company's publications. In 1942 Johnson
was assigned to glean news about blacks for the insurance company
officers. Believing he could market such news to the public, he started
Negro Digest in November 1942, and within eight months it had a national circulation of 50,000. When circulation growth stalled, however,
Johnson searched for a way to draw attention to his publication.

He found the answer when he asked ER to contribute a guest essay
to one of the magazine's regular features entitled, "If I Were a Negro,"
written by prominent whites who each received an honorarium of fifteen
dollars. After declining two of Johnson's earlier requests, ER received a
telegram from Johnson while she was in Chicago for a speaking engagement, again appealing for a contribution. She responded by immediately
dictating and sending him an article, which was featured in the October
1943 issue of *Negro Digest*. ER's assertion that if she were black in 1940s
America, she would have both great bitterness and great patience was
picked up by the national press and offended segregationists as well as
some black leaders. The controversy, however, boosted the fortunes of
Johnson's new publication. Circulation doubled to 100,000. Johnson said
that the article "marked a major turning point in the fortunes of *Negro
Digest*. . . . After that we never looked back" (Johnson, 132).

Johnson went on to establish *Ebony*, a monthly photo magazine, in
1945 and *Jet*, a weekly news magazine, in 1951. *Negro Digest* was discontinued with the debut of *Jet*.

SELECTED BIBLIOGRAPHY

Black, Allida M. *Casting Her Own Shadow: Eleanor Roosevelt and the Shaping of
Postwar Liberalism*. 1996.
Ingham, John N., and Lynne B. Feldman. *African American Business Leaders: A
Biographical Dictionary*. 1994.
Johnson, John H. *Succeeding Against the Odds*. 1989.

Zangrando, Joanna Schneider, and Robert L. Zangrando. "ER and Black Civil Rights." In Joan Hoff-Wilson and Marjorie Lightman, eds., *Without Precedent: The Life and Career of Eleanor Roosevelt*. 1984.

Mary Jane Alexander

K

KENNEDY, JOHN F. (29 May 1917, Brookline, MA–22 November 1963, Dallas, TX).

Prior to the nomination of John F. Kennedy (JFK) as the Democratic presidential candidate in 1960, Eleanor Roosevelt had exhibited a keen distrust of, and sometimes overt antagonism toward, the Massachusetts politician. Suspicious of the Kennedy family's political aspirations and backroom maneuvering as well as harboring doubts about JFK's lack of experience and refusal to espouse ER's brand of liberalism, the former First Lady had thought JFK lacking in the qualities she believed essential for a successful presidency. JFK, on the other hand, needed ER's support because in the late 1950s and early 1960s she commanded power and respect within the Democratic Party,* especially among its more liberal factions. With JFK's capture of the Democratic nomination and subsequent election as president, however, ER began increasingly to praise him, although she never fully ceased her criticism of some of his policies.

ER's wariness about JFK and his family existed long before he began his successful drive for the presidential nomination. She shared the anger of her late husband, Franklin D. Roosevelt,* toward JFK's father, Joseph Kennedy, who served in the Roosevelt administration as chairman of the Securities and Exchange Commission from 1934 to 1935 and as ambassador to England beginning in 1937. Resigning his ambassadorship in November 1940, the elder Kennedy publicly had joined the isolationist cause and disapproved of FDR's decision to run for a third term. As a result of FDR's contentious relationship with Joseph Kennedy, ER evinced a distrust of the family that predated JFK's entry into the political arena.

For ER, the Kennedy family also symbolized the corruption that plagued certain segments of the Democratic Party. In a 1958 ABC-TV interview, ER asserted that Joseph Kennedy spent "oodles of money in the country on his [JFK's] behalf" and that the Kennedys had "paid representatives in every state" (Berger, 129). ER believed that the elder Kennedy hoped to purchase the presidency for his son.

Most galling to ER was Kennedy's response to McCarthyism* in the early 1950s. ER condemned McCarthy and his tactics and looked for political leaders from both parties to make a principled stand against the Wisconsin senator's Red-baiting. ER castigated JFK both for refusing to condemn McCarthy and for missing the Senate's 1954 vote to censure him. JFK and his supporters responded by pleading that he had been hospitalized at the time of the censure movement. ER refused to accept this excuse largely because JFK had ample time before and after the vote to condemn McCarthy publicly. Pragmatic politics, in fact, may have guided JFK's actions; Arthur Schlesinger Jr., a JFK confidant, wrote in 1967 that the president had told him, "Hell, half of my voters in Massachusetts look on McCarthy as a hero" (Berger, 128). It was this type of crass politicking, however, that ER detested when it came to what she considered issues of conscience.

ER not only questioned JFK's defense of civil liberties, but found his lukewarm endorsement of greater civil rights* for African Americans wanting. Kennedy's refusal to push civil rights, specifically, his failure to condemn the anti-integrationist Southern Manifesto and his moderation on the 1957 Civil Rights Act, caused ER much consternation. These schisms between ER and JFK concerning anticommunism and civil rights signified their divergent conceptions of American liberalism. ER championed an activist agenda and searched for new leaders capable of reigniting the idealism and energy of the New Deal.* In Kennedy, she, too, often saw a cautious and conservative politician whose utmost concern was winning the highest office in the land.

These schisms, especially the controversy concerning McCarthy, played a role in ER's refusal to support JFK for the vice presidential nomination at the Democratic convention in 1956, despite his intense courtship of her. Instead, she endorsed Senator Estes Kefauver of Tennessee, who won the nomination and ran on the ticket with Adlai Stevenson,* whose campaign ER championed. In spite of her efforts, Stevenson and Kefauver lost to the incumbents, President Dwight D. Eisenhower* and Vice President Richard Nixon in November 1956, guaranteeing four more years for Republicans in the White House. As Kennedy geared for another run at the Democratic presidential nomination in 1960, ER continued to belittle him. Commenting in December 1958 on JFK's Pulitzer Prize–winning book, *Profiles in Courage*, ER found it ironic that JFK understood "what courage is and admires it but has not quite the independence to have it" (Berger, 129). As Kennedy closed in on the 1960 nomination, ER emerged as the leading spokesperson for a movement to draft Adlai Stevenson. She thought that Stevenson's maturity and experience in foreign affairs, attributes she believed Kennedy lacked, made him the best candidate; Kennedy was instead a good choice for the second spot on the ticket, where he would receive, according to ER, "the opportunity to grow and learn" (Berger, 130). Kennedy's momentum, however, could not be stopped, and the convention chose JFK on the first ballot; ER was unenthusiastic about his victory.

Kennedy's supporters immediately began to recruit ER, who informed them (and the public) that she would support the ticket but would not campaign for JFK. JFK's strategists realized, however, that their candidate needed her support. They understood that ER's participation would ensure a large turnout of liberal Democrats. Their participation was essential for a Kennedy victory because JFK and Nixon, the Republican presidential nominee, were running neck and neck in a number of vital states, including New York, Illinois, and California.

On 15 August JFK traveled to Hyde Park* to request that ER campaign for him. After learning of the death of her granddaughter, Sarah Roosevelt, who lived next door, in a horseback riding accident the previous day, JFK offered to postpone the scheduled visit. ER, ever the political player, told him to come ahead and exacted a price for her support: the involvement of Stevenson in the campaign on foreign policy issues. She surprised Kennedy, however, by not demanding that he promise Stevenson the position of secretary of state in his administration should he win; instead, she informed JFK that she felt it inappropriate to dictate who his advisers should be and who should be appointed to his cabinet—ultimatums to which Kennedy, in fact, never would have agreed. Following the meeting, she wrote in her "My Day"* column on 17 August that she had found JFK "anxious to learn" and possessing "a quick mind"—but feared "that he might tend to arrive at judgements almost too quickly" (Emblidge, 253). ER actively campaigned for JFK in the fall of 1960, appearing in his radio and television advertisements and traveling to California, Illinois, New York, and Indiana on his behalf.

ER expressed a number of misgivings about the course of Kennedy's presidency. While she liked the eloquence and vision of his inaugural address and believed it portended the possibility of a successful term, his policies sometimes disappointed her. In his conduct of Cuban–American relations, she opposed the Bay of Pigs invasion to overthrow Fidel Castro and argued that the Cuban people had legitimate grievances that justified their revolt against the previous dictator, Batista. She questioned Kennedy's program of military aid to the South Vietnamese. In domestic affairs, she continued to press JFK to move faster in civil rights, particularly in sending federal marshals to protect civil rights workers in the South and carrying out a campaign promise to sign an executive order banning discrimination in federal housing.

Yet, there were instances of cooperation and agreement. Of Kennedy's New Frontier programs, the establishment of the Peace Corps, with its call for sacrifice and its goal of peaceful international relations, impressed ER the most. She supported JFK's Alliance for Progress, a 1961 program that promoted social and economic development in Latin America. She lobbied for a nuclear atmospheric test ban treaty that JFK eventually did sign.

In December 1961 JFK appointed ER to chair the President's Commission on the Status of Women*; earlier that year he had named her to the U.S. delegation to the United Nations*. Declining health, however, soon began to limit her activities. Upon her death on 7 November 1962, Kennedy released a judicious official statement that appeared in the *Washington Post* the next day lauding the "tireless idealism" and "wise counsel" of "one of the great ladies in the history of the country." Ironically, ER's brand of liberal idealism and her attempts at advising the younger Democrat often placed Kennedy and the former First Lady at odds.

SELECTED BIBLIOGRAPHY

Berger, Jason. *A New Deal for the World: Eleanor Roosevelt and American Foreign Policy*. 1981.
Black, Allida M. *Casting Her Own Shadow: Eleanor Roosevelt and the Shaping of Postwar Liberalism*. 1996.
Emblidge, David, ed. *Eleanor Roosevelt's "My Day."* Vol. 3. 1991.
Parmet, Herbert S. *The Presidency of John F. Kennedy*. 1983.

Jason Berger

KERR, FLORENCE STEWART (30 June 1890, Harriman, TN–6 July 1975, Washington, DC).

Florence Stewart Kerr, an official involved in New Deal* women's relief programs, attended Grinnell College (1908–1912), where she was a classmate of Harry L. Hopkins.* After her marriage in 1915 to Robert Y. Kerr, she taught English in the Iowa public schools and at Grinnell except for a period of wartime service in the South with the American Red Cross,* which placed her again in association with Hopkins. At the advent of the Great Depression,* she was appointed to the Iowa Governor's Commission on Unemployment Relief in 1930.

In 1935, when Harry Hopkins created an administrative staff for the Women's Division of the Works Progress Administration* (WPA), Kerr became one of five regional supervisors and moved to Chicago to oversee the women's work relief program in thirteen midwestern states. Eleanor Roosevelt's practice of visiting offices of the regional supervisors placed her in contact with Kerr, whose headquarters were a frequent stop for the First Lady.

When Ellen S. Woodward* resigned late in 1938 as director of the

WPA's Women's and Professional Projects, Kerr became her successor and retained the position until final liquidation of the WPA in 1943. In February 1939, soon after she assumed the position, Kerr was an invited speaker at one of ER's press conferences.* ER's backing was especially crucial to Kerr when executive reorganization caused the WPA to be reconstituted as the Works Projects Administration within the new Federal Works Agency. Women's and Professional Projects became the Division of Professional and Service Projects in April 1939.

After 1940 a new focus mandated by the general shift in most New Deal programs toward national defense threatened women's programs. Faced with budget cuts as well, Kerr relied on ER to help maintain community service projects that had been the mainstay of the women's program. In April 1940 ER spoke by radio* to more than 600,000 project workers attending local dinners throughout the nation that concluded a weeklong demonstration and display of the women's service projects in a "This Work Pays Your Community" promotion. In a further effort to protect nonconstruction WPA projects, Kerr's allies among women close to ER urged the latter to assume chairmanship of a women's volunteer defense committee that would utilize the WPA Community Service projects under Kerr's jurisdiction.

That plan did not materialize, but Kerr herself took steps to convert women's work relief into civilian defense. She vigorously defended daycare centers before congressional committees on labor and education. She also kept alive programs in clothing and food production as well as public health projects and expanded training for housekeeping aides, continuing to enlist ER's help until the demise of the WPA in 1943.

In 1944 Kerr was named director of war public services under the Federal Works Agency. At the war's end, she left government to become an executive with Northwest Airlines and moved to Minneapolis. In the mid-1950s she returned to Washington, where she remained until her death.

SELECTED BIBLIOGRAPHY
Columbia Oral History Collection, Florence Kerr interview (1974), Columbia University, New York.
Record Group 69 (WPA), National Archives, Washington, DC.
Swain, Martha H. *Ellen S. Woodward: New Deal Advocate for Women.* 1995.

                                                         Martha H. Swain

KING, MARTIN LUTHER (15 January 1929, Atlanta, GA–4 April 1968, Memphis, TN).

Martin Luther King and Eleanor Roosevelt emerged in the 1950s as key leaders in the effort to bring civil rights* to African Americans. King, a preacher in Montgomery, Alabama, gained national attention in 1955, when he organized the Montgomery bus boycott. ER, concerned with the condition of black Americans since her years in the White House, became in the 1950s perhaps the preeminent white supporter of civil rights. With this common passion and determination, the two formed a respectful friendship as they battled, often within separate circles, for a cause that both believed essential to America's future.

The affinity between King and ER grew out of their belief that non-violence and passive resistance to segregation were the most effective strategy for the Civil Rights movement. For King, this tactic involved peacefully protesting the South's segregationist policies, thereby risking a confrontation with racist southern police and government officials. If attacked, and this often occurred, the protesters were not to retaliate. King utilized this strategy throughout the South, most prominently and effectively in Montgomery in 1955 and 1956 and in Birmingham, Alabama, in 1960. ER wrote in her "My Day"* column of 24 May 1957 that while all people possess a "breaking point" at which violent reaction to oppression becomes a possibility, "I hope that I am wrong and that we will see a continuation of the staunchness shown by the citizens in Montgomery, Ala., who under the leadership of the Rev. Martin Luther King, Jr. have adhered to non-violence" (Emblidge, 131).

In pursuing their common goal of civil rights for African Americans, King and ER worked together in a number of different settings. ER used her considerable clout to help the Southern Christian Leadership Council (SCLC), of which King was the first president, raise much-needed funds to run the Student Nonviolent Coordinating Committee (SNCC). Both appeared at a sold-out rally in New York City's Madison Square Garden to honor Autherine Lucy, the first black woman to seek admission at the segregated University of Alabama. Both nurtured an interest in Africa and the continent's travails in escaping colonialism while serving on the American Committee on Africa.

Most important, ER served as an intermediary between President John F. Kennedy* and King when relations between the two leaders broke down due to Kennedy's concern that too close a relationship with King would alienate his core support within the Democratic Party.* ER made certain that the president was aware of King's viewpoints on the various civil rights issues facing the nation. Not surprisingly, King and ER earned the ire of those opposed to their efforts in support of civil rights: the South detested both, labeling them communists; the FBI collected massive files on their civil rights activities.

As ER neared the end of her life, she expressed the admiration she had for the Reverend King. "Dr. King is a very moving speaker," she wrote in her "My Day" column of 6 February 1961. "He is simple and direct, and the spiritual quality which has made him the leader of non-violence in this country touches every speech he makes" (Emblidge, 270). King revealed his respect for ER in a heartfelt remembrance of the former

First Lady for the *New York Amsterdam News* on 24 November 1962. Describing ER as a "Humanitarian," a "Friend of the fallen," and a "Foe of injustice," King remarked, "The courage she displayed in taking sides on matters considered controversial, gave strength to those who risked only pedestrian loyalty and commitment to the great issues of our times."

SELECTED BIBLIOGRAPHY

Black, Allida. *Casting Her Own Shadow: Eleanor Roosevelt and the Shaping of Post War Liberalism*. 1996.

Emblidge, David, ed. *Eleanor Roosevelt's "My Day."* Vol. 3. 1991.

King, Martin Luther. "Epitaph for Mrs. FDR." *New York Amsterdam News*. 24 November 1962.

Oates, Stephen B. *Let the Trumpet Sound: The Life of Martin Luther King, Jr.* 1982.

Zangrando, Joanna S., and Robert L. Zangrando. "ER and Black Civil Rights." In Joan Hoff-Wilson and Marjorie Lightman, eds., *Without Precedent: The Life and Career of Eleanor Roosevelt*. 1984.

Dianne Lynch

L

LABOR. Eleanor Roosevelt, First Lady of the United States from 1933 to 1945 and political ambassador on behalf of liberalism until her death in 1962, firmly supported the philosophy and goals of the organized labor movement. Conscious of the troublesome and often wretched conditions of working-class life and desirous of refashioning the political system with the onset of the Great Depression,* ER insisted that labor could help build a strong, prosperous, and democratic America. She did not believe, as many on her left did, that conflict between labor and management was inevitable, and she often spoke out against the heavy-handed tactics of such union leaders as the long-serving head of the United Mine Workers (UMW), John L. Lewis. But ER did believe that in a modern capitalist society, unions had a fundamental role to play in achieving a more just political order and that unions protected individuals from both the vagaries of the marketplace and the power of big business. In 1941 in a magazine published by the American Federation of Labor, she declared, "The ideals of the organized labor movement are high ideals. They mean that we are not selfish in our desires, that we stand for the good of the group as a whole, and that is something which we in the United States are learning every day must be the attitude of every citizen" (*The American Federationist*, March 1941).

ER began to develop a deep interest in the labor movement after the end of World War I. In 1922 she established what proved to be a long and sustaining friendship with Rose Schneiderman,* a Jewish immigrant and a socialist who educated ER and her husband, Franklin D. Roosevelt,* on working-class issues. That same year, at Schneiderman's urging, she joined the Women's Trade Union League* (WTUL) and quickly proved to be one of the organization's most active and intelligent campaigners, as well as a crucial source of financial support. While a member of the WTUL, ER campaigned for female workers and acted to improve the onerous working conditions prevalent in American factories. ER was particularly enraged over the widespread use of child labor. In 1924 she successfully prodded the New York state Democratic Party to accept a plank at its convention that called for its abolishment. In 1927, as the chair of the legislative committee of the New York Women's City Club,* ER issued proposals for compulsory school attendance and strict enforcement of a fourteen-year-minimum age law for working boys.

The onset of the Great Depression in the fall of 1929 jolted ER's belief in the ability of progressive reformers like herself to improve the conditions of the nation's laborers through the prevailing means. The endless lines of unemployed workers milling outside the factory gates, the raw misery, and the apparent loss of hope among millions convinced her that America's political system had to change in fundamental ways. Our nation, she declared, needs a "spirit which is not afraid of new difficulties and new solutions, not afraid to stand hardships" (Cook, 423). She became convinced that the federal government now had to play a positive role in securing both social justice and economic security. Without either, America could not pretend to be a democracy. "It is not a true democracy," she insisted, "when some people cannot eat unless the government provides the food" (Hareven, 134).

During the depression, ER proved to be a constant voice of compassion for the downtrodden, as well as a main pillar of support for New Deal* liberalism. The unemployed, she affirmed in 1936, "are not a strange race" but are "like we would be if we had not had a fortunate chance at life" (Black, 29). ER strove to ensure adoption of liberal programs and laws that would bring a measure of security and justice to workers, the unemployed, and the aged. So, too, did she continue her campaign to end child labor. "No civilization," she argued, "should be based on the labor of children" (Hareven, 135). She urged upon her husband an expansive definition of liberalism and rallied support for such crucial legislation as the Social Security Act of 1935 and the Fair Labor Standards Act of 1938, which established a minimum wage and a forty-hour workweek and also abolished child labor. Finally, ER set a personal example of support for the labor movement during the 1930s by refusing to cross any picket lines while serving as First Lady. In 1939, for instance, she declined an invitation to attend a birthday celebration for the president at a hotel in Alexandria, Virginia, because the waitresses at the hotel were on strike.

During World War II* ER attempted to balance her support for organized labor with her commitment to the war effort. In 1941, when the president of the Brotherhood of Sleeping Car Porters, A. Philip Randolph, protested discriminatory hiring practices in defense industries and threatened a protest march on Washington, she attempted to persuade Randolph to call off the demonstration. At the same time, however, the First Lady called attention to Randolph's demands and prodded her husband to take effective action to help black workers. On 25 June 1941 FDR issued Executive Order 8802, which created a Committee on Fair Employment Practices (FEPC) and banned discrimination on the basis of "race, creed, color, or national origin" in government agencies and among businesses that held defense contracts. In 1943 ER faced a more serious challenge when John L. Lewis led the UMW in a series of strikes in the bituminous coal industry. Like most other Americans, ER was enraged over Lewis' actions and believed, erroneously, that the strikes threatened the war effort. Nonetheless, she refused to let her distaste for Lewis obscure her concern over the dangerous working conditions in the mines, and, unlike most politicians, she opposed the punitive 1943 Smith-Connally Act, which granted the president authority to seize plants threatened by strikes, required a thirty-day cooling-off period after a union called a strike, and prohibited union contributions to political candidates. Finally, during the war ER developed close relationships with younger labor leaders, notably, the rising star of the United Automobile Workers (UAW), Walter Reuther,* and Congress of Industrial Organizations (CIO) secretary-treasurer James C. Carey. Indeed, according to one account, she was Reuther's "secret weapon" (Black, 67) in the White House.

After the death of her husband in April 1945, ER continued her outspoken support for the labor movement. If anything, in the postwar world she became more adamant in her insistence that America's political and economic system be more responsive to the needs of the nation's workers. "If we really believe in Democracy," ER contended in 1945, then "we must face the fact that equality of opportunity is basic" (Black, 93). In postwar America, she argued, the nation's business leaders have got to look beyond the bottom line and consider the good of the whole nation. Even when undertaking the most basic decisions governing technology and production, industrialists, she held, should act in such a way that they benefit their workers and their communities as well as their stockholders.

Throughout the tumultuous years that President Harry S Truman* was in office (1945–1952), ER proved to be one of labor's most forceful supporters. In 1946 she offered broad support for the 4.5 million workers who participated in nearly 5,000 strikes, the greatest number of strikes in one year in American history. She insisted that companies could afford to raise wages, and she resoundingly defended the right of workers to strike "against the very great powers in the hand of industrial associations and organizations" (Black, 72). Indeed, ER backed labor's whole agenda of an expanded New Deal and vigorous public action in behalf of workers and minorities. She urged Truman to continue to support price controls, rebuked him for his threats to draft striking workers, and called upon Congress* to pass a strong full employment law and permanent Fair Employment Practices legislation. After Republicans gained control of both houses of Congress in 1946, ER cautioned conservatives to avoid harsh, antilabor measures. In 1947, when the eightieth Congress did pass the Taft-Hartley Act—which banned sympathy strikes, allowed the president to issue an eighty-day cooling-off period before strikes began, and permitted states to pass legislation proscribing union shops—she denounced conservatives for seeking to undo the New Deal. Labor's opponents, she claimed, argued that they opposed "socialism," but what they really were against were "old age pensions, Social Security, unemployment insurance," and "efforts to improve housing" (Emblidge, 244). In the newspaper of the Amalgamated Clothing Workers of America, ER stated that instead of clamping down on the labor movement, Americans "should be extremely grateful to unions," which had given workers a sense of decency by reducing poor working conditions "and by so doing have helped the country and all the workers" (*The Advance*, 1 September 1950). After Truman's presidency, ER continued to work closely with the labor movement and to advance its progressive agenda on civil rights,* social legislation, and civil liberties.

Though ER and organized labor usually agreed on most political questions, she dissented from the uncompromisingly hard-line Cold War* stance of key labor leaders. Led by George Meany, president of the American Federation of Labor (AFL), 1952–1955, and of the AFL-CIO, 1955–1979, organized labor was militantly anticommunist in the postwar era. Labor spokesmen often testified before the House Committee on Un-American Activities* (HUAC), called for stiff measures against members of the Communist Party, and insisted, in Meany's words, that "no country, no people, [and] no movement, can stand aloof and be neutral in this struggle" (Goulden, 272). In contrast, ER felt uneasy with these hard-line Cold War views, and she agreed with Meany's critics* in the labor movement that anticommunism had to be tempered with efforts to dampen Cold War tensions. True, she regularly spoke out against the evils of the Soviet system, and she supported most of the anticommunist foreign policy initiatives of the Truman administration. But she opposed measures to ban the Communist Party and joined liberal laborites in condemnation of anticommunist hysteria. She was particularly uncomfortable with the sweeping, moralistic language in which Meany and his supporters spoke. Thus, for example, in 1955, after Meany insisted that neutrality was not an acceptable position to take during the Cold War, ER personally rebuked him for being heavy-handed and "for a certain lack of recognition in this speech . . . that leadership requires an acceptance of one's own shortcomings and a constant effort to improve at home" (Goulden, 272).

Despite their differences over the issue of communism, ER and organized labor sustained a fruitful relationship right up to her death on 7
November 1962. Indeed, on her passing, few mourned her loss as much
as laborites. At the 1963 AFL-CIO convention, delegates respectfully
passed a resolution praising her for being "a noble woman whose mind
and heart were constantly devoted to those humanitarian causes to
which men and women in organized labor are likewise deeply dedicated." Mrs. Roosevelt, Walter Reuther added, has "more than any
woman who has lived in the last hundred years . . . symbolized the hopes
and aspirations of working people all over the world" (1963 AFL-CIO
Convention Proceedings, 524–27).

SELECTED BIBLIOGRAPHY

Black, Allida. *Casting Her Own Shadow: Eleanor Roosevelt and the Shaping of Modern
    Liberalism.* 1996.
Cook, Blanche Wiesen. *Eleanor Roosevelt.* Vol. 1. 1992.
Emblidge, David, ed. *Eleanor Roosevelt's "My Day."* Vol. 2. 1990.
Goulden, Joseph C. *Meany.* 1972.
Hareven, Tamara K. *Eleanor Roosevelt: An American Conscience.* 1968.
Scharf, Lois. *Eleanor Roosevelt: First Lady of American Liberalism.* 1987.

                                              Robert H. Zieger and Anders G. Lewis

LADIES' HOME JOURNAL. As a writer, Eleanor Roosevelt had a long
association with the *Ladies' Home Journal*, the nation's leading monthly
women's magazine in paid circulation in the middle decades of the twentieth century. It ended unhappily for the *Journal*, which underestimated
her appeal to its audience, chiefly housewives, and let ER move to its
chief competitor, *McCall's.** Nevertheless, ER's work for the *Journal*,
owned by the influential Curtis Publishing Company, helped establish
her credentials as a magazine journalist and make her a role model for
American women.

It was in the *Journal* that ER, tentatively moving into public life, first
made her journalistic debut before a national audience. In 1923 as a
spokesperson for the Bok Peace Prize,* a competition funded by former
Journal editor Edward Bok, to choose the best plan for world peace, ER
announced the details in the *Journal*. In her article she called attention to
the then-novel idea of soliciting expressions of public opinion via mass
communication. In the years to come her personal interaction with the
public would mark her *Journal* contributions.

ER's next major connection with the *Journal* came in 1937, when it
serialized the first volume of her autobiography,* *This Is My Story*, which
took her life from birth through her marriage to Franklin D. Roosevelt*
up until 1924. Contacted by ER's agent, George Bye, the *Journal's* new
editors, Bruce Gould and Beatrice Gould, eager to bolster sagging circulation, snatched up the rights to the book for $75,000. An enormous

sum for the times, this was an amount equal to FDR's annual salary as president. Other executives at Curtis, whose leading publication was the strongly anti-Roosevelt *Saturday Evening Post*, criticized the Goulds, but their action brought favorable attention to the *Journal* from liberal New York columnists and critics.

Years later, the Goulds recalled how ER had confided to them, "I can't tell you how happy this makes me, to receive all this attention for something I've done by myself and not because of Franklin" (Beasley, 110). This overlooked the fact that it was her husband's position that made her memoir so salable, but it showed ER's hunger for recognition. The serialization was highly successful, with readers sweeping 250,000 copies of the first installment off the newsstands, a significant factor in allowing *Journal* circulation to overtake that of its chief rivals, *Woman's Home Companion** and *McCall's*. According to the Goulds, they made "the exciting discovery that Eleanor Roosevelt's autobiography was read, in effect, by everyone—in government, parlors, and slums" (Gould, 198).

Although the editors did not think ER was a good writer, they bought three articles by her after the book series ended (on divorce, April 1938— she thought it necessary under some circumstances—on the need for good manners, June 1939, and on her busy days, October 1940). At the same time she sold articles to various publications including *Journal* rivals *McCall's*, *Good Housekeeping*, and *Woman's Day*.

In 1941 Bye suggested that ER write a monthly page for the *Journal*. The Goulds quickly accepted the idea but with editorial control to avoid what they saw as the "inanity" of some of her "My Day"* columns (Gould, 214). They agreed to pay her $2,500 per month for a question-and-answer column, "If You Ask Me," in which she would answer questions selected by the editors from those sent in by readers. The column allowed her to speak directly to millions of readers about topics of concern to them, enhancing her stature as a political figure and celebrity.

She launched the column in May 1941 with a call for compulsory national service by women as well as men, an idea rapidly shot down by critics, even though ER proposed women would not have to go outside their local communities. Subsequent columns covered a wide range of topics, as ER answered eight to ten questions per issue, following a format similar to her question-and-answer column in the *Democratic Digest** from 1937 to 1941. She gave advice on personal relationships, explained her husband's policies, and explored issues about which she herself felt strongly.

The Goulds called it "an instantaneous hit" and praised her "succinct" answers to questions such as, "Do you mean by 'racial equality' intermarrying of the races?," to which she replied, "Not of necessity. Marriage is an individual thing and each person must decide for himself. Equality of the races, however, can be established whether individuals decide to marry or not" (Gould, 215). Sometimes she showed flashes of humor, as when asked, "What do you think of the increasing tendency of novelists to use so many 'four-letter-words' not spoken in polite society?" and she responded, "I did not know there were any words left that were not spoken in polite society" (Gould, 215).

In the midst of answering innocuous queries, ER discussed controversial topics: abortion (not a good solution but not a question for legislation, May 1942); planned parenthood (carefully supported in terms of a couple's decisions when to have children, July 1944); representation of women at the peace table when World War II* ended (yes, but they should be younger and have more government experience than she herself, December 1943). Her forthright comments made the column required reading for liberal columnists—and opponents, who criticized her opinions. Yet, drawing on her personal experiences, as in August 1944, ER sometimes expressed melancholy over women's roles: "[L]ike many other women, very little that I have done in life seems to have been done as a matter of choice."

In 1942 ER journeyed to England on an official morale-building mission that also provided material for *Journal* articles. Her travels* there were the basis for a *Journal* article in February 1943 praising the British for kindness to American troops as well as one two months later on British women coping with wartime conditions. On the trip she was joined by the Goulds at the suggestion of FDR, who encouraged their frequent visits to the White House as a way of establishing relations with Republican editors. The British trip helped the Goulds make contacts that led to one of their most successful series—the story of the British princesses, Elizabeth and Margaret Rose, by their former governess.

ER had an agreeable working relationship with the *Journal* until 1949. In December 1943 the magazine carried an article on her trip to the South Pacific as an American Red Cross* representative and in February 1944 a companion piece on the war work of Australian and New Zealand women. Selected columns were published in a book in 1946. When she presented the second volume of her autobiography to the *Journal*, however, the relationship soured.

The *Journal* was given first option on serialization rights to *This I Remember*, but Bruce Gould was not pleased with the manuscript, telling her, "You have written this too hastily—as though you were composing it on a bicycle while pedaling your way to a fire" (Lash, 285). When Gould wanted her to work extensively with a collaborator, ER and her son, Elliott Roosevelt,* decided to look elsewhere, even though Gould warned that if another publisher accepted the manuscript, he would drop her question-and-answer page.

ER paid little attention to the threat. Elliott took the manuscript to *McCall's*, which jumped at the chance to it, sight unseen, for $150,000 and happily took the column, too, paying her $500 more per page than had the *Journal*. It also gave her a five-year contract, while the *Journal* had insisted on a month-to-month one. After the autobiography turned out to be a tremendous critical and commercial success, the Goulds admitted they had been "at least half in the wrong" (Gould, 285). The *Journal* had lost one of its valuable assets to the competition.

SELECTED BIBLIOGRAPHY

Beasley, Maurine H. *Eleanor Roosevelt and the Media: A Public Quest for Self-Fulfillment.* 1987.
Gould, Beatrice, and Bruce Gould. *American Story.* 1968.
Lash, Joseph P. *Eleanor: The Years Alone.* 1972.
Roosevelt, Eleanor. *If You Ask Me.* 1946.
Zuckerman, Mary Ellen. *A History of Popular Women's Magazines in the United States: 1792–1995.* 1998.

Kathleen L. Endres

LAPE, ESTHER EVERETT (8 October 1881, Wilmington, DE–17 May 1981, New York).

Esther Lape, an activist for various progressive causes, including world peace and national health care, served for over thirty years as director of the American Foundation, a private, public-interest organization. She was an important influence on Eleanor Roosevelt's developing interest in political causes. Lape stood at the center of "the world of postsuffrage feminists" (Cook, 6), who gave ER the support to follow her own vision.

Eleanor Roosevelt met Lape in 1920 after ER joined the board of the New York state League of Women Voters.* Persuaded to monitor the progress of the league's legislative program, ER received help from Elizabeth Read,* an attorney. Read was the life partner of Lape, a Wellesley graduate who had taught English at various colleges, including Swarthmore and Barnard, before establishing a career as a journalist and publicist. The three women became lifelong friends, working closely together on a range of political issues and sharing other interests. Like Madame Souvestre,* the headmistress of Allenswood, the school in England that ER had attended, Lape and Read were stylish and cultivated. ER enjoyed dining and reading literature in French with them one night each week at their home in New York's Greenwich Village in the 1920s. She later wrote of Lape and Read: "Their standards of work and their interests played a great part in what might be called 'the intensive education of Eleanor Roosevelt' during the next few years" (Roosevelt, 325).

They, in turn, admired ER's emerging ability as an organizer. Their respect and friendship helped restore ER's confidence in herself in the aftermath of her discovery of her husband's relationship with Lucy Mercer (Rutherfurd*). Through Lape, ER became involved in the Bok Peace

Eleanor Roosevelt appears with Esther Lape in Washington, D.C., in 1924 for hearings by a Senate committee investigating the Bok Peace Prize. *Courtesy of Franklin D. Roosevelt Library*

Prize* competition, funded by Edward Bok, the former editor of the *Ladies' Home Journal.** Impressed by articles that Lape had written on woman's rights and immigrants, in 1923 Bok asked her to direct his contest to select the best plan to preserve world peace. The winner was to receive an initial $50,000 and an additional $50,000 if the plan was accepted by the U.S. Senate.

Lape agreed only after obtaining approval to invite two associates from the League of Women Voters, ER and Narcissa Cox Vanderlip,* to work with her on the prize committee. The winning entry called for U.S. membership in the World Court* and conditional support for the League of Nations,* arousing hostility from isolationists. The competition, which generated massive amounts of publicity, became the subject of a Senate investigation, although Bok and Lape, who went to the Capitol in ER's company, testified so effectively that the inquiry was dropped.

Lape continued to work for U.S. participation in the World Court as member-in-charge of the American Foundation, which Bok founded in 1924 to address public policy issues, particularly support of the World

Court. In 1927 President Calvin Coolidge sent her to Europe as an unofficial envoy to study how best to present the World Court in the United States.

After Franklin D. Roosevelt* was elected president in 1932, ER rented a small apartment above Lape and Read's own quarters in the building they owned on East Eleventh Street. She retreated there from the White House, taking comfort in the fact that Lape and Read were loyal, trusted friends who did not seek to benefit personally from their relationship with her. When Lape finally revealed in 1937 that she and Read were Democrats, ER replied, "I have never cared what you and Lizzie were politically. . . . It does not make the slightest difference unless either of you were trying for a Democratic party job. I know that isn't even a remote possibility" (ER to Lape, 8 July 1937). Malvina Thompson* (Scheider), ER's secretary, also became a close friend of Lape, carrying on a candid personal correspondence that included comments on ER's career, friends, and family.

Lape and ER conferred from time to time on political issues. Lape turned to ER as an intermediary in an effort to gain FDR's backing for membership in the World Court. Despite FDR's belated support in 1935, the U.S. Senate did not ratify U.S. participation in the court until it became the International Court of Justice of the United Nations* in 1945.

Lape also supported U.S. recognition of the Soviet Union, serving as member-in-charge of the American Foundation Committee on Russian–American Relations. In the fall of 1933, Lape wrote to ER asking if publication of the committee's *The United States and the Soviet Union* would cause any embarrassment for FDR. ER wired back, "Franklin says go ahead with release any time you want" (ER to EL, 19 October 1933). The report favoring recognition was published 1 November 1933. FDR announced resumption of diplomatic relations between the United States and the Soviet Union seventeen days later.

After the Social Security Act of 1935 failed to address health care, Lape worked with ER to arrange a meeting in 1937 between FDR and a committee of physicians who advocated federal aid for medical education, research, and hospitals to raise standards and provide medical attention for the indigent. Their proposals reflected some of the conclusions set forth in *American Medicine: Expert Testimony Out of Court*, a two-volume report edited by Lape and published in 1937 by the American Foundation. It summarized the views of 2,100 doctors who disagreed with the assertion of the American Medical Association (AMA) that American health care was adequate. Expressing concerned about the lack of medical care available to an estimated one-third of Americans, FDR supported a National Health Conference held in January 1938. This led to the Wagner health bill of 1939, but the AMA fought against it. In the face of this opposition, FDR did not endorse the bill, and the approach of World War II* soon drew his attention to other issues. Continuing her interest in health care, Lape later prepared *Medical Research: A Midcentury Survey*, a study of trends in medical research, issued in two volumes by the American Foundation in 1955, when ER was a board member.

As her own career expanded, ER carefully maintained ties with Lape and Read. Correspondence between Lape and ER touched not only on political issues but also on plans for visits (often postponed by changes in ER's schedule), the exchange of small gifts, and solicitude about the other's welfare. Lape once insisted that an indisposition ER considered minor was "pneumonia—special walking type 'Anna Eleanor Roosevelt ambulous'" (EL to ER, 16 May 1934). ER often saw Lape and Read at their Westbrook, Connecticut, country retreat, Salt Meadow, which they had purchased in 1927. She wrote a number of her "My Day"* newspaper columns there. After Read's death in 1943, ER made time to visit the lonely survivor there.

In a letter to ER on Election Day in 1944, Lape commiserated, "Of the outcome of this election I cannot feel the slightest doubt—you are in for it." She urged ER, however, "to take time to think out the best ways to make available—in the places and to the persons best able to use it—the tremendously increased powers that are so peculiarly now yours." She concluded on a lighter note, "The Connecticut Light and Power man told me my social position had suffered by reason of [my] Democratic enrollment in this particular place. But when I said I never had any (social position) he had no answer" (EL to ER, 8 November 1944).

ER visited Lape for the last time in 1962, a few months before her own death. Lape, along with Helen Rogers Reid, the former publisher of the *New York Herald Tribune*, and Lady Stella Reading, an English friend of ER, organized a committee to ask the Nobel Committee to consider a posthumous award of the Peace Prize in 1965 to ER. The prize that year, however, went to the United Nations International Children's Emergency Fund.

In her later years Lape befriended Lorena Hickok,* ER's close friend, and served as a source of information for Joseph P. Lash* when he wrote his biographies of ER. In 1972 Lape donated Salt Meadow, a 147-acre property, to the federal government to be maintained as a wildlife refuge.

SELECTED BIBLIOGRAPHY
Cook, Blanche Wiesen. *Eleanor Roosevelt*. Vol. 1. 1992.
Eleanor Roosevelt Papers, Franklin D. Roosevelt Library, Hyde Park, NY.
Lash, Joseph P. *Eleanor and Franklin*. 1971.
———. *Eleanor: The Years Alone*. 1972.
———. *Love, Eleanor: Eleanor Roosevelt and Her Friends*. 1982.
Roosevelt, Eleanor. *This Is My Story*. 1937.

Kristie Miller

LASH, JOSEPH P. (2 December 1909, New York–22 August 1987, Boston).

A onetime radical who later became a liberal journalist and political activist, Joseph Lash was best known for his biographies of Eleanor Roosevelt—one of which, *Eleanor and Franklin* (1971), received the Pulitzer Prize. Lash was more than ER's biographer, however. Friends for more than thirty years and sharing complementary political opinions, Lash looked to ER for personal and professional guidance. ER, in turn, considered Lash one of her inner circle of liberal advisers and confidants. Even after her death in 1962, Lash and ER continued to benefit from their relationship: ER's life story provided Lash with much of his professional acclaim; Lash, as ER's biographer, shaped America's memory of "the First Lady of the World"—in stunning, intimate, and accurate detail.

Born in New York City in 1909 to Russian Jewish immigrants, Joe Lash graduated in 1931 from the City University of New York, where he majored in English. He proceeded to Columbia University, earning a master's degree in literature and philosophy. In 1932 he began looking for work, but the Great Depression* limited his employment options and disillusioned him with capitalism. Lash began participating in a variety of leftist American student movements, all of which sought greater economic and political justice and rights. In 1932 he became secretary of the Socialist Party's Student League of Industrial Democracy (SLID) and editor of its periodical, *Student Outlook*. Three years later, a Lash-led SLID merged with its rival, the Communist National Student League, to form the American Student Union* (ASU). Lash served as the ASU's national secretary from 1935 to 1939, during which time the ASU (and the American student Left) began to fracture as factions of socialists, communists, and liberals expressed different opinions concerning the New Deal* and the Spanish civil war.

In the mid-1930s a Popular Front of these three groups attempted to work together for progressive causes but ultimately could not breach their differences. Lash's ASU, in particular, struggled over the role of communists in the partnership. The 1939 Nazi–Soviet Pact effectively ended the Popular Front and horrified Lash, who had admired communism's antifascist stand in Spain.* He abandoned his plans to join the Communist Party and instead became a leading noncommunist within the ASU and the student Left. As the decade ended, Lash was increasingly embroiled in, and personally conflicted about, internal ASU political conflicts between communists and noncommunists.

In 1939 the House Committee on Un-American Activities* (HUAC) investigated communist activities within American youth* groups. HUAC summoned Lash and representatives from the American Youth Congress* (AYC) to answer charges that their organizations were communist-dominated. On the train ride to Washington, Lash and his compatriots met Eleanor Roosevelt by chance. The First Lady, a supporter of progressive student activism, attended the HUAC session to show support for the students and invited several, including Lash, to the White House. ER was intrigued by Lash's attempts to stymie the HUAC committee's Red-baiting, while still expressing his heartfelt disagreements with communists in the student movement. She asked Lash to stay in touch, offering him the use of her Val-Kill* cottage for rest and contemplation of his political future.

Later in life, Lash speculated about why his friendship with ER blossomed during the late 1930s. "What deep needs within her nature I answered I could never quite fathom," he admitted, but he believed that he and ER shared "a moral affinity" and a "real sense of kinship and understanding." Above all, according to Lash, ER needed her own friends. "She had a compelling emotional need to have people who were close, who in a sense were hers and upon whom she could lavish help, attention, tenderness," Lash wrote. "Without such friends, she feared she would dry up and die" (Lash, *A Friend's Memoir*, 140–41).

Lash's disappointment with the communist-influenced ASU led to his resignation from the group in 1940 and his full embrace of New Deal liberalism, a conversion aided by ER. Lash devoted himself to the 1940 presidential campaign of Franklin D. Roosevelt,* directing the Youth Division of the Democratic National Committee. In 1941 Lash organized a youth leadership institute at the Roosevelt summer home at Campobello,* New Brunswick. From 1940 to 1942, he was general secretary of the International Student Service (ISS), which assisted foreign students visiting the United States.

ER's friendship and assistance helped Lash in each of these endeavors. ER, in turn, benefited from Lash's savvy political advice; the former radical educated (and warned) ER about communist factions in the youth movement. Their friendship, however, elicited criticism from both the Left and the Right. Communists contended Lash had sold out to the Establishment, while conservatives thought Lash a dangerous radical who possibly shared the First Lady's bed. These false rumors of a salacious relationship between Lash and ER flourished during World War II,* appearing in ER's confidential Federal Bureau of Investigation* (FBI) file kept by J. Edgar Hoover.

Lash's political past stymied his attempt to gain a commission in U.S. Naval Intelligence in 1941; his application, using ER as a reference, became controversial when conservative members of Congress* and the press used it to criticize FDR's defense plans and to castigate ER's friendship with a former student radical. Lash was drafted into the army in April 1942. Stationed in the South Pacific for eighteen months, he and

ER engaged in frequent correspondence, and she visited him on her 1943 American Red Cross* tour of the South Pacific. ER encouraged Lash's roromantic relationship with another ISS organizer and liberal activist, Trude Pratt, and was pleased when she became Trude Pratt Lash* in 1944.

After leaving the military at the end of the war, Lash resumed his involvement in the liberal politics that he shared with ER. He and ER were founding members of the Americans for Democratic Action* (ADA), an anticommunist liberal organization; Lash was New York ADA director from 1946 to 1948. In 1950 Lash joined the staff of the *New York Post* and covered the United Nations* (UN) at the time ER served on the U.S. delegation to the organization. Their relationship helped Lash write his 1961 laudatory biography of UN secretary-general Dag Hammarskjold; Lash dedicated the book to ER. From 1960 to 1966, Lash was the assistant editor of the *Post*'s editorial page, writing columns as well as editorials.

During the 1950s Lash began his most famous pursuit, acting as chronicler of the Roosevelt years in the White House. In 1952 he helped Elliott Roosevelt* edit two volumes of FDR's letters. After ER's death in 1962, Lash wrote a short biography, *Eleanor Roosevelt: A Friend's Memoir*, which appeared in 1964. Two years later, Franklin Roosevelt Jr. chose Lash to write his mother's definitive life story, allowing him sole access to ER's files. Lash published *Eleanor and Franklin* in 1971 to tremendous critical acclaim, including a National Book Award as well as the Pulitzer Prize. A sequel, *Eleanor: The Years Alone*, followed. By that time Lash had established himself as the leading authority on the Roosevelts, and several other books followed, including two volumes based on ER's correspondence.

Lash's portrayal of the former First Lady was accurate and detailed, befitting the author's unparalleled knowledge of ER's life, while remaining humane and believable; Lash wrote biographies, not hagiographies. In Lash's *New York Times* obituary of 23 April 1987, the Pulitzer jurors were quoted as noting in their 1971 citation for *Eleanor and Franklin*, "It is a sharp, vivid yet kindly recreation of the loves of a famous couple, shedding new insights on their sometimes inspired, sometimes deeply troubled relationship."

At Lash's death, his place in American journalism and history seemed secure. His career as a political activist, journalist, and author had engaged him with ER as a friend, mentor, political ally, and historical subject who shaped his life in innumerable ways. At the same time, Lash influenced ER's life, making it richer, warmer, and more stimulating. As ER wrote to Lash in a birthday letter in 1956, "I love you very dearly & to see you interested & content inwardly means much to me" (Lash, *A World of Love*, 453).

SELECTED BIBLIOGRAPHY
Joseph P. Lash Papers, Franklin D. Roosevelt Library, Hyde Park, NY.
Lash, Joseph P. *Eleanor Roosevelt: A Friend's Memoir.* 1964.
————. *Eleanor: The Years Alone.* 1972.
————. *Love Eleanor: Eleanor Roosevelt and Her Friends.* 1982.
————. *A World of Love: Eleanor Roosevelt and Her Friends, 1943–1962.* 1984.

Veronica A. Wilson

LASH, TRUDE PRATT (13 June 1908, Germany–   ).

Best known as the wife of political activist and Eleanor Roosevelt biographer Joseph P. Lash,* Trude Lash is a professional woman whose support and leadership of social causes brought her to the forefront of liberalism in New York state during the twentieth century's middle decades. During the 1940s she and Eleanor Roosevelt developed a close, personal friendship, built, in large part, from their mutual devotion to Joe Lash, which lasted until ER's death in 1962.

Trude Lash and ER also shared a zeal for advocating an activist liberal political agenda. In the political arena, ER's stature as the "First Lady of American Liberalism" offered Lash a role model and provided her with links to influential persons. Lash skillfully used these connections to forward her own causes in the fields of child care and welfare.

Born Gertrude von Adam Wenzel in the Black Forest section of Germany, she is the daughter of a chemist and engineer who hoped she would follow in his footsteps. Instead, she studied philology, philosophy, and literature in Germany and Paris, earning a Ph.D. in philosophy from the University of Freiburg in 1930. In 1931 she came to the United States and taught at Hunter College in New York for one year; she also served as a delegate to the World Conference of the International Student Service (ISS), an organization dedicated to solving the problems faced by university students that met at Mt. Holyoke College in Massachusetts.

In the fall of 1932, she returned to Germany and began writing for a liberal newspaper that the Nazis suppressed when Adolf Hitler came to power in 1933. By then, however, she had married U.S. citizen Eliot D. Pratt, whom she had met through her ISS work, and left Nazi Germany for New York City. Pratt, a member of a prominent New York family with a history of philanthropy, provided her with an early entrée into the elite liberal circles with which she would associate for the rest of her life.

In the 1930s Trude began working for organizations of students and refugees,* most prominently the ISS, which had transformed itself into a refugee aid group. During World War II* she succeeded Joseph Lash as the general secretary of the ISS. She helped organize the 1942 International Student Assembly of youth representatives from the Allied nations fighting the Axis powers of Germany, Italy, and Japan. It met at the Roosevelts' summer home in Campobello,* New Brunswick.

While involved in the ISS in the late 1930s, she met Joe Lash and his close friend and mentor ER. After considerable soul-searching and counsel by ER, Trude divorced Eliot Pratt, with whom she had three children, and married Lash in November 1944. She gave birth to their son, Jonathan, in 1945. Trude's relationship with ER became an integral part of her life during the 1930s and World War II. "It was the kind of relationship in which one had daily contact," Trude recalled. "Unless Mrs. Roosevelt was abroad in Asia* or Europe we would telephone each other every morning. There were few days without at least a voice contact" (McDonald, 153). In 1945 Trude introduced ER to David Gurewitsch,* a physician, who became ER's closest friend in the last years of her life.

In the postwar years, Trude Lash managed to balance marriage, children, and career as she continued to work, often with ER, for progressive political causes. She was secretary for the United Nations' Human Rights Commission, headed by ER, worked with the former First Lady on behalf of Israeli children during the mid-1950s, and was active in the Democratic Party* with ER. She earned public acclaim as the executive director of the Citizen's Committee for Children (CCC), a New York City–based child welfare advocacy group whose support largely came from New York's philanthropies that had connections with ER. Lash led the CCC from 1953 to 1972, its most important and successful years, launching fund-raising and publicity drives, efficiently managing a growing staff, and bringing the organization's work to the attention of sympathetic New York politicians, especially New York City mayor Robert Wagner. ER provided a powerful political presence in the organization and helped bring it publicity.

When Lash retired from the organization in 1972, numerous New York political and civic leaders lauded her "unmatched contributions to the welfare" of the city (*New York Times*, 26 May 1972). She, in turn, credited ER with providing the personal guidance and assistance needed to achieve the organization's objectives. Lash now divides her time between Martha's Vineyard, Massachusetts, Key West, Florida, and New York City. She has served since 1987 as cochair of the Franklin and Eleanor Roosevelt Institute, Hyde Park,* New York, dedicated to preserving the ideals of the Roosevelts and applying them to current problems.

SELECTED BIBLIOGRAPHY

Lash, Joseph P. *Love, Eleanor: Eleanor Roosevelt and Her Friends*. 1982.

———. *A World of Love: Eleanor Roosevelt and Her Friends, 1943–1962*. 1984.

McDonald, Mary J. "The Citizen's Committee for Children of New York and the Evolution of Child Advocacy, 1945–1972." Ph.D. dissertation. New York University. 1993.

Veronica A. Wilson

LATIN AMERICA. From the 1920s until her death in 1962, Eleanor Roosevelt's interactions with Latin America were conducted in the context of furthering U.S. policy goals in the region. She served as a highly successful goodwill ambassador; an interpreter of Pan-Americanism to the U.S. public; and a critic of Republican interventionist policies in the Caribbean and Central America.

ER's January 1927 editorial for the *Women's Democratic News,** "Our Foreign Policy—What Is It?," charged that there was no "constructive effort to build up good feeling" with our hemispheric neighbors. ER's concern with creating "good feeling" among the nations of the Western Hemisphere was part of the rethinking of U.S. relations with Latin America that became the Good Neighbor Policy, formally announced by Franklin D. Roosevelt* in his first inaugural address in 1933.

During her years in the White House, ER maintained a public position of neutrality on women's issues raised in the inter-American arena. Within the United States, ER's support of protective legislation for women workers put her at odds with the advocacy of equal rights by the National Woman's Party (NWP), but in the inter-American arena ER's antipathy toward Doris Stevens, a leader of the NWP and chair of the Inter-American Commission of Women, was subsumed to the diplomatic goal of creating hemispheric solidarity. At the Seventh International Conference of American States held in Montevideo, Uruguay, in December 1933, the Inter-American Commission of Women introduced a treaty entitled "The Convention on the Nationality of Women" that endorsed women's equality. Both opponents and advocates of the treaty sought the support of the First Lady; in a 20 December 1933 United Press story from Washington journalist Ruby Black* reported: "Mrs. Franklin D. Roosevelt firmly refused to participate in the feminist controversy which ended today when the U.S. delegation at Montevideo agreed to sign the equal nationality treaty."

As war neared, ER played an active role in promoting hemispheric cooperation. In 1941 she accepted the offer of the Pan American Coffee Bureau, comprised of Brazil, Colombia, Costa Rica, Cuba, the Dominican Republic, El Salvador, Mexico, and Venezuela, to give a series of Sunday evening radio broadcasts.* ER opened the program on 28 September 1941 with a salute to the mutual desire of the nations of the Americas to build a defensive unit based on economic cooperation and cultural understanding. ER primarily addressed her remarks to the American homemaker, but the Pan-American broadcasts also provided a forum for the discussion of inter-American policy. On 1 December 1941 Nelson Rockefeller, federal coordinator of inter-American affairs, described the contributions U.S. hemispheric allies were making to the defense effort and publicized the availability of cultural educational programs. ER's 22 February 1942 guest, Leo S. Rowe, director-general of the Pan-American

Eleanor Roosevelt chats with U.S. enlisted men on 27 March 1944 at a base in the Galapagos Islands off the coast of Ecuador during her morale-building trip to military installations in Central and South America. *Courtesy of Franklin D. Roosevelt Library*

Union, explained the history of inter-American mutual defense agreements and reported the results of the meeting of the ministers of foreign affairs of the American republics in Rio de Janeiro, 15–28 January 1942, at which nineteen of the twenty-one American nations agreed to break diplomatic relations with the Axis powers. The twin themes of the Good Neighbor Policy and coffee, "the Good Neighbor Drink," framed the spokesman's thanks to ER in the final broadcast 5 April 1942.

In her role as First Lady, ER hosted receptions, dinners, and luncheons attended by Latin American visitors as well as the resident diplomatic community. Her calendar revealed continual contact with Latin Americans through her attendance at Pan-American conferences on children, labor,* and health; during the drafting of the charter of the United Nations* she worked closely with Berta Lutz of Brazil, Minerva Bernardino of the Dominican Republic, and Mexican Amalia Castillo de Ledón, all Latin American members of the Inter-American Commission of Women. ER took Spanish lessons, which she put to effective use at a dinner with Mexican president and Mrs. Manuel Avila Camacho in Monterrey, Mexico, 19 April 1943. In June 1943 she flew with world-renowned Brazilian aviator Anesia Pinheiro Machado to publicize the joint program of the U.S. Civil Aeronautics Administration and the Office of the Coordinator of Inter-American Affairs in which women were trained to teach other women and army and navy pilots to fly.

In March 1944 ER undertook a goodwill trip to U.S. military bases in the Caribbean and Central and South America. Ruby Black, who was a correspondent for the Puerto Rico newspaper *La Democracia*, had proposed as early as 1940 that the First Lady undertake a goodwill trip to Latin America. In 1944 Black, who had taken a job in the Office of the Coordinator of Inter-American Affairs, was instrumental in designing ER's mission, which quickly expanded beyond boosting the spirits of American service personnel. The South American portion of the trip included stops at Natal, Belem, and Recife in Brazil and visits to Caracas, Venezuela, and Guayaquil, Ecuador. The public and press greeted her with exuberance: "Mrs. Roosevelt: Good Neighbor Ambassador" proclaimed the 21 March 1944 edition of *Acción Democrática* (Caracas, Venezuela); in Ecuador, *La Prensa* dedicated its 24 March issue "to the United Nations and Mrs. Roosevelt, symbol and spirit of the American women engaged in war work." She completed her tour with stops at U.S. bases in Panama, Puerto Rico, and Cuba.

ER's familiarity with Latin America served U.S. interests well at the first meeting of the United Nations in London, January 1946. John Foster Dulles* asked her to speak for the U.S. delegation to the General Assembly on the issue of forced repatriation of refugees,* which the United States opposed. ER wrote of the experience in *On My Own*: "I knew we must, if possible, hold our South American colleagues until the vote was taken . . . So I talked about Simon Bolivar and his stand for the freedom of the people of Latin America . . . to my joy the South American representatives stayed with us to the end, and when the vote came, we won" (Roosevelt, 51).

In 1952 President Harry S Truman* asked ER to head the American delegation to the inauguration of Chilean president-elect Carlos Ibáñez, who had campaigned on an anti-American, pro-Peronist platform. With typical energy and lack of pretense, ER eschewed all nonessential social functions and spent her time in Santiago touring housing projects and health and hospital centers and, to the delight of the Chilean people, held a wide-open press conference. The rumored anti-American fervor never developed, and Ibáñez made a point of being seen on cordial terms with her. The Chilean mission, ER's last as an ambassador *extraordinaire*, was a resounding diplomatic success.

ER was steadfast in her opposition to U.S. intervention in the affairs of other American republics. During the presidential debates in August

1960 she wrote John F. Kennedy* to caution him against giving the impression that, if elected, he would act unilaterally, rather than in concert with the other American states, vis-à-vis Cuba.

Through the radio broadcasts, the 1944 goodwill trip, and state visits and as hostess at meetings, receptions, and conferences, ER made a significant contribution to U.S. efforts to bind the nations of the hemisphere into a defensive whole during the war years. Later, her understanding of the nuances of inter-American relations proved valuable to the Truman and Kennedy administrations and in her work at the United Nations.

SELECTED BIBLIOGRAPHY

Beasley, Maurine, and Paul Belgrade. "Eleanor Roosevelt: First Lady as Radio Pioneer." *Journalism History* 11 (Autumn/Winter 1984): 3–4.
Doris Stevens Collection, Schlesinger Library, Radcliffe College, Cambridge, MA.
Miller, Francesca. *Latin American Women and the Search for Social Justice.* 1991.
Roosevelt, Eleanor. *On My Own.* 1958.
Ruby Black Collection, Manuscript Division, Library of Congress, Washington, DC.
Transcripts of the Pan American Coffee Bureau Broadcasts, Manuscript Division, Library of Congress, Washington, DC.

Francesca Miller

LEAGUE OF NATIONS. Eleanor Roosevelt, who showed little interest in the peace movement* or collective security measures before World War I, became an ardent supporter of the League of Nations. Created after World War I at the Paris Peace Conference (1919), the league was the first international security organization. President Woodrow Wilson, the world's leading proponent of the idea by 1918, convinced negotiators for the other major Allied powers—England, France, and Italy—to include the league Covenant in the Treaty of Versailles, which ended World War I. But when Wilson returned home to sell the idea to the American people and the U.S. Senate, he met firm resistance.

ER visited devastated regions in Europe in early 1919 and returned home committed to the league and to American participation in the organization. She did not, however, offer unqualified support for the Versailles treaty, which she believed excessively favored Britain and France's harsh settlement demands. Ultimately, the Senate failed to ratify the treaty because of the inclusion of the league Covenant. The resulting lack of formal U.S. participation in the 1920s and 1930s weakened the organization severely. Throughout the years between World War I and World War II,* however, ER remained one of the nation's most prominent pro-league advocates. In the early years of the Cold War* after World War II, ER's continued confidence in the effectiveness of collective security organizations led to her devoted support of the League of Nation's successor institution, the United Nations.*

SELECTED BIBLIOGRAPHY

Cook, Blanche Wiesen. *Eleanor Roosevelt.* Vol. 1. 1992.
Hoff-Wilson, Joan, and Marjorie Lightman, eds. *Without Precedent: The Life and Career of Eleanor Roosevelt.* 1984.
Lash, Joseph P. *Eleanor and Franklin.* 1971.

John M. Craig

LEAGUE OF WOMEN VOTERS. Eleanor Roosevelt joined the New York state League of Women Voters in 1920 and remained active in the organization throughout her life. She stayed in touch with the organization's leaders and activities because of the role the league had played in her life and her belief in its significant role in citizen's political education.

Carrie Chapman Catt,* who became a cherished friend of ER, organized the nonpartisan League of Women Voters as an outgrowth of the National American Woman Suffrage Association in 1919, when the passage of the Nineteenth Amendment became apparent. The league's objectives were to educate women on voting, implement a program of desired legislative reform, and promote active interest in public policy on federal and state levels.

ER's first responsibility for the New York state league was to chair its legislative committee in 1921. With the assistance of Elizabeth Read,* a lawyer with whom she developed a lasting friendship, ER studied the *Congressional Record*, investigated pending bills, and prepared a report on her findings for league members.

In January 1921 ER represented Dutchess County at the annual state convention of the League of Women Voters at Albany, New York. She heard a speech by Nathan L. Miller, the Republican governor, who condemned the league and castigated its lobbying agenda for welfare legislation as detrimental to American institutions. Narcissa Cox Vanderlip,* chair of the New York League, invited Catt to respond, and she promptly denounced the governor's remarks. His assault backfired and helped to increase the league's membership. Catt's fearlessness in challenging the governor impressed ER, who became Catt's admirer.

ER also attended the second annual national convention of the league in Cleveland in April 1921 as a New York delegate. Through her work with the league, ER met women who emotionally supported and educated her as she began a public life, giving presentations to league members on issues such as the Sheppard-Towner Maternity and Infancy Act to promote the welfare of mothers and babies. From league colleagues, ER learned about the intricacies of public policy, advocacy, and politics.

In the process, she raised her self-esteem and developed leadership abilities and organizational skills that she employed in later endeavors. ER's work with the league was temporarily disrupted in August 1921, when her husband, Franklin D. Roosevelt,* was stricken with polio, but in December of that year she resumed her attendance at state league board meetings.

At the New York league's convention in January 1922, ER was elected to the board of directors and chaired the committee to revise the organization's constitution. Although her contribution to the league's political work was recognized, it was her mediation of an internal dispute that boosted her esteem within the organization when struggles between early leaders threatened the league's success. Margaret Norrie and Rosalie B. Edge, two board members dissatisfied with the administration of Vanderlip, challenged the convention voting proceedings conducted by Esther Lape.* ER chaired a committee to investigate the charges and found that they were unsubstantiated. On the advice of FDR, she moved to table the issue, thereby foreclosing discussion of the matter. To maintain unity, she urged board members to keep their differences private.

ER rapidly progressed to an even more active role in the league. In 1922 the New York state league's goal was to organize a league in every county; ER helped establish a league in Greene County. In 1923–1924 ER held the office of vice-chair of the New York state league. She concentrated her efforts on advocating an international peace plan, women's right to jury service, and the equal prosecution of women and men in prostitution cases.

In 1924 ER resigned from office as she became more active in the Democratic Party.* She, however, remained a visible figure at league conventions. From 1925 to 1928 ER participated in league activities as a speaker on foreign affairs, social legislation, and pacifism and as a hostess for teas in support of U.S. entry into the World Court.* At many of the league's conventions, ER presented the Democratic Party's position on social legislation in her capacity as one of the leaders of the Women's Division of the New York state Democratic Committee.

After FDR's election as governor of New York in 1928, she regularly entertained league women at the governor's mansion and held fundraising socials for the organization. She also helped publicize league concerns such as disarmament, the World Court, and women's responsibility in a democratic society.

During her White House years, Roosevelt continued to support the league's endeavors and spoke regularly at league conventions. She championed the league as a primary source for nonpartisan information on government issues and credited it with educating citizens on their responsibilities in a democracy.

SELECTED BIBLIOGRAPHY

Black, Allida. *Casting Her Own Shadow: Eleanor Roosevelt and the Shaping of Postwar Liberalism.* 1996.

Goodwin, Doris Kearns. *No Ordinary Time: Franklin and Eleanor Roosevelt: The Home Front in World War II.* 1994.

League of Woman Voters of New York State Collection, Columbia University, NY.

League of Woman Voters of the U.S. Collection, Library of Congress, Washington, DC.

Watrous, Hilda R. *In League with Eleanor.* 1984.

Young, Louise M. *In the Public Interest.* 1989.

Julieanne Phillips

LEHAND, MARGUERITE "MISSY" (13 September 1898, Potsdam, NY–31 July 1944, Somerville, MA).

Marguerite LeHand, called "Missy" as the result of a nickname given her by the Roosevelt children, was the confidential private secretary of Franklin D. Roosevelt.* Totally loyal to her employer, the exact nature of whose relationship with her remains unclear, she and Eleanor Roosevelt maintained an outward show of warm friendship, although ER apparently held ambivalent feelings toward her. LeHand worked for FDR for twenty-one years, including nine years in the White House, until incapacitated by illness in 1941.

While ER treated LeHand like a member of the family, occasional comments revealed some tension in the relationship. Women reporters, for example, detected hints of jealousy when LeHand was given flattering newspaper coverage after FDR's election as president in 1932, although she was paid only half of what FDR's male secretaries made. ER told women attending her press conferences* that they should write about her secretary, Malvina Thompson* (Scheider), "who is equally important" (Beasley, 104).

Born in Potsdam, New York, LeHand graduated from high school in 1917, attended secretarial school, and went to work. Employed at the national headquarters of the Democratic Party,* she was involved in FDR's campaign for vice president in 1920. Following his defeat, LeHand was hired as his personal secretary. After he was stricken with infantile paralysis in 1921, she accompanied FDR to the run-down health resort at Warm Springs, Georgia, in which he had invested as part of his effort to fight the effects of the disease. ER, who did not like life in the rural South, spent little time at Warm Springs, leaving LeHand to perform hostess and housekeeping duties typically carried on by a wife, along with her secretarial chores. LeHand also took trips with FDR on his houseboat, *Larooco*, enjoying leisurely cruises that ER disliked.

After FDR was elected governor of New York in 1928, LeHand moved

(l. to r.) Earl Miller, "Missy" LeHand, Franklin D. Roosevelt, and Eleanor Roosevelt enjoy the swimming pool at Val-Kill about 1930. *Courtesy of Franklin D. Roosevelt Library*

into the governor's mansion at Albany. LeHand offered FDR companionship that the career-minded ER did not or could not provide—presiding over dinner parties, writing checks and paying bills, playing poker, helping sort stamps for his collection, reading his favorite books, and supervising the housecleaning. Her presence made it possible for ER to continue to teach at the Todhunter School* in New York for part of each week, with LeHand acting as official hostess in her absence.

When the Roosevelts moved to the White House in 1933, ER, having given up her teaching position, asked FDR if she could take care of his correspondence. He dismissed her request with a comment that LeHand might think ER was interfering. LeHand had her own room in the White House and started her day's routine in her housecoat in FDR's bedroom, where he breakfasted and prepared for his appointments. As a key member of FDR's intimate circle, she unfailingly joined in FDR's cocktail hours, which ER avoided, and was sought after by those who wanted access to the president.

In June 1941 LeHand, who had suffered rheumatic fever as a child and was somewhat frail, collapsed at a White House dinner party and two weeks later suffered a major stroke that left her partially paralyzed with little speech function. A factor that may have led to her illness was stress stemming from fears that the exiled Princess Martha of Norway, a

Washington-area resident during World War II,* had replaced her as FDR's favorite companion, occupying the seat next to him that had long been hers on automobile rides. After treatment at Warm Springs, Le-Hand, who remained an invalid, was taken to the home of her sister, where she died. FDR paid her medical bills and made provision in his will for her care. ER attended her funeral, but FDR, off on a wartime trip, did not.

Historians question whether LeHand and FDR had a sexual relationship. One Roosevelt son, Elliott Roosevelt,* contended that they did. His brother, James Roosevelt,* disagreed, arguing that the effects of the polio would have made it difficult for FDR to engage in sexual activity. Yet, according to Earl Miller,* ER's confidant and bodyguard, he, Miller, carried on a two-year dalliance with LeHand in the early 1930s to break up her intimacy with FDR because it hurt ER.

Blanche Cook, a current biographer of ER, concluded that ER's "public attitude toward LeHand was that of first wife to second wife in the culture of extended ruling families" (Cook, 2, 38). She pointed to a passage in one of ER's last books that advised that if you were not able to fulfill the need of a loved one, "You must learn to allow someone else to meet the need, without bitterness and envy, and accept it" (Roosevelt, *You Learn by Living*, 67).

SELECTED BIBLIOGRAPHY

Beasley, Maurine H. *Eleanor Roosevelt and the Media: A Public Quest for Self-Fulfillment*. 1987.
Cook, Blanche Wiesen. *Eleanor Roosevelt*. Vol. 2. 1999.
Goodwin, Doris Kearns. *No Ordinary Time: Franklin and Eleanor Roosevelt: The Home Front in World War II*. 1994.
Roosevelt, Eleanor. *This I Remember*. 1949.
———. *You Learn by Living*. 1960.
Roosevelt, James. *My Parents: A Differing View*. 1976.

Ginger Rudeseal Carter

LONGWORTH, ALICE ROOSEVELT (12 February 1884, New York–20 February 1980, Washington, DC).

Alice Roosevelt Longworth, the oldest daughter of Theodore Roosevelt,* was the first cousin of Eleanor Roosevelt, with whom she had a conflicted relationship. When his first wife, Alice Lee Roosevelt, died two days after giving birth to Alice, Theodore turned his daughter over to the care of his sister, Anna Roosevelt (Cowles*). Theodore Roosevelt's remarriage forced three-year-old Alice to leave her "Auntie Bye" to join her father and stepmother, Edith Kermit Carow Roosevelt, at their Sagamore Hill estate at Oyster Bay, Long Island. Alice grew up with five half siblings and she often felt like the outsider in the nursery.

Although Alice and ER played together as small children and saw each other frequently at the home of Auntie Bye (who wielded a strong influence over both cousins), visits between the two were restricted after the death of Eleanor's father, Elliott Roosevelt,* Theodore's brother. Eleanor's maternal grandmother, Mary Ludlow Hall, with whom she lived in New York's Hudson River Valley, did not approve of the boisterous Oyster Bay Roosevelts, and Alice's stepmother, Edith, wary of the possible influence of alcoholism in Eleanor's family, extended only occasional invitations. Still, Eleanor's son, James Roosevelt,* believed that Alice "was the best friend" ER had as a child (Roosevelt, 13). After one visit Edith wrote of her niece, "Poor little soul, she is very plain. . . . But the ugly duckling may turn out to be a swan" (Brough, 63).

Alice, christened "Princess Alice" by an adoring popular press after Theodore Roosevelt assumed the presidency in 1901, became a youthful celebrity. Unlike Eleanor, Alice was more interested in fun than in good works. The "First Daughter" had her debut in the White House when she was seventeen and soon flouted tradition by riding in an automobile unchaperoned and openly smoking cigarettes. Such high jinks masked a deep intelligence and an increasing interest in politics, heightened when she served as an unofficial goodwill ambassador for her father on a six-country congressional junket in 1905. While Alice's madcap adventures alienated her cousin, Eleanor asked Alice to be one of her six bridesmaids at her wedding on 17 March 1905 to her fifth cousin, Franklin D. Roosevelt* of Hyde Park,* New York.

One year after ER's wedding, Alice married Republican representative Nicholas Longworth, a playboy congressman from Cincinnati, in a spectacular White House ceremony. After FDR and ER moved to Washington in 1912, when FDR became assistant secretary of the navy, Alice and ER moved in the same social circles, but they were not close. In 1917, when ER took the Roosevelt children to Campobello* for the summer, Alice encouraged a romance between FDR and Lucy Mercer (Rutherfurd*), ER's social secretary, which would jeopardize, but not end, ER's marriage.* Alice thought FDR deserved the affair because "he was married to Eleanor" (Cook, 1:222).

In 1925 Republican Nicholas Longworth became Speaker of the House, and Washingtonians of both parties were attracted to Alice's salon by the sophisticated political debate that took place there. By this time, the Hyde Park Democratic Roosevelts and the Oyster Bay Republican Roosevelts were political opponents. In 1920 Alice's half brother, Theodore Roosevelt Jr., shadowed FDR when he was the Democratic candidate for vice president, opposing him with speeches that described FDR as "a maverick" lacking "the brand of our family" (Brough, 265). In 1924, when Theodore Roosevelt Jr. was the Republican gubernatorial candidate in New York, ER turned the tables. Joining other members of the Women's Division of the New York state Democratic Party, she traveled about the state with an oversized tea kettle attached to a car to connect the Republican candidate to the Teapot Dome scandal of former president Warren G. Harding's administration. When her brother lost the election, Alice was furious. She believed her brother should follow in his father's presidential footsteps and saw ER's actions as a betrayal of the family.

Throughout FDR and ER's stay in the White House, Alice, widowed in 1931, kept up a barrage of criticism. In 1936 she began a syndicated column that was a direct competitor of ER's "My Day."* Alice's unabashedly political and partisan writing, however, was neither as popular nor as long-lasting as the First Lady's, lacking the rapier-sharp wit that marked Alice's dinner-table conversation. Although Alice was known for entertaining her guests with an imitation of ER's high-pitched voice, she was invited regularly to White House social occasions.

Alice outlived her cousin by nearly two decades, remaining a celebrity and the grand dame of Washington society. At the age of forty-one, she gave birth to a daughter, Paulina, who died in 1957, leaving a ten-year-old child, Joanna Sturm, whom Alice reared. Although Alice opposed much of what ER advocated, from American entry into the League of Nations* to federal intervention to address economic ills, Alice ultimately concluded that ER's career had been extraordinary.

Historians and journalists have been fascinated to contrast the two cousins—picturing ER as the beneficent, activist First Lady with a social conscience and Alice as the caustic "saloniste" who pulled political strings behind the scenes. As with most generalizations, the reality was more complex. In 1943 ER wrote about an encounter with Alice to a friend, saying, "I enjoyed her. She is a vivid & amusing creature no matter how unkind at times! She [Alice] remarked that no matter 'how much we differed politically there was always a tribal feeling between us'!" (Lash, 85).

SELECTED BIBLIOGRAPHY

Brough, James. *Princess Alice: A Biography of Alice Roosevelt Longworth*. 1975.
Caroli, Betty Boyd. *The Roosevelt Women*. 1999.
Cook, Blanche Wiesen. *Eleanor Roosevelt*. Vols. 1, 2. 1992, 1999.
Lash, Joseph. *A World of Love: Eleanor Roosevelt and Her Friends, 1943–1962*. 1984.
Longworth, Alice Roosevelt. *Crowded Hours: Reminiscences of Alice Roosevelt Longworth*. 1931.
Roosevelt, James. *My Parents: A Differing View*. 1976.

                                                              Stacy A. Cordery

LOWENSTEIN, ALLARD (16 January 1929, Newark, NJ–14 March 1980, New York).

During the course of her lifetime, Eleanor Roosevelt developed a series of intense relationships with various men and women. Oftentimes, these individuals occupied positions outside the mainstream of ER's primary social group. Sometimes, like Rose Schneiderman,* they were trade union women who came from an immigrant background; at other times, they included maverick journalists, such as Lorena Hickok.* Frequently, they were men much younger than she, often of Jewish background, whose attachment to her led to powerful and profound interactions. In almost all cases, what characterized these relationships most was an imbalance of power, status, and authority and—on the other side—a deep emotional attachment.

Of the many younger men with whom ER developed such ties, Allard Lowenstein—national student leader, congressman from New York, and Democratic Party* and liberal activist—was one of the most extraordinary. As a very young student at the University of North Carolina in Chapel Hill, Lowenstein first came into contact with ER at the Ethical Culture Encampment for Citizenship, which occurred each year outside New York City. At the time he met her in 1948, Lowenstein was a student leader coming into his own at Chapel Hill. A New York Jew who felt significant ambivalence about his own ethnic and cultural roots, Lowenstein had risen to prominence at Chapel Hill as a result of his leadership in fighting the Jim Crow system of the South and in advocating student government positions noted for their liberalism and internationalism. The Encampment for Citizenship that Lowenstein attended was designed to help reinforce the political and educational values that Lowenstein had come to represent.

Lowenstein developed a growing relationship with ER. After he was elected president of the National Student Association in 1950, he went to Yale Law School in the early 1950s and arranged for her to come visit in New Haven. He served as her driver as she went to local engagements. In performing that role, he practiced a pattern that he himself had learned by driving the president of the University of North Carolina at Chapel Hill—Frank Porter Graham*—to various meetings and also anticipated his own future pattern of having younger students drive him to speeches and events. For Lowenstein—and evidently ER as well— these encounters provided an opportunity to deepen their friendship and enhance their sense of confidence and trust in each other.

The special nature of the relationship between Lowenstein and ER became clear when Lowenstein served in the armed forces during the 1950s in Europe. ER arranged for him to be given a special leave so that he could meet her in Paris. ER was helpful, as well, in arranging for Lowenstein to play a major role in the Students for Stevenson* campaign in 1956. The two remained close until ER's death in 1962, especially around issues involving civil rights* and student activism.

Although Lowenstein's relationship with ER did not approach the intense level of intimacy that was reflected in her relationship with Joseph

Lash* and David Gurewitsch,* there was about their communications a similar pattern of his veneration for a saintly political figure and her devotion and affection, often of an almost maternal nature, for her younger charge.

In the Lowenstein–Roosevelt relationship, as in other relationships that ER developed, complexity rather than simplicity was a key. Equally important, it is critical to remember the degree to which the personal and political were tied together in a harmonious and mutually fulfilling partnership.

SELECTED BIBLIOGRAPHY

Chafe, William H. *Never Stop Running: Allard Lowenstein and the Struggle to Save American Liberalism.* 1993.

William H. Chafe

M

MARRIAGE. Through more than four decades, Eleanor and Franklin D. Roosevelt* remained together in an unconventional marriage that vastly enriched both partners, even though it failed to provide either of them with steady emotional support or intimate companionship. From the outset, with President Theodore Roosevelt* on hand to give the bride away on 17 March 1905, it was a marriage of opposite temperaments played out on a public stage.

"You couldn't find two such different people as Mother and Father," FDR and ER's daughter, Anna Roosevelt Halsted,* mused. Whereas FDR, Halsted thought, had "too much security and too much love" (Goodwin, 373), with parents, relatives, and servants all doting on him, ER seemed forever starved for love. During their courtship, it seemed that each had found in the other a complementary aspect of something lacking in his or her self. For ER, FDR's confidence, charm, and sociability stood in welcome contrast to her own insecurity and shyness. For FDR, ER's sincerity, honesty, and high principles stood in contrast to his guileful manner and all-too-easy charm. Over the years, however, the very qualities that had first attracted FDR and ER to one another became sources of conflict as ER came to see FDR's sociability as shallow and duplicitous, while he redefined her honesty as stiffness and inflexibility. "It is very hard to live with someone who is almost a saint," Roosevelt's labor adviser Anna Rosenberg observed. "He had his tricks and evasions. Sometimes he had to ridicule her in order not to be troubled by her" (Goodwin, 373).

The springs of ER's insecurity disrupted the marriage from the very beginning. Though there were many good days, ER's fear of failure prompted her again and again to give up too soon on a variety of activities that would have allowed an easy companionship with her husband.

Newlyweds Franklin D. and Eleanor Roosevelt stand beside Sara Delano Roosevelt, Franklin's mother, on a visit to Newburgh, New York, in May 1905. *Courtesy of Franklin D. Roosevelt Library*

After days of practicing golf on her own, she allowed FDR's teasing remarks about her awkwardness to turn her away from trying to play again. A minor crash into a gatepost kept her from driving for more than a decade. Terror of the water ruled out the pleasures of swimming or sailing for years. Nor, for reasons that even she did not understand, did ER ever allow herself to learn enough about FDR's stamp collection to share the fun of it. "If I had it to do over again," ER confessed years later, "I would enter more fully into FDR's collecting enthusiasm. I would learn all I could about stamps. Every collector appreciates the real interest of his family in what he is doing" (Goodwin, 374).

Perhaps, everything would have eventually worked out had ER been able to derive confidence and comfort as a mother. Surely, she possessed the warmth, sensitivity, and insight that should have allowed her to be a compassionate mother. But from the moment her children were born, the rivalry with FDR's mother, Sara Delano Roosevelt,* was transformed into a battle over the children, a battle so fierce that the children ultimately became an additional force pulling FDR and ER apart. Lacking confidence in her mothering skills, ER allowed her ever-confident mother-in-law to take charge of hiring the nurses and setting up the nursery, accepting Sara's intervention both grudgingly and gratefully. A heavy price was paid, for as it turned out, ER later admitted, "FDR's children were more my mother-in-law's children than they were mine" (Lash, 56).

Nor did FDR make it easy for ER to find her own way as a wife and mother, for he was never able to limit the intrusive role his own mother insisted on playing in their marriage. For ER, the strain of accommodating herself to Sara's wishes finally proved too much. A few weeks after she and FDR had moved into a new house on East 65th Street that Sara had bought for them, ER broke down. "I did not quite know what was the matter with me," she recalled years later, but "I sat in front of my dressing table and wept, and when my bewildered young husband asked me what on earth was the matter with me, I said I did not like to live in a house which was not in any way mine, one that I had done nothing about and which did not represent the way I wanted to live. Being an eminently reasonable person, he thought I was quite mad and told me so gently" (Roosevelt, *This Is My Story*, 162).

This tangled web of relationships provided the fertile soil that produced FDR's relationship with Lucy Mercer (Rutherfurd*), a young woman in Washington whom ER had hired to help with her correspondence while FDR was assistant secretary of the navy. The exact nature of FDR's relationship with Lucy has never been confirmed. We know only that in 1918, while ER was unpacking FDR's suitcase after his return from a visit to the European front, she discovered a packet of letters from Lucy to her husband. At this moment, ER later admitted, "the bottom dropped out of my own particular world and I faced myself, my surroundings, my world honestly for the first time" (Lash, 66).

ER told her husband she would grant him a divorce, but after much discussion, FDR promised never to see Lucy Mercer again, and the marriage resumed. For ER, however, the marital crisis proved to be a turning point, opening up for her a new path, creating the possibility of standing apart from FDR. No longer did she define herself solely in terms of his wants and his needs. Before the crisis, though marriage had never fulfilled her prodigious energies, she had no way of breaking through the habits and expectations of a proper young woman's role. To explore her independent needs and to journey outside her home for happiness were perceived as dangerous and wrong. With the discovery of the affair, however, she was free to define a new and different partnership with her husband, free to seek new avenues of fulfillment.

In the years that followed, ER poured all her pent-up energies into a variety of reformist organizations dedicated to the abolition of child labor,* the establishment of a minimum wage, and the passage of protective legislation for women workers. In the process she became involved with a circle of women activists who taught her that she had a range of talents she had never exercised before—for public speaking, for organizing, for articulating social problems. Then, when FDR was paralyzed from polio in 1921, ER's political activism and newfound confidence became a vital force in his life as well as hers. Unable to travel easily on his own, he encouraged her to become his eyes and ears, traveling the state of New York and then the country on his behalf, gathering the grassroots knowledge he needed to understand the people he governed. Under FDR's tutelage, ER learned how to inspect state institutions with the eye of an investigative reporter, bringing her husband reports of which institutions were working and which were failing. In time, she became so thorough in her inspections that FDR set great value in her reports. "Much of what she learned and what she understood about the life of the people of this country rubbed off onto FDR," labor secretary Frances Perkins* said. "It could not have helped to do so because she had a poignant understanding. Her mere reporting of the facts was full of a sensitive quality that could never be escaped. Much of his seemingly intuitive understanding—about labor situations . . . about girls who worked in sweatshops—came from recollections of what she had told him" (Goodwin, 28).

"The polio was very instrumental in bringing them much closer into a very real partnership," Halsted observed. "They were finding mutual interests on a totally different level than they had been before" (Goodwin, 98). ER's astonishing travels,* her strong convictions, her perceptive reports on almost every phase of the nation's life, from slum clearance to experimental beehives, from rural electrification to country dances, provided fascinating material for endless conversations, arguments, and debates.

They made an extraordinary team. She was more earnest, less devious, less patient, less fun, more uncompromisingly moral; he possessed the more trustworthy political talent, the more finely tuned sense of timing, the better feel for the citizenry, the smarter understanding of how to get things done. She could speak her mind without the constraints of public office. He had to calibrate his words. She was dedicated to what should be done; he was concerned with what could be done. She was the agitator; he was the politician.

Through it all, they were linked by indissoluble bonds, and they drew strength from each other. "The truth of the matter is that a deep and unshakable affection and tenderness existed between them," James Roosevelt* said. The fact that "certain parts of their marriage were not as happy as one would have hoped," Halsted later said, did not mean that

ER didn't love FDR. "She did love Father. There wasn't any doubt" (Goodwin, 629). ER's close friend, Esther Lape,* agreed. "I don't think she ever stopped loving him. That was why he always had the ability to hurt her" (Goodwin, 629).

James Roosevelt, the Roosevelts' oldest son, observed that his father always said that ER was "the most remarkable woman he had ever known, the smartest, the most intuitive, the most interesting, but because she was always going somewhere, he never got to spend time with her" (Goodwin, 371).

"He might have been happier with a wife who was completely un-critical," ER observed in her memoirs. "That I was never able to be, and he had to find it in other people. Nevertheless, I think I sometimes acted as a spur, even though the spurring was not always wanted or welcome. I was one of those who served his purposes" (Roosevelt, *This I Remember*, 349).

"She had indeed served his purposes," historian Lois Scharf wrote, "but he had also served hers. He furnished the stage upon which her incomparable abilities and human qualities could gain the widest audi-ence and respect. Few Presidents and no other first ladies have ever used the platform to such effect. In less obvious ways he was her spur as much as she was his." Together, they "created a far different political and social landscape than the one that had existed when they entered the White House" (Scharf, 140–41).

If ER brooded over her husband's shortcomings while he was alive, once he died, she chose, her son, Elliott Roosevelt,* observed, "to re-member only the lovely times they had shared, never the estrangement and pain" (Goodwin, 633). She loved to quote word for word the things they had told one another. Maureen Corr,* ER's secretary during the 1950s, remembered her "constantly talking about what Franklin did or what Franklin said or . . . how Franklin thought about this or that. And every time she mentioned his name you could hear the emotion in her voice and see the glow in her eyes" (Goodwin, 633).

SELECTED BIBLIOGRAPHY

Goodwin, Doris Kearns. *No Ordinary Time. Franklin and Eleanor Roosevelt: The Home Front in World War II.* 1994.

Lash, Joseph. *Love, Eleanor: Eleanor Roosevelt and Her Friends.* 1982.

Roosevelt, Eleanor. *This I Remember.* 1949.

———. *This Is My Story.* 1937.

Scharf, Lois. *Eleanor Roosevelt: First Lady of American Liberalism.* 1987.

Ward, Geoffrey. *A First Class Temperament.* 1989.

Doris Kearns Goodwin

MARSHALL, GEORGE CATLETT (31 December 1880, Uniontown, PA– 16 October 1959, Washington, DC).

In one sense both Eleanor Roosevelt and general of the army George

C. Marshall were raised to prominence by President Franklin D. Roosevelt,* his wife by virtue of her status as First Lady and Marshall because the president had selected the aloof soldier to be chief of staff on the eve of World War II.* But if ER and the chief of staff were anointed by FDR, their fierce independence from that selfsame president raised them to greatness.

Career soldier George Marshall had earned a wide reputation in the army for his abilities as a staff officer. He weathered the doldrums of America's peacetime army after World War I to rise slowly to the army's highest position on 1 September 1939, coincidentally the day World War II began.

As chief of staff—with the considerable aid of White House intimate Harry Hopkins* and later Secretary of War Henry Stimson—Marshall demonstrated the selfless leadership that would make him indispensable to the Allied war effort. He became, in the phrase of Winston Churchill,* "the true 'organizer of victory' " (Cray, 515). In his capacity as chief of staff General Marshall apparently first engaged ER's attention. The United States was mobilizing with the first peacetime draft in its history, rushing to rearm, while supplying beleaguered Great Britain through FDR's Lend-Lease program.

As the nation's unofficial ombudsman, ER took to forwarding to Marshall and the War Department letters of complaint she had received from citizens. ER's correspondence to "Dear General" began before the war and dealt with subjects as far-ranging as the durability of army uniforms, the death of a soldier from pneumonia, the induction of eighteen-year-olds, and, most often, the treatment, training, and assignments accorded Negro troops—particularly those sent to southern training camps. Approximately twenty of ER's invariably polite letters are to be found in various archives.

If her letters seemed to be no more than nuisances to the War Department staff, overwhelmed by vast draft levies, with the need to construct training camps and buy or build everything from mops to B-17 bombers, Marshall himself was careful to investigate the questions ER raised.

He came to appreciate that ER's concerns for morale were genuine and neither politically nor publicity-driven. In time, he reached out to her, inviting ER to visit a basic training camp. In mid-1942 her name was added to the recipient list of the War Department's secret summaries sent daily to the White House. By mid-1944 the chief of staff was forwarding reports on the entertainment of troops and the availability of correspondence courses. Eventually, the usually reserved soldier would send her a leather-bound copy of his final report as chief of staff.

If anything brought their respectful relationship close to friendship, it was the death of the president. Apparently, the only letter ER wrote the night of the military funeral at Hyde Park,* New York, was a handwritten note to "My dear General," who had arranged the ceremony: "My husband would have been grateful and I know it was all as he would have wished it" (ER to GM, 15 April 1945). Even as they grew closer, they remained "General" and "Mrs. Roosevelt." Only Mrs. Marshall and a handful of comrades from World War I dared call the austere general by his first name.

Marshall and ER would again join forces when President Harry S Truman* named the former army chief of staff to be secretary of state in 1947. ER, earlier tapped by Truman to be a delegate to the United Nations* (UN), was delighted with the choice. These were pivotal years in shaping the future of a Europe ravaged by war. To meet the increasingly grave situation, Marshall proposed in June 1947 a European Recovery Program (later dubbed "the Marshall Plan"—a term he never used). Not only did ER back the plan, but her outspoken support was important in muting the Democratic Left's criticism of the "capitalist" proposal.

As a UN delegate, ER was a forceful spokesman for the Truman–Marshall foreign policy. In the midst of the 1947 UN session, Marshall told the president's cabinet that "the most intelligent, cooperative and effective assistance came from Mrs. Eleanor Roosevelt" (Lash, 102).

Marshall deliberately chose ER to be the U.S. spokesperson in drafting a declaration on human rights.* Who better than the woman who had campaigned for civil rights* at home so often and so publicly? Her firm leadership and authority, through no less than eighty-five wearying sessions, eventually overpowered Soviet bloc opposition during the Paris meetings. Ultimately, the United Nations on 10 December 1948 would approve a Universal Declaration of Human Rights* 48–0, with two absent and eight largely Soviet bloc abstentions.

With that, the United States had proclaimed itself the unswerving advocate of human rights and scored a significant victory in the escalating Cold War* rivalry with the Soviet Union. Marshall's faith in ER had been justified.

On only one significant issue did Marshall and ER disagree: partition and recognition of the state of Israel* in 1948. ER wholeheartedly endorsed the proposal, arguing that it was the just thing to do. Marshall firmly opposed it, fearing the Arab states would retaliate by cutting off sales of vital crude oil needed for national defense. Harry Truman opted to back ER's position and grant American support of the new state.

The decision did nothing to diminish Marshall's stature. By then, he, like ER, had become an icon of American strength, resolve, and compassion. Neither did it rupture their relationship. Marshall and ER would remain friends and sometime correspondents until Marshall's death in 1959.

SELECTED BIBLIOGRAPHY
Cray, Ed. *General of the Army*. 1990.
George C. Marshall Papers, George C. Marshall Research Library, Lexington, VA.
Lash, Joseph P. *Eleanor: The Years Alone*. 1972.
Pogue, Forrest. *George C. Marshall: Statesman*. 1987.

Ed Cray

MASON, LUCY RANDOLPH (26 July 1882, Alexandria, VA–6 May 1959, Atlanta, GA).

Lucy Randolph Mason, a labor publicist and friend of Eleanor Roosevelt, had the blood of Virginia's most illustrious sons in her veins. One of five children of the Reverend Landon and Lucy Ambler Mason, she was related to George Mason, John Marshall, and Robert E. Lee, the second cousin of her father. He was an Episcopal minister with strong social gospel leanings, and his daughter shared both his religious convictions and desire to bring about the Kingdom of God on earth. Like ER, Mason was a member of the Episcopal Church and had a commitment to better the world.

Educated at Richmond's most exclusive private school for girls, Mason worked first as a legal stenographer before accepting a position in 1914 as industrial secretary of the Richmond Young Women's Christian Association (YWCA). She became its general secretary in 1923. There she developed programs of such innovation that she came to the attention of several of the nation's prominent women reformers, including Florence Kelley, secretary of the National Consumers' League* (NCL). Mason was Kelley's personal choice to succeed her, and on her death in 1932 the board acceded to her wish. Accordingly, Mason left the South for the first and only time in her life, for New York.

She served with the NCL for five years, during which time she aimed to focus its attention more closely on industrial matters, as well as to work with the social reformers in the myriad New Deal* agencies. Her reputation as an advocate for the rights of labor* drew her to the attention of John L. Lewis, head of the fledgling Congress of Industrial Organizations (CIO), who in 1937 offered her the job of public relations representative in the Southeast, working out of Atlanta. Lewis hoped that her lineage and her decidedly nonthreatening appearance would at least get labor a hearing in communities where more typical union organizers would be given short shrift. The experiment succeeded. For the rest of her working life, until her retirement in 1953, Lucy Mason tirelessly represented the cause of organized labor in a region increasingly hostile to union activism.

Lucy Mason's relationship with Eleanor Roosevelt started when she went to New York and lasted the rest of her life. She first wrote to the president's wife even before meeting her, recognizing in her someone who shared her social concerns. Soon, ER had become Mason's most important reference point. She looked forward tremendously to their occasional meetings, and she wrote to her often, seeking advice and assistance, reposing confidences in her, and regularly proclaiming her admiration and love. At times they collaborated on enterprises, such as the organization of the first meeting of the Southern Conference for Human Welfare* in 1938, which ER attended. Mostly, however, their relationship was carried out by mail. In 1952 ER wrote a brief foreword to Mason's autobiography, *To Win These Rights*, paying tribute to her courage and acknowledging her pride in having known her. There is no doubt that these sentiments were entirely genuine.

SELECTED BIBLIOGRAPHY

Lader, Lawrence. "The Lady and the Sheriff." *New Republic* (5 January 1948): 17–19.
Lemons, J. Stanley. *The Women Citizen: Social Feminism in the 1920's.* 1973.
Mason, Lucy Randolph. *To Win These Rights.* 1952.
Salmond, John Alexander. *Miss Lucy of the CIO: The Life and Times of Lucy Randolph Mason, 1882–1959.* 1988.

John A. Salmond

MCBRIDE, MARY MARGARET (16 November 1899, Paris, MO–7 April 1976, West Shokean, NY).

Mary Margaret McBride, a journalist who gained fame as a radio talk show pioneer, was an admirer of Eleanor Roosevelt, who appeared repeatedly on McBride's radio shows. A 1919 graduate of the University of Missouri School of Journalism, McBride attained success in New York as a magazine writer and author before being hired in 1934 by radio station WOR to host a daytime women's program. Soon tiring of pretending to be a grandmother named Martha Deane, the persona the station wanted her to assume, McBride confessed to her listeners that she was a single, thirty-five-year-old journalist who wanted to tell them about interesting places and people.

The response was overwhelming, and McBride was launched on a spectacular radio career that capitalized on her down-home style, interviewing skills, and ability to sell products by ad-libbing advertisements that constituted personal endorsements. In 1937 she went from WOR to the Columbia Broadcasting System (CBS) and, in 1941, to WEAF, flagship station of the National Broadcasting Company (NBC), where she attracted a daily audience of some 6 million fans for a forty-five-minute show. After a contract dispute, in 1950 she moved to the American Broadcasting Company (ABC) for four years. Although she tried television, it was not her forte, as radio was.

ER had a standing commitment to appear once a year on McBride's shows. A large woman who loved to discuss food, McBride chatted with her guests, who ranged from zookeepers, to General Omar Bradley and President Harry S Truman,* while dispensing mouth-watering recipes and household hints along with an extraordinary number of commercials. Her unique formula made her the most successful woman radio personality of her day.

In 1960 McBride picked ER as the most outstanding among her thousands of radio guests because she "has something important to say, . . . is frank, gracious and giving, has a good vocabulary, is quick on the uptake, talkative but not loquacious, and tells a story well" (McBride, *Out of the Air*, 323). Although McBride once stayed overnight at the White House as ER's guest, and the two occasionally lunched together, McBride lamented that she did not feel close to ER: "[H]ow I long to be able to talk to her not as an interviewer, but as a friend" (McBride, *Out of the Air*, 331).

The two women had a professional association that started when McBride interviewed ER while Franklin D. Roosevelt* was governor of New York. In a 1933 article for *Good Housekeeping*, McBride described ER's leadership in the Mobilization for Human Needs conference at the White House, which urged women to organize in their communities to relieve distress during the Great Depression.* In 1944, when McBride celebrated her tenth anniversary with a broadcast before 20,000 in Madison Square Garden, ER flew up from Washington to open the program, an event that publicists portrayed as "[t]he first Lady of the Land pays tribute to Lady No. 1 of the Radio" (Cerf, 6).

In her remarks ER urged women to join the armed services during World War II* and thanked McBride for advancing women's position in society: "I'm always happy when a woman succeeds, but when a woman succeeds superlatively she helps all other women" (*New York Times*, 1 June 1944). Writing about the event in her "My Day"* column the next day, ER said, "I have seen the Garden filled for important meetings, but never have I seen it as full as it was yesterday for just one woman and a program of radio interviews." Four years later McBride filled Yankee Stadium to celebrate her fifteenth year on radio. Some 300 dignitaries attended the event in observance of McBride's commitment to racial understanding. Her main guest was ER.

After McBride left WEAF, the station countered by hiring ER for *Mrs. Roosevelt Presents*, a series of women's radio broadcasts* copying the McBride formula and airing from 12:30 to 1:15 P.M., Monday through Friday, which meant the program cut into the first fifteen minutes of McBride's ABC show. If NBC executives intended to worry McBride, they apparently failed. McBride said of her new competitor, "I love her to death. I think she's the greatest woman in the world" ("Opposites," 58). Likewise, Mrs. Roosevelt, in her premier broadcast on her sixty-sixth birthday, 11 October 1950, paid a generous tribute to McBride. ER's program, however, did not find commercial sponsorship and was dropped. Elliott Roosevelt,* ER's son, who was the announcer, was ridiculed for using the Roosevelt name in product advertising; critics said ER herself simply could not compete with McBride as an entertaining saleswoman.

In 1954 McBride retired to upstate New York, where she conducted an interview program three times a week over WGHQ at Kingston until her death. ER made three appearances on the program, broadcast from a renovated barn on McBride's property. McBride also recorded programs from ER's Val-Kill* cottage. McBride was a charter member of the New York Newspaper Women's Club* to which ER also belonged.

McBride wrote a total of fifteen books by herself and with others, four of which were autobiographical. She also wrote a daily column for the Associated Press from 1953 to 1956. In her last autobiography, she credited ER with appearing "on every radio and television program I've ever asked her to be on" (McBride, *Out of the Air*, 331).

SELECTED BIBLIOGRAPHY
Cerf, Bennett. "Here Comes McBride." *Saturday Review of Literature* (1 March 1947): 6.
Heggie, Barbara. "Mary Margaret's Miracle." *Woman's Home Companion* (April 1949): 36–39.
McBride, Mary Margaret. "Lest We Forget." *Good Housekeeping* 97 (November 1933): 40–41, 139.
———. *Out of the Air*. 1960.
Mary Margaret McBride Papers, Manuscript Division, Library of Congress, Washington, DC.
"Opposites." *Time* 56 (9 October 1950): 58.

Beverly G. Merrick

MCCALL'S. Eleanor Roosevelt was a prominent writer for *McCall's* magazine from 1949 until her death in 1962, during a period when it became the top-selling women's magazine in the nation. When Otis Weiss, the editor, purchased serialization rights to the second volume of ER's autobiography* and took her monthly question-and-answer column away from the rival *Ladies' Home Journal,* it marked the start of a harmonious relationship between ER and the magazine.

Weiss promoted ER's move in June 1949 to *McCall's*, a magazine owned by the McCall Company and that was begun to sell dress patterns. Her picture graced the cover, and the first installment of her autobiography, *This I Remember*, appeared along with her column, "If You Ask Me." The book, which ran in seven installments, proved an overwhelming success and became a Book-of-the-Month-Club selection. ER herself proved popular within the magazine's editorial offices. According to Herbert R. Mayes, who took over as editor in 1958, no columnist "was prompter than Mrs. Roosevelt about turning in copy" (Mayes, 15).

Following the pattern that had been established at the *Journal*, in her column she forthrightly answered readers' questions selected by the editors on political and social concerns as well as personal matters. She denied that she and Franklin D. Roosevelt* ever had been separated (October 1949); devoted an entire column to a defense against charges that she and other liberals connected to the Roosevelt administration had been communists (July 1953); urged that the controversial Kinsey report on sexual behavior be made available (December 1953); said that women were not making progress in seeking equality with men in politics ("They are not equal nor are they in comparable posts when it comes to policy decisions," August 1954); advocated nursery schools for the children of working mothers (June 1955); and backed tax policy that would let working women deduct the costs of household help (March 1959).

Taken as a whole, her columns presented a running commentary on mid-twentieth-century issues. Responding to Cold War* concerns, she warned readers in 1955 and 1956 that outlawing communism would be "very dangerous" (Black, 156). She frequently answered questions about the United Nations* and defended that organization against charges of communist control.

As a Democrat, she repeatedly commented on Republican president Dwight D. Eisenhower,* contending he had not done a good job on either foreign or domestic issues (October 1957), and said that Vice President Richard M. Nixon would not be an acceptable president (June 1960). After President John F. Kennedy* was elected on the Democratic ticket in 1960, she wrote that he had a praiseworthy approach to his office that reminded her of FDR's (July 1961), but she criticized Kennedy for shortcomings in areas of education and medical care for the elderly as well as for the failure of his foreign policy on Cuba (April 1962).

Yet, she still portrayed herself as a wife and mother, a message that fitted well with the magazine's overall approach to its readers. She said she would not consider running for president herself because no woman was ready for that office (October 1958). While many columns defended FDR and his administration against criticism, she said that she might consider remarrying (February 1956) and that she did not feel qualified to write his biography (November 1957). Asked what her greatest accomplishment was, she answered, "I have not the remotest idea. . . . I suppose the greatest contribution any woman makes is her children" (January 1959). A compilation of her columns from 1946 to 1949 in the *Journal* and from 1949 to 1954 in *McCall's* appeared in 1954, pointing out that many subjects addressed were personal, not political.

In an effort to balance ER's liberal stances and not alienate conservative readers, in 1960 Mayes persuaded the best-known Republican woman of the era, Clare Booth Luce, former congresswoman and ambassador, to write a monthly column that he could run with ER's. While he hoped the two would spar and attract publicity to the magazine, he soon was disappointed. In her first column Luce recommended two vice presidents of the United States, one a man and one a woman, and named ER as especially qualified for the post.

ER's final column ran in November 1962, the month of her death. This was not the last time, however, she wrote for *McCall's*. Her article, "I Remember Hyde Park,"* appeared in February 1963, a bittersweet account of life in the home of her mother-in-law, Sara Delano Roosevelt,* which stated, "For over forty years I was only a visitor there" (Mayes, 16). ER had asked Mayes not to publish the article until after her death. It ran in the same issue in which *McCall's* editors said their farewell to their longtime columnist.

SELECTED BIBLIOGRAPHY

Black, Allida M. *Casting Her Own Shadow*. 1996.
Edens, John A. *Eleanor Roosevelt: A Comprehensive Bibliography*. 1994.
Mayes, Herbert R. *The Magazine Maze*. 1980.
Roosevelt, Eleanor. *It Seems to Me*. 1954.
Zuckerman, Mary Ellen. *A History of Popular Women's Magazines in the United States, 1792–1995*. 1998.

Kathleen L. Endres

MCCARTHYISM. Eleanor Roosevelt felt distaste for both communists and Red-baiters, particularly Republican Senator Joseph R. McCarthy of Wisconsin, whose wild charges of communist influence led to the derogatory term "McCarthyism." She had an aversion to the authoritarianism that accompanied communist rule, but she warned that excessive anticommunism produced a parallel menace to American democracy.

Despite her anticommunism, she was a constant target of Red-baiters. They viewed her early connections with feminist and other reform causes and her later identification with the New Deal,* civil rights,* and other social movements as confirmation of her membership in what shrill right-wing critics saw as "Red networks."

Her most significant run-in with the Red-hunters embroiled her with Congressman Martin Dies' House Special Committee to Investigate Un-American Activities* (HUAC). In 1939 Dies summoned leaders of the American Youth Congress* (AYC), including several protégés of hers, to testify about communist influences in that organization. She met their train, fed them lunch at the White House, heard their testimony, and, when questioning took a hostile turn, took a seat purposefully at the press table. The AYC's subsequent gravitation toward pro-Soviet positions as World War II* approached proved disillusioning for her. The Soviets' brutal occupation of Eastern Europe and her experience with their obstructionism during her United Nations* work further stoked her mistrust.

Yet the tightening grip of Cold War* politics disturbed ER. She expressed misgivings about the 1947 loyalty program of President Harry S Truman* (though Franklin D. Roosevelt* had approved a similar, if less drastic, program during World War II). She defended Alger Hiss and other New Dealers accused before HUAC in 1948. She was critical of Hiss' indictment on charges of perjury and dubious about the guilty verdict against him. This prompted critics to question her judgment on matters relating to communism.

Though never directly embroiled with Senator McCarthy, she was his frequent critic. She ridiculed his early charges against her friend, Dorothy Kenyon, who had been a municipal court judge in New York City and a U.S. delegate to the United Nations Commission on the Status of Women. In 1951 she termed him "the greatest menace to freedom" (Black, 168). A 1953 trip around the world occasioned a discovery made by such other American travelers as Adlai E. Stevenson*: a sense of the damage that McCarthy's antics, which included attacks on the Voice of America and overseas libraries, were doing to America's prestige abroad. She punctuated her journey with expressions of her worries.

During this period she also remarked that "the time to have stopped Hitler was when he went into the Rhineland" (Reeves, 497). She often expressed concern over McCarthyism's impact on the nation's colleges and freedom of thought and warned of the harm produced by overwrought fears of communism. Because they were so consistent with her well-established political position, however, her criticisms of McCarthy surprised no one and had limited effect on public debate.

After McCarthy's censure by the Senate, she continued to resist anticommunist excesses. In 1955 she signed a petition seeking amnesty for communists jailed under the Smith Act, which made it a crime to advocate the violent overthrow of the U.S. government, a law she had always deplored. In 1959 she joined the theologian Reinhold Niebuhr and others in a petition to abolish HUAC. As Senator John F. Kennedy* positioned himself to run for president, she made barbed references to his invisibility in the battle over McCarthyism.

Although militant anticommunists harshly criticized her, her great prestige prompted elected politicians to treat her with caution. When Congressman Harold Velde of HUAC assailed her in 1951, he was forced to remove the offending words from the *Congressional Record*.

Her distaste for communism was deeply held, but in the nation's domestic affairs she found it more often an annoyance than a clear and present danger. During the Cold War she stood among a handful of liberals who, while consistently avowing anticommunism, at the same time resisted surrender to its more extreme expressions, which she thought the graver menace.

SELECTED BIBLIOGRAPHY

Black, Allida M. *Casting Her Own Shadow: Eleanor Roosevelt and the Shaping of Postwar Liberalism.* 1996.

Lash, Joseph P. *Eleanor and Franklin.* 1971.

————. *Eleanor: The Years Alone.* 1972.

Reeves, Thomas C. *The Life and Times of Joe McCarthy: A Biography.* 1982.

Richard M. Fried

MEMORIALS. Since Eleanor Roosevelt's death in 1962, a variety of memorials have commemorated her achievements. These range from statues and monuments to commemorative stamps and plaques, to schools, buildings, institutions, awards, and even streets named in her honor. (For example, there is an Eleanor Roosevelt Street in Hato Rey, Puerto Rico.) In addition, publications, exhibits, posters, and dramatic reenactments have honored her work on behalf of civil rights,* woman's rights, international human rights,* labor,* education, and other progressive causes. Funds for these memorials have come from both public and private sources.

On 23 April 1963 President John F. Kennedy* signed Public Law 88-11 chartering the Eleanor Roosevelt Memorial Foundation as a vehicle for private donations to support projects in her honor. Memorials to ER that the foundation helped fund include a monument at the United Nations* (UN), two wings in her memory at the Franklin D. Roosevelt Library and Museum in Hyde Park,* New York, and the Eleanor Roosevelt Institute for research in Denver. The UN memorial, which was dedicated 24 April 1966, consists of a curved bench and ten-foot-high granite slab carved with a flame and a quotation from a eulogy to ER by Adlai Stevenson*: "She would rather light a candle than curse the darkness and her glow has warmed the world" (*New York Times*, 24 April 1966). With the opening in 1972 of the new wings at the Roosevelt Library and Museum, additional space was provided for ER's personal papers as well as for a gallery with exhibits illustrating her life and achievements, making this site the first presidential library to have a section devoted to a First Lady. The Eleanor Roosevelt Institute in Denver, which studies the genetic basis of disease, received support initially from the Eleanor Roosevelt Cancer Foundation, to which ER had lent her name in 1959, and later from the Eleanor Roosevelt Memorial Foundation.

In 1972 the Eleanor Roosevelt Memorial Foundation was terminated, and its resources were transferred to a newly established Eleanor Roosevelt Institute in Hyde Park. That institute and the Franklin D. Roosevelt Four Freedoms Foundation merged in 1987 into the Franklin and Eleanor Roosevelt Institute, a private, nonprofit corporation that supports scholarship on the Roosevelt era and informs new generations of the ideals of both Roosevelts. The institute initially sponsored the Eleanor Roosevelt Better Schools Project, which worked to strengthen educational opportunities at three public schools in New York City. Among its ongoing projects is the Roosevelt Study Center in Middleburg, the Netherlands,* which provides a research library for European scholars of American studies.

Val-Kill* cottage in Hyde Park, which became ER's principal home after 1945, was designated a National Historical Site by the U.S. government in 1977. That same year the Eleanor Roosevelt Center at Val-Kill (ERVK) was established as a private, nonprofit organization, based at the Val-Kill site. It conducts educational programs designed to further ER's humanitarian ideals.

In 1984 the U.S. Congress* established an Eleanor Roosevelt Centennial Commission to honor her legacy with numerous special events and publications. Included was an Eleanor Roosevelt stamp issued by the U.S. Postal Service, which had previously issued an Eleanor Roosevelt Commemorative Stamp in 1963. In 1998 the Postal Service as part of a series on the 1930s issued a stamp portraying ER talking with a young African American girl.

The Franklin Delano Roosevelt Memorial in Washington, D.C., dedicated in 1997, is the first presidential memorial to include a sculpture of a First Lady. ER's statue in the fourth room of the memorial stands in front of a symbol of the United Nations, reflecting her role in drafting the Universal Declaration of Human Rights.* In Riverside Park in New York City, a bronze memorial statue, depicting ER leaning contemplatively against a boulder, was unveiled on 5 October 1996 with First Lady Hillary Rodham Clinton at the dedication ceremony. A statue of ER in a niche of the Washington National Cathedral in Washington, D.C., was dedicated on 5 December 1998 in conjunction with an Eleanor Roosevelt Exhibition at the cathedral celebrating the fiftieth anniversary of the Universal Declaration of Human Rights.

Numerous awards for accomplishment have been named for ER. The American Association of University Women (AAUW) gives the biennial Eleanor Roosevelt Fund Award to recognize an individual, project, organization, or institution for contributions to gender equity in education. The AAUW also awards Eleanor Roosevelt Teacher Fellowships to public school teachers who design projects to stimulate girls' interest in math, science, and technology. Among other honors named for her is the Eleanor Roosevelt Humanitarian Award, presented annually by the League for the Hard of Hearing.

Educational institutions named for ER include the Eleanor Roosevelt High School in Greenbelt,* Maryland—the largest secondary school in the state. One of the five undergraduate colleges on the campus of the

University of California, San Diego, was named for ER in 1994. Roosevelt University in Chicago now is named for both Eleanor and Franklin D. Roosevelt.* When this independent, nonsectarian university opened in 1945 to promote equal educational opportunity and social justice, the school was named in memory of Franklin D. Roosevelt. ER served on its early advisory board, along with Albert Einstein, Thomas Mann, Pearl Buck, and Marian Anderson.* In 1959 the university was rededicated to honor ER as well as FDR. It sponsors a yearly lecture exploring the progressive legacies of both Roosevelts.

Such a broad spectrum of recognition extends into the future the collective memory of ER's activism and humanitarian idealism.

SELECTED BIBLIOGRAPHY

Anna Roosevelt Halsted Papers, Franklin D. Roosevelt Library, Hyde Park, NY.
Eleanor Roosevelt Papers, Franklin D. Roosevelt Library, Hyde Park, NY.
Hershan, Stella K. *A Woman of Quality.* 1970.
James Roosevelt Papers, Franklin D. Roosevelt Library, Hyde Park, NY.

Lynn Y. Weiner

MERCER, LUCY. See RUTHERFURD, LUCY MERCER.

MILLER, EARL (9 May 1897, Schenectady, NY–2 May 1973, Hollywood, FL).

Squire, companion, confidant, Earl Miller had a unique place in Eleanor Roosevelt's heart. There was room for him wherever she lived; regular times were reserved for him in her hectic schedule.

Until the long and detailed letters to Earl that ER referred to in other correspondence are found, the basic facts of their friendship, which began in 1928 and continued until her death in 1962, are located only in their visits, home movies, Miller's guarded memories shared with a few others, and ER's many references. A New York state trooper assigned to protect ER when Franklin D. Roosevelt* was elected governor of New York in 1928, Miller worked to serve her best interests.

Homeless at the age of twelve, tall and athletic, Miller took a series of odd jobs—as a contortionist, stuntman, and circus acrobat—before joining the navy and winning its Atlantic middleweight boxing championship. A chief petty officer in 1918, he escorted FDR during his European battlefield tour as assistant secretary of the navy. In 1928 FDR was delighted to see Miller, then a New York state trooper detailed to the Executive Mansion in Albany.

Miller became ER's bodyguard and accompanied her on inspection tours of prisons and public institutions. He suggested investigative techniques she used and refined throughout her public life. Like Louis Howe,* he encouraged her to smile for photographers and relax in the company of reporters. After FDR was elected president in 1932, he ap-

Eleanor Roosevelt takes part in a skit, "Kidnapping the First Lady," with Earl Miller while relaxing at Chazy Lake, New York, in August 1934. This photograph is made from a home movie taken by Marion Dickerman. *Courtesy of Franklin D. Roosevelt Library*

pointed Miller director of personnel for New York state's Department of Correction—which meant that Earl would not be part of ER's entourage in Washington. Nevertheless, Miller, whose second marriage was annulled in 1933, continued to play a special role in ER's life during the White House years.

When ER refused Secret Service protection, Miller taught her to shoot a pistol. They played billiards and lighthearted games; they sang while Miller played the piano. He helped her perfect her dive, a physical feat that somehow mattered to her. He also gave her the two horses she most loved and rambunctious dogs he trained to guard her. He introduced her to show business people like Mayris Chaney, a dancer with whom ER maintained a lifelong friendship. He monitored her checkbooks and sought to protect her from chiselers and cheats. Interviewed by Joseph Lash,* Miller stressed that ER "was never one to check on those dunning her. I would say, 'People aren't all good.' She would say, 'They don't ask for very much.'" Earl lamented: "It was not easy to protect the Lady." His warnings were often rejected by ER, who said: "The trouble with you, Earl, is you're too much of a cop. You don't trust anybody" (Lash, *Love, Eleanor*, 120).

ER and Earl Miller agreed on most political issues. Miller deplored the Red Scare strategy that condemned opposition to racial injustice and concern for "the underdog" as "pink or radical" (Cook, 1:439). He was proud of his work on behalf of those in want and in trouble. Appointed by FDR to inspect southern prisons in the 1940s, he was often accompanied by Lucy Mercer (Rutherfurd),* who had come between ER and FDR during World War I. Now a philanthropist married to Winthrop Rutherfurd, she and Miller exposed brutal conditions endured by black prisoners in Georgia and Florida, and their work led to significant reforms.

Miller and ER shared many interests. We know about their walks in the woods when the snow reached their knees and the poems ER read aloud during long winter nights; we know that she enjoyed fussing over Earl's houses, and we have a record of the many presents she gave him. But we know very little about the secrets they shared, the words and feelings they exchanged, which marked one of ER's most abiding friendships.

Earl Miller was much involved in the game of hearts, but his three marriages failed—perhaps because of ER's presence in his life. But there were other troubles. In February 1938 Miller was ill at ER's New York apartment in Greenwich Village. ER wrote her daughter, Anna Roosevelt Boettiger (Halsted*): "I'm really worried about him but I think his trouble is being unable to find peace & no one can do that but the individual themselves" (Asbell, 97).

For many years, ER's correspondence with her daughter included references to visits and holidays with Earl that were tranquil and satisfying. One evening, Esther Lape,* who lived with Elizabeth Read* at 20 East 11th Street in Greenwich Village and rented ER a hideaway apartment there, went upstairs to visit unannounced. She rang the bell and heard ER hurry to the door. Dressed elegantly, ER flung open the door with excitement. Her great warm smile disappeared instantly, Lape recalled: ER could hardly conceal her disappointment. She said, "Oh, I was expecting Earl, but do come in" (Cook, 1:434). Unlike Marion Dickerman* and Nancy Cook,* Lape was more impressed than disapproving of the ER-Miller friendship. Lorena Hickok* also disapproved. But she was more specifically jealous.

ER's champion and defender, Miller provided a safe port in major storms. In February 1940 ER left for an unusual midwinter holiday in Florida with Earl, Tommy (ER's secretary and assistant, Malvina Thompson*), and Tommy's longtime companion, Henry Osthagen. She was exhausted after her support for the members of the American Youth Congress* (AYC) resulted in vicious press criticism and public acrimony.

The young people of the AYC had been her political allies and personal friends until the Nazi–Soviet Pact of August 1939. When they were hauled before Martin Dies' House Committee to Investigate Un-American Activities* during hearings to prove communist domination of the AYC, she had sat with them and invited them to the White House. Then, AYC members booed her husband when he lectured them while they stood in the rain on the White House lawn.

After bitter weeks of recriminations and press abuse, ER went to a private home owned by Miller's friends in Golden Beach, Florida. She wrote her daughter a long letter in which she defended the politics of the AYC, criticized her husband's speech, "though I wish they (AYC members) had better manners about it!," and concluded: "I'm getting a good tan & doing nothing social. Henry & Earl are having some friends for cocktails today & yesterday Tommy, Earl & I went to see 'Grapes of Wrath,' otherwise I've lived on the beach in a bathing suit" (ER to ARB, 21 February 1940).

During World War II,* Miller served as a lieutenant commander in the navy and succeeded Gene Tunney as director of physical training at the Naval Air Station at Pensacola, Florida. Reassigned to a naval base in New York, he spent much of the war camped in ER's new and larger apartment off Washington Square Park.

After FDR's death in 1945, ER'S international career and campaign for human rights* resulted in world travels* and new adventures. But some part of Miller's life remained entwined with his great friend. His last wife, Simone Miller, sued for divorce—implying that the couple's marital woes were caused by her husband's primary attachment to ER. On 18 August 1948, the *New York Mirror* featured the story: "The attractive, young Upstate matron, who has accused Miller of 'consorting with a woman of prominent reputation,' steadfastly refused to disclose the identity of the woman in question."

On 26 October 1948 Simone Miller was granted custody of their two children, named Eleanor and Earl, and a settlement of an undisclosed amount. Her attorney told reporters that "we could not sustain" the allegation concerning "a woman of prominent reputation" (International News Service dispatch, Albany, 26 October 1948). The separation was granted on grounds of cruelty. In 1950 the case was rehashed in three nasty columns by Westbrook Pegler.* Tommy wrote ER's daughter, Anna, that Pegler's column got Miller into "a lather but it didn't bother your mother or me." Still, Tommy thought Pegler was "pretty bad" and "stopped just short of naming names" (Lash, *World of Love*, 317).

During the 1950s Earl Miller moved to Hollywood, Florida, and ER concentrated on her work at the United Nations.* They continued to correspond until her death.

For more than twenty years Miller and ER shared pleasure in each other's company and a generous, public-spirited ethic. When he was informed, incorrectly, that he was named in ER's will, he wrote his friends and neighbors, Miriam and Robert Abelow, that "whatever it might be I shall donate it to her favorite charities, of which I'm well acquainted" (EM to MA and RA, 16 December 1962). When he agreed to give *Life* and *Look* magazines access to his motion picture films for still pictures, and they offered to pay him fifty dollars for each picture used, he wrote that he "told them to donate it to 'Boys Athletic League, Inc' N.Y. City. Many of those kids (all underprivileged) never saw a live cow. . . . I still to this day send a boy to camp for 2 wks each summer" (EM to MA, 12 June 1965).

Miller remained anonymous and silent until his death. He avoided the press and all publicity. "I've never told a new acquaintance of my relationship. I haven't fraternized with any tenant here . . . none have been in my apt so the R[oosevelt] pics [pictures] on my walls have been for my pleasure only" (EM to MA, 5 August 1972).

Without correspondence or testimony, we know only that Earl Miller was one of the most intense and enduring figures in ER's life, a source of security, joy, and romantic adventure.

SELECTED BIBLIOGRAPHY

Anna Roosevelt Halsted Papers, Franklin D. Roosevelt Library, Hyde Park, NY.
Asbell, Bernard. *Mother and Daughter*. 1982.
Cook, Blanche Wiesen. *Eleanor Roosevelt*. Vols. 1, 2. 1992, 1999.
Lash, Joseph P. *Love, Eleanor: Eleanor Roosevelt and Her Friends*. 1982.
———. *A World of Love: Eleanor Roosevelt and Her Friends, 1943–1962*. 1984.
Miriam S. Abelow Papers, Franklin D. Roosevelt Library, Hyde Park, NY.

Blanche Wiesen Cook

MILLS, HARRIET MAY (9 August 1857, Syracuse, NY–16 May 1935, Syracuse, NY).

Harriet May Mills was the leading woman in the Democratic Party* in New York state at the time Eleanor Roosevelt first became active in politics. A member of an abolitionist family, Mills was an early woman graduate of Cornell University (in 1879) and devoted three decades to working for woman suffrage on the local, state, and national levels as an orator, lobbyist, and suffrage association official. In 1920 she was the first woman candidate from a major party for statewide office in New York, unsuccessfully running for secretary of state on the Democratic ticket. After her defeat, she became the first director of the Women's Division of the New York state Democratic Committee in 1922.

Although she admired Mills, initially, ER thought that she was too strong a feminist. According to ER, she met Mills through Nancy Cook,* who, as Mills' assistant, invited ER to speak at a Democratic fund-raising luncheon. Although the politically inexperienced ER thought Mills too militant, she appreciated her political skills. She later credited Mills with starting "all the work among the women" in the New York Democratic

Party. Although Mills left the director's post in 1923, she "responded to every call for assistance," ER continued (Roosevelt, 124).

Mills was a member of the electoral college that voted for Franklin D. Roosevelt* in 1932 and was a guest of the Roosevelts at the White House, making her the first Syracuse woman to be invited to visit there. In 1934 ER, at Mills' invitation, spoke in the new Women's Building at the New York state fairgrounds in Syracuse. The building subsequently was named for Mills. After Mills' death, ER lectured in Syracuse to help raise funds for the Syracuse Museum of Fine Arts in Mills' honor.

SELECTED BIBLIOGRAPHY

Eleanor Roosevelt Papers, Franklin D. Roosevelt Library, Hyde Park, NY.
Lash, Joseph P. *Eleanor and Franklin.* 1971.
Roosevelt, Eleanor. *The Autobiography of Eleanor Roosevelt.* 1961.
Watrous, Hilda R. *Harriet May Mills 1857–1935.* 1984.

Hilda R. Watrous

MORGENTHAU, ELINOR F. (19 February 1892, New York–21 September 1949, New York).

The second most important thing in Elinor Morgenthau's life was her friendship with Eleanor Roosevelt, exceeded only by her devotion to her own nuclear family. In this respect she was perhaps unique among a tight circle of intimates—mostly single, divorced, and widowed women and both men and women who were between relationships—whose lives were firmly in orbit circling around ER, the queen bee.

Elinor Morgenthau met ER and Franklin D. Roosevelt* shortly after she married Henry Morgenthau Jr. in 1916. He was managing his cattle and apple farm in southern Dutchess County and was one of the few active Democrats in this upstate New York Republican stronghold. The first known reference to the Morgenthau–Roosevelt liaison appears in a letter Sara Delano Roosevelt,* FDR's mother, wrote from Hyde Park* to her daughter-in-law in Washington. "Young Morgenthau and his wife called this PM, and while they were here Mrs. F.W.V. [Frederic W. Vanderbilt] came bringing 5 people, and we had a pleasant tea. Young Morgenthau was easy and yet modest and serious and intelligent. The wife is very Jewish but appeared very well" (Lash, *Love, Eleanor,* 76). At this point ER was accustomed to exchanging remarks with Sara that reflected the anti-Semitism ingrained in the upper-class America of her day. But not long afterward, ER outgrew such sentiments.

Elinor Morgenthau was a determined assimilationist, bent on breaking out of the German Jewish gilded ghetto in which she had been raised. Indeed, the Morgenthaus were the only Jewish family the Roosevelts were intimate with socially. Henry, Elinor, and their three children were frequently invited to attend picnics at Hyde Park, where ER grilled the hot dogs. In the winter the Morgenthaus vacationed aboard the Roosevelt houseboat, the *Larooco*, off Key West, Florida.

ER and Elinor were drawn together by similar interests and tastes. Both rather plain by conventional standards of beauty, they had learned to attract men by their wits rather than appearance. Elinor was short and plump. Her most striking features were her deep-set, piercing, dark brown eyes and clear, alabaster skin. Both women were conservatively well groomed and found little time to waste keeping up with fashion. Both had been brought up to keep out of their own kitchens. But while the meals served at the Roosevelts under ER's supervision were generally frugal and tasteless, the Morgenthau repasts were consistently ample and appetizing; and on occasions when FDR came to dine, an opulent spread was designed to satisfy his epicurean taste.

Elinor was the daughter of Morris Fatman, a woolen manufacturer, and Lisette Lehman, whose father had been a founding partner in the banking house of Lehman Brothers. After graduating from Vassar College in 1913, where she had been president of the dramatic society, Elinor continued her involvement in theater, teaching and directing plays at the Neighborhood Playhouse, an adjunct of the Henry Street Settlement House, located in the impoverished Jewish quarter of Manhattan's Lower East Side. When she was twenty-four, Elinor married Henry Morgenthau Jr., the only son of Ambassador Henry Morgenthau, President Wilson's emissary to Turkey. After two unhappy years at Cornell University, young Morgenthau had settled down as a farmer in Dutchess County, New York, and immersed himself in local politics.

After her marriage, Elinor's life in the theater ended; within six years she had become the mother of three children, Henry III, Robert, and Joan. In the mid-1920s she refocused her energies. Striving to advance her husband's political ambitions, she became a key associate of ER in the Women's Division of the New York state Democratic Committee, while her husband secured his role as an able and trusted FDR cohort.

That both Morgenthaus retained footholds in the separate and sometimes rivalrous Roosevelt camps can be attributed largely to Elinor Morgenthau's diplomatic finesse. In addition, ER was impressed by Elinor's tightly knit family, which ER wistfully observed in stark contrast to her own dysfunctional clan. Given the difference in the way FDR and ER conducted themselves as public personages, the Morgenthaus' sustained balancing act was a remarkable achievement. ER, always hungry for affection, became emotionally entangled with the people she worked with, at the same time hating the jealous contest for her favor she unconsciously fostered. When one of the aggrieved parties confronted her with complaints, she could become uncharacteristically angry. FDR, on the other hand, distanced himself from his key appointed officials, encouraging bitter rivalries while he remained jauntily above the fray. But it was soon apparent that Henry, when he was in difficulty or wanted to float a trial balloon, was assured special access to "the boss" via the Elinor–ER linkage.

After FDR was crippled by polio in 1921 ER, under the tutelage of Louis Howe,* kept the Roosevelt political presence alive. When Alfred E. Smith,* a promising New York City Tammany Hall politician, decided to run for governor in 1922, he sought the support of the Roosevelts and the clout of their name upstate. With FDR largely out of action, ER, as a leader in the Women's Division, began organizing on his behalf. The enthusiastic young Morgenthaus followed her lead, with Elinor doing most of the speaking.

The Morgenthaus' family friendship with the Roosevelts flourished. In the summer of 1928 the Morgenthaus, as the only husband-and-wife delegates, joined the Roosevelts in the insufferably hot (pre-air-conditioning) convention hall in Houston, Texas, where Al Smith won the Democratic presidential nomination. ER wrote FDR, "Elinor and Henry are like children in their joy that she should be made a delegate at large—I never realized anyone could care so much" (Lash, *Love, Eleanor,* 107). FDR was nominated to succeed Smith as governor of New York, and Elinor's uncle, Herbert Lehman, was nominated for lieutenant governor.

During the campaign Henry served as FDR's advance man while Elinor worked under ER, proving herself an able cohort as an organizer and writer for the *Women's Democratic News,** published monthly by the Women's Division. Yet, their relationship was never easy. Elinor was keenly aware that she was playing a political game for very high stakes—the favor of the Roosevelts—and with the passionate rivalries that ER unwittingly encouraged, a player could be bumped out of the game at any time.

During the twelve years of the Roosevelt presidency, both ER and Elinor Morgenthau served primarily as their husbands' mates, but in very different ways. ER, feeling trapped in the White House, was eager to roam the country in the mutually satisfying role of the president's eyes and ears. In contrast, when Henry Morgenthau Jr. became secretary of the treasury, Elinor withdrew from public life to nurture her husband's fragile ego and counsel him on human relations, making sure he kept the direct access to "the boss" that he had long enjoyed. At the same time she performed the prescribed duties of a cabinet wife with great aplomb. Her personal association with ER became stronger than ever. With Elinor's emotional center rooted in her own family, she was able to distance herself from the storms of passions that consumed ER's more rootless favorites.

As the First Lady's companion rather than dependent, Elinor was ever enthusiastically available, and her association with ER ranged from early morning horseback rides in Washington's Rock Creek Park, to excursions to the theater in New York. On these occasions they often dined at the Colony Club, the city's most exclusive women's club. In 1937 ER proposed Elinor for membership. When she was blackballed because she was Jewish, much to the shock of both women, ER quietly resigned.

Elinor also accompanied ER on visits to New Deal* projects such as Arthurdale,* a West Virginia resettlement community for unemployed miners. When ER held a festive costume party for "Gridiron widows," women excluded from the all-male Gridiron dinners where elite journalists razzed the president face-to-face, Elinor planned and staged the skits. ER insisted on having a debut for Elinor's daughter, Joan, when she was eighteen, holding a dance at the White House on 26 December 1940.

As World War II* threatened to engulf the United States, FDR appointed the charismatic mayor of New York City, Fiorello LaGuardia, to establish the Office of Civilian Defense* (OCD), with ER serving as his deputy and Elinor as her associate. This was the one and only time each held down federal jobs, albeit unpaid and on a part-time basis. After the Japanese attack on Pearl Harbor and U.S. entry into the war in 1941, OCD faced enormous demands. ER's efforts, which included putting some personal friends—like a dancer, Mayris Chaney—on the payroll, opened her to vicious personal attacks. Frustrated in her attempts to establish order and discipline in the chaos left in ER's wake, Elinor prudently backed out before becoming involved in the disaster, pleading poor health. Shortly thereafter, both ER and LaGuardia resigned, turning their responsibilities over to a full-time staff. In a short time the two women once again resumed their companionable personal relationship. Elinor, however, began to suffer from illnesses caused by a congenital tendency to multiple thrombosis, for which there was then no effective treatment.

One of her last journeys with ER, in September 1941, was a visit to a camp in upstate New York at Fort Ontario in Oswego that housed 982 refugees.* Most were Jews who had escaped the Holocaust.* Throughout their relationship Elinor had fought against being labeled ER's "Jewish friend." But on this occasion her presence was important for just that reason. Both women were sadly aware that this "token payment to decency" was, in fact, the sum total of the U.S. government's commitment to provide a safe haven for Jewish refugees (Morgenthau, 334). They departed feeling profoundly disheartened.

In April 1945 Elinor and Henry were on vacation in Florida when Elinor suffered severe damage to her heart. Thus ended her days of trailing in ER's footsteps. Her health increasingly frail, Elinor kept the remaining four years of her life, for the most part, family-centered. Loyal to her dear friend, ER called on Elinor frequently while the two of them continued to exchange gifts and greetings. At her funeral ER delivered the eulogy. In her autobiography she had written: "Elinor Morgenthau and I ... thrown together by our common interests ... became warm friends. She is a sensitive generous person whose qualities I recognized and appreciated and our relationship developed with the years" (Roosevelt, 31).

SELECTED BIBLIOGRAPHY
Eleanor Roosevelt Papers, Franklin D. Roosevelt Library, Hyde Park, NY.
Lash, Joseph P. *Eleanor and Franklin.* 1971.
———. *Love, Eleanor.* 1982.
———. *A World of Love.* 1984.
Morgenthau, Henry, III. *Mostly Morgenthaus, a Family History.* 1991.
Roosevelt, Eleanor. *This I Remember.* 1949.

Henry Morgenthau III

MOSKOWITZ, BELLE LINDNER (ISRAELS) (5 October 1877, New York–2 January 1933, New York).

Belle Moskowitz, a social worker and public relations counselor who became a close adviser of Alfred E. Smith,* worked closely with Eleanor Roosevelt during Smith's tenure as governor of New York during the 1920s. While ER regarded Moskowitz as highly competent, she influenced Franklin D. Roosevelt* against hiring Moskowitz as his private secretary when he was elected governor in 1928 on grounds she was too attached to Smith to render faithful service to FDR.

The daughter of an immigrant Polish Jewish family, Moskowitz attended Teachers College at Columbia University for a year and studied acting privately before becoming a social worker at the Educational Alliance, a settlement house that served Jewish immigrants on New York's Lower East Side. After leaving the alliance to marry Charles Israels, an architect, in 1903, she continued to be active in social causes, particularly the licensing of dance halls to protect young women, and helped found the New York Travelers Aid Society. Left a widow in 1911 with three small children to support, she eventually became manager of the labor department of the Dress and Waist Manufacturers' Association, where she settled labor disputes from 1914 to 1916.

Following her marriage in 1914 to Henry Moskowitz, a settlement house head who ran unsuccessfully for Congress* on the Progressive ticket, she joined with him in the new field of public relations. Committed to woman suffrage and reform, she, like her husband, believed in the organization of public opinion to improve society. Meeting Smith during his first gubernatorial campaign in 1918, Moskowitz encouraged him to bring women who had just received the vote in New York state, into the Democratic Party.* After his election Smith appointed her executive secretary of the Reconstruction Commission, a group set up at her suggestion to study governmental organization and other issues of public concern, including the rising cost of living, housing, health care, unemployment, and labor and industrial relations. Progressive measures proposed by the commission became the basis for many of Smith's legislative initiatives as well as his platform in later election campaigns.

ER and Moskowitz, who shared the belief that women entered politics to advance ideals rather than their own careers, worked together in several organizations in the 1920s, both partisan and nonpartisan. They both participated in activities of the Women's Division of the New York state Democratic Committee and were involved in Smith's 1922 gubernatorial campaign. After his election, ER and Moskowitz joined forces in various women's groups to push for passage of his legislative program.

Both were part of the inner circle of the Women's City Club,* which attracted most of the politically active women in New York. Moskowitz was elected to the board in 1922, and ER in 1924. They met at board and committee meetings and often lunched together. Each campaigned for Smith in 1924, consulting on tactics and strategy. From 1925 to 1928, each lobbied for Smith's reform legislation, including improved administration of government, housing for the poor, and limitation on women's working hours. ER thought Smith a good man, but she attributed to Moskowitz the social welfare programs for which he was generally given credit. Some of these programs were similar to those later adopted by FDR as governor and president. When Smith became the Democratic candidate for president of the United States in 1928, Moskowitz took charge of his publicity, while ER directed women's activities in the national campaign, reporting to Moskowitz and keeping in close touch with her.

After Smith's defeat and Roosevelt's election as New York governor, Moskowitz's political career ended. At the time of her death, she was described as "having wielded more political power than any other women in the United States" during Smith's ascendancy in the Democratic Party, and her role was summarized as a remarkable triumph of behind-the-scenes influence: "Holding no public office she occupied a unique position during Mr. Smith's four terms as Governor of New York. She was his advisor on matters of statecraft as well as politics and many times she was the unseen advocate of progressive legislation which he sponsored" (*New York Times*, 3 January 1933).

SELECTED BIBLIOGRAPHY
Cook, Blanche Wiesen. *Eleanor Roosevelt*. Vol. 1. 1992.
Perry, Elisabeth Israels. *Belle Moskowitz: Feminine Politics and the Exercise of Power in the Age of Alfred E. Smith*. 1987.
Roosevelt, Eleanor. *This Is My Story*. 1937.

MOTION PICTURES. Eleanor Roosevelt was both a fan and an admirer of the power and influence of motion pictures. Indeed, she had significant personal ties to the Hollywood movie business. In 1939 the legendary movie producer Sam Goldwyn hired her son, James Roosevelt,* in large part so that Goldwyn could brag that the son of President Franklin D. Roosevelt* worked for him. James, in turn, drew his mother into Hollywood society. Through him, she was a special guest at the premiere of William Wyler's *Wuthering Heights* at the Pantages theater in Los Angeles on 13 April 1939.

In 1940 James tired of being a "trophy executive" and moved on to create his own independent motion picture production company, Globe Productions. His controversial British film *Pastor Hall* told the tale of a German pacifist. United Artists distributed the film, and *Pastor Hall* premiered on 13 September 1940. It featured ER herself narrating the prologue written by Robert Sherwood, the playwright turned FDR speechwriter and Roosevelt family friend.

To the general public, however, ER was best known as the highly visible First Lady who frequently appeared in the weekly newsreels that accompanied feature films in the cinema theaters of the day. These showed her by FDR's side as well as engaged in extensive travel to serve as the eyes and ears of her husband. Her warm, charming, and often amusing personality seemed naturally to come across in these productions, making her come alive for the millions of Americans who flocked to the era's films. So, for example, for a 9 July 1938 picnic held at Hyde Park,* New York, the leading Hollywood star of the day, Shirley Temple, was filmed with ER by Fox Movietone Newsreel cameramen. ER probably appeared in at least one newsreel a month during FDR's terms in the White House. She continued to appear in newsreels, albeit less frequently, until they disappeared from movie theaters around 1960 with the advent of television.

ER developed close friendships with a number of Hollywood notables. First among these was Helen Gahagan Douglas,* a former Hollywood actress who went on to become a member of the U.S. House of Representatives and was married to a major Hollywood star, Melvyn Douglas.* ER's son, Elliott Roosevelt,* was married from 1944 through 1950 to actress Faye Emerson, another movie star, with whom ER had cordial relations.

Moreover, her various charitable activities, in particular for the March of Dimes, a campaign to raise money to fight infantile paralysis, enabled her to regularly mingle with some of Hollywood's leading stars. She was regularly photographed with box office favorites, like Robert Taylor, Jean Harlow, Judy Garland, and Mickey Rooney, at "Birthday Ball" fundraisers, events held annually on FDR's birthday to benefit the March of

Dimes in tribute to the president's battle against the disease. So, for example, on 30 January 1936 ER, arm in arm with Harlow and Taylor, visited every "Birthday Ball" in the nation's capital, producing pages of positive publicity in newspapers and magazines and raising record sums of contributions. More than any other means—save newsreels—these occasions made ER a notable figure to the American moviegoing public.

As First Lady ER also was regularly invited to movie premieres. She attended, for example, the well-publicized openings of *Snow White and the Seven Dwarfs* in 1938 and *The Grapes of Wrath* in 1940. (In May 1938 *Snow White and the Seven Dwarfs* was shown after dinner in the White House at the request of FDR, who had seen it once and wanted to see it again.) Of *The Grapes of Wrath*, a dramatization of migrants' lives, ER wrote in her "My Day*" column of 23 February 1940: "I think it is well done, but I wonder if it will convey to many people the reality of what they are seeing" (Chadakoff, 161).

ER wrote movingly of events surrounding the January 1940 world premiere of Robert Sherwood's film adaptation of his play *Abe Lincoln in Illinois*, which was held in Washington as a benefit for the Children's Hospital. She told her "My Day" readers on 24 January that when she reached the Keith's theater in the center of the capital, she found marching African American protestors, who had been barred from attending because of laws requiring segregation, blocking the way to the lobby. Although she entered the theater, she wrote of the irony of attending a segregated showing that celebrated the life of the Great Emancipator, while the descendants of those he had freed were kept from viewing it. It was, she said, a "symbol of the fact that Lincoln's plea for equality of citizenship and for freedom, has never been quite accepted in our nation" (Chadakoff, 155).

As her fame grew, ER inspired moviemakers. The fictional film *Great Day* (1946), for example, recounted how a small British community overcame its internal feuds preparing for a visit by ER. When Katharine Hepburn began filming *The African Queen* (1952), she asked director John Huston how she should portray her character, Rose, the sister of a missionary; Huston told Hepburn to become "Eleanor Roosevelt." Thirty years later in her autobiography, Hepburn thanked ER for inspiring her performance in this classic movie role.

ER has been directly portrayed on the movie screen countless times. A number of documentary films on ER have been produced, including *Eleanor Roosevelt* (1956), *The Eleanor Roosevelt Story* (1965), and *First Lady of the World: Eleanor Roosevelt* (1974). In the 1960 Hollywood feature film *Sunrise at Campobello*, adapted by Dore Schary from his Broadway play, Greer Garson played ER. In a later made-for-television movie, *Eleanor, First Lady of the World*, which was first shown on 12 May 1982, Jean

Stapleton played ER. Thus, her image has really never been absent; there can be no doubt that capturing her on-screen will challenge many more actresses in the future.

SELECTED BIBLIOGRAPHY

Berg, A. Scott. *Goldwyn: A Biography*. 1989.
Chadakoff, Rochelle, ed. *Eleanor Roosevelt's My Day*. Vol. 1. 1989.
Douglas, Helen Gahagan. *A Full Life*. 1982.
Hepburn, Katharine. *Me: Stories of My Life*. 1991.
Roosevelt, Eleanor. "Film Folk I Have Known." *Photoplay* (January 1939): 10–11, 83.

Douglas Gomery

MURRAY, ANNA PAULINE ("PAULI") (20 November 1910, Baltimore– 1 July 1985, Pittsburgh).

Pauli Murray, who achieved distinction as a writer; labor,* civil rights,* and woman's rights pioneer; legal scholar; and theologian, became a friend of Eleanor Roosevelt in the early 1940s. Earning a bachelor's degree from Hunter College in 1933, Murray received a law degree cum laude from Howard University in 1944, a master's degree in law from the University of California, Berkeley, one year later, and a doctorate in law from Yale University in 1965. After practicing law and teaching at the University of Ghana, Benedict College, and Brandeis and Boston universities, she received a master's degree in divinity from the General Theological Seminary in 1976. In 1977 she became the first African American woman to be ordained as a priest in the 200-year history of the Protestant Episcopal Church. She also was a cofounder of the National Organization for Women (NOW) in 1966.

Twenty-six years junior to ER, Murray, who was raised by relatives in Durham, North Carolina, had a qualitatively different relationship with the First Lady than did veteran African American leaders such as Mary McLeod Bethune.* Founder and president of the National Council of Negro Women, Bethune was an experienced politician whose dealings with the First Lady and President Franklin D. Roosevelt* were always calculated and never impulsive. By contrast, Murray was an impatient, independent thinker-activist, determined to share her opinions with FDR and ER no matter how impractical or rash they sounded.

At first glance, a genuine friendship between the granddaughter of former slaves and the First Lady would seem unlikely. Yet Murray and ER had several things in common. Both were orphaned before adolescence; both were raised primarily by older women kinsfolk and nurtured throughout their lives by significant friendships with women; both were intelligent and temperamentally shy; both were Episcopalians; and both became activists in the civil and woman's rights movements.

The first time Murray saw ER was in the winter of 1934–1935 at Camp

Tera in the Bear Mountain area of upstate New York. Named initially for the Temporary Employment Relief Administration and later in honor of Jane Addams,* this was the first camp to be established for unemployed women and girls and was the result of efforts by ER and Frances Perkins,* secretary of labor in the Roosevelt administration, to create a female counterpart to the CCC (Civilian Conservation Corps) camps for men. From the beginning, ER showed interest in the camp, urging that it be racially integrated and visiting periodically to talk with its residents and staff. On this particular visit ER spoke to an assembly and passed through the social hall where Murray and other residents were seated. Shy and overwhelmed by the First Lady's presence, Murray did not stand up and introduce herself.

Their actual introduction was occasioned four years later by a letter that Murray wrote to FDR on 6 December 1938. It was prompted by a speech he had given at the University of North Carolina at Chapel Hill, praising the institution for its liberalism and commitment to social progress. Murray, then a teacher on the rolls of the Works Progress Administration* (WPA), had applied to North Carolina's graduate school, fearing that she would be rejected because of its whites-only admission policy. She was irritated by FDR's rhetoric and wrote to challenge his sincerity. Hoping to ensure that her letter would actually be seen by the president, she sent a copy with a covering note to ER.

There were two responses to Murray's letter, neither directly from FDR. The official response came on 23 January 1939 from Hilda Worthington Smith,* a WPA administrator, to whom Murray's letter had been referred. But the first response, a sympathetic personal note, came from ER on 19 December 1938, a few days after Murray was officially rejected by the university. In the letter ER counseled patience and offered hope. So began the seeds of a friendship that later included visits to Hyde Park* and ER's New York apartment and lasted until ER's death in 1962.

The early years of the friendship were characterized by generational and political differences associated with Murray's desire for dramatic social change and the First Lady's appeals for gradualism. For example, in the spring of 1940, when Murray was arrested in Petersburg, Virginia, for violating state law that required segregated seating on public buses, ER advised against breaking the law but also wrote local authorities inquiring about the incident. Later that year the First Lady became involved, at the urging of Murray, now working for the Workers Defense League, in a national campaign to save the life of Odell Waller,* a Virginia sharecropper convicted of first-degree murder in the death of his white landlord by an all-white jury. ER lobbied both FDR and Governor Colgate W. Darden Jr. of Virginia without success to commute Waller's sentence to life imprisonment.

In the 1950s and the early 1960s, their friendship deepened, and ideological conflicts softened, with Murray moving toward the political center. Although Murray once professed little faith in political parties, she agreed to work in the 1952 and 1956 Democratic presidential campaigns of Adlai Stevenson* as a result of ER's influence. They both were appointed by President John F. Kennedy* to the President's Commission on the Status of Women*—ER as chair and Murray as a member of the Committee on Civil and Political Rights.

Like an obedient daughter supported by the unconditional acceptance of a mother's love, Murray measured herself by the ideals and spirit of ER. In her unpublished essay, "A Stormy Relationship with Mrs. Roosevelt," she wrote of the emotional meaning of this friendship: "She gave me a sense of personal worth [and] she warmed me with a maternal quality which made me want to strive to walk in her footsteps" (31). Of the relationship, ER wrote in a 1953 *Ebony* magazine article: "One of my finest young friends is a charming woman lawyer—Pauli Murray, who has been quite a firebrand at times but of whom I am very fond" (Roosevelt, 172–73). That she personally responded to the protestations of a young African American woman was symbolic of ER's compassion.

Stating that she sought to honor the work ER began with the commission, Murray focused her later work largely on woman's rights. As a legal theorist, she helped lay the framework for Title VII of the 1964 Civil Rights Act, which forbade employment discrimination against women, and joined Betty Friedan in organizing NOW. At heart a writer, she wrote landmark essays and briefs on gender and racial discrimination; a family biography, *Proud Shoes: The Story of an American Family* (1956); *Dark Testament and Other Poems* (1970), a collection of poetry dedicated to ER; and *States' Laws on Race and Color* (1956), a critical compilation that Thurgood Marshall called a bible for civil rights attorneys. Her award-winning autobiography (1989) was published posthumously.

SELECTED BIBLIOGRAPHY
Pauli Murray Papers, Schlesinger Library, Radcliffe College, Cambridge, MA.
Murray, Pauli. *Pauli Murray: The Autobiography of a Black Activist, Feminist, Lawyer, Priest, and Poet*. 1989.
Roosevelt, Eleanor. "Some of My Best Friends Are Negro." Reprinted in Allida M. Black, ed., *What I Hope to Leave Behind: The Essential Essays of Eleanor Roosevelt*. 1995.

Patricia Bell-Scott

"MY DAY." Eleanor Roosevelt wrote a syndicated column for daily newspapers, "My Day," a diary-like account of her activities, which continued from 1936 until shortly before her death in 1962. One of the first and longest-running columns to capitalize on public interest in the lives of celebrities, "My Day" served various purposes during its twenty-six-year history. It humanized the New Deal,* featured the achievements of women, presented political messages attuned to the Democratic Party,* and promoted the United Nations.* Toward the end of ER's life it evolved from a rambling daily chronicle into a somewhat more focused commentary on current issues.

More important, "My Day" helped enlarge the boundaries for women, particularly First Ladies,* in American life. Although ER always pictured herself within the setting of the Roosevelt family, the column was instrumental in establishing her as having an identity separate from that of her husband, President Franklin D. Roosevelt.* The product of an era when woman had few role models except movie stars, "My Day" presented ER as the most notable exception to stereotypical portrayals of actresses, wives, and mothers. It showed her as a middle-aged woman who pursued her own interests, earned an independent income, and raised her own voice on contemporary issues.

Over the years "My Day" gave ER control, to some extent, over her own public image. It charted her growth as a public figure, as she moved from a representative of her husband attempting to remedy ills of the Great Depression,* through the turbulent years of World War II,* when she visited military installations all over the globe, to her emergence as a world-renowned diplomat at the United Nations. In "My Day" in 1939 she announced her resignation from the Daughters of the American Revolution when it refused to let the African American singer Marian Anderson* give a recital in Constitution Hall (although she did not name the organization in keeping with the column's noncontroversial tone at the time). In later years, when she became more vocal, the column gave her a venue to speak out against McCarthyism* and for civil rights,* support the state of Israel,* and endorse political candidates.

"My Day" had an unpretentious, simplistic quality that critics* parodied but readers liked. It remained viable for many years as a testimony to ER's ability to touch others with personal reactions to her own experiences, even though they took place in a milieu far different from that in which her readers lived. The first "My Day" column was released in haste on 30 December 1935 to compete with a political column being started by ER's tart-tongued cousin, Alice Roosevelt Longworth,* a Republican. In spite of ridicule by Westbrook Pegler,* another columnist, and others for shallowness and lack of literary merit, "My Day" long outlasted the Longworth effort and drew a respectable audience. By 1938, for example, it appeared in sixty-two newspapers, with a total circulation of more than 4 million.

This gave ER exposure to more readers than popular political pundits like David Lawrence, although she lagged far behind Dorothy Thompson, most important of the few women columnists, who reached 7.5 million in 1940. The Scripps-Howard newspaper chain carried "My Day" in

the *New York World-Telegram* and other newspapers until 1956, when it
dropped the column, contending that ER had been too partisan in the
presidential election by using the column to campaign for Adlai Stevenson.* It then was picked up by the liberal *New York Post*, which continued
to feature it prominently for the remainder of its existence.

In contrast to weighty columns by political insiders, ER wrote informally about where she went and what she did—in her first columns she
mentioned plays, books,* movies, the weather, housekeeping at the
White House, her family, and her travels* along with references to figures in the New Deal, particularly women, and current issues. As an
indication of "My Day" 's early popularity, ER received more than 1,000
letters a week, mainly from housewives who found her day not so very
different from their own. According to ER's friend, journalist and novelist Martha Gellhorn,* the "artless" columns proved ER was not a
writer, but they showed she had an ability to communicate: "Her mass
audience was ordinary people. . . . In language they would understand,
she talked to them rather than wrote for them" (Chadakoff, xi). The syndicate promised her $1,000 a month for the column, although her profits
varied with the number of newspapers subscribing.

Distributed by the United Features Syndicate, "My Day" replaced a
weekly column that ER had unsuccessfully attempted for another syndicate on topics such as White House china and food for state functions.
Promised to be livelier and more personal than its predecessor, the daily
column succeeded, in part, because of economic factors that made columns popular during the depression era, when newspapers cut back
expenditures and laid off employees. Advertised as a personal chat with
the First Lady, it was offered on a sliding scale, making it available to
small papers for a few dollars a week. Even then, it never appeared in
more than a minority of the nation's 1,800 daily newspapers.

Aimed at women readers whom newspapers wanted to draw to attract
department store advertising, "My Day" generally ran on women's
pages, staples of newspapers of that day, although some newspapers
treated it as a political column. It fluctuated in readership from a high
of ninety newspapers following the death of Franklin D. Roosevelt in
1945, when readers presumably were curious about ER's reaction to her
widowhood, to fewer than forty toward the end of her life when it was
reduced from a six-day-a-week feature to a three-day-a-week feature.

Written in a rush, generally in a half hour per day, the column usually
was dictated to ER's secretary, Malvina Thompson* (Scheider), although
sometimes ER typed it herself. She dashed it off in trains, planes, cars,
and ships, on picnics and in hotel rooms, taking pride in the fact that
she never missed her deadline for sending it off by telegraph. In the
habit of writing a record of her engagements in her daily letter to her
close friend, journalist Lorena Hickok,* ER found that it was relatively

easy to write a column based on her activities. As a former teacher at the Todhunter School,* she used a bland, somewhat preachy tone for commonplace topics, which her syndicate editors tactfully urged her to replace with mention of "more serious subjects" that would "present a fuller picture of you and your mind" (Beasley, 90). Grammatical problems crept up, as one editor pointed out in a memo on corrections to the column: "I note with sorrow that the first lady has turned cannibal. Her lead sentence in her story is 'We had a lunch of some 50-odd ladies yesterday . . . ' and a little further down she goes on with the fearful orgy as evidenced by 'We returned in time for lunch and had a very distinguished group of doctors. . . . ' I have carefully changed these two sentences lest we lose our vegetarian readers" (Beasley, 91).

The column offered a picture of White House life that made it an effective political tool in a low-keyed way. For example, when the U.S. Supreme Court invalidated the Agricultural Adjustment Administration, a key New Deal program, in 1937, ER pictured FDR accepting the decision gracefully, swimming as usual, and bantering good-naturedly at the dinner table.

Occasionally, "My Day" floated trial balloons for the administration. When Hickok, in her role as an undercover investigator of relief programs for the New Deal, prepared a confidential report on technological unemployment in steel mills that was unfavorable to Republican industrialists, FDR told ER to run the information without attribution in her column. In a note of apology to Hickok, ER said, "I wanted to wait for your consent but Franklin won't let me. I think he wants me to be whipping boy and tho' he can't bring the question out he wants it out" (ER to LH, 7 May 1936).

Perhaps forgetting about the incident, however, ER denied to her press conference* members on 27 September 1939 that FDR ever had tried to influence what she wrote: "He has never called me in and said he wished I had said this or that or the other thing" (Beasley, 94). When she became ill in September 1936, FDR offered to write the column for her, but ER refused the offer on grounds the column belonged to her alone. FDR himself made slighting references to "My Day," telling reporters that ER was not a true columnist but simply wrote a diary.

Yet, the column was required reading by those seeking insight into administration policies, according to Arthur Krock of the *New York Times*. He pointed out in 1939 that ER had raised the issue of cutbacks in Works Progress Administration* (WPA) jobs for the unemployed in her column before FDR had addressed it. Krock made his comment three months after the *Times* itself had carried "My Day" for a brief period—when ER reported in it on the visit of the king and queen of England to Washington and the Roosevelt home at Hyde Park,* New York.

In commenting on literary and theatrical works, ER showed herself to have somewhat unsophisticated tastes, which may have been in line with those of many of her readers. Brooks Atkinson, drama critic for the *New York Times*, took her to task after she chastised him and other critics for preferring Thornton Wilder's notable play *Our Town* to a mediocre romance, which ER had found more pleasant. Atkinson observed: "Mrs. Roosevelt is there in the paper to soothe the tired head. No country ever had a sweeter mother" (Atkinson, 89). But he chided her for doing "less than justice to a distinguished work of art" (Atkinson, 91).

During World War II ER used "My Day" to report on her extensive travels to visit military facilities and to back the war effort. No longer concerned with administration policy after FDR's death in 1945, "My Day" became a platform for ER to endorse the Americans for Democratic Action* and to give her views on the Communist Party, which she did not trust, although she expressed the hope that the United States could cooperate with Russia. This attitude distressed some who feared accommodation toward communists might menace U.S. security. Some of her closest readers were agents of the Federal Bureau of Investigation* who monitored "My Day" carefully, reporting to J. Edgar Hoover on its contents. Among her most notable columns was one (17 August 1960) endorsing John F. Kennedy* as the Democratic candidate for president.

In her later years, "My Day" provided ER with both a personal forum and extra income that furthered her ability to function in public life at an age when many persons had retired. In 1952 the Advertising Research Council said the column was read by 37 percent of women newspaper readers and that ER was the columnist with the most appeal to women. In 1954 the column brought her $28,000 a year. "My Day" succeeded, as George A. Carlin, her syndicate editor expressed it, because it was "an honest projection of one of the great personalities of our own time" (Lash, 565).

SELECTED BIBLIOGRAPHY

Atkinson, Brooks. *Broadway Scrapbook*. 1947.
Beasley, Maurine H. *Eleanor Roosevelt and the Media*. 1987.
Chadakoff, Rochelle, ed. *Eleanor Roosevelt's My Day*. Vol. 1. 1989.
Emblidge, David, ed. *Eleanor Roosevelt's "My Day."* Vols. 2, 3. 1990, 1991.
Lash, Joseph P. *Eleanor and Franklin*. 1971.
Lorena Hickok Papers, Franklin D. Roosevelt Library, Hyde Park, NY.

                                                                   Alf Pratte

N

**NATIONAL ASSOCIATION FOR THE ADVANCEMENT OF COL-
ORED PEOPLE.** Founded in 1909, the National Association for the Advancement of Colored People (NAACP) was the most prominent civil
rights* organization in the United States during the twentieth century.
Eleanor Roosevelt became involved with the NAACP around 1934, as
the organization expanded its lobbying activity in Washington, and remained associated with the NAACP until her death in 1962.

There is little evidence of exactly how and when ER developed an
interest in race relations and civil rights. Indeed, as biographer Blanche
Wiesen Cook has observed, ER "began her public career steeped in the
sensibilities of the Old South, filled with distorted and ugly images of
blacks" (Cook, 6). Her engagement with racial issues, however, was
clearly an outgrowth of her fundamental commitment to human dignity
and social justice and the efforts of NAACP executive secretary Walter
White* to cultivate the First Lady's interest and support. During the early
years of the New Deal,* ER developed a bond with White, as well as
several other black civil rights activists, particularly Mary McLeod Bethune* and, later, Pauli Murray.* Moreover, the democratic rhetoric and
reform initiatives of the New Deal engaged the hopes and aspirations of
African Americans throughout the nation. Their appeals for fair treatment found a receptive proponent in ER.

During the 1930s the NAACP succeeded in drawing national attention
to lynching as the most revealing symbol of the lawlessness, terror, and
political impotence endured by African Americans in the Jim Crow
South. The association had been lobbying for antilynching* legislation
since the early 1920s. With the New Deal and the expansion of federal
power into many areas of national life, the NAACP intensified its efforts
to secure federal action against lynching. ER became a primary focus of

Walter White's lobbying efforts. Roy Wilkins, White's assistant, recalled that White "bombarded Mrs. Roosevelt with letters and telegrams and appeals for interviews," and, in the end, "he prevailed" (Wilkins, 129).

ER and White established a working relationship around the drive for antilynching legislation. The NAACP leadership had helped to draft a bill that was introduced early in 1934 by Senators Edward P. Costigan and Robert F. Wagner, both Democrats. By the time the Senate Judiciary Committee reported favorably on the Costigan–Wagner Anti-Lynching bill in April 1934, ER had already discussed the bill at length with Franklin D. Roosevelt* and had arranged for White to meet with the president. The president privately assured White of his support for the bill, but, in the face of a dominant southern leadership in Congress, he proved unwilling to expend any political capital pushing for the legislation. Despite the fact that, according to Walter White, a majority of the senators favored the bill, Senate majority leader Joseph Robinson of Arkansas stalled the bill and did not allow it to come to the floor of the Senate for a vote. With a southern Democratic bloc united against the antilynching bill, victory on the legislative front failed to materialize during the peak years of the New Deal.

While ER was sensitive to FDR's efforts to placate the southern wing of the Democratic Party,* she continued to aid the NAACP's cause with a steady flow of information and sustained a high level of personal support. In the winter of 1935, when Walter White invited the First Lady to an NAACP-sponsored art exhibit on lynching, she hesitated, expressing concern that her appearance would only stiffen opposition to the bill. Yet she finally did attend, though she carefully avoided publicity. In the late 1930s ER attended a fund-raiser in Harlem for the NAACP's magazine, *The Crisis*. Black people packed into the Mother AME Zion Church, spilling over onto the side streets. In what was her first public appearance in Harlem as First Lady, she proclaimed that "we should all have equal rights, and minorities should certainly have them exactly as majorities do" (Wilkins, 131). She also acknowledged that New Deal reforms were still just "a drop in the bucket" (Wilkins, 131) compared to what needed to be done for Harlem and other urban communities.

On the eve of America's entry into World War II,* the relationship of blacks to the war effort emerged as one of the major civil rights issues. In the spring of 1940, Walter White joined A. Philip Randolph in demanding that the president desegregate the armed forces and the defense industries or risk having thousands of African Americans march on the nation's capital to demand fair treatment. Arguing that political realities would not allow him to make such a bold move, FDR refused, and ER worked on her husband's behalf, urging White and Randolph to drop their plans for a march. They would not consider backing down. Roosevelt finally agreed to issue an executive order banning discrimination in federally funded defense industry programs and establishing the Fair Employment Practices Committee (FEPC) to monitor compliance, a compromise that ER was instrumental in securing.

In 1945, shortly after FDR's death, ER accepted nomination to the NAACP's board of directors. One of the first major debates she took part in concerned the FEPC and efforts to ensure its continuation. Several board members thought it should be treated exclusively as an NAACP issue, while others argued that the Council for a Permanent FEPC, a coalition of liberal and labor groups, should also be encouraged to continue its work. ER supported a broad-based fight for fair employment, arguing at the NAACP directors meeting, 14 October 1946, that the "FEPC should never be considered solely as a piece of Negro legislation because there are many other people who are discriminated against, and should work for passage of [legislation creating a permanent] FEPC" (NAACP Papers). In July 1947 ER proudly appeared with President Harry S Truman* when he addressed an NAACP rally in front of the Lincoln Memorial. The first president to address the NAACP, Truman pledged that the federal government would act as "a vigilant defender of the rights and equalities of all Americans" (Wilkins, 198).

In the post–World War II era, ER's relationship with the NAACP and the civil rights struggle was tempered by her involvement with the United Nations* (UN) as a representative of the United States and by the impact of the Cold War* on domestic politics. After ER became chair of the UN Commission on Human Rights early in 1947, W.E.B. Du Bois* met with her twice to discuss plans for a petition the NAACP planned to submit to the United Nations regarding the condition of African Americans. The document, entitled, "An Appeal to the World: A Statement on the Denial of Human Rights to Minorities in the Case of Citizens of Negro Descent in the United States of America and an Appeal to the United Nations for Redress," outlined the history of racial discrimination in the United States and its impact on African Americans in the midtwentieth century. When a draft was submitted during the summer of 1947, the report caused a minor furor among U.S. representatives. ER refused to introduce it and, according to Du Bois, threatened to resign from the NAACP if the matter was brought up by any other nation. Surprised and disappointed by ER's reaction, Du Bois concluded that she was following State Department orders. Walter White distanced himself from the appeal and tried to prevent any further distribution of the report through the NAACP.

ER informed the NAACP board of directors at its meeting 5 January 1948 that she planned to spend most of her time in Hyde Park* and with her UN work and, therefore, would not be able to attend meetings regularly. If the board so desired, she explained, she would submit her resignation. Walter White quickly responded at the meeting that she was one of the board's "most valuable members" and that the association "would suffer irreparable loss if you were to resign" (NAACP Papers). ER continued to attend board meetings occasionally. As one NAACP official observed, her participation was, for the most part, ritualistic. But her membership on the board during these years kept her associated with the NAACP's fight against racial segregation on multiple fronts, and she often spoke out in support of desegregation efforts around the country.

In 1954 the NAACP's twenty-year-long legal challenge to unequal education culminated with the Supreme Court's decision, *Brown v. Board of Education*. As white southerners pledged resistance to the Court's ruling, ER argued that "understanding and sympathy for the white people of the South is as important as understanding and sympathy for the colored people" (Gillon, 94). ER's gradualist approach reflected a belief that she had expressed in 1943, in response to black pressure for desegregation of the armed forces. "This change has to come slowly from the human heart and it takes a long while to bring about great changes" (Kirby, 84). Her appeal for moderation in 1956, however, also conveyed the sentiments of a national Democratic Party anxious not to alienate its southern wing.

ER actively supported the presidential candidacy of Adlai Stevenson* in 1956, a cautious liberal who was determined to preserve party unity by keeping civil rights out of the 1956 campaign. Roy Wilkins, who had succeeded Walter White as executive secretary of the NAACP, wanted a plank in the Democratic Party platform supporting the enforcement of the *Brown* decision. He tried to pressure Stevenson, warning that his waffling on civil rights might cost him the black vote. In response to Wilkins' veiled threat, ER told an intermediary that Wilkins was pursuing a reckless course and hinted that she would resign from the NAACP board if he persisted. Wilkins met with ER, and they worked out their differences; Wilkins' criticism of Stevenson ceased. In a feeble effort to ensure that the issue was not completely ignored during the 1956 campaign, the NAACP organized a national rally for civil rights in Washington, attended by 2,000 people.

It can be concluded that ER played a critical role at a pivotal time in the history of the NAACP. It was during the New Deal era that the organization established a permanent presence in Washington and, through the tireless lobbying efforts of Walter White, became part of the emerging liberal–labor coalition that eclipsed the singular dominance of the southern Democrats. The active and very public support of ER enhanced White's efforts and helped give the NAACP legitimacy in Democratic political circles and among liberals in the national political arena. Moreover, Roy Wilkins recalled, it was her "personal touches and . . .

personal fight against discrimination" (Hareven, 124) that helped rally black support to the New Deal and, in turn, the Democratic Party.

By the 1950s, however, when the NAACP's victory in the Supreme Court had opened the way for a direct challenge to the segregation system in the South, the constraints of Cold War liberalism and consensus politics had vastly narrowed the scope of Democratic Party activism. ER's approach to racial reform had changed very little since the days of the New Deal, but, in the context of the 1950s, it lacked the boldness and imagination that had secured for her a distinguished and undiminished role in the struggle for civil rights some twenty years earlier.

SELECTED BIBLIOGRAPHY
Cook, Blanche Wiesen. *Eleanor Roosevelt*. Vol. 1. 1992.
Gillon, Steven M. *Politics and Vision: The ADA and American Liberalism*. 1987.
Hareven, Tamara K. *Eleanor Roosevelt: An American Conscience*. 1986.
Kirby, John B. *Black Americans and the Roosevelt Era: Liberalism and Race*. 1980.
National Association for the Advancement of Colored People (NACCP) Papers, Library of Congress, Washington, DC.
Wilkins, Roy. *Standing Fast: The Autobiography of Roy Wilkins*. 1982.

Patricia Sullivan

NATIONAL CONSUMERS' LEAGUE. Eleanor Roosevelt began to work with the New York City Consumers' League in 1903, when she sought interests beyond social activities following her debut into society the previous year. Documented in her correspondence with Franklin D. Roosevelt,* her reform work with both the movement for social settlements* and the Consumers' League carried her into working-class immigrant neighborhoods, where she observed sweatshops and poverty firsthand.

She was drawn into the league through a network that began with her debutante group and the Junior League for the Promotion of Settlement Movements, cofounded by Mary Harriman Rumsey.* The settlement movement was part of a broader network of reform organizations that included the Women's Trade Union League* and the Consumers' League. Since the mother of one of her debutante friends, Helen Cutting, and the head of the Rivington Street settlement, where ER volunteered, were both active in the Consumers' League, ER soon shifted her activism to that venue. When the league sent her to investigate the sweatshops in which artificial feathers and flowers were being made, she was appalled. "In those days, these people often worked at home, and I felt I had no right to invade their private dwellings, to ask questions, to investigate conditions. I was frightened to death." Still, she thought, "this was what had been required of me and I wanted to be useful." When she entered "my first sweatshop and walked up the steps of my first tenement," she saw "little children of four or five sitting at tables until they dropped with fatigue" (Roosevelt, 103–4).

Through both its practical and theoretical perspectives, the league introduced ER to the power that was part of Progressivism.* Practically, it introduced her to strategies that emphasized a four-stage legislative reform process: investigate, educate, legislate, and enforce. Theoretically, the league taught her about the potency of gender as a principle of organization in American political culture. Although after her marriage in 1905 she withdrew to devote herself to her family, and when she returned to political activism in the 1920s, she focused on other organizations, her early years with the Consumers' League lent a seriousness of purpose to her participation in American political culture that informed her public persona throughout her life.

When ER joined the Consumers' League movement in 1903, the organization was young, having been launched in New York City in 1891 by Josephine Shaw Lowell in cooperation with striking women hatmakers to combat sweatshops and other exploitative labor practices. The national league was founded in 1898, uniting local leagues in New York, Massachusetts, Illinois, New Jersey, Ohio, and Pennsylvania. Most important for ER, league membership brought her into contact with the national league's secretary general, Florence Kelley, who had spent the 1890s with the remarkable group of women reformers whom Jane Addams* attracted to Hull House in Chicago and in 1903 lived at the Henry Street Settlement, founded by Lillian Wald* on Manhattan's Lower East Side. Kelley had been hired to head the Consumers' League movement and implement its crusade against sweatshops. As the chief factory inspector of the state of Illinois between 1893 and 1897, Kelley had exercised power through state office; in 1904 she orchestrated the power of middle-class women's activism.

When ER joined the Consumers' League, she enlisted in its primary activity, the promotion of the Consumers' White Label campaign. Reflecting the diversity and geographic breadth of American political culture, that campaign forged a network of local leagues that raised members' consciousness of the way that consumer goods were produced and provided effective strategies for improving working conditions.

To qualify for the Consumers' White Label, manufacturers had to submit to an inspection and meet minimum standards as defined in the National Consumers' League annual reports. Qualifying manufacturers promised to obey state factory laws, shun subcontracting, eliminate overtime work, and employ no one under sixteen years of age. In the first years of the campaign, Florence Kelley herself performed the inspections necessary to enforce these standards.

The National Consumers' League left a tripartite legacy to ER. Through it she witnessed the ability of women to launch local political initiatives, to use publicity effectively, and to make political goals personally meaningful. These lessons about the importance of grassroots support, of effective publicity, and of personal involvement in reform goals were not lost on the young ER, and in later years she applied them well.

SELECTED BIBLIOGRAPHY

Cook, Blanche Wiesen. *Eleanor Roosevelt*. Vol. 1. 1992.
Hoff-Wilson, Joan and Marjorie Lightman, eds. *Without Precedent: The Life and Career of Eleanor Roosevelt*. 1984.
Lash, Joseph P. *Eleanor and Franklin*. 1971.
Roosevelt, Eleanor. *You Learn by Living*. New York. 1960.

Kathryn Kish Sklar

NATIONAL HEALTH INSURANCE. Although sympathetic to the cause, Eleanor Roosevelt was never a champion of the movement for national health insurance. In 1935, when the Roosevelt administration was considering Social Security proposals, members of the American Medical Association accused her of being an advocate in disguise of national health insurance. This was not true. She deliberately kept a low profile on the issue, and health insurance was not included in the Social Security Act of 1935.

In 1937 at the request of her close friend, Esther Lape,* ER arranged a meeting between President Franklin D. Roosevelt* and a small group of medical specialists, who called for a partnership between government, medical schools, and hospitals. The physicians argued that federal subsidies for medical care and research would raise all medical standards and guarantee medical attention for the indigent, but they did not advocate national health insurance. Their views reflected the conclusions set forth in *American Medicine: Expert Testimony Out of Court*, a two-volume report edited by Lape for the American Foundation, a private organization that studied public issues. It summarized the comments of 2,100 physicians on the organization of medical care in the United States. Due to ER's mediating role, the advocates of national health insurance believed that ER had convinced her husband to support the subsidizing of medical research and education instead of a national health insurance program. FDR himself, however, long had been ambivalent on the subject, considering it only one option to improve medical care.

After meeting with the physicians, FDR sought a recommendation from the federal Interdepartmental Committee to Coordinate Health and Welfare Activities, chaired by Josephine Roche, a former assistant secretary of the treasury. At the National Health Conference in July 1938 the committee presented a proposed national health plan that included federal grants to encourage states to develop health insurance for the indigent. ER did not attend the conference but was kept posted on the proceedings by Roche. FDR's response was to call for careful study of the issue, rather than immediate action. While national health insurance bills were later introduced, without the endorsement of FDR all failed to get through Congress.

After leaving the White House, ER supported the national health insurance proposals of President Harry S Truman* through her "My Day"* columns and radio broadcasts.* She was also a member of the Committee for the Nation's Health, a private organization to promote national health insurance that was financed by Mary Lasker, a philanthropist and personal friend. The committee published newspaper endorsements of Truman's national health plan signed by prominent public figures, including ER.

In her "My Day" column of 24 December 1952, ER stated that health services were a "basic human right" (Emblidge, 2:281). Although she backed national health insurance in principle, she, like FDR, favored other options for improved medical care, advocating federal subsidies for medical research and education as the best way to raise standards and guarantee access to care. In "My Day" on 7 September 1945, she argued that "research and training are two things which are essential to the health of the nation" (Emblidge, 2:30). On 4 April 1946 she rebutted attacks on a national health bill that opponents claimed was "socialistic," saying she was sure people wanted "not only more medical facilities but more doctors, scientists, dentists, nurses and other specialists" (Emblidge, 2:55).

ER repeatedly emphasized the need for extending public health service programs for the elderly, mothers, and children. Her enthusiasm for national health insurance increased when the Democrats in Congress introduced legislation during the administration of President Dwight D. Eisenhower* to provide coverage for those sixty-five years and older as part of Social Security. ER spoke out in favor of this plan, which became known as Medicare. In "My Day" of 9 April 1960 she emphasized the need for rapid enactment since "the help must be given now and not after the people are dead" (Emblidge, 3:241). On the twenty-fifth anniversary of the Social Security Act in 1960, presidential candidate John F. Kennedy* endorsed Medicare at Hyde Park* in ER's presence. Medicare was eventually enacted in 1965, three years after her death.

SELECTED BIBLIOGRAPHY

Emblidge, David, ed. Eleanor Roosevelt's "My Day." Vols. 2, 3. 1990, 1991.
Kooijman, Jaap. And the Pursuit of National Health: The Incremental Strategy Toward National Health Insurance in the United States. 1999.
———. "Soon or Later On: Franklin D. Roosevelt and National Health Insurance, 1933 to 1945." Presidential Studies Quarterly 29 (June 1999): 336–350.
Lape, Esther Everett, ed. American Medicine: Expert Testimony Out of Court. Vols. 1, 2. 1937.
Lash, Joseph P. Eleanor and Franklin. 1971.

Jaap Kooijman

NATIONAL YOUTH ADMINISTRATION. In May 1934 Eleanor Roosevelt confessed to experiencing "moments of real terror," as she confronted the possibility that the United States could well be losing "this generation" (Kearney, 23). Certainly, the question of unemployed and unemployable youth* was a crucial concern for many New Dealers, including President Franklin D. Roosevelt* and his wife. Young people were among the worst casualties of the Great Depression.* Denied work, unable to complete their education, they were in danger of becoming a generation of misfits, incapable of participating in social and economic recovery, if and when it came.

The new administration moved swiftly to deal with the problem. Within weeks after Roosevelt's inauguration, the Civilian Conservation Corps had been created, putting thousands of unemployed young men to work on conservation tasks throughout the land. One of the most popular of all the New Deal* measures, it was also the president's personal creation, and yet it was clearly a palliative, catering to the worst cases only. Most young people were unable to leave their homes in order to work in the woods. A much more wide-ranging youth program was needed, one located in communities that would provide training as well as work.

The National Youth Administration (NYA) was the New Deal's attempt to fill this need, and ER was closely involved with the agency from its inception. Indeed, she had been part of a discussion group on youth problems that had considered the first blueprints of what was to become the NYA, and she certainly lobbied her husband on its behalf. FDR referred to it as "the missus organization" (Salmond, *Case Study*, 138), in recognition of the depth of her commitment.

Created in June 1935 and originally part of the new work-relief scheme of that year, exemplified by the Works Progress Administration* (WPA), the NYA became a fully independent agency in 1939. Headed from the start by the WPA's deputy director, Aubrey Willis Williams,* a passionate, liberal Alabamian, the new agency's task was twofold. First, it had to develop programs for those currently in high school or college, providing grants in return for work on the campus sufficient to enable them to stay in school. Its second job, the more difficult one, was to aid those unemployed young people who were no longer in school, providing work relief but also job training of permanent value.

ER constantly demanded progress reports from Williams in NYA's early days, she studied work project proposals, she advised him as to policy and personnel problems, and she frequently visited projects—in short, she acted as both an adviser to the agency and its White House advocate-in-residence. Moreover, she provided Williams with useful advice and unswerving support when he and the agency came under attack

Eleanor Roosevelt addresses the national conference on the problems of the Negro and Negro youth on 12 January 1939 in Washington, sharing the platform with Aubrey Williams and Mary McLeod Bethune of the National Youth Administration. *Courtesy of National Archives*

in its last years. When Williams needed to see the president, for example, ER arranged it, even if it meant disrupting carefully planned dinner table seating schedules. The NYA had no better friend than the First Lady, for it reflected both her concern for America's young people and her deepening sense of social justice.

After a slow start, the NYA proved to be one of the New Deal's success stories, touching the lives of more than 5 million young Americans before it was terminated in 1943. Williams had no desire to run a tightly centralized agency. Consequently, the program was organized by state and local officials, with the central office providing broad policy guidelines only. Though a southerner, Williams did not share his region's racial views. One of his top assistants was the black educator Mary McLeod Bethune,* who was in charge of Negro affairs at the NYA. Young black men and women were enrolled in the NYA, as far as possible, according to need, not population ratio. Furthermore, Williams insisted that the training requirement be rigorously met and that the skills learned be relevant to the enrollees' home communities. "Make-work" projects, therefore, were kept to a minimum.

When Williams moved full-time to the NYA in 1939, it was a well-established, thriving agency, democratic in its organization, decentralized in its operation. As the threat of World War II* grew, however, he changed its focus, deciding that the agency should concentrate on training young people for defense industry work, teaching them welding and other industrial skills before sending them to individual plants. The transformation was accomplished swiftly. In its last years the NYA was solely a defense training agency, giving its participants shop skills, transporting them to areas of labor shortage, and finding them jobs before letting them go. That it did this work well is evidenced by the thousands of letters of support from local businessmen to be found in its files. Though it was eliminated in 1943, the victim of partisan congressional infighting, it stands as an example of one of the most successful and enlightened of New Deal agencies.

SELECTED BIBLIOGRAPHY

Kearney, James R. *Anna Eleanor Roosevelt: The Evolution of a Reformer.* 1968.
Lindley, Betty, and Ernest K. Lindley. *A New Deal for Youth: The Story of the National Youth Administration.* 1938.
Reiman, Richard A. *The New Deal and American Youth. Ideas and Ideals in a Depression Decade.* 1992.
Salmond, John A. *The Civilian Conservation Corps: A New Deal Case Study.* 1967.
————. *A Southern Rebel. The Life and Times of Aubrey Willis Williams.* 1983.

John A. Salmond

NATIVE AMERICANS. Eleanor Roosevelt was a genuine champion of New Deal* Indian policy because it addressed her two major concerns about Native people—the economic conditions on reservations and the preservation of cultural traditions. Congress established an Indian New Deal in 1934 through passage of the Wheeler–Howard Act, also known as the Indian Reorganization Act. This act ended the destructive policy of allotment, which had divided Indian land previously held in common and distributed tracts to individual owners. Under the direction of John Collier, commissioner of Indian affairs for President Franklin D. Roosevelt,* the Indian New Deal also sought to rectify the disastrous economic and cultural effects of allotment by promoting a return to traditional Native practices and values.

The Indian Arts and Crafts Board, created by Congress* in 1935, attracted ER's attention, and she became an advocate for the exhibition and marketing of Native arts. After visiting the Indian Arts and Crafts Board's display at the 1939 San Francisco World's Fair, she wrote in her "My Day"* column on 23 March 1939: "I was deeply impressed by the attitude of the Indians themselves. They have had a share in this exhibition and they are very happy over the result and proud to show some of their most beautiful work. . . . A big basket, rugs, tiles, etc., shown in a room with modern furniture, prove how well these Indian things are adapted to modern living" (Chadakoff, 114). The sale of handicrafts, she believed, promised one solution to the desperate poverty of many Native communities.

In 1941 she visited the House Indian Affairs Committee room to see a display of crafts by Native peoples from the Northwest, including the Coeur d'Alenes of Idaho, who had taken advantage of the leather glove shortage created by the war in Europe to market their gloves through a Spokane department store. ER supported the Arts and Crafts Board's 1941 exhibit at the Museum of Modern Art in New York and wrote in the foreword of the catalog, *Indian Art of the United States*: "In appraising the Indian's past and present achievements, we realize not only that his heritage constitutes part of the artistic and spiritual wealth of this country, but also that the Indian people of today have a contribution to make toward the America of the future" (8).

ER realized that the economic future of Native people had to rest on a broader foundation than the marketing of arts and crafts. Consequently, she became an advocate of incorporating Indians into public works programs. She became personally involved in promoting construction of the Tonawanda Indian Community House for Senecas living near Akron, New York. Built almost exclusively with Native labor, the structure housed an auditorium, library, museum, and rooms for adult education. Its construction provided job training in carpentry, masonry, and other building trades. On 13 May 1939, the First Lady attended the community house's dedication. Her photograph, inscribed "To my friends on the Tonawanda Reservation," remains today at the community house, which one historian has called "a living legacy of the New Deal" (Hauptman, 126).

An incident that occurred during the planning of the Tonawanda Indian Community House, however, pointed to the tunnel vision of New Dealers when it came to implementing Indian policy. Wary of tribal factionalism and assertions of sovereignty, promoters of the community house bypassed the tribal council. When Chief Aaron Poodry and members of the council learned about the plans, they took offense. Ultimately, Poodry and others came to support the community house, but their dilemma in accepting a project foisted on them, however worthy, was one shared by Native people throughout the United States.

Like other New Dealers, ER believed that the federal government could help individuals solve their problems, including the problem of poverty on Indian reservations. In 1941 two groups of Navajos from Arizona, New Mexico, and southern Utah visited ER to acquaint her with the Bureau of Indian Affairs' stock reduction program, which they believed was making them even poorer by killing thousands of sheep on which they depended for subsistence. ER summoned Collier, who told her, as she reported in her "My Day" column on 18 June 1941, that "the land on the reservation, in more than 81 years, has completely changed because of overgrazing . . . [and] in order to bring it back, there must be a dramatic curtailment of cattle, wild horses, goats and sheep." She recognized that the loss of livestock meant that the Navajos "must either go on relief, which they want at all costs to avoid, or starve to death" (Chadakoff, 209). Another solution, she believed, was a federally funded irrigation project, and she urged its consideration. At no point did ER question government intervention or the possibility, now suggested by scholars, that the stock reduction program was unfair, excessively harsh, poorly administered, and perhaps motivated by concern over silt collecting behind dams downstream rather than Navajo poverty.

At the same time, ER was a defender of Native American sovereignty. In "My Day," she urged President Harry S Truman* to veto two bills that jeopardized the gains Native people had made under the Indian New Deal. The Butler–D'Ewart bill, which was under consideration in Congress, authorized an individual Indian to sell his equity in tribal landholdings. ER, in her "My Day" column on 5 October 1949, accurately placed this bill in the context of the "constant effort going on to transfer Indian property to whites." The Navajo–Hopi Rehabilitation bill, which lay on Truman's desk, extended state law over these people. ER charged that through "this new bill we will interfere with all the things that are important to them—their religion, their art, their self-governing arrangements. The very things that those who study Indian life consider most important, this bill would destroy." In addition, ER argued that to deny Native Americans their civil rights* weakened the United States at a time when the nation needed to strengthen its "governmental household so that it will not be vulnerable to attack by the Communists" (Emblidge, 182–83). This use of the exigencies of the Cold War* to justify improving Native American civil rights echoed ER's tactics in arguing for African American civil rights. ER's criticisms were successful; neither bill became law.

While ER never really rose above the paternalism inherent in New Deal Indian policy, she did become a person to whom Native people felt comfortable addressing their concerns. Not only did Native artists, proponents of the Tonawanda Community House, and the Navajo delegation protesting stock reduction seek her out, but Indians throughout the nation felt comfortable writing her about their children's education, their economic problems, and their concern that government had forgotten them. Like many silenced Americans, Native peoples sought a voice in ER.

SELECTED BIBLIOGRAPHY

Chadakoff, Rochelle, ed. *Eleanor Roosevelt's "My Day."* Vol. 1. 1989.

Emblidge, David, ed. *Eleanor Roosevelt's "My Day."* Vol. 2. 1990.

Hauptman, Laurence M. *The Iroquois and the New Deal.* 1981.

Philip, Kenneth R. *John Collier's Crusade for Indian Reform.* 1977.

Schrader, Robert Fay. *The Indian Arts and Crafts Board: An Aspect of New Deal Indian Policy.* 1983.

White, Richard. *Roots of Dependency: Subsistence, Environment, and Social Change among the Choctaws, Pawnees, and Navajos.* 1983.

Theda Perdue

NESBITT, VICTORIA HENRIETTA KUGLER (12 March 1874, Duluth, MN–16 June 1963, Bethesda, MD).

When Henrietta Nesbitt, a neighbor of Eleanor Roosevelt in Hyde Park,* New York, arrived at the White House in 1933, she had little preparation for the job of official housekeeper, which she held throughout ER's years as First Lady. At age fifty-nine, Nesbitt's job experience had consisted mainly of keeping books for family businesses and running a home bakery. ER, however, offered Nesbitt the position, knowing that she needed work and confident that she could maintain accurate accounts. Nesbitt had been treasurer of the League of Women Voters* in Hyde Park, a group that ER had organized. Both women also were members of St. James Episcopal Church in Hyde Park.

Growing up in Minnesota, Nesbitt learned to bake. She put this skill to use when her husband, Henry Nesbitt, who had been a salesman for whaling and cooperage businesses, became unemployed. The Nesbitts, who had two sons, moved to a farm near Hyde Park in 1929 and began selling goods baked in their kitchen with ER as their chief customer. After ER had tasted a freshly baked loaf of Nesbitt's whole wheat bread at a league event, she asked her to bake large numbers of bread and tea cakes for guests at the Roosevelt home.

On duty at the White House, Nesbitt initially felt intimidated by the enormity of her housekeeping task, but she quickly adjusted to planning an array of meals—family dinners, teas for thousands, and dinner parties for hundreds of dignitaries—and overseeing accommodations for visiting royalty. Her husband assisted her as White House custodian, a post he held until his death in 1938. ER looked over menus and, in keeping with the frugality of the Great Depression* era, experimented with the serving of seven-and-one-half-cent-per-person meals developed by home economists at Cornell University. Nevertheless, almost all domestic decisions were left to Nesbitt. She had full charge of buying and preparing food and supervised a staff of about thirty African American servants, many of whom had worked for the Roosevelt family for years. Under Nesbitt the cooking was simple American fare, with some dishes detested by Franklin D. Roosevelt* and the Roosevelt children, who often complained about Nesbitt's uninspired cuisine. On one occasion FDR wrote ER, "Do you remember that about a month ago I got sick of chicken because I got it . . . at least six times a week? . . . for the past month I have been getting sweetbreads about six times a week. I am getting to the point where my stomach positively rebels and this does not help my relations with foreign powers. I bit two of them today" (FDR to ER, 29 April 1942). A determined individual, Nesbitt continued to serve the president broccoli, even though he disliked it, on the grounds it was good for him.

ER, who apparently considered conversation, instead of food, of primary importance at meals, paid little heed to unfavorable comments about Nesbitt's culinary offerings. She applauded her for being economical and told her she was "a wonder" (Nesbitt Diary, 5 December 1933). Nesbitt remained as White House housekeeper until ER's successor as First Lady, Bess Truman, fired her.

Nesbitt subsequently wrote two books, *White House Diary* (1948) and *The Presidential Cookbook* (1951). She admired ER and considered her a wonderful friend.

SELECTED BIBLIOGRAPHY
Cook, Blanche Wiesen. *Eleanor Roosevelt*. Vol. 2. 1999.
Goodwin, Doris Kearns. *No Ordinary Time: Franklin and Eleanor Roosevelt: The Home Front in World War II*. 1994.
Henrietta Nesbitt Papers, Manuscript Division, Library of Congress, Washington, DC.
Nesbitt, Henrietta. *White House Diary*. 1948.
President's Secretary's File, Franklin D. Roosevelt Library, Hyde Park, NY.
Truman, Margaret. *First Ladies*. 1995.

Marilyn Elizabeth Perry

THE NETHERLANDS. Queen Wilhelmina of the Netherlands and her daughter, the Crown Princess Juliana, numbered among the royalty who visited the Roosevelts at both the White House and Hyde Park* during World War II.* After the Nazi invasion of the Netherlands, the Dutch queen, who had set up a government-in-exile in London, also maintained a summer home at Lee, Massachusetts, close to Juliana, who had sought refuge in Canada. In the summer of 1942 the queen visited the Roosevelts at Hyde Park, prompting Eleanor Roosevelt to write approvingly in her "My Day"* column of 16 July, "One senses [in the queen] a deep concern and constant anxiety over what is happening to the people of her country" (Chadakoff, 250).

The next month Wilhelmina made a state visit to Washington, where she became the first reigning sovereign to address Congress on 6 August. Before her address ER used her press conferences* to assist the queen and the Roosevelt administration in making the visit a success. On 5 August ER called for "courtesy to the stranger" and told reporters to discount unflattering news reports that the queen had demanded air-conditioned rooms and wasted scarce gasoline by driving fast in New England ("First Lady Asks Courtesy to Queen," *New York Times*, 6 August 1942). The following day she presented Wilhelmina herself to the press conference group, where she answered questions, stressing the fortitude of the Dutch people. The occasion was the queen's first press conference and the first press conference to be held in Washington by a reigning monarch.

In her speech to Congress Wilhelmina emphasized the war effort of the Allies in defense of democracy, but she also spoke of the Dutch colonies and their place in the framework of the Dutch Kingdom. While ER did not approve of colonialism, she came increasingly to respect the queen's concern for the welfare of her European subjects. ER called on Wilhelmina in London in November of that year, and the queen returned to Washington and Hyde Park in June 1943. In the course of their visits, the two women discussed war and peace aims. In *On My Own*, ER commented that she had always admired Queen Wilhelmina "for her staunch courage and her insistence upon being a good Dutch housewife as well as a capable ruler" (Roosevelt, 176–77).

Several of ER's many postwar travels* were European tours, during which she visited the Netherlands four times and was a guest of the royal family. In 1948 the University of Utrecht awarded ER an honorary doctorate, an unusual recognition for a woman, and she made good use of her stay by observing conditions in Europe, on which she reported back to President Harry S Truman.* Although perhaps not as interested as FDR in family history and the Dutch origins of the Roosevelt family, ER, accompanied by her son, Elliott Roosevelt,* accepted an invitation in 1950 to visit the Roosevelts of Tholen Island from which Claes Martenszen van Rosenvelt, a farmer, was said to have emigrated around 1650 to found the Roosevelt family in the United States.

ER developed a special fondness for Juliana during World War II when, as crown princess, she stayed several times in the White House; it was an affection that endured over the years and was extended to Juliana's daughter, Beatrix. In 1952 Juliana, who had followed her mother as queen in 1948, addressed the U.S. Congress, expressing Dutch gratefulness for American assistance in war and reconstruction. ER and Juliana shared a common interest in humanitarian efforts, such as support of development projects for newly sovereign states, that promoted international democratic cooperation. When Crown Princess Beatrix visited the United States in 1959, ER invited her to visit Val-Kill.* In 1982, twenty years after ER had died, Queen Beatrix maintained the tradition of her predecessors by speaking to the U.S. Congress, celebrating 200 years of American–Dutch diplomatic relations.

ER's friendship with the reigning monarchs of the Netherlands helped to cement the American wartime and postwar alliance with Western Europe. It was one example of the way ER supported American foreign relations by acting initially in the First Lady's ceremonial role* and then as an unofficial ambassador for the United States.

SELECTED BIBLIOGRAPHY
Chadakoff, Rochelle, ed. *Eleanor Roosevelt's "My Day."* Vol. 1. 1989.
Eleanor Roosevelt Papers, Franklin D. Roosevelt Library, Hyde Park, NY.
Emblidge, David, ed. *Eleanor Roosevelt's "My Day."* Vol. 2. 1990.
Minnen, Cornelis A. van, ed. *A Transatlantic Friendship: Addresses by Queen Wilhelmina, Queen Juliana and Queen Beatrix of the Netherlands to the Joint Sessions of the United States Congress.* 1992.
Queen Wilhelmina. *Eenzaam maar niet alleen.* 1959.
Roosevelt, Eleanor. *On My Own.* 1958.

Mieke van Thoor

NEW DEAL. When Franklin D. Roosevelt* accepted the Democratic presidential nomination for president in June 1932, he pledged himself to a "New Deal" for the American people, providing the label quickly applied to Great Depression*–era programs instituted after his election. Eleanor Roosevelt had no policy role in her husband's administration, yet she exerted considerable influence on the New Deal. As First Lady, she served as both an advocate for, and a critic of, FDR's developing reform program. While she neither drafted legislation nor held elective office, ER worked with other reformers outside and inside the administration to shape the contours of the New Deal. In many instances, her influence was extremely important. "It would be impossible," marveled Rexford G. Tugwell,* "to say how often and to what extent American governmental processes have been turned in new directions because of her determination" (Black, 47).

ER cannot be described as an ideologue, but she had a philosophy of reform based on the fundamental belief that an enlightened government should promote human welfare and social justice. Raised in an upperclass home in which a noblesse oblige attitude toward social reform prevailed, she participated little in the Progressive movement of the pre–World War I era, although she had volunteered at the Rivington Street settlement house in New York City and joined the National Consumers' League* before her marriage in 1905. In the 1920s, however, ER became active in a number of reform and political groups, including the League of Women Voters,* the Women's Division of the New York state Democratic Committee, the Women's City Club of New York,* and the

Eleanor Roosevelt and Lorena Hickok (in her capacity as an investigator for the New Deal) inspect conditions in a poverty-stricken area of San Juan in March 1934. *Courtesy of Franklin D. Roosevelt Library*

Women's Trade Union League.* She came to know a network of reform-minded women ranging from settlement house leaders Lillian Wald* and Mary Simkhovitch and trade unionist Rose Schneiderman,* to political activists like Nancy Cook,* Molly Dewson,* Marion Dickerman,* and Caroline O'Day,* with whom she worked to bring women into the Democratic Party* and give them greater influence. As a result, ER went to the White House in 1933 as a savvy politician and a seasoned representative of New York's reform community.

Unlike previous First Ladies* who shied away from political and policy issues while assuming traditional domestic roles, ER moved boldly into the public eye to mobilize support for her husband's programs. She publicized them in countless speeches,* press conferences,* and newspaper columns. As the president's roving ambassador, she traveled widely, providing the administration with descriptions of conditions that proved invaluable in assessing the effectiveness of New Deal initiatives. Never before had a First Lady been so visibly associated with her husband's policies, a degree of involvement that proved unsettling to New Deal opponents as well as to those who thought ER's activism unseemly for a woman.

In addition to her role as popularizer of the New Deal's image, ER called attention to aspects of programs that she deemed inadequate. She became an unofficial ombudsman or intermediary between troubled citizens and the government, receiving a large volume of correspondence*—300,000 pieces in 1933—and referring appeals for assistance to relief agencies. She kept in touch with New Deal administrators about citizens' concerns, and became a special advocate for the needs of women, youth,* and minorities. She became, according to presidential speechwriter Robert Sherwood, "the keeper and constant spokesman for her husband's conscience" (Biles, 182).

From the outset of the New Deal, ER endeavored to ensure that women were included in government programs. She backed Molly Dewson, head of the Women's Division of the Democratic National Committee, in seeking patronage for women in the New Deal, an effort that led to the appointment of an unprecedented number of talented women to federal administrative positions. At the center of an unofficial women's network, ER provided access to the White House for women officials and continually worked to expand women's participation in Democratic Party affairs. ER, in addition, sought to include more women in New Deal relief programs. She held a series of White House conferences* on women's economic plight (in 1933 addressing the emergency needs of unemployed women, in 1934 considering proposals for camps for unemployed women, and in 1938 focusing on concerns of black women and children). In short, women's influence in the New Deal and participation in its programs were greatly heightened because of ER's efforts.

ER's intervention also appeared clearly in the case of the National Youth Administration* (NYA). Established within the Works Progress Administration* (WPA) in June 1935, the NYA provided grants to students in return for part-time work so they could stay in school and job training for young people not in school. Initially, WPA administrator Harry Hopkins* discussed a proposal for the youth agency with ER, who urged FDR to take action. ER constantly monitored the implementation of NYA programs, seeking to make them nondiscriminatory. ER's influence led to the appointment of the black educator Mary McLeod Bethune* in 1935 to the NYA National Advisory Committee. In 1936 Bethune became director of Negro affairs for the NYA. Supported by ER, she advocated for black people not only there but also in other New Deal agencies.

ER's interest in minority youth mirrored a larger concern with the plight of the nation's entire African American population. Civil rights* became one of her major and most controversial causes. Repeatedly, she tried to persuade her more cautious husband to support civil rights legislation, working, in particular, with Walter White,* secretary of the National Association for the Advancement of Colored People* (NAACP), in an attempt to secure presidential endorsement of a proposed federal antilynching* law. The effort failed because of FDR's refusal to alienate southern Democrats, whose support he thought essential for the passage of other legislation. Although the New Deal stopped well short of challenging the prevailing societal norms on racial inequality and segregation, ER's role in facilitating access by blacks to officials and scrutinizing the implementation of relief programs was instrumental in allowing blacks to share in the benefits of government programs. It contributed to the revolutionary political shift of black voters from the Republican to the Democratic Party.

ER's concern for society's downtrodden also surfaced in her efforts on behalf of the rural poor. Having witnessed firsthand the chronic unemployment and wretched living conditions at the destitute mining community of Scott's Run, West Virginia, she expedited the relocation of that population to Arthurdale,* the first planned community of the new federal subsistence homestead program. She visited Arthurdale repeatedly and contributed her own funds to the community prior to its sale by the government to private owners. Despite Arthurdale's failure to achieve self-sufficiency and protracted political opposition to what critics called "communist towns," ER remained a dedicated supporter of resettlement communities.

ER's interests in relief measures extended to her earnest support of the WPA's programs for unemployed actors, artists, musicians, and writers. She publicized their achievements, defended their value, and opposed action by Congress* in 1939 that reduced funding for the WPA Federal Writers', Arts, and Music Projects and ended the WPA Federal Theater Project. Interested in preserving history, folk art, and local and regional culture, she backed the WPA Writers' Project (including its collection of folklore and slave narratives as well as its publication of local guides and an Index of American Design). The productions of the WPA's Theater and Music Projects, which staged hundreds of performances nationwide, appealed to her populist view of the arts, which called for a rediscovery of the common man as a cultural force.

By the late 1930s, a rising conservative coalition in Congress and an increasing preoccupation with affairs in Europe led to a declining spirit of reform in Washington, but ER remained steadfast in her commitment to social legislation. During World War II* and in the following decades, she continued to defend the New Deal's achievements against a growing and influential cadre of critics. For example, she argued fervently for commitment to public housing construction during wartime as a means of improving the nation's housing stock in the long run. FDR, on the other hand, sided with those who championed the hasty building of temporary structures that could be disposed of immediately after the war. As a partisan Democrat, ER forcefully argued for the rest of her life that the New Deal had done much to better the lives of countless Americans. She rued the reluctance of some in her party to continue to advance reform legislation. Even more than FDR himself, she could accurately be termed the preeminent New Dealer.

SELECTED BIBLIOGRAPHY

Biles, Roger. *A New Deal for the American People*. 1991.

Black, Allida M. *Casting Her Own Shadow: Eleanor Roosevelt and the Shaping of Postwar Liberalism*. 1996.

Hareven, Tamara. *Eleanor Roosevelt: An American Conscience*. 1968.

Hoff-Wilson, Joan, and Marjorie Lightman, eds. *Without Precedent: The Life and Career of Eleanor Roosevelt*. 1984.

Scharf, Lois. *Eleanor Roosevelt: First Lady of American Liberalism*. 1987.

Ware, Susan. *Beyond Suffrage: Women and the New Deal*. 1981.

Roger Biles

NEWSPAPER WOMEN'S CLUB OF NEW YORK. Eleanor Roosevelt became a member of the Newspaper Women's Club of New York, an organization that included influential women in journalism, based on the fact that she wrote her syndicated column, "My Day."* The club, founded in 1922 to cement ties among women journalists who had covered the suffrage campaign, provided an encouraging professional and social atmosphere for women at a time when they faced discrimination in pay, promotions, and assignments. Membership initially was limited to women working on New York daily newspapers or wire services. ER qualified because her column was carried in New York newspapers, first the *World-Telegram* and then the *Post*.

According to her financial records, ER apparently joined the club in 1947, when it had about 100 members, and remained a member until her death in 1962. Her application may well have been sponsored by Emma Bugbee,* a founding member, who covered ER's White House press conferences* for the *New York Herald Tribune* and became a close friend even though her newspaper favored the Republican Party editorially. Other prominent club members included Helen Rogers Reid, publisher of the *Herald Tribune*; Anne O'Hare McCormick of the *New York Times*, first woman to win a Pulitzer Prize for foreign correspondence; Alicia Patterson, publisher of *Newsday*; Dorothy Schiff, publisher of the *New York Post*; and Dorothy Thompson, syndicated political commentator.

ER certainly was aware of the group for years before joining. For example, in 1934 she contributed a jingle for a mock newspaper that was passed out at the club's annual Front Page ball. At the 1935 ball she was the subject of a skit, led by Bugbee and first put on at the Women's National Press Club* in Washington, that portrayed the Eleanor Roosevelt Home for Tired Newspaper Women, fatigued from keeping up with the First Lady. Speaking at the ball, ER said that sympathy should not go "to the ladies of the press but [to] the lady who has to be hare for all the hounds" (*New York Herald Tribune*, 27 April 1935).

By affiliating with the club as an active member and attending club events after leaving the White House, ER showed her desire to be taken seriously as a woman journalist. The club offered her a way to maintain contacts with Bugbee and other women who had covered her press conferences. Her presence enhanced the group's visibility and helped in the recruitment of members.

Following ER's death the club set up a fund named in her honor that has been used for scholarships for women interested in journalism from developing countries. In 1971 the club changed its name to the Newswomen's Club of New York and broadened membership requirements to take in women employed on weekly newspapers, on national news or news-feature magazines or trade publications, and in radio and television.

SELECTED BIBLIOGRAPHY

Historical Records, Newswomen's Club of New York, National Arts Club, 15 Gramercy Park S., New York 10003.

Beverly G. Merrick

NEW YORK CITY REFORM MOVEMENT. No campaign, maintained Eleanor Roosevelt, "ever meant more to me than this present struggle to bring real democracy into the Democratic party* of this state" (*New York Times*, 12 June 1959 p. 18). She was referring to the efforts of New York City's political reform movement to unseat Carmine De Sapio, the last boss of the Tammany Hall Democratic Party organization in New York County. Long known for its influence in New York City and state politics as well as for its corruption, the Tammany organization had declined in the 1930s and 1940s as its control over patronage was reduced by anti-Tammany officials such as Fiorello LaGuardia, mayor of New York from 1933 to 1945.

Tammany was further challenged after World War II* by citizens who agitated for openness in government and founded new political clubs of their own. It regained influence, however, when De Sapio in 1949 became the first Italian American to be selected as the leader of the Democratic Executive Committee of New York County. He supported some reforms, welcoming African Americans and Hispanics into the organization and backing popular measures such as rent control. Most important, he favored the election rather than the appointment of the district leaders who, like himself, served on the executive committee. As a result, De Sapio's own position now rested with the electorate. He would not or could not expunge organized crime, however, and in other ways ruled like an old-fashioned Tammany boss.

DeSapio's decisions in selecting and assisting candidates for political office led to conflict with ER. She saw De Sapio's hand in the maneuvering that led the New York state Democratic Convention in 1954 to select Averell Harriman* rather than her son, Franklin D. Roosevelt Jr.,* as its candidate for governor. In 1956 De Sapio backed Harriman's bid for the Democratic presidential nomination, and when ER's choice, Adlai Stevenson,* won the nomination, De Sapio offered only lukewarm assistance in the campaign. In 1958 he handpicked New York district attorney Frank Hogan for the Democratic senatorial nomination, angering not only ER but also former senator Herbert Lehman, who had supported former U.S. Air Force secretary Thomas K. Finletter.

In January 1959 ER, Finletter, and Lehman created the New York Committee for Democratic Voters (CDV), dedicated to reforming Tammany "rather than to serve the urge for personal power by party professionals" (Nevins, 378). ER campaigned vigorously for the reformers, climbing ladders to sound trucks and speaking in hot summer weather in spite of her advancing age. Within a year CDV candidates won in several assembly districts, giving them a voice in the Democratic New York County Executive Committee. In 1961 New York mayor Robert Wagner broke with De Sapio, calling for him to step down, and in the 1961 election De Sapio was defeated as district leader in his home base in lower Manhattan, thus ending his reign as the last Tammany boss.

SELECTED BIBLIOGRAPHY

Allen, Oliver E. *The Tiger: The Rise and Fall of Tammany Hall*. 1993.
Black, Allida M. *Casting Her Own Shadow: Eleanor Roosevelt and the Shaping of Postwar Liberalism*. 1996.
Eisenstein, Louis, and Elliot M. Rosenberg. *A Stripe of Tammany's Tiger*. 1966.
Lash, Joseph P. *Eleanor: The Years Alone*. 1972
Nevins, Allan. *Herbert H. Lehman and His Era*. 1963.

Karen E. Robbins

NEW YORK CITY RESIDENCES. During most of her life, Eleanor Roosevelt maintained a home in New York City, even though she often lived elsewhere. Following are her New York City addresses and the period of time she was associated with each location.

- 56 West 37th Street (1884–1891). ER's parents, Anna Hall Roosevelt* and Elliott Roosevelt,* lived here at the time of her birth on 11 October 1884.

- 54 East 61st Street (1891–1892). Anna moved with her children into a new home at this location in November 1891, while Elliott was in Paris being treated for alcoholism. After Anna's death in December 1892, ER remained in the care of her maternal grandmother, Mary Ludlow Hall.

- 11 West 37th Street (1893–1902). ER's Grandmother Hall maintained a town house at this address in New York City and a country home on the Hudson—

Oak Terrace, near Tivoli, New York. (From 1899 to 1902 ER attended Allenswood, a girls' boarding school near London, England.)

- 8 East 76th Street (1902–1905). The town house at this address belonged to her
  godmother and cousin, Mrs. Henry Parish, known as Cousin Susie, who provided ER a New York City home after Grandmother Hall closed her West 37th
  Street home in the fall of 1902. ER and Franklin D. Roosevelt* were married
  here on 17 March 1905.
- Hotel Webster, 40 West 45th Street (Spring 1905). ER and FDR lived in a small
  apartment in this hotel while FDR finished the term at Columbia Law School.
- 125 East 36th Street (1905–1907). On returning from a summer-long honeymoon
  in Europe, FDR and ER moved into this town house, which was rented, furnished, and staffed by his mother, Sara Delano Roosevelt.*
- 47–49 East 65th Street (1908–1928). In 1908 Sara Roosevelt gave one of the twin
  town houses at this address to ER and FDR and moved into the other herself.
  She had them designed with a common vestibule and connecting doors on
  three floors. After 1928 ER and FDR lived there only for brief periods, while
  Sara occupied her house until her death in 1941. The building now belongs to
  Hunter College.
- 20 East 11th Street (1932–1945). During the White House years, ER rented a
  small hideaway apartment in this Greenwich Village brownstone, owned by
  her friends Esther Everett Lape* and Elizabeth Fisher Read.*
- 29 Washington Square West (1945–1949). This large Greenwich Village apartment building served as ER's home in New York City when she was appointed
  U.S. delegate to the United Nations.* She made Val-Kill* cottage at Hyde Park,*
  New York, her principal residence for the remainder of her life.
- Park-Sheraton Hotel, 870 Seventh Avenue (1949–1953 and 1958). Seeking to
  simplify housing arrangements, ER maintained an office-apartment for several
  years at this hotel.
- 211 East 62nd Street (1953–1959). ER rented a small duplex located for her by
  Esther Lape. It had a garden for her dog, Duffy, and was closer to her office
  at the American Association for the United Nations* than the Park-Sheraton
  Hotel.
- 55 East 74th Street (1959–1962). ER shared a brownstone townhouse with David
  Gurewitsch,* her personal physician, and his wife, Edna. She had separate
  quarters within the building, which she purchased with the Gurewitsches. She
  died there on 7 November 1962.

SELECTED BIBLIOGRAPHY
Cook, Blanche Wiesen. *Eleanor Roosevelt.* Vols. 1, 2. 1992, 1999.
"Eleanor Roosevelt in New York," exhibit description by Stuart Desmond, cu-
     rator. New York Historical Society, New York City. 1996.
Lash, Joseph P. *Eleanor: The Years Alone.* 1972.
Roosevelt, Eleanor. *This Is My Story.* 1937.

                                                            Mary A. Hamilton

O

O'DAY, CAROLINE LOVE GOODWIN (22 June 1875(?), Perry, GA–4 January 1943, Rye, NY).

Caroline O'Day was New York's congresswoman at large from 1935 until the day before her death on 4 January 1943. She was a close friend and associate of Eleanor Roosevelt, who as First Lady participated actively in O'Day's initial congressional campaign in 1934, making speeches* on her behalf, as did President Franklin D. Roosevelt.* As an advocate of the social and economic betterment of working people, O'Day consistently supported major New Deal* measures. A dedicated pacifist, however, she broke with the Roosevelt administration prior to the entry of the United States into World War II,* hoping to keep this country out of the conflict. In 1939 she voted against portions of the Neutrality Act to allow arms sales to nations fighting against Nazi Germany and in 1940 against the Selective Training and Service Act, the first peacetime program of compulsory military service in the United States.

Born on a Georgia plantation to a prominent family that had been active in the Confederacy, she attended private schools and is known to have graduated in 1886 from the Lucy Cobb Institute in Athens, Georgia, which indicates her actual year of birth may have been 1869 rather than 1875, the date that she gave for her birth. After studying art briefly in New York, she left for Europe to pursue artistic training, remaining there eight years and helping support herself as a magazine illustrator and costume designer.

In Europe she met Daniel T. O'Day, heir to a Standard Oil fortune. The couple married in 1901 after her return to the United States and settled in Rye, New York. They were the parents of three children, a daughter and two sons. Her husband supported her activities on behalf of the woman suffrage movement. After his death in 1916, she devoted much of her time to issues of peace and political and social reform, volunteering the use of her estate as a site for peace meetings and trade union conferences.

O'Day's commitment to pacifism stemmed from her childhood memories of Civil War devastation in Georgia. She opposed American involvement in World War I and later was a vice-chair of the Women's International League for Peace and Freedom. The war also developed her interest in social welfare work. After doing volunteer work in the movement for social settlements* on New York's Lower East Side, she became a member of the New York Consumer's League,* the Women's Trade Union League,* and the board of the Henry Street Settlement founded by Lillian Wald.* She joined the Democratic Party* when women were given the vote, becoming active in both the League of Women Voters* in New York's Westchester County and the Westchester Democratic Committee. In 1923 she was appointed by Governor Alfred E. Smith* to the State Board of Charities (later the Board of Social Welfare), a position she held until 1935, which gave her sensitivity to the needs of poor farmers and workers.

ER became a close friend of O'Day through their mutual friends and coworkers in the Democratic Party, Nancy Cook* and Marion Dickerman.* When O'Day succeeded Harriet Mills* as chair of the Women's Division of the New York Democratic Committee in 1923, she set to work with ER, Cook, and Dickerman to organize women's units in every county in the state. Traveling 8,000 miles by automobile, the four women, often in groups of two, visited each one of New York's counties annually. They met with local politicians, gave talks, recruited members in traditionally Republican strongholds, and built an effective organization in upstate New York that made women an important part of the Democratic Party. In addition, they led delegations of women to the state capital at Albany, seeking to push through Smith's legislative agenda. They advocated worker's compensation, an end to legal discrimination against women, and state action to implement federal programs for maternal and child health.

"Trooping for Democracy" was the way the quartet reported its organizing forays in the *Women's Democratic News*,* the newspaper they published monthly for the Democratic committee. The first issue, which appeared in May 1925, listed O'Day as the president of the publishing corporation, with ER as editor and treasurer. When ER resigned due to FDR's election as New York governor in 1928, O'Day became the editor. Described as a calm, sweet person who was not domineering, O'Day was said to be well liked by both men and women and a natural campaigner, willing to talk to groups no matter how small.

The ties between the four women extended far beyond the political arena. While O'Day was personally closer to Dickerman than to Cook or to ER, she was a frequent visitor at ER's Val-Kill* cottage on the Roosevelt estate at Hyde Park.* O'Day herself had no part in building the cottage, designed as a vacation spot for ER, Dickerman, and Cook, but O'Day's cousin, Henry Toombs, an architectural draftsman, assisted FDR in designing the building. Later O'Day was made an honorary vice president of Val-Kill Industries, which consisted mainly of a furniture factory set up by ER, Dickerman, and Cook at Val-Kill in 1926 to employ local artisans to make reproductions of early American furniture. O'Day helped publicize the venture, writing about it, for example, in 1928 for the magazine published by the Women's City Club of New York.* The factory, however, was not profitable. Although O'Day has been said to have contributed to it, no record of any financial involvement on her part can be found in ER's personal papers relating to finances.*

O'Day was a delegate to the Democratic National Conventions of 1924, 1928, 1932, and 1936 and was elected chair of her state delegation in 1924. She worked hard in the presidential campaigns of both Smith in 1928 and FDR in 1932. The large majorities by which she was elected to Congress* in 1934, 1936, 1938, and 1940 may be traced, in part, to the grassroots organizing she pursued with ER, Cook, and Dickerman in the 1920s as well as to the help she received from ER and FDR in her first race.

As an at-large candidate (a position that no longer exists), O'Day ran for Congress in the entire state of New York on a platform promising to look after the interests of wage earners, taxpayers, and consumers and to back wider opportunities for women. Although it was unprecedented for a First Lady to campaign for a candidate, ER made as many as five speeches a day on O'Day's behalf in 1934, drawing loud outcries from Republicans who contended campaigning was inappropriate for a First Lady. O'Day was the first candidate for whom ER campaigned while in the White House.

In Congress, O'Day sponsored numerous bills for relief for individual immigrants, fought to outlaw child labor,* spoke out against lynching, and advocated on behalf of women. Nevertheless, she was the only congresswoman to oppose the Equal Rights Amendment,* which she believed would lead to the loss of protective legislation for working women. Although she became extremely ill early in 1942, Democratic leaders asked her not to resign but to finish her term. According to ER, her long friendship with O'Day contradicted the "theory that women cannot work together or for each other" (Cook, 2:222).

SELECTED BIBLIOGRAPHY

Cook, Blanche Wiesen. *Eleanor Roosevelt*. Vols. 1, 2. 1992, 1999.
Davis, Kenneth S. *Invincible Summer: An Intimate Portrait of the Roosevelts*. 1974.
Ware, Susan. *Beyond Suffrage: Women in the New Deal*. 1981.

Ginger Rudeseal Carter

ODELL WALLER CASE. In the fall of 1940, Anna Pauline ("Pauli") Murray* wrote Eleanor Roosevelt on behalf of Odell Waller, a young black sharecropper from Gretna, Virginia, who had killed his white landlord, Oscar Davis, in a dispute over a wheat crop they jointly owned. Responding to federal crop allotments, Davis had cut to two acres the land he rented to Waller. In the spring of 1940, while Waller was away working in Maryland, Davis had seized the entire wheat harvest and evicted Waller's foster mother, Annie, and his wife, Mollie, from their shack on the Davis property. On his return, Waller went to see Davis to demand his rightful share of the crop. They argued, and when Davis, who usually carried a gun, reached for his pocket, Waller shot him. Waller fled to Ohio, where he was caught and extradited to Virginia.

After being tried by an all-white jury, Waller was convicted of murder in the first degree and sentenced to die in the electric chair. Because of evidence supporting Waller's belief that he had shot Davis in self-defense, and because Waller was denied a jury of his peers, since only persons who had paid a poll tax were eligible for jury service in Virginia, his trial ignited a two-year debate about the interconnections of race, poverty, political disfranchisement, and treatment by the U.S. justice system.

The campaign to save Waller's life was directed primarily by the Workers Defense League (WDL). Pauli Murray, a young African American activist and friend of ER, was the WDL's field secretary for the Odell Waller case. At Murray's urging the First Lady wrote letters to Governor James H. Price and his successor, Governor Colgate W. Darden Jr. Although ER persuaded President Franklin D. Roosevelt* to write Governor Darden, FDR refused to appoint a presidential inquiry commission or to meet with a delegation of black leaders who had come to Washington on Waller's behalf. On the eve of Waller's execution, the president also refused to ask the governor to commute Waller's sentence, despite the pleas of the First Lady and the delegation. Shaken by FDR's decision, ER called A. Phillip Randolph, international president of the Brotherhood of Sleeping Car Porters and leader of the delegation, with the bad news. In her autobiography* Murray wrote that she, along with others who listened on a telephone extension, heard the First Lady say in a trembling voice that almost broke: "I have done everything I can possibly do. I have interrupted the President twice. He has said this is a matter of law and not of the heart. It is in Governor Darden's jurisdiction and the President has no legal power to intervene" (Murray, 173).

Despite ER's efforts to keep her advocacy on Waller's behalf private, word leaked to the press. Conservative southerners complained that the First Lady was treading on state matters, that her pleas for clemency were unwarranted, that she was soliciting the black vote, and that her sympathy for Waller would incite racial conflict.

The Odell Waller case was an explosive issue that challenged states' rights, Jim Crow politics, and economic discrimination. It also exposed the shameful conditions in which tenant farmers lived and demonstrated that the poll tax made most blacks and many poor whites ineligible to serve on juries or to vote. Despite the valiant efforts of the WDL, ER, and many prominent Americans, Odell Waller was executed on 2 July 1942. While black leaders condemned FDR for his inaction, the First Lady's behind-the-scenes support earned her the trust of many progressives.

SELECTED BIBLIOGRAPHY

Eleanor Roosevelt Papers, Franklin D. Roosevelt Library, Hyde Park, NY.
Murray, Pauli. *Pauli Murray: The Autobiography of a Black Activist, Feminist, Lawyer, Priest, and Poet*. 1989.
Pauli Murray Papers, The Schlesinger Library, Radcliffe College, Cambridge, MA.
Sherman, Richard B. *The Case of Odell Waller and Virginia Justice, 1940–1942*. 1992.

Patricia Bell-Scott

OFFICE OF CIVILIAN DEFENSE. On 22 September 1941, Eleanor Roosevelt became the first wife of a U.S. president to hold a formal office in the federal government when she accepted the post of assistant director of the Office of Civilian Defense (OCD). She took the unsalaried position reluctantly, hoping to use it to build civilian morale and to further her ideals of public service and social justice. Although ER was eminently qualified to serve, her dual role as First Lady and government official caused controversy and criticism that nearly wrecked the agency. When she resigned the post five months later on 20 February 1942, she concluded that a president's wife could not be judged as an individual and that by taking the post, she had allowed New Deal* opponents to attack the commander in chief indirectly by aiming their fire at her.

In May 1941, before the United States entered World War II,* President Franklin D. Roosevelt* had appointed New York City mayor Fiorello LaGuardia as OCD director. The energetic mayor, who also was running his city as well as running for reelection, concentrated primarily on recruiting volunteer air raid wardens and firefighters and acquiring firefighting equipment in anticipation of the air raids that had devastated European cities during the war. He dismissed other volunteer activities as "sissy stuff" (Lingeman, 34).

LaGuardia delegated responsibility for other civilian efforts to two assistant directors. Former Olympic athlete John B. Kelly headed a physical training program, Hale America, to improve national physical fitness in case of invasion; while ER took charge of all volunteer participation. ER envisioned marshaling wartime patriotism to better social conditions in the United States. She especially sought to integrate women and African

Eleanor Roosevelt holds a Washington press conference with women reporters in the spring of 1942 in her role as assistant director of the Office of Civilian Defense at the start of World War II. *Courtesy of Ann Cottrell Free*

Americans into a broad range of activities on the home front. Her object was not simply to raise an army of volunteers, but to ensure that the jobs for which they volunteered would be useful to their communities.

Poor management hindered OCD operations from the start. Any program that LaGuardia did not want to handle he thrust into ER's division. Since the mayor spent most of his time in New York and was rarely available for consultation, he left the agency with little coherent leadership. Despite these irritations, ER continued to admire LaGuardia's enthusiasm and courage. She herself devoted long hours to the job, in part as a distraction from her grief over the recent death of her brother, G. Hall Roosevelt,* and her disappointment over the congressional dismantling of many liberal New Deal programs. ER juggled her work for the OCD, her regular responsibilities as First Lady, and her family obligations.

Concerned for the well-being of her staff, ER organized lunchtime recreational dancing on the roof of the OCD's Washington headquarters. News of the rooftop dancing caused Republicans and conservative southern Democrats to ridicule both her and the agency. The furor swelled when her critics learned that the OCD had hired her friend, the dancer Mayris Chaney, to develop a recreational program for children in bomb shelters. Congressional antagonists mislabeled Chaney as a "fan dancer" and a "stripteaser" and complained that she received a higher salary than many military officers—charges widely reprinted in newspaper editorials (Representative Thomas Ford, quoted in Lingeman, 37). Other Roosevelt friends in the agency, notably Joseph Lash* on the advisory committee on youth and the actor Melvyn Douglas on the arts council, came under similar fire as beneficiaries of government "boondoggling" (Goodwin, 324). The House of Representatives voted to ban any use of civilian defense funds for "instructions in physical fitness by dancers" and considered transferring all civilian defense responsibilities to the War Department (Lingeman, 37).

On 8 December 1941, the day after Japan bombed Pearl Harbor, ER joined Mayor LaGuardia on a flight to the West Coast after hearing FDR ask Congress* for a declaration of war. Merely by going there, she hoped that they might quell some of the public hysteria over a possible Japanese invasion. She traveled the length of the coast, from San Diego to Seattle, in a train with its lights concealed to meet blackout conditions. In her public appearances, she took the unpopular stand of calling for tolerance toward Japanese Americans and the maintenance of civil liberties during wartime.

American entry into the war made administrative reform of the OCD essential to reverse its negative public image. Shocked by LaGuardia's lax managerial style, Bureau of the Budget officials urged the president to appoint a new director. Also keenly aware of the agency's internal problems, ER recommended Harvard Law School dean and current regional director of the OCD for New England James M. Landis (a dedicated New Dealer) as LaGuardia's replacement. In January 1942 FDR declared LaGuardia overworked at the OCD and suggested that he devote himself to speaking tours around the country to boost public morale. The president then appointed Landis as executive of the OCD to handle its managerial affairs. LaGuardia recognized this as a face-saving gesture, and within a month he resigned from the agency.

Landis immediately shifted the controversial physical fitness division out of the OCD. He fired all the former mayors whom LaGuardia had appointed to the agency, and he demanded that Mayris Chaney resign. In February he accepted ER's resignation. Well aware of the political nature of the attacks against her, she had tendered her resignation on the day Landis became director to allow the agency to resume its mission unhindered, but he had hesitated before acting on it. Personally, Landis admired ER and observed that she never attempted to outrank him. She insisted on holding all their conferences in his office, rather than making him go downstairs to her office. He also appreciated her drawing away from him most of the hostile fire from Congress and the press. Yet in spite of their ability to work together, Landis concluded that it was "a perfectly impossible situation, to have as an assistant director the wife of the President of the United States" (Ritchie, 108). As for ER, she described her short tenure with the OCD as one of the experiences she least regretted putting behind her.

SELECTED BIBLIOGRAPHY
Goodwin, Doris Kearns. *No Ordinary Time: Franklin and Eleanor Roosevelt: The Home Front in World War II*. 1994.
Lash, Joseph P. *Eleanor and Franklin*. 1971.
Lingeman, Richard R. *Don't You Know There's a War On? The American Home Front, 1941–1945*. 1970.
Polenberg, Richard. *War and Society: The United States, 1941–1945*. 1972.
Ritchie, Donald A. *James M. Landis: Dean of the Regulators*. 1980.
Roosevelt, Eleanor. *This I Remember*. 1949.

Donald A. Ritchie

OFFICE OF WAR INFORMATION. Eleanor Roosevelt played a minor, but symbolically important, role in the history of the Office of War Information (OWI). OWI was the World War II* propaganda agency of the United States. Established in 1942 out of a series of predecessor agencies and organized into two branches—domestic and overseas—OWI had a stormy existence. In the course of a series of political squabbles, it experienced the cutback of some of its component parts. By the end of the war it had scaled down its liberal aspirations and learned to conform to the psychological warfare programs the military allowed.

OWI had its origins in the efforts of liberals, such as poet Archibald MacLeish and playwright Robert Sherwood, who supported a war that would result not in mere victory but in a stronger and more democratic world order. They worked with CBS radio announcer Elmer Davis, who headed the new organization begun six months after American entrance into the war in December 1941. By mid-1943, however, the OWI found itself under attack from all sides as opponents teamed up to eliminate its domestic branch and circumscribe the overseas branch.

ER worked with OWI in ways that were typical of her mode of operation. She sent appeals and suggestions she received to OWI, and she responded to requests when Elmer Davis made them of her. A typical letter from ER to Davis was one in which she recommended a young man "who was born in Germany and who lived in Russia," pointing out that "if any of your people need a young person for research work," he would be useful (ER to Davis, 23 July 1942). In the spring of 1942 she worked with the OWI to construct a letter to the families of sons killed in war. It should be a letter, she explained, "which would give the same feeling that President [Abraham] Lincoln's letter [to a grieving mother in the Civil War] gave," one that could be "framed and hung with a picture of the son" (ER to Frank Knox, 11 March 1942).

Davis called upon her for help. He asked her to speak at rallies and to make broadcasts for the domestic branch. At his request she hosted a visit from British and American war workers on a tour promoted by OWI. She worked with the overseas branch as well, as when Davis asked her to record a broadcast to Sweden inaugurating a radio exchange series between the United States and Sweden. In December 1943 Davis asked her to write a piece for a Swedish women's publication on "What I Hope the Peace Will Bring." "I hesitate to intrude on your time in this way," Davis wrote the First Lady, "but feel that a short piece by you would be helpful in our program for promoting mutual friendship and under-standing" (Davis to ER, 10 December 1943). She contributed a short piece to the magazine.

Not all of the demands made upon her were so easy to fill, however. When in 1943 the Emergency Conference to Save the Jewish People of Europe asked ER to broadcast a message of encouragement to European Jews* she was unwilling to counter administration policy regarding war-time assistance to Jews. She first refused. "I have your telegram," she responded, "and cannot see what can be done until we win the war" (Wyman, 145). Under the auspices of OWI, however, she agreed to give the requested broadcast, but she kept it short; it was under two minutes.

ER thus worked with OWI when she felt she could be helpful—either to members of the American public or OWI itself. The occasions were infrequent, but the ways in which she operated shed light on the ways in which she served the nation during World War II.

SELECTED BIBLIOGRAPHY
Eleanor Roosevelt Papers, Franklin D. Roosevelt Library, Hyde Park, N.Y.
Office of War Information Records, RG 208, National Archives and Records Ad-
    ministration, Washington, DC.
Winkler, Allan M. *The Politics of Propaganda: The Office of War Information, 1942–
    1945.* 1978.
Wyman, David S. *The Abandonment of the Jews: America and the Holocaust 1941–
    1945.* 1984.

Allan M. Winkler

OPINION POLLS. Eleanor Roosevelt was the highest-rated woman of the twentieth century, according to surveys taken of Americans ("People, Opinion and Polls," 33). ER was the most admired woman in her lifetime and continued as the highest-rated woman—and one of the highest-rated Americans—over thirty years after her death. In 1993 the Siena Institute conducted a survey of historians and professors of American and women's history, which rated her as the most influential American woman of the twentieth century. This survey categorized women in sev-enteen categories. ER finished ahead of Jane Addams,* Rosa Parks, and Margaret Sanger to top the general list (Walters, 13).

In terms of polling, the wives of presidents since ER's day have not had the lock on the title of "Most Admired Woman" that their husbands have had on "Most Admired Man," mainly because of ER's continued dominance of the list of admired women after she left the White House in 1945—a feat unmatched by any other former First Lady. None of her successors as First Lady topped the list until after her death in 1962. Only then did Jacqueline Kennedy become the first incumbent First Lady since ER to be the country's "Most Admired Woman." In more recent years, presidents' wives have had to compete—often unsuccessfully— with Margaret Thatcher and Mother Theresa for the title of "Most Admired Woman." Mother Theresa has run second only to ER in the number of appearances at the top of Gallup's list of "Most Admired Woman."

ER has received her highest poll rankings when surveyed in comparison to other women (such as heading lists of "Most Admired Women") or in surveys taken of women's opinions on Americans in general. For example, in February 1948, readers of the *Woman's Home Companion** selected her as their "favorite American" over Generals Dwight D. Eisenhower,* George C. Marshall,* and Douglas MacArthur and President Harry S Truman,* in that order.

During her White House years, ER's ratings were often higher than those of Franklin D. Roosevelt,* in keeping with the fact that presidents' wives usually have higher approval ratings than do their husbands. (Rosalyn Carter, Nancy Reagan, and Hillary Clinton, however, have been exceptions to this pattern.) In December 1938 ER had an approval rating of 67 percent, while FDR's was 58 percent. Her support was strongest among Democrats, with an approval rating of 81 percent, compared to 43 percent among Republicans.

In a 1940 survey, the Gallup poll asked, "Do you approve of the way Mrs. Roosevelt has conducted herself as 'First Lady'?" Sixty-eight percent said yes, while 32 percent said no. Her approval rating was 73 percent among women and 62 percent among men. Her ratings differed from FDR's in that her support was fairly evenly distributed around the country, while his was significantly lower in New England (Gallup, 1:135). This survey also showed that her support was highest among middle- and lower-income groups. Fifty-six percent of upper-income respondents approved of her conduct, while 68 and 75 percent of middle- and lower-income respondents, respectively, approved of her conduct.

Polls showed that ER had strong public support on one of her more controversial actions as First Lady—her decision to resign as a member of the Daughters of the American Revolution. In March 1939 Gallup asked, "The Daughters of the American Revolution would not allow a well-known Negro singer to give a concert in one of their halls. As a protest against this, Mrs. Roosevelt resigned from the organization. Do you approve of her action?" Sixty-seven percent supported her, while 33 percent disapproved of her action—numbers almost identical to her overall approval ratings (Gallup, 1:142).

Although ER received strong approval ratings for her White House activities, there was uncertainty as to how people would react to her continued presence in public life if FDR left office. In May 1940, *Fortune* magazine conducted a survey (by the Roper organization) that gave readers a chance to voice opinions on ER's post–White House activities if FDR did not successfully seek a third term. *Fortune* asked its readers, "What do you think Mrs. Roosevelt should do if she does not return to the White House next year?" Overall, 44 percent agreed with the statement "She should continue with various activities like writing and lecturing." Fifty percent of women and 39 percent of men agreed with this statement. Since this survey was conducted in an era when the vast majority of Americans did not think women were suitable candidates for public office, only 7 percent of women and 6 percent of men said ER should be elected or appointed to an office. Thirty percent of men and 17 percent of women agreed with the statement that she should "retire completely from the public eye" (*Fortune*, 77).

Unlike the Gallup surveys, this poll found her support evenly distributed among income groups. *Fortune*'s editors noted, "There are very small variations by income levels; the rich, who generally disapprove of Mrs. Roosevelt's husband, seem just as friendly toward her as the poor. Moreover, a cross-tabulation shows that people who believe the President's usefulness is now over apparently think, as the nation does, that his wife's usefulness is not over" (*Fortune*, 77). The publication noted that the survey's results suggested "that Mrs. Roosevelt's incessant goings and comings and her "[My] Day"* have been accepted as a rather welcome part of the national life" (*Fortune*, 160). This was high praise from a magazine known for conservative views. England's *The Spectator* noted on 30 October 1942 that "more than once, it was apparent that the President's wife, far from being a parasite on her husband's popularity and prestige, was able to lend him, at low moments, some of the political capital she had accumulated."

During World War II,* ER's approval ratings lost ground as FDR's ratings increased. One aspect of her activities that received mixed reviews was her wartime travels.* In April 1944, on the eve of her trip to South America—her third major trip during the war, when gasoline rationing kept most Americans from traveling—the Gallup organization took a survey that showed only 36 percent of Americans approved of ER's trips, while 45 percent disapproved, and 19 percent had no opinion. More men than women were critical of the trips, with only 33 percent of men approving and 50 percent disapproving. Among women the ratings were 40 percent approving and 39 percent disapproving (Gallup, 1:445).

In December 1945, eight months after FDR's death, the Gallup organization asked, "It is often said that many people who have not held public office would make good Presidents. Can you think of anyone in this state or nation who you think might make a good president?" (Gallup, 1:550). Generals Douglas MacArthur and Dwight D. Eisenhower finished first and second, with industrialist Henry Kaiser in third place. ER tied for fourth with automotive industrialist Henry Ford and financier Bernard Baruch.*

Throughout the 1950s, ER continued to dominate the "Most Admired Woman" lists, but polls showed she held her own even when competing against men. In May 1958 the Gallup organization asked, "If you could invite any three famous persons in history—from the present or the past—to your home for dinner, which three would you like to have?" (Gallup, 2:1560). ER came in sixth, following, in order, Abraham Lincoln, FDR, Eisenhower, George Washington, and Harry Truman. She was the highest ranked nonpresident, finishing ahead of Douglas MacArthur, Mamie Eisenhower, and Winston Churchill.*

That her children usually stood in her shadow was demonstrated when the Gallup organization asked those who identified themselves as Democrats, "Is there any other person not on the list whom you would like to see as the Democratic candidate in 1956?" ER consistently finished ahead of her sons except in mid-1955, when she was overtaken by Franklin D. Roosevelt Jr.* (Gallup, 2:1373).

ER's domination of the "Most Admired" lists continued for decades after her death. For example, in 1982 the Siena Institute asked historians to rank the performance of the wives of the presidents. ER came in first, ahead of Abigail Adams, who was in second place, by nearly ten points (Nelson, 1051). In September 1988 the *Ladies' Home Journal** commissioned Roper to do a nationwide survey of women's opinions on First Ladies.* When respondents were asked, "Which First Lady do you admire most?," ER came in first with 28 percent of the vote, and Nancy Reagan, the incumbent First Lady, came in second with 26 percent. ER was most popular with Democrats and women over the age of forty-five. Yet, even though ER, with her activist approach to her duties as First Lady, topped the poll, responses to questions showed most women still favored a traditional role for the First Lady. For example, respondents were asked, "Do you think that a First Lady should ever publicly disagree with the president on controversial issues?" Sixty-nine percent said the First Lady should not publicly disagree with the president. Only 25 percent said she had a right to speak out ("The First Lady," 90).

SELECTED BIBLIOGRAPHY

"The First Lady." *Ladies Home Journal* (September 1988): 90.
"Fortune Survey." *Fortune* (May 1940): 76–77, 160, 168–171.

Gallup, George. *The Gallup Poll: Public Opinion, 1935–1971*. Vols. 1, 2, 3. 1972.

Nelson, Michael, ed. *Guide to the Presidency*. Vol. 2. 1996.

"People, Opinion and Polls: 'Most Admired' Man and Woman." *The Public Perspective* (February/March 1995): 33.

Walters, Laurel Shaper. "Survey Names Notable Women." *Christian Science Monitor*, 22 March 1993, 13.

Tracey A. Johnstone

P

PEACE MOVEMENT. Once dominated by a predominantly male elite, the U.S. peace movement grew increasingly diverse in membership and goals over the course of the 1920s. While some peace advocates limited their involvement to antiwar activities aimed at ending specific conflicts, others followed notions of absolute pacifism, and still others connected peace advocacy to interests such as socialism, feminism, or racial justice. After World War I, the most powerful wing of the movement became the liberal internationalists, who believed in the need for a strong international organization and sought a greater commitment to social justice throughout the world. Eleanor Roosevelt fell squarely in this last group.

ER noted in her autobiography that although she was sympathetic to antiwar advocates such as secretary of state William Jennings Bryan, she publicly supported U.S. preparations for, and later American involvement in, World War I, whatever her private misgivings. Influenced by her uncle, Theodore Roosevelt,* she believed that the United States had to take a side in the conflict. Her husband, Franklin D. Roosevelt,* as assistant secretary of the navy, assumed the strongest pro-preparedness stance among President Woodrow Wilson's advisers, and ER loyally followed his lead. During the war, she helped organize the American Red Cross* operations in Washington, knitted and distributed wool on behalf of the Navy League, and visited wounded sailors.

After the war, two experiences moved ER in the direction of peace activism. First, a visit to war-torn Europe in 1919 brought the plight of women and children directly to her attention in ways that she could not ignore or forget. She became a firm supporter of both the League of Nations* and U.S. adherence to the World Court,* hoping that these institutions could help to secure peace in the aftermath of destruction wrought by World War I. Second, in 1923 she joined Esther Lape* and

Narcissa Vanderlip,* colleagues from the League of Women Voters,* on the committee that administered the Bok Peace Prize.* Over the course of the 1920s, ER became increasingly linked to several women's peace organizations, including the National Conference on the Cause and Cure for War (NCCCW), organized by Carrie Chapman Catt,* and the Women's International League for Peace and Freedom (WILPF) associated with Jane Addams.* She wrote extensively on peace-related issues and foreign affairs, though her expressed views were always tempered by her close connection to the Democratic Party.*

When she assumed duties as First Lady in 1933, she remained concerned with social justice throughout the globe and the role of peace in bringing this about. During her twelve years in this highly visible position, she championed internationalist and anti-imperialist positions. In addition to the WILPF and the NCCCW, she supported the work of the Fellowship of Reconciliation, the American Friends Service Committee, and other leading peace organizations of the era. She lent her name to honorary boards of these groups and spoke regularly at peace conferences. In print and in radio* addresses, she often focused on the role of women within the movement. As she said in a radio address in 1937, women could end war if properly organized because "a woman's will is the strongest thing in the world" (Cook, "Turn toward Peace," 113).

If ER became one of the nation's most prominent liberal internationalists, she was, however, hardly an absolute pacifist. She opposed isolationist sentiment that sought to avoid foreign influences and entangling alliances and maintain neutrality in European conflicts. She spoke out against the America First Committee, founded in 1940 to advance isolationist positions. An early and staunch opponent of Nazi Germany, by the late 1930s she believed the United States could not avoid war with Hitler. She advocated lifting the arms embargo against republican forces during the civil war in Spain.* Before the United States entered World War II,* she supported Lend-Lease, a program under which the United States transferred military equipment and supplies to countries fighting the Axis powers, as well as conscription.

While favoring military preparedness, she also became active in efforts to assist refugees,* many of whom were Jewish, from Nazi Germany. Her behind-the-scenes campaign in 1939 for the Wagner–Rogers bill,* which would have allowed 20,000 German refugee children entry into the United States, was beaten back by isolationist and anti-Semitic forces. Later, personal encounters with survivors revealed the enormity of the Holocaust* to ER, spurring her devotion to human rights* after the war.

President Harry S Truman* appointed ER as a member of the U.S. delegation that attended the first meeting of the United Nations* (UN) General Assembly in London in January 1946. Assigned to the social, humanitarian, and cultural committee, she helped transform it into an important UN committee. Her success earned her the position of chair of the Human Rights Commission, which she held from 1946 to 1952. Under her leadership, the commission produced the Universal Declaration of Human Rights,* approved by the UN General Assembly in December 1948. Understanding that the declaration could not be "a U.S. document" if fifty-eight nations were to approve it, ER refused to simply take only the point of view of the U.S. State Department on what it should contain. When it won passage, she received a spontaneous standing ovation from the assembly. U.S. peace organizations, many of which were concerned about the orientation of the United Nations to major national powers, hailed the declaration as potentially a great force for peace.

After President Dwight D. Eisenhower* replaced ER as a UN delegate in 1953, she traveled extensively, speaking for the American Association for the United Nations.* Though not tied closely to any particular peace or antinuclear organization, she was widely recognized as "a living symbol of world understanding and peace," as President John F. Kennedy* noted in 1962 (Lash, *Eleanor: The Years Alone*, 335). Nominated for the Nobel Peace Prize several times, she never received the honor of winning it, although the first UN Human Rights prize went to her posthumously in 1968.

SELECTED BIBLIOGRAPHY
Cook, Blanche Wiesen. *Eleanor Roosevelt*. Vols. 1, 2. 1992, 1999.
———. "Turn toward Peace." In Joan Hoff-Wilson and Marjorie Lightman, eds., *Without Precedent: The Life and Career of Eleanor Roosevelt*. 1984.
Lash, Joseph P. *Eleanor and Franklin*. 1971.
———. *Eleanor: The Years Alone*. 1972.
Roosevelt, Eleanor. *The Autobiography of Eleanor Roosevelt*. 1961.

John M. Craig

PEGLER, FRANCIS WESTBROOK (2 August 1894, Minneapolis–24 June 1969, Tucson, AZ).

From the late 1930s until the mid-1960s, Westbrook Pegler periodically criticized, derided, and ridiculed Eleanor Roosevelt in his nationally syndicated newspaper column. ER's social activism and her work with the United Nations* created polemical opportunities for Pegler, who continued to disparage ER after her death. Pegler's persistent diatribes began when his "Fair Enough" column appeared in perhaps 150 newspapers with a total daily circulation of 4–5 million copies. Eventually, the vitriol that Pegler directed at ER, the Roosevelt family, and others caused most newspaper editors to drop the column. By the mid-1960s, Pegler lost his last national outlet when *American Opinion*, the John Birch Society magazine, decided that Pegler too often wrote about "his personal peeves," of which ER was one, and ceased publishing his essays (Farr, 219).

Throughout the thirty-year campaign conducted by Pegler, readers of his column saw ER referred to as "La Boca Grande," "the Gab," and "the Widow" (Pilat, 11). When she and other advocates of civil liberties opposed efforts during the late 1940s to deport or imprison members of the Communist Party of the United States, Pegler described her as "the madam of the [communist] whorehouse" and "the chief prostitute of those who pretend to extol the First Amendment" (Black, 154). ER generally ignored Pegler, once telling an interviewer she considered him "a little gnat" (Pilat, 11). Occasionally, she referred sarcastically to "the virtuous" Pegler in her own syndicated column, "My Day"* (Pilat, 184). Before Pegler started his campaign of vilification, the syndicated columns written by him and ER often appeared together on the same page of the *New York World-Telegram*, whose editor encouraged diversity of opinion.

Pegler and ER were on friendly terms until 1938. That spring Pegler called her "the greatest American woman" and declared, "She knows the country better than any other individual including her husband" (Farr, 148). But soon he published a widely quoted parody of her column, making fun of her chats with acquaintances on social issues. By 1946 Pegler had grown totally hostile, insisting ER was not qualified to be a U.S. delegate to the first United Nations General Assembly. His vituperative opposition separated him from other journalists, who believed ER exceptionally qualified. Biographers of Pegler suggest he became Roosevelt's nemesis because he preferred to take the contrary side; thus, because she generally was popular among reporters and columnists, Pegler chose to attack her.

Taking the contrary side had brought Pegler wealth and fame. The son of a newspaper rewrite man who later became an editor for Hearst newspapers, Pegler started working as an office boy for United Press (UP), a wire service, before high school graduation in Chicago in 1912. He covered World War I in Europe but ran afoul of military censorship and was forced to leave the front. During the 1920s UP assigned him to cover sports, and he developed a reputation for colorful writing and was promoted to columnist. He moved to the *Chicago Tribune* News Syndicate in 1925 and in 1933 to United Features, owned by Scripps-Howard newspapers, the same syndicate for which ER began writing her column in 1935. His depression-era income was thought to be $50,000 to $60,000 a year (the equivalent of $562,000 to $674,000 in today's money).

Pegler considered himself a populist, a champion of mainstream American political and social standards. Although he was an early member of the Newspaper Guild,* a trade union for journalists, his "Fair Enough" columns regularly bashed union-organizing efforts and strikes. He won the Pulitzer Prize for reporting in 1941 for columns exposing labor racketeers in Hollywood.

Pegler's involvement with the guild may have made him vehemently anticommunist and also contributed to his animosity toward ER. Because of her column, ER was eligible to join the guild, which she did in 1936. Pegler resigned a year later in a dispute over organizing tactics and a belief, shared by some other journalists, that communists had influenced guild policy. By contrast, ER's reaction was that noncommunists should not quit but should be more active in union business and vote the communists out.

By 1944 Pegler had grown increasingly reactionary. When United Features did not renew his contract, he moved to King Features, a Hearst subsidiary. Since all Hearst newspapers published the column, this guaranteed Pegler exposure in most major American cities. King Features canceled the contract in 1962 after Pegler publicly denounced Hearst executives.

Pegler's increasingly extremist viewpoints prompted media critics to question his good sense. A. J. Liebling commented on the persistent attacks on ER by Pegler and another Hearst columnist in the *New York Journal-American*: "The two would toss Mrs. Roosevelt from page 2 to page 3 and back again, like the girl in an adagio act" (Liebling, 119). Pegler's obsession during the 1950s with the Roosevelts caused many people to wonder about his motives. A question-and-answer sketch in *Esquire* in 1962 conveyed this response: "I did not hate Roosevelt and do not hate his widow, but I despise their pretense of humane motives. Contempt rather precludes the fine spiritual emotion of hatred" (Pegler, 58). In his last years he grew paranoid and was published infrequently.

SELECTED BIBLIOGRAPHY
Beasley, Maurine H. *Eleanor Roosevelt and the Media*. 1987.
Black, Allida M. *Casting Her Own Shadow: Eleanor Roosevelt and the Shaping of Postwar Liberalism*. 1996.
Farr, Finis. *Fair Enough: The Life of Westbrook Pegler*. 1975.
Liebling, A. J. "The Wayward Press: Peg and Sol." *New Yorker* (18 November 1950): 119–120.
Pegler, Westbrook. "Self-Portrait: Westbrook Pegler." *Esquire* (January 1962): 68.
Pilat, Oliver. *Pegler: Angry Man of the Press*. 1963.

James C. Landers

PERKINS, FRANCES (10 April 1880, Boston–14 May 1965, New York).

Frances Perkins, secretary of labor in the Roosevelt administration and the first woman in history to serve in the cabinet, maintained a long-term friendship with Eleanor Roosevelt. Both women admired the political ideas of Franklin D. Roosevelt* and each other's personal and professional attributes, but the closeness and scope of their relationship varied over the years.

Perkins, a social reformer, graduated in 1902 from Mount Holyoke College. While teaching school in Illinois, she volunteered for social service and worked with Jane Addams* at Hull House. She earned a masters' degree in social economics in 1910 from Columbia University after doing graduate work at the University of Pennsylvania and was secretary of the New York Consumers' League from 1910 to 1912. Perkins was married in 1913 to Paul Wilson, a financial statistician, and gave birth to two children, one of whom died in infancy, but she kept her maiden name. Wilson, who suffered from depression, lost most of his money in 1918, prompting Perkins to give up volunteer work and seek paid employment. From the 1920s until his death in 1952, Wilson frequently was confined to institutions, where Perkins oversaw his care.

The Roosevelts first met Perkins in 1911 during a campaign for factory safety in New York state that followed the Triangle Shirtwaist Company fire in which 146 workers, mainly women, died because exit doors had been blocked. A witness to the tragedy, Perkins, a suffragist, campaigned for measures to safeguard the health and safety of workers, including passage of a state law to regulate wages and hours. ER initially impressed Perkins as a quiet homemaker, but as ER blossomed into a political force, the two women repeatedly crossed paths, and their friendship grew.

When FDR became governor of New York in 1928, he appointed Perkins state industrial commissioner. Previously, she had been named by Governor Alfred E. Smith* as the first woman member of the state industrial board. During FDR's tenure as governor, ER and Perkins often rode the train together from New York City to Albany, the state capital, and sometimes shared a bedroom at the Executive Mansion when the guest rooms overflowed. One night, Perkins heard ER confide her life story, focusing on her problems with her marriage* and her mother-in-law, Sara Delano Roosevelt.* Perkins sympathized, but she never reciprocated by confiding in ER. When ER published her memoirs, Perkins was appalled that she would share such intimacies with the public.

Contrary to popular belief, ER did not suggest Perkins, who was referred to as "Madame Perkins," for the post of secretary of labor, but she was pleased with her husband's choice. As a cabinet member, Perkins contributed substantially to the shaping of legislation dealing with unemployment insurance and workmen's compensation, and she was the chief architect of Social Security. She credited ER's keen observations with convincing FDR of the need for social change, even though she disagreed with some causes that ER championed. In 1934 ER encouraged Perkins to appoint an African American woman to the Women's Bureau, but Perkins refused, citing the prevailing climate of prejudice. Despite their disagreements, Perkins admired ER's political savvy and straightforward manner.

In return, ER defended Perkins, who was unpopular with the press, to her critics. A controversial figure in Washington, Perkins, customarily seen in a black dress and tricorn hat, became a symbol of discontent with New Deal* labor policies. Although accused of condoning union violence, she showed little patience with arrogant unionists and was frequently criticized by industrialists and labor leaders alike. In 1938 Representative J. Parnell Thomas, a Republican, called for Perkins' impeachment because she had postponed deportation hearings for Harry Bridges, a radical leader of the Pacific Coast's longshoremen. Inspired by Representative Martin Dies, chair of the House Committee to Investigate Un-American Activities,* the General Federation of Women's Clubs labeled Perkins, an Episcopalian of New England Puritan background, a communist and alleged falsely that she was of Russian Jewish ancestry. ER dismissed the charges against Perkins as politically motivated and reassured her of FDR's support. After Perkins appeared voluntarily before the House Judiciary Committee, the impeachment move died.

Following FDR's death, ER and Perkins maintained an ambivalant relationship. ER criticized President Harry S Truman* for eliminating Perkins from the cabinet. To appease the New Deal wing of the Democratic Party,* Truman appointed Perkins to the Civil Service Commission, where she served until 1953. ER complimented Perkins on her book about FDR, *The Roosevelt I Knew* (1946), but she also claimed the book contained errors. After ER left the White House, Perkins publicly called ER a great person, but she confided to her colleagues at the Cornell School of Industrial Relations, where she taught from 1958 until 1965, that ER did not have an intellectually organized mind. Roosevelt and Perkins parted ways as Perkins retreated to a quiet life at Cornell, while ER grew in stature as a world figure.

SELECTED BIBLIOGRAPHY

Columbia Oral History Collection, Frances Perkins interview, Columbia University, New York.
Frances Perkins Papers, Columbia University, New York.
Lash, Joseph P. *Eleanor and Franklin*. 1971.
Perkins, Frances. *The Roosevelt I Knew*. 1946.
Roosevelt, Eleanor. *This I Remember*. 1949.
Steinberg, Alfred. *Mrs. R.* 1958.

Julieanne Phillips

PETERSON, ESTHER (9 December 1906, Provo, UT–20 December 1997, Washington, DC).

For the better part of her long career as an advocate for women, labor,* and consumer interests, Esther Peterson cherished Eleanor Roosevelt as a political mentor and role model for women in the twentieth century. Greatly influenced by the labor movement, each developed an earnest concern for the plight of poor and working women.

Peterson received a bachelor's degree from Brigham Young University and attended Teachers' College, Columbia University, where she met and married Oliver Peterson and become active in the labor movement. As a union organizer and lobbyist in the 1930s and 1940s, Peterson became a supporter of the politics of Franklin D. Roosevelt* and an admirer of ER's character and egalitarianism. For many years, both ER and Esther Peterson favored labor laws that protected women from harsh working conditions but also limited their opportunities for advancement.

Spurred by the political discontent of women in the 1960s, President John F. Kennedy* appointed Peterson assistant secretary of labor and director of the Women's Bureau. In that role, she guided the creation of the President's Commission on the Status of Women.*

At Peterson's suggestion, the president appointed ER chair of the twenty-six-member commission that would become the first forum for the burgeoning women's movement. ER presided over its first meeting in February 1962, when it began its work by endorsing equal pay legislation. By then she had moderated her forty-year opposition to the Equal Rights Amendment.* Already ill in June, she hosted the members of the commission and their families for a weekend at her home in Hyde Park,* New York. After her death in November, the chair remained empty in ER's honor.

From the Women's Bureau, Peterson continued to nurture the work of the commission. The commission's 1963 report, *American Women*, documented the extent to which women were denied equal rights and opportunities.

Peterson continued to work for labor, consumer, and women's interests for another thirty years, serving as special assistant for consumer affairs under Presidents Lyndon Johnson and Jimmy Carter.

SELECTED BIBLIOGRAPHY

Davis, Flora. *Moving the Mountain: The Women's Movement in America since 1960.* 1991.

Harrison, Cynthia. *On Account of Sex: The Politics of Women's Issues, 1945–1968.* 1988.

Lash, Joseph P. *Eleanor and Franklin.* 1971.

Paterson, Judith. *Be Somebody: A Biography of Marguerite Rawalt.* 1986.

Peterson, Esther, with Winifred Conkling. *Restless: The Memoirs of Labor and Consumer Activist Esther Peterson.* 1995.

                                                                Judith Paterson

PICKETT, CLARENCE (14 October 1884, Cissna Park, IL–17 March 1965, Boise, ID).

Clarence Pickett served as executive secretary of the American Friends Service Committee (AFSC) from 1929 until 1950, providing the leadership that made the organization a corecipient of the Nobel Peace Prize in 1947. After retirement he was cochairman with Norman Cousins of the National Committee for a SANE Nuclear Policy, sat on the national advisory council for the Peace Corps, and was a director of the U.S. Committee for Refugees.* He met Eleanor Roosevelt in 1933 and thereafter worked closely with her on a number of humanitarian issues of critical importance to them both.

Pickett, who had a background in theological studies, believed in a practical, action-oriented approach to social betterment that appealed to ER. A graduate of the Hartford Theological Seminary who also had studied at the Harvard Divinity School, Pickett left a professorship at Earlham College, a Quaker school, to take the AFSC position. In 1931 at the request of the Committee on Unemployment Relief, set up by President Herbert Hoover,* and the U.S. Children's Bureau, the AFSC under Pickett began relief and rehabilitation work in the coalfields of West Virginia, Maryland, Kentucky, Tennessee, Illinois, and Pennsylvania—feeding children and relocating miners on subsistence farms. He first met ER when she visited the coalfields in Morgantown, West Virginia, within weeks after the inauguration of President Franklin D. Roosevelt.* She quickly became committed not only to helping the miners temporarily but to backing a government-sponsored subsistence homestead project for long-term alleviation of their distress.

Appointed assistant administrator of the newly created federal Division of Subsistence Homesteads, Pickett worked closely with ER on construction of Arthurdale,* a homestead project that became one of her most cherished endeavors. She came increasingly to rely on Pickett, whom she found an adviser without vanity or personal ambition. In 1934 she arranged for the AFSC to investigate the appeals of the numerous people asking her for money. Thereafter, she used the AFSC as one route through which she donated to charitable causes part of the money she received from her radio broadcasts.*

In 1936, when the AFSC initiated an Emergency Peace Campaign to promote pacifism as the worldwide pressure for war heightened, Pickett persuaded ER to launch the campaign with a nationwide radio broadcast. A year later Pickett, working with Anna Louise Strong,* established a Joint Committee for Spanish Children to help relieve what he described as the "shocking homelessness and misery of throngs of children who themselves were neither Nationalist nor Loyalist" in the Spanish civil war (New York Times, 18 March 1965). ER helped by prodding the U.S. State Department to persuade Francisco Franco, the fascist leader of the Nationalist forces rebelling against the republican Loyalist government, to permit children to be taken to safety.

By 1938 Pickett had turned his attention to the plight of European Jews* and worked with an interim committee formed to mobilize public opinion of their behalf. Members included ER, as well as Benjamin Cohen, who had helped draft the Securities Exchange Act of 1934 and other

New Deal* legislation, Justine Wise Polier,* and Marshall Field, a newspaper publisher. In June 1940 ER agreed to Pickett's request to convene a meeting to set up the U.S. Committee for the Care of European Children, an effort to aid youthful refugees.

In the postwar years ER joined Pickett in working for the National Committee for a SANE Nuclear Policy. They also worked together on the U.S. Committee for Refugees. Pickett received numerous humanitarian awards, including the Bok* Award in 1939 and the World Brotherhood Award of the Jewish Theological Seminary in 1951.

SELECTED BIBLIOGRAPHY
Berger, Jason. *A New Deal for the World: Eleanor Roosevelt and American Foreign Policy.* 1981.
Lash, Joseph P. *Eleanor and Franklin.* 1971.
Pickett, Clarence. *For More than Bread.* 1953.
Roosevelt, Eleanor. *This I Remember.* 1949.
Sutters, Jack, ed. "American Friends Service Committee." In Henry Friedlander and Sybil Milton, eds., *Archives of the Holocaust.* 1990.

PICTURES. One of the great ironies of Eleanor Roosevelt's life was that an individual so self-conscious about her own appearance would become one of the most photographed women of the twentieth century. Dissatisfaction with her appearance was noted by her and others. In her autobiography* ER described herself as being a child with "plain looks and lack of manners" (Roosevelt, 6). Shy and serious, she was teasingly referred to as "Granny" by her own mother, Anna Hall Roosevelt* (Roosevelt, 9). When she grew into adolescence, she felt too tall and was unfashionably dressed by her grandmother, Mary Hall. An early biographer noted that in her mature years she referred to her youthful self as "an ugly little thing, keenly conscious of her deficiencies" (Kearney, 239).

Not surprisingly, the camera recorded something of ER's insecurities, particularly when she was under stress. For example, after she discovered love letters from Lucy Mercer* (Rutherfurd) to her husband, Franklin D. Roosevelt,* in September 1918, ER was unable to look directly at a camera for months. During the period of emotional turmoil caused by FDR's betrayal, she was often photographed with eyes averted.

When FDR was elected governor of New York, ER found herself frequently in the camera's eye, to her great discomfort. Her bodyguard and friend, Earl Miller,* sought to lessen the burden that photographers unintentionally imposed upon her and went so far as to stand in the background and make comical faces intended to put her at ease. Rarely did she photograph to the satisfaction of those who had an opportunity to meet her in person. As one *New Yorker* correspondent remarked, the camera seemed to deal "unjustly" with her because it could not capture her charm, her intelligence, or her forceful personality (Lash, 341).

Even when ER lived in the White House and became an expert at dealing with print journalists, she was a reluctant subject for the photographer's lens. According to Grace Tully, one of FDR's secretaries, "It was a misfortune that the first lady was such a poor subject before the camera and the results were consistently evident. . . . [her] vivacity and sparkle never seemed to register on film" (Tully, 118). When FDR would "twit" her about some "fantastic camera recording," she would laugh it off, Tully continued, by saying, "Oh, dear, it's just the usual. Isn't it terrible?" (Tully, 119). FDR's preferred photographs of ER were her formal portraits in evening dresses.

After years in the public eye, ER became more relaxed in photographs, although she never fully overcame her discomfort with photographers. Thousands of photographs of her, however, captured aspects of her personality to a considerable degree, creating a public face that was helpful to the New Deal* and to other causes in which ER believed. Photographs gave her an image that emphasized substance over the superficialities of social position, which long had been associated with First Ladies.

Instead, photographs of ER depicted her as a woman of remarkable social commitment and curiosity, traveling the country, stopping to talk to ordinary people, and generally serving as the auxiliary eyes and ears of the president. Later, photographs of ER at the United Nations* and campaigning for the Democratic Party* spotlighted her activism in the public realm and made her one of the relatively few positive role models for older women in the middle period of the twentieth century.

SELECTED BIBLIOGRAPHY

Cook, Blanche Wiesen. *Eleanor Roosevelt*. Vol. 1. 1992.
Kearney, James R. *Anna Eleanor Roosevelt*. 1968.
Lash, Joseph P. *Eleanor and Franklin*. 1971.
Roosevelt, Eleanor. *Autobiography*. 1961.
Tully, Grace. *F.D.R. My Boss*. 1949.

Randolph Lewis

POLIER, JUSTINE WISE (12 April 1903, Portland, OR–31 July 1987, New York).

Daughter of Rabbi Stephen and Louise Wise, Justine Wise Polier was a lawyer, New York City children's court judge, and advocate for children's rights and refugees* from political and religious persecution. Polier, who first met Eleanor Roosevelt as a volunteer for the Women's Trade Union League* in the 1920s, worked with her on refugee issues in the 1930s while attempting to aid victims of Nazi persecution. Subsequently, in 1941–1942, she served as counsel to ER in the Office of Civilian Defense* (OCD). Polier also engaged ER in the support of the

Wiltwyck School,* the first racially integrated residential school for disturbed boys from New York City. It initially was located at Esopus, New York, across the Hudson River from the Roosevelt home at Hyde Park,* New York.

Polier and ER became political allies when a group was formed in December 1938 to mobilize public opinion to expand the immigration quotas for German—mostly Jewish—children fleeing Nazi persecution. ER served as its liaison to the White House and, through undersecretary of state Sumner Welles,* the Department of State. In this capacity she advised on ways to frame legislation and lobby Congress.* In February 1939 the group's effort culminated in the Wagner–Rogers bill.*

In the fall of 1941 ER asked Polier to work with her at the Office of Civilian Defense. Polier temporarily moved from New York to Washington, D.C., and, as Polier remembered years later, "that was really when Mrs. R. and I became close friends" (Polier, 23). In 1942 Polier appealed to ER for financial support for the Wiltwyck School. The First Lady became an enthusiastic benefactor and remained so until her death. In 1956 Polier suggested that ER act on behalf of Jewish refugees who were trying to leave Morocco for Israel. ER wrote to the king of Morocco on 31 July 1956 on the Jews'* behalf. As Polier later wrote Joseph Lash,* "within a few days the Jews in Casablanca were released" (JP to JL, 29 February 1972).

The enduring Polier–ER friendship was an example of the way in which ER often mixed work and companionship into binding relationships. It was with Polier and her husband, Shad Polier, a lawyer, that ER spent the evening after the funeral of Franklin D. Roosevelt.* Polier's last visit to ER was shortly before she died. In describing the way in which ER endeavored to help many children, Polier recalled how ER received individual requests, evaluated them, and then acted. "They were like small mosaics that helped build a larger picture of the needs of children" (Polier, 12).

SELECTED BIBLIOGRAPHY

Eleanor Roosevelt Oral History Project, Interview with Justine Wise Polier (1977), Franklin D. Roosevelt Library, Hyde Park, NY.
Justine Wise Polier papers, American Jewish Historical Society, Waltham, MA.

PRESIDENT'S COMMISSION ON THE STATUS OF WOMEN. In December 1961 Eleanor Roosevelt accepted the request of President John F. Kennedy* to chair the President's Commission on the Status of Women (PCSW), undertaking her last official duty prior to her death on 7 November 1962. The proposal for the commission had come from Esther Peterson,* a former labor* lobbyist, whom Kennedy had appointed director of the Women's Bureau in the Department of Labor and assistant secretary of labor. Concerned about criticism that his administration was

Eleanor Roosevelt presides at a press conference in January 1962 to announce plans for President Kennedy's Commission on the Status of
Women, a group that she headed as one of her last major activities
before her death on 7 November 1962. *Courtesy of Franklin D. Roosevelt
Library*

not doing enough for women, Kennedy by executive order 10980 on 14
December 1961 established the PCSW "to review progress and make
recommendations for constructive action" concerning women in areas
related to employment, legislation, political, civil and property rights,
family relations, and "new and expanded services that may be required
for women as wives, mothers, and workers" (*American Women*, 76).
Through her work on the commission, ER made a final effort to advance
the interests of women on the national political front. Her presence gave
the commission immediate credibility, recognition, and visibility.

Peterson, who was named executive vice-chair of the commission, saw
it as a way not only to improve the status of women but also to counterbalance pressure for an Equal Rights Amendment* (ERA) to the Constitution, an issue that had divided women's advocates. Supporters of

the ERA argued that the amendment was needed to end inequities between men and women, while organized labor* and some women's organizations claimed the ERA would eliminate protective legislation for
women. By the time the commission was established, ER had moderated
her long-held opposition to the ERA, but she became ill before the commission took up the issue and did not take part in its substantive discussions of the ERA.

The commission was composed of the secretaries of the departments
of commerce, agriculture, labor, and health, education and welfare, the
attorney general, the chairman of the Civil Service Commission, and
twenty members appointed by the president, including representatives
of industry, labor, Congress,* the media, religious groups, women's associations, and academe. It included fifteen women and eleven men.

Recognizing the importance of publicity, ER explained the importance
of the commission to the press shortly after President Kennedy announced its creation. She also helped recruit members for the seven
working committees that explored the areas within the commission's
charge, the most sensitive of which were civil and political rights. Personal invitations in ER's name—telegrams signed "Eleanor Roosevelt"—
encouraged busy individuals to serve on the committees, which included
technical experts and leaders of women's groups, business, and labor.

ER chaired the commission's first meeting, a two-day event in Washington, which was opened by the president at the White House on 12
February 1962. Immediately thereafter she flew to Europe for a month-
long trip, but from Paris on 16 February she gave readers of "My Day"*
her views on the commission's work: "The effort, of course, is to find
how we can best use the potentialities of women without impairing their
first responsibilities, which are to their homes, their husbands and their
children" (Emblidge, 299). In April she testified at a congressional hearing on behalf of equal pay legislation for women, which was endorsed
by the PCSW. On 16–17 June she hosted the commission's members at
a meeting at the Roosevelt home in Hyde Park,* New York, showing
them the family mansion and grounds. She also invited the commission
to a supper at her Val-Kill* residence, where she personally served stew
to the group.

In August 1962 ER submitted a progress report from the commission
to the president. The commission noted its gratification at Kennedy's
directive that appointments or promotions in the federal civil service
were to be made without regard to sex. It reported it was seeking the
cooperation of a wide variety of individuals and groups to promote the
idea of equal pay for equal work by women as well as further extension
of minimum wage legislation to both men and women. The commission
asserted that improved education was needed for women of all ages to
realize their fullest potential. It also noted that "many women must work
outside the home . . . [and] genuine equality of economic opportunity re-

quires that they be judged and rewarded on the basis of what they show themselves able to do" (Progress Report, 20560).

By fall of 1962, ER's failing health limited any further work as the chair of the commission. After her death in November, the administration did not appoint another chair, stating there could be "no adequate replacement" (Harrison, 112). Thus, the commission proceeded with its work under Peterson's leadership.

On 11 October 1963, ER's birthday, the commission submitted its final report to the president with a tribute to ER, noting that "her devotion to fuller realization of the abilities of women in all walks of life and in all countries raised the status of women everywhere in the world" (*American Women*, 1). The report outlined the limitations imposed on women by custom, law, employment discrimination, and inadequate support services. Recommendations to address these inequities reflected both the commission's assumption that women had the primary responsibility for care of the home and children and its recognition that women were joining the labor force in increasing numbers, with one out of three married women in paid employment.

The commission recommended that women receive training in child care and homemaking, as well as counseling about broader opportunities. It called for expanded day-care services. It advocated the principle of equal opportunity for women in hiring, training, and promotion at work, with equal pay for comparable work. It generally looked for such results to be achieved through moral suasion rather than legislative action.

It did state its belief, however, that the "principle of equality (of men and women) is embodied in the 5th and 14th Amendments to the Constitution of the United States" and that "there exist some laws and official practices which treat men and women differently and which do not appear to be reasonable in the light of the multiple activities of women in present day society" (*American Women*, 44). Rather than pursue the ERA, it called for interested groups to seek court review of discrimination and urged all branches of government to eliminate archaic discriminatory standards. Finally, to implement its recommendations, the commission called for the appointment of a federal interdepartmental committee and a citizens advisory committee. These groups were established by executive order on 1 November 1963.

The report received extensive press coverage; the year after it was released, the government distributed some 80,000 copies. By 1967 every state had formed commissions patterned on the PCSW. While its recommendations were cautious, the PCSW heightened awareness of sex discrimination issues and proved to be "the opening salvo of a reborn women's movement" (Scharf, 173). According to Katherine P. Ellickson, who served as the commission's executive secretary, ER "had assured its success," by enlisting the cooperation of more than a 1,000 influential persons (Ellickson, 96).

SELECTED BIBLIOGRAPHY

American Women: Report of the President's Commission on the Status of Women. 1963.

Ellickson, Katherine P. "Eleanor Roosevelt and the Commission on the Status of Women." In Jess Flemion and Colleen M. O'Connor, eds., *Eleanor Roosevelt: An American Journey.* 1987.

Emblidge, David, ed. *Eleanor Roosevelt's "My Day."* Vol. 3. 1991.

Harrison, Cynthia. *On Account of Sex: The Politics of Women's Issues, 1945–1968.* 1988.

"Progress Report to the President on the President's Commission on the Status of Women." *Congressional Record* 108 (24 September 1962): 20559–20560.

Scharf, Lois. *Eleanor Roosevelt: First Lady of American Liberalism.* 1987.

Kelly A. Woestman

PRESS CONFERENCES. As First Lady, Eleanor Roosevelt held 348 press conferences in the White House, from 6 March 1933 to 12 April 1945, making a small amount of front-page news, but—more significantly—making history for presidents' wives and women journalists. Save for one wartime exception, ER held fast to her rule that only women journalists could attend the weekly events.

The conferences reflected patterns of gender separation that found many women journalists covering a relatively narrow array of topics considered suitable for women readers. Because men were not admitted to the gatherings, a few news organizations employed women to cover them. Consequently, the conferences widened opportunities for women reporters, although women were active in journalism long before ER's arrival in Washington. ER allowed men to cover her press conferences when she was away from the capital and also when she met the press at the Office of Civilian Defense* (OCD) as its assistant director in 1941–1942. She refused to have men at the White House conferences except once, when she returned from the Pacific war zone.

By functioning as a focal point on occasion for ER's concern with youth,* the aged, and the poverty-stricken, the conferences called attention to inequitable socioeconomic conditions, particularly in the District of Columbia,* and helped spur corrective action through public and political channels. For example, in 1940 the administration's interest in Social Security and the welfare of elderly indigents was reflected in press conference discussions of substandard conditions at the District of Columbia* Blue Plains home for the aged poor. ER also testified about Blue Plains before a committee in Congress,* and improvements were made.

Of equal importance, however, the press conferences brought increased recognition to some women journalists, whose articles usually were relegated to society and homemaking pages, by giving them a source of news from the White House, which sometimes was printed in main news sections. A symbiotic relationship soon developed between ER and the women reporters, with the conferences providing valuable visibility to both the First Lady and the women covering her.

The press conferences' claim to historical significance was based on the rarity of meetings between previous First Ladies and the press. ER's predecessors had only limited contact with reporters in accord with the Victorian idea that ladies should not seek the public eye. ER was the first to recognize that regular conferences could enhance the newsmaking capabilities of the First Lady's role and serve a public purpose. Like her uncle, President Theodore Roosevelt,* she found the White House a "bully pulpit" for her own activist agenda as she sought to improve conditions during the Great Depression.* Her immediate predecessor, Lou Henry Hoover,* had made radio broadcasts urging individuals to help others, but she had been so uncooperative with the press that one reporter, Bess Furman* of the Associated Press, was forced to disguise herself in a Girl Scout uniform to cover a White House Christmas party.

Women reporters welcomed ER's willingness to facilitate opportunities for them to gather news without any male interference. They also enjoyed the prestige and exhilaration of frequenting the White House, however limited their contact there might be. By banning men, ER made sure that women would have news unavailable to male competitors and a forum for subjects of special interest to women.

The idea for the press conferences originated with Lorena A. Hickok,* an Associated Press reporter who became ER's intimate friend while covering her in 1932. Hickok, referred to as "Hick," recognized that women reporters needed their own news sources for added job security during the depression and that it would be more convenient for ER and the reporters to meet at one time and place rather than to schedule individual appointments. Hickok left the AP because she felt her intense closeness to the First Lady would color her news judgment, so she did not cover any of the conferences.

Her successor, Furman, however, along with a small group of other journalists, developed a friendly relationship with ER, forming an inner circle of conference allies. The group included Ruby Black,* United Press, May Craig,* Guy Gannett newspapers of Maine, Emma Bugbee,* *New York Herald Tribune*, Genevieve Forbes Herrick, *Chicago Tribune*, and Martha Strayer, *Washington Daily News*. Furman chose ER as godmother for one of her twins, Black took her daughter to play with the First Lady's granddaughter, Strayer honored ER with an annual birthday party, and Craig often had her to dinner at the Craig home. Members of this circle also received invitations to visit the Roosevelt homes at Hyde Park*, New York, and Campobello.*

Craig was among a few feminists who argued against excluding men when women were fighting for opportunities to cover news on an equal

footing with men. Most of the women reporters, however, saw the conferences as a way to improve their professional stature and did not worry
about questions of equality. Like Craig, Black, the first woman hired by
the United Press in Washington as a result of ER's insistence on women-
only coverage, and several other women journalists also attended the
press conferences of President Franklin D. Roosevelt,* which had no gender criteria.

About thirty-five women attended ER's first press conference on 6
March 1933. Slightly nervous, ER passed around a box of candied fruit
to the "newspaper girls," as she called them, even though some were in
their forties, fifties, and sixties. This gathering took place two days after
FDR's inauguration as president on 4 March 1933 and two days before
the first of his 998 press conferences.

Some male competitors scoffed at the idea of the conferences and
dubbed the attending reporters "incense burners" because a posed picture of ER's second press conference showed some of the women sitting
on the floor at ER's feet (Beasley, *Eleanor Roosevelt and the Media*, 49).
Male editors inaccurately predicted that the conferences would not last.
The conferences gained more respect after women reporters roundly
scooped the men when ER announced on 3 April 1933 and 29 January
1934 that alcoholic beverages, first beer and then wine, would be served
in the White House following the end of Prohibition.* Reporters thought
that this news break was planned by Stephen T. Early,* the president's
press secretary, because he, along with Louis Howe,* the Roosevelts'
political strategist, thought it would be more politically appealing to
have ER release this news rather than FDR. Known to be against the use
of alcoholic beverages, as were many other women of the era, ER emphasized that she personally did not drink but that alcoholic beverages
would now be offered to those who wished them.

The conferences were held in the Monroe Room on the second floor
of the living quarters. Although there were sufficient chairs, the reporters, in an unseemly dash, rushed up the stairs for front-row seats. (The
author, the youngest member of the group when she started covering
the conferences at age twenty-four in 1941, remembers that she was
never able to outrun the older women and was relegated to the second
row.) Initially, Early certified forty representatives of press associations,
Washington bureaus of metropolitan dailies, and Washington newspapers, which were limited to one reporter each, to attend the conferences.
Early's involvement showed that the conferences were part of the overall
White House political communication effort.

Once the women were assembled, ER entered, followed by her private
secretary, Malvina "Tommy" Thompson* (Scheider), who took shorthand notes, and her social secretary, Edith B. Helm. After ER's customary
"Good Morning, Ladies," the First Lady shook each woman's hand, an-

nounced her schedule of activities, and entertained questions on a variety of subjects, ranging from her wardrobe and her children to her own personal and women's general role in war and peace. Like FDR, she limited the use of direct quotations, initially requiring reporters to obtain her permission and to check their notes for accuracy with Thompson, who kept a shorthand record, as did Strayer.

Most conferences lasted more than an hour, and there were some grumbling and criticism among the experienced reporters about ER's tendency to meander, making it difficult to take notes. They were also annoyed by what they considered "silly and useless" questions about trivial matters (Beasley, *Eleanor Roosevelt and the Media*, 49). Nevertheless, other questions dealt with substantive issues, although ER was careful not to tread on ground that she considered her husband's territory and declared she would not answer political questions.

Yet, she repeatedly violated her own rule, as when she made a statement in 1933 protesting the administration's dismissal of married women from the federal workforce as a budget-cutting measure. Sometimes she floated trial balloons for the New Deal,* as when she promoted work camps for unemployed women in 1933, which resulted in complaints that women would be taken from their homes. In response, the camps were limited to single women only. On occasion, she used conferences to answer critics,* like those who claimed in 1934 that she was involved in a communistic project to resettle unemployed miners in Arthurdale,* West Virginia.

ER used the conferences to publicize other leading women whom she invited to meet the reporters. Her guests included women from within the administration like Mary Anderson,* head of the Women's Bureau, as well as White House guests like Madame Chiang Kai-shek.* Sometimes ER arranged special parties for the reporters and opportunities to meet visiting royalty like King George VI and Queen Elizabeth of England in 1939 and Queen Wilhelmina of Holland in 1942.

At times social queries related to political issues, such as whether Marian Anderson,* an African American contralto, would be presented to the king and queen of England after performing at the White House. ER's affirmative reply represented a symbolic statement of support for civil rights,* as had her 1939 resignation from the Daughters of the American Revolution because of its denial of Anderson's use of the organization's Constitution Hall.

Prior to U.S. entry into World War II* in 1941, the number of women admitted to the conferences grew to more than 100, mainly by the inclusion of correspondents who wrote weekly Washington columns for out-of-town newspapers. A few women employed in public relations for federal agencies also were admitted. Starting in 1939, radio reporters were allowed in, but not photographers or newsreel representatives. No

African American reporters attended; according to Early's papers, inquiries regarding their admission were rebuffed by Early on grounds that black reporters were not admitted to FDR's press conferences since they did not represent daily newspapers.

During World War II, the scene changed for ER and the press. As assistant director of OCD, she held press conferences open to men at OCD headquarters. Her White House press conferences focused on women's participation in the war effort as well as that of her four in-uniform sons. After ER's travels* to England in 1942, she reported at her press conference on the war's effect on the embattled British people. In 1943 ER used the conferences to deny stories about immorality among servicewomen, which she said originated in a Nazi-inspired whispering campaign.

A drastic cut in attendance marked wartime conferences. Due to Secret Service security concerns, new accreditation policies were drawn up by the women journalists themselves, who organized as Mrs. Roosevelt's Press Conference Association in 1942. A five-member standing committee was elected, and attendance was limited to full-time, accredited editorial representatives in reputable standing of daily newspapers, weekly newsmagazines, press associations, and broadcasting companies. The tightened criteria were designed not only to keep out security risks but to prevent the recurrence of an incident in which a manufacturer's representative had obtained a press card by saying she wrote for a newspaper and thereby improperly claimed White House access.

The new admission policy reduced the conference size from 115 reporters in 1941 to 33 in 1942, increasing to 56 by 1945. Many of those dropped were correspondents for out-of-town newspapers. Eighteen government public relations and information officers were admitted but were not allowed to ask questions. Special admission cards were issued, as well as official Secret Service White House cards, which bore individuals' photographs and fingerprints. Application fees and annual dues were one dollar each.

At its monthly meetings, the standing committee voted on new applications, which were then passed on to Thompson, who in turn, passed them on to Early, who continued to keep his eye on all press contact with the White House. The committee also expressed a wish that reporters would ask ER sharper questions and that ER would relax the ban on direct quotation. The First Lady relented, provided she had the right to put certain remarks off-the-record.

As a self-governing body, the association elected its own officers. The first chair was Mary Hornaday,* *Christian Science Monitor*, 1942, followed by Ann Cottrell Free, *New York Herald Tribune*, 1943; Isabel Kinnear Griffin, *Springfield (Massachusetts) Union*, 1944; and Ruth Montgomery, *New York Daily News*, 1945.

Its most publicized challenge was posed by an application for membership from Gordon Cole of the Washington bureau of *PM*, a New York daily, who accurately noted there were no written gender criteria. The committee referred his request to ER. On 11 December 1942 it issued a statement, saying Cole had been turned down because "Mrs. Roosevelt considers this a woman's conference dealing with questions of interest to women, from a woman's point of view." On 27 September 1943 ER and the committee temporarily reversed this policy by admitting men to her press conference on her trip to the South Pacific war zones. The conference was moved to the Green Room to accommodate the men; twenty attended, but only one asked a question.

The association's ban on allowing government public relations and information representatives to ask questions at the conferences brought a painful moment. Two representatives of the Office of War Information* and one from the office of the Coordinator of Inter-American Affairs directly requested ER to ask the association to exempt them from the rules. They claimed that their knowledge of counterpropaganda needs put them in a better position than other reporters to ask questions so that ER's answers could be broadcast over government-leased shortwave stations. Two of these three were ER's old friends, Furman and Black, who had recently taken government jobs to increase their incomes. Nonetheless, their request was denied.

In keeping with the White House Press Correspondents Association annual black-tie dinner for the president, the First Lady's press conference association honored ER with a formal dinner in 1944 at the Statler Hotel at which she made an off-the-record speech. Her last conference was held on 12 April 1945, a few hours before FDR's sudden death. A small, but unresolved, dispute ensued over whether ER had been misquoted at a previous conference. This issue was to be reviewed by the association, but the organization ended with the president's death since Bess Truman, ER's successor, declined to hold press conferences.

Before leaving the White House, ER invited association members to a farewell tea and said she would be joining their journalistic ranks—even though she was already a syndicated columnist as author of the daily "My Day"* column and a member of the Women's National Press Club.* In response, the association presented a scroll to "Eleanor Roosevelt, a Pioneer," bearing words of appreciation for her faith in the integrity of the press, her far-reaching activities for good, her creation of news for and by women, and her awareness of their professional goals. It called her "our friend."

SELECTED BIBLIOGRAPHY

Beasley, Maurine H. *Eleanor Roosevelt and the Media.* 1987.
———, ed. *The White House Press Conferences of Eleanor Roosevelt.* 1983.

Free, Ann Cottrell. "Eleanor Roosevelt and the Female White House Press
    Corps." *Modern Maturity* (October-November 1984): 98–102.
Mrs. Roosevelt's Press Conference Association Papers, Franklin D. Roosevelt Li-
    brary, Hyde Park, NY.
Roosevelt, Eleanor. *This I Remember*. 1949.
Winfield, Betty Houchin. "Mrs. Roosevelt's Press Conference Association: The
    First Lady Shines a Light." *Journalism History* 8 (Summer 1981): 54–55,
    63–67.

Ann Cottrell Free

PROGRESSIVE PARTY. The Progressive Party has been the name used by three separate, short-lived U.S. political parties in the twentieth century. Eleanor Roosevelt took an active position on only one—the Progressive Party formed in 1948, which she opposed. That year the party, which was made up mainly of dissident Democrats, fielded Henry A. Wallace* as its candidate for president. Although ER and Wallace once had been close, she had strong differences with him over the inclusion of communists within his party's liberal coalition.

In choosing its name, the Wallace party attempted to draw on progressive traditions associated with the earlier parties. The first Progressive Party, commonly called the Bull Moose Party, was created after a split in the Republican Party in 1912 and nominated ER's uncle, Theodore Roosevelt,* for president. Despite her fondness for her uncle, ER stood by her husband, Franklin D. Roosevelt,* who actively supported the winning Democratic candidate, Woodrow Wilson. Neither ER nor FDR had any connection with the second Progressive Party, made up mainly of farm and labor leaders organized formally as the League for Progressive Political Action. It nominated Wisconsin senator Robert M. La Follette for president in 1924 but carried only Wisconsin and soon faded from the national scene.

The Progressive Party of 1948 was concerned with both Cold War* and economic issues stemming from New Deal* ideology. ER and Wallace had been allies when he served as vice president during FDR's third term. Only three days after the death of FDR on 12 April 1945, she wrote to Wallace, "I feel that you are peculiarly fitted to carry on the ideals which were closest to my husband's heart and which I know you understand" (Walton, 34). Less than two years later, however, each was a key figure in political organizations with opposing views on how to accomplish those ideals.

In December 1946 Wallace was the featured speaker at the organizational meeting of the Progressive Citizens of America (PCA), which was willing to work with communists in efforts to build a strong liberal movement. In January 1947 ER was the keynote speaker at the founding convention of the Americans for Democratic Action* (ADA), which rejected the possibility of achieving liberal goals in alliance with communists.

The PCA was formed by a merger of the Independent Citizens' Committee of the Arts, Sciences, and Professions (ICCASP) and the National Citizens Political Action Committee (NCPAC)—organizations that had worked in the 1944 election to rally support among independent liberal groups for FDR. The PCA provided the nucleus of the 1948 Progressive Party, which nominated Wallace for president and Idaho Democratic senator Glen H. Taylor for vice president. Among other initial adherents was Rexford G. Tugwell,* former undersecretary of agriculture under FDR.

Announcing his candidacy on 29 December 1947, Wallace said that both the Democrats and the Republicans "stand for a policy which opens the door to war [with Russia] in our lifetime" (Walton, 181). He predicted that military spending would create domestic economic distress and called for new efforts by the United States and Russia to reduce tensions and work toward peace.

"Oh, dear, oh dear" (Lash, 143) was ER's initial response to the Wallace candidacy. She was distressed with Wallace's decision to run because she feared it would hurt the elections prospects of the Democratic Party.* Although she herself was never a Red-baiter who denounced individuals for alleged communist ties, she disliked the tactics of the U.S. Communist Party, which supported the Progressive Party and what she perceived to be its influence within the new party. Immediately after Wallace announced his candidacy, ER in her "My Day"* columns on 29, 30 and 31 December 1947 assailed him, concluding that "he has never been a good politician, he has never been able to gauge public opinion, and he has never picked his advisers wisely" (Lash, 143). Charges of communist influence in the Progressive Party were the basis of repeated attacks on Wallace by the ADA and labor leaders supported by ER.

Wallace received only 2.38 percent of the national vote in 1948, and the Progressive Party again faded into insignificance. In a letter dated 10 July 1956 to his main supporter in the commercial press, J. W. Gitt, publisher of the *Gazette and Daily* newspaper in York, Pennsylvania, Wallace said, "What a shambles the Communists made out of a movement which would have been a strong and helpful influence in American life!" (Hamilton, 35). Too easy an explanation for his resounding defeat perhaps, but no doubt ER would have agreed.

SELECTED BIBLIOGRAPHY
Hamilton, Mary A. "A Pennsylvania Newspaper Publisher in 'Gideon's Army':
        J. W. Gitt, Henry Wallace and the Progressive Party of 1948." *Pennsylvania
        History* 61 (January 1994): 18–44.
Lash, Joseph P. *Eleanor: The Years Alone.* 1972.

MacDougall, Curtis D. *Gideon's Army*. Vols. 1, 2, 3. 1965.

Markowitz, Norman D. *The Rise and Fall of the People's Century: Henry A. Wallace and American Liberalism, 1941–1948*. 1973.

McAuliffe, Mary Sperling. *Crisis on the Left, Cold War Politics and American Liberals, 1947–1954*. 1978.

Walton, Richard J. *Henry Wallace, Harry Truman and the Cold War*. 1976.

Mary A. Hamilton

PROGRESSIVISM. Beginning in the 1890s and reaching a climax in the years preceding World War I, a political and social movement known as progressivism made itself felt on the local, state, and national level. While its participants often had different priorities and sometimes were in conflict with each other on various issues, all shared a conviction that the new needs of the increasingly urbanized, industrializing, and very diverse society required a move away from the strict adherence to laissez-faire and limited government. These reformers promoted government regulation and a new sense of corporate responsibility in order to ensure societal progress. Progressives embraced the American ideal of individual liberty, but they advocated some restrictions on the exercise of those rights, in order that the very powerful not threaten the freedoms of the society at large. While Eleanor Roosevelt was only a very limited participant in this movement during her young adult years, the early interest in some important progressive issues was a harbinger of the causes she was to champion once she moved into public life.

As an adolescent, ER's training at the English boarding school Allenswood, particularly her close relationship with headmistress Marie Souvestre,* first exposed her to women who were deeply committed to political issues of the day. Souvestre spoke with her students about the evils of European imperialism, the problems of anti-Semitism, the issues of race. ER returned home at eighteen, truncating her education to take up the proper life of a debutante. She was meant to be a woman undisturbed by the political problems of the day, but she channeled her continuing interests in social issues through settlement house work. At that time, the movement for social settlements* was in full swing in America's cities, and the interest in working with the immigrant poor had moved beyond the world of middle-class and prosperous college graduates, such as Jane Addams* of Hull House, who were making a career of such endeavors, to the most elite circles of society, of which the Roosevelts were so much a part. In 1903 ER, along with friends in New York's Junior League, volunteered at the College Settlement House on Rivington Street. There, she taught dancing and calisthenics to neighborhood girls. She journeyed to and from the settlement by public transportation so that she could get a sense of the local neighborhood but did admit to feeling "a certain amount of terror" as she walked the streets; while very flattered that one young woman's father invited her to his home to thank her for providing such joy to his daughter, she refused to go (Roosevelt, 108). Like other young people of her day interested in the relationship between social reform and social scientific investigation, she took a course in practical sociology. Finally, in 1903 ER joined the New York Consumers' League, headed by Maude Nathan. This quintessential progressive organization, which in 1898 had joined with leagues in other states to form the National Consumer League,* investigated working conditions, especially for women and children, and agitated for state laws to regulate conditions of labor.* ER herself surveyed both garment factories and department stores.

At the time, ER was being courted by her cousin Franklin D. Roosevelt,* and she knew that he did not take her volunteer efforts seriously. Once married in 1905, she focused for the next fifteen years on her role as wife and, to some extent, mother. But as FDR embarked on a political career, so, too, did ER become increasingly aware of progressive politics. In 1910, as Democratic state senator from Dutchess County, New York, FDR became a member of the anti-Tammany Hall faction, and ER was drawn into state politics. According to the biographer Blanche Cook, while FDR concentrated on issues of good government, a high priority of many progressives, ER was more attracted to the Albany politicians such as Alfred E. Smith* and Robert Wagner, who were interested in improving working conditions for New Yorkers. Convinced that increasing women's political power would help the cause of progressive legislation, many activists were ardent supporters of woman suffrage, but at the time, ER had not viewed the vote as important and, indeed, was surprised when in 1911 her husband came out in support of the suffrage cause. She, in turn, then supported her husband's position.

One year later, at the height of progressive agitation, ER's uncle, Theodore Roosevelt,* ran again for president, at the helm of the Progressive Party.* In that three-way race, FDR was an ardent supporter of Woodrow Wilson and his Democratic version of progressivism; ER, though a great admirer of her uncle and many of his supporters, followed her husband's lead. For one, she believed Wilson had the better chance of succeeding, and, like many of her contemporaries, she feared that given the social problems of the day, "If we are not going to find remedies in Progressivism then I feel sure the next step will be Socialism" (Lash, 63). With Wilson the victor over both President Taft and Roosevelt, FDR was well rewarded for his support with the appointment as assistant secretary of the navy.

ER's first years in Washington in the Wilson era* were taken up with the duties of political wife, socializing and entertaining in Washington government circles. With the outbreak of World War I in Europe, many progressive reformers became outspoken opponents of American military preparedness, but not so assistant secretary of the navy Roosevelt. Like "Uncle Teddy," well known for his interventionist views on World War I, FDR argued for greater efforts to build up America's military in preparation for entry into the war on behalf of the Allies. It was logical, then, that ER would remain well away from the antimilitarist movement.

U.S. entry into the war in 1917 actually provided ER with the most extensive public activity of her young adult life. The war, which, ironically, ushered in the end of the Progressive Era, provided opportunities for the great leap forward in organization and bureaucratization so often admired by progressive activists. For ER and other women volunteers, the massive social service efforts connected to the war effort offered new possibilities for their participation in the civic arena. ER worked regularly at the American Red Cross* Canteen in the District of Columbia* railway yards, a job she took very seriously and one that clearly invigorated her; she also visited the Naval Hospital regularly. Horrified by the conditions she found at the federal hospitals, she lobbied the government for improved conditions, just as she lobbied the Red Cross to expand recreational facilities for the soldiers. (See also Wilson Era Sunday Evening Suppers.)

The social reform agenda of the progressives faded in the 1920s, to reemerge in new forms during the New Deal.* But during those more conservative years, when ER moved determinedly into public life, she sought out men and women who had begun their careers in the reform movements of the exciting progressive years, and she remained committed to the social welfare activities that had first challenged her in 1903 and then again during the war.

SELECTED BIBLIOGRAPHY

Cook, Blanche Weisen. *Eleanor Roosevelt*. Vol. 1. 1992.
Lash, Joseph P. *Love, Eleanor: Eleanor Roosevelt and Her Friends*. 1982.
Roosevelt, Eleanor. *This Is My Story*. 1937.

Miriam J. Cohen

PROHIBITION. Eleanor Roosevelt epitomizes the complex relationship between the American reform tradition and Prohibition, the antialcohol movement that culminated in a national ban on the manufacture and sale of intoxicating drink from 1920 to 1933. Certainly, alcohol played a tragic role in her personal life. Her father, Elliott Roosevelt,* profoundly alcoholic, was secluded from public view during part of her childhood and died of alcohol-related illness before ER's tenth birthday. During her adolescence, ER witnessed the dissipation of her mother's two brothers, Valentine and Edward Hall, while living with her grandmother, Mary Livingston Ludlow Hall. ER's brother, G. Hall Roosevelt,* became an alcoholic. Not surprisingly, ER objected to the casual drinking of her husband, Franklin D. Roosevelt,* particularly when family members snidely made comparisons between "poor Eleanor's father" and "poor Eleanor's husband" (Cook, 304). Her intimate friend, Lorena Hickok,* noted that ER "once told me that the very smell of alcoholic beverages was distasteful to her" (Hickok 65). Yet, ER did not demand abstinence from her guests, and she herself shared a rare glass of wine with company.

ER's personal sentiments related integrally to the public debates surrounding Prohibition, which was a dominant movement in American state and national politics in the early twentieth century. Prohibition, so its advocates believed, would not only eliminate drunkenness, but end the vote-tampering of saloon keepers, the poverty and violence within drinkers' families, the prostitution and backroom machinations of the "vice interests." Women's groups, in particular, supported Prohibition because they believed its promised benefits would affect them and their families positively.

World War I, with its demands for grain conservation and its anti-German, antibrewer sentiment, increased the "dry" enthusiasm of the general populace. By 1920, thirty-three of the forty-eight states had some form of Prohibition. In January of that year the Eighteenth Amendment to the U.S. Constitution, having passed Congress* and an overwhelming majority of states, went into effect, banning the manufacture, transportation, or sale of intoxicating beverages within the United States. During the 1920s Prohibition certainly reduced alcoholism. But it also glamorized drinking and the lawbreaking associated with it and threatened to overwhelm the legal system. By the 1930s Prohibition was widely considered a national joke, if not a national disgrace. Women reformers such as ER saw the noble and progressive intentions of Prohibition undermined by bootlegging criminals, rural bigotry, and flaunting disregard for the Constitution.

As a social activist and political insider, ER confronted repeatedly the dilemmas posed by Prohibition. In the 1920s New York contained a formidable dry population upstate, and the issue remained at the forefront of state politics throughout the decade. ER refrained from joining women's dry organizations such as the Woman's Christian Temperance Union and the Woman's National Committee for Law Enforcement (WNCLE). Yet she was a prominent member of the League of Women Voters* in New York, which strongly supported Prohibition. Her dry sympathies were nationally recognized in a *North American Review* article in 1928. Her role within the Democratic Party* as the representative of dry womanhood had particular importance given the traditional connection between Prohibition and the Republican Party. When Democrat Alfred E. Smith* ran for governor of New York in 1926, ER campaigned for him in the dry Republican counties upstate. She took this role nationwide in 1928 during Smith's presidential campaign against Herbert

Hoover.* ER spearheaded the attack against dry women Democrats who supported Hoover. Stating that she was "personally absolutely dry," she accused the National Woman's Democratic Law Enforcement League of racism in calling for enforcement of the Eighteenth Amendment but not the Fourteenth and Fifteenth Amendments, which gave voting rights to African Americans (*New York Times*, 30 January 1928). Following Hoover's election, she praised his efforts to enforce Prohibition law.

In 1932 ER again served as a balance to the repeal sentiments of her party and her husband. But by 1932 the dry forces were so embattled, if not irrational, that they brooked no criticism whatsoever of the Prohibition amendment. Even though ER continued to describe herself as dry, prohibitionists excoriated her because she would not unconditionally support the law. As First Lady-elect, ER criticized Prohibition in a radio* speech for exposing young women to alcohol more than in previous generations, contending, "Nowadays a girl who goes out with a boy must know how to handle her gin" (Hickok, 66). A flurry of criticism followed. Norman Vincent Peale, a well-known minister, replied that ER was a "child of the rich who doesn't understand anything about American life"; Lucy Peabody, head of WNCLE, considered ER just as "abnormal" as other wet women (*New York Times*, 15 January 1933).

In April 1933 the New Deal* Congress legalized 3.2 percent beer, handing ER the delicate task of reintroducing alcohol to the White House. The national press reported that "the personal views and tastes of the first lady . . . notwithstanding," beer would be served in the White House, in iced-tea glasses (*New York Times*, 4 April 1933). Following repeal of the Eighteenth Amendment in late 1933, the First Lady also served wine and hard liquor, though she continued to object to FDR's afternoon martini rituals.

ER demonstrates the nuanced, often strained position of women reformers in the waning years of Prohibition. In announcing that beer would return to the White House, she stated that "no matter what the legislation, I myself do not drink anything with alcoholic content, but that is purely an individual thing" (*New York Times*, 4 April 1933). In saying this, she was implicitly criticizing the moralistic bullying of the prohibitionists, presenting herself as moderate, flexible, and open-minded. Her views on alcohol, however, represented the reaction of a woman defined by her childhood and committed to a female reform tradition far different from the exuberant personal liberalism of modern America.

SELECTED BIBLIOGRAPHY

Barnard, Eunice Fuller. "Madame Arrives in Politics." *North American Review* 226 (1928): 1–3, 20.
Clark, Norman. *Deliver Us from Evil: An Interpretation of American Prohibition.* 1976.

Cook, Blanche Wiesen. *Eleanor Roosevelt*. Vol. 1. 1992.
Hickok, Lorena A. *Eleanor Roosevelt*. 1962.
Jackson, William John. "Prohibition as an Issue in New York State Politics, 1836–
    1933." Ph.D. dissertation. Columbia University. 1974.

                                               Catherine Gilbert Murdock

R

RADIO BROADCASTS. Eleanor Roosevelt had a successful career as a radio broadcaster that spanned much of her public life. One of the first notable women in radio, she delivered news commentary and human interest material and backed causes in which she believed. Her sponsored broadcasts over major networks both enlarged the concept of radio performance by individuals in public life and affirmed the right of married women to earn money on their own.

ER's radio career began in the 1920s, when she spoke occasionally over New York stations, giving, for example, a talk in 1925 in praise of the civic ideals of the Women's City Club.* It expanded after Franklin D. Roosevelt* was elected president in 1932. In the preinaugural period between 9 December 1932 and 24 February 1933, ER delivered a series of twelve radio commentaries sponsored by Pond's, a cold cream manufacturer, chiefly on child raising and family relations. After the Pond's radio series generated newspaper criticism that the future First Lady was using her name "for commercial purposes," she announced that she intended to accept no more radio contracts (Beasley and Belgrade, 42).

In 1934, however, ER resumed commercial broadcasting. Going off-the-record at one of her women-only press conferences,* she expressed her determination to "get the money for a good cause [charity] and take the gaff" (Beasley and Belgrade, 42). She broadcast first for a roofing company, which paid her $500 per minute, the same amount earned by the highest-paid radio stars, and then for the Simmons Mattress Company at the same rate for five commentaries on highlights of the week's news. After that contract ended, she presented six fifteen-minute talks on education for the American typewriter industry, and in 1935 the Selby Shoe Company sponsored her broadcasts. Speaking in a personal, con-

Eleanor Roosevelt in widow's black speaks to the people
of the United States over the CBS radio network on 19
August 1945, the day of prayer proclaimed by President
Harry S Truman in thanksgiving for the cessation of hos-
tilities in World War II. *Courtesy of Franklin D. Roosevelt
Library*

versational style, ER delivered listeners for her sponsors and proved that
she was worth large sums to advertisers.

In public ER justified her commercial contracts on grounds of earning
money for good purposes. She announced that payments for her broadcasts would go directly to the American Friends Service Committee,
which channeled proceeds to Arthurdale,* a resettlement community in
West Virginia, and other projects in which ER took a special interest. Yet,
deductions for her agent's commission and other expenses reduced the
amount that went to charity.

The pay issue involved symbolic as well as ethical considerations. ER
believed that she and other women had a right to engage in careers and
to be compensated for their work. In the opinion of her son, Elliott Roo-

sevelt,* ER wanted a career to justify her own self-worth and to satisfy a need for "power and influence, provided it was in her own right and her own name" (Roosevelt, 299). Viewed in this light, ER's radio broadcasts can be seen as beacons to other women who wished to break into the male-dominated domain of commercial radio broadcasting.

At the same time, however, the broadcasts obviously depended heavily on ER's position as the wife of the president of the United States. ER spoke generally on noncontroversial topics like typical days in the White House, the life of the wife of a public official, and official life in Washington. Yet, some broadcasts related to political concerns: she repeatedly emphasized the need for women to take part in civic affairs and spoke out on the issues of education, youth,* and world peace.* While somewhat high-pitched, her voice had a patrician quality and carried well on the radio; she had clear, upper-class, East Coast diction.

After a hiatus during the election year of 1936, ER returned to sponsored radio broadcasts over the National Broadcasting Company (NBC) network. In 1937 the Pond's company paid her $3,000 for each of thirteen weekly broadcasts. She received the same fee for a series of fifteen-minute talks sponsored for twenty-six weeks by Sweetheart Soap in 1940. In 1939 WNBC called her the "First Lady of Radio" (Lash, 419).

Her most significant commercial broadcast as First Lady, however, was a series of twenty-six Sunday evening broadcasts for the Pan-American Coffee Bureau, which represented eight coffee-exporting nations in Latin America.* The broadcasts began in October 1941 and ran through April 1942, covering the period immediately before and after U.S. entry into World War II,* when ER served as assistant director of the Office of Civilian Defense.* By today's standards, it would be almost inconceivable for a president's wife to receive payments from foreign governments, particularly during a war, but the series was well accepted at the time it was broadcast. *Time* magazine said that the programs were carried by more NBC outlets than the popular *Fibber McGee and Molly* comedy show.

The programs, for which ER received a total of $28,000, helped prepare American women for war, praising homemakers as "the first line of defense" (Beasley and Belgrade, 43). Before the United States entered the conflict, ER promoted the administration policy of aiding the British in spite of opposition from isolationists. On the fateful Sunday, 7 December 1941, when the Japanese bombed Pearl Harbor, she changed her prepared remarks to urge listeners to rally behind the administration as it led the nation into war. She called on women and young people to aid the war effort; such appeals continued on subsequent broadcasts.

Eleanor Roosevelt's radio career was supported by her husband and others within his administration who thought it good politics to reach a large audience of women voters. In her radio broadcasts, as in her daily newspaper column, "My Day,"* she consistently plugged FDR's New

Deal* programs and defense policies. In her broadcast for the Coffee Bureau on 15 February 1942, she defended the administration's decision to proceed with Japanese American internment.* Although not characteristic of her attitudes toward civil rights,* this broadcast illustrated the way she supported her husband politically.

The Pan-American series ended ER'S career as a paid radio commentator while acting as First Lady, but she continued her broadcasting career after leaving the White House. During and following her years as a United Nations* delegate, she appeared as an unpaid guest on many radio and television* news and public affairs programs. While she was at the United Nations (UN), she delivered broadcasts on U.S. policy in French, in which she was fluent, German, Spanish, and Italian for the Voice of America.

ER also engaged in more commercial radio work, primarily to help her children financially. In 1948–1949, she cohosted a daily radio talk show on the American Broadcasting Company (ABC) with her daughter, Anna Roosevelt (Halsted*), to help both Anna after her second marriage had failed and her son, Elliott, who had begun a radio broadcasting business in Los Angeles. Her correspondence with Anna during this period reflected both Anna's and ER's preoccupation with the money Anna would earn from the radio program. Eleanor often recorded her part of the program from Europe, where she was engaged in her UN duties, and included serious commentary on world affairs. Anna broadcast her part of the show live from Hollywood and concentrated more on soft news. Although the show was dropped after thirty-nine weeks for lack of commercial sponsorship, it won praise for intelligent content.

In 1950 she signed a contract Elliott had negotiated with WNBC in New York for a daily radio program to replace the successful Mary Margaret McBride* program, which had moved to ABC. Elliott coproduced *The Eleanor Roosevelt Show* and read the commercials. Columnists were troubled by his willingness to exploit his mother's name. The *New Republic* complained that "when Elliott reminds listeners that 'mother' uses a certain kind of bobby-pin and that further information about a soup may be obtained by dropping a card 'to the Roosevelts,' he is trading on his name—and on hers" ("On the Air," 21). The program left the air in less than a year.

ER's radio career illustrated her growth as a public figure and helped establish a woman's right to comment on substantive issues. She herself saw her radio career as important because of its potential for educating women about issues beyond the confines of the home. Joseph P. Lash,* ER's friend and biographer, summarized her dedication to her large audience of women: "She tried consciously to envision the women who were listening . . . on lonely ranches, in mountain cabins, in tenements and to remember that they were weighing her words against their own experience" (Lash, 419).

SELECTED BIBLIOGRAPHY

Asbell, Bernard, ed. *Mother & Daughter: The Letters of Eleanor and Anna Roosevelt*. 1982.

Beasley, Maurine. *Eleanor Roosevelt and the Media*. 1987.

Beasley, Maurine, and Paul Belgrade. "Eleanor Roosevelt: First Lady as Radio Pioneer." *Journalism History* 11 (Autumn/Winter 1984): 42–45.

Lash, Joseph P. *Eleanor and Franklin*. 1971.

"On the Air: Soap and the Roosevelts." *The New Republic* (25 December 1950): 21.

Roosevelt, Elliott, and James Brough. *An Untold Story*. 1973.

Paul S. Belgrade

READ, ELIZABETH FISHER (8 September 1872, New Brighton, PA–13 December 1943, New York).

A scholar and lawyer, Elizabeth Fisher Read met Eleanor Roosevelt in 1920, when Read agreed to help ER direct the national legislation committee of the League of Women Voters.* Describing the meeting, ER said, "I felt very humble and inadequate to the job when I first presented myself to Elizabeth Read, but I liked her at once and she gave me a sense of confidence. It was the beginning of a friendship with her and with her friend, Miss Esther Lape"* (Roosevelt, 324). Read helped ER by combing through the *Congressional Record* and marking the bills that she believed might be of interest to the league. ER and Read then met each week to discuss the various pieces of legislation that Read had highlighted, and ER prepared a monthly report that was distributed to league members. In ER's view Read and Lape "came to feel an affection and a certain respect for me because I was willing really to work on these reports" (Roosevelt, 325).

The weekly meetings evolved into a close personal and professional association. Read and Lape, her life partner, maintained an apartment in New York City and in 1927 began to acquire the woodlands and meadows in Connecticut that became their country retreat, Salt Meadow. Playing what ER described as a major role in her "intensive education" during the 1920s, they became the core of her female support network as she began her public career (Roosevelt, 325). Intensely interested in legal issues, Read was a graduate of Smith College, held a master's degree from Columbia University, and had graduated with distinction from the law school of the University of Pennsylvania at a time when few women were lawyers. She and Lape encouraged ER, promoted her work, and welcomed her into their circle of college-educated, ambitious, and accomplished women.

Throughout the 1920s, ER spent one evening a week with Read and Lape at their Greenwich Village apartment. The three had dinner together and then read French poetry aloud. They also discussed political reforms and strategies, as well as the contents of *City-State-Nation*, a weekly review without editorial comment of pending legislation from the local to the national level. Read and Lape edited the publication in the early 1920s, directing it at both men and women voters.

In February 1923 ER joined the committee that published the review in cooperation with the New York state League of Women Voters. Along with Narcissa Vanderlip* and Helen Rogers Reid, later president of the *New York Herald Tribune*, ER provided the review's financial support. In the company of Read and Lape, ER learned how to maneuver in league politics, with the three women receiving advice from Franklin D. Roosevelt* on how to assure Vanderlip's leadership of the state organization. Years later Lape noted that ER and Read, "both with more time available than I could have . . . often communicated to each other on rather difficult points of social and political interest" ("Salt Meadow," 24).

Read practiced law in New York City for many years. She also served as director of research for the American Foundation, a private organization directed by Lape that focused on international as well as national public affairs issues. Read's major scholarly efforts included writing a book, *International Law and International Relations* (1925), which was used as a college text to stimulate interest in international law as an area of study. She also translated and edited a volume titled *The World Court** (1926) and assisted Lape in editing a book titled *American Medicine: Expert Testimony out of Court* (1937). According to Lape, ER was impressed by Read's "clear thinking and her stern intellectual values" ("Salt Meadow," 8–9). At ER's request Read and Lape sent her memorandums on issues of interest to FDR.

Read and ER remained close friends during the White House years, with ER renting an apartment in the building that Read and Lape owned and where they also lived at 20 East Eleventh Street in New York City. Read and Lape frequently visited ER both at the White House and at Hyde Park* during the summer. ER, often joined by her secretary, Malvina Thompson* (Scheider), made numerous trips to Salt Meadow, where Read practiced forestry, laid out trails, and constructed rustic bridges.

On a professional level, Read became ER's personal attorney, counseling her on a variety of investments and property matters. She served as the First Lady's financial adviser, a responsibility that became increasingly important and complex in the late 1920s, when ER became involved in the Todhunter School,* Val-Kill* Industries, and her work as a writer and lecturer. Read handled ER's income taxes beginning in the 1920s and continuing into the 1940s.

After Read's death following years of ill health, ER wrote Joseph Lash* that "Elizabeth always subordinated anything to Esther's interests tho' she had the stronger character & tho' less brilliant, she had better judgment & in some ways a better mind than Esther's. . . . it is Elizabeth one would talk to & be sure of understanding" (Lash, 101). When Read's ashes were buried at Salt Meadow, ER planted bulbs over the grave for the following spring.

SELECTED BIBLIOGRAPHY

Beard, Rick, and Leslie Cohen Berlowitz, eds. *Greenwich Village: Culture and Counterculture*. 1993.

Cook, Blanche Wiesen. *Eleanor Roosevelt*. Vol. 1. 1992.

Hoff-Wilson, Joan, and Marjorie Lightman. *Without Precedent: The Life and Career of Eleanor Roosevelt*. 1984.

Lape, Esther. "Salt Meadow: From the Perspective of a Half Century." Unpublished memoir. The Esther Lape Papers, Franklin D. Roosevelt Library, Hyde Park, N.Y.

Lash, Joseph P. *A World of Love: Eleanor Roosevelt and Her Friends, 1943–1962*. 1984.

Roosevelt, Eleanor. *This Is My Story*. 1937.

Rodger Streitmatter

REFUGEES. A leading advocate for refugees from the 1930s until her death in 1962, Eleanor Roosevelt alerted Americans, as well as people all over the world, to the plights of displaced peoples and helped transform this awareness into concrete programs. American assistance primarily took two forms. In some instances, the U.S. government offered entry visas to the refugees. In other cases, organizations—charitable, humanitarian, federal, or international, often acting in concert with each other—provided aid to the suffering. ER championed and facilitated both types of refugee policy.

Yet to describe ER as merely a supporter of refugees misses the complexity of her involvement, ultimately diminishing her achievements. Although at times she wished to make an explicit case for refugee relief, several factors limited her ability to speak and act candidly. First, the American public's anti-immigrant stance, which contained strong xenophobic and restrictionist sentiments, propagated ambivalence and apathy toward refugees. This discouraged American involvement, especially when the proposed solutions involved immigration. Second, U.S. foreign policy objectives often determined the extent of American aid to refugees and the degree to which ER advocated on their behalf. Especially while First Lady, ER was confronted by serious political implications when commenting on refugees, reducing her latitude in grappling with these issues.

Despite these factors, ER supported refugee relief causes, and her involvement can be divided into two periods. The first was from the mid-1930s to 1945, when ER was First Lady and the United States confronted the European fascist threat, which produced a series of refugee crises. The second period was from 1945 to 1962, after ER left the White House but remained active in public affairs as a U.S. delegate to the United Nations* from 1945 to 1952 during the Cold War* between America and the Soviet Union.

ER first displayed a commitment to refugees during the civil war in Spain* (1936–1939). This brutal conflict between the Spanish republican government and the rebel fascist forces led by General Francisco Franco, who were armed by Hitler's Germany and Mussolini's Italy, forced thousands of Spanish civilians to flee in search of safety, precipitating a humanitarian crisis that received worldwide attention. In the United States, several institutions, including the American Friends Service Committee (AFSC), the American Red Cross,* the Joint Committee for Spanish Children (JCSC) and, eventually, the U.S. government, organized relief efforts. ER served as an informal adviser to the AFSC and JCSC, apprising them of shifts in official American policy and building support among her influential contacts and friends for their endeavors.

ER's first foray into refugee affairs highlighted several dynamics that recurred in the future, the most important being her precarious positions as both refugee advocate and wife of the president. Because of her status, ER received many requests asking for her assistance in easing the plight of Spanish refugees, yet her public position as a representative of the administration limited her ability to respond vigorously. She simply could not afford either to inflame isolationist sentiment or to offend either her husband's political allies or opponents by pushing a refugee agenda. Moreover, given America's official neutrality in the Spanish civil war, she could not disturb the nation's precarious geopolitical position by advocating an aggressive American response.

Many of these political and geopolitical concerns reappeared during the numerous refugee crises produced by the sweep of German and Italian fascism across Europe, which especially endangered Jews.* ER did her best to aid Jewish and child refugees by supporting various activities, including the Emergency Rescue Committee (ERC), which used her name to expedite the processing of immigrant refugees, the U.S. Committee for the Care of European Children (USCCEC), of which she was honorary chairwoman, and the rescue work of Varian Fry.* She supported the passage of the Wagner–Rogers bill* of 1939, which would have permitted the entry of 20,000 German child refugees into America over a two-year period, but this bill, despite repeated attempts by supporters, did not secure a much-needed endorsement from President Franklin D. Roosevelt* and was withdrawn. In contrast to her role as an unofficial lobbyist for the Wagner–Rogers bill and her ceremonial and behind-the-scenes work for the ERC and the USCCEC, ER formally participated in the Children's Crusade for Children (CCFC) in 1939 and 1940, an organization whose nonpartisan and nonpolitical agenda permitted ER to engage more actively in its cause. Headed by the novelist

Dorothy Canfield Fisher, this group sought student donations to provide "help for refugee children from American schoolchildren" (DCF to ER, 10 January 1940). ER served on the CCFC's award jury, which decided to whom and to which nations this aid was to be given. Most importantly, with members of the Roosevelt administration, such as assistant secretary of state Breckinridge Long, often obstructing aid efforts, ER stood out as a friend of refugee relief causes, lobbying her husband, building alliances with sympathetic government figures (most prominently Sumner Welles*), and providing her allies in the relief community with insights concerning government policy. But, as her involvement with the Wagner–Rogers bill and the CCFC demonstrated, ER still needed to pick her battles carefully for fear of offending her husband's and her own powerful enemies. Finally, America's entry into World War II* made maintaining a united homefront and winning the war her most important priorities; once again, larger American foreign policy goals distracted ER's attention from refugee issues. Some scholars, most notably, David Wyman, have criticized ER's refugee activities during this period, decrying her efforts and the overall American response as ineffective.

The postwar years produced a different set of refugee issues and a new role for ER, the private citizen. The disastrous economic and social consequences of the war in Europe generated a large refugee problem. The Soviet imposition of communist governments in Eastern Europe exacerbated these crises as thousands fled harsh political conditions behind the Iron Curtain for the already overburdened nations of Western Europe. At the newly formed United Nations, leaders from the Soviet Union, Europe, and the United States heatedly debated solutions to these issues. ER's role as a member of the U.S. delegation to the United Nations from 1946 to 1952 placed her in the middle of these Cold War refugee controversies, allowing her to continue her advocacy efforts begun in the late 1930s. Even after leaving the United Nations in 1952, ER's extensive international travels* and her ties to liberal American politicians and activists kept her at the forefront of international refugee problems. While certainly still involved in refugee issues, ER during the post-1945 period acted more as a voice of conscience and as a policy ombudsman rather than as the political insider that she had been from 1937 to 1945.

As a member of the U.S. delegation to the first meeting of the United Nations (UN) General Assembly in early 1946 in London, ER was assigned to Committee Three, which addressed the fate of European displaced persons in the post–World War II era and the approaches governments should take in dealing with them. The Soviets took a hard line and demanded the forced repatriation of refugees to their countries of origin, believing that many refugees were traitors either to the anti-fascist or pro-communist causes. ER articulated the American response:

refugees had the right to political and religious asylum and thus should be treated sympathetically and given aid. In contrast to her efforts during the Spanish civil war and World War II, which involved specific programs and organizations, her approach was largely part of an ideological contest centered upon human rights.* While unable to change the Soviet position, ER helped define the relatively liberal and compassionate Western stance on refugees, which ultimately manifested itself in the worldwide relief and emigration efforts of the late 1940s and 1950s.

Refugee issues, however, were not confined to Europe or to the burgeoning American–Soviet competition; the creation of Israel* induced another crisis. ER supported Israel as a safe home for European Jews. Yet, its creation displaced the sizable Arab population living in what was now deemed Israeli territory. Thus, she supported relief efforts for these refugees, beginning in 1948 with a UN resolution that allocated over $29 million to Arab refugee assistance. In 1952, during a tour of the Middle East, ER visited Arab refugee camps in Jordan. While shocked by the abject poverty and hopelessness she found, ER steadfastly refused to find Israel responsible for the well-being of these Arab refugees. For ER, the fate of the Jewish Israeli state was more important than the fate of Arab refugees.

In the postwar years and especially after leaving the United Nations in 1952, ER continued to draw attention to the suffering of refugees and the worthiness of relief efforts. In her October 1955 "If You Ask Me" column for *McCall's,** ER criticized American apathy toward refugees, highlighting relief organizations' struggles to generate support for their operations. ER also continued to publicize and critique the American government efforts to aid refugees; in 1955 she joined other liberals in decrying the restrictions of the Refugee Relief Act of 1953, which only very slowly and inefficiently granted entry visas to European refugees.

ER's efforts on behalf of refugees spanned the last twenty-five years of her life. As First Lady, UN delegate, and private citizen, she worked to aid refugees who, in a world torn apart by violence or geopolitical conflict, often became little more than objects or, worse yet, problems in the eyes of policymakers. While not always successful in achieving her goals, her basic understanding of human needs was a much needed tonic in an era often lacking in compassion for the suffering. As ER recognized in her foreword to Lyman C. White's *300,000 New Americans*, "This is still the age of the uprooted man, the man who seeks to build a new life in a new land and who needs our help to do so."

SELECTED BIBLIOGRAPHY

Eleanor Roosevelt Papers, Franklin D. Roosevelt Library, Hyde Park, NY.
Feingold, Henry L. *The Politics of Rescue: The Roosevelt Administration and the Holocaust: 1938–1945.* 1970.
Roosevelt, Eleanor. "If You Ask Me." *McCall's* 83 (October 1955): 72.

White, Lyman C. *300,000 New Americans*. 1957.
Wyman, David. *Paper Walls: America and the Refugee Crisis, 1938–1941*. 1985.

Carl Joseph Bon Tempo

RELIGION: EPISCOPALIAN. Eleanor Roosevelt had a lifelong association with the Episcopal Church, which included frequent church attendance. She was baptized 21 January 1885 as an infant in her parents' home by Henry Yates Satterlee, the rector of Calvary Episcopal Church, 61 Gramercy Park, North, New York City. The church was located near the home of her uncle, Theodore Roosevelt,* who was her godfather. Her family had been part of Calvary for years. Both her mother, Anna Hall Roosevelt,* and her father, Elliott Roosevelt,* were members there, as was her grandmother, Mary Ludlow Hall, with whom ER lived after the death of her mother when ER was eight. Her grandfather, Valentine Hall, had been a Sunday school teacher there.

Grandmother Hall maintained a town house in New York City and a summer home near Tivoli in the Hudson River Valley. She made sure ER attended church in both the city and the country. For Grandmother Hall, Sunday was a day set apart, when in addition to attending church, ER had to learn Bible verses and hymns, was allowed to read only special books, and could not play games. ER resented some of these restrictions and found the four-mile ride in the small seat of a horse-drawn coach to the Episcopal church at Tivoli very uncomfortable. What she remembered as "a joy to me" was the family's practice of singing hymns around the piano on Sunday evenings (Roosevelt, *This Is My Story*, 45).

After ER returned in 1902 from a three-year stay at Allenswood School in England, she attended the Episcopalian Church of the Incarnation at 209 Madison Avenue, New York City, where she was confirmed on 3 May 1903. Her marriage* to Franklin D. Roosevelt* on 17 March 1905 was recorded in the church's parish register, although the wedding actually took place at 8 East Seventy-sixth Street, the home of her cousin, Susan Parish, and her husband, Henry. During their early married life in New York City, ER and FDR were parishioners of the Church of the Incarnation along with FDR's mother, Sara Delano Roosevelt,* who attended services there when she was living in Manhattan. The funeral of the Roosevelts' infant son, Franklin D. Roosevelt Jr., who died when he was seven months old, was held at the church on 3 November 1909.

After her marriage, ER also began an association with St. James Episcopal Church in Hyde Park,* New York. This was the church to which she would in time form the strongest ties, first, as a frequent visitor during periods when she and FDR lived with his mother on her Hyde Park estate and eventually as a resident of Hyde Park herself after FDR's death in 1945.

When the Roosevelts moved to Washington after FDR was appointed assistant secretary of the navy from 1913 to 1920, they attended St. Thomas Episcopal Church. The Roosevelt children were enrolled in its Sunday school, since FDR insisted that ER take the children to church, even though he sometimes opted to play golf instead of accompanying the family. During World War I ER helped with suppers and entertainment at the church for soldiers. St. Thomas also was the family church during FDR's presidency from 1933 to 1945, although he preferred to have monthly Episcopal services at the White House rather than go to the church because of the attention his presence drew.

After leaving the White House, ER made Val-Kill* cottage in Hyde Park her principal home. She soon became one of the most faithful parishioners and supporters of St. James Episcopal Church, attending on Sundays even in the final weeks of her life, when she was too weak to rise during the service. ER did not like to go to church alone and often took with her not only grandchildren and relatives but visiting dignitaries such as Queen Juliana of the Netherlands* and the labor leader Walter Reuther.* When ER was in New York City, where she maintained an apartment, she at times attended Calvary Episcopal Church in the company of her grandson, Curtis Dall Roosevelt, remembering her religious experience there as a child.

ER made only limited public comment on matters of theology. In a book written for young people the year before her death, she affirmed a belief in God, as "my greatest source of strength" (Roosevelt, *Your Teens and Mine*, 37). Her minister, the Reverend Gordon Kidd, rector of St. James Episcopal Church from 1946 to 1966, however, said, "She [ER] didn't believe in a life after death" (Kidd, 19). ER's niece, Eleanor Roosevelt Wotkyns, summed up ER's views on life hereafter as, "I'm interested in what's going to happen, but I'm too busy to worry about it. I'll find out soon enough" (Wotkyns, 58–59).

Doctrine and dogma were not matters that ER dwelled on. Her granddaughter, Nina Roosevelt Gibson, believed ER's interest in taking her to church stemmed from a desire to provide a worthwhile educational experience: "I think it was the tradition and the stories and the literature and the music; I think all those things she [ER] felt you needed to be exposed to" (Gibson, 6–7).

In a 1932 magazine article, "What Religion Means to Me," ER wrote: "I am an Episcopalian, as I was as a child, but I feel this makes me neither better or worse that those who belong to any other church. I believe in habits of regular church going and regular work for the church. . . . But these are the outward symbols which should proclaim inner growth. . . . If people can attain it without the help of what might be called religious routine, that is for them to decide. The fundamental vital thing which must be alive in each human consciousness is the religious teaching that we cannot live for ourselves alone, and that as long as we are here on this earth we are all of us brothers, regardless of race, creed, or color" (Black, 4–5).

Reflecting this ecumenical approach, ER endorsed the teachings of Gandhi in her "My Day"* column of 27 January 1953 and cited the prayer of a Native American in the "My Day" column of 10 February 1956. In her "My Day" column of 25 August 1954, she said that for humankind to achieve world peace, people needed "to get rid of feelings of hate and to try to develop charity and understanding in the circles that they individually touch" (Emblidge, 42).

Yet, there was no doubt she remained a Christian. In answers to questions from readers of her *Ladies' Home Journal** column, she named Christ as the greatest man of all time. She expressed agreement with a sermon by an Episcopalian clergyman who said "the most revolutionary doctrine in the world was the way of life preached by Christ himself," although she added, "Almost any other religion, if you lived up to the ideals of the founders, would lead you to what might be termed a revolutionary way of living" (Roosevelt, *If You Ask Me*, 122–123). Such was ER's personal faith in religion and her fellow human beings.

SELECTED BIBLIOGRAPHY

Black, Allida M., ed. *What I Hope to Leave Behind: The Essential Essays of Eleanor Roosevelt.* 1995.
Eleanor Roosevelt Oral History Project, Interviews with Nina Roosevelt Gibson (1979), the Rev. Gordon Kidd (1978), and Eleanor Wotkyins (1978), Franklin D. Roosevelt Library, Hyde Park, NY.
Emblidge, David, ed. *Eleanor Roosevelt's "My Day."* Vol. 3. 1991.
Roosevelt, Eleanor. *If You Ask Me.* 1946.
———. *This Is My Story.* 1937.
——— with Helen Ferris. *Your Teens and Mine.* 1961.

Robert W. Morrow

RELIGION: GROWTH IN. Eleanor Roosevelt's religious beliefs started conventionally. She was taught to worship in Protestant Christian Sunday church services, pray at home, and listen regularly to her mother reading the Bible. As a teenager, she carried this moral set with her to England where she attended Allenswood, a private school for the daughters of upper-class European and American families. There she began to develop her own pattern of interaction, nurturing and comforting first her schoolmates and thereafter nearly everyone she associated with. In the last three decades of her life, her religion developed into a real fusion of her earliest principles with her continuous social interactions. She never forswore her faith, but she merged her abstracted Episcopalian* Christian beliefs with her humane actions. The result was strong reliance, confidence, and faith in her own ability to work with and nurture people of any religion, skin color, or politics.

Eleanor Roosevelt, an experienced rider, takes to the trail with a ranger during a camping trip with Lorena Hickok in Yosemite National Park in July 1934. *Courtesy of Franklin D. Roosevelt Library*

ER has sometimes been regarded as a poor little aristocrat, orphaned when she was nine, depreciated by her mother and rejected or traduced by others of the social set from which she emerged. This is an exaggeration. Her mother, Anna Hall Roosevelt,* indeed didn't know what to make of this solemn child who lacked the physical beauty of both her mother and her grandmother. But ER's mother did instill in her eldest child a sense of duty to obey those biblical moral imperatives that she learned from her own parents. The sense of duty to obey moral principles stayed with her, but over the nearly eight decades of her life, the moral principles became more elemental as ER matured. Without ever abandoning her Christianity, she integrated it in her dealings with others, not as fellow Christians but as fellow human beings.

The slow and long process of her religious evolution merits mention of specific events in her life that deepened and strengthened her self and her actions. She truly wondered how Jonah got inside the biblical whale and, when she came to disbelieve the story, wondered how she should tell her children. Her husband, Franklin D. Roosevelt,* told her the children would eventually find out by themselves and not to worry about disillusioning them. Her growth came partly from her experience with FDR as a husband and as a man who disillusioned her, while he also was establishing strong, enduring bonds with others. She began establishing her own strong, sometimes passionate, bonds with others.

She got to the bottom of things, not by rationalizing an ideology but by interacting with people. Early on she opposed women's suffrage, was at least conventionally anti-Semitic, and patronizing of black people. Yet as she emerged as an individual she became concerned with equalizing respect and dignity and with integrating religious words and deeds.

Getting to the bottom of things meant looking beneath the surface of individuals. She admired her beautiful mother but not her inability to identify with her daughter and to see the world as ER saw it. She adored her father, Elliott Roosevelt,* the brother of Theodore Roosevelt,* and judged him by the spontaneous, warm affection he showed to her. She did not learn about his alcoholism and philandering until she was sixteen, seven years after his death.

After she returned from Allenswood in 1902, FDR pursued her and finally won her hand. FDR overcame her puzzlement that such a handsome man should want her. After six pregnancies, she made herself ignore the rumors of his infidelity when they were in Washington during the World War I, and her husband was assistant secretary of the navy. When he returned from the European theater of war in the fall of 1918, she took out of his luggage and read the letters that he had received from Lucy Mercer (Rutherfurd*). She realized the rumors were true. What could she make of love—Christian, sexual, maternal, or otherwise?

These events, so close to ER, presented face-to-face confrontations with the conventional moral standards of her childhood Christianity. Having been taught as a child how people are commanded by God to behave, she perhaps sensed only dimly her father's deficiencies. He was forever beloved. But as a woman, she did not ignore her husband's adultery: rather, she confronted him, commiserated with her husband's redoubtable mother, Sara Delano Roosevelt, and agreed to stay married.

Three years after she had discovered her husband's infidelity, his terribly crippling attack of polio made inevitable a further confrontation in her own mind between her faith and her actions. As she helped him to return to an active political life, her dedication and generosity were related to the teachings of Jesus. But at that stage of her life, they were perhaps more the products of her perception of duty than of love.

Two people she met in the 1920s and 1930s rather profoundly affected her. One of these was the bodyguard whom her husband assigned to her when he became governor of New York in 1929. The other was the news reporter who covered her when her husband was campaigning for the presidency in 1932. The first of these, Earl Miller,* a lusty and direct person, saw through her politesse and engaged her as a woman. The second of these, Lorena Hickok,* a very gifted news reporter and the abused daughter of a heavy-drinking midwestern butter-maker, got through ER's defenses to form an intense relationship.

ER established bonds with her bodyguard and her reporter that elicited from within her an intense, intimate emotionality, after it had been nearly destroyed by her Victorian and very human reaction to her husband's faithlessness. Both intimate friends succeeded in making it clear by their interaction that, even though they were not New York aristocrats, they were very real human beings. She began to identify with people outside her aristocratic origins, not as plebeian unfortunates who were deserving objects of her aristocratic grace and kindness but as human beings.

One of the many results was that ER's religious beliefs became steadily closer to her practices: people became individuals to interact with rather than objects to act upon. Christianity for her was no longer a class-based religion admonishing aristocrats to be benign: it was a set of beliefs and values that facilitated her daily life.

Her intensive work in the United Nations,* notably on the Universal Declaration of Human Rights,* and her worldwide travels* served to establish human bonds that were not limited by differences in race, religion, or ideology. She remained a regular churchgoing Episcopalian, but she integrated her Christianity with actions that were at once consistent with it and with her identification with all people as human beings.

SELECTED BIBLIOGRAPHY
Cook, Blanche Wiesen. *Eleanor Roosevelt*. Vols. 1, 2. 1992 and 1999.
Goodwin, Doris Kearns. *No Ordinary Time*. 1994.
Lash, Joseph P. *Eleanor and Franklin*. 1971.
————. *Eleanor: The Years Alone*. 1972.
Roosevelt, Eleanor. *The Autobiography of Eleanor Roosevelt*. 1960.
Scharf, Lois. *Eleanor Roosevelt: First Lady of American Liberalism*. 1987.

James Chowning Davies

REUTHER, WALTER PHILIP (1 September 1907, Wheeling, WV–9 May 1970, Pellston, MI).

To Eleanor Roosevelt, Walter Reuther, president of the United Automobile Workers (UAW) from 1946 to 1970, embodied all that was progressive and exciting in American unionism and in labor*-liberal politics. They developed not only an effective political partnership but a friendship that lasted more than twenty years. Since she passed on his views to her husband, Franklin D. Roosevelt,* Reuther called her "my secret weapon," once commenting, "Every time I had an idea, good or otherwise, I always talked to her" (Cormier and Eaton, 211).

Reuther first came to ER's attention during the months before Pearl Harbor, when, as a rising leader in the UAW, he sought a voice for organized labor in the wartime agencies dealing with defense production. ER championed, within the White House and at the Office of Production Management, Reuther's plan for "500 Planes a Day," to be manufactured in converted auto factories of the Midwest (Lichtenstein, 154). Like many liberals, ER was skeptical of business control of the war production effort; with Reuther, she favored labor's participation, along with business executives and government officials, in the management of America's wartime economy. She supported Reuther's proposal, ultimately unsuccessful, for "equality of sacrifice," which included a $25,000 cap on executive salaries; in her "My Day"* column, she called it "a constructive suggestion showing that someone is doing some thinking" (Cormier and Eaton, 200).

With his boyish enthusiasm, flair for publicity, and growing influence in the labor movement, Reuther held ER's interest. Trained as a tool-and-die maker, he had been hired at the Ford River Rouge automobile plant just outside Detroit in 1927. After travel through Europe in 1933 followed by work at a Soviet auto plant for two more years, he had returned to "New Deal"* America, where he was a founder of the UAW in 1935 and participated in sit-down strikes in the auto industry.

As American victory in World War II* neared, Reuther's attention turned to postwar economic development and the conversion of war plants to civilian production. ER shared this interest and fought for Reuther's inclusion in the government's postwar economic planning councils, praising him to FDR's advisers as "this rather intelligent labor leader" (Lash, 701). In the long UAW strike against General Motors (GM) in 1946, the year Reuther was elected president of the million-member union, ER, along with Henry R. Luce, Harold Ickes,* and Henry Morgenthau Jr., supported the UAW, which sought wage increases without a boost in GM car prices. She became a leading member of a citizens' committee to assist families of union members.

During the post–World War II years, Reuther and ER continued to support many of the same foreign and domestic policy issues. In Cold War* foreign affairs, they defined a liberal anticommunism that nevertheless sought to moderate American–Soviet tensions. They helped found the Americans for Democratic Action* (ADA) and led the fight against Progressive Party candidate Henry Wallace,* who held the support of some liberals as well as the Communist Party. In the 1950s ER and Reuther both strongly supported the United Nations,* defended the nonaligned neutralism of Jawaharal Nehru, prime minister of India,* and criticized the foreign policies of John Foster Dulles,* secretary of state under President Dwight D. Eisenhower.* In 1953 Reuther became president of the Congress of Industrial Organizations (CIO). After it merged with the American Federation of Labor (AFL) in 1955, as an influential AFL-CIO vice president, he battled to expand the scope of collective bargaining and tilt the Democratic Party* toward a more consistent liberalism.

With the labor movement at its zenith during the 1950s and 1960s, ER saw progressive unionists like Reuther as key allies in the construction of a socially liberal and racially egalitarian Democratic Party. ER and Reuther both served on the board of the National Association for the Advancement of Colored People* (NAACP), both supported the presidential campaigns of Adlai Stevenson* in 1952 and 1956, and both criticized Eisenhower's domestic policies. Reuther, however, was an early supporter of John F. Kennedy* for the Democratic presidential nomination in 1960, while ER offered JFK only a lukewarm endorsement.

Pleasant contacts underlay this political alliance—with ER inviting Reuther and his family for annual visits to Hyde Park,* New York, until her death in 1962. Reuther commented, "Mrs. Roosevelt and I became really very, very close and warm friends" (Cormier and Eaton, 211). The political and personal aspects of their relationship tellingly merged in ER's and Reuther's annual meeting to exchange newspaper clippings of the most hostile attacks from their critics during the past year.

SELECTED BIBLIOGRAPHY
Cormier, Frank, and William J. Eaton. *Reuther*. 1970.
Lash, Joseph. *Eleanor and Franklin*. 1971.
Lichtenstein, David. *The Most Dangerous Man in Detroit*. 1995.

William J. Eaton

ROBINSON, CORINNE ROOSEVELT (27 September 1861, New York–17 February 1933, New York).

Youngest of four children born to Theodore Sr. and Martha Bulloch Roosevelt, Corinne, the aunt of Eleanor Roosevelt, married a Scottish-born businessman Douglas Robinson in 1882. Robinson owned a large tract near Abingdon, Virginia, where Elliott Roosevelt,* Corinne's brother and ER's alcoholic father, was sent by the Roosevelt family in 1892 in hopes of his rehabilitation.

The Robinsons, who were Republicans, had four children, two of whom became active in government. The eldest, Theodore Douglas Robinson, served in the New York state legislature and as assistant secretary of the navy; daughter Corinne Robinson Alsop* was both a political wife and a legislator herself, serving two terms in the Connecticut state legislature. Joe Alsop* and Stewart Alsop, two of her sons, became syndicated columnists, and a third son, John, was credited with originating the term "egghead," a slang term for an intellectual that was used against Adlai Stevenson,* Democratic candidate for president in 1952.

Corinne began writing poetry as a child. In her mid-forties, she submitted poems to magazines under an assumed name so as to conceal her relationship with her other brother, Theodore Roosevelt,* then president of the United States. When they were accepted, she acknowledged authorship. These and other poems were later collected in five volumes: *Call of Brotherhood* (1912); *One Woman to Another* (1914); *Service and Sacrifice* (1919); *Poems of Corinne Roosevelt Robinson* (1921); *Out of Nymph* (1930). Her book, *My Brother Theodore Roosevelt*, and her articles on subjects ranging from politics to divorce and art appeared well before ER ventured into print.

Corinne became a good friend of Republican senator Henry Cabot Lodge and took enthusiastic part in derailing Woodrow Wilson's plan for U.S. participation in the League of Nations.* In 1920 Corinne seconded the nomination of Leonard Wood at the Republican convention in Chicago, becoming the first woman to give a nomination speech at a major party convention. Her activities were among the family influences* stimulating ER to pursue her own career.

SELECTED BIBLIOGRAPHY
Caroli, Betty Boyd. *The Roosevelt Women*. 1998.
Robinson, Corinne Roosevelt. *My Brother Theodore Roosevelt*. 1921.

Betty Boyd Caroli

ROOSEVELT, ANNA HALL (17 March 1863, New York–7 December 1892, New York).

Anna Hall Roosevelt, mother of Eleanor Roosevelt, was a New York socialite whose life reveals the imperatives and weaknesses of conventional society in Victorian America. On her mother's side Anna was a Livingston, descended from land-rich colonial grandees who had ruled the Hudson River Valley like feudal barons. Her ancestors signed the Declaration of Independence and administered the oath of office to President George Washington. Anna's upbringing was characterized by tradition and supervision. Every morning and evening the family prayed together, and on Sunday afternoons they sang hymns. Her father, Valentine Hall, required Anna to take daily walks with her shoulders held back by a stick in the crook of her arms. When she entered society, Anna was frequently praised for her upright bearing. The training in posture could be enlarged into a lesson on life: success came through self-discipline.

In 1881, when she met Elliott Roosevelt,* Anna was one of the most popular debutantes in New York, admired for her beauty and charm. Elliott was a dashing young man, recently home from a world tour. He courted her with bouquets bearing the message, "Even the flowers are happier at being your servants" (ER to AH, n.d.). They soon fell in love. In a letter redolent of her character she wrote him, "All my love and ambition are now centered in you and my objects in life are to keep and be worthy of your love, to aid you in the advance of all your projects in life, and to lead myself and aid you in leading a life worthy of God's children" (Roosevelt, 148–50).

Anna and Elliott were married on 1 December 1883 at New York's Calvary Church. A reporter would call this "one of the most brilliant social events of the season" (Lash, 20). After a brief honeymoon the couple settled into a brownstone house in mid-Manhattan. Theirs was one of many fine houses clustered around Fifth and Madison Avenues between Washington Square and Central Park. In these houses and in larger mansions built by business tycoons lived the elegant members of an increasingly select New York society. Elliott and Anna enjoyed the fruits of $15,000 per year from inherited wealth. This income provided a fine house well staffed with servants, imported dresses for Anna, and polo ponies for Elliott.

The Roosevelts became leaders in the young social set known as the "swells." Anna quickly established herself as one of society's most admired ornaments. Her "presence was a blessing," one friend declared. "She never entered a room as others did—she seemed almost to float forward with upraised hand in cordial greeting" ("Three Friends," 12, 15–17). Her smile was described as "the sweetest play of light upon the features . . . an expression of sweetness and of sympathy sometimes so intense that one knew it was never to be forgotten" ("Three Friends," 21–22).

Anna bore three children: Eleanor in 1884, Elliott Jr. (known as "Ellie") in 1889, and Hall in 1891. Like other parents of their social class, the Roosevelts left much of the raising of their children to servants, but they were devoted parents. Eleanor became a little girl with light brown hair cut straight across her forehead and rolling in long waves to her shoulders. Her large blue eyes were quizzical and alert. As she grew older, she worshiped her mother but was somewhat awkward with her.

Anna Roosevelt grew to be an ideal Victorian wife. Her friends said of her: "She ever strove to be faithful to God," and "She grew into lovely and noble womanhood" ("Three Friends," 7). She fitted the mold of Victorian respectability. But unfortunately, Elliott did not. After a few years of marriage, Anna Roosevelt faced a problem for which her upbringing had not prepared her—the psychological and moral collapse of her husband. Elliott had always been uncomfortable in the world of commerce, but he tormented himself with his failure to be a successful businessman. To this weakness was added the impact of drugs: he injured his ankle while practicing for an amateur circus and took morphine and laudanum to ease the pain, became addicted, and also drank heavily. In December 1889 he abruptly left the family, ostensibly to seek a rest cure in the South. Anna wrote him, "Dearest, Throw your horrid cocktails away and don't touch anything hard. . . . Remember that your little wife and children love you so tenderly and will try to help you in every possible way in the hard fight" (AHR to ER, n.d.).

Elliott did come home to Anna that winter, but soon indulged in one more temptation. He had an affair with one of the household servants, Katy Mann. Elliott was in Europe when Katy Mann gave birth to an illegitimate child; his brother Theodore Roosevelt* visited the infant and recognized an unwanted nephew. Elliott's dissipations continued in Europe, and at Theodore's urging Anna agreed that he should be separated from his family. Reluctantly, Elliott went to Virginia to work to try to redeem himself. In the meantime, Anna and the children stayed in New York.

Anna had not wanted to give Elliott up, but once she and her husband were separated, she became more conscious of having been wronged. She was now a woman living alone in a society where almost all her peers were married. How should she behave? Could she give dinner parties without Elliott? Should she accept invitations to go driving with men? She felt "desperately lonely and wildly furious" at the circumstances that robbed her of the fun of youth (Lash, 40).

At home with her children she still had a conventional role to play. Every morning the children, even baby Hall, came into Anna's room for prayers before breakfast. Anna's relationship with her little girl was in some respects more formal than warm. Eleanor received the impression that she had disappointed her mother by failing to be suitably beautiful. In later years ER portrayed her mother as sometimes insensitive and remote, a cold person who embarrassed her daughter by referring to her in company as shy and solemn. As a child, she apparently felt left out of an intimate circle that seemed to revolve around her mother and her two brothers. Whether she really was overlooked or was simply experiencing an older child's normal jealousy of two younger siblings is hard to gauge.

A friend left an account of an afternoon's visit to Anna that provides an indelible image of a Victorian mother at home—and suggests that her daughter was hardly ignored. Anna was seated at the tea table in a cozy upstairs room. The sun had just set, and the curtains were drawn. A wood fire burned brightly on the hearth, the gas lamps were lighted, and the silver teakettle steamed. Anna wore a pink silk wrapper with white lace. The two women sat near the fire, and "a sense of rest, of womanly refinement, of sympathetic intelligence, pervaded the room," as they met to discuss a course of studies for the winter. "Why we must know about the moon, and all the recent discoveries in the planets!" Anna exclaimed. "I must know all this for my children's sake at least" (Youngs, 40).

While Anna and her friend were talking, the children ran in for a visit with their mother. Anna kissed her three-year-old, Ellie, and placed young Hall in her lap; she brought a footstool for Eleanor and gave each child a biscuit. This was the hour that she wanted the children to remember as "mother's hour." The visitor remembered Anna that evening as "sweet and loving and playful" (Youngs, 41). She left Anna a copy of Horace Bushnell's *Christian Nurture*, a highly respected treatise on child raising. Anna began reading that night and came to cherish the book, which contains passages such as this: "The Christian life and spirit of the parents, which are in and by the spirit of God, shall flow into the mind of the child" (Bushnell, 22).

Separated from her husband, Anna Roosevelt sought to inculcate in her children a sense of what she and her companions referred to as "the Right." But the terrible toll on her of her husband's downfall was apparent a few weeks later, when she went into the hospital for an operation. Under ether she revealed things she had never admitted before: Elliott had made her utterly miserable and she had nothing to live for. Following the operation she contracted diphtheria, and on 7 December 1892 Anna died.

Soon afterward several of her friends published a collection of their memories of Anna Roosevelt. The friend who had joined Anna a few months before by the fireside remembered her last glimpse of her friend that evening. As she left, she turned to see Anna at the top of the stairs, framed in the soft light of the sitting room. Eleanor stood shyly behind her mother in the doorway. "It was a home picture," the friend recalled, "with an earnest, sweet mother, rarely to be equaled, never to be excelled" (Youngs, 41). The description of that evening was undoubtedly true, but it is an incomplete picture, omitting the torment of Anna's marital life. Both serenity and turmoil were in the legacy Anna Hall Roosevelt left to her daughter, Eleanor.

SELECTED BIBLIOGRAPHY

Bushnell, Horace. *Christian Nurture*. 1871.
Eleanor Roosevelt Papers and Roosevelt Family Papers, Franklin D. Roosevelt Library, Hyde Park, NY.
Lash, Joseph P. *Eleanor and Franklin*. 1971.
Roosevelt, Eleanor, ed. *Hunting Big Game in the Eighties: The Letters of Elliott Roosevelt, Sportsman*. 1933.
"Three Friends." *In Loving Memory of Anna Hall Roosevelt*. 1893.
Youngs, J. William T. *Eleanor Roosevelt: A Personal and Public Life*. 1985.

J. William T. Youngs

ROOSEVELT, ELLIOTT (father) (28 February 1860, New York–14 August 1894, New York).

Eleanor Roosevelt's relationship with her father, Elliott Roosevelt, was as close as circumstances would allow. ER's writings attest to the uncritical love she bore her father. Elliott's sicknesses—perhaps epilepsy, probably depression, alcoholism, and drug addiction—led to a series of separations from his wife and children, and finally caused his premature death at the age of thirty-four.

The second son of Theodore Roosevelt Sr. and Martha Bulloch Roosevelt, Elliott was noted for his charm and congeniality. As a young teenager, however, he began having unaccountable spells of nervous sickness that kept him out of school. His parents sent him to Texas in hopes that an outdoor life would strengthen him. Shortly after he returned to New York City in somewhat better health, his father, to whom he had been devoted, became ill and died of cancer in 1878. A legacy of about $125,000 from his father helped Elliott indulge his growing interest in sport, society, and drink as well as occasionally patronize his father's charitable causes.

In November 1890 he embarked on a round-the-world trip that took him first to London and then to India* and Ceylon. His shipmates for the voyage to England included the newly married Sara Delano Roosevelt* and James Roosevelt of Hyde Park,* New York. He would later be the godfather for their son, Franklin D. Roosevelt,* who became ER's husband. Years later ER edited his accounts of his travels in her first book, *Hunting Big Game in the Eighties: The Letters of Elliott Roosevelt, Sportsman.*

Soon after Elliott's return in March 1982 he met Anna Rebecca Hall (Roosevelt*). They were married in New York City in 1883 and became leaders of the city's trendsetting young socialites. As the couple's three children arrived, Elliott found it increasingly difficult to adhere to the role of a stable, Victorian father, although Eleanor always remembered him as the most caring and important figure of her childhood.* She was born in 1884; Elliott, Jr.,* in 1889; and Gracie Hall Roosevelt,* in 1891.

When Anna was pregnant with Eleanor, Elliott's mother died. He turned to drink to assuage his grief, alienating Anna and beginning a deadly pattern for their marriage. In 1887 the couple traveled to Europe in an attempted reconciliation. They left Eleanor with relatives because she feared the ocean following an earlier steamship accident. The trip was a failure, and upon their return, Elliott rededicated himself to yachting, polo, and hard drinking. In 1889 Elliott suffered a broken leg, which did not heal properly and led him to use morphine, laudanum, and large quantities of alcohol to ease the pain. Depression set in. During this time, Eleanor frequently lived apart from her father.

In 1890 the family tried another trip abroad. While ER remembered wonderful times with her father in Italy, her child's eyes could not see how sick he was. She tended to blame herself for family tensions and tried harder to keep her father's affection. In Europe the family's deterioration continued. Anna took to her bed; Eleanor was sent to a convent school. The family placed an unwilling Elliott in a French asylum for

medical treatment and sailed for home. In New York his siblings negotiated a settlement with Katy Mann, a domestic worker in Elliott's household who said he fathered her son.

In 1892 Elliott, at the insistence of his brother, Theodore Roosevelt,*
committed himself to the Keeley Center for the treatment of alcoholism
in Dwight, Illinois, and then in the spring of 1892 went to work in Abingdon, Virginia, helping to develop a mining property owned by his
brother-in-law, Douglas Robinson. During this period, Theodore barred
Elliott from seeing his family. In December 1892 Anna died following an
operation, giving custody of the children to her mother, Mary Ludlow
Hall. In 1893 Elliott Jr. died.

Sunk in despair, Elliott moved in with his New York mistress. He
rarely saw Eleanor and Gracie Hall, but Eleanor lived for short visits
with her father and treasured his letters, which she kept for the rest of
her life. Spurred by Elliott's vague promises of a future life with her,
Eleanor fantasized that someday she would make a home for her father.
Elliott's childhood nickname had been Nell; he addressed her as "Little
Nell," and she signed her letters to him using that term. In 1894 Elliott
died, delusional and miserable, at his mistress' home.

In spite of Elliott's failings, ER's recollections of him were almost completely laudatory. She considered him to be the only person in her family
who really loved her. In her book of his letters, she wrote that his death
took away "all the realities of companionship which he had suggested
for the future, but . . . he lived in my dreams and does to this day" (Roosevelt, *Hunting Big Game*, 181). His behavior toward Eleanor was mostly
tender but sometimes cruel, such as the time when he left her outside
his club for hours while he drank. That she loved him so fiercely was
probably an indication of how difficult ER's childhood truly was.

SELECTED BIBLIOGRAPHY

Cook, Blanche Wiesen. *Eleanor Roosevelt*. Vol. 1. 1992.
Lash, Joseph P. *Eleanor and Franklin*. 1971.
McCullough, David. *Mornings on Horseback*. 1981.
Morris, Edmund. *The Rise of Theodore Roosevelt*. 1979.
Roosevelt, Eleanor. *This Is My Story*. 1937.
Roosevelt, Eleanor, ed. *Hunting Big Game in the Eighties: the Letters of Elliott Roo-
sevelt, Sportsman*. 1933.

Stacy A. Cordery

ROOSEVELT, ELLIOTT (son) (23 September 1910, New York–27 October 1990, Scottsdale, AZ).

Elliott Roosevelt, the second surviving son of Franklin D. Roosevelt*
and Eleanor Roosevelt, was named for ER's beloved father. A delicate
child, he was restless as an adult, moving in and out of a long series of
ventures and frequently changing his residence. Like his namesake, he
had considerable charm and a special claim on ER's affection.

The closest and most strained association between Elliott and ER came after FDR's death in 1945, when Elliott moved to Hyde Park,* New York, to became his mother's business partner. From 1946 to 1952 he lived at Top Cottage, which FDR had built for a retreat near ER's Val-Kill* residence. During this period ER helped finance a Hyde Park farming operation for Elliott on land bought from FDR's estate, gave him the rights to publish FDR's letters, and for a time allowed him to act as her agent. This arrangement ended unhappily in 1952, when Elliott moved away after selling Top Cottage and other Roosevelt land, ending most of his business connections with ER and loosening their family ties.

Prior to moving to Hyde Park, Elliott had been a source of concern to his mother. After graduation from Groton School in 1929 and a preparatory school in Princeton, New Jersey, the following year, he broke a family tradition and refused to attend college. His name, however, opened many doors. In the years before World War II,* he moved through a series of jobs, including assistant advertising account executive, aviation editor for the Hearst newspapers (political opponents of FDR), vice president and lobbyist for an aeronautical association, manager of a small airline owned by his mother's friend, Isabelle Greenway,* and vice president of a Hearst radio network in the Southwest.

In 1940 Elliott narrowly avoided a political conflict with his parents. As a member of the Texas delegation to the Democratic National Convention, Elliott was prepared to second the nomination for vice president of Jesse Jones, chairman of the Reconstruction Finance Corporation, when ER arrived at the convention on 18 July 1940 to speak in favor of Henry Wallace,* whom FDR insisted should be his running mate. It was James Farley,* chairman of the Democratic National Committee, who convinced Elliott not to participate in the nomination of Jones.

Soon Elliott enlisted in the U.S. Army and in a short time was commissioned a captain in the Army Air Force. His appointment as an officer generated charges of favoritism, although he became a decorated pilot, flying various combat missions during World War II and receiving the rank of brigadier general in 1945. Nevertheless, an episode in which an enlisted man was bumped off a plane to make room for Elliott's dog generated unfavorable publicity.

Elliott was present with FDR at several wartime meetings, including the Tehran Conference in 1943 with Winston Churchill* and Joseph Stalin. In 1946, the year he moved to Hyde Park, Elliott published a controversial book entitled *As He Saw It*, giving his interpretation of the conferences and perspective on FDR's plans for the postwar world. ER wrote an introduction for the book and defended it against those who attacked it as inaccurate. She also wrote introductions for four volumes of FDR's letters, edited by Elliott with her permission and published in 1946, 1947, and 1950.

ER initially saw Elliott's presence in Hyde Park as facilitating her desire to remain there, although her assistance to him generated some resentment among her other children. In 1947 she purchased over 800 acres of farmland, woods, and buildings from FDR's estate for $85,000 to establish Val-Kill farms in partnership with Elliott, to whom she deeded the property. He assumed responsibility for operating the farm and took over a $37,000 mortgage from her. In a letter to Trude Lash* on 10 March 1947, defending the help she was giving her children, ER said, "I surmise Elliott has to be established and encouraged & become more secure" (Lash, *A World of Love*, 232). Unfortunately, the farming venture was not profitable, leading Elliott to sell much of the property.

In 1949 Elliott began acting as ER's agent. That year he arranged with *McCall's** for serialization of the second volume of her autobiography,* *This I Remember*. The next year Elliott sold a Sunday afternoon television* show to NBC featuring his mother in an informal setting interviewing guests such as Albert Einstein and the duke and duchess of Windsor. The program, which started 12 February 1950, ran until 15 July 1951 but failed to obtain a commercial sponsor. Elliott also contracted with WNBC for ER to host a daily radio* program of forty-five minutes at midday. It ran from her birthday, 11 October 1950, to 31 August 1951, when it also was discontinued for lack of sponsorship. Elliott coproduced the show and served as its announcer but drew criticism for using his mother's name in commercials.

ER generally ignored criticism of Elliott, but she was hurt by his sale of Top Cottage without her knowledge prior to his departure from Hyde Park in 1952. By that time ER's youngest son, John Roosevelt,* had moved into Stone Cottage, which was next door to her Val-Kill cottage, and friction had developed between the two brothers. ER made a final, unsuccessful effort to patch things up, writing Elliott, "I've always loved you dearly, wanted you near and been proud of the fine things you have done. . . . You have weaknesses and I know them, but I never loved you less because I understand so well" (Roosevelt and Brough, 202).

During the next four decades, Elliott engaged in numerous activities. He raised Arabian horses in Portugal, served as mayor of Miami Beach, Florida, from 1965 to 1969, and collaborated with James Brough on three books about his parents. The first, *An Untold Story*, covering the period 1916–1932, offered Elliott's view of his parents' relationship and his father's extramarital interests, presenting FDR as a dominant figure and his mother as a fault-finding introvert. Elliott's book, which was published in 1973, generated further conflict with his sister and brothers, who immediately disavowed it. Nevertheless, Elliott and Brough continued the series, publishing *A Rendezvous with Destiny* (1975) about FDR and ER during the White House years, and *Mother R.* (1977), on ER's post–White House activities. In his final years, Elliott portrayed his mother as an amateur detective in mystery novels. Eight such books were published under his name between 1984 and his death in 1990, and several more appeared after his death.

Elliott's varied professional career was matched by an unsettled personal life. He was married five times: to Elizabeth Browning Donner, a steel heiress, in 1931 (divorced 1933), with whom he had one child, William Donner; to Ruth Josephine Googins, a Texas socialite, in 1933 (divorced 1944), with whom he had three children, Ruth Chandler, Elliott Jr., and David Boynton; to Faye Emerson, a well-known actress, in 1944 (divorced 1950); to Minnewa Bell, an oil heiress, in 1951 (divorced 1960); and to Patricia Peabody Whitehead, a real estate agent, in 1960, whose four children he adopted.

SELECTED BIBLIOGRAPHY
Collier, Peter, and David Horowitz. *The Roosevelts*. 1984.
Lash, Joseph P. *Eleanor and Franklin*. 1971.
———. *Eleanor: The Years Alone*. 1972.
———. *A World of Love*. 1984.
Roosevelt, Elliott, and James Brough. *Mother R*. 1977.
Roosevelt, Patricia Peabody. *I Love a Roosevelt*. 1967.

Leonard Schlup

ROOSEVELT, FRANKLIN DELANO (30 January 1882, Hyde Park, NY– 12 April 1945, Warm Springs, GA).

The upbringing of Franklin D. Roosevelt, husband of Eleanor Roosevelt and four times president of the United States, was as tranquil and secure as ER's was turbulent and insecure. His father was James Roosevelt, a sometime-attorney and full-time country gentleman, twenty-six years older than his second wife, Franklin's mother. She was Sara Delano Roosevelt,* regal, supremely self-assured, and single-mindedly devoted to her only child, whom she insisted be the center of the universe at Springwood, the family's estate at Hyde Park,* New York. He was deferred to as "Master Franklin" by his father's tenants, educated by nurses and tutors, dressed and bathed by his mother until at least the age of eight.

He was taught by his parents to be stoical and avoid unpleasantness, to consider as his duty helping those less fortunate than he, and to believe that he could succeed at anything to which he put his hand. But he also learned from his mother's fond, but often overbearing, interest in the most minute details of his life the uses of charm and misdirection to get what he wanted and the necessity of keeping his own emotional counsel. All these lessons would affect his political career—and his marriage to ER. He attended Groton School (1896–1900), then went on to Harvard University. His father died during his first year in college, and his bereft mother turned to her son for solace, further strengthening the

Eleanor and Franklin D. Roosevelt sit in the president's study in the White House in 1933 during FDR's first presidential year. *Courtesy of Franklin D. Roosevelt Library*

bond between them. In his second year at Harvard, FDR secretly proposed marriage to Alice Sohier, a beautiful Boston heiress, who turned him down. Five weeks later, without his mother's knowledge, he began to court his distant cousin, ER. He was drawn to her serious, sympathetic nature. She seemed far more substantive than the other young women he knew—and she was the niece of the man he admired most in the world, his distant kinsman, Theodore Roosevelt.* FDR was an ebullient, attentive suitor and deeply smitten: "E. Is an Angel" (Ward, *Before the Trumpet*, 308), he noted in his diary, carefully disguising the entry in code so that his mother could not decipher it. His attentions overwhelmed ER at first, but she seems to have seen in him some of the same qualities her beloved father was said to have had—enormous energy, charm, gregariousness—combined with a sense of purpose she found reassuring. She was pleased when he seemed impressed with the work she was doing at the Rivington Street Settlement House on the Lower East Side: "My God," he told her after his first visit to the neighborhood. "I didn't know anyone lived like that" (Ward, *Before the Trumpet*, 319).

But she also remained fearful for the future: after they were engaged, a cousin found ER sobbing: "I shall never be able to hold him," she said. "He is so attractive" (Ward, *A First-Class Temperament*, 412).

When FDR finally confessed his love for ER to his mother in 1904, she insisted the couple wait a year to marry—her son was only twenty-one, his intended bride just eighteen. She hoped FDR's ardor would cool, but he would not be denied, and ER did her best to reassure her prospective mother-in-law that she was gaining a daughter, not losing a son. They were married on 17 March 1905. Theodore Roosevelt himself gave the bride away and congratulated FDR for "keeping the name in the family" (Ward, *Before the Trumpet*, 340).

Even when they were young and in love, the Roosevelts were very different people, with very different hopes for their marriage. FDR was self-confident and outgoing; he loved good times and had hoped for a high-spirited companion to share them with, something his serious-minded wife could never be. ER was self-conscious and shy and wished for someone with whom to share her deepest feelings, something FDR's boyhood training had made impossible for him.

For the first fifteen years of their marriage, seeing after FDR and their five children (a sixth died in infancy) and negotiating with her mother-in-law consumed most of ER's energies. FDR was an affectionate but distracted, father, fond of romping with his five children but incapable of disciplining them. He was also unable ever to decide to which of the two strong women in his life he owed his primary allegiance, a failure that made his marriage far more difficult than it might otherwise have been.

FDR was graduated from Harvard in 1906, spent two years at Columbia Law School, then went to work for a Wall Street law firm. But he yearned to try politics—already dreamed of being president one day, in fact—and when he was offered a chance to run for the state Senate as a Democrat in 1910, he jumped at it and never looked back. He served one term, was reelected in 1912, and then joined the Woodrow Wilson administration as assistant secretary of the navy. In Albany and Washington, ER's activities outside the home were largely limited to the traditional role played by an official's wife. But when the United States entered World War I in 1917, she threw her enormous energies into working for the American Red Cross.*

Then, in September 1918, ER discovered a bundle of love letters to her husband written by her own social secretary, Lucy Mercer (Rutherfurd*). They seemed to confirm her worst fears—about herself as well as FDR. Reading those letters, she would one day confide to a friend, "the bottom dropped out of my own particular world and I faced myself, my surroundings, my world, honestly for the first time" (Ward, *A First-Class Temperament*, 412).

She confronted her husband and told him she was willing to grant him a divorce if that was what he wanted. It was. But his mother threatened to disinherit him if he dared bring scandal to the family by leaving his wife and children. His political strategist, Louis Howe,* warned that divorce would end his promising political career. It took him at least two weeks to make up his mind, but he finally agreed to remain married and pledged never to see Lucy Mercer again. (Mercer eventually married an elderly widower, Winthrop Rutherfurd.)

Neither her husband's affair nor his subsequent crippling by polio drove ER to reemerge as a public figure, but the first forced her to reexamine her life, and the second would provide her with the public rationale she needed to begin to build an independent life of her own outside the home. ER once claimed to have forgiven but not forgotten her husband's transgression; in fact, she was never able to do either. From 1918 on, the Roosevelts would sleep—and for the most part live—apart; they would become hugely effective and sometimes affectionate political partners, rather than husband and wife.

On the strength of his famous name and wartime record, FDR was nominated to run for vice president of the United States on the 1920 Democratic Party* ticket headed by James Cox. Cox and FDR were soundly defeated by Warren Harding and Calvin Coolidge, but riding the candidates' campaign train across the country gave ER her first taste of national politics.

In the summer of 1921, FDR was stricken with infantile paralysis at the Roosevelt summer home on Campobello* Island. This crisis brought husband and wife back into close proximity for a time—she bravely nursed him through the first agonizing weeks—but she soon found caring for him as onerous as he found her exhortations to do his exercises. He was irritated, too, by her plainspoken realism about his condition: she told his doctor that she was "not sanguine" (Ward, *A First-Class Temperament*, 647) about his ever regaining the use of his limbs. She was right, but her bluntness threatened the buoyant optimism to which he desperately clung. He spent several months each year from 1923 through 1928 away from his wife and children, seeking unsuccessfully to strengthen his legs—aboard a yacht off Florida, at a Massachusetts seaside cottage, and in Warm Springs, Georgia, where, in the face of initial opposition from ER (who thought he was throwing his money away), he spent nearly two-thirds of his fortune to establish a center for the treatment of polio. Wherever FDR went, Marguerite "Missy" LeHand* went, too, serving as his hostess as well as his secretary, often occupying the cabin or room adjoining his. ER made no objection.

Similarly, FDR rarely interfered with his wife's hard-won autonomy. It was his idea to design and have built for her a Hyde Park home of her own at Val-Kill,* out from under his mother's watchful eye. He was invariably cordial to her friends, no matter what rumors about the supposed "unsuitability" of some of them may from time to time have reached his ears. He took genuine pride in the political and social work "My Missus" was doing on her own; besides, it kept her happily occupied and indirectly kept his name alive in the political world.

But if FDR did not personally seek to limit her independent career, she feared his political career—which resumed with his unexpected nomination for governor of New York in 1928—would derail it. As the governor's wife, she was afraid she would be reduced once again to pouring tea and seeing to seating arrangements. She campaigned hard for Alfred E. Smith,* the Democratic nominee for president, but only rarely appeared alongside FDR. "No, I am not excited about my husband's election," she told reporters after the votes were in. "I don't care. What difference can it make to me?" (Lash, 320). (She would make similar remarks about all of her husband's subsequent campaigns.) In fact, the four years she spent as the governor's wife proved a good training ground for the twelve years as First Lady that were to follow. She devised ways to pursue her own interests, both personal and political, while acting as her husband's hostess as well as his "legs and ears." She also mastered the art of the inspection tour, remembering FDR's exhortation to lift the lids on cooking pots in state institutions to check whether "the contents corresponded with the menu" (Roosevelt, 56).

Her fears of being sidelined nonetheless resurfaced when FDR ran for president in 1932. She suggested that she be given "a real job" this time, seeing to some of his mail, and was rebuffed; Missy LeHand would consider it "interfering," FDR said. "I knew he was right," she remembered, "but it was a last effort to keep in close touch and to feel that I had a real job to do" (Roosevelt, 76). With her husband's active encouragement she would take on a thousand unpaid real jobs over the next dozen years, of course, transforming the role of the president's wife in the process. She was a tireless public advocate of her husband's programs when she believed them right and a no less tireless private critic when she thought them misguided or too timid. "No one who ever saw Eleanor Roosevelt sit down facing her husband, and, holding his eyes firmly, say to him, 'Franklin, I think you should' . . . or 'Franklin, surely you will not' . . . will ever forget the experience" (Lash, 457–458), wrote Rexford Tugwell.*

The Roosevelt partnership was complex. Each was fiercely proud of the other's achievements—and each was sometimes irritated by elements of the other's personality. Political and personal differences between the Roosevelts caused there to assemble around them two rival groups of intimates. ER's closest friends, echoing her own private frustrations, deplored FDR's sometimes unsteady views, his reluctance to champion causes he believed lost, his fondness for being surrounded by admiring women. The president's closest aides, in turn, were put off by what they saw as his wife's unrelenting earnestness, by her reluctance to compromise, and, above all, toward the end of his life, by her seeming inability to see how exhausted he was, how badly he needed simply to rest.

"He might have been happier with a wife who was completely uncritical," ER admitted later. "That I was never able to be, and he had to find it in other people" (Roosevelt, 349). Over the years, those other people would include Marguerite LeHand, his distant cousin, Margaret Suckley,* Crown Princess Martha of Norway, his own daughter, Anna Roosevelt (Halsted*), and—toward the end of his life—Lucy Mercer (Rutherfurd) again.

The presence of Rutherfurd at Warm Springs at the time of FDR's fatal cerebral hemorrhage was deeply wounding to ER, a betrayal of her husband's long-ago pledge never again to see his onetime lover. His death, therefore, left her with an "almost impersonal feeling," she wrote, in part, because "much further back I had to face certain difficulties until I decided I had to accept the fact that a man must be what he is, life must be lived as it is . . . and you cannot live at all if you do not learn to adapt yourself to your life as it happens to be" (Roosevelt, 348–349). Yet despite this wound that never closed, ER never ceased to be proud of the great things she and her husband had done together. She would resolutely remain "Mrs. Roosevelt" to the end of her long life, often crediting him with good works her persistence alone had encouraged him to undertake.

SELECTED BIBLIOGRAPHY

Burns, James MacGregor. *Roosevelt: The Lion and the Fox*. 1956.
Davis, Kenneth S. *FDR*. Vols. I, 2, 3, 4. 1972–1993.
Lash, Joseph P. *Eleanor and Franklin*. 1971.
Roosevelt, Eleanor. *This I Remember*. 1949.
Ward, Geoffrey C. *Before the Trumpet: Young Franklin Roosevelt*. 1985.
———. *A First-Class Temperament: The Emergence of Franklin Roosevelt*. 1989.

Geoffrey C. Ward

ROOSEVELT, FRANKLIN D., JR. (17 August 1914, Campobello Island, Canada–17 August 1988, Poughkeepsie, NY).

Franklin D. Roosevelt Jr., the fifth child born to Eleanor and Franklin D. Roosevelt,* was a lawyer and businessmen who served in the U.S. Congress,* held posts in the John F. Kennedy* and Lyndon B. Johnson administrations, and ran twice for governor of New York. Bearing a striking resemblance to his father, he sought with limited success to make his mark in public life.

Following an illustrious navy career in World War II,* Franklin was elected in 1949 to the first of three terms in Congress from New York, defeating a Tammany Hall Democrat to represent Manhattan's Upper

West Side. In spite of a record of poor attendance in Congress, he clearly had the inside track for New York's Democratic Party* gubernatorial nomination in 1954. But Carmine De Sapio and the Tammany Hall organization, which thought Roosevelt too independent, denied him what had seemed certain party endorsement for a governorship thought to be a stepping-stone to the White House, choosing to back Averell Harriman* instead.

ER, her son's strong political ally, never forgave De Sapio and actively worked in the New York City reform movement,* which led to the demise of Tammany and de Sapio's leadership. Deprived of the nomination, Franklin ran for attorney general but was defeated by Republican Jacob Javits. In 1966 he made a surprising last bid for elective office by unsuccessfully running for governor on the Liberal Party ticket.

Keeping with family tradition, Franklin attended the Groton School and Harvard University. In one of the year's most notable weddings, in 1937 he married Ethel du Pont, whose family despised the New Deal* and financed its opponents. He then went to the University of Virginia Law School, where he received a law degree in 1940.

Rising to the rank of lieutenant commander in World War II,* he was stationed on destroyers and won the Navy Cross, Legion of Merit, Purple Heart, and a Commendation Medal. Following the war, he practiced law in New York City and was elected vice-chairman of the Americans for Democratic Action,* a liberal, noncommunist group that ER helped found.

After 1954 Franklin buried his political frustrations and entered the business world, becoming a principal importer of Fiat and Jaguar automobiles into the United States and later going into banking. At the time of his death he was chairman of the Mickelberry Corporation, a holding company, and of the Park Avenue Bank. He also bred cattle at his showplace Clove Creek Farm located, like Hyde Park,* in Dutchess County, New York. Residents of the area recall that he provided ER with little two-seat convertibles in which she took trips with her rotund driver, Charles "Tubby" Curran, at the wheel.

In common with other family members, Franklin joined in political discussions at ER's Val-Kill* cottage that were lively, loud, and sometimes acrimonious, with ER placed in an uncomfortable role of mediator. Yet, Franklin admired his mother's achievements and had encouraged her to accept her appointment from President Harry S Truman* as a U.S. delegate to the United Nations.*

Unlike ER, who supported Adlai Stevenson,* Franklin was an early backer of Kennedy for the 1960 Democratic presidential nomination. He campaigned tirelessly for Kennedy in the crucial West Virginia primary, where voters' reverence for both FDR and ER helped Kennedy win. Roosevelt subsequently was named undersecretary of commerce and frequently visited the White House. Under President Lyndon B. Johnson, he was named the first chairman of the Equal Employment Opportunity Commission.

As chairman of the executive committee of the Franklin and Eleanor Roosevelt Institute, Franklin, who was ER's literary executor, furthered causes in which his parents believed. He also was involved in the development of the Roosevelt Campobello International Park.

His marriage to Ethel du Pont, by whom he had two sons, Franklin D. Roosevelt III and Christopher du Pont Roosevelt, ended in divorce in 1949. In 1949 he wed Suzanne Perrin, who shared his interest in farming. They had two daughters, Nancy Suzanne Roosevelt Ireland and Laura Delano Roosevelt, and divorced in 1970. That year he married Felicia Warburg Sarnoff, the former wife of Robert Sarnoff, head of Radio Corporation of America; they divorced in 1976. In a horseback ceremony in 1977 he married Patricia Louise Oakes, by whom he had a son, John Alexander Roosevelt; they divorced in 1980. His final marriage was to Linda Stevenson Weicker in 1984.

SELECTED BIBLIOGRAPHY

Collier, Peter, with David Horowitz. *The Roosevelts: An American Saga*. 1994.
Lash, Joseph P. *Eleanor: The Years Alone*. 1972.
———. *A Friend's Memoir*. 1964.

Donald R. Larrabee

ROOSEVELT, GRACIE HALL (28 July 1891, Paris, France–25 September 1941, Washington, DC).

G. Hall Roosevelt, the brother of Eleanor Roosevelt and nephew of President Theodore Roosevelt,* was seven years younger than his sister. Hall and ER were the children of Elliott Roosevelt,* Theodore's brother, and Anna Hall Roosevelt.* In 1892, when Eleanor was eight years old, and Hall was two, their mother died of diphtheria, and in 1894 their father died. The two children went to live with Grandmother Hall. Before he died, Elliott Roosevelt exhorted Eleanor to take care of her brother, Hall. Eleanor took her adored father's request seriously and from that day until the day he died, she undertook to be Hall's family for him. In 1905, when Franklin D. Roosevelt* and ER were married, Hall was invited to live with them.

After elementary school in New York City, Hall went to the Groton School in Massachusetts. From Groton he went on to Harvard University, where he earned a bachelor's degree in three years and a Phi Beta Kappa key followed by a master's degree in engineering.

In 1912 Hall married Margaret Richardson of Boston. ER was delighted that her brother would now have a home of his own to make up for his lonely childhood. In 1917 he joined the newly organized U.S. Air Force and was a flying instructor in Florida during World War I. For fifteen years, interrupted by his military service, he worked for General Electric in Schenectady, New York, and other cities. Hall and Margaret had three children, Henry Parish, Daniel Stewart, and Eleanor, but Hall was unhappy and eager to get a divorce. ER was finally persuaded to accept his decision, although divorce was anathema in the society of those days.

In 1925 Hall married Dorothy Kemp of Detroit and moved to that city, where in 1929 he became vice president of the Detroit United Railways. During the Great Depression,* Frank Murphy, mayor of Detroit (later U.S. Supreme Court justice) appointed Hall city controller (a post in which he sought bank credit for the city) as well as chairman of the Detroit Unemployment Bureau. Hall was a bright and energetic organizer and innovator, but Murphy eventually found him too headstrong and too socialistic in his views. Hall was dismissed.

He returned to New York state. He divorced his wife in 1937, leaving her with their three small daughters, Amelia, Diana and Janet. By then he was a confirmed alcoholic and unable to hold a job, although he attempted to work as a consulting engineer and banker. ER tried to invent work for him to do. He wrote the story of the first Roosevelts to come to this country, *Odyssey of an American Family.*

During the last years of his life, ER put him up in a small outbuilding on the Roosevelt estate at Hyde Park.* Hall was devastated by the untimely death of his favorite child, Danny, in an airplane crash in 1939, and his health deteriorated. In September 1941 he was taken to Walter Reed Hospital, where he died of cirrhosis of the liver. His funeral was held at the White House.

ER had mixed feelings about her brother. As a young child, he was a favorite with older people, while she stood by, feeling shy and awkward, but her father's request was sacred to her. All his life Hall went to her with his problems. He knew he could count on her support, and he respected her. If he ever loved anyone, it was ER, even though he knew he often disappointed her. She deplored his drinking but envied his ease in social situations. She felt she had failed him, that it was somehow her fault he was addicted to drink. It was a deep sorrow and frustration to her because he had been a brilliant young man. When he died, ER had yet one more reason to turn to her own work in an effort to ease the ache in her heart.

SELECTED BIBLIOGRAPHY
Cook, Blanche. *Eleanor Roosevelt*. Vol. 2. 1999.
Lash, Joseph P. *Eleanor and Franklin*. 1971.
Roosevelt, Hall, with Samuel D. McCoy. *Odyssey of an American Family*. 1939.

Eleanor Roosevelt

ROOSEVELT, JAMES (23 December 1907, New York–13 August 1991, Newport Beach, CA).

Eleanor Roosevelt's second child, James, a war hero, U.S. representative, and delegate to the United Nations* whose business dealings sometimes caused controversy, was named after his paternal grandfather. An illness-prone child, he and his siblings were raised, as was the custom in their social circle, by a succession of governesses—at least one of whom physically and psychologically tormented the children. ER generally deferred to the governesses and Sara Delano Roosevelt,* her mother-in-law, in child-raising decisions, lacking the confidence to do otherwise. In later years Roosevelt blamed his mother's inattention for his early bouts with pneumonia and his premature baldness. After attending Groton School, he graduated from Harvard University in 1930 and became a successful insurance broker in Boston.

Active in his father's political career, Roosevelt managed the 1932 presidential campaign of Franklin D. Roosevelt* in Massachusetts. He often was pictured beside FDR; he helped his father stand and give the appearance of walking. In 1937 Roosevelt resigned from his insurance firm, Roosevelt and Sargent, becoming first an assistant and then secretary to the president.

He took the post over the objections of ER, who anticipated, correctly, that both men would face criticism from opponents in Congress and the press on grounds of use of political connections to further James' business interests. Although these allegations were never proven, Roosevelt quit the post in 1938 after recuperating from surgery for stress-related ulcers. His first marriage failed to survive the White House, where tension arose between his attractive wife, Betsey, who was a favorite of FDR, and ER, who thought her daughter-in-law tried to usurp the First Lady's role. Still, FDR regularly depended on his eldest son for emotional and physical support.

Subsequently, James was a motion picture executive in Hollywood before appointment as a captain in the U.S. Marines in 1940. He sponsored the American release of an English anti-Nazi film, for which he persuaded his mother to read the prologue, and produced one film of his own. Serving in the Pacific during World War II,* he won both the Navy Cross and the Silver Star and was promoted to colonel. His mother's newspaper column, "My Day,"* mentioned him more during that period than during any other, perhaps partly as a means of helping other mothers endure—and support—the war effort. After the war he returned to the West Coast and resumed his insurance business. He continued in the Marine Corps reserve, becoming a brigadier general.

The domestic lives of "Jimmy"—as his mother always referred to him, even in print—and all of his siblings frequently troubled ER, although she rarely intruded (in later years, she did financially help some of the children, including James). He was married four times: to Betsey Cushing, daughter of a well-known surgeon, in 1930 (divorced 1940), with whom he had two children, Sara Delano and Kate; to Romelle Schneider, who had been his nurse, in 1941, with whom he had three children, James Jr., Michael Anthony, and Anna Eleanor (divorced 1955); to Irene Owens, his former receptionist, with whom he adopted a son, Hall Delano, in 1956 (divorced 1969); and to Mary Lena Winskill, former teacher of his son Hall, in 1969, with whom he had a daughter, Rebecca Mary.

Roosevelt's support of Dwight D. Eisenhower* for the Democratic 1948 presidential nomination probably cost him the endorsement of President Harry S Truman* when he unsuccessfully ran for California governor in 1950. In response, angry at Truman, ER considered resigning from the United Nations (UN). In 1954 Roosevelt won the first of his six terms in Congress. He and ER usually agreed politically, but not always: ER supported Adlai Stevenson* for president in 1952, 1956, and 1960, but Roosevelt supported Estes Kefauver in 1956 and was an early backer of John F. Kennedy* in 1960.

After an unsuccessful Los Angeles mayoral bid, Roosevelt left Congress in 1965 to become U.S. delegate to the UN Economic and Social Council. Financial problems led him to resign in 1966 to join a troubled international firm—Investors Overseas Services, where his associates included Robert Vesco, against whom criminal charges were brought; Roosevelt was not implicated. His third wife, Irene, who was unhappy living in Geneva, where the firm was located, stabbed him in a 1969 dispute that drew international attention.

Roosevelt returned to California, where he became one of the leaders of "Democrats for Nixon" in 1972. He endorsed the Democratic candidate, Jimmy Carter, for president in 1976 but backed Republican Ronald Reagan in 1984. He lectured at the University of California-Irvine and Chapman College, served as a business consultant, and joined the Orange County Transportation Commission. In 1983 he founded the National Committee to Preserve Social Security and Medicare, a nonprofit organization later criticized for frightening the elderly as a means of soliciting funds, partly through mailings that looked like official government documents.

Roosevelt authored three books: *Affectionately, F.D.R.* (1959), *My Parents: A Differing View* (1976), and *A Family Matter* (1979). ER offered a mixed review of the first in her "My Day" column of 19 November 1959, defending, in particular, her White House housekeeper, Henrietta Nesbitt,* whom Roosevelt had criticized. The second was kinder to both parents than—and written partly in response to—books by his brother, Elliott Roosevelt,* with whom he openly disagreed. The third combined fact and fiction in a cloak-and-dagger novel, featuring James Roosevelt as its hero. In *My Parents*, he lamented his parents' lack of closeness but was more critical of his mother's lack of warmth than of his father's extramarital affairs. He also suggested that his mother may have had an affair with Earl Miller,* her bodyguard.

SELECTED BIBLIOGRAPHY

Chadakoff, Rochelle. *Eleanor Roosevelt's "My Day."* Vol. 1. 1989.
Cook, Blanche Wiesen. *Eleanor Roosevelt.* Vol. 2. 1999.
Emblidge, David, ed. *Eleanor Roosevelt's "My Day."* Vols. 2, 3. 1990, 1991.
Parks, Lillian Roger, with Frances Spatz Leighton. *The Roosevelts: A Family in Turmoil.* 1981.
Roosevelt, James, and Sidney Shalett. *Affectionately, F.D.R.: A Son's Story of a Lonely Man.* 1959.
Roosevelt, James, with Bill Libby. *My Parents: A Differing View.* 1976.

James B. McPherson

ROOSEVELT, JOHN ASPINWALL (13 March 1916, Washington, DC– 27 April 1981, New York).

The youngest child of Eleanor Roosevelt and Franklin D. Roosevelt,* John A. Roosevelt was a businessman and a Republican in a Democratic family. Unlike his brothers, he never ran for political office. From 1952 until after ER's death in 1962, he lived with his family in Stone Cottage, adjacent to ER's Val-Kill* country home in Hyde Park,* New York.

After FDR's polio attack in 1921, ER tried to assume some of the responsibilities traditionally within a father's domain, taking John and his brother, Franklin D. Roosevelt Jr.,* on an extended summer camping trip through New England and Quebec in 1925 and a tour of Europe in 1929. John graduated from Groton School in 1934 and Harvard University in 1938. That year he married a Boston debutante, Anne Lindsay Clark. They had four children, Haven Clark, Sara Delano, Anne Sturgis (Nina), and Joan Lindsay.

John began his business career as a clerk at Filene's department store in Boston. He served in the U.S. Navy from 1941 to 1946, spending time on an aircraft carrier in the Pacific and rising to the rank of lieutenant commander. He was decorated with the Bronze Star. After he left military service, John and his family settled on the West Coast, where he was involved in several business and financial concerns, including the operation of a department store in Los Angeles.

After moving to Stone Cottage in 1952, he eventually acquired what remained of the Hyde Park property his brother Elliott Roosevelt* had operated as a farming venture in partnership with ER. Since 1946 Elliott had lived in Top Cottage, the hilltop retreat FDR had built near Val-Kill. The two brothers, however, bickered continuously, and Elliott, who had become restless at Hyde Park, left the area soon after John's arrival.

John continued to pursue various business activities, becoming a consultant to the investment firm of Bache and Company in 1956, and retiring in 1980 as a senior vice president of Bache, Halsey, Stuart, Shields, and Company. He also engaged in voluntary fund-raising for various philanthropies, including the National Foundation for Infantile Paralysis, founded by his father, and served on the Greater New York Council of the Boy Scouts of America.

After Elliott left Hyde Park, ER said she would not remain in her Val-Kill home—a center for family reunions and visiting grandchildren—if John and his family moved away. Nevertheless, there were strains and boisterous arguments at times at family gatherings. One source of tension was John's conversion in 1947 to Republicanism, which ER saw as an identification with his wife's family. In the 1952 presidential campaign he became chairman of Citizens for Eisenhower, while ER supported the Democratic candidacy of Adlai E. Stevenson.* John also defended vice presidential nominee Richard M. Nixon, whom ER distrusted.

Proximity gave John's children ready access to their grandmother. His daughter, Nina, later said that "as children we were in Grandmere's house as much as we were in the Stone Cottage" (Gibson, 10). She remembered long walks and picnics with ER, who took pleasure in recalling the memories she associated with various places in Hyde Park. In 1956 ER took John's son, Haven, and another grandson, John Boettiger, on a trip to Europe. In 1959 she took Nina to visit Turkey, Iran, Israel,* France, Italy, and England. ER also tried to help the family cope with the death of John's daughter, Sara, who was killed in a riding accident in 1960.

John and Anne Roosevelt were divorced in 1965. That same year he married Irene Boyd McAlpin, with whom he lived on an estate at Tuxedo, New York. After ER's death, John sold the Val-Kill properties in 1970. Seven years later federal legislation authorized the creation of the Eleanor Roosevelt National Historic Site at Val-Kill. Today ERVK* (the Eleanor Roosevelt Center at Val-Kill) occupies Stone Cottage.

SELECTED BIBLIOGRAPHY
Collier, Peter, with David Horowitz. *The Roosevelts.* 1994.
Cook, Blanche Wiesen. *Eleanor Roosevelt.* Vol. 1. 1992.
Eleanor Roosevelt Oral History Project, Interviews with Nina Roosevelt Gibson (1979) and Haven Roosevelt (1979), Franklin D. Roosevelt Memorial Library, Hyde Park, NY.
Goodwin, Doris Kearns. *No Ordinary Time.* 1994.
Lash, Joseph P. *Eleanor and Franklin.* 1971.
———. *A World of Love* 1984.

Leonard Schlup

ROOSEVELT, SARA DELANO (21 September 1854, Newburgh, NY–7 September 1941, Hyde Park, NY).

Sara Delano Roosevelt, the mother of Franklin Delano Roosevelt,* was,

Eleanor Roosevelt participates in a presidential visit to a battleship with Franklin D. Roosevelt, his mother, Sara Delano Roosevelt, and their oldest son, James Roosevelt, and his wife, Betsy Cushing Roosevelt, before World War II. *Courtesy of Library of Congress*

during his presidency, the nation's first dowager queen. Her stately appearance and royal manner made her the undisputed monarch of her estate at Hyde Park* on the Hudson River in New York, which became the summer White House. But by the time FDR achieved the country's highest office, her attempts to dominate his and his wife's lives had failed. Although they spent their summers with her, their lives and their work were elsewhere, out of her reach. For the mature Eleanor Roosevelt, her mother-in-law was a cross she bore with dignity; early in her married life, however, she had reacted more often with tears and silent anger.

Sara Delano Roosevelt was an authentic American aristocrat who could claim some degree of kinship with seven passengers on the *Mayflower* as well as with a French Huguenot, Phillipe de la Noye, who crossed the Atlantic only a year later on a Dutch ship. Born on 21 September 1854 at Algonac, an estate near Newburgh, New York, about twenty miles south of Hyde Park but on the opposite side of the Hudson, she was the middle child among nine brothers and sisters. Her father,

Warren Delano, like his father before him, had made his fortune in the China trade, and her mother, Catherine Lyman Delano, was the daughter of a Massachusetts judge.

Her family called her Sallie to distinguish her from the aunt for whom she was named. Like her six sisters, she was taught at home in the family mansion by tutors and governesses. While absorbing countless lessons in proper decorum, she displayed an active mind and a strong sense of duty, leavened in private by a zesty sense of humor; long afterward, when she was over eighty, she sometimes astonished Hyde Park guests by offering her own jaunty version of the sea chantey, "Blow, my bully boys, blow!," which she remembered from the clipper-ship voyage to China she had been taken on during her girlhood (Kleeman, 47).

As her sisters and brothers began making suitable marriages,* Sallie gave no sign of wishing to follow their example. With congenial friends and a wealthy father she idolized, she seemed content to remain single. Handsome, haughty, and also exceptionally tall—by the time she reached marriageable age she stood a full five feet and ten inches—it appeared less and less likely that she would ever find a husband of whom both she and her father could approve.

But as Sara approached her twenty-sixth birthday in 1880, on a visit to the family home of Theodore Roosevelt Sr., ER's paternal grandfather, in New York City, she met a distant cousin of the Roosevelts and fell in love. James Roosevelt was a whiskered widower of fifty-two; although twice Sallie's age, he was remarkably like her own father, and the pair suited each other splendidly. After their wedding on 7 October 1880, they resided at her husband's estate, Springwood, in Hyde Park. Theirs was a notably happy marriage, lasting until his death in 1900.

Their only child, FDR, was born on 30 January 1882. His mother devoted an extraordinary amount of attention to her son, keeping him at her side until he was fourteen years old and went off to Groton School. Four years later, shortly after he entered Harvard University, Sara's devotion to FDR became single-minded following the death of her husband. She rented a house in Boston so he could spend his weekends with her.

Sara was confronted by a distressing threat to her maternal sway, however, when FDR in his junior year fell in love with his fifth cousin, Eleanor Roosevelt. When told by the young couple that they wished to marry, Sara tried to make them break their engagement on the grounds that they were too young, although she insisted she had no personal objection to ER. The year's delay they reluctantly agreed upon proved only a temporary impediment; ER and FDR were married on 17 March 1905.

During the first year of their marriage, "My mother-in-law did everything for me," ER later wrote with careful restraint (Roosevelt, *This Is*

My Story, 140). When Sara rented, furnished, and staffed the couple's first New York home while they were honeymooning abroad, the twenty-year-old bride, who was completely lacking in domestic training, felt truly grateful. But within three years, after Sara had designed and built a brand-new house at 45 East Sixty-fifth Street for her son and his wife that adjoined a twin residence for her own use, the insecure ER felt helplessly oppressed by her husband's domineering mother: "You were never quite sure when she would appear, day or night" through the connecting doors, ER wrote much later (Lash, 162). Since FDR always joked away the family management ER found so burdensome, he could not understand his young wife's periodic weeping spells over her mother-in-law.

Throughout the rest of Sara's life, her indulgence of ER and FDR's five children would cause much family friction. From their infancy to their adulthood, Sara persisted in providing them with expensive presents without remembering to consult their parents beforehand; parental discipline was repeatedly undercut by her gifts of ponies or trips, then cars or apartments. As James Roosevelt,* the eldest son, put it long afterward: "Granny's ace in the hole . . . was the fact that she held the purse strings in the family" (Lash, 162).

Still, Sara's efforts to exert day-by-day control over her daughter-in-law could not continue after her son became Woodrow Wilson's assistant secretary of the navy in 1913 and moved his family to Washington. During the ensuing eight years the mature ER began emerging. Yet, the major battle between Sara and ER came when FDR, at the age of thirty-nine, was stricken with infantile paralysis in 1921.

For Sara this was an opportunity to reclaim her son. She wanted him to live as a pampered invalid in Hyde Park, puttering with his stamps, collecting ship models, and, if that were not enough, serving on local boards such as the hospital committee. This time ER fought back—and won, encouraging FDR to continue in politics. Nevertheless, Sara used her daughter-in-law's alliance with FDR's political adviser Louis Howe* to exacerbate ER's difficulties with her daughter, Anna Roosevelt (Halsted*). Granny encouraged Anna's teenage resentment at being dispossessed from her choice bedroom in the family's Manhattan home by Howe, who moved in to help FDR but who was referred to by Sara as "that ugly, dirty little man" (Lash, 274). The ensuing tension did much to make the initial months after FDR's illness the most trying winter of ER's life.

Although Sara despised politics as an unseemly occupation for a gentleman, she eventually learned to accept her son's career. By the time he ran for president in 1932, she collaborated on a campaign book about him, *My Boy Franklin*, and she graciously received his political friends at her Hyde Park home whenever he was there. As president, he preferred spending Christmas and most other holidays at the White House, so Sara would join her family there, becoming accustomed to posing regally for news photographers. She enjoyed being driven down to New York City behind an escort of motorcycle police to appear at some function as the mother of the president. She reveled in entertaining the king and queen of England at Hyde Park in 1939.

When Sara died in 1941, ER in her "My Day"* column on 7 September 1941 described her mother-in-law as "a very vital person [whose] strongest trait was loyalty to her family. . . . She was not just sweetness and light, for there was a streak of jealousy and possessiveness in her where her own were concerned." Less guardedly, in a letter to her close friend, Joseph Lash,* ER wrote: "I looked at my mother-in-law's face after she was dead & understood so many things I'd never seen before. It is dreadful to have lived so close to someone for 36 years & feel no deep affection or sense of loss. It is hard on Franklin however" (Lash 643).

SELECTED BIBLIOGRAPHY

Faber, Doris. *The Presidents' Mothers*. 1978.
Kleeman, Rita Halle. *Gracious Lady: The Life of Sara Delano Roosevelt*. 1935.
Lash, Joseph P. *Eleanor and Franklin*. 1971.
Leighton, Isabel, and Gabrielle Forbush. *My Boy Franklin as Told by Mrs. James Roosevelt*. 1933.
Roosevelt, Eleanor. *This Is My Story*. 1937.
———. *This I Remember*. 1949.

Doris Faber

ROOSEVELT, THEODORE (27 October 1858, New York–6 January 1919, Oyster Bay, NY).

Eleanor Roosevelt's only paternal uncle was Theodore Roosevelt, the twenty-sixth president of the United States and elder brother of ER's father, Elliott Roosevelt.* Theodore's relationship with his niece was somewhat distant but warm. Theodore undoubtedly influenced ER's interest in social justice. In this regard Theodore modeled himself on his father and ER's grandfather, Theodore Sr., known as "Greatheart," a political reformer and philanthropist renowned for his activities on behalf of New York's poor. The family valued intellectual endeavor, and Theodore graduated from Harvard University in 1880. That same year, he married Alice Hathaway Lee, who died in 1884, two days after the birth of their only child, Alice Roosevelt (Longworth*). Two years later, Theodore married his childhood companion, Edith Kermit Carow. They had five children.

When ER was young, she occasionally visited her cousins at their Oyster Bay home on Long Island but found the family games less decorous than those she was used to. Nevertheless, in her autobiography* she said, "In some ways I remember these visits as a great joy, for I loved chasing through the haystacks in the barn with Uncle Ted after us, and going up to the gun room on the top floor of the Sagamore House where he would read aloud, chiefly poetry" (Roosevelt, 19).

As he ascended to the presidency, Theodore charted a course that was to be followed, in part, by ER's husband and fifth cousin, Franklin D. Roosevelt* on his path to the White House, although Theodore, unlike FDR, was a Republican. Theodore served in the New York state Assembly (1882–1884) and as U.S. Civil Service commissioner (1889–1895), president of the Board of Police Commissioners in New York City (1895–1897), assistant secretary of the navy (1897–1898), and the colonel in charge of the famous "Rough Riders," a U.S. volunteer cavalry regiment during the Spanish-American War in 1898.

Displaying a flair for showmanship that both FDR and ER also demonstrated, Theodore attracted favorable attention from the press and the public as a politician and war hero. He was elected governor of New York in 1898 and vice president in 1900. Following the assassination of President William McKinley, Theodore became president in 1901 and was elected in his own right in 1904. As chief executive, he extended the power of the presidency, intervening in disputes between capital and labor on behalf of the public, broadening federal regulation of business, and expanding holdings of public lands to provide parks and resources for future generations.

Theodore was also an author, naturalist, explorer, and hunter well known for championing the strenuous life. When he stepped down in 1909 as president, he went on a safari in Africa, toured Europe, and returned in 1910 to political activity in the United States. In 1912 he ran for president as the candidate of the Progressive Party* and lost.

ER visited her uncle in the White House and with FDR attended Theodore's inauguration in 1905. When the president wrote to congratulate FDR on his engagement to ER, Theodore stated that he was "as fond of Eleanor as if she were my daughter" (Lash, 138). Theodore and his wife offered to give ER a White House wedding, but she declined. "Uncle Ted," however, gave ER away at her wedding in New York City on St. Patrick's Day, 17 March 1905, a date picked for his convenience. His presence upstaged the bride and the groom, who were left alone while the guests surrounded the president.

FDR consciously looked to Theodore as a role model and followed in his footsteps as assistant secretary of the navy and governor of New York before being elected president. ER also looked to Theodore for inspiration. Both ER and Theodore had a strong moral core that guided their politics and their friendships. Both considered it their duty to right myriad wrongs. Both learned how to use the fame that accompanied their positions for worthy causes, and both inspired fanatically devoted followers.

There were also differences between them. ER, as the loyal wife of a Democratic appointee, supported President Woodrow Wilson's persistent efforts to keep the United States out of World War I, while her uncle urged a more militant approach. Her admiration for her uncle, however, was reflected in her reaction to his death: "I knew what his loss would mean to his close family, but I realized even more keenly that a great personality had gone from active participation in the life of his people. The loss of his influence and example was what I seemed to feel most keenly" (Roosevelt, 98). Toward the end of her life when family and friends urged her to slow down, her response was, "I think I must have a good deal of my uncle Theodore Roosevelt in me because I enjoy a good fight and I could not, at any age, really be contented to take my place in a warm corner by the fireside and simply look on" (Roosevelt, 428).

SELECTED BIBLIOGRAPHY

Brands, T. H. *T.R.: The Last Romantic*. 1998.
Gould, Lewis L. *The Presidency of Theodore Roosevelt*. 1991.
Harbaugh, William H. *The Life and Times of Theodore Roosevelt*. 1975.
McCullough, David. *Mornings on Horseback*. 1981.
Miller, Nathan. *Theodore Roosevelt: A Life*. 1982.
Roosevelt, Eleanor. *The Autobiography of Eleanor Roosevelt*. 1961.

Stacy A. Cordery

RUMSEY, MARY HARRIMAN (17 November 1881, New York–18 December 1934, Washington, DC).

Mary Harriman Rumsey, the eldest of six children of railroad financier Edward H. Harriman and philanthropist Mary Williamson Averell Harriman, cofounded the Junior League, a voluntary social service organization for debutantes that introduced ER into the world of social settlements.* Started by New York debutantes of the 1900–1901 season under the leadership of Mary Harriman and Natalie Henderson, the group, originally called the Junior League for the Promotion of Settlement Movements, chose the College Settlement on Rivington Street as a major project.

In the winter of 1903–1904, when she was nineteen, Eleanor Roosevelt joined the league and taught calisthenics and dancing at the Rivington Street settlement. Her awareness of the league's activities had been heightened when an elderly male relative criticized the group for drawing young women into public activity. Describing her involvement, ER said, "It [the Junior League] was in its very early stages. Mary Harriman . . . was the moving spirit. There was no clubhouse; we were just a group of girls anxious to do something helpful in the city in which we lived" (Roosevelt, 107). ER was the secretary of the league in 1904. Mary chaired the organization, later called the Junior League of New York, until 1905, the year she graduated from Barnard College, where she had studied biology and sociology.

After the death of her father in 1909, she helped manage her family's farms and promoted agricultural and livestock cooperatives. Her marriage to Charles Cary Rumsey, a sculptor, took place in 1910; he was killed in an automobile accident in 1922. The couple had three children. In 1928 she and her brother, Averell Harriman,* broke with her family's traditional allegiance to the Republican Party to support the presidential campaign of Alfred E. Smith,* for which ER headed women's activities at the Democratic National headquarters.

After FDR's election, Rumsey was appointed chair of the Consumers' Advisory Board of the National Recovery Administration (NRA), a group made up mainly of economists and clubwomen, to see that consumers' interests were considered when the NRA industrial fair practices codes were established. To reinforce these efforts, she advocated establishing consumer councils throughout the country. Rumsey also persuaded Averell Harriman to accept an administrative position in the NRA. In addition, she brought consumer concerns to the National Emergency Council, a coordinating body for New Deal* agencies. She served there along with Frances Perkins,* an old friend and associate in social reform with whom she shared a house in Washington.

ER worked to help Rumsey get consumer representation at the state level and to strengthen the national consumers' board. "I wish . . . that *you knew* how much you have helped the whole range of consumer problems and policies" (Lash, 383), Rumsey wrote her. Sometimes, though, the First Lady's efforts were less helpful, as when, trying to help Rumsey with public relations difficulties, ER suggested to women journalists that they moonlight doing work for the Consumers' Advisory Board, not realizing that this would be viewed as a conflict of interest and could cost them their full-time jobs.

Rumsey's work in the New Deal was foreshortened by her death in 1934 from injuries received in a fall from a horse while foxhunting in Virginia.

SELECTED BIBLIOGRAPHY
Cook, Blanche Wiesen. *Eleanor Roosevelt*. Vol. 1. 1992.
Lash, Joseph P. *Eleanor and Franklin*. 1971.
Roosevelt, Eleanor. *This Is My Story*. 1937.
Ware, Susan. *Beyond Suffrage: Women in the New Deal*. 1981.

RUTHERFURD, LUCY MERCER (26 April 1891, Washington, DC–31 July 1948, Allamuchy, NJ).

Lucy Page Mercer (later Rutherfurd), who served as Eleanor Roosevelt's part-time social secretary in the World War I era, played a pivotal role in changing the nature of the marriage* of Eleanor and Franklin D. Roosevelt.* Employed from 1914 to 1917 to assist ER with her social responsibilities when FDR served as assistant secretary of the navy in Washington, D.C., Mercer drew favorable attention for her elegant good looks and pleasing personality. In 1918 ER discovered that FDR was in love with Mercer. The event rocked her world and marked the major turning point in the Roosevelts' marriage.

Born to a well-connected Washington family that had fallen into straitened circumstances, Mercer, who was educated in private schools, began her work with ER when she was twenty-two. ER's cousin, Alice Roosevelt Longworth,* remembered Mercer as "beautiful, charming, and absolutely delightful" (Ward, 359). Efficient, organized, and cheerful, she soon proved invaluable to ER with her knowledge of Washington society. Mercer came to be considered almost one of the family.

It is not known when the relationship between Mercer and FDR began, but it was well established by 1917, when ER discharged her secretary, citing a need for economy during World War I. Mercer then enlisted as a yeoman for the Navy Department, working as a secretary in the same building where FDR had his office. While ER and the children were away at the Roosevelts' summer home on Campobello* Island, New Brunswick, Canada, Mercer continued to be part of FDR's social circle, accompanying him on outings and seeing him privately. While their relationship was gossiped about in Washington, ER apparently did not know what was taking place, even though she may have harbored suspicions.

In September 1918, however, ER unpacked FDR's bags when he came home ill after an inspection trip in Europe and discovered love letters from Mercer. ER felt deeply betrayed. Not only had her husband fallen in love with a woman whom Eleanor had treated as a member of the family, but he had humiliated her by seeing Mercer in the company of others. The affair also resurrected ER's childhood fears that she was unlovable because she was not as beautiful as her mother. She offered FDR his freedom, but after careful consideration, he rejected the idea of a divorce. According to biographers, pressure from his mother, Sara Delano Roosevelt,* who controlled the family finances, concern over his children, and admonitions from Louis Howe* that a divorce would ruin his political career all contributed to FDR's decision to remain with his wife. In addition, Mercer was a Catholic and would not have been able to marry a divorced man in her church. ER, however, obtained from FDR a promise that he would never see Mercer again.

After the affair, the Roosevelts attempted to recover some of the closeness of their marriage, although their children claimed that they never resumed a sexual relationship. At the same time, ER remade the marriage on her own terms by developing an independent life. She now took a stronger stand with her mother-in-law. She also began to devote time to her own circle of friends. In her work for social causes and in her friendships, ER found a way to restore her battered self-esteem.

After leaving the Navy Department, Mercer had become a governess for the six children of Winthrop Rutherfurd, a wealthy widower nearly twice her age who owned estates at Allamuchy, New Jersey, and Aiken, South Carolina. She and Rutherfurd married in 1920, and she devoted herself to her family, raising her stepchildren and a daughter born to the couple.

Yet, FDR and Lucy Rutherfurd continued to maintain some contact. According to biographer Doris Kearns Goodwin, in 1941 Rutherfurd, using an assumed name, apparently saw FDR at the White House to explore the possibility of medical care for her husband at Walter Reed Army Hospital. Subsequently, she saw the president occasionally when she visited Washington. Soon after her husband died in 1944, Rutherfurd visited FDR at the South Carolina estate of Bernard Baruch.*

During the summer of 1944, when the Roosevelts' daughter, Anna Roosevelt Boettiger (Halsted*), was acting as FDR's assistant, he sometimes asked her to invite Rutherfurd to dine at the White House when ER was away. Although Anna knew that ER would be hurt if she found out, she thought her father needed pleasant companionship and agreed to make arrangements for Rutherfurd's secret visits, some dozen of which took place in the following nine months. Rutherfurd and FDR also met late in 1944 at the little White House in Warm Springs, Georgia.

Rutherfurd was among those present when FDR suffered a fatal cerebral hemorrhage at Warm Springs on 12 April 1945. At the time he was stricken, her friend, Madam Elizabeth Shoumatoff, was painting his portrait at Rutherfurd's request. When ER learned of Rutherfurd's return to FDR's life, her old wound was revived. She accused Anna of conspiring with FDR against her, and relations were strained for a period between the mother and daughter.

Nevertheless, when ER was going through her husband's belongings at Hyde Park,* New York, and found a small watercolor of FDR painted by Madam Shoumatoff, she had it sent to Rutherfurd. In a letter of appreciation to ER on 2 May 1945, Rutherfurd said: "Thank you so very much . . . you must know that it will be treasured always. I have wanted to write you for a long time to tell that I had seen Franklin and of his great kindness about my husband when he was desperately ill in Washington, and of how helpful he was too, to his boys—and that I hoped very much that I might see you again. . . . I think of your sorrow—you whom I have always felt to be the most blessed and privileged of women must now feel immeasurable grief and pain and that must be almost unbearable. . . . As always, Affectionately, Lucy Rutherfurd" (Goodwin, 631).

The relationship between FDR and Rutherfurd became a matter of public knowledge in 1966, some years after the death of all of the principals, when Jonathan Daniels, the son of Josephus Daniels, who had been FDR's superior as secretary of the navy in 1913–1920, described the affair in his book, *The Time between the Wars.*

SELECTED BIBLIOGRAPHY

Asbell, Bernard. *Mother and Daughter: The Letters of Eleanor and Anna Roosevelt.* 1982.

Cook, Blanche Wiesen. *Eleanor Roosevelt.* Vols. 1, 2. 1992, 1999.

Daniels, Jonathan. *The Time Between the Wars.* 1966.

Goodwin, Doris Kearns. *No Ordinary Time: Franklin and Eleanor Roosevelt: The Home Front in World War II.* 1994.

Lash, Joseph P. *Eleanor and Franklin.* 1971.

Ward, Geoffrey C. *A First Class Temperament: The Emergence of Franklin Roosevelt.* 1989.

Melissa Walker

S

SCHEIDER, MALVINA THOMPSON. See THOMPSON, MALVINA (SCHEIDER).

SCHNEIDERMAN, ROSE (6 April 1882, Saven, Poland–11 August 1972, New York).

Rose Schneiderman, a labor* leader and reformer, is credited with educating Eleanor and Franklin D. Roosevelt* about the labor union movement. Born in Poland, Schneiderman came with her family to the United States in 1890, and began working when she was thirteen, first as a sales clerk, and then in a cap factory, where she helped organize the women in her shop and led a strike for a union shop.

In 1905 she joined the Women's Trade Union League* (WTUL), in which workers and upper-class reformers joined efforts to improve conditions for working women. In 1910 she became a full-time organizer for the New York branch of the WTUL. She participated in drives to bring women workers into the International Ladies Garment Workers' Union, taking a position as a national organizer for that union in 1915–1916. She also spoke out for woman suffrage, believing voting rights would help working women achieve protective legislation. In 1917 Schneiderman returned to the WTUL as an organizer, and in 1918 became president of the New York league. She remained in that position until 1949 and also served as president of the national WTUL from 1926 until it disbanded in 1950.

Schneiderman acquired a strong supporter as well as a personal friend when ER joined the league in 1922, shortly after talking with Schneiderman at a fund-raising tea for the league at the home of Dorothy Whitney Straight (Elmhirst*). When ER asked why women should join unions, Schneiderman told her about the treatment of women workers—that they remained unskilled because employers showed no interest in training them, worked nine- or ten-hour days and frequently longer for low wages of three dollars a week and could be fired if they complained.

In 1922 the New York league bought a clubhouse in New York City, which Schneiderman made into both a social and educational center for working women. For a number of years, ER went once a week to the league clubroom in a renovated brownstone to read poetry or a novel aloud to the women and to take cookies and hot chocolate for the group. From 1925 until the beginning of World War II,* ER gave a Christmas party for children of unemployed WTUL members. FDR attended the first party and enthralled the children with his reading of "A Christmas Carol."

FDR, in turn, heard about the history, struggles, and achievements of the trade unions from Schneiderman and her friend, Maud Swartz, national president of the WTUL in 1922–1926, who were frequent guests of ER in the Roosevelt homes. Frances Perkins* attributed FDR's understanding of the trade union movement to "the knowledge he had gained from these girls" (Perkins, 32).

FDR appointed Schneiderman in 1933 to the labor advisory board of the National Recovery Administration (NRA), where she served until the NRA was declared unconstitutional in 1935. Schneiderman was secretary of labor for New York state from 1937 to 1943. During this period she remained president of both the national WTUL and the New York league.

In addition to offering moral support and a conduit to FDR, ER, as chair of the WTUL'S finance committee, raised funds to pay off the remaining portion of the New York clubhouse mortgage in 1929. Schneiderman appealed to ER for further help in fund-raising as the Great Depression* deepened. ER responded with appeals to friends for contributions. From her radio broadcast* earnings in 1932–1933, ER personally donated $300 per week for each of twelve weeks, which enabled the league to continue in the depths of the depression.

Throughout her years in the White House, ER continued to respond to a wide variety of requests from Schneiderman, ranging from further assistance with fund-raising, to sending a statement on the achievements of the league for a WTUL Thanksgiving Day radio broadcast on 24 November 1938. She spoke personally on 5 February 1941 at a strike meeting of women electrical workers in Long Island.

In 1949, when Rose Schneiderman retired as president of the New York league, ER was among the 300 guests attending her retirement luncheon. In her autobiography, Schneiderman wrote that ER, in spite of her privileged upbringing and lifestyle, was "a born trade unionist" (Schneiderman, 251). During a union conference in San Francisco, ER told the audience that Schneiderman had taught her all she "knew about trade unionism" (Schneiderman, 257).

SELECTED BIBLIOGRAPHY
Eleanor Roosevelt Papers, Franklin D. Roosevelt Library, Hyde Park, NY.
Orleck, Annelise. *Common Sense and a Little Fire: Women and Working-Class Politics in the United States, 1900–1965.* 1995.
Perkins, Frances. *The Roosevelt I Knew.* 1946.
Schneiderman, Rose, with Lucy Goldthwaite. *All for One.* 1967.

Barbara Straus Reed

SEXUALITY. A commentator on Eleanor Roosevelt's sexuality immediately encounters two basic problems: the definition of sexuality and the lack of unequivocal evidence to support an argument. While ER treated so many areas of her life in her various books,* newspaper columns, and magazine articles, she was basically silent on the subject of sex and sexuality. It would never have occurred to her to share that aspect of her life with her readers. Whether or not she thought much about her own sexuality and talked about it with others close to her and how she acted on what she discovered are all unknown and unknowable. So if one is going to limit the definition of sexuality to what some call the pursuit of genital pleasure, there is nothing at all to say. Only if one defines sexuality more broadly as a force for pleasure, tenderness, and human relatedness, derived from bodily processes but extending to the most attenuated expression of emotional attachment, can one make an argument about sexuality in ER's life.

For many years, a more limited definition of sexuality led ER's family and her biographers to regard her as asexual. The only evidence cited was the recollection of Anna Roosevelt Halsted* of her mother's instruction to her about sex as a wife's marital duty (with the plain implication that it was no pleasure) and the assertion of James Roosevelt* that ER's discovery of the infidelity of Franklin D. Roosevelt* (with Lucy Mercer [Rutherfurd*]) put an end to the sexual relationship between his parents. While children are not the most trustworthy commentators on the sexual lives of their parents, these assessments did not seem off the mark. In his authoritative biography, Joseph Lash* endorsed the grandmotherly and asexual character of ER, a view that most of his audience was happy to share. He did note, but only in passing, the occasional raised eyebrows and gossip about her association with Earl Miller,* who treated ER in an openly affectionate manner and traveled frequently with her when he served as bodyguard-cum-chauffeur. Not until the Lorena Hickok* papers were mined for evidence of a frankly lesbian relationship between Hickok and ER did the possibility of ER as sexed and sexual receive real scrutiny. Blanche Weisen Cook, in her biography of ER, admits the unknowable sexual character of the ER–Hickok relationship but then makes much of Earl Miller as a source of pleasure, intimacy, and physical affection (noting pictures showing his hand on her knee).

This range of equivocal evidence taken from the observations and judgments of others can be rendered coherent by modern-day commentators only when they bring their own values and theories to make sense of what they find. To the degree that values and biases differ, people of goodwill may come to different conclusions in reading the same evidence. Thus, Kenneth Lynn took Doris Faber, Hickok's biographer, to task for what he considered her preoccupation with the question of overt lesbianism. In retrospect, her treatment of that relationship seems less focused on the question of sexuality than the more recent book of ER–Hickok letters edited by Rodger Streitmatter. Another approach to the subject is taken by Susan Ware, who argues that ER's deep, successive attachments to four individuals, Miller, Hickok, Lash, and finally, David Gurewitsch,* show that she gained emotional sustenance from people of both sexes.

The question of sexuality requires a different context for a personality psychologist who has spent some time trying to understand how ER developed as a child and adolescent into a predictable young matron but then was able to transform herself in totally unpredictable ways in her middle age and beyond. The larger understanding of who she was by temperament, by training, and by sheer bad luck in the choice of her parents renders some interpretations of the available evidence more valid than others. From this perspective, several factors would push ER toward repression and suppression of her sexuality—the times, her temperament, her deep-seated conviction of her plainness, and her terror of loss of control.

The idealization of beauty by ER's mother, Anna Hall Roosevelt,* who saw it as the defining characteristic of successful womanhood, marked ER as unfeminine from the beginning. The affection and attention she received from her father, Elliott Roosevelt,* were marred by his increasing problems with alcohol, which led to his abrupt departure from her life. ER's attachment to her father lasted her whole life; in fantasy, if not in fact, she was attractive to a man. By temperament, ER seems to have been a shy and fearful child who worked to overcome the inhibitions that kept her from meeting her father's expectations for physical bravery. But there is little indication that she ever was very comfortable in her body, that she dressed in ways that were appealing, or that she expressed other physical appetites for food or exercise that would support a sense of being grounded physically. Abraham Maslow draws a connection between a woman's enjoyment of her sexuality and her relish of good food, and ER's disdain for even paying attention to what she was eating, much less enjoying it, was well known.

One can imagine that her discovery of FDR's relationship with Lucy Mercer struck at the heart of her insecurities about herself as a woman. But that discovery did lead eventually to an extraordinary transformation from a conventional, upper-class wife, to an increasingly independent, intelligent, and engaged mature woman. That transformation may well have included new understandings and new expressions of her sexuality. Blanche Cook argues that ER's relationships with lesbian couples in the 1920s broadened her understanding of the expression of sexuality, and that may be so. The physical expression of emotional intimacy explicit in the Lorena Hickok letters—where touching, kissing, and lying together in each other's arms are clearly part of the relationship in its early and most intense phase—raises the question of this relationship as lesbian. Cook's characterization of the relationship with Earl Miller in its affection and its attenuated physical intimacy, which some found improper because she was a lady and he clearly was not a gentleman, introduces the possibility of heterosexual gratification outside the marriage relationship. There can be no doubt of the emotional benefits to ER of loving and being loved by both Earl Miller and Lorena Hickok with an intensity and exclusivity that she had not known before. They provided the base from which she could move out with increasing confidence into the wider world, pursuing both FDR's work and her own. Any further characterization—whether of ER as lesbian or bisexual—moves beyond the available data.

SELECTED BIBLIOGRAPHY

Cook, Blanche Weisen. *Eleanor Roosevelt*. Vols. 1, 2. 1992, 1999.
Faber, Doris. *The Life of Lorena Hickok, ER's Friend*. 1980.
Lynn, Kenneth S. "The First Lady's Lady Friend." In *The Air-line to Seattle*. 1983.
Maslow, Abraham. *The Farther Reaches of Human Nature*. 1971.
Streitmatter, Rodger. *Empty without You: The Intimate Letters of Eleanor Roosevelt and Lorena Hickok*. 1998.
Ware, Susan. *Letter to the World*. 1998.

Anne Constantinople

SMITH, ALFRED EMANUEL (30 December 1873, New York–4 October 1944, New York).

Four-time governor of New York state and 1928 Democratic presidential nominee, Al Smith was strongly supported by Eleanor Roosevelt as a prominent reform leader of his era. Smith transformed New York State government, in terms of both efficiency and creating the forerunner of the welfare state. Coming from the dockside, Brooklyn Bridge district of New York City, Smith left school and went to work when he was twelve after the death of his father. He became active in a church-sponsored amateur theater group and through friendship with Tom Foley, a Tammany Hall Democratic precinct leader, secured an appointment in 1895 as a court processor server and was elected in 1903 to the state Assembly. After a few years in the legislature he became a leading spokesman for a new generation of Americans, the mass of recent urban citizens from immigrant backgrounds. His presidential bid in 1928 was marked by virulent attacks on his Roman Catholicism, which, to a large extent, caused his defeat.

Smith also was instrumental, albeit reluctantly, in choosing Franklin D. Roosevelt* to succeed him as governor of New York that year. Shortly after that, however, relations between the two men began to cool, and after FDR's election to the presidency in 1932, Smith began to turn on the New Deal.* The climax of this feud came in 1936, when Smith, who had joined the ultra-right-wing Liberty League, delivered a blistering attack on the Roosevelt administration, branding it as communist-inspired. Their relationship improved, however, in the late 1930s and early 1940s, when Smith joined in the campaign against Nazism.

Relations between Smith and ER were always warmer and closer than they had been with FDR. ER had maintained a long-standing interest in Smith's career, stemming from the many interests and causes that they shared. For example, she was impressed by Smith's fight for the rights of women and children in the industrial slums of New York City. He served as vice-chairman of the New York state legislative committee, chaired by Robert Wagner, that investigated the Triangle Shirtwaist Company fire in 1911, which took 146 lives, mostly of working women. As a result, Smith and Wagner became champions in New York state politics of protective legislation. They secured major improvements in fire inspection and prevention and also fought to better conditions in factories, advocating safety measures, a minimum wage, and restrictions on hours for women. ER also was impressed with Smith's warmth and down-to-earth qualities, his ability to reach out to the common woman and man in a way that even her husband could never do (as FDR would ruefully note when the two became rivals).

ER first became actively involved in Smith's political career in 1924 during his successful bid for a third term as governor, even though his opponent was Theodore Roosevelt Jr., ER's cousin. Publicizing the latter's participation in the Warren G. Harding administration with its Teapot Dome oil scandal, ER joined in a motorcade against him known as the "teapot tour"* because it featured a replica of a teapot mounted on the lead car. Her activities took on special significance because they represented the first time that she became involved in politics on her own terms; she was working for Smith, a candidate of her choosing, rather than simply supporting FDR's career.

After 1924, ER remained in touch with Smith and wrote him frequently regarding women's issues. In 1928 she played a key role in his presidential campaign; her commitment was so strong that she refused to become involved in her husband's quest for the governorship, dedicating her efforts solely to Smith's presidential bid. She was director of women's activities for the Democratic National Committee, reporting directly to

Belle Moskowitz,* Smith's principal political adviser, who was in charge of national campaign publicity. ER's role restricted her activities primarily to New York City, but she also made a few speaking trips to other areas. Besides organizing women's Smith Clubs around the country, ER wrote articles detailing Smith's positions on foreign affairs and on Jeffersonian democracy, respectively. These appeared in both party and popular publications and gave her initial exposure to what it would be like to function as a journalist/advocate, a role she would take up much more extensively later in life.

After 1928 ER remained in touch with Smith, even when his contacts with FDR became icy. In 1936, when Smith arrived in Washington to deliver his attack on the New Deal, ER offered to let him stay at the White House. Smith turned her down, leading to a painful exchange of letters about how hard it was to maintain friendship amid political differences. In 1944, when Smith died, ER represented her husband at the funeral.

SELECTED BIBLIOGRAPHY
Cook, Blanche. *Eleanor Roosevelt*. Vol. 1. 1992.
Finan, Christopher. "Fallen Idol: Alfred E. Smith in the Thirties." Ph.D. Dissertation. Columbia University. 1992.
Morrison, Glenda. "Women's Participation in the 1928 Presidential Campaign." Ph.D. Dissertation. University of Kansas. 1978.
Roosevelt, Eleanor. "Governor Smith and Our Foreign Policy." *Woman's Journal* 13 (October 1928): 21.
———. "Jeffersonian Principles the Issue in 1928." *Current History* 28 (June 1928): 354–57.

                                                        Robert A. Slayton

SMITH, HILDA WORTHINGTON (19 June 1888, New York–3 March 1984, Washington, DC).

Hilda Worthington Smith, an advocate of workers' education programs, received a liberal arts education at Bryn Mawr College, where she obtained a bachelor's degree in 1910 and a master's degree in 1911. She also earned a master's degree in 1915 from what is now the New York School of Social Work. From 1919 to 1922 she served as dean of Bryn Mawr College, where from 1921 to 1933 she directed the Bryn Mawr Summer School for Women Workers, combining her interest in social work and adult education. In 1925 Eleanor Roosevelt visited the school where her friend, Marion Dickerman,* was teaching during that summer and found common ground with Smith in the belief that workers' education could help foster responsible citizenship.

ER's interest and support proved valuable after Smith, who had become director of a group of labor* schools called the Affiliated Schools for Workers, accepted an appointment in 1933 as a specialist in workers' education in the Federal Emergency Relief Administration (FERA). In 1935 she became director of the federal Workers' Education Program (WEP) under the Works Progress Administration (WPA).* To combine relief and education, Smith put jobless teachers to work offering economics, government, English, and other general education classes to unemployed industrial workers with the goal of making them informed and self-supporting citizens. As Smith diligently promoted workers' education, she provided progress reports to ER and increasingly turned to her for support when her program came under budgetary pressure in the late 1930s. In her 29 January 1936 "My Day"* column, ER described a visit to the White House of WEP supervisors and noted the importance she attached to workers' education, "especially at this time, when so many people seem to be beset by fears of socialism and communism." In her 27 June 1939 "My Day" column she expressed concern that as a result of cutbacks in the WPA "the adult education program in which I have been very much interested, may suffer."

Smith also was given the task of drawing up plans for a network of residential camps for needy women, which became known as the "she-she-she" camps to distinguish them from the Civilian Conservation Corps (CCC) camps for young men. To push Smith's proposal forward, ER hosted a White House Conference* on Camps for Unemployed Women on 30 April 1934. Due largely to her sponsorship, the program was approved. Unlike CCC camps, the women's camps did not offer residents a chance to earn wages or engage in physical work (which was not considered appropriate for women). Instead, during short stays at the camps, women received free housing, experience in group living, much-needed moral support, limited vocational counseling, and short-term educational opportunities. By 1936 ninety camps provided services for 5,000 needy women. In spite of Smith's reports on the improved health and mental outlook of participants and strong support from ER, the women's camps, which were transferred to the National Youth Administration* (NYA) in 1935, closed when federal relief agencies faced budget cuts in 1937.

Smith continued to advocate workers' education and the importance of an enlightened citizenry in a democracy until the WPA phased out the program in 1943. She then moved to the Federal Public Housing Administration, where she worked on education and recreation programs for war workers. After leaving this position in 1945, she continued her involvement with workers' education in a series of lobbying, writing, and consulting activities.

In 1946 ER and Smith sat next to each other at a dinner in New York honoring the twenty-fifth anniversary of the Bryn Mawr Summer School, and they kept in touch through holiday and birthday greetings until ER's death. In 1965 at the age of seventy-six, Smith returned to Washington and worked at the Office of Economic Opportunity until retiring in 1972.

SELECTED BIBLIOGRAPHY

George, Elsie L. "The Women Appointees of the Roosevelt and Truman Administrations: A Study of Their Impact and Effectiveness." Ph.D. dissertation. The American University. 1972.
Hilda Smith Papers, Franklin D. Roosevelt Library, Hyde Park, NY.
Swain, Martha. *Ellen S. Woodward: New Deal Advocate for Women.* 1995.
Ware, Susan. *Beyond Suffrage: Women in the New Deal.* 1981.

June Hopkins

SMITH, LILLIAN EUGENIA (12 December 1897, Jasper, FL–28 September 1966, Atlanta, GA).

Internationally acclaimed for her novel *Strange Fruit* (1944), a bestselling interracial love story, and *Killers of the Dream* (1949), an autobiographical critique of southern race relations, Lillian Smith was the foremost southern white liberal writer of the mid-twentieth century. Eleanor Roosevelt first knew Smith as coeditor with Paula Snelling of *The North Georgia Review*, a journal of literary and social commentary noted for its sharp critique of the South's poverty and social inequities. Smith and ER developed a friendship whose importance is reflected in their personal correspondence from 1938 to early 1962 and in their respective newspaper columns (ER's "My Day"* and Smith's "A Southerner Talking," *Chicago Defender*, 1948–1949). Their shared commitment to liberal democratic values, especially their strong support of full civil rights* for African Americans, survives in their correspondence with such mutual friends as Mary McLeod Bethune,* Pauli Murray,* Virginia Durr,* and Walter White,* as well as in their work for the Rosenwald Fund, the National Association for the Advancement of Colored People,* the Southern Conference for Human Welfare,* and Americans for Democratic Action.*

ER's political influence first proved helpful to Smith in 1943, after postmasters in Atlanta and Clayton, Georgia, tried to prevent the mailing of Smith's magazine, *The North Georgia Review*. Through the auspices of Bethune, Smith visited ER in Washington. ER, in turn, phoned Attorney General Frances J. Biddle, and the postmasters backed down. Smith again benefited from ER's assistance in May 1944, when the Post Office Department barred *Strange Fruit* from the mails on grounds of obscenity. After the publisher spoke to ER, President Franklin D. Roosevelt* had the order lifted. ER also turned to Smith for assistance, especially in regard to requests for help from white southerners; for example, in 1961 she asked Smith to protest against a twenty-five-year sentence in a Georgia prison given to a man charged with homosexuality.

Beyond documenting incidents of their shared values and political activism, their correspondence demonstrates the critical importance of women's friendships, especially for those fiercely independent and outspoken women, like Smith and ER, who challenged cultural norms of race and gender. "You have created a new kind of woman," Smith wrote on her 1958 Christmas card to ER; "You have shown us feminine possibilities that did not exist before. . . . Please, mam, take care of you for the rest of us."

SELECTED BIBLIOGRAPHY

Blackwell, Louise, and Frances Clay. *Lillian Smith.* 1971.
Gladney, Margaret Rose, ed. *How Am I to Be Heard? Letters of Lillian Smith.* 1993.
Loveland, Anne C. *Lillian Smith: A Southerner Confronting the South.* 1986.
White, Helen, and Redding S. Sugg Jr., eds. *From the Mountain: An Anthology of the Magazine Successively Titled Pseudopodia, the North Georgia Review, and South Today.* 1972.

                                             Margaret Rose Gladney

SOCIAL SETTLEMENTS. In the 1930s, Eleanor Roosevelt achieved enormous popularity by visiting the homes and workplaces of ordinary Americans. Her passion for firsthand knowledge of average citizens' lives developed long before her husband's presidency and, indeed, characterized two generations of elite and middle-class women who came of age around the turn of the century. As early as 1903, while still a teenager, ER began to venture beyond her elite New York neighborhood by volunteering at the College Settlement on Rivington Street.

Like hundreds of other social settlements, the College Settlement took its inspiration from Toynbee Hall, the first social settlement, which was founded by the Anglican priest Samuel A. Barnett in 1884 within one of London's most impoverished districts. Barnett's innovative institution was a place where young, university-educated men lived and hoped, by living among working-class families, to close the gap that separated workers from their wealthier countrymen. At the very least, these earnest youth hoped to bring the benefits of middle-class life—especially education—to those less fortunate. Almost immediately, Barnett's experiment became a routine stop on the European tours of America's college graduates. Many determined to create similar class-bridging institutions in American cities.

Women dominated the settlement movement in the United States. By 1911, when over 400 settlements served urban neighborhoods in the United States, 53 percent of those surveyed housed women only; 2 percent, men only. Moreover, the most important leaders of the settlement movement were women. Jane Addams,* cofounder of Hull House in Chicago, proved the movement's most renowned representative, with Lillian Wald,* founder of Henry Street Settlement in New York, a distant second. In contrast to these leaders, most women worked only briefly in a settlement—two or three years—and, in this, ER was not unique.

While longing for vivid and challenging experience characterized both women and men of ER's generation, America's first cohort of college-educated women flocked to urban, working-class neighborhoods because settlement life offered them new opportunities that, nevertheless, met some of the standard expectations for Victorian ladies. By venturing into the slums, a middle-class woman could appear to be providing charitable service to the needy. This made the move seem to fulfill the obligations of Victorian womanhood. At the same time, settlements promised independence, adventure, and meaningful work to women barred from many of the mainstream professions that offered their brothers autonomy and status. Settlements, then, embodied a blend of convention and innovation that eased many American women into powerful, independent lives without tarnishing their respectability.

When ER volunteered at the College Settlement, she thus entered a community of women dedicated to creating new possibilities for educated women by improving the conditions of America's working class. Opened in 1889 by a group of female college graduates, the College Settlement began with seven original residents, who within a year received applications from more than eighty other women wishing to join their middle-class outpost on New York's Lower East Side. As the settlers got acquainted with their immigrant neighbors—mostly from Southern and Eastern Europe—they created services to meet the most obvious needs: a kindergarten, after-school classes and clubs for children, lecture series and study groups for adults, health services, and playgrounds.

By the time that ER joined the movement, residents were also involved in local politics. Like settlement residents the country over, they now believed that only government could provide the services necessary to ameliorate the inequities of urban, industrial life. Consequently, they gathered and published information about the living conditions of their impoverished neighbors and agitated for better social services from the municipal, the state, and, eventually, the national government. In this way, many settlement residents became part of the Progressive reform movement that swept the United States early in the twentieth century, and the values of that movement clearly shaped those of ER.

Along with many elite volunteers, ER chose not to reside in the settlement. She continued to live with her family while traveling to Rivington Street to teach dance and exercise to the neighborhood's girls. In contrast to many young women of her class, however, ER refused the protection of her own carriage for transportation to the settlement. Instead, she took a streetcar to the infamous Bowery and walked to her classes. She later wrote: "I often waited on a corner for a [street]car, watching, with a great deal of trepidation, men come out of the saloons or shabby hotels nearby, but the children interested me enormously" (Roosevelt, 108). Indeed, her immigrant students introduced ER to their families and to their difficult lives, inspiring in the future First Lady a comfort with working-class people and a commitment to making their lives better that would be hallmarks of her long public career.

SELECTED BIBLIOGRAPHY

Davis, Allen F. *Spearheads for Reform: The Social Settlements and the Progressive Movement, 1890–1914.* 1967.

Muncy, Robyn. *Creating a Female Dominion in American Reform, 1890–1935.* 1991.

Roosevelt, Eleanor. *This Is My Story.* 1937.

Rousmaniere, John P. "Cultural Hybrid in the Slums: The College Woman and the Settlement House, 1889–1894." *American Quarterly* 22 (Spring 1970): 45–66.

Sklar, Kathryn Kish. "Hull House in the 1890's: A Community of Women Reformers." *Signs* 10 (Summer 1985): 658–77.

Robyn Muncy

SOUTHERN CONFERENCE MOVEMENT: THE SOUTHERN CONFERENCE FOR HUMAN WELFARE AND THE SOUTHERN CONFERENCE EDUCATIONAL FUND. In the spring of 1938 Eleanor Roosevelt began working with a group of southern liberals to create an organization with the broad goal of challenging the existing economic, political, and racial order of the South. A major meeting held 20–23 November 1938 in Birmingham, Alabama, led to the creation of the Southern Conference for Human Welfare (SCHW), which continued until 1948. Initially begun as a committee of the SCHW, the Southern Conference Educational Fund (SCEF) carried on in its place from 1948 until it declined in the 1970s. ER remained faithful to the conference and the fund from 1938 until her death.

The original goal of the SCHW was to shake the South into a consciousness of what conference leaders defined as the region's own best interests: to use to the fullest extent possible its human and natural resources without regard to race, creed, or color and to make the South a healthier, better educated, less violent, and more democratic place. To this end the SCHW held its meetings in southern cities that did not adhere strictly to segregationist practices and strongly supported federal antilynching* legislation, goals that resembled those of the National Association for the Advancement of Colored People.* The SCHW also formed the National Committee to Abolish the Poll Tax, which operated between 1938 and 1948.

The SCHW broke with the notion that blacks were to blame for southern poverty. Southerners who claimed such a connection steadily spoke out against the organization. Accusations of communist infiltration dogged both the SCHW and the SCEF; as Frank Porter Graham* wrote to ER on 21 March 1940, the conference "was smeared as being both red and black."

Following publication of a study that President Franklin D. Roosevelt* had commissioned—the National Emergency Council's "Report on Economic Conditions of the South"—that labeled the region as the nation's number one economic problem, the November 1938 meeting created a kind of summit of southern activists. It brought together an interracial alliance of New Dealers, labor* leaders, business executives, members of Congress, newspaper editors, sharecroppers, and college professors. The coalition was broad and deep, but even at its most expansive, the SCHW represented a minority southern viewpoint. The issues discussed included public health, education, child labor, youth* in the South, race relations, farm tenancy, suffrage, constitutional rights, and labor relations. Resolutions called for passage of the Costigan–Wagner antilynching* bill and abolition of the poll tax, as well as a number of agricultural reforms.

ER played an important role from the very beginning. Not only did she support the idea of the SCHW, but she attended their meetings, gave political advice, and contributed money. Offering her symbolic presence as First Lady, ER agreed not only to attend but also to give a speech at the initial November meeting. While between 1,200 and 1,500 delegates had assembled for that conference, about 7,000 people, of whom 3,000 were African American, crowded into Birmingham's Municipal Auditorium to hear ER speak on 22 November 1938. "Justice begins at home" (*Washington Post*, 22 November 1938), she told the crowd. But, in response to a question from the audience, she said: "What do I think of the segregation of white and Negro here tonight? Well, I could no more tell people in another state what they should do than the United States can tell another country what to do. . . . The answer to that question is not up to me but up to the people of Alabama" (Egerton, 194).

But if her words were temperate, her actions were not. Birmingham's police chief ordered the interracial crowd to seat themselves in accordance with their race. Earlier that day, arriving late for a conference session, ER sat in the black section of the hall. When ordered to move, she shifted her chair to the line that divided the two sections. The response was electric. As one columnist wrote, "It may not be too much to say that not since Scottsboro [a reference to a case in which African Americans were unjustly sentenced to death] has anything so upset . . . sectional feelings in the Deep South" (Carroll Kilpatrick, *Washington Post*, 30 November 1938).

The number of liberals in the South was so small that the SCHW was bound to bring together people with whom ER had already worked or who knew, or knew of, each other. Thus, the SCHW leadership included such friends and colleagues as Mary McLeod Bethune,* Virginia Durr,* Aubrey Williams,* Walter White,* Frank Porter Graham,* Lillian Smith,* and Lucy Randolph Mason.* James Dombrowski, who had been active in the Highlander Folk School* for a period in the 1940s, administered both the SCHW and the SCEF. As Graham wrote ER when he invited her to speak at a meeting in Chattanooga, Tennessee, "You can be assured that the Southern people want you, [and] that you will be in the hands of your friends" (Graham to ER, 21 March 1940), thus reassuring the First Lady that she would be protected from any southern hostility.

As her ties were close to the SCHW, so were her connections to the SCEF and its sustained commitment to issues of race, gender, and class equality. In 1955 she spoke out with the SCEF against the lynching of Emmett Till, a fourteen-year-old African American youth who allegedly whistled at a white woman in Mississippi. She supported the fund's request for an investigation by the Senate Subcommittee on Human Rights into the need for federal intervention to protect the civil rights* of black Mississippians and their white supporters. She upheld SCEF pressure on the New Orleans School Board in the spring of 1956 to hold public hearings on school desegregation. She wrote for the SCEF's monthly publication, the *Southern Patriot*.

In her "My Day"* column on 17 October 1952, she recorded her thoughts about the SCEF: "Through pamphlets and publications, conferences and opinion polls, the SCEF seeks to achieve a more equitable sharing of our democratic heritage." She listed a few particulars and then concluded that "it is such organizations as the Southern Conference Educational Fund that will really bring about the changes all of us hope for—not only in the South but throughout our country. Then we can say with truth and conviction that we move forward to ever better conditions for all of our people" (Emblidge, 277–78).

For over two decades the members of the SCHW and its successor, the SCEF, publicized the effects of segregation and discrimination in the South. They kept issues of equality and the promise of the American ideal before the nation for years before the major legislative breakthroughs for civil rights of the 1960s. By lending her name to these organizations, ER helped legitimate the efforts of the SCHW and SCEF to accomplish these goals.

SELECTED BIBLIOGRAPHY

Black, Allida. *Casting Her Own Shadow: Eleanor Roosevelt and the Shaping of Postwar Liberalism*. 1996.

Dunbar, Anthony P. *Against the Grain: Southern Radicals and Prophets*. 1981.

Egerton, John. *Speak Now against the Day*. 1994.

Emblidge, David, ed. *Eleanor Roosevelt's "My Day."* Vol. 2. 1989.

Reed, Linda. *Simple Decency and Common Sense: The Southern Conference Movement.*
    1991.
Sullivan, Patricia. *Days of Hope: Race and Democracy in the New Deal Era.* 1996.

                                                                            Linda Reed

SOUVESTRE, MARIE (1830?, France—30 March 1905, London, England).

Eleanor Roosevelt was just turning fifteen when her grandmother and guardian, Mary Ludlow Hall, sent her to England in the fall of 1899 to attend Allenswood, an exclusive girls' finishing school near Wimbledon Common on the outskirts of London. ER would remember her three years at Allenswood as "the happiest of my life" (Lash, 87). She would always regard Marie Souvestre, the school's charismatic founder and headmistress, as the most influential figure of her youth,* after her father, Elliott Roosevelt.*

Mademoiselle Souvestre had been educating young women from prominent European and American families for several generations, first at Las Ruches, her school in Fontainebleau outside Paris, and subsequently in England, where she settled in the early 1880s. The daughter of Emile Souvestre, a noted French novelist and philosopher, she was well connected and highly regarded throughout liberal intellectual circles. Henry James, the writer, urged his philosopher brother, William, to send his daughter to Allenswood, because of Souvestre's personality and accomplishments.

ER's beloved "Auntie Bye" (Anna Roosevelt Cowles,* sister of Theodore Roosevelt*) had been sent to Las Ruches in 1869, before it was closed at that location during the Franco-Prussian War, and ER's parents had met and liked Marie Souvestre while traveling in Europe in 1891. So it was with some confidence that Mrs. Hall commended her tall, diffident granddaughter to Mlle. Souvestre's care, writing ahead to tell the headmistress about Eleanor's troubled past and uncertain future.

ER went to Allenswood as a solemn, insecure adolescent starved for love and approval. Looking back, she wrote, "I see that I was always afraid of something; of the dark, of displeasing people, of failure" (Roosevelt, *Autobiography*, 12). Marie Souvestre recognized in the girl reserves of strength and special qualities of mind and spirit that Mrs. Hall's letter had not mentioned. She welcomed ER warmly and worked hard to encourage her. It was the first time since her infancy that an adult had been truly interested in ER for herself, and she responded by living up to Souvestre's expectations. She discovered that she could succeed and be noticed and that she could make friends easily, and she began to gain a new sense of confidence and poise. "This was the first time in all my life that all my fears left me," she recalled (Roosevelt, *Autobiography*, 24).

Allenswood was no ordinary fin de siècle finishing school but, rather, a serious collegiate environment that set high standards of instruction. Souvestre, now approaching seventy, personally taught history and literature in her flower-filled library, daring her students to open their minds and think for themselves. A short, stout, imperious woman with piercing gray eyes, silvery hair drawn back in the manner of a Greek statue, and outspoken liberal views, she was an eloquent and witty lecturer, a passionate advocate of the underdog, and a champion of unpopular causes.

Even though she was operating a school in England, she sided with the Boers against the British in the Boer War in South Africa. While she did not attempt to convince her English students of the correctness of her views, she "gathered around her the Americans and the other foreign girls. To them she expounded her theories on the rights of the Boers or of small nations in general. . . . echoes of [these talks] still live in my mind," ER wrote years later (Roosevelt, *Autobiography*, 26).

Souvestre also favored trade unions, defended the innocence of Alfred Dreyfus, a Jewish French army officer unjustly accused of spying, long before he was vindicated, and upset her students by calling herself an atheist. Rarely, if ever, had ER heard such opinions expressed at home. "Mlle. Souvestre shocked me into thinking" (Roosevelt, *This Is My Story*, 71), she remembered.

A vivid portrait of Marie Souvestre can be found in *Olivia*, a roman à clef written in 1933 by Dorothy Strachey Bussy, sister of Lytton Strachey, the biographer, and published anonymously in 1948. Bussy attended Las Ruches as a student and later taught classes in Shakespeare at Allenswood. Bussy's mother, Lady Jane Strachey, had become friendly with Souvestre in 1870 in Florence, Italy, where she had moved her school temporarily to escape the Franco-Prussian War, and eventually helped her relocate in England. The schoolmistress was close to the entire Strachey family, helped educate Lytton, and influenced what became known as the Bloomsbury Group of writers and artists, which included Virginia Woolf.

Olivia suggests that Las Ruches finally closed its doors after a bitter quarrel between Souvestre (the novel's Mademoiselle Julie) and the woman who was her partner at the French school and evidently her lover; years of sadness followed before Souvestre founded Allenswood. ER received a copy of the published book from a former Allenswood classmate, and while she acknowledged the gift with thanks, she left no record of any comment on the novel's erotic themes. There is no evidence that Eleanor, as a student, was aware of her teacher's personal life, although she was considered Souvestre's favorite pupil, and their correspondence shows that she confided in Souvestre about her family affairs.

During school holidays, ER joined Souvestre as her traveling companion on trips to France and Italy, "one of the most momentous things that happened in my education" (Roosevelt, *Autobiography*, 29–30). They stayed in modest hotels that saw few foreigners, ate the local food, went off the beaten track, and changed plans on the spur of the moment, a style of travel that came as a revelation to Eleanor. "She did all the things that in a vague way you had always felt you wanted to do," she wrote (Roosevelt, *Autobiography*, 30). "Never again would I be the rigid little person I had been before" (Roosevelt, *Autobiography*, 31).

ER wanted to stay on at Allenswood for a fourth year, but Mrs. Hall summoned her home in 1902 to make her formal debut in New York society. She had arrived at Allenswood feeling "lost and very lonely" (Roosevelt, *Autobiography*, 20) and left in triumph, having won the affection and esteem of her classmates, her teachers, and her headmistress. She believed that her encounter with Souvestre's "liberal mind and strong personality" had changed her life (Ward, 303). Souvestre, in turn, told Mrs. Hall that her granddaughter had "the warmest heart I have ever encountered" (Lash, 82).

ER and Marie Souvestre corresponded until Souvestre's death from cancer two weeks after Eleanor's marriage to Franklin Delano Roosevelt.* ER kept Souvestre's portrait on her desk and carried her letters with her throughout her life.

SELECTED BIBLIOGRAPHY

Bussy, Dorothy Strachey. *Olivia*. 1948.
Cook, Blanche Wiesen. *Eleanor Roosevelt*. Vol. 1. 1992.
Lash, Joseph P. *Eleanor and Franklin*. 1971.
Roosevelt, Eleanor. *The Autobiography of Eleanor Roosevelt*. 1961.
———. *This Is My Story*. 1937.
Ward, Geoffrey C. *Before the Trumpet*. 1989.

Russell Freedman

SPAIN, RELATIONS WITH. For liberals in the democracies of Western Europe and the United States, the Spanish civil war (1936–1939) was the defining political event of the years between World War I and World War II.* Accordingly, the postwar survival of the victorious rebel, the Spanish dictator General Francisco Franco, remained a critical reminder of the rise of fascist regimes that had been instrumental in propelling Western Europe into World War II. Opposition to Franco stood out as a touchstone of liberalism on both sides of the Atlantic and was a cause that drew Eleanor Roosevelt.

By 1937 ER had become a supporter of the beleaguered Spanish Republican government, which lost to Franco's forces. On her visit to England in 1942, ER told British Prime Minister Winston Churchill* that the United States and Britain ought to have helped the Spanish Republicans. A person's position on Franco became one of ER's tests of political trustworthiness. In 1944 she wrote her husband, President Franklin D.

Roosevelt,* that she considered a particular individual at the U.S. State Department unreliable because of his position on Spain. FDR, she suggested, should oppose this man's candidacy for a higher position in the departmental bureaucracy—then undergoing extensive reorganization—because "we know he backed Franco and his regime in Spain" (Lash, 713).

Like many American liberals, ER remained a staunch supporter of the Spanish Loyalists and a committed opponent of Franco after World War II. The swiftly unfolding Cold War,* however, placed liberals increasingly on the defensive as American relations with the Union of Soviet Socialist Republics*—the most important foreign ally of the republican government during the Spanish civil war—became increasingly hostile. In the climate of the late 1940s and early 1950s it became easy to link the Spanish republicans with the USSR and thus see its enemy, Franco, as an American ally, who had achieved international legitimacy by opposing Stalin and international communism.

In 1949 ER found herself actively involved in relations between Spain and the United States. During the spring of 1949, the U.S. government was searching for a way to include Spain in the North Atlantic Treaty Organization (NATO)—an alliance of nations created to staunch the spread of communism into Western Europe. President Harry S Truman* signed the treaty for NATO on 3 April 1949 and sent it to the Senate for ratification, knowing that a number of key senators wanted the strategically placed Spain included in the organization. The State Department therefore welcomed an opportunity to support a United Nations* (UN) motion by Brazil designed to remove most of the sanctions the international community had imposed on Franco's government in 1946. These proscriptions included the withdrawal of ambassadors, an arms embargo, and a condemnation of the Spanish regime as a fascist state. The State Department therefore advised the American delegation to the United Nations—of which ER was an important member—to quietly support Brazil's motion, thus reinstating Spain in world affairs.

ER and her UN colleague, John Foster Dulles,* both vigorously opposed this State Department policy directive. ER opposed any concessions to Franco until the generalissimo agreed to domestic democratic reform. Both ER and Dulles saw dangers in this change in U.S. policy and considered it an ill-conceived plan, almost certain to alienate American labor* unions and other Left-leaning U.S. organizations, whose support in 1949 was critical to the passage of NATO.

Secretary of State Dean Acheson heeded their advice and accordingly revised State Department policy, rejecting the Brazilian plan. The Soviet propagandists flung howls of outrage and vituperation against ER—whose prominent voice had been powerful and effective in defending the fledgling NATO—as the Soviets realized that they could not use support for Franco to demonstrate the "fascistic" nature of the current American and British governments and the aggressive, imperialistic nature of NATO itself. ER's continuing opposition to Franco also fed her ongoing disagreement with policies of the Catholic Church, a key supporter of Franco, which she most publicly articulated as an argument over federal funding of parochial schools through a dispute with Francis Joseph Cardinal Spellman.*

As ER had disapproved of Franco since his rise to power during the Spanish civil war, the Cold War fight against including Spain among the NATO treaty nations finally offered her an opportunity to wage an effective and successful battle against his government. It was a political battle in which her judgments proved right and finely tuned on the side of the United States against the Soviet Union.

SELECTED BIBLIOGRAPHY

Arend, Anthony C. *Pursuing a Durable Peace: John Foster Dulles and International Organization.* 1988.
Edwards, Jill. *Anglo-American Relations and the Franco Question.* 1998.
Lash, Joseph. *Eleanor and Franklin.* 1972.
Roosevelt, Eleanor. *On My Own.* 1958.
———. *This I Remember.* 1949.
U.S. Department of State. *Foreign Relations of the United States, 1949.* Vol. 4: *Western Europe.* 1975.

Jill Edwards

SPEECHES. Eleanor Roosevelt's public speaking career spanned forty years and earned her the distinction of being one of the most widely heard women in American history. ER achieved this distinction by giving thousands of speeches ranging from short talks for local Girl Scout troops, to orations on human rights* that reached a worldwide audience. Public speaking helped ER establish a distinct public identity separate from that of her husband, President Franklin D. Roosevelt.* At the same time her addresses furthered FDR's political aims.

ER relied on public speaking as one of the most effective ways to disseminate her ideas. Delivering an estimated 1,400 speeches during her years as First Lady from 1933 to 1945, ER spoke to millions of people in the United States and abroad. Unlike many modern political figures, she composed all of her own speeches when she was in the White House, only occasionally asking others to provide statistics and supporting material. ER frequently delivered addresses from minimal notes and rarely followed a fully prepared manuscript. Only when she served as a U.S. delegate to the United Nations* from 1945 to 1952 did she frequently deliver speeches from a written manuscript.

Ironically, ER suffered stage fright for most of her public life. Shyness as a young woman might have prevented her from participating in politics altogether had it not been for two influential factors: the disability of FDR after his attack of infantile paralysis in 1921 and her own involvement in women's civic and reform organizations. After FDR contracted polio, ER was strongly encouraged by Louis Howe,* FDR's chief political adviser, to serve as her husband's surrogate in Democratic politics while he recuperated. ER also began to associate with public-minded women in the League of Women Voters* and other organizations who helped her gain the self-confidence and political savvy needed for a public role.

Consequently, ER's speaking career grew out of social reform activities that shaped her political conscience and eventually developed her strong sense of a public identity. She delivered her first address, a fund-raising speech, in 1922 at a luncheon for the newly formed Women's Division of the New York state Democratic Committee. ER's memory of her public speaking debut reflected her initial tentativeness and inexperience. She wrote, "I had never done anything for a political organization before nor had I ever made a speech in any sizable gathering. Here I found myself presiding at a luncheon, without the faintest idea of what I was going to say or what work the organization was really doing" (Roosevelt, *Autobiography*, 121). In spite of self-doubts about her ability, ER soon joined other members of the women's division, Nancy Cook,* Marion Dickerman,* and Caroline O'Day,* in a statewide tour to encourage the formation of additional Democratic women's clubs. By 1926 ER had became a leading speaker for the New York senatorial campaign of Robert Wagner. In 1928 she headed women's activities for the national Democratic Party* and campaigned vigorously for the presidential bid of Alfred E. Smith.* As a result, ER had achieved greater recognition among party activists than FDR at the time he received the Democratic nomination for governor of New York in 1928. Her prominence as a public figure continued to rise after FDR won the gubernatorial election and became the Democratic nominee for president in 1932.

Yet, public speaking remained something of a chore for ER. According to the journalist Lorena Hickok,* ER's intimate friend, ER did not present herself to advantage during the 1932 campaign. "She was not a good speaker. Her voice, normally soft and pleasant, would become shrill when she was making a speech, and she hated making speeches. She also had a nervous habit of laughing when there wasn't anything to laugh at" (Hickok, 45–46).

Although ER did not work directly in FDR's campaign, she did address groups of women in New York state on behalf of Democratic candidates. At the time, the American public and press debated (and in many cases still do) the issue of how outspoken a First Lady should be in the public arena. Prevailing social norms of femininity and definitions of womanhood frequently relegated women's communicative activities to the private sphere of home and family. Many Americans expected First Ladies to fulfill their responsibilities and enhance their husbands' careers discretely and privately. ER was keenly aware of these role expectations: "I knew what traditionally should lie before me. I had watched Mrs. Theodore Roosevelt and had seen what it meant to be the wife of a President, and I cannot say that I was pleased at the prospect" (Roosevelt, *Autobiography*, 163).

Realizing the limitation of the First Lady role, ER nevertheless engaged in public communication on a far greater scale that any of her predecessors. She developed her public speaking to further the causes in which she believed. On occasion she appeared to differ with her husband, speaking out, for example, more strongly than FDR in the area of civil rights.* In her addresses, she insisted that education, housing, employment, and voting were basic human rights that society was morally and politically obligated to provide all of its citizens. As early as 1934, she asserted in a speech that "we must learn to work together, all of us, regardless of race or creed or color; we must wipe out, wherever we find it, any feeling that grows up, of intolerance, of belief that any one group can go ahead alone. We go ahead together or we go down together, and so may you profit now and for the future by all that you do in this conference" (Speech, National Conference on Fundamental Problems in the Education of Negroes, 11 May 1934).

As a speaker, she received a mixed critique from the press and public. While they complimented ER for her graceful hand gestures, they criticized her for being verbose and having a high-pitched voice, frequently mimicked at Washington parties by her cousin, Alice Roosevelt Longworth.* As a result ER employed Elizabeth von Hesse, a speech teacher, to help lower her voice and improve her tone and resonance.

From 1935 to 1941 she traveled the country for the W. Colston Leigh Bureau of Lectures and Entertainments, giving over 700 paid lectures. Throughout this time, ER's popularity on the lecture circuit never waned. She undertook two long tours each year until 1941, when she ceased lecturing to devote her time to the Office of Civilian Defense* as U.S. entry into World War II* loomed on the scene. She undertook her lectures, ER wrote, because they afforded her a "wonderful opportunity to visit all kinds of places and to get to know a good cross section of people" as well as to tour federal projects of various kinds (Roosevelt, *This I Remember*, 152). In addition, she explained, the lectures "gave me more money for things I wanted to do than my husband could afford to give me" and also provided information that FDR used "as a check against the many official reports he received" (Roosevelt, *Autobiography*, 131).

ER's audiences ranged from 2,000 to 15,000 as she spoke to college students, Rotary clubs, teachers' conventions, and religious groups. Although no payment was involved for the majority of her speaking engagements, she charged a sizable fee of $1,000 per lecture for Leigh's bureau. Sponsoring groups were offered a choice of hearing her speak on any one of six general topics: "Relationship of the Individual to the Community," "Problems of Youth," "The Outlook for America," "The Mail of a President's Wife," "Peace," and "A Typical Day at the White House." The lectures usually lasted one hour and were followed by a question-and-answer period. Although she gave stock speeches, ER often infused them with spontaneity and adapted them to her particular audience.

ER's frequent travels* and earned income raised the question of whether the wife of a president should be free to pursue her own career. Resentment of ER's activity included complaints that she should stay home and care for her family. Many critics, including some congressional representatives, accused her of commercializing her position. According to her first biographer, Ruby Black,* ER received less than half of the proceeds from her lecture tours after the agency commission and expenses were deducted. While some of the proceeds went to charity, the entire amount did not, and ER received some criticism that she was exploiting and cheapening her role as First Lady.

In her speaking career ER adopted a variety of persuasive strategies that permitted her to overcome the tensions between role expectations and feminine stereotypes, on one hand, and political expedience, on the other. She generally addressed socially acceptable topics, but at times she touched on controversial ones. She used personal anecdotes to illustrate her arguments. In addition, she often explained her activities as deriving from a civic/moral imperative to speak out because of the extraordinary time in which she lived. Finally, she adopted a modest and ingratiating tone and relied on a traditionally feminine delivery style to generate a nonthreatening public image.

Often ER's topics and speaking engagements were consistent with social expectations for middle-class women. Initially, ER spoke only to women's organizations and clubs. Many of her speeches focused on traditional concerns of clubwomen: protective legislation for women workers, laws against child labor,* the improvement of education, and the need for women to exercise their newly earned voting rights. Her focus on civic responsibility also allowed her to introduce more controversial issues such as federal support of public housing and civil rights* for African Americans.

To develop her ideas ER used personal stories and examples from her interactions with other citizens. She acknowledged the impact of listener beliefs on her own thinking with regard to public policy, explaining that "I read so many human lives every day in their letters; but I do get from those letters a very good picture of the conditions throughout the country and I realize more and more how important it is that we, as individuals, actually shall take an interest in our government" (speech, the Institute of Women's Professional Relations, 28 March 1935).

A recurring theme in ER's speeches was civic and moral duty. Couched in such terms as "responsibility," "citizenship," "patriotism," and "service to the country," this ethic undergirded virtually all of her arguments. In 1936, for example, she entreated members of her audience to invest themselves in their communities: "Wherever we live, wherever we are, let us put down roots. We may not live there always, but while we are there we may mean something in that community so that we may really leave a mark on the people that we have associated with, because we have stood for the things we believed in with all our might, and so we shall be a part of the consciousness of that community" (speech, Cause and Cure of War Convention, 23 January 1936).

At the 1940 Democratic National Convention, which nominated FDR for an unprecedented third term, ER became the first wife of a president ever to address a major political party conclave. Her speech, considered one of her greatest successes, was credited with helping unite the delegates, who were divided over FDR's insistence that Henry A. Wallace* be his vice presidential candidate. To motivate them to rally around FDR's controversial choice, she invoked the idea of civic duty. Alluding to the prospect of U.S. involvement in World War II, ER stated, "We cannot tell from day to day what may come. This is no ordinary time, no time for thinking about anything except what we can best do for the country as a whole, and that responsibility is on each and every one of us as individuals" (speech, Democratic National Convention, 18 July 1940).

With her listeners ER adopted a modest, ingratiating tone. In an address to the Chicago Civil Liberties Committee, she commenced by noting that "I imagine a great many of you could give my talk far better than I could" (speech, "Civil Liberties and the Individual and the Community," 14 March 1940). ER's modesty worked to her advantage, especially when she wished to address controversial topics and/or admonish her audience for particular actions. For example, in her 1934 address to African Americans advocating the improvement of their educational opportunities, she used the inclusive pronoun "us," faulting herself and others for a lack of initiative: "We have also been slow, many of us who are of the white race, in realizing how important . . . it is, . . . that you should have the best educational advantage." (speech, National Conference on Fundamental Problems in the Education of Negroes, 11 May 1934).

ER communicated messages, even on commonplace subjects, with genuine conviction and a personal style that made her audience responsive. Her striking physical presence (she was nearly six feet tall and weighed

about 160 pounds in 1940) and her energetic demeanor conveyed enthusiasm and sincerity on the public platform. At the same time her appearance and mode of dress were consistent with prevailing norms of
femininity. ER's wardrobe, which often consisted of her trademark fox
fur collar and matronly dresses, reinforced her unassuming manner. In
addition, she often carried a bag of yarn and knitted while she attended
conferences and rallies. This nonverbal image of a grandmother, which
she was at this point, helped fulfill audience expectations of womanhood.

ER's public speaking career expanded after she left the White House.
Her success as a public speaker while First Lady, along with freedom
from the constraints imposed on her by her role in the White House,
allowed her to broaden activities as a social advocate. She was especially
outspoken about postwar politics that she believed threatened civil rights
and liberties. She spoke frequently at conventions of the National Association for the Advancement of Colored People* and rallies advocating
the rights of African Americans. She also spoke out against McCarthyism* and activities of the House Un-American Activities Committee.* In
1946 she became the first woman to keynote the New York state Democratic Convention. She also addressed the Democratic National Convention two more times—in 1952 and 1956. While traveling to the
Middle East and India* in 1952, she addressed the Indian Parliament.

As U.S. delegate to the United Nations and the guiding spirit behind
the Universal Declaration of Human Rights,* ER spoke often in the
United States and abroad to promote the role of the United Nations in
world affairs. For example, appearing before the Democratic National
Convention, she urged continued support of the United Nations to ensure national security: "Without the United Nations our country would
walk alone, ruled by fear instead of confidence and hope. To weaken or
hamstring the United Nations now, through lack of faith and lack of
vision would be to condemn ourselves to endless struggle for survival
in a jungle world" (speech, Democratic National Convention, 23 July
1952). As the leading volunteer of the American Association for the
United Nations,* ER made the United Nations a central focus of her
speaking engagements for the last decade of her life.

During four decades of public speaking, ER matured from an individual who "was quite certain I could never utter a word aloud in a public
place" (Roosevelt, *Autobiography*, 54), to a revered political figure heard
all over the world. ER's modesty, strategic use of topics related to human
welfare, personal style of presentation, and emphasis on a civic and
moral imperative all combined to allow her to overcome barriers to public communication that faced women speakers in general and First Ladies
in particular. Furthermore, her success as a public speaker both expanded the public role of the First Lady and advanced ER's impact as a
social activist and U.S. political representative abroad.

SELECTED BIBLIOGRAPHY
Eleanor Roosevelt Papers, Franklin D. Roosevelt Library, Hyde Park, NY.
Gutin, Myra. "Political Surrogates and Independent Advocates—Eleanor Roo-
    sevelt." In *The President's Partner: The First Lady in the Twentieth Century.*
    1989.
Hickok, Lorena A. *Reluctant First Lady.* 1962.
Petersen, Debra L. "Anna Eleanor Roosevelt." In Karlyn Kohrs Campbell, ed.,
    Women Public Speakers in the United States: A Bio-Critical Sourcebook. 1993.
Roosevelt, Eleanor. *Autobiography.* 1961.
————. *This I Remember.* 1949.
              Diane M. Blair, Lisa M. Gring-Pemble, and Martha S. Watson

SPELLMAN, FRANCIS JOSEPH (4 May 1889, Whitman, MA–2 December 1967, New York).

In 1949 Cardinal Francis J. Spellman publicly and bitterly fought with
Eleanor Roosevelt over the issue of federal funding of primary and secondary education, a battle still remembered for its vehemence and
hostility. Their relationship, however, was more complex than simple
disagreement over public moneys and the Catholic Church. Their acquaintance dated back to the mid-1930s. Spellman, who had been ordained a priest for the archdiocese of Boston in 1916 and appointed to
the secretariat of state at the Vatican in 1925, returned to the United
States in 1932 as auxiliary bishop to Boston's archbishop, Cardinal William O'Connell. He was at that time instructed by Cardinal Eugenio
Pacelli, papal secretary of state and a personal friend, to work toward
establishing diplomatic relations between the Vatican and the United
States.

President Franklin D. Roosevelt* took with him to Washington a new
openness toward American Catholics, derived, in large measure, from
the president's understanding of the importance of the Catholic vote for
the Democratic Party.* Two-thirds of the judges FDR appointed during
his first term were Catholic. His private secretary, Marguerite "Missy"
LeHand,* was Catholic, as were important and close advisers such as
Thomas Corcoran and FDR's ambassador to Great Britain, Joseph P.
Kennedy. At the same time, the American Catholic Church was in the
process of change, emerging from a church of immigrants to a fully
American institution of second- and third-generation Americans who
had assimilated to the national culture—in a Protestant-led America still
marked with animosity toward Catholics. The goal of the American
Catholic Church was both to become fully American and yet to remain
distinctive. Spellman was well placed for this task. He had spent years
at the Vatican and had growing power and prestige in America. Thus,
it was typical of both his assignments and his contacts that when asked
to arrange a meeting between Cardinal Pacelli and the president in late

1936, Spellman went to Kennedy and through him arranged for the president to host a luncheon at Hyde Park.* Shortly thereafter ER paid a visit to Boston, and Spellman noted on 26 December 1936, "Miss LeHand and Mrs. Roosevelt are using my car" (Spellman diary). It was a triumphant moment for Spellman, and his later dispute with ER must be seen against this backdrop, as well as the broader context of his dealings with FDR.

Spellman's relationship with the president grew closer in 1939, after Spellman became archbishop of New York, a post that carried with it ecclesiastical jurisdiction over Catholics in the military services. In December 1939 he was largely responsible for FDR's appointment of Myron C. Taylor as the president's "personal representative" to Pope Pius XII, a decision about which ER was not enthusiastic, because the appointment represented a compromise between politics and diplomacy. While Spellman continued to enjoy close relations with the president, their association became strained after 1943. They differed over the Allied selection of bombing targets (which included both Rome itself and the papal villa outside Rome), the meaning of "unconditional surrender," the future of Germany, and the president's accommodation of Stalin at Yalta.

In 1946 Spellman was named a cardinal and emerged as the principal American Catholic spokesman, the American Catholic Church's most public and influential prelate on domestic issues and in its campaign against communism. Indeed, Spellman became increasingly preoccupied with the diabolical nature of the communist foe while defending the "Americanness" of the American Catholic Church against an outbreak of anti-Catholicism led by Paul Blanshard and his organization, called Protestants and Other Americans United for the Separation of Church and State (POAU). While Spellman became increasingly identified with anticommunism, ER emerged as a liberal voice for progressive causes. While certainly not pro-Soviet or pro-communist and a founder of the liberal-centrist Americans for Democratic Action,* she opposed the hunt for communists that dominated American politics in the late 1940s and early 1950s. It seems likely that Spellman frowned on ER's support of such measures as the resolution of the United Nations* calling for member nations to sever diplomatic ties with Franco's Spain* and that he suspected her of leftist leanings. These then were the two issues—anti-Catholicism and anticommunism, within the matrix of an increasingly American, yet still insecure, church and mounting communist hysteria— that provided the context of Cardinal Spellman's attack on Eleanor Roosevelt.

The specifics of the battle were over the limits of federal aid to education. Congress* had only begun to consider the use of federal funds to support education—traditionally, a state and local issue—in 1937, but in the intervening decade it had become a hotly contested issue. On 11 May 1949 Representative Graham Barden (D-NC) introduced a bill to appropriate $300 million to the states for public elementary and secondary schools. The proposed legislation specifically excluded aid to parochial schools, even for transportation, despite the fact that the Supreme Court had declared such funding constitutional in *Everson v. Board of Education* in 1947. The Barden bill added fuel to the fire. Spellman urged Catholics to pray for the soul of Congressman Barden and his "disciples of discrimination," who vented "venom upon children" and who was committing a "sin shocking as it is incomprehensible" (Lachman, 41). The cardinal summed up his attitude succinctly in an address entitled "Barden Bill—Brewer of Bigotry." "Congressman Barden," Spellman wrote, "claiming to be a loyal American, holding a key position in our democratic government, is in truth violating, and inciting others to violate, the very rights and freedoms upon which our democratic government was founded" (Centola, 460). Making matters more incendiary, waving a red flag at Catholic fears, the POAU, albeit along with liberal Protestant denominations, wholeheartedly supported the bill and sent out mailings in its support.

ER entered the fray with three articles in her "My Day"* column: 23 June, 8 July, and 15 July 1949. In the first of these columns she specifically cited Spellman's efforts to obtain a portion of federal aid for Catholic schools. She proceeded to explain her views that direct federal aid to religious schools violated the Constitution—and would bring these schools under federal control.

Spellman wrote her a blistering letter, which was published in the press even before ER had received it. He not only argued that the Supreme Court had upheld support for ancillary services such as transportation, health care, and nonreligious textbooks but broadened his attack to accuse her of anti-Catholicism, of condemning him personally, and of ignorance (she had admitted to not reading the text of the Barden bill). He declared he would never again publicly acknowledge her, observing that "for whatever you may say in the future, your record of anti-Catholicism stands for all to see." It was, he continued, a record "unworthy of an American mother" (Cooney, 177–178).

ER upheld her position that public funds should be restricted to public schools and went on to assert that "spiritual leadership should remain spiritual leadership and the temporal power should not become too important in any church" (Lash, 159). While Spellman had been intemperate in his language, ER implied that a church or its spiritual leader should take no position in temporal matters. As for her being an unworthy American mother, she declared, the "final judgement, my dear Cardinal Spellman, of the worthiness of all human beings is in the hands of God" (Cooney, 178–179).

The controversy became page-1 news across the nation. While prominent bishops and many Catholic leader defended the cardinal, ER received enormous support from Protestants, Jews,* and even some Catholics, ranging from the American Civil Liberties Union to the Catholic congressman Andrew Jacobs (D-IN). Former New York governor Herbert H. Lehman, who was considering a run for the Senate, issued a statement affirming his shock at Spellman's attack on ER, "whose life has been dedicated to a constant fight for tolerance and brotherhood" (Lachman, 49). Lehman was shortly thereafter nominated for the U.S. Senate by the Democratic Party and won handily, including in heavily Catholic areas. On 3 August the mayor of New York, William O'Dwyer, himself an Irish Catholic, issued a statement holding ER free of any type of bigotry and regretting the entire controversy.

Spellman realized that he could hurt only himself and the American Catholic Church by carrying on the controversy and wrote a statement clarifying his beliefs. He telephoned ER and asked her to review it. She agreed to accept publicly his principal position: that the Catholic Church was asking for federal support only of auxiliary services. The day after his statement was published in the *New York Times*, ER declared the new statement to be "clarifying and fair" (Lachman, 49). Two weeks later Spellman traveled to Peekskill, New York, to dedicate a new chapel and made an unannounced stop at Hyde Park* to pay a social call on ER. "We had a pleasant chat," she wrote in her "My Day" column on 24 August 1949, "and I hope the country proved as much of a tonic for him as it always is for me" (Lash, 165).

The trajectory of Spellman's attitude toward ER between 1936, when he wrote in his diary that he was pleased that ER, along with Missy LeHand, was willing to borrow his car, to his anger at her thirteen years later says much about Spellman and ER. In 1936 Spellman was thrilled at his own influence within the federal government. By the later years of World War II,* however, it was already becoming clear that deep issues would continue to divide many Protestants and the Catholic Church. With the coming of the Cold War,* Catholic leaders, led by Spellman himself, had taken up the cause of anticommunism as a way of reconciling their faith with their patriotism. Their outspokenness demonstrated both how far they had come from an immigrant community afraid to voice publicly its concerns and how profoundly separate they still were from some elements of mainstream America. In her dedication to the separation of church and state, ER represented what seemed to Spellman to be an anti-Catholic bias in American society. ER, after all, had been born into a class whose members at that time found anti-Catholicism, along with racism and anti-Semitism, acceptable. He may well have resented the fact that she had done so much to alter her attitudes toward African Americans and champion their cause and made so many friends among the American Jewish community and had fought anti-Semitism—without seeming to recognize the reality of anti-Catholicism in America or doing anything to attack it. Spellman, however, was an excellent politician. He knew when to withdraw from battle.

For ER the issues were quite different. Like many liberal members of her generation, the causes she had taken up and the beliefs she held seemed often to be at odds with those held by the Catholic Church. The church, after all, had supported Franco in Spain, while Spellman—together with the majority of Americans—had declared war on communists at home after World War II. For ER the issue of public aid to education threatened the U.S. Constitution and the principle of the separation of church and state. But she never considered herself anti-Catholic.

SELECTED BIBLIOGRAPHY
Centola, Kathleen G. "The American Catholic Church and Anti-Communism, 1945–1960: An Interpretive Framework and Case Studies." Ph.D. Dissertation. State University of New York at Albany. 1984.
Cooney, John. *The American Pope: The Life and Times of Francis Cardinal Spellman.* 1984.
Francis J. Spellman Diary, Archives of the Archdiocese of New York, New York City.
Gannon, Robert. I. *The Cardinal Spellman Story.* 1962.
Lachman, Seymour P. "The Cardinal, the Congressmen, and the First Lady." *Journal of Church and State* 7 (Winter 1965): 35–66.
Lash, Joseph P. *Eleanor: The Years Alone.* 1972.

                                                              Gerald P. Fogarty, S.J.

STEVENSON, ADLAI EWING, II (5 February 1900, Los Angeles–14 July 1965, London, England).

Adlai Ewing Stevenson II, a close personal and political friend of Eleanor Roosevelt, was elected governor of Illinois in 1948, became the Democratic nominee for president of the United States in 1952 and 1956, and served as U.S. ambassador to the United Nations* (UN) from 1961 until his death. He first met ER in 1942, when he was working as a personal assistant to secretary of the navy Frank Knox. In 1946 he was an adviser to the U.S. delegation at the first meeting of the UN General Assembly in London and in March 1947 an alternate delegate, when ER was a U.S. delegate. He came to admire her work on UN Committee Three and the Human Rights Commission. Their most significant contact occurred during his presidential campaigns of 1952 and 1956, when ER actively supported Stevenson.

Throughout their important personal and professional association, they shared similar views on domestic politics and foreign affairs. They also enjoyed each other's company, with ER playing the maternal role of suggesting headache pills and cold remedies to a younger confidant.

Eleanor Roosevelt and Adlai E. Stevenson meet in New York with Polly Cowan, a key figure in the women for Stevenson organization set up to back Stevenson's campaign for president in 1956. *Courtesy of Cowan family.*

While ER admired Stevenson's humility and speaking ability, he was impressed with her intelligence, diligence, and sensible perspectives on postwar America. To a man who found public service an important goal in his own life, ER's dedicated attendance at long UN sessions became a model.

Meanwhile, she responded that he had a better understanding of the world, so necessary during the perilous early days of the Cold War,* than anyone in American politics. ER also admired his eloquence, even as she acclaimed his progressive views promoted in the 1956 presidential campaign on ending hydrogen bomb testing in the atmosphere and replacing the draft with a volunteer army.

When Stevenson was nominated as the Democratic presidential candidate in the spring of 1952, ER was impressed by his famous charge to the Democratic National Convention in Chicago, "Let's Talk Sense to the American People." In her subsequent campaign appearances for him, she emphasized his internationalism. She also paid tribute to his experience in foreign affairs through his early service as an adviser to the U.S. delegation to the United Nations. An inveterate traveler herself, she located in his overseas trips a shared experience that she believed brought insight to his views on foreign policy.

ER shared with Stevenson his intense anger at the witch-hunting of Republican senator Joseph R. McCarthy and the complacent approach of Dwight D. Eisenhower,* the Republican presidential candidate, to the Wisconsin senator's unsubstantiated charges that government agencies were harboring communists. During the 1952 campaign, Eisenhower sat on the same platform with McCarthy's supporter, Indiana's Republican senator William Jenner, even though Jenner had attacked Eisenhower's friend and patron, General George Marshall.* In response, both Stevenson and ER spoke out against the surrender of the Republicans to McCarthyism.*

In the election that followed, Eisenhower easily defeated Stevenson, carrying 55 percent of the vote to Stevenson's 44 percent. But ER consoled Stevenson with the thought that almost no one could defeat an American hero like Eisenhower. In the years that followed ER turned to her work promoting the United Nations, to which Eisenhower had not reappointed her. As a private citizen, Stevenson traveled, served as a sometimes reluctant head of the Democratic Party,* and met, in his frequent trips to New York, with ER, who was rapidly emerging as one of his most important counselors. The two continued to share similar views on the Red-baiting of Joseph McCarthy as well as on the challenges of the nuclear age to the survival of humanity.

In 1956 ER took a much more active role in Stevenson's nomination and campaign. By this time she was an elder spokesperson of the Democratic Party, of which he was the titular leader. Stevenson needed less encouragement to run in 1956, but ER worked hard for his nomination over that of Senator Estes Kefauver and New York's Averell Harriman.* In 1956 the primaries emerged as important in the process of obtaining the nomination, and ER provided important advice to Stevenson about his tactics and strategy, sending names of possible donors and influential supporters to him.

ER was particularly helpful in soliciting the African American vote. As a board member of the National Association for the Advancement of Colored People,* she lost some of the support of black activists, such as Roy Wilkins, who were disgruntled with Stevenson's cautious approach to desegregation. ER also acknowledged in private letters to the candidate what many of Stevenson's inner circle knew well—that he spent too much time working on his speeches and did not put enough energy into engaging the common people.

When Stevenson lost this election, he announced that he would not run again. But he did permit a group of volunteers to work for him. By the spring of 1960, ER called on Stevenson to clarify his position, and in her "My Day"* column of 17 April 1960, she noted his maturity and experience, characteristics that, in her judgment, John F. Kennedy,* the principal Democratic contender for the nomination, did not have. When Kennedy easily obtained the nomination, ER promoted the idea of Stevenson as secretary of state. After Kennedy finally appointed Stevenson ambassador to the United Nations, in turn Stevenson encouraged Kennedy's appointment of ER as a delegate to the special UN session meeting in March 1961.

After ER's death in November 1962, Stevenson in a moving eulogy at her memorial service and also at the United Nations, paid tribute to the woman who throughout her life, in his words, had lit candles rather than cursed the darkness.

SELECTED BIBLIOGRAPHY
Baker, Jean H. *The Stevensons: Biography of an American Family.* 1996.
Black, Allida. *Casting Her Own Shadow: Eleanor Roosevelt and the Shaping of Post-War Liberalism.* 1996.
Lash, Joseph P. *Eleanor: The Years Alone.* 1972.

Jean Harvey Baker

STRONG, ANNA LOUISE (24 November 1885, Friend, NE–29 March 1970, Peking, China).

Eleanor Roosevelt invited the radical journalist Anna Louise Strong to lunch at the White House on 26 January 1935, at the suggestion of the social reformer Lillian Wald,* who wrote ER that Strong "knows Russia now better than anyone else.... It occurred to me that you might like to see her informally" (LW to ER, 17 January 1935). Questions raised at the meeting about the Soviets by ER and President Franklin D. Roosevelt* led Strong to follow up with a lengthy letter to ER, extolling the Soviet system and predicting difficulties for the New Deal.* ER's brief acknowledgment and comment that "we are more hopeful than you are" (ER to ALS, 5 February 1935) began an association that was sustained largely through correspondence. It was a lively exchange that illustrated ER's tolerance of differing political views and commitment to the free expression of ideas but was strained by ER's criticism of the Soviet Union after the Russian–German nonaggression pact in August 1939 and later deteriorated to animosity during the Cold War* years.

A minister's daughter who held a doctorate in philosophy from the University of Chicago, Strong was influenced by the progressive social politics and labor union activity of the early 1900s. In the 1920s she began a series of extended stays in Russia and China, becoming acquainted with the communist leaders in both countries. Perceiving their revolutionary movements as a quest for equality and justice, she became their enthusiastic advocate in a series of lecture tours in the United States, as well as in books and articles.

In her letters to ER in 1937 and 1938, Strong advocated various causes such as aid for children affected by the civil war in Spain* and U.S. assistance to China for industrial development. ER was impressed by Strong's dedication, energy, and compassion, observing that Strong's unofficial status allowed her to go places and write observations that Roosevelt in her official capacity could not. ER passed some of Strong's letters to FDR, who on one occasion wrote ER, "Will you tell the lady (Strong) that as far as the financing of China goes, the Government has no legal authority to do it?" (FDR to ER, 5 July 1938).

In 1937 Strong wrote to ER with a more optimistic view of the New Deal: "I have been ever more and more impressed by the tremendous historic significance of what the President is doing. The climax came when I read that wages and hours bill" (ALS to ER, 29 May 1937). In 1939 ER suggested Strong use her skill and energy toward promoting New Deal reforms. Strong traveled across the United States, visiting the Tennessee Valley Authority at ER's specific suggestion; the following year Strong published her observations in the book *My Native Land*.

In 1939 and 1940, however, Strong's letters defending Russia's actions in signing the Stalin–Ribbentrop nonaggression pact with Germany on 23 August 1939, invading Poland on 17 September 1939, and attacking Finland on 30 November 1939 provoked increasingly critical replies from ER. They came at a defining moment that divided American liberals from American radicals and ended the period of democratic–socialist–communist cooperation known as the Popular Front (1936–1939). Predictably, ER and Strong fell on two sides of the dividing line.

Thus, ER responded to Strong after the Russian–German agreement: "This treaty does not seem to me to be in the interest of peace. It simply says to Hitler 'We will not attack you, so you are sure of having one less enemy. . . . As far as we are concerned you can go ahead and take possession of any of other countries that you choose without our help.' . . . Of course, it seems quite possible that there may be in addition to this some secret agreement by which Russia will take her share of any particular country she is interested in controlling" (ER to ALS, 28 August 1939). After Russia joined with Germany in defeating and occupying Poland, ER wrote Strong that "there is a Polish officer who was taken prisoner in the part of Poland taken over by Russia, who escaped. He reports that every little land owner and every priest was shot by the Russian army. I realize that these things happen in war and soldiers can not be controlled, but they do not make the picture as charming as you would seem to make it" (ER to ALS, 17 October 1939).

Shortly thereafter ER criticized Americans who followed the Soviet party line, writing Strong, "The thing which is doing Russia the most harm in this country . . . is the fact that Earl Browder and various other American Communists, are discovered not to have been acting as free agents, but as directed ones. . . . It is one thing to have American citizens believe in a theory of government and argue for it on a perfectly independent basis, but to have it fostered by another country is not looked upon with favor over here" (ER to ALS, 25 October 1939). After Strong defended Russia's invasion of Finland, ER replied, "Everything else seems to be immaterial just now except the fact that Russia with 180,000,000 people, attacked a small country like Finland and which makes me feel that the leaders have in some way lost their first ideals" (ER to ALS, 20 January 1940).

By mid-1940 ER wrote Strong, "All you say is of course Nazi and Communist propaganda, as they want us to stay out of war. However, we are going ahead getting ready to prevent them from going any further. We are determined to protect our democratic forms of government and liberties" (ER to ALS, 17 June 1940). After visiting ER in early 1941, Strong began a letter to ER, "[I]t [the meeting] left me deeply unsatisfied; you seem to have changed so much" (ALS to ER, 12 February 1941). Shortly thereafter, Strong's letters to ER began to draw only brief acknowledgments.

During an extended visit to China in 1946–1947, Strong interviewed and publicized the Chinese communist leader, Mao Tse-tung; she lived in China from the late 1950s until her death. In 1959, when Strong criticized U.S. policy toward communist China, ER in her "My Day"* newspaper column of 21 December 1959 denounced Strong's views. ER commented, "I am not at all convinced by what she writes, and I am more than ever appalled by the closed-mind attitude of the really convinced Communist."

SELECTED BIBLIOGRAPHY

Anna Louise Strong Papers, Manuscripts and University Archives, University of Washington Libraries, Seattle.

Eleanor Roosevelt Papers, Franklin D. Roosevelt Library, Hyde Park, NY.

Strong, Anna Louise. *I Change Worlds: The Remaking of an American*. 1935. Reprinted 1979.

———. *My Native Land*. 1940.

Strong, Tracy B., and Helene Keyssar. *Right in Her Soul: The Life of Anna Louise Strong*. 1983.

Janet M. Cramer

SUCKLEY, MARGARET (20 December 1891, Rhinebeck, NY–29 June 1991, Rhinebeck, NY).

A distant cousin of both Eleanor and Franklin D. Roosevelt,* Margaret Suckley became one of FDR's least-known but most intimate confidantes during the presidential years. She was born and brought up at "Wilderstein," her family's country home, in the same rarified Hudson River atmosphere from which the president sprang. Margaret—known as

"Daisy" from girlhood—first got to know FDR in 1922, when he returned to his boyhood home in Hyde Park,* crippled by polio, and his mother, Sara Delano Roosevelt,* asked her to come and keep her son company as he did his exercises on the lawn. That summer, she developed a deep affection for her gallant, glamorous kinsman that never left her.

She was witty but quiet and undemanding, unqualifiedly admiring, and as delighted as was FDR by the Hudson River gossip, which ER found wearying. She was also utterly discreet: surviving letters suggest that her relationship with the president was chaste but distinctly flirtatious during the 1930s, yet no one—including the president's wife and mother—seems ever to have suspected it. Suckley helped FDR plan Top Cottage, his Hyde Park private retreat overlooking Val-Kill,* hoping to share it with him after he left the White House in 1941.

When he ran for a third term, instead, and won, she settled for a new role as his companion and sometime nurse. After his mother's death in 1941, with his secretary, Marguerite LeHand,* incapacitated by a stroke and his wife often occupied elsewhere, the president felt increasingly isolated. "His wife is a wonderful person," Suckley wrote, "but . . . [s]he is away so much, and when she is here she has so many people around— the splendid people who are trying to do good and improve the world— 'uplifters,' the [president] calls them—that he can not relax and really rest" (Ward, 148). Suckley filled as much of the vacuum as she could, and FDR gave her a job as archivist with his presidential library, in part, to provide a public explanation for her frequent presence at his side. She fed him his pills, made sure he ate his lunch, listened to his stories, sometimes traveled aboard his private railroad car, and, beginning in 1944, worried constantly over his declining health. She also gave FDR his celebrated Scotty, "Fala,"* and after his death only reluctantly relinquished the dog's care to ER.

Suckley was at the president's bedside, holding his hand, when he died at Warm Springs on 12 April 1945. She went on working at the Roosevelt Library in Hyde Park until her retirement in 1963 and died in her 100th year, in the house in which she had been born. Only afterward was it discovered that she had kept voluminous journals and scores of letters chronicling her days with FDR.

SELECTED BIBLIOGRAPHY

Ward, Geoffrey C. *Closest Companion: The Unknown Story of the Intimate Friendship between Franklin Roosevelt and Margaret Suckley.* 1995.

                                                               Geoffrey C. Ward

T

"TEAPOT TOUR" OF 1924. During the 1920s the New York state Democratic Committee's Women's Division, in which Eleanor Roosevelt played a leading role, made automobile campaign tours around the state. In 1924 Governor Alfred E. Smith* ran for reelection against ER's cousin, Theodore Roosevelt Jr. To remind voters that Roosevelt had been linked to the Teapot Dome oil scandals of the Harding administration, the women constructed a large replica of a tea kettle, which they mounted on top of their automobile, and when they arrived in a town, they would make it spout steam. ER later regretted this "rough stunt" at her cousin's expense, but it helped the Smith ticket win the state in another national Republican victory year (Lash, 291).

SELECTED BIBLIOGRAPHY
Lash, Joseph P. *Eleanor and Franklin*. 1971.

Elisabeth Israels Perry

TELEVISION. Eleanor Roosevelt skillfully used television as a means of mass communication during the last thirteen years of her life. She understood the great potential of the new medium to reach out to Americans across the nation, and she stood out as an industry defender—at least to a limited degree. In 1959 she published an article, "Television's Contribution to the Senior Citizen," in the most widely circulated television magazine, *TV Guide*. While ER admitted that she did not have much time to watch television, preferring to read newspapers instead, she expressed an appreciation for television's vast, although sometimes underutilized, social and cultural power. She praised its capacity to act as a companion to the elderly—to keep them informed and to assist them in understanding the nation's youth.* While many television shows were not to her liking, she said that "[when] a sense of loneliness comes over them [the elderly], they can turn on television, see people and hear them talk, listen to beautiful music. . . . Thus the responsibility of those who make and air the programs is great. They [the producers and network executives] ought to have in mind their most constant audiences—children and older people and housewives. . . . Whether programs are good or bad or offer opportunities for work or service, just as they are now there is no question in my mind that to our older citizens television is one of the blessings of our period of history" (Roosevelt, 7–8).

ER's television career began in 1949 on *Meet the Press*, in the days when there were only 106 television stations operating in the United States. At first she was represented by her son, Elliott Roosevelt.* Later, in 1955, she hired an agent, Thomas L. Stix, who had started a talent agency for radio* commentators in the early 1940s and whose clientele included contemporary news stars such as Elmer Davis, Edward R. Murrow, and Howard K. Smith. "You are going to have a bad time trying to sell me because I'm so controversial," she told Stix at the beginning, and he soon learned she was right, Stix wrote, because she "bore a well-hated name" (Stix, 104).

On 12 February 1950 she premiered her own live Sunday afternoon half-hour program, *Mrs. Roosevelt Meets the Public*, on the National Broadcasting Company (NBC). Elliott Roosevelt sold the show on the basis that few celebrities would turn down an invitation to appear with his mother. Formatted as if the viewer were a guest in ER's living room, the program did draw major figures during its seventeen-month run. Albert Einstein, for example, spoke during a rare appearance on television. But the show did not attract a sponsor in an era when advertisers were under pressure to avoid being associated with alleged communists. One manager for an advertising agency reported that he was visited by a delegation of women armed with a list of suspected communists and their sympathizers; ER's name was at the top.

Controversy over the program erupted in March 1950, when Elliott Roosevelt invited Paul Robeson, an African American actor and singer committed to political action, to appear along with U.S. representative Adam Clayton Powell, a New York Democrat, and Perry Howard, a Republican committeeman from Mississippi, to discuss African Americans in political life. Although ER's path had crossed Robeson's in connection with civil rights* issues since 1940, she was an open critic of his communist sympathies. As she wrote in her "My Day"* column of 2 November 1949, "Mr. Robeson does his people great harm in trying to line them up on the Communist side of the political picture" (Duberman, 361). Despite her public denouncement of Robeson's politics, NBC refused to allow Robeson on the air. After receiving more than 100 phone calls condemning Robeson in less than twenty-four hours, the network announced that "no good purpose would be served in having him speak on the issue of Negro politics" (Foner, 39). Dedicated as she was to free speech, ER did not defend Robeson's right to appear on her program. She refused to comment except to say that he would have been only one of a number of speakers and would not have been able to determine the program's point of view.

Throughout the 1950s ER regularly appeared on a wide variety of public affairs programs, such as the 11 May 1950 broadcast where she helped present the Four Freedoms Awards on the Columbia Broadcasting System (CBS). In 1954 Edward R. Murrow booked her as a special guest on the CBS *Person to Person* show, one of the most prestigious interview forums of that era. Her appearance on NBC's equally prestigious *Meet the Press* became almost commonplace: she was on 11 April 1954, 16 September 1956, 20 October 1957, and 26 October 1958. During her 1956 appearance ER played the role of the partisan Democrat as she bluntly challenged the qualifications of President Dwight D. Eisenhower* and Vice President Richard M. Nixon to lead the nation for a second term. Her 1957 appearance drew attention because she discussed her trip to the Union of Soviet Social Republics,* climaxed by an interview with Nikita Khrushchev.

In 1960 ER made frequent television appearances in support of Senator John F. Kennedy,* the Democratic presidential candidate. In that campaign, she filmed a sixty-second television advertisement praising Kennedy's character in contrast to that of Nixon. In particular, she praised Kennedy's grasp of history as an essential trait for a great man like her late husband. Her support may have helped Kennedy win the race by the thinnest of margins.

In the late 1950s ER became more broadly popular; the distaste for her held by some conservatives seemed to drain away as concerns about communists somewhat abated. She selectively ventured into avowedly entertainment shows, although initially she had refused to appear on game and quiz shows. Her agent, Stix, arranged for her to be a celebrity guest on *The Comedy Hour* with Bob Hope and a central figure in Frank Sinatra's show, *Here's to the Ladies*. He tried to arrange a guest shot on Ed Sullivan's popular variety show—before and after a trip to Israel by ER—but Sullivan deemed her too political because she wanted to present appeals for Israel,* and he rejected the idea.

According to Stix, the turning point in ER's acceptability to advertisers came when she agreed to do a commercial for Good Luck margarine in 1959. Initially advised to reject the idea by Maureen Corr,* her confidential secretary, and her close friends Joseph Lash,* and his wife, Trude Lash,* ER was persuaded to do the commercial when Stix told her it would prove "she would no longer be 'poison' to sponsors" (Stix, 105). She used her $35,000 fee for the margarine commercial on CARE packages for the relief of hungry children.

ER also participated in programming for National Education Television, the forerunner of public broadcasting. From 1959 to 1962 she moderated a public affairs documentary series, *Prospects for Mankind*, for Brandeis University and WGBH in Boston. It was produced by Henry Morgenthau III, the son of her old friends Henry and Elinor Morgenthau.* On the show ER talked with friends including President Kennedy, Murrow, Adali Stevenson,* and Bertrand Russell. At the time of her death in November 1962, she was working on plans to expand the program, which was filmed in Waltham, Massachusetts, before a live studio audience.

After ER died, CBS broadcast a half-hour special, *The Death of Eleanor Roosevelt*. In 1977 the American Broadcasting Company (ABC) broadcast the miniseries *Eleanor and Franklin*. For decades ER has remained in the public eye on network, public, and cable television as part of both documentaries and docudramas.

SELECTED BIBLIOGRAPHY
Black, Allida M. *Casting Her Own Shadow: Eleanor Roosevelt and the Shaping of Postwar Liberalism*. 1996.
Duberman, Martin B. *Paul Robeson*. 1988.
Foner, Philip S. *Paul Robeson Speaks: Writings, Speeches, Interviews, 1918–1974*. 1978.
Lash, Joseph P. *Eleanor: The Years Alone*. 1985.
Roosevelt, Eleanor. "Television's Contribution to the Senior Citizen." *TV Guide* (17 October 1959): 6–8.
Stix, Thomas L. "Mrs. Roosevelt Does a TV Commercial." *Harper's* 227 (November 1963): 104–106.

Douglas Gomery

THOMPSON, MALVINA (SCHEIDER) (8 January 1893, New York–12 April 1953, New York).

Malvina "Tommy" Thompson (Scheider) served as Eleanor Roosevelt's personal secretary and confidant for thirty years. More than that, according to ER, Thompson was "the person who makes life possible for me" (Beasley, 137). "She wanted to be useful and in many, many ways she not only made my life easier but gave me a reason for living," ER wrote after Thompson's death (Roosevelt, 107). The relationship ER had with Thompson was one of the closest of her adult life. When she first started work for ER, Thompson acquired the nickname "Tommy" from the Roosevelts' daughter, Anna (Halstead),* and it stayed with her for the rest of her life.

A native of the Bronx, Thompson was the daughter of a locomotive

Malvina Thompson, Eleanor Roosevelt's dedicated
secretary, is at her side during a trip to Illinois on
24 September 1939. *Courtesy of Franklin D. Roosevelt
Library*

engineer. After high school she taught herself typing and began her secretarial career. Employed by the American Red Cross from 1917 to 1922,
she moved on to the New York state Democratic Committee, where she
worked for ER on a part-time basis when she organized women's campaign activities for Governor Alfred E. Smith.* In the beginning, ER did
not know how to give dictation, and Thompson did not know how to
take it. In fact, Thompson never learned formal shorthand, so her notes
were unreadable by others. She continued part-time work for ER while
employed full-time by Louis M. Howe,* the political adviser to both
Eleanor and Franklin Delano Roosevelt.*

In 1921 she married Frank Scheider, an industrial arts teacher in the
New York City school system. When ER became First Lady in 1933,
Thompson moved to Washington as her secretary, leaving Scheider be-

hind. The marriage ended in divorce in 1938 on grounds of voluntary separation. Thompson had a long-term relationship with Henry Osthagen, an engineer with the U.S. Treasury Department, but did not marry him because of the demands of her job.

More than a secretary and friend, Thompson was an extension of ER. Like Marguerite "Missy" LeHand,* secretary to FDR, Thompson was offered living quarters in the White House. Despite working hours that often crowded midnight, however, she chose to live in a nearby apartment. Thompson handled ER's personal correspondence and, in fact, wrote many letters for ER's signature, working with the White House social office* that handled routine mail. She attended all ER's press conferences* and took notes during her speeches,* highlighting passages that were well received by the audience. She also acted as an informal editor for her magazine articles and books* and helped with political activities.

In addition to her secretarial duties, Thompson deftly juggled and mediated among the competing friends and factions that vied for ER's attention. Thompson was no fawning sycophant. "In almost anything I did, she was a help but she was also a stern critic," ER commented (Roosevelt, 107). Nevertheless, Thompson was a staunch defender of her boss. She once said, "People who criticize her simply don't know what they're talking about. They don't understand the meaning of her activities. Or they just unconsciously resent her being so different from other Presidents' wives. Or they insist on looking at her from their special political viewpoint" (Adamic, 108). Thompson told journalist Lorena Hickok,* ER's close friend, "My boss is a very big person, just about the biggest person in the world. Anything I can do to help her—no matter what— justifies my existence" (Lash, *Eleanor: The Years Alone*, 237).

One of Thompson's most valuable roles was as gatekeeper for ER. Since ER was reluctant to turn down requests, it was often up to Thompson to do so or to prevent requests from getting to ER in the first place. She also paved the way for access to ER; it was Thompson who initially arranged for Hickok to develop a reportorial relationship with a reluctant ER (Beasley, 29). FDR himself appreciated her talents. According to Margaret Suckley,* a Roosevelt cousin, "F[DR] says Tommy is the wonder of the age. She works steadily 18 hours a day, flying with Mrs. R., arranging accommodations, typing, etc., etc. He said she saves Mrs. R. from many unscrupulous people who get around Mrs. R. through sympathy" (Ward, 218). In order to remain independent, it was Thompson's practice not to go out socially with individuals who might try to use her as a conduit to the White House.

In an era when the job of confidential secretary was one of the highest to which a woman could aspire, Thompson herself received press attention, which ER wanted her to have. For instance, Thompson was featured in a lengthy article headlined "Keeping Up with Mrs. Roosevelt a Joy, Not a Job" by Emma Bugbee* in the *New York Herald Tribune* on 18

December 1939. In it Thompson explained how she conformed to ER's grueling work and travel schedule: "Everything I do is conditioned by her needs. . . . The real reason I have stood all this travel and all these letters is that I thoroughly enjoy my job. I couldn't endure it unless I did." In return, ER treated her as a member of the Roosevelt family, building an apartment for Thompson in 1938 at her own Val-Kill* cottage and including her in social activities. Thompson's ability to see the humorous side of situations made her an entertaining companion who often caused ER to burst into laughter. Still, Thompson never addressed her employer by her first name despite ER's repeated invitations to do so.

Thompson accompanied ER on most of her travels* as First Lady, including her wartime trips to Britain and South America. More often than not, Thompson was ER's only traveling companion. The two crossed the nation by train and air countless times, averaging some 40,000 miles per year during FDR's first two terms. Thompson carried a portable typewriter so she could keep up with ER's correspondence and type her "My Day"* newspaper column, which ER dictated in planes, trains, and automobiles.

Thompson was known for being selfless. Her colleague, Edith Helm, who served as ER's social secretary and often poured tea with Thompson at White House functions, said about Thompson, "I felt that her death was partly because she gave herself so unstintedly in service to others—including me" (Helm, 143). After Thompson died on the eighth anniversary of FDR's death, ER wrote, "I learned for the first time what being alone was like" (Lash, *Eleanor: The Years Alone*, 237).

SELECTED BIBLIOGRAPHY
Adamic, Louis. *Dinner at the White House*. 1946.
Beasley, Maurine. *Eleanor Roosevelt and the Media*. 1987.
Helm, Edith Benham. *The Captains and the Kings*. 1954.
Lash, Joseph P. *Eleanor: The Years Alone*. 1972.
Roosevelt, Eleanor. *On My Own*. 1958.
Ward, Geoffrey. *Closest Companion*. 1995.

Tracey A. Johnstone

TODHUNTER SCHOOL. In 1927 Eleanor Roosevelt began an association with the Todhunter School. A small, private school in New York City offering primary and secondary education for young women from well-to-do families, the school attempted to combine progressive teaching methods with traditional testing and grading standards. Not just a finishing school, Todhunter emphasized art, music, and dramatic activities as well as a college preparatory program, drawing students primarily from the area between Park Avenue and Central Park. Unlike many other elite schools, it admitted Jewish girls, although "not too large a proportion" (Cook, 2, 316).

ER and her friends Marion Dickerman* and Nancy Cook* purchased

Eleanor Roosevelt, fourth from left, associate principal, joins Marion Dickerman, principal, third from left, and teachers and students at the Todhunter School for girls for this photograph taken about 1929. *Courtesy of Franklin D. Roosevelt Library*

the school in 1927 from Winifred Todhunter, the owner, an Oxford graduate who had decided to return to her native England. ER, Dickerman, and Cook were also partners in Val-Kill* Industries in Hyde Park,* New York, which made handcrafted replicas of early American furniture. Dickerman took over as principal of Todhunter School, having taught there since 1922, and ER, at the age of forty-three, started a teaching career there, later becoming associate principal, although she had never attended college.

As a teacher ER patterned herself after Marie Souvestre*, headmistress of Allenwood School, an exclusive finishing school in England for daughters of the wealthy, which she had attended from 1899 to 1902, when her formal education ended. A liberal with an interest in social causes, Souvestre, whom ER credited with being one of the people who had most influenced her life, had attempted to acquaint her pupils with broad social issues and make them aware of the plight of the underprivileged.

With Souvestre as a model, ER tried to challenge her own students and widen their horizons. She wrote, "I gave courses in American history and in English and American literature and later we tried some courses in current events. . . . We visited the New York City Courts. . . . Those whom their parents allowed to go I took to see the various kinds of tenements . . . and various other places. All this made the government of the city something real and alive, rather than just words in a textbook" (Roosevelt, *Autobiography*, 146). She soon established herself as a commanding figure in the classroom, covering classical readings and trying to give students an appetite for lifetime learning.

After her husband, Franklin D. Roosevelt,* was inaugurated as governor of New York in 1929, ER continued to teach at Todhunter three days a week, commuting by train from Albany to New York City every Sunday evening and returning on Wednesday afternoon to resume her responsibilities at the state capital. She graded papers diligently on her train trips and wrote lesson plans.

Describing her work at Todhunter to a reporter in 1932, she said, "I like it better than anything else I do" (Cook, 1, 399). That year she enrolled her five-year-old granddaughter, Anna Eleanor "Sisty" Dall, in the school. On her 1932 income tax return, she listed her occupation as "teacher, writer and editor." She was pleased when her friend Wall Street financier Bernard Baruch* supported her interest in Todhunter and sent his niece there.

ER resigned from her teaching responsibilities at Todhunter when she took on the role of First Lady in 1933. For several years, however, she continued a close association with the school, appearing at its commencement exercises, hosting an annual weekend visit by the senior class to the White House, and arranging an annual lecture series on civic affairs for Todhunter graduates. The 1934–1935 series consisted of fourteen presentations by federal officials on New Deal* recovery efforts, and the 1935–1936 series, arranged with the help of New York City mayor Fiorello LaGuardia, focused on municipal government.

With the friendship between Dickerman, Cook, and ER beginning to fray during ER's White House years, Dickerman did not express total appreciation for ER's involvement in Todhunter. She complained that its identification as "ER's school" was a handicap in recruiting students because most of the pupils came from Republican families (Cook, 2, 360).

Nevertheless, in 1937 Dickerman sought ER's help in raising funds to acquire a larger building necessary for the school's growth. ER merely provided a mild statement of support for a fund-raising brochure. She declined Dickerman's request that she say Todhunter would be one of her chief interests after leaving Washington, advising the school's fund-raising firm that she had "no definite idea of what my other interests will be or where they will take me" (Lash, 476). The expansion plans were dropped in the recession of 1937–1938.

After a final break in her close friendship with Dickerman and Cook in the summer of 1938, ER wrote to Dickerman on 9 November 1938, withdrawing from her interests in Todhunter. In a separate letter written on the same day ER described a conversation with Cook the previous summer: "She told me, for instance, that while we were working in the [Women's Democratic] committee, in the school, and in the [Val-Kill] industries together, you had always felt that whatever was done was done for the sole purpose of building me up. My whole conception was entirely different. . . . I went into the school because I had an interest in education and in young people and being fond of you I was anxious to help you in what you wanted to do. It gave me an opportunity for regular work which I was anxious to have" (Cook, 2, 534). Dickerman reluctantly accepted ER's resignation on 14 November 1938.

For financial reasons, the Todhunter School merged in 1939 with the Dalton School in New York City, where Dickerman held an administrative position until resigning in 1942.

SELECTED BIBLIOGRAPHY
Cook, Blanche Weisen. *Eleanor Roosevelt*. Vols. 1, 2. 1992, 1999.
Davis, Kenneth S. *Invincible Summer: An Intimate Portrait of the Roosevelts*. 1974.
Eleanor Roosevelt Papers, Franklin D. Roosevelt Library, Hyde Park, NY.
Lash, Joseph P. *Eleanor and Franklin*. 1970.
Roosevelt, Eleanor. *The Autobiography of Eleanor Roosevelt*. 1960.
————. "The Seven People Who Shaped My Life." *Look* 15 (19 June 1951): 54–56, 58.

TRAVELS. Travel was essential to Eleanor Roosevelt's long career. It made her the physical embodiment of the Roosevelt administration, and it led to her worldwide fame. It was the good fortune of Franklin D. Roosevelt* that ER was a tireless traveler, and it was her good fortune that love of traveling helped establish her as a journalist, political leader, and world figure. ER traveled about 300,000 miles during the first eight years she was First Lady, flew across the Atlantic and Pacific during World War II,* and maintained a demanding travel schedule after leaving the White House. Traveling almost constantly, she appeared in many roles: political campaigner, fact-finder for her physically handicapped husband, publicist for the New Deal,* paid lecturer, goodwill ambassador, diplomat at the United Nations,* and global symbol of democratic values.

Yet, her traveling life had an inauspicious start when, at the age of two, she embarked on her first transatlantic journey aboard the ship *Britannic*. The ship collided with another vessel, the *Celtic*, and, amid much terror, little Eleanor was thrown from the *Britannic* to her father in a lifeboat below. After the *Celtic* returned the family to New York, her parents soon sailed again for Europe, but her fear of the ocean was so great that they left her behind with relatives. Nevertheless, when she was five, she went with her family for her first tour of Europe. In France Eleanor attended a convent school and spoke French, which she had first learned from her governess.

Eleanor Roosevelt, an early enthusiast of air travel for women, knits while seated in an airplane in this rare color photograph, originally taken by her son, John Roosevelt, about 1936, and later used in advertising. *Courtesy of Franklin D. Roosevelt Library.*

Between 1899 and 1902, ER again crossed the Atlantic to spend three adolescent years at Allenswood, an elite boarding school for girls near London. During holidays she frequently traveled in England and on the continent, visiting friends and relatives and at times accompanying the school's headmistress, Mlle. Marie Souvestre* on tours of Italy, France, Belgium, and Germany. Souvestre relaxed the careful chaperonage to which ER had been subjected and sent her forth with a Baedeker guidebook to explore the cities of Europe. This increased ER's self-confidence and led to her lifelong belief that traveling was both a liberating and educational experience.

Although ER and Franklin D. Roosevelt* enjoyed a honeymoon trip to Europe in the summer of 1905, ER's overseas voyages were soon curtailed by the raising of her five children. Nevertheless, by 1911 she had become an expert at family travel—moving her growing family every year between their New York City home and Albany, where FDR was serving in the state Senate, and for vacations to their summer home on Campobello* Island, New Brunswick, as well as to the estate of Sara Delano Roosevelt,* her mother-in-law, at Hyde Park,* New York. After the family moved to Washington, D.C., in 1913, when FDR became assistant secretary of the navy, ER accompanied him on some official travel, including an inspection trip to the Pacific Coast in 1914, a visit to the San Francisco World Fair in 1915, and a trip to postwar Europe in 1919. In the fall of 1920, she was the only woman aboard FDR's train for four weeks as it made a western campaign trip during his unsuccessful bid for the vice presidency.

Following FDR's polio attack in 1921, New York state became the locus of much of ER's travel as she emerged as a public figure. Becoming active in the Women's Division of the New York state Democratic Party,* she toured the state by car, campaigning for Governor Alfred E. Smith* in 1924. After FDR became governor himself in 1929, ER commuted by train from Albany to New York City every Sunday evening during the school year to teach at the Todhunter School* and returned on Wednesday afternoon to resume her responsibilities as the governor's wife. These included inspection trips to state-run hospitals, prisons, and other government institutions as a representative of her husband, who could not walk unaided. In the summer of 1929, she took her youngest sons, Franklin D. Roosevelt Jr.* and John Roosevelt,* on a tour of Europe.

Following FDR's inauguration as president in March 1933, fact-finding travels and appearances on behalf of the administration took ER to every state in the union except one, South Dakota, by 1940. A *New Yorker* cartoon of 3 June 1933 summed it up, showing two miners looking up from their shovels and saying, "For gosh sakes, here comes Mrs. Roosevelt!" Providing tangible evidence of New Deal concern for the unfortunate, by plane, train, car, and boat, ER visited Indian reservations, slums in Puerto Rico, schools, mines, factories, migrant camps, and federal projects of every description and attended civil rights* conferences and national political conventions. Visits with her children, who were scattered about the country, meant more travel. Unlike previous First Ladies, ER refused Secret Service protection, although she carried a gun in the glove compartment of her car when she went off on vacation trips to New England and Canada in 1933 and to Yosemite National Park in 1934 with her intimate friend Lorena Hickok.*

From 1936 until World War II,* ER also undertook two paid lecture tours a year, one in the spring and one in the fall, each of which required about two to three weeks of grueling travel. Often she was accompanied only by her secretary, Malvina Thompson* (Scheider). She learned to travel lightly, carrying dresses that did not wrinkle easily and two hats, one for good weather and one for bad. Her knitting went along, too, to occupy her en route.

Rarely did FDR and ER travel together, except when on the campaign trail, partly because of differences in their attitudes toward travel. While FDR relished taking the long way to a destination by train or ship, ER preferred getting there as quickly as possible. Although she depended on trains for her lecture tours because of their reliability, she loved flying.

ER was one of the first prominent women to boost commercial aviation in an era when many women were afraid to take to the skies. In 1933 Amelia Earhart* took ER on her first night flight from Washington, D.C., to Baltimore and back. ER had wanted to take flying lessons herself the previous year, but FDR had forbidden it. In 1939 ER was shown knitting on a plane in a handsome colored photograph (see page 519) used in national magazine advertising by the Air Transport Association, which said she had flown almost 100,000 miles in the previous four years.

During World War II, ER undertook notable international journeys at FDR's request. To foster goodwill in Anglo-American relations,* she flew to England, accompanied by Thompson, in October 1942 and spent three weeks touring the country, seeing bombed-out sections of London, hospitals, factories, shipyards, and military bases. She met with King George VI and Queen Elizabeth, Prime Minister Winston Churchill,* and members of Parliament, as well as American servicemen and British women defense workers. She broadcast over the BBC to the British people and filed her "My Day"* newspaper column from London, praising the spirit of her hosts in meeting wartime challenges.

In August and September 1943, traveling by herself as a representative of the American Red Cross,* she undertook a five-week, 25,000-mile trip to the South Pacific, visiting Australia and New Zealand as well as numerous islands, including Guadalcanal, Bora Bora, Samoa, Fiji, New Caledonia, and Christmas Island. Most of her time was spent at military camps, hospitals and Red Cross clubs where she saw an estimated 400,000 servicemen and women. She reported her experiences in her "My Day" column, typing it herself and donating the proceeds from it to the American Red Cross and the American Friends Service Committee. It was an arduous experience; she lost some thirty pounds.

By March 1944 ER was in the air again on another international mission. This time with Thompson by her side, ER made a 10,000-mile trip to visit troops at army and navy bases in Latin America.* She went to Brazil, Ecuador, Venezuela, Colombia, Panama, Guatemala, Cuba, Puerto Rico, the Virgin Islands, and several other Caribbean islands.

Although ER was generally described by her hosts as an excellent morale builder, her wartime travels were controversial. Gasoline was rationed in the United States, and civilian travel was limited. Shortly after her return from Latin America, a Gallup poll of Americans in May 1944 on the propriety of her trips reported "45 percent opposed on the grounds she had claimed travel privileges denied to most Americans, 36 percent in favor, 6 percent without opinion, and 13 percent claiming it was none of their business" (Beasley, 159).

ER's travels continued when she left the White House after the death of FDR on 12 April 1945. Upon being appointed a U.S. delegate to the United Nations* (UN) by President Harry S Truman* in December 1945, she began "bustling back and forth across the Atlantic Ocean rather like a harassed commuter for six years" (Roosevelt, 324). She went to London in January 1946 for the first meeting of the UN General Assembly and briefly visited refugee camps in Frankfurt and Berlin, Germany. Her UN responsibilities took her to Geneva in 1947 and 1951 and Paris in 1948 and 1951–1952. When her flight to Geneva in 1947 was delayed in both Newfoundland and Ireland, she and her physician, Dr. David Gurewitsch,* who was traveling on the same plane to Switzerland to seek medical care for himself, became close friends and in later years often traveled together.

Some of ER's post–White House travel was to commemorate the achievements of FDR. In the spring of 1948 she went to London as the guest of the king and queen of England to unveil a statue of FDR in Grosvenor Square. She then stopped briefly in Switzerland to see Gurewitsch, who was still recovering from tuberculosis, and in the Netherlands,* where she was the guest of Princess Juliana and received a doctor of laws degree from the University of Utrecht. In 1950, accompanied by Thompson, Elliott Roosevelt,* and two of his children, Chandler and Elliott Jr. (Tony), ER went to Oslo, Norway, for the unveiling of a statue of FDR and traveled on to visit Sweden, Finland, Denmark, the Netherlands, and Belgium.

After the UN General Assembly in Paris concluded in February 1952, ER, as a leading figure in world affairs, accepted a number of invitations to visit various countries. Accompanied by Maureen Corr,* who had replaced Thompson as her secretary, ER decided to "go home the long way—around the world" (Roosevelt, 324). The trip took her first to the Arab countries of Lebanon, Syria, and Jordan, where she found the refugee* camps for Palestinians displaced from Israel* "distressing beyond words" (Roosevelt, 326). She next visited Israel and was impressed by desert reclamation projects. Joined by Gurewitsch in Israel, ER went on to Karachi, Pakistan, where she was the guest of the All Pakistan Women's Association.

The next stop was New Delhi, India,* where she was met on 27 February 1952 by Prime Minister Jawaharlal Nehru and Madame Vijaya Pandit, the head of India's delegation to the United Nations, and other officials. During a thirty-day tour of India she saw most of the important cities of the country and made a brief side trip to Nepal, catching a glimpse of Mount Everest. From India she headed home, stopping for brief visits in Indonesia and the Philippines. Another overseas trip took place in December 1952, when she headed a U.S. delegation to Chile for the inauguration of President Carlos Ibanez.

Some of her most extensive travels occurred after leaving the United Nations in 1953. Her work as a volunteer helping organize new chapters of the American Association of the United Nations* (AAUN) took her throughout the United States. She also increased her paid speaking engagements. She noted in her *Autobiography*, "During the winter, I am on the road perhaps one week and sometimes two weeks in every month, including fairly regular trips abroad. Many of these [domestic trips] to deliver lectures (I give about 150 a year) or to work for the AAUN are quick ones. . . . I try to arrange it so I can go by plane, arriving just in time to keep my engagement, and return the same evening or at least early the next morning" (Roosevelt, 291).

In late May 1953 ER, with Corr again accompanying her, began another round-the-world trip as an unofficial ambassador of U.S. culture. During the first leg of the journey—a five-week stay in Japan as part of a cultural exchange program—ER was joined by her daughter-in-law, Minnewa Roosevelt, then the wife of Elliott. In Japan ER visited Hiroshima, where the United States had dropped the first atom bomb, met with Emperor Hirohito and Empress Nagako, and talked with government ministers, college professors, students, and women's groups. They discussed not only changes in Japan but also racial discrimination and McCarthyism* in the United States.

Continuing westward, she stopped briefly in Hong Kong and Istanbul, Turkey, before arriving in Athens, where she saw the Acropolis and had lunch with King Paul and Queen Fredericka. Gurewitsch met ER and Corr in Athens and traveled with them to Yugoslavia, for ER's first visit to a communist country. There she interviewed President Josip Tito on his country's efforts to develop as a nonaligned state after its break with the Soviet Union. ER returned home by way of Vienna, Paris, and London. As in the case of her trip to India, she used material gained from her travels for her column, magazine articles, and books.*

In 1955 ER fulfilled a desire to see the island of Bali in Indonesia, arranging a stop there while traveling to a meeting in Bangkok of the World Federation of United Nations Associations. With Gurewitsch as her companion, she also made a brief visit to Cambodia to see the Angkor Wat temple and a weeklong stop in Japan, where ER found economic conditions improving and democracy taking hold.

As she aged, ER showed no signs of slowing down her travels. At seventy-one in the summer of 1956 she spent three weeks in Europe with two grandsons, John Roosevelt Boettiger and Haven Clark Roosevelt. In the spring of 1957, ER accepted an invitation from the sultan of Morocco and spent several days touring Morocco along with Elliott Roosevelt and Gurewitsch. Morocco had been granted independence from France the previous year, and ER was struck by the development needs of the country.

In September 1957 ER, as an accredited journalist, made the first of two long-anticipated trips to the Union of the Soviet Socialist Republics,* flying to Moscow by way of Frankfurt, Berlin, and Copenhagen with Corr and Gurewitsch. Among the places she visited in the Soviet Union were Tashkent, Moscow, Leningrad, and Yalta on the Black Sea, where she interviewed Soviet premier Nikita S. Khrushchev on the arms race and other Cold War* issues. In her "My Day" column, she reported extensively on her impressions of the Soviet Union, noting its advances in education and medical care, as well as the depressing aspects of life there under a totalitarian system. A year later, in the fall of 1958, along with Gurewitsch, his wife, Edna, and Corr, ER made a second visit to the Soviet Union, after first attending a conference in Brussels of the World Federation of the United Nations Associations. While in Brussels, she had lunch with Queen Elizabeth of Belgium.

In 1959 ER took her granddaughter, Nina Roosevelt, to Iran and Israel. The trip gave ER an opportunity to visit her daughter, Anna Halsted,* whose husband, Dr. James Halsted, was helping establish a medical school in Shiraz, Iran. In September 1960 ER went to Warsaw, Poland, for a meeting of the World Federation of United Nations Associations. Upon her return, she traveled to several states to campaign for the Democratic presidential candidate, John F. Kennedy.*

Although her health was failing, ER made a last trip to Europe in February 1962, accompanied again by Corr and David and Edna Gurewitsch, showing them some of her favorite places. She stopped in London to make a recording for her television* series, *Prospects for Mankind*, and visit old friends, before continuing on for short stays in France, Israel, and St. Moritz, Switzerland.

In August 1962, although seriously ill, ER flew with the Gurewitsches and Corr to Campobello Island, New Brunswick, for the dedication of the FDR Memorial Bridge between the island and Lubec, Maine. She drove back to Hyde Park with Trude Lash,* with stops along the way to see her old friends, Molly Dewson* and Esther Lape.* It was her final trip before returning to New York, where she died. In many ways ER's entire life had been a journey, both literally and figuratively, as she had sought to learn and to tell others about the world around her.

SELECTED BIBLIOGRAPHY

Beasley, Maurine H. *Eleanor Roosevelt and the Media*. 1987.

Eleanor Roosevelt Papers, Franklin D. Roosevelt Library, Hyde Park, NY.

Lash, Joseph P. *Eleanor and Franklin*. 1971.

———. *Eleanor: The Years Alone*. 1972.

Roosevelt, Eleanor. *The Autobiography of Eleanor Roosevelt*. 1961.

Ruby Black Papers, Manuscript Division, Library of Congress, Washington, DC.

Kelly A. J. Powers

TRUMAN, HARRY S (8 May 1884, Lamar, MO–26 December 1972, Kansas City, MO).

It was Eleanor Roosevelt who informed Harry Truman that Franklin D. Roosevelt* had died. A graduate of the public schools of Independence, Missouri, a former farmer and haberdasher, and a veteran of World War I, Truman had moved up from local politics and government to the U.S. Senate. Serving there for ten years and then briefly as vice president, he became FDR's successor on 12 April 1945.

Harry had not been ER's choice, but she tried to shape his presidency, while he, aware of her great prestige and large following and admiring much about her, did what he could to get and hold on to her support. She wrote to him and visited with him frequently, devoted some of her "My Day"* newspaper columns to him, and gave him advice on a wide range of issues. Although sometimes resenting her pressure, he encouraged her to contact him, responded carefully in an effort to hold the New Deal* coalition together, and praised her for the advice she gave. Above all, late in 1945, he appointed her to the U.S. delegation to the United Nations,* and thereafter, he regularly reappointed her.

The appointment did not prevent her from criticizing Truman. Sometimes during 1946, her criticism focused on the people around him; often, it dealt with domestic policies; frequently, it suggested that the administration should rely more heavily on the United Nations and seek better relations with the Soviet Union. Truman treated her criticisms with respect and tried to persuade her that he was doing what her husband would have done. Restrained by her position in the United Nations, she often concealed her unhappiness from the public.

In 1947, a pivotal year in American foreign policy, ER swung from criticism to support. Her discontent had soared when Truman called for economic and military aid to Greece and Turkey, for the "Truman Doctrine," in her view, linked the United States with an undemocratic regime in Greece and bypassed and thus weakened the United Nations, but he responded with an elaborate defense of the policy. He also defended his loyalty program (requiring investigations of the loyalty of government workers) against her criticism and praised her work in the United Nations. He did more for himself in her eyes by endorsing a program of American aid for European economic recovery (the Marshall Plan) and drawing her into the campaign for it. She now defended him against supporters of her former ally, Henry A. Wallace.*

The new Truman–Roosevelt relationship did not last. By early 1948, ER was convinced that the influence of Wall Street and the military was on the rise and that Truman was weakening the United Nations, bungling in the Middle East, and moving toward war with the Soviet Union. She felt so at odds with the administration, especially on policy toward Palestine, that she offered to resign from the United Nations so as to be free to express her opinions.

ER also feared the president was leading the Democratic Party* and liberalism toward a serious defeat in the presidential election of 1948. She did not join her sons in efforts to substitute Dwight D. Eisenhower* for Truman, but, although the latter persuaded her not to resign, she also resisted pressure to endorse him. In defense of her neutrality, she argued that her United Nations post made it inappropriate for her to participate in party politics. After the Democrats nominated Truman, she told him she would do no more than inform her readers of her intention to vote for the Democratic ticket. Truman replied that she had done yeoman service for the party in her column, but she saw her efforts as designed mainly to elect liberals to Congress.* (See "My Day," 11 August 1948 and 10–11 September 1948.)

Late in the campaign, ER reluctantly endorsed the president, doing so after an appeal from Frances Perkins.* ER explained to Perkins that Truman had been "such a weak and vacillating person" and had "made such poor appointments" that she could not give "any good reasons" for being for him (ER to Perkins, 4 October 1948). Nevertheless, she found persuasive Perkins' view that, although Truman would surely lose, ER should do all she could for her party's choice.

Thus, ER sent a letter to Truman. Noting speculation that her silence meant she favored Tom Dewey, she insisted that she was "unqualifiedly" for "the Democratic candidate" (ER to Truman, 4 October 1948). Needing her help, Truman obtained permission to release her endorsement to the public, and she reinforced it with a radio broadcast.*

Truman's surprising victory raised his status. ER continued to regard him as "easily fooled in spite of his good intentions," but she gave his spirited campaign most of the credit for his win (ER to Joseph Lash,* 5 November 1948). When he maintained that her endorsement had been invaluable, she insisted that he was elected on his own.

After the election, the two continued to press one another. He advised her that he needed liberal support to carry out the wishes of the American people, and she told him that the United States must prove to the poverty-stricken all over the world that democracy betters the lot of all people. In line with her advice, he reappointed her to the United Nations and sent her on trips to the Third World. She supported the North Atlantic Treaty Organization and his Korean War policy, and he backed her in her clash with Cardinal Spellman.* He angered her by not endorsing her son, James Roosevelt,* for governor of California; she continued to believe that he should fire some of the people around him, and, before he decided not to run again in 1952, she favored Adlai Stevenson* as the Democratic candidate. Nevertheless, she accepted Truman's request that she address the Democratic National Convention and wrote him a generous letter when he left office.

Out of office, ER and Truman maintained a complex relationship. Not always political allies, they clashed on political issues more than once, yet she attended the dedication of the Truman Library and the celebration of his seventy-fifth birthday, and he came to her funeral and endorsed her for the Nobel Peace Prize.

SELECTED BIBLIOGRAPHY

Black, Alida M. *Casting Her Own Shadow: Eleanor Roosevelt and the Shaping of Postwar Liberalism.* 1996.

Hamby, Alonzo L. *Beyond the New Deal: Harry S. Truman and American Liberalism.* 1973.

Kirkendall, Richard S. "ER and the Issue of FDR's Successor." In Joan Hoff-Wilson and Marjorie Lightman, eds., *Without Precedent: The Life and Career of Eleanor Roosevelt.* 1984.

Lash, Joseph P. *Eleanor: The Years Alone.* 1972.

Richard S. Kirkendall

TUGWELL, REXFORD GUY (10 July 1891, Sinclairville, NY–21 July 1979, Santa Barbara, CA).

Rexford G. Tugwell, who held a doctorate in economics from the University of Pennsylvania, was one of the Columbia University professors known as the "brains trust" who advised Franklin D. Roosevelt* on economic recovery programs during his 1932 presidential campaign. Discussions of the group often began at the dinner table, where Tugwell found that Eleanor Roosevelt always had some good cause to further and was deeply concerned about the worsening effects of the depression. As ER sought to gain a better understanding of the economic crises, her comments annoyed some of the advisers, but Tugwell concluded that "even if not profound, and somewhat platitudinous, they went cautiously in the right direction" (Tugwell, 86).

FDR appointed Tugwell assistant secretary of agriculture in 1933, undersecretary of agriculture in 1934, and administrator of the Resettlement Administration in 1935. Tugwell offered FDR advice on a broad range of New Deal* policies. In 1933 he helped prepare legislative proposals for the Agricultural Adjustment Act, which aimed to curb overproduction and raise farm commodity prices, and the National Industrial Recovery Act, which called for industrial self-regulation in an attempt to expand production and purchasing power. Tugwell advocated limits on the planting of surplus staple crops like cotton and wheat and championed planning as a cure for economic ills, contending that business cooperating with government could produce successful results. Like ER, he wanted everyone to share in America's abundance.

ER had cordial, but limited, contacts with Tugwell in 1933–1934. She endorsed a bill developed by Tugwell and introduced in Congress* in June 1933 to strengthen consumer protection under the Pure Food and Drug Act of 1906, even though it was strongly attacked and blocked by industry. In December 1933 Tugwell took ER for a tour of the federal agricultural research center at Beltsville, Maryland, to show her marginal land where one of the Resettlement Administration's greenbelt towns* would later be built.

Coincidence placed them in Puerto Rico at the same time in March 1934, when ER was reviewing depressed conditions on the island, and Tugwell was seeking ways to improve its agriculture. After Tugwell sent ER copies of two of his speeches, including one promoting American wines, but unfortunately entitled "Wine, Women, and the New Deal," ER replied, "I think you did a swell job in both of these speeches. However, I think I would be a little more conservative in my use of words and titles. . . . Your sense of humor does lead you into traps" (ER to RT, 3 May 1934). On 19 May 1934, after a dinner with ER, Tugwell noted in his diary, "My admiration for her grows all the time. She is always concerned in good causes and has boundless energy in furthering them" (Namorato, 119).

ER's dedication to furthering the Arthurdale* subsistence homestead project near Reedsville, West Virginia, for displaced coal miners, however, created a challenge for Tugwell after it came under his Resettlement Administration, established by executive order in May 1935. Unlike Secretary of the Interior Harold L. Ickes,* who, when he oversaw Arthurdale, resented ER's involvement, Tugwell was more sympathetic in addressing her concerns. Arthurdale accounted for a small part of Tugwell's $375 million first-year budget for the new agency, but it took a disproportionate amount of his time. ER sometimes bypassed Tugwell and took Arthurdale problems directly to FDR. Arthurdale residents, in turn, sometimes tended to go over Tugwell's head to ER. She was persistent with suggestions and requests to Tugwell for expedited action on a range of Arthurdale issues such as building barns, providing construction materials, setting up a committee of businessmen to advise on attracting small industries for the community, and finding ways to satisfy the settlers' expectations of eventually owning their houses.

Tugwell, whose main interest was in urban greenbelt communities, questioned the practicality of the Arthurdale project. As early as 1932 he had debated with the Roosevelts the feasibility of rural resettlement for displaced industrial workers, since he believed people "go to employment, not employment to people" (Lash, 409). Efforts to attract industry to Arthurdale did not succeed until World War II.* Nevertheless, Tugwell attempted to be responsive to ER's involvement in the community.

Tugwell also provided ER with summary information on other activities of the Resettlement Administration. By 1, November 1936, the new agency had (1) made loans totaling almost $94 million to 386,000 needy farm families who could not get credit elsewhere; (2) made small grants to meet emergency needs of 468,000 farm families amounting to over $19 million; (3) purchased 9,100,000 acres of substandard land to convert it to forests, parks, and other noncrop uses; (4) completed nineteen rural resettlement projects (inherited from other agencies) and continued work on forty-four additional rural communities for displaced or impoverished families; and (5) started building three greenbelt suburban communities to provide low-income housing for increasing urban populations.

New Deal critics labeled the supporters of the Resettlement Administration as collectivists, a term associated with communism, and stepped up their attacks on Tugwell. He resigned at the end of 1936. The Resettlement Administration was absorbed the following year into the Farm Security Administration, and the resettlement communities were eventually liquidated.

Tugwell subsequently held a variety of positions. These included the vice presidency of the American Molasses Company in 1937, the chairmanship of the New York City planning commission from 1938 to 1940, and the governorship of Puerto Rico from 1941 to 1946. He was a professor of political science at the University of Chicago from 1946 to 1957 and a senior fellow and associate of the Center for the Study of Democratic Institutions from 1964 to 1979.

In a reminiscence for a journal prepared for the 1958 Americans for Democratic Action* Convention, Tugwell said, "No one who ever saw Eleanor Roosevelt sit down facing her husband and holding his eye firmly, say to him 'Franklin, I think you should . . . ' Or, 'Franklin surely you will not . . . ' will ever forget the experience. . . . It would be impossible to say how often and to what extent American governmental processes have been turned in new directions because of her determination that people should be hurt as little as possible and that as much should be done for them as could be managed."

SELECTED BIBLIOGRAPHY
Eleanor Roosevelt Papers, Franklin D. Roosevelt Library, Hyde Park, NY.
Lash, Joseph P. *Eleanor and Franklin*. 1971.
Namorato, Michael V., ed. *The Diary of Rexford G. Tugwell: The New Deal. 1932–1935*. 1992.

Rexford G. Tugwell Papers, Franklin D. Roosevelt Library, Hyde Park, NY.
Sternsher, Bernard. *Rexford Tugwell and the New Deal*. 1964.
Tugwell, Rexford G. *The Brains Trust*. 1968.

Leonard Schlup

U

UNION OF SOVIET SOCIALIST REPUBLICS, TRIPS TO. For decades, Eleanor Roosevelt had wanted to travel to the Soviet Union, only to have her plans canceled. ER's chance to visit finally came in the late 1950s. "I do not feel," she wrote in her autobiography,* "that we, as individuals, or as a nation, gain either in dignity or in prestige by refusing to know the people who lead the great opposition to our way of life" (Roosevelt, 435). Acting on her own advice, ER made two trips to the Soviet Union, one in 1957 and the other in 1958. These visits afforded her the opportunity to draw her own conclusions about the Soviet Union, the nation that dominated American foreign policy considerations in the post–World War II* years.

ER's first visit, in 1957, was as a journalist reporting for the *New York Post*, which had purchased the flagship rights to her "My Day"* column the previous year. The trip made an indelible impression. Like all American travelers to the Soviet Union, ER found the clothes drab and tourist schedules rigid. Like all tourists, her ability to meet typical Soviet citizens was severely limited. In addition to the standard tourist sites such as Lenin's mausoleum and Moscow State University, Roosevelt visited state farms and a Baptist church in Moscow, as well as many educational and medical facilities. Upon the advice of Supreme Court justice William O. Douglas, ER also traveled to Soviet Central Asia.

But it was clear ER was no ordinary tourist. Her arrival was noted on the front page of all the major Soviet newspapers, and she was given the same furniture and translator Franklin D. Roosevelt* had used at the Yalta Conference in 1945. Few tourists or even journalists could aspire to interview Premier Nikita Khrushchev or Andrei Gromyko, the minister of foreign affairs. The culmination of ER's trip was a three-hour interview with Khrushchev at his vacation home in Yalta—his first major interview by a westerner. The interview rated front-page headlines in Soviet papers, with *Pravda* declaring on 28 September 1957 that "the conversation took place in a warm and brotherly atmosphere." In fact, it was amiable but thorny, covering controversial topics such as the arms race and the treatment of Soviet Jews.* As Khrushchev joked, "At least we did not shoot each other" (Lash, 271). ER reciprocated Khrushchev's hospitality by inviting him to visit Hyde Park,* which he did during his first visit to the United States in 1959.

ER's second trip occurred in the fall of 1958, when she visited the Soviet Union for three weeks after attending a meeting of the World Federation of United Nations Associations at the World's Fair in Brussels as a delegate representing the American Association of the United Nations.* Traveling with her friends David and Edna Gurewitsch,* ER again toured a variety of educational and health care institutions. She devoted her "My Day" columns of 3 October and 6 October 1958 to the visit, detailing the accommodations afforded her in Russia and the merits of the United States' opening full diplomatic and economic relations with both Russia and China.

ER came away from her visits impressed by the progress that had been made in housing and medical care since the 1920s and the Soviet's post-war building efforts. These were all efforts that ER identified with and supported, not only in underdeveloped nations but also in America. Yet, it was clear to ER that the Soviet people paid a high personal and political price in accomplishing these goals.

For ER, the most memorable feature of the trips was the sober nature of Soviet life. Hardened by the war and cowed by a repressive government that neglected basic civil and human rights, citizens seemed to live in a state of fear. Her comment upon her return home, "The people there spend their lives frightened, and everything in the newspapers is done to frighten them," was reported by the *New York Times* on 1 October 1958. This distaste for the Soviet system, reinforced by her experiences and travels during the Cold War,* appeared in the last portion of her autobiography: "I think I should die if I had to live in Soviet Russia" (Roosevelt, 369).

SELECT BIBLIOGRAPHY
Gurewitsch, David. *Her Day*. 1973.
Lash, Joseph. *Eleanor: The Years Alone*. 1972.
Roosevelt, Eleanor. *The Autobiography of Eleanor Roosevelt*. 1992.

Tracey A. Johnstone

UNION OF SOVIET SOCIALIST REPUBLICS, VIEWS ON. Through-out the last forty years of her life, Eleanor Roosevelt dealt with the Union of Soviet Socialist Republics from a variety of positions: First Lady, delegate to the United Nations,* world traveler, and unofficial U.S. goodwill ambassador. Her opinions of the Soviet Union can be divided into two periods with distinctly different tones: from 1933 to 1945 (characterized largely by acceptance and alliance) and from 1945 until her death in 1962 (characterized by more stringent anticommunism and a growing distrust of Soviet intentions). ER's commitment to human rights,* world peace, and the suffering of the poor in underdeveloped and war-ravaged nations (including the Soviet Union) never wavered. Yet, the geopolitical realities brought on by World War II* followed by the Cold War* forced her to accommodate her humanitarian concerns about the Soviet Union with the realpolitik considerations of U.S. foreign policy.*

ER made her first critical public statement regarding the Soviet Union while addressing the question of the Soviet invasion of Finland at a press conference* on 12 February 1940. ER stated that she saw no justification for this act of aggression. This criticism, however, was brief, for with the German invasion of the Soviet Union in June 1941, the Soviets joined the Allied cause. In her "My Day"* column of 16 September 1942, she commended Soviet bravery at the Battle of Stalingrad. "There is no retreat for the defenders of Stalingrad," she wrote. "As we read this morning that their lines stiffen, I think everyone in this country must want to express his admiration for their extraordinary ability to stand and to take it" (Chadakoff, 254). In common with other Americans, any questions she might have had concerning human rights and the justness of the Soviet system were subordinated to the common American and Soviet goal: the defeat of Hitler's Germany.

During the postwar years, ER, as an American delegate to the United Nations, participated in heated debates over the reconstruction of Europe in the wake of the deterioration of American–Soviet relations. As head of the United Nations Human Rights Commission, she clashed with the Soviets over the citizenship rights of war refugees* and the tenets of the Universal Declaration of Human Rights.* After completing the negotiations that led to the adoption of the declaration, she displayed a hardening attitude toward the Soviets. On 15 January 1949 the *New York Herald Tribune* reported her comment: "I don't think I will ever compromise again even on words. The Soviets look on this as evidence of weakness rather than as a gesture of good will." Because of her opposition to Soviet initiatives, the Soviet press derided her as a "hypocritical servant of capitalism . . . a fly darkening the Soviet sun" (Lash, 106).

ER's view of the Soviet Union during the Cold War years fell between the two extremes present in American society: that of the unabashed cold warrior and that of the Soviet sympathizer and apologist. ER was not the archetypal American cold warrior. She often clashed with U.S. and Allied officials over policies toward the Soviet Union that she regarded as too confrontational; she saw Churchill's "Iron Curtain" speech as ill timed and incendiary. Additionally, she lauded the Soviet Union for the great advances it had made in recovering from the massive destruction of World War II. Consequently, many Republicans and conservatives criticized her and fellow Roosevelt–Truman Democrats as soft on communism, labeling them "socialists or 'commicrats' " (Cook, 118).

ER, on the other hand, refused to align with American liberals who viewed the Soviet Union as benign. She rejected the ideas of the Progressive Citizens of America, a group associated with Henry Wallace* that welcomed communist political support at home and idealized the Soviet Union. Instead, she favored membership in the Americans for Democratic Action,* a group that generally supported a confrontational foreign policy toward the Soviets. As a liberal cold warrior, she saw the conflict between the United States and the Soviet Union as more of an economic and political struggle than a military one. While she supported the Marshall Plan, which was designed to aid Europe as a way of counterbalancing the threat of Soviet expansion, she continued to be concerned about broad issues closer to her heart, such as world peace and human rights. Moreover, she refused to consider a policy of disengagement, instead hoping that continued contact with the Soviets would bring world peace and stability.

SELECTED BIBLIOGRAPHY

Chadakoff, Rochelle, ed. *Eleanor Roosevelt's "My Day."* Vol. 1. 1989.

Cook, Blanche Wiesen. " 'Turn toward Peace': ER and Foreign Affairs." In Joan Hoff-Wilson and Marjorie Lightman, eds., *Without Precedent: The Life and Career of Eleanor Roosevelt*. 1984.

Janeway, Elizabeth. "First Lady of the U.N." *New York Times Magazine*, 22 October 1950.

Lash, Joseph. *Eleanor: The Years Alone*. 1972.

Roosevelt, Eleanor. *The Autobiography of Eleanor Roosevelt*. 1992.

Tracey A. Johnstone

UNITED NATIONS. Eleanor Roosevelt's commitment to an international organization dedicated to human rights* and world peace predated the creation of the United Nations in 1945. In the 1930s she spoke out for peace and opposed what she considered the glorification of war and the establishment of a military culture in the United States. A supporter of the League of Nations,* ER also advocated American membership in the World Court,* an organization that the United States never joined. Many of her friends, such as Esther Lape* and Elizabeth Read,* were well-known peace advocates, and ER contributed a chapter to *Why Wars Must Cease* by the suffrage leader Carrie Chapman Catt.*

Identifying herself as a "realistic pacifist" (Black, 138), ER shifted her perspective during the late 1930s, when totalitarian regimes in Germany, Spain,* and Italy began to challenge democratic societies. The aggressiveness of fascism and the bitter struggle of World War II* only re-

Eleanor Roosevelt listens over headphones along with John Foster Dulles (l.) and Adlai Stevenson to proceedings at the United Nations in 1946. *Courtesy of Franklin D. Roosevelt Library*

inforced her conviction that a United Nations—as the planned world organization was dubbed by her husband, Franklin D. Roosevelt*—was essential to prevent future conflicts.

ER was appointed to the first American delegation to the United Nations by her husband's successor, President Harry S Truman,* in December 1945. Given her interest in world affairs and her reputation for diligent public service, she was a logical choice. But there were more practical reasons. Truman, aware of ER's standing with African American voters and the progressive wing of the Democratic Party,* sought her political support. Characteristically self-deprecatory, ER initially hesitated to accept the position because of her diplomatic inexperience but then accepted it.

Sixty-one years old, she joined a bipartisan, all-male, five-person delegation (plus five alternates) led by Secretary of State James Byrnes and former secretary of state Edward Stettinius at the historic first meeting of the General Assembly in London in January 1946. She began her conscientious service by immersing herself in State Department reports on the voyage across the Atlantic. ER already had personal experience in international affairs. More than most delegates, she had observed the challenges of the period firsthand through her wartime travels* overseas. She remained a delegate until President Dwight D. Eisenhower* replaced her in 1953.

ER made three major contributions to the United Nations at a time when its future was uncertain. First, her unflagging optimism for, and unending confidence in, the United Nations and her highly tuned ethical and moralistic perceptions, which never seemed selfish demonstrations of personal ego, made her a significant advocate for the organization. ER also added her international reputation to the new organization's credibility. In her travels at the end of the United Nations sessions, she carried throughout the world the message of the necessity for an international organization dedicated to collective security and world peace.

Second, she chaired the Human Rights Commission, which in 1948 drafted an international document called the Universal Declaration of Human Rights.* As the elected chair of this eighteen-member commission, for over five years she presided over divisive debates among the representatives of three blocs in the United Nations—the Western democratic-capitalistic societies, the Eastern bloc of communist nations, and the Third World nations, many of the latter newly freed from colonialism. Frequently, ER clashed with the Soviet representative, A. P. Pavlov, over the proper definition of what constituted human liberties. The Soviets, while lambasting the Americans for their denial of rights to African Americans, concentrated on economic entitlements delivered by the state to society. They insisted on articles in the declaration guaranteeing health care, housing, and full employment, while the British and Americans demanded the protection of individuals from repressive governments.

At issue was the definition of what constituted the kinds of liberties and rights that an international organization should guarantee to citizens of nation-states at the end of the twentieth century. As ER and her nation drifted into a Cold War* mentality, she still recognized that her frustrations with the Russians at the United Nations were the result of their following orders from Moscow. Though never simply the voice of U.S. State Department policy developed in Washington, she realized she was never completely autonomous either.

Even as ER supported the inclusion of principles for individual liberty and freedom on the order of the Bill of Rights, she reminded her colleagues that the declaration must be acceptable to all religions, ideologies, and cultures and that it must be written promptly. Throughout she insisted on brevity and simple language. She demanded hard work and prompt action, and under her leadership the committee's draft of a pre-amble and thirty articles was completed in 1948.

On 10 December of that year, a proud ER presented the final document to the General Assembly and listened to the overwhelming support of the delegates for the declaration. In an eloquent speech, she compared the declaration to the American Bill of Rights and the French Declaration of Rights. Forty-eight nations voted in the affirmative, two were absent, and there were eight abstentions from the communist bloc.

In an address delivered in French at the Sorbonne University in Paris before the final vote, ER, the least anti-Russian of the American dele-gates, told her audience, with the communist nations foremost in her mind, that on the observance of human rights rested the world's future hopes for peace. Yet, as it stood, the declaration was not legally binding.

ER and the Human Rights Commission next tackled the necessary task of developing some form of enforcement mechanism so that nations would be bound to respect the principles to which they had agreed. Directed by the U.S. State Department, she earlier had separated enforce-ment from definition. Although the British had insisted that the decla-ration be accompanied by some provision for implementation before it was voted on, ER had carried the day. She continued her work on the commission until the bulk of the work on two covenants or treaties was finished by which ratifying nations would be obligated to implement the rights enunciated in the declaration.

In these postwar actions by the Human Rights Commission chaired by ER came the modern definition of human rights and the essential stan-dards required of all nations in their treatment of their citizens. The declaration was one of the first steps taken in the field of human rights. The document has become the measure for establishing obligatory norms to govern international behavior insofar as the rights of individuals are concerned.

ER's third major contribution to the United Nations involved work on Committee Three, which dealt with humanitarian, social, and cultural affairs. Her colleagues on the American delegation felt such matters were the female's sphere and so, meeting without ER, assigned her to that committee. As she noted in *On My Own*, her account of her life after her husband's death, the male delegates believed that she would do the least harm on Committee Three.

Although John Foster Dulles* and other members of the American delegation came to respect ER, they were always suspicious of her ability and patronizingly dismissive of her contributions. On the other hand, she distrusted the grandstanding of several members, felt that James Brynes was frightened of his own delegation, and disliked the unilateral press conferences held by ambitious members of the delegation. It was

ER's own lack of personal ambition that brought her stature as the "First Lady of the World."

To the surprise of everyone, Committee Three quickly emerged as one of the most important structures in the United Nations when it was assigned the issue of the refugees.* Throughout Europe, over 1 million displaced persons were living in western detention camps. Homeless as a result of the war, some were former prisoners of war; others were survivors of concentration camps; many, as ER recognized, had lived in countries that no longer belonged to them. Some wanted to return to their native lands, but others feared the new communist regimes installed after the war.

Again she faced the Soviets, this time over the issue of repatriation, which as sharply as any other in the early days of the United Nations divided the East and West. ER, espousing the view that individuals should choose for themselves, confronted Andrei Vishinsky, who had been the legendary lead prosecutor in Stalin's purge trials in Moscow. Vishinsky and the Yugoslavian delegate Ales Beber rejected the Western proposal that there should be an international authority established under the auspices of the United Nations to deal with the refugee issue. Nor did they believe that these displaced persons should be permitted to choose where they would go. According to the Eastern bloc delegates, the refugees were no more than traitors and war criminals who had been stirred up by the West. The problem could easily be solved by repatriation, not, as ER proposed, by an International Refugee Organization.

In time ER's view was accepted by the General Assembly during a period in United Nations history when the views of the United States generally prevailed. But in the course of the debates, ER, one of the important spokespersons for civil rights* in the United States, was frequently assailed for her nation's failure to afford the political rights she sought for displaced persons to its own population of African Americans.

These long, acrimonious arguments with the Russians intensified ER's understanding that the United States would have to stand firm against the Soviets and argue tenaciously but reasonably with the Eastern bloc in the forum of the United Nations. A committed internationalist and a lifetime proponent of the necessity of global cooperation, ER was increasingly caught between the cold warriors of her nation and the conciliatory spirit that she believed to be the essence of any international organization. In her public statements ER cautioned moderation and understanding, even as she vociferously opposed McCarthyism* and the violations of the rights of Americans smeared as communists by Senator Joseph McCarthy.

On the other hand, by 1946 ER was comparing Soviet parliamentary tactics and propaganda to those of the Nazis. She also supported a unilateral instrument of American foreign policy—the Marshall Plan—arguing that either the Americans or the Russians would rebuild Europe. Initially, she could not bring herself to sanction the North Atlantic Treaty Organization, the Western bloc military alliance, because she thought it violated the essence of the United Nations, but she later defended it. During her seven-year tenure at the United Nations, the balance and moderation that had always marked ER's approach to postwar events became more difficult for her to maintain.

In 1953 President Eisenhower replaced ER as a delegate to the United Nations, and now sixty-eight years old, she returned to private life. But her personal commitment to the United Nations continued. Immediately, she joined the American Association of the United Nations* and as a volunteer traveled throughout the United States promoting the United Nations. At the time, the organization was under attack from right-wing Republicans and neoisolationists in the United States who believed it a communist-front organization. In response ER argued for its growing importance as a forum in which Cold War issues could be discussed.

In 1961, when Adlai Stevenson* became the United Nations ambassador in the administration of President John F. Kennedy,* he recommended that ER be reappointed to the organization she had served so well from 1945 to 1953. Now seventy-six, ER served as a delegate to the special March 1961 session. She became a special adviser to the U.S. delegation in 1962 while suffering from the bone marrow disease that contributed to her death on 7 November 1962. Two days later in an extraordinary session of the United Nations, her friend Adlai Stevenson offered an eloquent eulogy to a woman of "tireless energy . . . [who] had breathed life into [the United Nations]" (Johnson, 339).

SELECTED BIBLIOGRAPHY

Berger, Jason. *A New Deal for the World: Eleanor Roosevelt and American Foreign Policy*. 1981.

Black, Alida. *Casting Her Own Shadow: Eleanor Roosevelt and the Shaping of Post War Liberalism*. 1996.

Cook, Blanche Wiesen. "Eleanor Roosevelt and Human Rights: The Battle for Peace and Planetary Decency." In Edward Crapol, ed., *Women and American Foreign Policy*. 1992.

Johnson, Walter, ed. *The Papers of Adlai Stevenson*. Vol. 8. 1979.

Lash, Joseph P. *Eleanor: The Years Alone*. 1972.

Scharf, Lois. *Eleanor Roosevelt: First Lady of American Liberalism*. 1987.

Jean Harvey Baker

UNIVERSAL DECLARATION OF HUMAN RIGHTS. As U.S. delegate to the United Nations* (UN), Eleanor Roosevelt was credited with being the leading spirit behind the adoption of the Universal Declaration of Human Rights, a document that has come to be recognized all over the world as a powerful statement of human equality. It serves today as the basis for efforts to internationalize the concept of human rights.*

Eleanor Roosevelt holds a poster in November 1949 at Lake Success, New York, showing her crowning achievement as U.S. delegate to the United Nations—the Universal Declaration of Human Rights. *Courtesy of Franklin D. Roosevelt Library*

Adopted without dissent by the United Nations General Assembly on 10 December 1948, the declaration proclaimed that all men and women everywhere were born free and equal in dignity, entitled to basic human rights and freedoms without discrimination. Consisting of a preamble and thirty articles, the declaration sets forth basic civil, economic, political, and social rights and freedoms of all persons. The preamble states that the declaration is intended to be "a common standard of achievement for all peoples and all nations."

In January 1947 ER was elected chair of the Human Rights Commission established to work on the declaration after chairing a temporary group that recommended the UN General Assembly set up the eighteen-member commission. As chair, ER split the commission into three committees. The committee that she led drafted the declaration, the statement of general principles that was ratified by the General Assembly.

The other two worked on two covenants, the International Covenant on Civil and Political Rights and the International Covenant on Economic, Social, and Cultural Rights, which represented somewhat different views on the issue of human rights. The covenants, legal documents to "bind" the countries that ratified them, required the signatory nations to honor the rights enumerated in the declaration. While the International Covenant on Civil and Political Rights grew out of the U.S. concept of individual freedom, the International Covenant on Economic, Social, and Cultural Rights stemmed from traditions associated with socialism. Taken together, the three separate documents—the declaration and the two covenants—came to be known as the International Bill of Rights.

Following adoption of the declaration, ER continued work on the covenants, although the General Assembly did not approve them until 1966, long after ER had left the United Nations and four years after her death. When Dwight D. Eisenhower* became U.S. president in 1953, ER turned in her resignation, which all ambassadors were required to do. Bowing to the Republican Right, Eisenhower immediately accepted her offer to step down. "During my years at the U.N., it was my work on the Human Rights Commission that I considered my most important task," ER wrote in her autobiography* (Roosevelt, 71).

SELECTED BIBLIOGRAPHY

Berger, Jason. *A New Deal for the World: Eleanor Roosevelt and American Foreign Policy.* 1981.

Burns, James MacGregor, and Stewart Burns. *A People's Charter: The Pursuit of Rights in America.* 1991.

Kahn, E. J. "The Years Alone." Part 1. *The New Yorker* (12 June 1948): 30–34, 36, 39–41.

Lash, Joseph P. *Eleanor: The Years Alone.* 1972.

Roosevelt, Eleanor. *On My Own.* 1958.

Jason Berger

V

VAL-KILL. Val-Kill is the modest country retreat Eleanor Roosevelt called home. Named after the Fallkill Creek or, as it was known to early Dutch settlers, the "Val-Kill," stream of falls, the property—now about 180 acres—was part of the Roosevelt landholdings in Hyde Park,* New York, and is about two miles east of Springwood, the Roosevelt family estate.

The area along the Fallkill was a favorite picnic spot for the Roosevelt family and friends. After a picnic in the fall of 1924, ER and her two friends Nancy Cook* and Marion Dickerman* lamented the fact that it would be their last opportunity to visit the site until the following spring. Franklin D. Roosevelt* then suggested that they build a cottage there and use it as a year-round retreat. He drew up a lease on a building site, giving them a life interest in the property, engaged a young architect, Henry Toombs, to plan a stone replica of a Dutch colonial Hudson Valley vernacular-style cottage, and appointed himself as general contractor. The three women shared the $12,000 construction cost, and Stone Cottage was completed in 1926.

From the beginning, Val-Kill was more than a simple holiday retreat. It was a place where the free exchange of ideas in a relaxed atmosphere turned conversations into pilot projects. As the cottage was being built, the three friends, joined by Caroline O'Day,* decided to establish Val-Kill Industries in order to construct finely crafted furniture based on early American designs. They were encouraged by FDR, who shared their interest in training rural youth* for off-season employment within their own communities. The undertaking quickly outgrew Stone Cottage, so a separate two-story cinder-block structure about 200 feet northeast of Stone Cottage was then built to house the venture. A two-story addition was added as the business expanded.

Eleanor Roosevelt oversees a workman, Frank Landolfa, at the Val-Kill furniture shop in July 1931. *Courtesy of Franklin D. Roosevelt Library*

The enterprise was not a financial success, but it continued through the worst years of the depression and provided some employment in the Hyde Park area. A pewter forge and a homespun weaving enterprise were added in 1934. The latter continued under Nellie Johanssen, a former Val-Kill housekeeper, into the 1940s in the Val-Kill Tea Room and Weaving Cottage, which was built by ER on the highway near the property entrance.

The furniture factory closed in May 1936. ER converted the building into living quarters for herself, with an apartment-office for her secretary, Malvina Thompson* (Scheider), and guest rooms. The pewter forge became the playhouse used for picnics or meetings in inclement weather. The pond, terrace, and pool continued to be used for outdoor entertaining of family, friends, and guests.

From 1945 until her death in 1962, ER made Val-Kill cottage her principal home, spending as much time there as her busy schedule allowed. John F. Kennedy,* Khrushchev of the Soviet Union, Nehru of India,* Haile Selassie of Ethiopia, Tito of Yugoslavia, and other world leaders, as well as troubled young boys from Wiltwyck School,* foreign students, and local groups, all enjoyed ER's unassuming hospitality at Val-Kill.

After his mother's death in 1962, John Roosevelt* became the owner of the property, and in 1970 he sold it to two Long Island doctors. In 1972 they sought to change the zoning to build a nursing home, other health care facilities, and senior citizen housing on the site. The Hyde Park Town Council denied the rezoning in January 1973.

Three years later local citizens who belonged to the Hyde Park Visual Environment Committee joined forces with a representative of the New York state lieutenant governor's office, members of the Roosevelt family, and the director and superintendent of the Franklin D. Roosevelt Library and National Historic Site in an effort to save ER's home at Val-Kill from commercial development. Growing support for a national memorial* led to federal legislation in 1977 creating the Eleanor Roosevelt National Historic Site at Val-Kill. Dedicated in 1984, it was the first historic site to honor a First Lady. (See Eleanor Roosevelt Center at Val-Kill.*)

SELECTED BIBLIOGRAPHY

Davis, Kenneth S. *Invincible Summer: An Intimate Portrait of the Roosevelts*. 1974.
Roosevelt, Eleanor. *This I Remember*. 1949.
Wright, Emily L. *Eleanor Roosevelt and Val-Kill Industries 1925–1938*. 1978.

Joyce C. Ghee and Joan Spence

VANDENBERG, ARTHUR HENDRICK (22 March 1884, Grand Rapids, MI–18 April 1951, Grand Rapids, MI).

While they served as members of the first U.S. delegation to the United Nations,* Eleanor Roosevelt developed a close working relationship with Senator Arthur Vandenberg, a Republican from Michigan. Vandenberg's opposition to the domestic and foreign policies of President Franklin D. Roosevelt* in the 1930s made their partnership at first seem unlikely, but it symbolized an attempt, led by the senator, to craft a truly bipartisan foreign policy during the early years of the Cold War.*

Born in 1884, Arthur H. Vandenberg attended public schools in Grand Rapids, Michigan, and studied law for one year at the University of Michigan. In 1906 he became editor of the *Grand Rapids Herald*, where his editorials marked him as a rising star in the Michigan Republican Party. Leaving the newspaper in 1928, he entered the Senate, a position he held for the remainder of his life.

Vandenberg's stand on domestic policy, especially FDR's New Deal* programs, evolved throughout the 1930s. He generally supported the early years of the New Deal in 1933 and 1934, earning a reputation as a "New Deal Republican" (Tompkins, 96). As the decade continued, however, his opposition grew; by the end of the 1930s, Vandenberg had emerged as one of the leaders of the conservative coalition that successfully thwarted many of FDR's domestic proposals.

Vandenberg's views on foreign policy underwent an even greater series of transformations. An ardent pro-expansion nationalist who endorsed the diplomatic initiatives of President Theodore Roosevelt,* he opposed President Woodrow Wilson's foreign policy until the United States entered World War I, whereupon he enthusiastically supported American involvement. Upon the war's conclusion, Vandenberg favored Senate ratification of the Treaty of Versailles and American participation in the League of Nations* but voiced reservations about the league's potential to infringe upon America's national interests.

The European turmoil of the 1930s moved Vandenberg toward isolationism, as did his experience as a member of the Nye Committee, which held hearings on the munitions industry. These convinced him that U.S. involvement in World War I had been a mistake. In the mid-1930s, he began championing the Neutrality Acts, defining himself as "one who wants to preserve all of the isolation which modern circumstances will permit" (Tompkins, 176). His criticism of FDR's speech in January 1941 on aid to England angered ER, who, as the senator noted in his private papers, charged Vandenberg with engaging in partisan politics.

Vandenberg's isolationist position again changed during World War II.* He emerged as an architect of an internationalist and bipartisan foreign policy* based on consensus between the president, congressional leaders, and the State Department. "I do not believe that any nation hereafter can immunize itself from its own exclusive action" (Tompkins, 239), he stated on 10 January 1945, in a widely reported and critically acclaimed speech. He outlined his postwar objectives, strongly supporting the creation of the United Nations (UN). A delighted FDR appointed Vandenberg to serve on the United Nations Conference on International Organization in San Francisco in April–June 1945, which drafted the organization's charter.

Vandenberg's relationship with ER warmed as they joined forces at the United Nations. At first alarmed by reports that ER would serve on the American delegation to the first meeting of the UN General Assembly in London in 1946, Vandenberg changed his opinion of the former First Lady after working with her. "Mrs. Roosevelt is doing a splendid job," he commented to fellow members of the U.S. delegation. "She has made a fine impression on all the other delegations. I want to say that I take back everything I ever said about her, and believe me it's been plenty" (Vandenberg, 8). He grew to admire and respect ER's good judgment and her diplomatic skills. For her part, ER reciprocated favorably, praising Vandenberg's contribution to the United Nations. "It was he who worked so hard to keep the budget moderate so that there would be no danger of driving out the smaller, weaker countries," she wrote in *On My Own*. "His influence meant much in the early years when support was badly needed for this bold new concept of an organization" (Roosevelt, 42).

Both Roosevelt and Vandenberg advocated international cooperation for world peace and recognized that the United States would have to assume bold leadership in world affairs during the Cold War.* By forming this partnership, ER and Vandenberg symbolized the bipartisanship that marked U.S. foreign policy during the early years of the Cold War.

SELECTED BIBLIOGRAPHY

Arthur H. Vandenberg Papers, Michigan Historical Collection, University of Michigan, Ann Arbor.

Moore, Newell S. "The Rise of Senator Arthur H. Vandenberg in American Foreign Affairs." Ph.D. dissertation. George Peabody College. 1954.

Roosevelt, Eleanor. *On My Own*. 1958.

Tompkins, C. David. *Senator Arthur H. Vandenberg: The Evolution of a Modern Republican, 1884–1945*. 1970.

Vandenberg, Arthur H., and Joseph A. Morris, eds. *The Private Papers of Senator Vandenberg*. 1952.

Leonard Schlup

VANDERLIP, NARCISSA COX (9 February 1879, Quincy, IL–5 March 1966, Scarborough, NY).

Narcissa Cox Vanderlip, chair of the League of Women Voters* in New York state from 1919 to 1923, helped involve Eleanor Roosevelt in politics by persuading her to chair a league committee in 1921. Although Vanderlip belonged to the Republican Party, she and ER shared much in common. Both were married to prominent men; both belonged to America's affluent class; and each had given birth to six children. Both held membership in the Women's City Club of New York.*

Vanderlip dropped out of the University of Chicago to marry in 1903, but she was a strong proponent of an expanded role for women in public life and in 1933 received her degree in recognition of efforts to advance the university. The wife of Frank Arthur Vanderlip, president of the National City Bank of New York from 1909 to 1919, Vanderlip worked for woman suffrage and with her husband founded the progressive Scarborough School in 1912. During World War I, the couple traveled throughout the nation advancing the sale of liberty bonds and encouraging garden and food conservation programs. In spite of patriotic activities, Vanderlip's husband, a liberal Republican, was attacked after the war for his global financial enterprises and labeled a Bolshevik by Edward L. Doheny, a petroleum producer who later figured in the Teapot Dome scandal.

ER was impressed with the couple's public service and admired Vanderlip for her leadership ability, which included upholding the nonpartisan character of the League of Women Voters. After FDR's overwhelming defeat as the vice presidential candidate on the Democratic national ticket in 1920, Vanderlip urged a shy and insecure ER to head the national legislative committee of the New York state League of

Women Voters, preparing monthly reports and recommendations on pending legislation. As her assistant Vanderlip designated Elizabeth Fisher Read,* an attorney. Their weekly meetings produced a warm and lasting rapport between ER, Read, and Read's partner, Esther E. Lape.*

ER and Vanderlip also were active in other endeavors. They worked to raise matching funds in New York for the Sheppard-Towner Maternity and Infant Protection Act, which set up clinics and health care programs for infants and mothers. To critics who questioned the law's constitutionality, Vanderlip observed there was nothing unconstitutional about spending federal funds to rescue cows from tuberculosis or save children from death.

In the 1920s Vanderlip and ER favored American membership on the World Court,* international justice and peace, and the abolition of child labor,* among other causes. On occasion they conferred at Beechwood, Vanderlip's estate along the Hudson River in Scarborough. Their most notable undertaking came in 1923, when, with Lape, they administered the Bok Peace Prize* to determine the winner of the best plan for world peace. The competition, which isolationists attacked, led to a congressional hearing and accusations that the women were involved in un-American activity.

When ER turned her attention to Democratic politics, she and Vanderlip no longer were so closely associated. Vanderlip continued her varied charitable pursuits and for thirty-seven years was president of the New York Infirmary for Women and Children. In tribute to her philanthropy, her portrait hangs in the National Portrait Gallery in Washington.

SELECTED BIBLIOGRAPHY
Cook, Blanche Wiesen. *Eleanor Roosevelt*. Vol. 1. 1992.
Narcissa Cox Vanderlip Papers, Frank A. Vanderlip Collection, Columbia University Library, New York.
Roosevelt, Eleanor. *The Autobiography of Eleanor Roosevelt*. 1961.
Watrous, Hilda R. *In League with Eleanor: Eleanor Roosevelt and the League of Women Voters. 1921–1962*. 1984.
———. *Narcissa Cox Vanderlip*. 1982.

Leonard Schlup

VIDEO MATERIAL. A variety of video material, based on award-winning motion pictures* and television* programs, depicts the career of Eleanor Roosevelt. Perhaps the best-known video is *The Eleanor Roosevelt Story*, made from a film first released in 1965, which received the Academy Award for Best Documentary Feature. Narrated by Eric Severeid, Archibald MacLeish, and Mrs. Francis Cole (ER's first cousin, Corinne Robinson Alsop*), this ninety-minute video was redone in 1997 with an introduction by Hillary Rodham Clinton. It describes ER as a lonely child who became the most respected woman in the world. Also focusing on ER's life is *First Lady of the World*, a twenty-minute production by the National Park Service. Another biographical video, first shown on cable television, is the fifty-minute *Eleanor Roosevelt: A Restless Spirit*, which shows her efforts in broadening the role of women in society.

Two videos picture ER in her work at the United Nations* (UN). *Eleanor, First Lady of the World*, stars Jean Stapleton as ER. The ninety-six-minute film covers the period from 1945 to 1948, concluding with passage of the UN Declaration of Human Rights.* Another, produced by the United Nations, *For Everyone Everywhere: The Making of the Universal Declaration of Human Rights*, describes how the international community overcame the barriers of language, culture, and the Cold War* to create a universal document.

Other videos deal with ER in the context of her relationship to her husband, Franklin D. Roosevelt.* The 1977 six-hour miniseries, *Eleanor and Franklin*, which won eleven Emmy awards, is available in two video volumes, tracing the impact of two dynamic personalities on history. It portrays their public and private lives through the eyes of ER. A four-volume series that first appeared on public television, *The American Experience: FDR*, contains significant references to ER. It features cameo appearances by Curtis Roosevelt, a grandson, Edna Gurewitsch, a friend, and four Roosevelt biographers, Geoffrey Ward, Doris Kearns Goodwin, Blanche Wiesen Cook, and Hugh Gallagher.

ER's interest in racial justice is dramatized in *Tuskegee Airmen*, a ninety-minute video based on the true story of the 332d Fighter Squadron in World War II,* which was the first squadron of African American pilots allowed to go into combat.

Two videos show the Roosevelt homes. *Franklin and Eleanor Historic Sites* offers an overview of the Roosevelt homes in Hyde Park,* New York, including Val-Kill,* ER's cottage. *American Castles: The Roosevelt Homes* shows family homes in Hyde Park and New York City as well as the Roosevelt summer home on Campobello* Island in Canada.

SELECTED BIBLIOGRAPHY

Additional information can be obtained from the Roosevelt-Vanderbilt Historical Association and the Franklin D. Roosevelt Library Museum Store, Hyde Park, NY.

W

WAGNER–ROGERS BILL. As the plight of German Jews* worsened in the 1930s, culminating in the burning of synagogues, looting of Jewish shops, and violent attacks against Jews throughout Germany on the night of 9–10 November 1938 (*Kristillnacht*), some Americans, including Eleanor Roosevelt, expressed growing concerns about the deteriorating situation. One response was the Wagner–Rogers bill of 1939, which attempted to aid the growing number of German child refugees* (a large percentage of whom were Jewish) by providing a special exemption to immigration quotas, thereby easing their entry into the United States. Introduced in a political climate unfavorable to the reduction of such quotas (two other bills introduced by Jewish congressmen that would have reduced immigration restrictions, one by Representative Samuel Dickstein and the other by Representative Emanuel Cellar, had already failed in 1938), the Wagner–Rogers bill was withdrawn by its sponsors after a bitter political debate. ER was closely associated with the bill, but her attempts to convince her husband, President Franklin D. Roosevelt,* to declare administration support for it failed. Still, FDR was not personally opposed to the legislation and suggested to ER in her role as liaison between the White House and those seeking the legislation the strategy of having a Catholic Democrat and a Republican jointly introduce the bill in Congress. In view of FDR's position, ER felt she could offer only a behind-the-scenes endorsement of the measure at a time when it would have needed strong backing from the president to survive the determined attacks of its enemies.

The legislation was proposed by an advocacy group in New York called the Non-Sectarian Committee for German Refugee Children. On 9 February 1939 Senator Robert Wagner of New York, a Catholic Democrat, and Representative Edith Nourse Rogers of Massachusetts, a Protestant Republican, introduced identical refugee bills in their respective chambers. The measures called for 10,000 children under the age of fourteen to be admitted into the United States during each of the two years 1939 and 1940. These children would not be counted against the previously established quotas for German immigrants (set at 25,000 per year by the Immigration Act of 1924). The child refugees would be the responsibility of private agencies, charities, or individuals and not the U.S. government.

Support for the bill was widespread, coming from religious leaders such as Catholic bishop Bernard James Sheil of Chicago, political figures such as former Republican president Herbert Hoover* and former Republican presidential candidate Alf Landon, and a variety of labor* representatives, including the leadership of both the American Federation of Labor and the Congress of Industrial Organizations. Notable among leaders who did not endorse the bill, however, was the leading Catholic prelate, Francis Cardinal Spellman.* ER, who had attended some of the early meetings of the Non-Sectarian Committee, declared her support at a 13 February 1939 news conference: "I hope the Wagner Act on Refugees will pass. I think it is a wise way to do a humanitarian act and it seems the fair thing to do" (Beasley, 90).

The forces allied against the Wagner–Rogers bill were no less powerful than those supporting the legislation. The American Legion, the Daughters of the American Revolution, and the Ladies of the Grand Army of the Republic, among others, all argued vociferously against the bill. Moreover, the measure faced stiff opposition in Congress,* especially in the Senate, where a poll conducted by the lobbying arm of the Non-Sectarian Committee discovered that a great majority of senators were unlikely to support it. A meager 25 percent of Senate Democrats and less than 10 percent of the Senate Republicans declared their support for the measure. Opponents argued that the situation in Germany was overstated, that the material aid and sentiment engendered by the bill should go instead to poor American children, and that the bill would, in fact, harm German children by taking them away from their parents.

The White House's lack of support for the bill contributed to its demise. President Roosevelt, despite his wife's prodding, refused to endorse the bill. Cabling ER from a Caribbean vacation about a week after her 13 February declaration of support, he said that "it is all right for you to support the child refugee bill but it is best for me to say nothing till I get back" (Wyman, 97). Confronting a hostile Congress that hoped to thwart his legislative goals and reassert congressional independence, FDR may have felt silence to be his only good option with regard to an unpopular bill. ER understood her husband's predicament; after FDR's refusal to endorse the bill, ER tempered her support for the measure. As she stated at a press conference* on 25 April 1939: "It is a matter of legislation, so until it is decided, I should make no official comment. I did, however, go on a committee in New York for arranging for the care of the children if they were allowed to enter. So you can draw your own conclusion" (Beasley, 100).

A conservative Congress, suspicious of FDR and his foreign policy initiatives that portended intervention in the European conflict, began to debate and mark up the legislation in committee in the spring of 1939. On 30 June the Senate Immigration Committee reported on the bill favorably, but only after amending it so that the 20,000 refugee children would be counted as part of the annual German quota. With this crushing amendment, Senator Wagner angrily withdrew his bill, calling it "wholly unacceptable" (Wyman, 91). Myriad causes contributed to the defeat of the bill. One may have been lack of support from Cardinal Spellman. According to Justine Wise Polier,* she and her father, Rabbi Stephen Wise, who played key roles in the Non-Sectarian Committee, believed that Spellman "had no feeling for helping or lifting his finger due to his own prejudices" (Berger, 24). Historian David Wyman, in assessing the demise of the Wagner–Rogers bill, identified the "strong currents of nativism, anti-Semitism, and economic insecurity" prevalent in American life in the late 1930s as the primary explanations for the failure of the relatively modest measure (Wyman, 94).

SELECTED BIBLIOGRAPHY

Beasley, Maurine, ed. *The White House Press Conferences of Eleanor Roosevelt*. 1983.

Berger, Jason. *A New Deal for the World: Eleanor Roosevelt and American Foreign Policy*. 1981.

Feingold, Henry. *The Politics of Rescue: The Roosevelt Administration and the Holocaust, 1938–1945*. 1970.

Morse, Arthur D. *While Six Million Died*. 1968.

Newton, Verne W., ed. *FDR and the Holocaust*. 1996.

Wyman, David S. *Paper Walls: America and the Refugee Crisis, 1938–1941*. 1968.

Jason Berger

WALD, LILLIAN (10 March 1867, Cincinnati, OH–1 September 1940, Westport, CT).

Lillian Wald was an early leader in the movement for social settlements,* a pioneer of public health nursing, and one of the prominent women social reformers who inspired Eleanor Roosevelt in the 1920s. Wald, daughter of a wealthy dealer in optical goods, had been born to a life of comfort but was drawn to a career in nursing. She graduated from the New York Hospital training school for nurses in 1891 and the following year enrolled in the Women's Medical College in New York City. After teaching a home nursing class for poor immigrant women, in 1893 she decided to leave medical school and with her friend, Mary Brewster, founded a settlement house for nurses, first in a tenement building and then at 265 Henry Street on New York's Lower East Side. From this base she organized the Henry Street Visiting Nurses Service, which brought health care to thousands of poor families and marked the beginning of the new profession of public health nursing. An excellent fund-raiser, Wald soon recognized the need for integrating health care with social services and made Henry Street Settlement the focus of a full range of community programs.

Wald also worked for broader reforms. She joined the Women's Trade Union League* (WTUL) in 1903, worked for a ban on child labor,* and is credited with the idea that led to the establishment of the federal Children's Bureau in 1912. After the outbreak of World War I, she joined Jane Addams* and others in urging peaceful resolution of the conflict. She served as president in 1915 of the newly formed American Union against Militarism, while also supporting American Red Cross* drives. In 1918 she coordinated the efforts of New York nursing agencies to address the influenza epidemic.

In the 1920s Wald remained committed to the Henry Street Settlement, while speaking out for child welfare legislation and international peace initiatives. As ER involved herself in Democratic Party* politics and the WTUL during this period, she became acquainted with Wald and a number of other reformers who, ER said, "had a great influence on me" (Roosevelt, *This Is My Story*, 347). Both ER and Wald were members of the Women's City Club of New York,* which provided a forum for accomplished women to address a broad range of social issues.

In 1933 Wald retired to Westport, Connecticut, but she kept in touch with ER through correspondence, addressing her as "Beloved First Lady." Their letters touched on plans for occasional visits, mutual friends such as Addams and Alice Hamilton,* and individuals ER arranged to see at Wald's suggestion, such as the journalist Anna Louise Strong,* following her travels in Russia, and Madeleine Slade, who had worked with Gandhi in India.* In December 1934 Wald was a houseguest at the White House. In declining health in the late 1930s, she appreciated ER's letters and flowers, as well as ER's favorable review of a 1938 biography, *Lillian Wald: Neighbor and Crusader*, in which ER said, "I have long paid homage to Lillian Wald's personality, to her amazing vitality and her love of people. . . . So many things which we accept today as a responsibility of government had their inception in her fertile brain" (Roosevelt, *Survey Graphic*, 616).

SELECTED BIBLIOGRAPHY
Cook, Blanche Wiesen. *Eleanor Roosevelt*. Vol. 1. 1992.
Roosevelt, Eleanor. "Henry Street's Pioneer." *Survey Graphic* 27 (December 1938):
      616.
———. *This Is My Story*. 1937.
Siegel, Beatrice. *Lillian Wald of Henry Street*. 1983.

Wald, Lillian. *The House on Henry Street*. 1915.
————. *Windows on Henry Street*. 1934.

WALLACE, HENRY A. (7 October 1888, Orient, IA–18 November 1965, Danbury, CT).

Eleanor Roosevelt had a significant impact on Henry A. Wallace's political career. A graduate of the Des Moines public schools and Iowa State College, he had become editor of the family agricultural newspaper, *Wallaces' Farmer*, in 1921, succeeding his father, who had moved to Washington as secretary of agriculture. In 1926 he founded a corporation that would rise to the top as a producer of hybrid corn seed, and in 1933 he accepted the invitation of Franklin D. Roosevelt* to serve as secretary of agriculture. While he shaped New Deal* agricultural policy, he and ER distrusted one another, but their relationship changed when he took on a new role.

They became political allies during World War II.* At the 1940 Democratic National Convention, ER worked for Wallace's nomination as vice president, and after he took on his new duties, his efforts to make the war serve democratic purposes drew them together. She came to think of him as the person best qualified to carry forward her husband's work and tried to persuade FDR to demand that the Democrats renominate Wallace in 1944. She failed; Harry S Truman* became vice president, and thus he, not Wallace, succeeded FDR at his death in 1945.

For a time, ER remained close to Wallace. She battled for his appointment as secretary of commerce in early 1945, pressed him to supply leadership for the liberal movement, and agreed with him on many points as he grew critical of Truman, especially his policy toward the Soviet Union. Although she was more skeptical than Wallace, they agreed the president should make new efforts to gain the confidence of the Russians. When the disagreement between Truman and Wallace led to the latter's forced resignation from the cabinet in September 1946, ER tried to function as peacemaker.

Three events in 1947 opened a wide gap between the former allies. First, Wallace upset ER by criticizing American foreign policy* while traveling in Europe. Then, he added to her unhappiness by rejecting the Marshall Plan to provide American aid for European economic recovery. Finally, his decision to run for the presidency on a third-party ticket alarmed her, for it appeared likely to damage the Democratic Party,* help reactionary Republicans, and hurt liberal Democrats.

ER now frequently criticized Wallace. She argued that he was a poor politician, did not have a realistic plan for peace, and was misleading some good Americans and alarming Western Europeans. Convinced that he lacked her understanding of communists, she insisted that they, not he, controlled the new Progressive Party.* No longer regarding him as the representative of her husband's principles, she welcomed his over-whelming defeat in the 1948 presidential election. To her, the outcome proved that the American people wanted "a progressive administration untinged with communism" (ER to Mr. Chute, 21 December 1948).

Because of her roles in the pivotal years of Wallace's political career, it appears that she hurt him more when he ran for the presidency than she had helped him earlier. After the late 1940s, the two were occasion-ally friendly, but the politics of 1947–1948 had opened a wound in their relationship that never closed.

SELECTED BIBLIOGRAPHY

Black, Allida M. *Casting Her Own Shadow: Eleanor Roosevelt and the Shaping of Postwar Liberalism.* 1996.

Eleanor Roosevelt Papers. Franklin D. Roosevelt Library, Hyde Park, NY.

Hamby, Alonzo L. *Beyond the New Deal: Harry S. Truman and American Liberalism.* 1973.

Kirkendall, Richard S. "ER and the Issue of FDR's Successor." In Joan Hoff-Wilson and Marjorie Lightman, eds., *Without Precedent: The Life and Career of Eleanor Roosevelt.* 1984.

Lash, Joseph P. *Eleanor and Franklin.* 1971.

———. *Eleanor: The Years Alone.* 1972.

Richard S. Kirkendall

WELLES, SUMNER (14 October 1892, New York–24 September 1961, Bernardsville, NJ).

A career diplomat whose primary importance lay in his contributions to U.S. policy toward Latin America* and the "Good Neighbor" policy of Franklin D. Roosevelt,* Sumner Welles was born into an upper-class New York family in 1892. He entered the Department of State in 1915, where he remained, with a few years' interruption in the 1920s, until he retired in 1943. Under Franklin D. Roosevelt he was ambassador to Cuba (April–December, 1933), assistant secretary of state (1933–1937), and un-dersecretary of state (1937–1943). He worked with Eleanor Roosevelt in three main areas of foreign policy: Latin America,* European refugees,* and the United Nations.*

Welles' relationship to ER dated back to their childhood.* The two families were close. ER's and Welles' mothers were good friends, and ER's younger brother, Hall Roosevelt,* attended the same schools as Welles, from grade school to Harvard University. When ER and FDR were planning their wedding, ER chose Welles as their page boy. Over the years the parallel structures of the Roosevelts and Welles family lives reinforced their ties as they sent their sons to school together, and the next generation became friends. As Welles' son and biographer, Benja-min Welles, recalled, "Sumner Welles grew up with a sense of Eleanor" (Welles interview).

Sumner Welles may have known ER first, but it was FDR who initially was in a position to help Welles, who was a decade younger. In 1915 Welles decided to go into the diplomatic service. Needing a patron from within the government, he went to FDR, who was then assistant secretary of the navy. FDR sponsored Welles, who quickly passed the exams with a near-perfect score. In the years before the Democratic Party defeat of 1920 the two men saw each other professionally—especially in relationship to Pan American affairs and U.S. efforts to keep Germany from establishing bridgeheads in the Caribbean—but Welles left no mention of ER, nor she of him, in this period of their lives.

The two men kept in occasional touch about Latin American politics in the 1920s. After Welles was forced out of the State Department in 1925—following his divorce and remarriage, behavior President Calvin Coolidge considered unacceptable for a gentleman and a member of his administration—Welles found himself in a political and professional wilderness. Although it is possible that ER was critical of Welles' divorce, she nevertheless became his sponsor and conduit to FDR. As FDR actively reentered New York state politics as the Democratic Party's candidate for governor, ER's support became increasingly vital.

After Welles wrote his first major policy paper for FDR, a twenty-four-page indictment of Republican policy toward Latin America containing the germs of the "Good Neighbor" policy, ER enthusiastically wrote Welles that his essay was the best thing she had ever read on the subject. FDR, influenced by his wife, came to share their enthusiasm for a policy in which the United States would treat Latin American nations as legal equals and regard them with the respect due to equals. As the 1928 gubernatorial contest heated up, FDR asked Welles to arrange speaking engagements with and through ER. Welles grasped the opportunity to help strengthen his ties to the Democratic Party.

By the time FDR ran for president, Welles had become an important supporter and foreign policy adviser. His ties with ER remained critical. It is indicative of their relationship that ER invited Welles and his wife to her box seat to hear FDR's first inaugural address. A few days later FDR appointed Welles assistant secretary of state for Latin America, and the two soon began implementing the Good Neighbor policy. As ER wrote enthusiastically a few years later in *This Troubled World*, the Roosevelt administration had given up a policy that seemed to Latin Americans to embody "a bullying, patronizing attitude." The new U.S. policy, she argued, had created a political and diplomatic environment that finally allowed the nations of the Western Hemisphere "to get together and discuss subjects of mutual interest with little or no sense of suspicion and fear" (Roosevelt, 11–12).

Welles became increasingly important in the State Department. His understanding of departmental management and bureaucratic efficiency was paralleled only by his profound understanding of foreign relations. Secretary of state Cordell Hull possessed neither of these qualities—but his grasp of national politics, his ties with the U.S. House and Senate from his years first as representative and then senator from Tennessee, and his relationship to the southern wing of the Democratic Party made him a politically powerful force within the administration. Nevertheless, for many years Welles virtually ran the department. When foreign ambassadors visited the State Department, they first paid a short call to Hull as a matter of protocol and then spent two hours or so with Welles.

ER and Welles began an active correspondence in the late 1930s over the issue of European refugees from fascism, especially European Jews.* As leaders of the various committees to help European refugees turned to ER, she, in turn, wrote to Welles. ER's familiarity with Welles, a correct and distant man in most of his bureaucratic dealings, broke through his formal barriers. When, for example, he replied to a letter she had written deploring the British refusal to allow Jews into Palestine with a heavily bureaucratic missive, she responded with a terse note declaring that the U.S. government had to take action. It was, in part, due to her that Welles came to see Zionism* as the only solution for the world's Jews.

Welles was central to the administration's wartime planning for an effective successor to the League of Nations*—the United Nations.* Whereas FDR preferred the diplomacy of realpolitik, Welles was a devoted idealist and Wilsonian. As he wrote in 1944, it was now the moment to reaffirm the Wilsonian ideals that had so thrilled his generation, the realization of which was now "well within human capacity" (Sumner Welles, 3). In this regard Welles was far closer to ER than to the president. ER thus became an important support for, and colleague of, Welles over the shape and powers of the United Nations. While FDR was wary of a chorus of little nations participating in global politics, ER and Welles shared a belief in the importance of including the smaller nations of the world in the global body politic. Welles drafted an institutional structure that combined FDR's wish for the "big four" with his and ER's belief in a general council open to all the nations of the world. It was a vision of the Good Neighbor policy extended to the globe.

Behind their collaboration lay a mutually shared vision of the world and their role in it. ER, Welles, and FDR all grew up believing that those who belonged to the privileged classes had a debt to those who were less fortunate and that they were obliged to discharge this debt through public service. It was a kind of missionary view of the world, a set of values known at the time as "ricebowl Christianity." For ER, Welles, and FDR it formed a pattern of life that dictated dress, demeanor, and deportment. When in *This Troubled World* ER wrote of how the world could peacefully resolve international conflict, she stated that "the first step . . . is self-discipline and self-control" (Roosevelt, 21). Within those conventions ER and Sumner Welles worked together on a few selected, but important, foreign policy issues. On 5 April 1941, after finding Welles a reliable ally for so long over so many issues when she was frustrated by State Department red tape, ER, speaking both for herself and her secretary, Malvina Thompson* (Scheider), wrote Welles a thank-you letter. "You are one of the grandest people in government," they said. "You can be reached on the phone without delay, you give an answer when you are reached and our many questions are settled quickly! With appreciation and, on my part, affection, Eleanor" (ER and MT to SW, 5 April 1941).

In August 1943, after a protracted and ugly fight between Hull and Welles became politically dangerous to the president, Welles was forced to retire. Welles' enemies successfully charged that he had solicited sex from sleeping car porters during a train ride back from the Alabama funeral of Speaker of the House William B. Bankhead in September 1940. FDR felt he had no choice and asked Welles for his resignation. But it was, wrote Robert Sherwood, playwright and presidential speechwriter, a great loss to FDR, who relied on Welles—"particularly in all matters relating to the framing of the ultimate peace" (Sherwood, 135). It was a loss to ER as well. In retirement Welles wrote seven books and commented on public affairs. He was married three times and had two sons.

SELECTED BIBLIOGRAPHY

Benjamin Welles interview with Holly Shulman, 13 April 1998.
Eleanor Roosevelt Papers, Franklin D. Roosevelt Library, Hyde Park, NY.
Roosevelt, Eleanor. *This Troubled World*. 1938.
Sherwood, Robert. *Roosevelt and Hopkins: An Intimate History*. 1948.
Welles, Benjamin. *Sumner Welles: FDR's Global Strategist*. 1997.
Welles, Sumner. *The Time for Decision*. 1944.

WEST VIRGINIA. See ARTHURDALE.

WHITE HOUSE CONFERENCES. On several occasions, Eleanor Roosevelt offered her prestige and the services of her staff to women in the New Deal* who sought an audience and publicity to promote their causes. The first, the White House Conference on the Emergency Needs of Women, assembled on 2 November 1933 to explore the plight of unemployed women and the imperative of quickly creating practical projects to employ them. Invitations prepared by Edith Helm, White House social secretary, ensured a warm response from a group of congresswomen and prominent leaders of women's clubs and professional associations. ER opened the proceedings but turned discussion over to Harry L. Hopkins,* head of the Federal Emergency Relief Administration (FERA), and Ellen S. Woodward,* director of the newly formed FERA

Women's Division. Woodward described women's emergency needs for food, housing, education, health care, recreation, and, above all, work. Hopkins pledged that at the year's end, 300,000 women would be assigned to work projects. On her own printed copy of the seventy-four-page official proceedings, Woodward penned, "Where the Women's Division was born."

Several months later, on 30 April 1934, ER hosted a White House Conference on Camps for Unemployed Women, based on proposals from Hilda Smith* at FERA. With the support generated by the conference, Hopkins quickly initiated funding for these camps.

During the second term of President Franklin D. Roosevelt,* ER and Woodward collaborated again to address the request of Mary McLeod Bethune,* president of the National Council of Negro Women, that the Democratic administration give greater attention to social programs for black women and children. Again, invitations to a conference were issued in ER's name, although Woodward's office formulated the program. Meeting in the morning at a Department of Interior auditorium and in the afternoon in the East Room of the White House, the Conference on Participation of Negro Women and Children in Federal Welfare Programs convened on 4 April 1938. More than fifty representatives of black women's clubs, sororities, and professional associations directed the attention of officials in the Works Progress Administration* (WPA), the Social Security Administration, the Women's Bureau in the Department of Labor, and like agencies to the health, employment, and training needs of minority women. In concluding remarks, ER recommended that local biracial committees emphasize the community good that would derive from increased attention to minorities. There is little evidence, however, that the conference produced significant results.

ER wrote in an article in the April 1944 *Reader's Digest*, entitled "Women at the Peace Conference," that women should be included in delegations to peace talks. Two months later, on 14 June, she opened a White House Conference on How Women May Share in Post-War Policy-Making. Delegates heard reports from six women who had represented the United States at recent international assemblies related to peacetime social programs. As a result of discussions, delegates determined to initiate and maintain a roster of able women from which the Department of State could make recommendations to the president for appointments. State Department officials expressed an interest but made no visible effort to expand the role of women in foreign affairs. Nonetheless, women's organizations, especially the American Association of University Women, continued to promote women's advancement to policy-making posts. Ultimate success came to advocates when President Harry S Truman* in 1945 named ER as U.S. delegate to the first meeting of the United Nations* General Assembly.

SELECTED BIBLIOGRAPHY

Proceedings, White House Conference on the Emergency Needs of Women, RG 69 (FERA, WPA), National Archives, Washington, DC.

Proceedings of Conference on Participation of Negro Women and Children in Federal Welfare Programs, Records of National Council of Negro Women, National Archives for Black Women's History, Washington, DC.

Proceedings, Conference on How Women May Share in Post-War Policy-Making, Papers of American Association of University Women (microfilm edition), Reel 122.

Roosevelt, Eleanor. "Women at the Peace Conference." *Reader's Digest* 44 (April 1944): 48–49.

Martha H. Swain

WHITE HOUSE SOCIAL OFFICE. On 4 March 1933, as the end of the inaugural parade was glimpsed from the presidential reviewing stand on Pennsylvania Avenue in front of the White House, First Lady Eleanor Roosevelt left her husband's side and hurriedly crossed the lawn to the North Portico entrance. Five hundred guests had been invited to tea in the East Room following the inauguration ceremonies at the Capitol. The occasion marked the first of countless White House functions at which ER would be hostess. The pattern of official events had been set long before, but ER introduced many large-scale teas, receptions, and garden parties where guests sometimes numbered in the thousands.

That same day ER's private secretary, Malvina Thompson* (Scheider) (named "Tommy" by the Roosevelt's only daughter, Anna Roosevelt [Halsted*] as a child), began answering the stack of unopened mail on her desk. Thompson did not know there was a small, permanent White House social office staff to help her. She soon found out, however, and ER made good use of it as she carried out her busy schedule of activities, including entertaining and answering correspondence.*

Government employees had been performing social duties for the First Lady since the Grant administration, when Octavius L. Pruden created guests' seating charts and addressed invitations in elegant calligraphy. When ER became First Lady, William Rockwell headed the White House Social Office. After his death in 1940, he was succeeded by Adrian B. Tolley. Ralph W. Magee was in charge of the White House social correspondence staff, supervising a handful of clerks housed in the Executive Office Building.

When ER learned that the form letters authorized by Frances Cleveland, wife of President Grover Cleveland, were still in use, she ordered them removed from the files and drafted new guidelines for the social staff in their place. Due to the large number of letters that were sent to her, by September 1933 the workload of Magee's staff had increased so dramatically that he asked for additional help and was loaned extra clerks from other government departments. During her first year at the White House, ER received some 300,000 pieces of mail, far more than her predecessors had received. By 1940 Magee had a staff that numbered twenty men and women. As ER's private secretary, Thompson worked closely with her in managing appropriate replies to the flood of correspondence and issued systematic instructions to Magee on how his staff should facilitate the process.

Also assisting the social office was Edith Benham Helm, an admiral's widow who was ER's social secretary. Thoroughly familiar with Washington society, Helm had served as the First Lady's social secretary during the Wilson administration and would stay on as social secretary for Bess Truman, ER's successor. Helm coordinated matters of protocol for official entertainments and arranged for invitations to be sent out by the social office.

Although precedent-breaking as a First Lady in many areas, ER bowed to convention when it came to official social events, accepting the White House calendar that was set by tradition. That first year the social season was from 16 November 1933 to 8 February 1934, with functions alternating between dinners and receptions. The dinners were for the cabinet, chief justice and associate justices of the Supreme Court, senior diplomats, the vice president, and the Speaker of the House. The receptions were for the diplomatic corps, the judiciary, members of Congress,* officials of federal departments and agencies, and the army and navy.

The most important official social event of the Roosevelt years was the visit of their Britannic Majesties King George VI and Queen Elizabeth to Washington from 8 to 10 June 1939 and then to Hyde Park,* New York, for a weekend. It was the first time the United States had received a reigning British monarch, and the social office worked diligently to cope with the extra pressures of the visit. As White House guests, the king and queen attended an elaborate state dinner and an elegant reception featuring American performers. At Hyde Park, by contrast, ER hosted a picnic. The night of 11 June, the royal couple departed by train as the crowd along the banks of the Hudson River sang "Auld Lang Syne."

As it turned out, in effect this marked the end of extraordinary social events during the Roosevelt administration, although several crowned heads, as well as heads of state, visited the White House during World War II.* After the Japanese attack on Pearl Harbor on 7 December 1941, the official White House social season was canceled, and the social staff's activities were severely curtailed for the reminder of ER's tenure as First Lady.

SELECTED BIBLIOGRAPHY

Helm, Edith Benham. *The Captains and the Kings*. 1954.
Roosevelt, Eleanor. *My Days*. 1938.
———. *This Is My Story*. 1937.

―――. *This I Remember*. 1949.

Somerville, Mollie. *Eleanor Roosevelt As I Knew Her*. 1996.

Mollie Somerville

WHITE, WALTER F. (1 July 1893, Atlanta, GA–21 March 1955, New York).

Exactly when in 1934 Walter White, executive secretary of the National Association for Advancement of Colored People* (NAACP), had his first communication with First Lady Eleanor Roosevelt is not clear. Having assumed leadership of the NAACP in 1929, White was familiar with the activities of ER while her husband, Franklin D. Roosevelt,* served as governor of New York. As did many, White sought—unsuccessfully—a meeting with the new president in January 1933 to discuss the worsening conditions facing black Americans. By early 1934 a central goal of the NAACP and White was securing passage of the Costigan–Wagner anti-lynching* bill, which was introduced in January. Continually rebuffed by the president's secretaries in seeking a meeting with FDR, White turned to ER. In April 1934 he had his first private conversation with her in the White House, and, the following month, she arranged for him to meet directly with the president. White failed then—as he did later—to persuade FDR to use his political influence in the cause of a federal antilynching bill, but over the next twenty years the personal and public friendship of ER and Walter White grew into a lasting collaboration.

White was born and raised in Atlanta, Georgia, by a mother who was a former schoolteacher and by a postman father. There were seven children in his family, and all were light enough to pass for white, although they identified themselves as African Americans. White graduated from Atlanta University in 1916 and worked for a short time for the Standard Life Insurance Company. Following his organizing of the NAACP branch in Atlanta, he went to New York City in 1918 as an assistant to James Weldon Johnson, field secretary for the NAACP. Posing as a white newspaper reporter during the 1920s, White investigated and later wrote about numerous race riots and lynchings in the South. He wrote two novels about racial issues and a sociological study about the horrors of lynching before becoming the head of the NAACP, first as acting secretary in 1929 and then from 1931 until his death in 1955 as executive secretary.

White was an important member of a group of prominent blacks that included Mary McLeod Bethune,* Robert Weaver, and the young activist Pauli Murray,* who with New Deal* race liberals like Harold Ickes,* Aubrey Williams,* and Will Alexander increased ER's knowledge of, and sensitivity to, black life and racial injustices. Like many of her background who had been raised in the racial climate of the late nineteenth and early twentieth centuries, ER held attitudes about race and African

Americans that were less than enlightened. Thus, by the early 1930s her close contact with blacks like Bethune and White was critical in her reeducation on racial matters.

Beginning with the antilynching campaign in 1934 and extending over the next two decades, Walter White encouraged ER's gradual evolution as a public advocate for racial equality. Although from early on, ER worked tenaciously behind the scenes to effect some change in the president's reluctance to challenge southern Democratic congressional opposition to proposed federal antilynching legislation, it was not until 1939 that she actually made a public statement in support of such a measure. In October 1934, following public disclosure of the brutal torture and hanging of a young black man, Claude Neal, White asked the First Lady to speak at an NAACP protest rally planned for Carnegie Hall. But after consulting with the president, she declined. Still, deeply disturbed by the lynching incidents she was made aware of by White, she persisted in passing on to FDR materials about the Neal atrocity and other killings. In January 1936 she made it possible for White to meet with attorney general Homer Cummings in the hope of encouraging the Justice Department to take action against lynchings like that of Neal. Cummings showed little interest.

Beyond lynching, a consistent concern of Walter White's NAACP and other black rights organizations during the 1930s and 1940s was finding ways to pressure government agencies and other federal departments to assure greater black participation in New Deal programs. Though ER was often quite visible in her numerous public visits to New Deal projects that included blacks, her greatest effectiveness was in being a source inside the administration through which White and others brought their ideas and concerns to the attention of administration agency and department officials.

Nowhere was this more evident than in the role she played in 1940 and 1941 in the controversies over racial segregation in the armed forces and discrimination in federal defense employment. In 1941, when labor* leader A. Philip Randolph proposed sending thousands of black people to march on Washington in a protest against inequities, ER served as a go-between for FDR and the black leaders. She helped secure the agreement of Randolph, White, and others to President Roosevelt's Executive Order 8802 of 25 June 1941. This created the Fair Employment Practices Committee to investigate complaints of discrimination in defense programs and served to persuade black leaders to call off the march.

Whether ER always supported or agreed with the civil rights* goals pursued by White and other black leaders is an important question. She often was uncomfortable with tactics that embraced public protests against segregation such as plans for the Washington march or proposals to picket the headquarters of the Daughters of the American Revolution when the organization refused to let Marian Anderson* sing in Constitution Hall. Certainly, she remained always acutely sensitive to the political considerations of her husband. It was also the case that neither the NAACP nor any other movement concerned with issues of black Americans had a comprehensive agenda during the l930s or 1940s. Yet people like White, with whom she developed an extraordinary mutual trust, helped ER to expand her understanding of race issues, which she consistently—often passionately—conveyed to the president and other responsible New Deal officials. Though she had been unwilling in the mid-l930s to speak at national NAACP conventions when requested to do so by White, by the end of the decade she not only spoke but became a member of the organization and served on its board after leaving the White House in 1945.

For White, ER was an indispensable part of his political and civil rights endeavors. She became a confidant, a friend to whom he could express some of his deepest feelings, hopes, and frustrations. As ER became more publicly involved in civil rights and participated more directly in activities within various African American communities, White's confidence grew in his ability to criticize the president's hesitant civil rights commitment. At times White also questioned some of ER's views. Yet, he later reflected that when he was in greatest despair over America's racial conflicts, the awareness of ER's presence in his life strengthened his faith and belief that there were white people who cared about black people and who could transcend the nation's racial phobias.

For both, their close private and public relationship carried with it certain burdens. ER's activities on behalf of African Americans often produced harsh personal attacks against her and political pressures on the president to still her voice. Although protests of her advocacy of African American causes came from all parts of the country, as well as from some within the administration (most notably, Stephen Early* and Marvin McIntyre, who were FDR's personal secretaries, and Secretary of War Henry L. Stimson), it was from the South that she experienced the most unkind criticism.

White also found himself being attacked for his close ties to the New Deal and the First Lady. For some African Americans like the black writer George Schuyler, White had sold out to the New Deal, becoming a politician trying to pack the administration with his own supporters. The president's failure to back antilynching legislation, to vigorously pursue black interests in government programs, or to embrace truly desegregated armed forces and black workers' rights in defense industries affected White's credibility as head of the NAACP and his leadership role within America's black communities.

In the end, however, whatever criticisms or even personal pain their friendship and political relationship created for them, whatever restrictions were imposed by their working so closely together during the difficult times of depression, war, and Cold War America, their gains from their relationship far exceeded their losses. Not only for ER and White but for the nation, their friendship enriched many lives, black and white alike.

SELECTED BIBLIOGRAPHY
Goodwin, Doris Kearns. *No Ordinary Time*. 1994.
Hareven, Tamara K. *Eleanor Roosevelt: An American Conscience*. 1968.
Kirby, John B. *Black Americans in the Roosevelt Era*. 1980.
Weiss, Nancy J. *Farewell to the Party of Lincoln*. 1983.
White, Walter. *A Man Called White*. 1948.
Zangrando, Joanna Schneider, and Robert L. Zangrando. "ER and Black Civil Rights." In Joan Hoff-Wilson and Marjorie Lightman, eds., *Without Precedent: The Life and Career of Eleanor Roosevelt*. 1984.

John B. Kirby

WILLIAMS, AUBREY WILLIS (23 August 1890, Springville, AL–3 March 1965, Washington, DC).

Aubrey Willis Williams was born in the north Alabama village of Springville. His father, Charles, was a blacksmith with a fondness for whiskey, and his mother, Eva, was a devoutly religious woman with a strong social conscience. The family moved to Birmingham when Aubrey was an infant, and it was there that he grew up, in poverty due mainly to his father's drinking. He had little formal schooling but in 1911 was admitted to Maryville College, a small Presbyterian seminary, to train for the ministry. Leaving there in 1915, he enrolled in 1916 in the University of Cincinnati. Because of growing concern over World War I, he went in 1917 to Europe, serving first as a recreation officer with the Young Men's Christian Association (YMCA) in Paris, then with the French Foreign Legion, and after 1917 with the U.S. Army. Following the armistice, he studied philosophy at the University of Bordeaux before returning home to complete a social work degree at the University of Cincinnati.

In 1922 he became executive secretary of the Wisconsin Conference of Social Work, remaining there until the New Deal* took him to Washington in May 1933 as southwest regional director of the Federal Emergency Relief Administration (FERA). He soon become deputy to Harry Hopkins* at FERA. In 1935 Williams became both deputy director of the Works Progress Administration* and executive director of the National Youth Administration* (NYA), holding the latter position until shortly before it ceased operation in 1943.

Through the NYA he first met Eleanor Roosevelt, who had made the youth* agency her special concern. Over the years they formed a bond that transcended their joint determination to do something for America's disadvantaged young people. They attended the inaugural meeting of the Southern Conference for Human Welfare* together in 1938, for both believed that the southern racial system had to be changed. Of all the relationships Williams developed while in Washington, that with ER was easily the most important. They worked as a team, pursuing the same egalitarian goals, exemplifying the social justice wing of the New Deal constellation. "I had great love for her," Williams once wrote, "not passionate but for her good sense and great know-how." She was "the greatest person I have ever known," he said (Salmond, 138).

On leaving federal service in 1943, he became an organizing director for the National Farmers Union and in 1945 returned to Montgomery, Alabama, where he edited a monthly publication, *Southern Farmer*. He continued to speak out for civil rights* and civil liberties, becoming president of the Southern Conference Education Fund, a militant antisegregation organization. Such activities not only put him in conflict with his southern neighbors but also led to his being investigated in 1954 by the Senate Internal Security Subcommittee. Nevertheless, he remained firm in his convictions and supported the Montgomery bus boycott in 1955, led by the Reverend Martin Luther King Jr.*

ER's death in 1962 shocked him profoundly, for they had continued their friendship and dined together only a few weeks previously. He watched her coffin being lowered into the grave and thought it "the saddest moment I have ever lived" (Salmond, 276). In 1963 he moved back to Washington, where he died two years later.

SELECTED BIBLIOGRAPHY

Kearney, James R. *Anna Eleanor Roosevelt: The Evolution of a Reformer*. 1968.
Lindley, Betty, and Ernest K. Lindley. *A New Deal for Youth: The Story of the National Youth Administration*. 1938.
Salmond, John Alexander. *A Southern Rebel. The Life and Times of Aubrey Willis Williams*. 1983.

John A. Salmond

WILSON ERA SUNDAY EVENING SUPPERS. In the autumn of 1913, after a summer at Campobello* Island, Eleanor Roosevelt and her children moved to Washington to join Franklin D. Roosevelt,* who the previous March had taken the oath of office as assistant secretary of the navy in the administration of Woodrow Wilson. The family remained in the nation's capital until 1920, enmeshed in a world of political intrigue, rigid protocol, and set social expectations. Yet, within the larger circle of Washington society, ER and FDR had their own intimate friends, a group that called itself informally "the Club." At least one contact made in "the Club" was to play a part in ER's eventual emergence into public life.

Washington society expected certain responsibilities from the wife of a subcabinet secretary, and ER dutifully carried them out. Systematically, she made sixty card calls a week, never exceeding six minutes a call, during which she left her calling cards at the homes of other women of similar or higher rank. On Wednesdays she remained at home to receive her own card callers. Other responsibilities included hostessing dinner parties and luncheons and attending diplomatic receptions, balls, and dinners. For her skill in these regards, ER won praise from society reporters and officials. Nevertheless, her obligations were so heavy that she had to hire a social secretary, Lucy Mercer (Rutherfurd*), with whom FDR fell in love, casting a shadow over the Roosevelt marriage* for the rest of ER's life.

Mercer, however, had no relationship to "the Club," for which ER and FDR reserved two Sunday evenings a month during the Wilson years. They enjoyed having "Club" members come to their home: the four-story brick house at 1722 N Street that they rented from ER's Auntie Bye (Anna Roosevelt Cowles*), the older sister of ER's Uncle Ted (Theodore Roosevelt*). Although ER had inherited important friends from Aunt Bye and Uncle Ted, including Henry Adams, Senator Henry Cabot Lodge and his wife, Nannie, and British ambassador and Lady Cecil Spring-Rice, who had known ER's parents, these were not the members of her small inner circle.

Instead, "the Club" consisted of Assistant Secretary of State William Phillips and his wife, Caroline Astor, of the socially prominent Astor family in New York and an old friend of ER, Secretary of the Interior Franklin Lane and his wife, Anne, and Adolph Miller, a member of the Federal Reserve Board, and his wife, Mary. ER was especially drawn to the Phillips and the liberal Lanes, who were from California.

For Sunday evening meetings of "the Club," ER served scrambled eggs from a chafing dish along with cold cuts. A cold dessert and cocoa completed the meal. Cooking was not ER's interest. Shared personal and political values and stimulating conversation, not food, sustained "the Club" and made the gatherings memorable.

When World War I reduced ER's social obligations, it gave her the opportunity to broaden her experience by serving others. As a volunteer for the American Red Cross* and the Navy Relief Society, she visited St. Elizabeth's Hospital, a federally owned mental asylum, where she found shell-shocked navy veterans locked in holding areas for lack of staff and facilities for rehabilitation. Horrified, she promised to have the Navy Red Cross provide a well-stocked recreation room, but she did not let the issue drop there. Aware that the hospital came under Lane's jurisdiction, she prevailed upon her friend to set up a committee to investigate conditions at the hospital. As a result of its report, Congress* increased the hospital's budget, giving ER a taste of what could be accomplished by a committed individual who understood the political system.

In early 1920 "the Club" broke up when Lane resigned from the cabinet, took a job with an oil company, and moved west. He left with ER's profound respect for his integrity and public career, and the two corresponded until his death in May 1921. ER never forgot "the Club." In 1936, when she was First Lady, she, Caroline Phillips, Mary Miller, and Anne Lane lunched together and revived their memories.

SELECTED BIBLIOGRAPHY

Cook, Blanche Wiesen. *Eleanor Roosevelt*. Vol. 1. 1992.

Lash, Joseph P. *Eleanor and Franklin*. 1971.

Lane, Anne Wintermute, and Louise Herrick Hall, eds. *The Letters of Franklin K. Lane: Personal and Political*. 1922.

Ward, Geoffrey C. *A First Class Temperament: The Emergence of Franklin Roosevelt*. 1989.

Keith W. Olson

WILTWYCK SCHOOL FOR BOYS. Eleanor Roosevelt had a long-standing interest in the Wiltwyck School for Boys, the first interracial residential treatment center for troubled New York City youth. She served as a member of the board of directors from 1942 until her death in 1962. ER helped with fund-raising, frequently visited its campus at Esopus, New York, just across the Hudson River from the Roosevelt estate at Hyde Park,* and personally hosted picnics at her Val-Kill* home for the students and staff. According to Dr. Viola Bernard, a child psychiatrist who was a Wiltwyck consultant, ER sent out "letters, many, many letters, in her terminal hospitalization [in 1962] trying to raise funds for the new campus for Wiltwyck" (Bernard, 30).

ER's involvement started in 1942, when she joined the board of directors of Wiltwyck at the request of Justine Wise Polier,* a New York City Children's Court judge, who had worked with ER on issues related to refugees.* Polier had been instrumental in reorganizing the institution in 1942, when it was about to close due to funding difficulties. Another of ER's close associates also was involved. Trude Lash,* the wife of ER's friend and later biographer Joseph Lash,* served as secretary of the board of directors during the 1940s.

The school had began in 1936, when the New York Episcopal City Mission Society started a summer camp for delinquent or homeless African American boys from New York City. The following year it expanded the camp into an all-year program, spurred by Polier and other judges who were concerned about a lack of facilities open to Protestant African American boys. It took its name from the place where it was located, the Wiltwyck estate at Esopus, which had been donated to the society.

In 1942 the Episcopal Society turned the school over to an independent board of directors. It became a nonsectarian, interracial facility for deprived and disturbed boys, aged eight to twelve, who were referred by the courts, hospitals, or welfare department of New York City. While the school received some public funding, a significant portion of its budget came from private donations.

Shortly after joining the Wiltwyck board, ER invited children from the school who had no homes to visit her at Hyde Park on Christmas Eve, where they heard President Franklin D. Roosevelt* read Christmas stories. The following year the timing of the visit to Hyde Park had to be changed, since the children who did have homes to go to did not want to miss this event.

For years after FDR died, she hosted an annual picnic for Wiltwyck boys on the grounds of her Val-Kill* country home. Describing the picnics, attended by about 100 persons, ER said, "I always try to enlist the help of my grandchildren, who wait on the guests and organize outdoor games. We feed the boys plenty and then they usually lie on the grass for a while and I read them a story such as Kipling's 'Rikki-tikki-tavi' or 'How the Elephant Got His Trunk'" (Roosevelt, 23). She served the boys ample fare. One of her shopping lists for a picnic read: "400 hot dogs, 200 rolls, 200 cup cakes, 50 quarts milk, 25 quarts ice cream, 100 bars candy, potato salad, mustard" (Lash, 307).

Wiltwyck offered therapeutic programs for deeply disturbed boys who came from poverty-stricken, disorganized families and were victims of racial prejudice. Bernard recalled that ER empathized with the children: "She was touched by the deprived lives of these kids" (Bernard, 15). Polier remembered that she became "a very familiar person whom the children loved" (Polier, 40). The institution had some notable successes. Among its former students were Floyd Patterson, who became heavyweight champion of the world, and Claude Brown, author of an acclaimed biography, *Manchild in the Promised Land*, which he dedicated to ER and the Wiltwyck School.

A committed fund-raiser, ER regularly gave her name to letters asking for contributions. Although she offered to resign from the Wiltwyck board of directors in 1956 because she was not able to attend all the board meetings, she was prevailed upon to remain. In 1962 she became chair of Wiltwyck's building and development fund committee. During the final months of her life she devoted time to a campaign to fund the relocation of the school to Yorktown Heights, New York, a community closer to Manhattan, to facilitate recruitment of professional staff as well as visits by members of the boys' families.

The campaign continued after her death, eventually raising over $4 million. In 1966 the school moved to its new campus at Yorktown, which was named in her honor. Problems with funding, however, eventually led to Wiltwyck's closure in 1981.

SELECTED BIBLIOGRAPHY

Brown, Claude. *Manchild in the Promised Land*. 1965.
Eleanor Roosevelt Oral History Project, Interviews with Justine Wise Polier

(1977), Viola W. Bernard (1977), and Eleanor Roosevelt Wotkyns (1978),
    Franklin D. Roosevelt Library, Hyde Park, NY.
Eleanor Roosevelt Papers, Franklin D. Roosevelt Library, Hyde Park, NY.
Lash, Joseph P. *Eleanor: The Years Alone.* 1972.
Roosevelt, Eleanor. *On My Own.* 1958.

WOMAN'S HOME COMPANION. Eleanor Roosevelt became the first president's wife to write a monthly magazine column when she signed a contract with the *Woman's Home Companion* after entering the White House. Seeking the First Lady's byline, the *Companion* offered her $1,000 per month for the column based on letters addressed to her in care of the magazine. It ran from 1933 to 1935 but apparently was ended because the *Companion*, then the top-selling women's periodical in the nation, did not want to appear to be too close to the Roosevelt administration.

"I want you to write to me," ER told readers as the column, "Mrs. Franklin D. Roosevelt's Page," was launched in the August 1933 issue. "I want you to tell me about the particular problems which puzzle or sadden you, but I also want you to write me about what has brought joy into your life." The public certainly responded—ER estimated she received a record number of some 300,000 letters in 1933, including those from readers.

Louis M. Howe,* chief political strategist for Franklin D. Roosevelt* and ER confidant, arranged the *Companion* contract, which also included an extra $325 per month for ER's daughter, Anna Dall (Halsted*), to handle the letters. The column was seen as a way for the administration to appeal directly to women, thereby strengthening ties between the White House and the public.

News of the financial arrangements brought some criticism that the First Lady was profiting from her position. Gertrude B. Lane, veteran editor of the *Companion*, which was owned by the Crowell Publishing Company, urged ER to respond by insisting the modern role of a president's wife was to maintain contact "between the White House and the public" (Beasley, 70). ER did not do so in the magazine, although she justified commercial contracts in general on grounds of earning money for charity. Perhaps she did not want Lane to dictate to her.

In her columns ER commented on selected letters from readers, speaking out on controversial issues during the fall of 1933. In September, in her second column, she complied with another request by Lane, urging readers to back a proposed constitutional amendment that ER had long favored to outlaw child labor* and that the *Companion* supported. In October ER urged women to exert their economic power to improve sweatshop conditions. In November she upheld the right of married women to work, a contentious issue in the Great Depression,* when women were being discharged in favor of male workers, even though she said it might be necessary for either men or women to give up their

jobs to needier persons. In December she explained various New Deal*
programs.

Subsequently, however, ER wrote mainly about noncontroversial
subjects—children's playthings, the need to prepare teachers better, vacations, national holidays, gardening. This may have stemmed from
Companion editorial policies. Lane opposed proposed New Deal legislation to strengthen governmental control on food and drugs because she
was afraid it would adversely affect advertising. She refused ER's request to write a column in support of it. According to Ruby Black,* ER's
first biographer, it was "common gossip in the publishing business that
the editors, fearful of political controversies, circumscribed her so she
could do little but write essays on the virtues of cleanliness, kindliness,
and perseverance" (Black, 110).

The *Companion* ended the column in the July 1935 issue. No announcement was made of why it was canceled, although the forthcoming presidential election probably was the reason. Like many women's
magazines, the *Companion* did not editorially support any candidate.
Lane may have discontinued ER's column to eliminate speculation that
the magazine was backing FDR in the 1936 election.

ER's magazine career by no means ended. She sold articles to numerous publications and became a mass-circulation magazine columnist
again in 1941 with a question-and-answer page for the *Ladies' Home Journal*.* Yet, she never again wrote for the *Companion*, which ceased publication in 1956.

SELECTED BIBLIOGRAPHY

Beasley, Maurine H. *Eleanor Roosevelt and the Media*. 1987.
Black, Ruby. *Eleanor Roosevelt: A Biography*. 1940.
Lash, Joseph P. *Eleanor and Franklin*. 1971.
Seeber, Frances M. " 'I Want You to Write Me': The Papers of Anna Eleanor
    Roosevelt." In Nancy Kegan Smith and Mary C. Ryan, eds., *Modern First
    Ladies: Their Documentary Legacy*. 1989.
Zuckerman, Mary Ellen. *A History of Popular Women's Magazines in the United
    States: 1792–1995*. 1998.

Kathleen L. Endres

WOMAN'S NATIONAL DEMOCRATIC CLUB. The Woman's National Democratic Club (WNDC) in Washington, D.C., was founded in
1922 as an educational, cultural, and social organization to facilitate gatherings of leading Democratic women, with Eleanor Roosevelt as a charter
member. Its organizational meeting was on 24 November 1922 at the
Washington home of Daisy Harriman.* In response to a request from
Harriman, who asked prominent Democratic women from around the
country to back the proposed organization, ER sent in nonresident membership dues even before the group received its charter from Congress.

Among the club's initial activities was fund-raising for purchase of a clubhouse to provide a meeting place for Washington residents and Democratic women visiting the capital. In 1927 the club moved into its present quarters, an imposing Victorian mansion near Washington's Dupont Circle. From 1926 to 1935 the club published the *Democratic Digest** and its predecessor, *The Bulletin*, which were magazines for Democratic women.

Although she attempted to help the WNDC recruit members in 1928 by publicizing the group at New York's Cosmopolitan Club, ER was not actively involved in the WNDC until after 1932, when members enthusiastically greeted her as the first Democratic First Lady in the club's history. She was prominently featured in its publication and participated in its programs, which she saw as important in building rapport among Democratic women.

In 1939 in her question-and-answer column for the *Democratic Digest*, ER explained the difference between the club and the Women's Division of the Democratic National Committee. She noted that the Women's Division worked to organize Democratic women for effective political action at both the local and national level, while the club "affords a delightful place for its weekly luncheon meetings . . . [it] is recognized by the Women's Division as the hostess organization in Washington. . . . Local clubs, organized in the early years as vehicles through which to work for the party . . . affiliated with the National Club by the payment of annual dues. Today, clubs supplement the work of women in the regular party organization."(Roosevelt, 8).

As First Lady, ER served as WNDC honorary president. She took part in club activities ranging from giving speeches,* to attending teas and garden parties and being photographed with Queenie, the Democratic National Committee's female donkey mascot. Some of her activities included:

• Introducing on 17 March 1936 a question-and-answer class on administration policies and New Deal* issues for wives of Democratic members of Congress who were running for reelection;

• Speaking on 26 September 1940 on the need for the draft and emphasizing preparedness, even though she expressed hopes that the United States would not become involved in war;

• Opening on 1 April 1941 a club lecture series on women's role in defense;

• Speaking on 30 November 1942, after her wartime visit to England, on the efforts of British women to win World War II*;

• Discussing in a final appearance on 25 May 1959 the communist threat to Iran, whose wealthy, educated elite she had found on a recent visit there to be indifferent to the plight of its rural poor. As a remedy ER proposed U.S. self-help assistance to village women.

572 WOMEN AND THE NEW DEAL

Her final talk was characteristic of her appearances at the club where she addressed U.S. interests at home and abroad and championed social reform before a sympathetic audience. Today the clubhouse has an Eleanor Roosevelt wing that contains mementos of her WNDC affiliation.

SELECTED BIBLIOGRAPHY
Roosevelt, Eleanor. "Dear Mrs. Roosevelt." *Democratic Digest* (December 1939): 8.
Scrapbooks of newspaper clippings, Woman's National Democratic Club Archives, Washington, DC.

Jewell Fenzi

WOMEN AND THE NEW DEAL. Just as the New Deal* exerted an enormous impact on American politics, economics, and culture in the 1930s, the New Deal had a large effect on the nation's women. But the category of women is too broad to permit easy generalizations: analysis of women and the New Deal depends very much on which women are under scrutiny. For some, the record of the New Deal was superlative; for others, only mixed. On the whole, however, the story was a remarkable one.

The level where the most progress undoubtedly occurred was for women who secured positions in the upper echelons of the New Deal. Experienced in social reform and welfare, these women administrators flourished in the experimental climate of the early New Deal. Many of these women had been friends and professional colleagues since the 1920s or earlier, and they shared common ideas about extending the role of the federal government in modern American life and expanding roles for women. Once in Washington, these women were part of a network of professional cooperation and personal friendship that was perhaps the most outstanding characteristic of women's participation in the New Deal.

The New Deal's record on opening opportunities to women to serve in major policy-making positions was not matched until the 1960s. Among the most important appointees were Secretary of Labor* Frances Perkins,* the first woman to serve in the cabinet; Ellen Sullivan Woodward,* head of the Division of Women's and Professional Projects for the Works Progress Administration* (WPA); Hilda Worthington Smith,* director of workers education for the WPA; Hallie Flanagan,* director of the Federal Theatre Project; Mary McLeod Bethune,* head of the Division of Negro Affairs for the National Youth Administration*; Clara Beyer, associate director of the Division of Labor Standards; and Josephine Roche, assistant secretary of the Treasury. Women also found larger roles in the Democratic Party* hierarchy under the leadership of social-worker-turned-politician Mary (Molly) Dewson,* who used her position at the Women's Division of the Democratic National Committee to become one of the prime movers of the women's network.

Eleanor Roosevelt, whose model of public-spirited womanhood was greatly admired and respected by women in Washington and throughout the nation, played a key role in facilitating the contributions of the women's network. She was especially useful in providing White House access to women administrators who had a program or idea that they wanted brought to the attention of the president or his aides. More than once, if a program was stalled, ER's offer to hold a conference at the White House magically broke the bureaucratic logjam. The First Lady also lent her support by inviting women administrators to discuss their programs at her press conferences* with women reporters. She also mentioned their activities in "My Day."* It is practically impossible to imagine so much progress for women occurring in the New Deal without ER in the White House.

These women administrators truly made a difference to the course of the New Deal, both as individuals assisting in the planning and administration of New Deal programs and as members of a network where cooperation on common goals enhanced their influence. The women's network had its greatest impact on two areas of the New Deal: Democratic Party politics and social welfare. Pushing an issue-oriented approach to politics, Molly Dewson built the Women's Division into a force of some 60,000 Democratic grassroots workers who publicized the accomplishments of the Roosevelt administration in communities across the nation. Women, especially Frances Perkins at the Department of Labor, supplied critical expertise and political clout in the drafting of major pieces of legislation such as the Social Security Act, which became the cornerstone of the modern welfare state for decades to come.

The same circumstances that facilitated the contributions of women in New Deal policy-making positions also worked to the benefit of a second tier of women scattered throughout the New Deal bureaucracy, many of whom were at the beginning of long careers in public life and government service. The experiences of women such as Caroline Ware on the Consumers' Advisory Board of the National Recovery Administration (NRA), Elinore Herrick at the National Labor Relations Board, and Florence Kerr* at the WPA remind us that not only eager young men but also young women flocked to Washington to staff New Deal agencies.

The New Deal's record on helping ordinary women was more checkered. Both as workers and as members of families disrupted by the Great Depression,* these women were in desperate straits. For the most part, however, whatever benefits women received from New Deal programs came about less because of specific attempts to single women out for special treatment than as part of a broader effort to improve the living conditions and economic security of all Americans.

The story of women on relief is one of gradual improvement after a dismal start. The popular image of an unemployed person was a man—

few recognized that more than 2 million women were out of work as well. Only after ER hosted a White House Conference* on the Emergency Needs of Women in November 1933 did federal relief agencies seriously begin to take the needs of women into account, but progress was still slow. The Civilian Works Administration gave women only 7 percent of its jobs, and the Federal Emergency Relief Administration did little better. Women workers did benefit from the minimum wage and maximum hours provisions of the NRA codes, yet one-quarter of the codes mandated a lower minimum wage for women than men in the same jobs. Many women, such as domestic workers, were left outside NRA protection entirely. The Civilian Conservation Corps, one of the New Deal's most popular programs, was limited by statute to men, although concerned administrators like Hilda Worthington Smith (with help from ER) did set up a limited number of camps (popularly referred to as "she-she-she" camps) for women.

The status of women on relief improved dramatically in 1935 with the establishment of the Works Progress (later, Projects) Administration. At its peak, more than 400,000 women were on the WPA rolls. Yet the WPA had its drawbacks for women, who found it harder to qualify for participation than men, since the WPA automatically assumed that men were the primary breadwinners. The WPA also continued the pattern of lower pay scales for women and placed the vast majority of women on relief jobs in sewing rooms and canning projects.

Like all Americans, women were affected by major pieces of New Deal legislation. The 1935 National Labor Relations Act (also known as the Wagner Act) with its federal guarantee of workers' right to organize encouraged a dramatic surge in union membership and made labor a major force in political and economic life. Women shared in this progress: by the end of the decade, some 800,000 women belonged to unions, a threefold increase over 1929. The Fair Labor Standards Act of 1938 made permanent the wage and hours standards first set forth in the NRA codes (which had expired in 1935, when the National Industrial Recovery Act was declared unconstitutional). As in the case of the NRA codes, however, those who did not work in interstate commerce were not covered by the standards. Major categories of women's employment were left outside the scope of the law; cannery workers, retail clerks, and domestic servants were not covered. Since minority women were concentrated in several of those areas, they were doubly disadvantaged.

The Social Security Act of 1935 was one of the New Deal's most lasting achievements, and yet discriminatory, indeed sexist, assumptions were written into the statute from the start. The operative assumption was that men were the primary breadwinners and heads of household, with women seen as secondary earners, less entitled to protection. Until the 1939 revisions, which shifted the emphasis from the individual worker to the worker's family, a wife was not even entitled to widow's benefits if her husband died. In addition to those discriminatory aspects, many groups of women, such as agricultural workers and domestic servants (large numbers of whom were minority women), were excluded from coverage entirely.

When making a general assessment of New Deal policies as they affected women, benefits and limitations must be weighed. Is it more important that one-quarter of the NRA codes discriminated against women or that three-quarters did not? Do we applaud the threefold increase in women in labor unions or bemoan the fact that so many women workers still lacked union protection? Whether one cheers the advances or harps on the drawbacks, in large part, comes down to an individual's ideological stance toward the New Deal itself, including the perennial question of whether the New Deal could have made more sweeping reforms than it did, or whether it pragmatically accomplished all it could within the context of American politics in the 1930s. For many historians, the New Deal provides more to praise than to condemn, and that judgment applies to women's treatment in the New Deal as well.

SELECTED BIBLIOGRAPHY

Blackwelder, Julia Kirk. *Women of the Depression: Caste and Culture in San Antonio, 1929–1939*. 1984.

Faue, Elizabeth. *Community of Suffering and Struggle: Women, Men, and the Labor Movement in Minneapolis, 1915–1945*. 1991.

Janiewski, Dolores E. *Sisterhood Denied: Race, Gender, and Class in a New South Community*. 1985.

Muncy, Robin. *Creating a Female Dominion in American Reform, 1890–1930*. 1991.

Scharf, Lois. *To Work and to Wed: Female Employment, Feminism and the Great Depression*. 1980.

Ware, Susan. *Beyond Suffrage: Women in the New Deal*. 1981.

Susan Ware

WOMEN'S CITY CLUB OF NEW YORK. The Women's City Club of New York, founded in 1915 by New York suffragists, served as an important training ground for Eleanor Roosevelt's public life. It was one of the city's leading forums for learning about the political process and organizing ways to influence it. After joining the club sometime about 1923, ER was elected to its board in 1924 and first vice president in 1925. In 1926 she took over leadership of the club's influential legislation committee, which recommended club positions on pending measures. In these capacities ER played many leadership roles, including investigating controversial issues, formulating club positions, organizing and taking part in public debates, and testifying before legislative committees at the state capital in Albany.

Yet, at the time ER joined the Women's City Club, she did not expect to reap such rewards in terms of self-development. She saw the club mainly as a way of educating women in the responsibilities of voting. Making her debut on the radio* in April 1925 on behalf of the club, she termed the organization a "clearing house for civic ideals" and called attention to its recent investigation of dance halls to determine if they were pernicious influences on young women patrons (Perry, *Training for Public Life*, 38).

Among the issues that engaged ER most were state-supported urban housing for low-income groups, protective legislation for working women, curbs on child labor,* the reorganization of state government, and the right of physicians to disseminate information on birth control* to married women. Both her radio broadcasts and her role in the club's effort to publicize the cause of women's access to birth control helped teach her how to handle the public spotlight. Club work developed her skills in making speeches,* organizing and chairing meetings, writing reports, political analysis, and working with people. When she first became legislative chair, ER appeared to push the agenda of the Democratic Party,* but as she gained more experience, she framed her efforts in less partisan terms.

Doubtlessly, the club's membership, which, after national woman suffrage in 1920, soared to almost 3,000, broadened ER's circle of acquaintances and provided her with contacts among many accomplished and professional women. These included, most prominently, Belle Moskowitz,* under whose direction ER later ran Democratic women's campaigns in support of Alfred E. Smith* for New York governor and president, and Mary (Molly) Dewson,* the club's first "civic secretary," who later took up national Democratic Party work under ER's guidance. During her White House years, ER would turn to others she had met at the club—lawyers, physicians, social reformers, businesswomen, and teachers—for help in promoting New Deal* programs or as candidates for government appointments.

With the election of Franklin D. Roosevelt* as governor of New York in 1928, ER resigned her club office. The club begged her to stay, but she felt that the office conflicted with her role as the state's First Lady. ER took with her valuable lessons for her subsequent career.

SELECTED BIBLIOGRAPHY
Perry, Elisabeth Israels. "Training for Public Life: Eleanor Roosevelt and Women's Political Networks in New York in the 1920s." In Joan Hoff-Wilson and Marjorie Lightman, eds., *Without Precedent: The Life and Career of Eleanor Roosevelt*. 1984.
———. "Women's Political Choices after Suffrage: The Women's City Club of New York, 1915–Present." *New York History* 62, no. 4 (October 1990): 417–34.

                                                              Elisabeth Israels Perry

WOMEN'S DEMOCRATIC NEWS. In 1925 members of the Women's Division of the New York state Democratic Committee began publishing a monthly newspaper, the *Women's Democratic News*. This paper, an enlargement of a mimeographed "News Bulletin" (first issued in 1922), appeared through 1935, when it merged with the *Democratic Digest*,* the publication of the Democratic National Committee's Women's Division. The idea for the newspaper originated in the 1924 campaign, when women party leaders, including Eleanor Roosevelt, toured the state to stump for Governor Alfred E. Smith* and met upstate Democrats who complained of feeling cut off from the party's center. After the campaign, the women pledged to visit annually every county organization and political club in the state. They also decided to use an enlarged newsletter as a means of strengthening bonds between the party's central and outlying organizations.

The newspaper's staff consisted of Caroline O'Day,* president; Elinor Morgenthau,* vice president; Nancy Cook,* business manager; ER, editor and treasurer (she resigned when her husband became New York state governor in 1928); and Marion Dickerman,* secretary. ER was active in all phases of the operation, from selling advertising to writing editorials. After resigning as editor, she continued to solicit articles for the paper. In February 1933, after the election of Franklin D. Roosevelt* as president, she began writing a monthly column in the form of a personal letter entitled "Passing Thoughts of Mrs. Franklin D. Roosevelt," which appeared in the paper until it ceased publication at the end of 1935.

The paper—nine by twelve inches in size, twelve pages long (by November 1925, sixteen pages), and printed on glossy paper—featured cartoons of two smiling donkeys flanking the masthead and a front page with an eye-catching party slogan, boldfaced message, political cartoon, or portrait of a prominent political figure. Stories appeared across three columns broken up by photographs, mostly of party leaders or authors of articles. Each issue contained regular features, such as reports from the female associate chairs of county organizations, explanations of major political issues or analyses of recent elections, and profiles of women prominent in government service or politics.

When the paper expanded, new features included drama and movie reviews and a tongue-in-cheek "Not in the Headlines" column containing stories of male bias against women in politics. A correspondent writing regularly as "Letty" commented on activities in the nation's capital, and Mrs. Frederick S. Greene, wife of the state superintendent of public works, reported on the Albany legislative scene. Major topics, such as child labor* laws, equal rights for women, U.S. policy in Central America, and state and national party conventions, received coverage. But the feature that best captured the spirit and purpose of the paper was "Trooping for Democracy," day-by-day reports on annual trips by Women's

Division members to rural party organizations. The feature illustrated how the *Women's Democratic News* helped forge a party unity that would lend support to FDR's New Deal* in the next decade.

SELECTED BIBLIOGRAPHY

Davis, Kenneth S. *Invincible Summer: An Intimate Portrait of the Roosevelts*. 1974.

Perry, Elisabeth Israels. "The Political Apprenticeship of Eleanor Roosevelt." In Jess Flemion and Colleen M. O'Connor, eds., *Eleanor Roosevelt, An American Journey*. 1987.

Women's Democratic News. 1925–1935. New York Public Library.

Elisabeth Israels Perry

WOMEN'S NATIONAL PRESS CLUB. As First Lady from 1933 to 1945, Eleanor Roosevelt formed close ties with the Women's National Press Club (WNPC) in Washington, an organization that brought together women journalists striving for recognition in a male-dominated field. Founded in 1919 by newspaperwomen and publicists involved in news coverage of the suffrage movement, the club offered professional and social contacts during the Roosevelt era to women excluded from membership in the male-only National Press Club.

While in the White House, ER maintained warm relationships with individual club members and the organization itself, which had about 150 members during the 1930s. She personally interacted with many WNPC members during her weekly press conferences.* Because ER would not allow men to attend these conferences, she forced several news organizations to hire women reporters, and, as a result some women journalists were grateful to her for their employment. For example, Ruby Black,* elected WNPC president in 1939, owed her job as the first woman hired by the United Press to ER's refusal to admit men to the press conferences.

Unlike her immediate predecessors as First Lady, Grace Coolidge and Lou Henry Hoover,* ER accepted invitations to the WNPC's yearly "stunt parties" that ridiculed the Washington political scene in song and skits. The chief subject of "stunt party" humor, ER laughed at parodies and gave humorous off-the-record reactions to skits that generally treated her with affection and respect; WNPC members did not forget her role in their own careers.

Although ER accepted club satire gracefully, it may have influenced her actions on at least one occasion: she gave up the job of editing a magazine for new mothers called *Babies-Just Babies** after the press women made fun of the new Roosevelt administration in a skit beginning, "We are new to the business of running the show. We're babies, just babies, just babies" (Lash, 373).

The "stunt parties" were the women's counterpart to the male-only banquets of the Gridiron Club, an organization of elite journalists whose annual events satirizing politics traditionally were attended by the president. Not to be outdone by men, ER held her own "Gridiron Widows" parties in the White House for women journalists and officials, including Secretary of Labor Frances Perkins,* who were excluded from the Gridiron dinners. Although many of the women journalists who were invited belonged to the WNPC, some were affiliated with another Washington group, the American Newspaper Women's Club, predominantly made up of society reporters. As First Lady ER was an honorary member of that organization and attended its functions.

In 1938 the WNPC voted to accept ER as an active member on the basis she was a professional journalist because she had written her syndicated column, "My Day,"* for two years. Her membership was proposed by Doris Fleeson, a political columnist for the *New York Daily News*, and seconded by Black and Bess Furman,* a former Associated Press reporter. Election was not unanimous; nine votes were cast against it, presumably because ER did not conform to a club requirement that membership go only to those who earn most of their living by writing.

Without doubt ER helped increase the organization's visibility. On the eve of the nation's entrance into World War II,* she was instrumental in arranging for Franklin D. Roosevelt* to speak at a club luncheon in 1941, the first time he had given a luncheon speech in Washington since his arrival as president in 1933. His topic: women's role in the national defense effort.

After leaving the White House, ER kept in contact with club leaders, like Furman, who admired her greatly. After ER's death, the WNPC set up a Golden Candlestick Award in her name to honor individuals for unselfish service. The club itself went out of existence in 1970, shortly before the National Press Club voted to accept women.

SELECTED BIBLIOGRAPHY
Beasley, Maurine. *Eleanor Roosevelt and the Media.* 1987.
———. "The Women's National Press Club: Case Study of Professional Aspirations" in Jean Folkerts, ed., *Media Voices: An Historical Perspective.* 1992.
Lash, Joseph P. *Eleanor and Franklin.* 1971.
Roosevelt, Eleanor. *This I Remember.* 1949.

Bonnie Brennen

WOMEN'S TRADE UNION LEAGUE. Founded in 1903 by settlement house workers and trade unionists, the Women's Trade Union League (WTUL) brought upper-class and working women together in efforts to improve conditions for working women. When she joined the league in 1922, Eleanor Roosevelt became a strong supporter of such alliances, which redirected the social uplift and charity tradition of her class into support work for trade unions. On 28 November 1932 she told a benefit for the league that "those of us to whom fortune has been kind . . . can

not enjoy life ourselves unless our sisters have something also to enjoy;
... we must have a greater spirit of cooperation, of interest in the daily
lives of those about us and a willingness to share our benefits, even if it
means that we have somewhat less ourselves in the way of ease and
pleasure" (Address by Mrs. Franklin D. Roosevelt).

Under the leadership of the wealthy progressive reformer Margaret
Dreier Robins, WTUL national president during 1907–1922, the league
set up branches in twenty-two cities by 1915, raised funds from bene-
factors, supported a cadre of labor organizers, and recorded some notable success in bringing women into labor* unions, particularly in the
garment industry.

ER first encountered league women at the 1919 International Congress
of Working Women in Washington, where she volunteered as a translator, since she was fluent in French. She became active in the New York
league in 1922 as part of her immersion in Democratic Party* and
women's reform politics. By this time working-class women, who had
assumed leadership of the WTUL, were encountering funding difficulties
and shifting their focus from organizing to lobbying for protective labor
laws for women, such as those setting minimum wages and maximum
hours. ER's friendship with Rose Schneiderman,* president of the New
York league from 1918 to 1949 and of the national WTUL from 1926 to
1950, led to opportunities for league officials to discuss labor issues with
Franklin D. Roosevelt* when he was governor of New York.

Referred to as a "fairy godmother" on the first page of the league's
annual report for 1932–1933, ER emerged as a major financial backer of
the New York league, raising the funds in 1929 to retire the debt on its
headquarters at 247 Lexington Avenue. She donated some of the earnings from her books* and radio* talks to pay league bills, singularly
maintaining the organization for three months during the winter of 1932–
1933 by giving it $3,600. That year the WTUL finance committee, which
she chaired, provided the staff, equipment, and supplies to open a clubroom for unemployed trade union women at the New York league headquarters. The women subsequently named their club after her.

Subscribing to WTUL philosophy that working-class women needed
"roses" as well as "bread," ER contributed to the union's education program. She gave weekly readings from American literature during the
1920s at the New York league, ending each session by serving cookies
and hot chocolate. From 1925 until the 1940s, she hosted an annual
Christmas party for children of league members. As late as 1946 she
taught a series of classes on current events for league members.

ER's parties, classes, and receptions for the league may have derived
from a sense of noblesse oblige, but, as the wife of the governor of New
York and later of the president of the United States, these events assumed a symbolic, even democratic meaning. At the New York league's

twenty-fifth anniversary in June 1929, over 200 members sailed up the Hudson to Hyde Park,* where ER's mother-in-law, Sara Delano Roosevelt,* and FDR entertained them on their estate. Never before, the *New York Times* reported on 9 June 1929, had a governor ever feted members of a labor organization in such a setting. During the 1936 national WTUL convention in Washington, ER invited working women delegates to stay at the White House. A New York dressmaker captured this use of presidential quarters when she recalled: "Imagine me, Feigele Shapiro, sleeping in Lincoln's bed" (Orleck, 158).

ER further provided the league with political access; leaders became New York state labor officials and held appointments under the New Deal.* Schneiderman served on the labor advisory board of the National Recovery Administration, traveling with ER in Puerto Rico in March 1934 to expose the exploitative conditions under which homeworkers made cotton garments there. ER pushed the league agenda for fair labor standards and an improved quality of life for working people in Albany and Washington and within the Democratic Party. She helped influence the party's platform planks on the eight-hour day, minimum wages, and a constitutional amendment banning child labor.

In line with league philosophy, she rejected the Equal Rights Amendment* for many years and was not above tying principle to party politics when she lobbied Robins against supporting Herbert Hoover* in the 1928 presidential election. By then ER had become a policy spokeswoman for the league. For example, on the league's behalf she debated the need for legislation to set maximum working hours at a Town Hall meeting in New York on 8 April 1929. When she was in the White House, she addressed league-supported Long Island electrical industry strikers on 5 February 1941.

The ties to the White House enjoyed by the WTUL during the Roosevelt administration, however, did not help prepare it for a sustainable role in the postwar years, when many established unions questioned the need for continuing an independent women's organization. Faced with declining membership and funding, the national WTUL held its last national convention in 1947 and closed its small national office in Washington in June 1950. The final dissolution came with the disbanding of the New York branch in 1955. Until her death in 1962, ER continued to promote the league's goal of education, serving as chair of the trustees administering college scholarships for women that derived from the remaining assets of the New York league.

SELECTED BIBLIOGRAPHY

"Address by Mrs. Franklin D. Roosevelt on 28 November 1932 at Benefit Concert, Women's Trade Union League." Eleanor Roosevelt Papers, Franklin D. Roosevelt Library, Hyde Park, NY.

Orleck, Annelise. *Common Sense and a Little Fire: Women and Working-Class Politics in the United States, 1900–1965.* 1995.
Papers of the Women's Trade Union League and Its Principal Leaders, Microfilm Edition, Library of Congress, Washington, DC.
Payne, Elizabeth Anne. *Reform, Labor, and Feminism.* 1988.
Schneiderman, Rose, with Lucy Goldthwaite. *All for One.* 1967.

Eileen Boris

WOODWARD, ELLEN SULLIVAN (11 July 1887, Oxford, MS–23 September 1971, Washington, DC).

Ellen Sullivan Woodward, an administrator of New Deal* women's relief programs, was educated in the Oxford, Mississippi, public schools and in Washington, D.C., where her father served briefly in the U.S. Congress. After one year at Sans Souci Academy in South Carolina, she returned to Mississippi and married at age nineteen. Widowed in 1925 and left with one son, she served out the term of her husband, Albert Y. Woodward, in the Mississippi legislature. Needing a reliable income, she began work in 1927 for the Mississippi state Board of Development and rapidly moved up to become its executive director. Concurrently, she developed close ties with the Democratic Party* and became Mississippi's National Committeewoman in 1932, the year that she first met ER, with whom she engaged in correspondence during the presidential campaign.

At ER's urging, Harry L. Hopkins,* head of the Federal Emergency Relief Administration (FERA), added a Women's Division to provide work relief for unemployed needy women. Aware of Woodward's past efforts to promote social welfare and public relief programs in Mississippi, Hopkins named her director of the new division in late August 1933. Almost immediately, Woodward sought the support of the First Lady, and together they conducted in November a White House Conference* on the Emergency Needs of Women. From then until Woodward left the Works Progress Administration,* the FERA's successor agency, in December 1938, ER was a close collaborator in maintaining a wide variety of projects that employed, at their peak, almost 470,000 women. She was especially important in protecting the women's program in the shift from the FERA to the WPA in 1935, when it appeared that the men's construction projects would be given disproportionate priority. Again, in 1938, when budget cuts threatened the women's institutional and service projects, Woodward hastened to Val-Kill* and gained ER's re-endorsement of the women's work program. ER was influential in the creation of the Four Arts projects for writers, artists, musicians, and theater personnel. She approved their transfer to Woodward in 1936, when the Women's Division was reconstituted as the Division of Women's and Professional Projects and championed them when they were in jeopardy by 1938.

ER was present when Woodward was sworn in as a member of the Social Security Board in late December 1938, and in her "My Day"* column of 31 December 1938 praised the new member for her "executive ability [and] tact." Woodward assisted ER in responding to inquiries about Social Security programs and continued, as she had done since 1933, to channel to appropriate officials the many demands made of the First Lady for personal assistance.

Woodward was the beneficiary of ER's insistence that women have a role in planning for post–World War II* peacemaking. In 1943 Woodward was named a delegate to the conference of the United Nations Relief and Rehabilitation Administration (UNRRA), the first of six that she would attend. Before leaving for the second UNRRA Assembly, she wrote her White House friend, "Most opportunities that come to me come through you" (EW to ER, 14 September 1944). After 1946, the year that Woodward was named a division director in the Federal Security Agency and when ER was no longer in the White House, the two saw less of one another. Extant records indicate no exchange between the aging veterans for women's welfare after a conference of Democratic women in 1958. Woodward's health declined after 1961; her death a decade later was attributed to arteriosclerosis.

SELECTED BIBLIOGRAPHY
Eleanor Roosevelt Papers, Franklin D. Roosevelt Library, Hyde Park, NY.
Ellen S. Woodward Papers, Mississippi Department of Archives and History, Jackson.
RG 69 (WPA) and RG 47 (Social Security Administration), National Archives, Washington, DC.
Swain, Martha H. Ellen S. Woodward: New Deal Advocate for Women. 1995.
———. "ER and Ellen Woodward: A Partnership for Women's Relief and Security." In Joan Hoff-Wilson and Marjorie Lightman, eds., Without Precedent: The Life and Career of Eleanor Roosevelt. 1984.
Ware, Susan. Beyond Suffrage: Women in the New Deal. 1981.

Martha H. Swain

WORKS PROGRESS ADMINISTRATION. Eleanor Roosevelt served as a dedicated supporter and major publicist of New Deal* programs, particularly the Works Progress Administration (WPA), which provided federally funded jobs instead of relief payments to the able-bodied unemployed. President Franklin D. Roosevelt* created the WPA by executive order on 6 May 1935, with the aim of phasing out the Federal Emergency Relief Administration (FERA), which gave grants to the states for direct relief payments. Harry Hopkins,* FERA administrator and a confidant of ER at the time, became the WPA administrator.

As a strong advocate of the WPA, ER frequently visited its projects during her travels.* She described them favorably in her lectures and

"My Day"* column and promptly referred concerns or problems that came to her attention to Hopkins and other officials. She acted as an invaluable ally for unemployed women, African Americans, and youth,* pressing for WPA programs to assist them and trying to make sure that they got fair treatment.

With ER's encouragement, Hopkins in 1936 selected Ellen S. Woodward,* director of women's programs in both FERA and the WPA, to head the Women's and Professional Division of the WPA, which made her a power in the agency. Woodward and ER had worked together on women's employment problems since the 1933 White House Conference* on the Emergency Needs of Women. At its peak the WPA employed more than 400,000 women on projects ranging from sewing, canning, and child care to library work, nursing, and teaching. In spite of ER's watchdog stance, however, efforts on behalf of women were only partially successful. Many unemployed women could not find WPA jobs due to preferential treatment given unemployed male heads of households. The jobs that were available to women were limited in both scope and salary.

ER's concern about the effect of the Great Depression* on young people led to her involvement with the National Youth Administration* (NYA). It was established in 1935 within the WPA to provide part-time employment for high school and college students that would allow them to stay in school, as well as job training for unemployed youth who were not in school. Hopkins and Aubrey Williams,* who became head of the NYA, discussed plans for the new agency with her, and she lobbied FDR on its behalf, keeping in close touch with Williams as he implemented NYA projects. This led FDR to refer to the NYA as "the missus organization" (Salmond, 138).

Another of ER's concerns was equitable treatment for African Americans in WPA projects. Mary McLeod Bethune,* who in 1936 was appointed director of the NYA Division of Negro Affairs, found ER to be a ready ally. She helped ensure that the NYA had the best record among New Deal agencies of including African Americans in its programs. At Bethune's request, ER on 4 April 1938 hosted a White House Conference on Participation of Negro Women and Children in Federal Welfare Programs. Nonetheless, like women, African Americans did not share fully in WPA programs.

The small, but controversial, WPA projects to provide work for unemployed actors, artists, musicians, and writers also found an advocate in ER. She wrote about their achievements and defended their value when Congress* threatened funding cuts, which in 1939 ended the WPA Federal Theatre Project and reduced allocations for the WPA Federal Writers', Art, and Music Projects. Budget-cutting came from conservative forces that disliked the projects' emphasis on social protest and opposed government support of the arts.

By the time the WPA (renamed the Works Projects Administration in 1939) terminated on 30 June 1943, it had provided employment at a cost of close to $11 billion for about 8.5 million needy individuals, who supported millions of other persons. WPA workers built roads, bridges, dams, and airports, created parks, gave concerts, painted murals, wrote guidebooks, produced plays, worked in schools, hospitals, libraries, offices, and museums, and carried out innumerable other projects.

When the Roosevelt administration created the WPA, it concluded that unemployment was a national problem that required federal action. The WPA, however, never employed more than one-third of the jobless. Detractors accused the agency of "make-work" programs and charged it with being wasteful and of exerting political influence on its employees. In a 1939 public opinion poll by the Institute of Public Opinion, the WPA topped the list as both the Roosevelt administration's greatest achievement and poorest accomplishment. Yet, the WPA improved the lives of millions of American families and assisted almost every community in the nation. ER remained its devoted champion.

SELECTED BIBLIOGRAPHY

Davis, Kenneth S. *FDR: The New Deal Years: 1933–1937*. 1979.
Hareven, Tamara K. *Eleanor Roosevelt: An American Conscience*. 1968.
Howard, Donald S. *The WPA and Relief Policy*. 1943.
Leuchtenburg, William E. *Franklin D. Roosevelt and the New Deal: 1932–1940*. 1963.
Salmond, John A. *A Southern Rebel. The Life and Times of Aubrey Willis Williams*. 1983.
Ware, Susan. *Beyond Suffrage: Women in the New Deal*. 1981.

June Hopkins

WORLD COURT. During the 1920s, Eleanor Roosevelt emerged as one of the nation's leading proponents of U.S. participation in the Permanent Court of International Justice, also known as the World Court. Rising isolationist sentiment in the United States, however, frustrated her efforts. The court was established pursuant to Article 14 of the Covenant of the League of Nations.* Approved by the league's Assembly in 1920, it opened in 1922 to hear any international dispute. Fifteen judges elected to nine-year terms decided cases based on majority votes. The court rendered thirty-one verdicts and handed down twenty-seven advisory positions between its creation and 1946, when it was succeeded by the International Court of Justice of the United Nations.

ER's leadership in the committee that administered the Bok Peace Prize* in 1923 thrust her into the forefront of the movement to secure U.S. participation in the court. The plan that won the prize called for immediate U.S. involvement in the court, so ER and her associates sought to use the extensive publicity surrounding the prize to promote the idea. The House of Representatives voted for U.S. participation in 1925, but the required two-thirds vote in the Senate for U.S. adherence to the court represented a monumental hurdle. ER urged her husband, Franklin D. Roosevelt,* to support the measure fully after his election as president in 1932, though he remained reluctant to do so until 1935 because of isolationist political pressure. Even when he finally pressed the issue, it still fell seven votes short in the Senate. Thus, the United States deferred participating in the World Court until after World War II,* when it became a party to the United Nations* Charter under which the International Court of Justice was established.

SELECTED BIBLIOGRAPHY
Cook, Blanche Wiesen. *Eleanor Roosevelt*. Vol. 1. 1992.
Dunn, Michael. *The United States and the World Court*. 1988.

John M. Craig

WORLD WAR II. "In the last war," Eleanor Roosevelt told an overflow crowd in February 1942, "we won . . . but we lost the peace." This failure, she continued, stemmed from the unfortunate fact that the nation "did not understand what it took to build a democracy." (*Chicago Defender*, 21 February 1942). Only a few months after the bombing of Pearl Harbor, the First Lady vowed do what she could to make sure that the United States did not repeat the mistakes of the past. Unless, she declared, America built democracy at home—a society that guaranteed to everyone the right to vote, a quality education, equal access to employment, and justice in the courts—then the gruesome sacrifices of war would be in vain. For ER, the challenge of World War II was to defeat fascism overseas, while extending the benefits of democracy at home to all of the nation's citizens regardless of color, creed, sex, or religion.

Personally, the war years were trying times for ER. Even before the United States entered the battle, her mother-in-law, Sara Delano Roosevelt,* and brother, G. Hall Roosevelt,* died in quick succession. The war brought more nerve-racking days to the Roosevelt family. All four sons of ER and Franklin D. Roosevelt* joined the armed services, and two of them faced enemy fire. With their children overseas, ER and FDR's relationship, long strained by infidelity and misunderstanding, grew chillier and more distant. ER complained that FDR had become too willing to sacrifice social concerns to mollify defense industries. The president, meanwhile, could not take what he saw as ER's constant hectoring about one cause or another. After a long day of meetings about this battle or that production problem, the president typically wanted to relax, mix a drink, and tell a few jokes. ER, however, had trouble relaxing. Increasingly during the war years, FDR avoided her. Yet ER and FDR never stopped respecting what the other thought or did.

The war changed ER's politics as well as her personal life. Horrified by the carnage of World War I, ER lent her support during the 1920s and 1930s to the nation's emerging peace movement.* She regularly spoke out in favor of disarmament and against militarism in her speeches* and newspaper columns. The threat of fascism, however, rattled her pacifist sentiments. Democracy, she feared, could not coexist with the kinds of malevolent forces taking shape in Europe. "You don't want to go to war," ER told a group of antiwar activists in 1940. "I don't want to go to war. But war may come to us" (Goodwin, 84). She added on another occasion, "If war comes to your own country, then even pacifists, it seems to me, must stand up and fight for their beliefs" (Scharf, 119).

With the coming of war to the United States, ER definitely stood up for her country. For a short time beginning in 1941, ER served as the deputy director of the Office of Civilian Defense (OCD),* the agency charged with boosting morale on the home front. Continuing to play the part of the eyes and ears of FDR, she traveled endlessly during the war. She went from one end of the country to another exhorting women and men, young and old, soldiers and civilians, to do their part to win the war. Always on the go, she visited defense plants and housing projects in military production centers. ER also went to see troops across the country, as well as at bases in England, Latin America,* and the South Pacific. Displaying her characteristically gracious manner, she chatted with soldiers from all walks of life, sharing with them the news from the home front, and asking them in a motherly sort of way how they were coping with their stressful situations.

Throughout her ceaseless travels,* ER forged a special bond with women, especially women war workers. As the country felt the first pinch of the war-induced labor shortage, the First Lady encouraged single and married women alike to seek work outside the home and contribute to their country. Many heeded her call, plus the lure of good wages, and threw on a pair of overalls and headed out to work each day with a lunch pail in their hands just as their fathers, brothers, and husbands did. Whenever ER visited defense plants, she made sure to ask the managers about the performance of female laborers, and she clearly delighted in hearing reports that they were "doing a swell job, better than expected" (Goodwin, 369).

ER took time to talk to these women workers as well. Walking through a Portland, Maine, shipyard late one cold night in January 1943, the First Lady sat down with a group of obviously tired women. She asked them what they did on the job, how they got to work, how they managed to take care of their children and keep up with the cooking and cleaning. In her widely circulated "My Day"* column and in speeches,* ER applauded public and private contributions of the many "Rosie the Riveters" to the war effort. At the same time, she highlighted the particular, gendered concerns of these women workers. Worried about the double burden faced by working women, she called on the government to build day-care facilities and establish community kitchens that would provide wives and mothers with hot meals they could take home after their shifts ended. ER also pressed store owners to open their shops to match the schedules of defense workers. Going one step further, she urged war plants to hire professional shoppers who would have bags filled with groceries waiting for women when they finished work. Finally, she demanded that women receive equal pay for equal work.

As war wound down in Europe and Asia, some people grew uneasy about women at work. What would happen, they wondered, when the soldiers returned home? Would Rosie give up her overalls for an apron and happily leave the shopfloor and return to the kitchen? Many insisted that women belonged back in the home. ER, however, refused to support the campaign to push women out of the factories. She argued that women deserved the right to decent jobs after the war if they needed the wages.

Defending the rights of women war workers was just part of ER's larger crusade to extend the benefits of democracy. "No one," she lamented, "can honestly claim that either the Indians or the Negroes of this country are free. . . . We have proverty which enslaves and racial prejudice which does the same" (Youngs, 185). Discrimination and segregation, ER insisted, were wrong, even un-American. Asked during the war if "Negroes should be admitted to the air corps without segregation," ER answered without hesitating, "Yes! I think Negroes should be admitted anywhere any other Americans are admitted" (*Chicago Defender*, 10 April 1943). Trying to lower exclusionary barriers, ER supported the efforts of the National Association for the Advancement of Colored People* to integrate the armed services and end job segregation. "It's not the color of your skin that makes you hirable," ER argued; "you've got to take a person, regardless of his race, creed, or color, when it comes to filling a job" (*Pittsburgh Courier*, 6 September 1941).

To ER, equality meant more than equal access to the army and war work. It also meant ending the disfranchisement of African Americans in the South. She asserted that all Americans must have the right to vote and that the poll tax, long used by southern states to deny black people access to the ballot, must be abolished. If we believe in democracy, she boldly declared, "we believe there should be no impediment which prevents any man from expressing his will through the ballot" (*Chicago Defender*, 24 July 1943).

Despite ER's widely publicized, stinging attacks on segregation, there were limits to her liberalism, even on the race question. Mostly, she refused to do anything that would compromise winning the war. As A. Philip Randolph, the head of the all-black Brotherhood of Sleeping Car Porters, geared up in the summer of 1941 to march on Washington to protest discrimination in defense industries, ER advised her longtime associate to call off the rally, fearing that it would trigger racial incidents. Asked a few years later how she would feel if she were a "Negro," the First Lady answered, "I should feel deeply resentful." She explained regretfully, "There are many things in our democracy which are not as yet democratic." But, ER was quick to add that "if I were either a colored soldier or his sweetheart, I should try to remember how far my race has come in some seventy-odd years" (Roosevelt, *If You Ask Me*, 137–38). She also advised caution when it came to social relations. "I have never," she assured an angry white southerner, "advocated social equality or intermarriage" (ER to L. W. Bates, 23 February 1942). Individuals, ER warned, could be pushed only so far, only so fast.

The limits of the First Lady's racial liberalism hardly mattered to her critics,* especially in the white neighborhoods of the South. "I don't mean to be rude," a woman began a letter to ER, but, she wondered, "do you have colored blood in your family as you seem to derive so much pleasure from associating with colored folks?" ER answered: "I haven't as yet discovered . . . any colored blood, but, of course, if any of us go back far enough, I suppose we can find that we all stem from the same beginnings. I have no feeling that the colored race is inferior to the white race" (Roosevelt, *If You Ask Me*, 68).

ER's racial politics gave rise to a host of wartime rumors. One of these stories had African American domestic workers joining "Eleanor Clubs."* According to these tales, club members vowed to stop working for whites and expected their ex-bosses to cook for them after the war. Others accused the First Lady of stirring racial tensions. Following the deadly Detroit race riot of 1943, a Richmond, Virginia, man wrote with disgust, "I suppose now you are satisfied." "YOU have been running all over the country sowing the seeds of discord and dissension. . . . Detroit . . . [is] the product of your endeavors." The editor of the *Jackson* (Mississippi) *Daily News* also pointed an accusing finger at ER. "It is blood on your hands, Mrs. Roosevelt," he wrote the day after the Detroit rebellion. "You have been personally proclaiming and practicing social equality at the White House. . . . What followed is now history" (Black, 285).

Conservatives from around the country joined white southerners in denouncing ER's wartime activities. Disturbed by what they saw as the First Lady's "unwomanly" public persona, some wanted her to stay at home. "I sincerely wish you would give Franklin a break and let him have the spot light," wrote a Mississippi woman (Audie Calvert to ER, 13 June 1942). ER was characterized as a "female-dictator" and urged "to keep Franklin company (as a real good woman should do)" and "tend to her knitting" (Youngs, 198).

Although ER was not impervious to attack, she did not wilt before the blistering criticism of her racial politics or public role. She did not drift into the background after FDR's death in April 1945. She continued in the postwar era to travel, write newspaper columns, and speak out in favor of democracy. Her continued activism made her one of the leading voices of a new brand of liberalism taking shape in America in the postwar era. While the New Deal,* especially in its early days, focused on economic issues and the distribution of wealth, the new liberalism fought to increase the civil rights* of individuals and social groups. Through her ceaseless wartime and postwar efforts, ER played a key role in shaping this vision of democracy dedicated to securing equal rights to all.

SELECTED BIBLIOGRAPHY

Black, Allida M. "Eleanor Roosevelt and the Wartime Campaign Against Jim Crow." *Social Education* (1996): 284–286.
Eleanor Roosevelt Papers, Franklin D. Roosevelt Library, Hyde Park, NY.
Goodwin, Doris Kearns. *No Ordinary Time: Franklin and Eleanor Roosevelt: The Home Front in World War II.* 1995.
Roosevelt, Eleanor. *If You Ask Me.* 1946.
Scharf, Lois. *Eleanor Roosevelt: First Lady of American Liberalism.* 1987.
Youngs, J. William T. *Eleanor Roosevelt: A Personal and Public Life.* 1985.

Bryant Simon

Y

YOUTH. No resident of the White House has ever approached the level of concern, activism, and empathy that Eleanor Roosevelt displayed for American youth. ER's willingness to work even with radical youth in the 1930s distinguishes her from any of her predecessors or successors. During eras of turbulence the White House tends to distance itself from its youngest critics. At the height of the Vietnam War era, for example, the administrations of President Lyndon B. Johnson and President Richard M. Nixon denounced leftist-led student protesters and supported government attempts to undermine the student movement of the 1960s. But when confronted with a similar movement in the 1930s, ER built bridges rather than barricades—befriending protest leaders, listening to their concerns, and helping to bring their key organizations, most notably, the American Student Union* and the American Youth Congress,* into the New Deal* coalition. She stood up for the right of youths to dissent during the Great Depression* and shielded them from the Red-baiting of the House Committee to Investigate Un-American Activities.* ER found areas of common ground with the student protesters, working with them on expanding federal aid to low-income students and unemployed youth as well as on such antifascist mobilizations as the World Youth Congress.

ER's friendliness toward the student movement was the most controversial—but by no means was it the only—facet of her involvement with youth and their problems during the depression decade. The First Lady's name is intimately connected with the history of the National Youth Administration* (NYA) and the whole effort to provide a New Deal—jobs, training, and student aid—for youth impoverished by the Great Depression. Historians disagree about the precise role that ER played in the NYA's creation. There is no question, however, that as the NYA

Eleanor Roosevelt participates in a session of the International Student Service summer leadership training institute held at the Roosevelt summer home on Campobello in July 1942 with (l. to r.) Mrs. Robert MacIver, wife of the institute director; Wilson Dizard, Fordham University; Walter Filley, Yale University; Mary Vallet, Hampton Institute; Harold Katz, Vanderbilt University; May Craig, correspondent for Maine newspapers; and Robert Marshall, Queens College. *Courtesy of Wilson Dizard*

began its work in 1935, she was the most persistent and effective champion of this new youth agency. The First Lady promoted the NYA through her syndicated newspaper columns, radio broadcasts,* and lobbying. Her role was acknowledged by President Franklin D. Roosevelt* himself, who referred to the NYA as "the missus organization" (Salmond, 138).

ER was more sensitive than her husband to issues of gender equity with respect to federal aid programs for youth. Dissatisfied with the Civilian Conservation Corps' males-only approach to youth relief, ER helped organize an effort that culminated in the Federal Emergency Relief Administration's funding in 1934 of camps for jobless young women known as "she-she-she" camps. These offered the participants short-term vocational counseling and educational programs.

Depression America was often reminded of ER's concern with problems of youth in her "My Day"* newspaper column. It included frequent references to her tours of NYA projects and other New Deal ventures on behalf of the young, meetings with administrators of federal youth programs, and talks with young people helped by these programs. The column also reflected ER's search for new solutions to the educational and job problems confronting the young, and if an author, youth commission, or activist had published something innovative in the field, it would almost inevitably attract at least a mention in "My Day."

Given all this work on behalf of the depression's young victims, it is little wonder that many impoverished children and teens regarded ER as the person in Washington most concerned with their plight. Thousands of these low-income children wrote to the First Lady, appealing for clothing, educational funding, and other forms of direct, personal assistance. Some told ER they thought of her as "a kind of fairy godmother," and others, that they loved her because she "looks [out] for the poor" (Cohen, "Dear Mrs. Roosevelt," 272, 295). Total strangers though they were, these youths felt that they could confide in her and shared their hard-luck stories of shame and deprivation—convinced that this singularly compassionate First Lady would care about, and help them solve, their problems.

ER's extensive involvement with youth issues during her years in the White House was obviously fostered by the severe economic crisis of the period. Its dimensions were suggested by a 1936 American Youth Commission study, which found that 40 percent of young people (sixteen to twenty-four years of age) were "neither gainfully employed nor in school" (Cohen, "Dear Mrs. Roosevelt," 271). But for ER the young were more than simply one of many groups victimized by the depression; they represented the future of America and as such could not be allowed to fade into joblessness and despair. Present in ER's rhetoric regarding youth was an element of guilt, which was common among Americans of her generation; it was a guilt that emanated from the failure of the older generation to provide jobs, education, and hope for the coming generation. Indeed, it was no accident that at the height of the depression decade Hollywood's top box office star was a child, Shirley Temple, whose motion pictures often featured her as an orphaned girl who succeeded despite poverty, hardship, and abandonment. Such films offered a sense of reassurance for Americans that although the depression had left them unable to provide for the young, all would turn out well anyway. Feelings of guilt were also expressed in some of ER's rhetoric regarding the international crisis wrought by fascism. In her "My Day" column of 31 August 1940, she wrote of children suffering because "of the sins of the elders"—who had made such a mess of international relations in the aftermath of World War I. This left her all the more determined to struggle for a warless world free from the threat of Hitlerism.

It would be a mistake, however, to see ER's activism on behalf of youth solely as a result of the crises of the 1930s. The political and psychological roots of that activism emerged decades before the Great Depression. Like many middle- and upper-class women of her generation, ER had become involved in the child-saving crusades of the Progressive Era. In 1903 she became interested in social settlements,* volunteering at the Rivington Street settlement house in New York City. That same year she joined the National Consumers' League,* and in 1922 she became a member of the Women's Trade Union League*—organizations active in the fight to abolish child labor and to improve the conditions of young women workers.

It is impossible to view ER's activism on youth issues without seeing its connection to her own youth. The daughter of an aloof mother and an alcoholic father—both of whom had died by the time she was ten years old—ER had a difficult childhood.* While ER's suffering in youth had been emotional rather than material, it helped to make her a person who took youth and their problems more seriously than did conventional politicians.

ER's own youth also gave her a positive model for activism on behalf the young. That model came from her enrollment at age fifteen in Allenswood, a private girls' school in England. There, ER came under the influence of the headmistress, Marie Souvestre,* who stressed the need for social and political activism as well as learning. Recalling Souvestre years later, ER noted, "Whatever I have become since had its seeds in those three years of contact with a liberal mind and strong personality" (Chafe, 366). Like many affected by an inspiring teacher, ER, out of gratitude, emulated her instructor. In much of her youth work, as well as in her teaching at the Todhunter School* prior to going to the White House, she sought to re-create for others what Souvestre had done for her.

There were other vital connections between ER's work with young people and her personal life. ER's relationship with her own children had been complicated by the constant intervention of her mother-in-law, Sara Delano Roosevelt.* Through her work with the student movement, ER was able to establish warm maternal relationships with a number of young activists, relationships that were in some ways closer than those with her own children.

The learning that came out of the relationships between ER and young people was not one-sided. ER taught young activists like Joseph Lash* and Pauli Murray* about the realities of American politics and the need for compromise and realism if positive reformist gains were to be won. In return, Murray helped educate ER about racial oppression and the impatience of young black intellectuals with racial gradualism; Lash taught ER about the byzantine politics of the American Left, so that she could recognize communist manipulations when she encountered them. The cumulative effect of her friendships with such young activists—most of whom were Jews,* the children of immigrants, or African Americans— was to help ER transcend the elitism, anti-Semitism, and racial prejudice of the upper-class culture into which she had been born. In this sense, ER's work with youth played a role in her emergence as one of the towering figures in twentieth-century American liberalism.

SELECTED BIBLIOGRAPHY

Chafe, William H. "Eleanor Roosevelt." In Linda Kerber and Jane Sherron De Hart, eds., *Women's America: Refocusing the Past.* 1991.

Cohen, Robert. "Dear Mrs. Roosevelt: Cries for Help from Depression Youth" and "To Mrs. Roosevelt Who 'Looks for the Poor': A Primary Source Teaching Segment." *Social Education* 60 (September 1996): 271–76, 295.

———. *When the Old Left Was Young: Student Radicals and America's First Mass Student Movement, 1929–1941.* 1993.

Jackson, Kathy M. *Images of Children in American Film: A Sociocultural Analysis.* 1986.

Kornbluh, Joyce L. "The She-She-She Camps: An Experiment in Living and Learning, 1934–1937." In Joyce L. Kornbluh and Mary Frederickson, eds., *Sisterhood and Solidarity: Workers Education for Women, 1914–1984.* 1984.

Salmond, John A. *A Southern Rebel: The Life and Times of Aubrey Willis Williams.* 1983.

Robert Cohen

Z

ZIONISM. Eleanor Roosevelt's view of Zionism, the modern political movement to reestablish a Jewish nation in Palestine, evolved over the years. Initially an anti-Zionist, she eventually became a steadfast supporter of the state of Israel.* With her death in 1962, Israel lost one of its most important American allies.

During her husband's presidency, ER's interest in Zionism was a direct outgrowth of her concern for Jewish refugees* fleeing Nazi persecution. In 1940 she became honorary chairwoman of Youth Aliya, which encouraged settlement of Jewish children in Palestine. Originally founded in Germany, it was in the United States a part of Hadassah, the Women's Zionist Organization of America. But ER considered Zionism itself an unfortunate example of Jewish particularism. She did not embrace the concept of a Jewish state. She believed that Jews* could maintain their separate religious identity and still be "natives of the land in which they live" (Lash, 109).

In World War II,* ER was exposed to widely divergent Jewish positions on Zionism through personal meetings with international Zionist leader Chaim Weizmann of Britain and anti-Zionist American Rabbi Morris Lazaron. ER, however, was most influenced by one of her husband's advisers, Isaiah Bowman, who was president of Johns Hopkins University and a State Department expert on the Middle East. Bowman asserted not only that Palestine would be unable to absorb a large influx of Jews but that Anglo-American forces would be required to protect the newcomers from an overwhelmingly hostile Arab world. He believed such military protection for Jews thousands of miles away would increase anti-Semitism in the United States. ER, after meeting with Bowman in 1944, agreed with him that Palestine could not be the national haven for Jews: "[T]he Jewish people must find homes in many places" (Penkower, 278).

Yet, as the war ended and the full horror of the Holocaust* became known, ER strongly backed the proposal to admit 100,000 European Jewish displaced persons into British-controlled Palestine. When Britain proved unwilling to do this, she advocated allowing the refugees to come to the United States. Still, she was against creation of a Jewish nation. Even a dramatic (and frequently quoted) 1946 encounter at a displaced person's camp in Germany with an old woman who hugged her and said repeatedly, "Israel! Israel!" (Roosevelt, 56), while eliciting ER's sympathy, did not alter her political evaluation. At the end of the year, she continued to favor a United Nations* trusteeship as the best outcome for Jews in Palestine.

But, when the British referred the Palestine question to the United Nations (UN), and the majority of a committee of that organization subsequently recommended partition of the territory into independent Jewish and Arab states, she became an ardent defender of that action within the U.S. delegation. When the General Assembly in late 1947 ratified partition, she was adamant in her view that the UN's viability rested on the implementation of its decision. Indeed, when her own government seemed to be moving away from partition toward temporary trusteeship in early 1948, ER informed both Secretary of State George Marshall* and President Harry S Truman* that she would resign her UN appointment in protest. Fearing the domestic political consequences of her angry departure, Truman begged her to stay, reaffirming his support for partition. So she remained a delegate and witnessed, from New York, the birth of the state of Israel in mid-May. Only days earlier, in siding with those around Truman supporting swift U.S. recognition as soon as Israel came into existence, she had urged the president not "to lag behind Russia" on this matter, declaring, "I personally believe in the Jewish State" (Cohen, 211). Finally, after much turmoil, she was a Zionist.

ER traveled to Israel in 1952, the first of several trips there. Entering the Jewish nation after visiting Lebanon, Syria, and Jordan was a relief, she wrote. Israel reminded her of America. She felt at ease with its citizens and respected its leaders. She was especially impressed with Israeli endeavors to reclaim desert areas for agricultural enterprise. She saw Israel as a model for the economic development of emergent nations and as a bulwark against Soviet designs in the Middle East.

She had been appalled at conditions in Palestinian refugee camps in Jordan. The refugees were a result of the war between Israel and invading Arab countries that resulted from the Jewish state's creation. ER had led the UN effort to aid the refugees, but she rejected their desire to return to their homes in Israel. She wanted them to be resettled in Arab lands and given meaningful employment. In time she hoped that with the refugee problem solved, Israel could assist other nations in the region. She exhibited what UN diplomat Ralph Bunche characterized as an almost "primitive" view of Arab people (Lash, 137).

ER feared that the Soviets would exploit the Arabs for their own purposes. Thus, communist arms sales to Egypt in September 1955 alarmed her. Early the following year, along with former president Truman and labor titan Walter Reuther,* she publicly exhorted the Eisenhower administration to provide defensive weaponry to Israel. Although this effort failed, she continued to press for such military assistance. She also advocated that UN peacekeeping forces protect Israel's borders. After Egyptian president Gamal Abdel Nasser's nationalization of the Suez Canal prompted an Israeli–British–French assault on his country in October 1956, ER claimed that Israel's participation had been an act of self-defense. Egypt's threats, its arms buildup, and Palestinian guerrilla raids from Egyptian-controlled territory all justified the Israeli response, she insisted.

ER was not uncritical of Israel. She did not approve of the power the rabbinate wielded in civil affairs. She expected that eventually Israel would adopt the secular governmental mode of the United States. She disagreed with that aspect of Zionist ideology that called for the mass emigration of the Jewish diaspora to Israel. Indeed, she once openly differed with Prime Minister David Ben-Gurion, a man she greatly admired, on this issue.

Still, ER worked tirelessly to help a multitude of Jews find refuge in Israel. During the 1950s she was instrumental in persuading Moroccan Sultan Mohammed V to allow more than 10,000 Jews to go there. Succeeding South African statesman Jan Christian Smuts as world patron of Youth Aliya, ER traveled widely and raised a considerable amount of money on its behalf. When she died, all the Youth Aliya centers in Israel held memorial* meetings. A number of Israeli public facilities already had been named in her honor.

SELECTED BIBLIOGRAPHY

Berger, Jason. *A New Deal for the World: Eleanor Roosevelt and American Foreign Policy.* 1981.

Cohen, Michael J. *Truman and Israel.* 1990.

Lash, Joseph P. *Eleanor: The Years Alone.* 1972.

Penkower, Monty Noam. *The Holocaust and Israel Reborn: From Catastrophe to Sovereignty.* 1994.

Roosevelt, Eleanor. *On My Own.* 1958.

Myron I. Scholnick

INDEX

Note: Encyclopedia entries and the pages where they appear are noted in **bold** type. Eleanor and Franklin D. Roosevelt are referred to by their full names in their primary entries; in other cases they are referred to as ER and FDR.

Abingdon, Virginia, 442, 448

Acheson, Dean, 35–36, 491

Addams, Jane, **1–3**, 196, 226, 364, 397, 401, 419, 483, 552

African Americans, 210, 267, 415, 535–36, 538, 584, 588–89, 594; American Red Cross and, 12; Arthurdale and, 33; District of Columbia and, 138–39. *See also* Anderson, Marian; Anti-lynching movement; Bethune, Mary McLeod; Civil Rights; Democratic Party; Du Bois, W.E.B.; Fair Employment Practices Committee; Great Depression; Johnson, John; King, Martin Luther; Murray, Anna Pauline; National Association for the Advancement of Colored People; National Youth Administration; New Deal; Press Conferences; Randolph, A. Philip; Smith, Lillian; Southern Conference; White, Walter; Wiltwyck School

Agriculture, 31–33, 527–28, 553

Allenswood, 4, 26, 67, 87, 437, 488–90, 516, 594. *See also* Souvestre, Marie

Alsop, Corinne Robinson, **3–4**, 169, 442

Alsop, John, 4, 442

Alsop, Joseph W., **4–5**, 170, 442

Alsop, Stewart, 4, 442

American Association for the United Nations (AAUN), **5–8**, 398, 497, 523, 532, 539

American Association of University Women, 558

American Broadcasting Company, 428

American Civil Liberties Union, 501

American Federation of Labor (AFL), 9, 441, 550

American Foundation, 301–4, 365

American Friends Service Committee (AFSC), 11, 31–33, 397, 403–4, 432; Emergency Peace Campaign and, 404; ER Transit Fund and, 181, 426

American Newspaper Guild, **8–10**, 117

American Red Cross, **10–14**, 228, 396, 421, 432, 453, 513, 521, 552

American Student Union (ASU), **14–16**, 17, 174, 251, 305–6, 591

American Women: Report of the President's Commission on the Status of Women, 403, 408, 410
American Youth Congress (AYC), 14, **16–19**, 104, 251, 305, 341–42, 591
Americans for Democratic Action (ADA), **19–22**, 71, 131, 150, 225, 418, 482, 529, 534; Reuther, Walter, and, 441, Roosevelt, Franklin D., Jr., and, 457
Ames, Jesse Daniel, 29
Anderson, Marian, **22–24**, 92, 267, 563
Anderson, Mary, **24–26**, 414
Anglo-American Relations, **26–28**. *See also* Churchill, Winston; England
Anticommunism, 102, 335–36, 499, 501–2; labor and, 297, 441
Antilynching Movement, **28–30**, 103, 359–60, 377–78, 485–86, 561–63
Anti-Semitism, 419, 596; ER and, 240, 275, 281–84, 344
Arab countries, 522, 597–98
Arthurdale, **30–35**, 103, 107, 161, 214, 236, 255, 414; ER's contributions to, 189, 426, 529–30; Ickes, Harold, and, 268, 528; Pickett, Clarence, and, 404; Tugwell, Rexford G., and, 268, 528–29
Asia, **35–37**
Autobiography, **37–41**, 55
Awards, ER's, **41–43**, 522

Babies-Just Babies, **44–46**, 61, 224, 234, 578
Banister, Marion Glass, 126
Barden, Graham, 499–500
Baruch, Bernard, 33–34, **46–47**, 281, 472, 517
Ben-Gurion, David, 284, 598
Bentley, Elizabeth, 252
Berger, Jason, 53, 58
Bernard, Viola, 567–68
Bethune, Albertus, 49
Bethune, Mary McLeod, **47–52**, 91, 93, 149, 352, 482, 487, 558, 561–62, 584; National Youth Administration and, 214, 368, 377, 572
Beyer, Clara, 572

Bibliographies (of works by and about ER), **52–54**
Biddle, Frances J., 482
Bilbo, Theodore, **54–55**, 104–5, 119
Biographers, ER's, **55–60**, 307
Birth Control, **60–62**, 576
Black, Allida M., 53, 60
Black, Ruby, 55–57, 59, 61, **62–66**, 72, 163, 202, 312, 412–13, 578–79
Black Cabinet. *See* Federal Council on Negro Affairs
Blair, Emily Newell, 125
Blanchard, Paul, 499
Boettiger, John (son-in-law), 224–25
Bok, Edward, 66–67, 298, 302
Bok Peace Prize, **66–67**, 196, 298, 301–2, 397, 547, 585
Bonus marchers, 212, 244, 255
Books by ER **67–70**, 514, 523
Bowles, Chester, **70–71**, 269, 272
Bowman, Isaiah, 596
Brandeis University, 512
Bricker, John W., 8, 259
Bridges, Harry, 402
Bromley, Dorothy Dunbar, 64
Broun, Heywood, 9
Browder, Earl, 175, 506
Brown, Claude, 568
Brown v. Board of Education, 21–22, 94, 362
Bryn Mawr Summer School for Women Workers, 480–81
Bugbee, Emma, 64, **71–72**, 202, 379–80, 412, 514
The Bulletin, 125–26, 571. *See also Democratic Digest*; Woman's National Democratic Club
Bunche, Ralph, 7, 92, 598
Bundles for Britain, **72–74**
Bush, Barbara, 187–88
Bye, George, 298–99
Byrnes, James, 535, 537

Cambodia, 37
Campobello, **75–76**, 107, 136, 412, 454, 458, 471, 520, 524
Carey, James C., 296
Carter, Jimmy, 259, 403, 461

Carter, Rosalyn, 188, 189–90,

Cartoons, ER's portrayal in, **78–79**, 118, 212

Cassin, Rene, 257

Catholic Church, 498–99; federal aid to parochial schools, 498–502

Catt, Carrie Chapman, 2, 5, **79–81**, 314, 397, 534

Cause and Cure of War: Committee on the, 2, 227; Conference on the, 80, 397

Celler, Emanuel, 164

Chafe, William H., 58–59

Chambers, Whittaker, 252

Chaney, Mayris, 104, 118, 340, 347, 388–89

Chiang Kai-shek, 81, 414

Chiang Kai-shek, Madame, **81–83**

Childhood, ER's, **83–87**

Children's Bureau, U.S. Department of Labor, 404, 552

Children's Crusade for Children, 432–33

China, 81–83, 505–7

Churchill, Winston, 26–27, **87–89**, 248, 449, 490, 521, 533

Civil Rights, **89–96**, 197, 238; Americans for Democratic Action and, 21–21; Bethune, Mary McLeod, and, 47–52, 93, 149, 352, 558, 561–62; Civil Rights Act of 1957, 95; Civil Rights Act of 1960, 95; Civil Rights Act of 1964, 354; Congress, U.S., and, 103–4; Du Bois, W.E.B., and, 119, 145–46, 361; Durr, Virginia, and, 147–150; ER and, 21–22, 89–96, 258, 288–89, 291–93, 353–54, 359–63, 494–97, 561–64, 565, 590; HUAC and, 253; Kennedy, John F., and, 288–89; King, Martin Luther, and, 291–93; Murray, Pauli, and, 352–54; NAACP and, 359–63, 561–64; Native Americans and, 371; Stevenson, Adlai, and 21–22, 362, 504; White, Walter, and, 23, 29–30, 91, 93, 359–62, 561–64; Williams, Aubrey, and, 368, 565. *See also* African Americans; Anderson, Marian; Antilynching

Movement; Fair Employment Practices; Japanese-American internment; Randolph, A. Philip; President's Commission on the Status of Women; Smith, Lillian; Southern Conference Movement

Civil Service Commission, 402

Civil Works Administration, 247, 574

Civilian Conservation Corps (CCC), 213, 255, 353, 367, 481, 574, 592

Clapp, Elsie, 34

Cleveland, Frances, 186

Clinton, Hillary, 188–89, 190

Clothing, ER's, **96–100**

Cohen, Benjamin, 149, 404

Cold War, **100–103**; Americans for Democratic Action and, 20; Arab-Israeli conflict and, 277; Asia and, 35, 37; ER and, 100–103, 197–98, 297, 491–92, 533–34, 536, 538–39; India and, 269, 271; labor and, 297; Spain and, 491–92; Stevenson, Adlai, and 503; Third World and, 71; Vandenberg, Arthur, and, 544–46

Cole, Gordon, 416

Collective security, 6–7, 14, 17–19, 313

College Settlement, 1, 452, 469, 483–84, 594

Collier, John, 369, 371

Colony Club, 228, 347

Committee for Refugees, U.S., 405

Committee for the Care of European Children, U.S., 239, 405, 432

Committee on Civil and Political Rights, 354

Committee on Unemployment Relief, 404

Committee to Defeat the Unequal Rights Amendment, 164

Communism: Cold War and, 101–2; HUAC and, 251–53

Communist Party: American Youth Congress and, 17–19; Progressive Party of 1948 and, 418

Communists, 150; American Newspaper Guild and, 9–10; American Student Union and, 14–15; American Youth Congress and, 16–18; FBI

and 173–74; Progressive Citizens of
America and, 417, 533
Condon, Edward, 252
Congress, U.S., **103–5**, 411; antilynch-
ing legislation and, 28–30. *See also*
specific acts
Congress of Industrial Organizations
(CIO), 9, 211, 251, 330, 441, 550
Congress of Racial Equality (CORE),
93, 95
Connor, Eugene, 149
Cook, Blanche Wiesen, 54, 59–60, 234,
476, 478
Cook, Nancy, **105–8**, 134–36, 234, 341,
343, 384–85, 493, 515–18, 577; Ar-
thurdale and, 33; Val-Kill industries
and, 107–8, 263–64, 516, 542
Coolidge, Calvin, 303, 454, 555
Coolidge, Grace, 186, 578
Corcoran, Thomas, 149, 498
Corr, Maureen, **108–10**; travels with
ER, 109–10, 220, 522–24
Correspondence of ER, **110–14**, 211,
514, 593
Costigan, Edward P., 29, 360
Covenant on Civil and Political
Rights, 147, 258, 540–41; women
and, 164
Covenant on Economic and Social
and Cultural Rights, 147, 258, 540–
41
Cowles, Anna Roosevelt "Bye"
"Bamie" (aunt), **115–16**, 168–9, 318–
19, 488, 586
Cox, James, 454
Craig, Elisabeth May, 10, 72, **116–17**,
123, 202, 412–13
Critics, ER's, **118–19**
Cunningham, Minnie Fisher, **120–21**

Dall, Anna Eleanor "Sisty" (grand-
daughter), 64, 224, 517
Dall, Anna Roosevelt. *See* Halsted,
Anna Eleanor Roosevelt
Dall, Curtis B. (son-in-law), 224
Dall, Curtis Roosevelt. *See* Roosevelt,
Curtis Dall (name changed)

Daniels, Jonathan, 473. Works: *The
Time between the Wars*, 473
Daughters of the American Revolu-
tion (DAR), 550; Marian Anderson
concert and, 22–24, 392, 562–63
Davis, Elmer, 390–91, 510
Davis, Norman, 11–12, 199
"Dear Mrs. Roosevelt" (Roosevelt,
Eleanor), *Democratic Digest*, 125
Death, ER's, **124–25**, 231–32, 290, 292,
298, 505, 539
Delano, Frederick, 137, 268
Democratic Digest, **125–27**, 142, 571,
577; ER's contributions to, 125–27,
299
Democratic National Committee, 129
Democratic Party, **127–132**; African
Americans and, 48, 378; Americans
for Democratic Action and, 21–22;
Catholics and, 498; Baruch, Ber-
nard, and, 46; Equal Rights Amendment and, 164; ER and, 21–22, 125–
127, 130–31, 254, 295, 449, 496, 535,
576, 580; Farley, James, and 170–71;
Kennedy, John F. and, 287–90;
Smith, Alfred, and 107, 129, 132;
Stevenson, Adlai, and, 131, 155–156,
503–5; Truman, Harry S and, 131,
526–27; Wallace, Henry A., and, 553;
women and, 129–30, 377, 582. *See
also Democratic Digest*; *Women's
Democratic News*; Women's Division
of the Democratic National Committee; Women's Division of the
New York State Democratic Committee; Woman's National Democratic Club
DeSapio, Carmine, 380–81, 457
Dewson, Molly, 126, 129, **132–34**, 213,
377, 524, 572, 576
Dickerman, Marion, 106–8, **134–37**,
234, 341, 384–85, 480, 493, 577; Todhunter School and, 135–36, 515–18;
Val-Kill Industries and, 136, 263–64,
516, 542
Dies, Martin K., 15, 18, 251, 335, 402
District of Columbia, 228; ER and,
137–40, 268, 411, 421

Dombrowski, James, 150, 487
Douglas, Helen Gahagan, 104, **140–44**, 212, 236, 350
Douglas, Melvyn, **140–44**, 350, 389
Dreier, Mary E., 25, **144–45**
Du Bois, W.E.B., 51, 119, **145–46**, 361
Ducas, Dorothy, 64, 203
Dulles, John Foster, **147–48**, 197, 259, 491, 537
Du Pont, Ethel (daughter-in-law), 457–58
Durr, Clifford, 148–50
Durr, Virginia Foster, **148–51**, 482, 487

Earhart, Amelia, 72, **152–53**
Early, Stephen "Steve," 91, 93, 119, **153–55**, 563; press conferences, ER's, and, 413, 415
Education, 481, 591–93; ER's personal, 160, 488–90 (*see also* Allenswood; Souvestre, Marie); ER's views on, 427, 481, 494–95, 580, 586. *See also* Arthurdale; National Youth Administration; Todhunter School
Eichelberger, Clark, 6
Eighteenth Amendment. *See* Prohibition
Einstein, Albert, 510
Eisenhower, Dwight David, 6, 36, 95, 122, 147, **155–57**, 259, 461; ER and, 155–57, 197; ER's resignation from United Nations and, 102, 156, 258, 536; McCarthy, Joseph, and, 156, 504; presidential campaigns and elections: (1952), 156–57, 504; (1956), 156, 288, 511
Eisenhower, Mamie, 186–87
Eisler, Hanns, 252
"Eleanor Clubs," 119, **157–58**, 174, 589
Eleanor Roosevelt Center at Val-Kill, **158–59**, 338, 463, 544
Eleanor Roosevelt High School, 216
Eleanor Roosevelt Memorial Foundation, 225, 337
Eleanor Roosevelt National Historic Site at Val-Kill, 463, 544

Eleanor Roosevelt Wings of the Franklin D. Roosevelt Library, **159–60**
Eleanor Roosevelt's Book of Common Sense Etiquette (Roosevelt, Eleanor with Robert Ballou), 70
Elizabeth, Queen of Belgium, 524
Elizabeth, Queen of England, 12, 26, 414, 467, 521–22, 560
Ellickson, Katherine P., 410
Elmhirst, Dorothy, 33, **160–61**, 474
Emergency Rescue Committee, 198–97, 432
Emerson, Faye (daughter-in-law), 350
England, 12, 26–28; U.S. aid during World War II to, 73–74. *See also* Anglo-American relations; Churchill, Winston
Equal Rights Amendment (ERA), **161–65**, 385, 403, 408–10, 581
Essary, Helen, 126
European Recovery Program ("Marshall Plan"), 329, 525, 534, 553

Faber, Doris, 59, 477
Fair Employment Practices Commission, recommendation for, 94
Fair Employment Practices Committee, establishment of, 93, 296, 360–61, 562
Fair Labor Standards Act (1938), 25, 163, 295, 574
Fala, **166–67**, 508
Family influences on ER, **167–70**
Farley, James, 129, **170–72**, 449
Fascism, 17–18, 432
Federal Bureau of Investigation (FBI), **172–76**; "Eleanor Clubs" and, 157; ER and, 102, 172–176, 306
Federal Council on Negro Affairs, 50
Federal Emergency Relief Administration (FERA), 34, 481, 583–84; African Americans and, 89–90, 584; Hickok, Lorena, and, 31, 89, 235; Hopkins, Harry, and, 247, 557–58; 582, 583–84; women's programs in, 213, 247, 557–58, 574, 582, 584; Woodward, Ellen, and, 582

Federal Public Housing Administration, 481
Federal Theatre Project, 194; HUAC and, 251
Ferguson, Robert Munro, 217
Fiction and ER, **176–80**
Field, Marshall, 405
Finances, personal, of ER, **180–84**, 430, 470, 475, 580
Finland, 19, 507, 533
First Ladies, ER's connections with, **184–89**
First Ladies, Rankings of, **189–90**
First Lady, Ceremonial Role of, ER and, **190–94**, 559–60
Fisher, Dorothy Canfield, 433
Fleeson, Doris, 579
Flanagan, Hallie, **194**, 251, 572
Ford, Betty, 187–88, 190
Foreign Policy, ER and, **195–98**, 553
Franco, Francisco, 14–15, 88, 196, 404, 432, 490–92, 499
Franklin and Eleanor Roosevelt Institute, 309, 337–38, 458
Franklin D. Roosevelt Library, 52, 159. *See also* Eleanor Roosevelt Wings of the Franklin D. Roosevelt Library
Frankfurter, Felix, 281
Fredericka, Queen of Greece, 523
Free, Ann Cottrell, 415
Fry, Varian, **198–201**, 432
Furman, Bess, 64, 72, **201–3**, 235, 412–16, 579

Gellhorn, Martha, **204–5**, 220
Genealogy, **205–9**
General Federation of Women's Clubs, 164, 402
George VI, King of England, 26, 414, 467, 521–22, 560
Georgia Woman's World, The, 91
Germany: Nazi regime, 226–27; USSR, invasion of, 533; USSR, nonaggression pact with, 15, 18, 505–6
Geyer, Lee, 150
Gibson, Nina Roosevelt (granddaughter), 436, 463

Gitt, J. W., 418
Good Housekeeping, 299
Goodwin, Doris Kearns, 56, 472
Gould, Beatrice, 298–301
Gould, Bruce, 298–301
Graham, Frank Porter, **210**, 486, 487
Grandchildren, ER and FDR's, 209, 451, 458, 224, 461, 462–63, 522–24
Great Depression, 3, **210–14**; African Americans and, 47, 89–91, 368; labor, and, 294–95; letters to ER about, 111–12, 114, 377; New Deal and, 375–79; women and, 211–13, 290–91, 481, 557–58, 569–70, 573–75, 582, 584; youth and, 14, 16–17, 367–68, 584, 591–93
Greenbelt, Maryland, 215–16
Greenbelt Towns, **214–17**, 528–29
Greenway, Isabella Selmes Ferguson, **217–19**; Wilkie, Wendell, and, 218
Gridiron Club, 255, 578
"Gridiron Widows," 255, 579
Griffin, Isabel Kinnear, 415
Gugler, Eric, 32, 193
Gurewitsch, A. David, **219–21**; ER and, 219–21, 309, 477, 522–24; Gellhorn, Martha and, 205, 220
Gurewitsch, Edna Perkel, 220–21, 524
Gutkind, Gabriele, 109

Hall, Edward (uncle), 421
Hall, Mary Ludlow (grandmother), 86, 167–68, 208, 319, 405, 448, 488, 490; religion and, 435
Hall, Valentine (uncle), 421
Hall, Valentine Gill, Jr. (grandfather), 208, 435, 443
Halsted, Anna Eleanor Roosevelt (daughter), 44–45, **222–26**, 512, 559, 569; ER and, 222–25, 428, 466, 472, 476, 524; FDR and, 222–24, 456, 472
Halsted, James A. (son-in-law), 225, 524
Hamilton, Alice, 3, **226–27**, 552
Harding, Warren, 454, 479
Hareven, Tamara, K., 53, 56–57
Harriman, Florence Jaffray Hurst ("Daisy"), 10, 160, **227–28**, 570

Harriman, William Averell, **228–30**, 381, 457, 470, 504

Health, ER's, **230–32**

Health care, 303–4, 365–66

Hearst, William Randolph, 224; Roosevelt, Elliott (son), employment by business interests of, 449

Helm, Edith, 174, 413, 515, 560

Hemingway, Ernest, 204–5

Henry Street Settlement, 364, 483, 552

Herrick, Elinore, 573

Herrick, Genevieve Forbes, 412

Hickok, Lorena A., 70, 143, 201, 204, 211, **232–37**, 341, 356, 476–78, 493; Federal Emergency Relief Administration and, 31, 89, 235; Lape, Esther, and, 304; Thompson, Malvina, and, 514; travel with ER, 64, 202, 236, 520

Highlander Folk School, 95, **237–39**

Hirohito, Emperor of Japan, 36–37, 523

Hiss, Alger, 252, 336

Hoey, Jane, 213

Holocaust, **239–41**, 256, 597; ER and, 239–41, 275, 283, 397; FDR and, 239–40, 282–83. *See also* Jews; Refugees

Hong Kong, 37

Hoover, Herbert, **241–45**, 550, 581; bonus marchers and, 244, 255; ER and, 242–45; executive branch of government and, 242; FDR and, 242–44; international relief programs and, 242–44

Hoover, J. Edgar: ER and, 172–76; FDR and, 173–74. *See also* Federal Bureau of Investigation

Hoover, Lou Henry, 185–86, 242, 244, **245–46**, 412

Hopkins, Charlotte, 138

Hopkins, Diane, 246, 248

Hopkins, Harry L., 90, 204, 229, 235, **246–49**, 584–85; ER and, 246–48; FDR and, 246–48; relief programs and, 246–47, 557–58, 582–84

Hornaday, Mary, **249–50**, 415

Horton, Myles, 237–38

House Committee to Investigate Un-

American Activities (HUAC), 15, 18, 103–4, 174, **250–53**, 269, 335, 497, 591; Federal Theatre Project and, 194

Housing, 378, 494–95, 576. *See also* Arthurdale; District of Columbia; Great Depression; Greenbelt towns; Ickes, Harold L.; New Deal; Resettlement Administration; Tugwell, Rexford G.

Howe, Louis, 32, 135, 153, 212, 222, **253–56**, 413, 466, 513; ER and 253–56, 569; FDR and, 253–56, 454, 471; Hickok, Lorena, and, 235

Hull, Cordell, 11, 556–57

Hull House, 1, 364, 401, 419, 483

Human Rights, internationalization of, ER and, 197, **256–60**, 329, 533–34, **536–37**, **539–41**. *See also* United Nations; Universal Declaration of Human Rights

Hunting Big Game in the Eighties: The Letters of Elliott Roosevelt, Sportsman (Ed. Roosevelt, Eleanor), 69

Hurst, Fannie, **260–62**

Hyde Park, N.Y., 135–36, **262–66**, 430, 457; ER and, 262–65, 409, 412, 449–50, 462, 501, 542–44; FDR and 262–64, 449, 451, 499, 542, 581; Khrushchev, Nikita, and 532; Roosevelt, Sara, and, 464–66, 520, 581

Ickes, Harold, L., 23, 32–33, 48, **267–69**, 441, 561

"If You Ask Me" (Roosevelt, Eleanor), *Ladies' Home Journal* (1941–49), *McCall's*, (1949–62), 299, 333–35, 434, 437

Illma, Viola, 16

India and Jawaharlal Nehru, 35–36, 69, 71, 148, 198, 210, **269–72**, 522–23

India and the Awakening East (Roosevelt, Eleanor), 69, 269

Indian Arts and Crafts Board, 369–70

Indian Reorganization Act, 369

Indonesia, 37

International Congress of Working Women, 580

International Court of Justice of the United Nations, 585–86
International Ladies Garment Workers' Union, 474
International Student Service, 16, 76, 174, 306
International Woman Suffrage Alliance, 79
Internet resources, ER and, **272–75**
Israel, 6, 69, **275–77**, 283–84, 329, 407, 434, 522, 524, 596–98. *See also* Jews; Zionism
It Seems to Me (Roosevelt, Eleanor), 70
It's Up to the Women (Roosevelt, Eleanor), 69

Japan, 36–37, 523
Japanese-American Internment, 197, 267, **278–81**, 389, 428
Jenner, William, 156, 504
Jews, 46, **281–84**, 347, 391, 404, 407, 434, 501, 549, 594, 596–98. *See also* Holocaust; Israel; refugees; Zionism
Johnson, John, 285–86
Johnson, "Lady Bird," 187
Johnson, Lyndon, 403, 458, 591
Jones, Jesse, 449
Juliana of the Netherlands, 373–74, 436, 522
Junior League, 469
Junior Literary Guild, 68

Kearney, James R., 53, 56–57
Kefauver, Estes, 288, 504
Kelley, Florence, 132, 330, 364
Kennedy, Jacqueline, 187, 392
Kennedy, John F., 71, 95 122, 197, **287–90**, 403, 512, 543; King, Martin Luther, and 292; presidential campaign and election (1960), 131, 457, 461, 505, 511; President's Commission on the Status of Women and, 407–8
Kennedy, Joseph, 287, 498–99
Kerr, Florence, 211, **290–91**, 573
Khrushchev, Nikita, 102, 122, 220, 511, 543; ER, interview with, 524, 531–32

Kidd, Gordon, 265, 436
King, Martin Luther, 94, **291–93**
Kingdon, Frank, 199–200
Korean War, 6, 526
Ku-Klux Klan, 238

Labor, **294–98**; child, 295, 385, 495, 547, 552, 569, 576–77, 581; FDR and, 294–96, 581; women and, 574–75. *See also* American Federation of Labor; American Newspaper Guild; Broun, Heywood; Congress of Industrial Organizations; Lewis, John L.; Mason, Lucy Randolph; Reuther, Walter; Schneiderman, Rose; Women's Trade Union League
Ladies of Courage (Roosevelt, Eleanor, and Lorena Hickok), 70
Ladies Home Journal, The, ER's writings in, 13, 61, 66, 70, **298–301**
La Follette, Robert M., 417
La Guardia, Fiorello, 380, 387–89, 517
Landis, James M., 389
Landon, Alfred, 550
Lane, Ann, 566–67
Lane, Franklin, 566
Lane, Gertrude, 569
Lape, Esther, 98, 237, **301–4**, 315, 341, 429–30, 524, 534; Bok Peace Prize and, 66–67, 196, 396, 547; medical care, U.S., and, 365
Lash, Joseph P., 12–13, 14–16, 18, 57–59, 65, 174–75, 184, **305–8**, 389, 476–77, 594
Lash, Trude Pratt, 219, 307, **308–10**, 524, 567
Latham, Natalie Wales, 73
Latin America, 554–55, 577; ER and, 13, **310–13**, 427, 515, 521, 523
League of Nations, 6, 67, 196, 256, **313–14**, 396, 443, 534, 545, 585
League of Women Voters (LWV), 7, 66, 79–80, 144, **314–16**, 384; Equal Rights Amendment and, 162–63; ER and, 36, 161, 263, 301, 314–15; New York League of Women Voters, 430, 546–47; Read, Elizabeth, and, 429

LeHand, Marguerite "Missy," 257,
  316–18, 455–56, 498–99, 514; ER
  and, 316–18; FDR and, 316–18, 454,
  508
Lehman, Herbert, 381, 501
Lend Lease, 397; Harriman, Averell,
  and 229; Hopkins, Harry, and, 248
Leslie Suffrage Commission, 80
Levermore, Charles, 66–67
Lewis, John L., 9, 296, 330
Linzer, Estelle, 6–7
Little, Herbert, 62–65
Lodge, Henry Cabot, 443
Long, Breckinridge, 239, 283, 433
Longworth, Alice Roosevelt, 318–20,
  355, 467, 471, 494
Longworth, Nicholas, 319
Lord, Mary Pillsbury, 147
Lowenstein, Allard, 320–22
Luce, Clare Booth, 334–35
Lucy, Autherine, 94, 292
Lynn, Kenneth, 477

Macfadden, Bernard, 44–45
Malik, Charles, 257
Mann, Katy, 85, 445, 448
Marriage, ER's, 323–27, 453–56, 470–
  72, 519–20, 586–87
Marshall, George C., 275, 327–30,
  504, 597
"Marshall Plan." See European Recov-
  ery Program
Martha, Princess of Norway, 228, 317,
  456
Maslow, Abraham, 57, 477
Mason, Lucy Randolph, 211, 330–31,
  487
McAllister, Dorothy, 141
McBride, Mary Margaret, 331–33, 428
McCall's, ER's writings in, 70, 244,
  300–301, 333–35, 450
McCarthy, Joseph R., 21, 253; Eisen-
  hower, Dwight, and 156, 197, 504;
  ER and, 102, 105, 197, 335–36, 504,
  538; Kennedy, John F, and, 95, 286;
  Stevenson, Adlai, and 504
McCarthyism, 335–37, 523, 538
McGill, Ralph, 29

McIntyre, Marvin, 563
Meany, George, 297
Medicare, 366
Meir, Golda, 284
Memorials, ER's, 337–39
Mercer, Lucy. See Rutherfurd, Lucy
  Mercer
Migrant camps, 141–42, 520
Miller, Adolph, 566
Miller, Earl, 234, 318, 339–43, 405,
  439, 462, 476–78
Miller, Mary, 566–67
Miller, Simone, 342
Mills, Harriet May, 343–44, 384
Mobilization of Human Needs, 213
Montgomery, Ruth, 415
Moral Basis of Democracy, The (Roose-
  velt, Eleanor), 69, 92–93
Morgan, Edith Hall "Pussie" (aunt),
  168
Morgenthau, Elinor, 3, 215, 226, 228,
  263, 281–83, 344–48
Morgenthau, Henry, Jr., 240, 281, 344–
  47, 441
Morgenthau, Henry, III, 512
Morgenthau, Joan, 192, 347
Morocco, 407, 523–24, 598
Mortimer, Elizabeth Hall "Tissie"
  (aunt), 97
Moskowitz, Belle, 348–49, 480, 576
Motion pictures, 350–52
"Mrs. Franklin D. Roosevelt's Page"
  (Roosevelt, Eleanor), Woman's Home
  Companion), 569–70
Murphy, Frank, 30
Murray, Anna Pauline "Pauli," 92,
  210, 352–54, 359, 386, 482, 561, 594
Murrow, Edward R., 510–12
"My Day," 354–59, 579; (references
  to): American Association for the
  United Nations, 6; Americans for
  Democratic Action, 20; Bethune,
  Mary McLeod, 52; blood donations,
  13; Daughters of the American Rev-
  olution, ER's resignation from, 23,
  92, 355; education, 481; England
  during World War II, 27, 521; Gan-
  dhi, 437; Hamilton, Alice, 227;

Hickok, Lorena, 235; Hoover, Herbert, 243–44; HUAC, 250, 252; India, 269, 271–72; Israel, 277; Japanese-American internment, 278–79; Jews, 241, 275, 283; Kennedy, John F., 289; King, Martin Luther, 292; motion pictures, 351; national health insurance, 366; Native Americans, 369, 371, 437; New Deal, 376, 584; parochial schools, federal aid to, 500; President's Commission on the Status of Women, 409; Robeson, Paul, 510; Roosevelt, James (son), 460–61; Roosevelt, Sara, 467; South Pacific during World War II, 13; Southern Conference Movement, 487; Stevenson, Adlai, 505; Truman, Harry S, 525; USSR, 524, 532, 533; Wallace, Henry A., 418; "We Will Never Die," 240; World War II, 588; youth, 592–93

Nagako, Empress of Japan, 523
Nathan, Maude, 420
National American Woman Suffrage Association (NAWSA), 79, 314
National Association for the Advancement of Colored People (NAACP), 28–29, 50–51, 93–95, 210, **359–63**, 482, 485, 497, 504, 588; Chiang Kai-shek, Madam, and, 82; Du Bois, W.E.B., and, 146–47; Reuther, Walter, and, 442; Truman, Harry S, and 94; White, Walter, and, 23, 561–63
National Association of Colored Women, 47, 50
National Broadcasting Company (NBC), 427
National Committee for a SANE Nuclear Policy, 404–5
National Committee to Abolish the Poll Tax, 149, 485
National Conference on Fundamental Problems in the Education of Negroes, 90
National Consumers' League, 132, 144, 226–27, 228, 330, **363–65**, 420,

594; Equal Rights Amendment and, 162–63; New York Consumers' League, 401, 420
National Council of Negro Women, 50–51, 558
National Emergency Council, 470
National Federation of Business and Professional Women, 163
National health insurance, 365–66
National Industrial Recovery Act, 32, 527
National Labor Relations Act (1935), 574
National Labor Relations Board, 573
National Press Club, 578–79
National Recovery Administration (NRA), 229; Consumers' Advisory Board, 470, 573; Labor Advisory Board, 475, 581, women and, 163, 574
National Woman's Democratic Law Enforcement League, 423
National Woman's Party, 63, 161–64
National Youth Administration (NYA), 14, 17, 247, **367–69**, 481; African Americans and, 47, 50–51, 368, 584; ER and, 213, 367–68, 377, 584, 591–92
Native Americans, 267, 369–72, 588
Neal, Claude, 29, 91, 562
Negro and Negro Youth, Conference on the Problems of the, 51
Nehru, Jawaharlal, 51, 69, 122, 269–72, 441, 522, 543
Nesbitt, Henrietta, 191, 264, **372–73**, 461
Netherlands, the, 338, **373–75**
New Deal, 375–79, 421, 479, 590; African Americans and, 47–51, 214, 368, 377–78, 561–64, 584; agriculture and, 527–28, 553; Americans for Democratic Action and, 19–20; anti-lynching movement and, 28–30, 377–78; Arthurdale and 30–31; education and, 367–68, 481, 591–93; ER's advocacy for, 295, 375–79, 406, 414, 518, 520–21, 576, 583–85; Fair Labor Standards Act and, 25, 163,

295, 574; Federal Emergency Relief Administration and, 89, 247, 481, 557–58, 574, 582–84; Hopkins, Harry L., and, 246–47, 557–58, 582, 583–84; labor policies of, 401–2; National Youth Administration and, 14, 17, 47, 50–51, 367–69, 377, 481; Native Americans and, 369–371; Strong, Anna, and, 505–6; Truman, Harry S. and, 525; Tugwell, Rexford G., and, 527–29; Vandenberg, Arthur, and, 544; Williams, Aubrey, and, 47, 367–69, 564; women and (*see* Women and the New Deal); Woodward, Ellen, and 582; Works Progress Administration, and, 583–85; youth and, 15, 16–19, 367–68, 591–93

Newspaper Women's Club of New York, 72, **379–80**

New York City reform movement, **380–81**, 457

New York City residences, ER's, **381–82**, 466

Nixon, "Pat," 187–88, 190

Nixon, Richard, 102, 143, 252, 463, 511, 591

Nonaggression Pact. *See* Germany; Union of Soviet Socialist Republics

Non-Sectarian Committee for German Refugee Children, 549–51

North Atlantic Treaty Organization (NATO), 6, 491–92, 526

O'Day, Caroline, 108, 135, **383–85**, 493, 542, 577

Odell Waller case, 92, 353, **386–87**

O'Dwyer, William, 501

Office of Civilian Defense (OCD), 347, **387–90**; Douglas, Melvyn, and, 142–143; ER and, 104, 130, 251, 347, 387–390, 494, 587; Polier, Justine Wise, and 406

Office of War Information, **390–91**

Olivia (Bussy, Dorothy Strachey), 489

On My Own (Roosevelt, Eleanor), 37, 40, 55, 69

Opinion polls, ER and, **391–95**

Osthagen, Henry, 514

Pacifists, 17–18, 134, 196, 383, 397

Pakistan, 35–36, 69, 198, 210, 522

Palestine, 241, 275, 283, 596–98

Palmer, A. Mitchell, 172

Pan-American Coffee Bureau, 310–11, 427

Pandit, Madam V., 271, 522

Parish, Susan (cousin), 223, 435

Parks, Rosa, 94, 238

Partners: The United Nations and Youth (Roosevelt, Eleanor, and Helen Ferris, 68)

Patterson, Floyd, 568

Paul, King of Greece, 523

Pavlov, A. P., 536

Peace Movements, 1, 3, 14, 66–67, 80, 195–96, **396–98**, 587

Pegler, Westbrook, 9, 12–13, 119, 251, 342, 355, **398–400**

Pehle, John, 240

Pepper, Claude, 149

Perkins, Frances, 25, 133, **400–402**, 470, 475; as Secretary of Labor, 401–402, 572–73. Works: *The Roosevelt I Knew*, 402

Peterson, Esther, 165, **402–3**; President's Commission on the Status of Women and, 407–8, 410

Phillips, Caroline Astor, 566–67

Phillips, William, 566

Pickett, Clarence, 11, 32–33, 199–200, **403–5**

Pictures of ER, **405–6**

Polier, Justine Wise, 282, 405, **406–7**, 551, 567–68

Poll tax, 92, 94, 149–50, 386, 485–86, 588

Popular Front, 18, 174, 305, 506

Powell, Adam Clayton, 510

President's Commission on the Status of Women (PCSW), 92, 131, 165, 290, 354, 403, **407–11**; education of women, and, 409–10

President's Committee on Civil Rights, 210

Press conferences, ER's, 54, 64–65, 201–3, 255, **411–17**, 514, 578; African Americans and, 154, 415; on American Newspaper Guild, 9; Anderson, Marion, and, 414; Anderson, Mary, and, 414; Chiang Kai-shek, Madame, and, 414; on Churchill, Winston, 88; on District of Columbia, 411; Early, Steve, and, 153–55; Elizabeth, Queen of England, and, 414; on Finland, 533; George VI, King of England, and, 414; Hickok, Lorena, and, 235, 412; Mrs. Roosevelt's Press Conference Association and, 415–16; Office of Civilian Defense and, 411, 415; Prohibition, on repeal of, 413; on radio broadcasts, 425; on Social Security, 411; "trial balloons" and, 414; Wilhelmina, Queen of the Netherlands, and, 374, 414; on women, camps for unemployed, 414; World War II and, 415

Progressive Citizens of America, 20, 417, 534

Progressive Party, **417–19**; Bull Moose Party, 1–2, 417, 468; League for Progressive Political Action, 417; Progressive Party of 1948, 146, 417–18, 553

Progressivism, 364, **419–21**, 594

Prohibition, 413, **421–24**; repeal of, 423

Protective legislation, 401, 479; for women, 164, 385, 403, 409, 474, 495, 576, 580–81. See also Equal Rights Amendment; President's Commission on the Status of Women

Protestants and Other Americans United for the Separation of Church and State (POAU), 499–500

Public Works Administration, 33, 267

Puerto Rico, 61, 64, 202, 236, 520, 528–29, 581

Radio broadcasts, ER's, **425–29**, 580; over BBC, 521; on education, 427; on family relations, 425; on Japanese-American internment, 428;

on Latin America, 310–311, 427; Mary Margaret McBride and, 331–33; on New Deal, 427–28; on Truman, Harry S, 526; on world peace, 427; on World War II, 427; on youth, 427

Randolph, A. Philip, 295–96, 360, 386, 562, 589

Rauh, Joseph, 22

Read, Elizabeth, 98, 196, 301, 303–4, 314, **429–31**, 534

Reagan, Nancy, 187–88

Reagan, Ronald, 461

Red Scare, 173, 252, 341

Refugees, 11–12, 37, 239–41, 277, 282–84, 347, 406–7, **431–35**, 556, 596–98; Arab, 434; United Nations and, 147, 197, 275, 312, 433–34, 533, 538, 597; Wagner-Rogers bill and, 397, 407, 549–51. See also Holocaust; Jews

Reid, Helen Rogers, 379, 430

Relief programs, 246–47, 557–58, 582, 583–84. See also individual agencies

Religion, Episcopalian, **435–37**, 437, 440; Calvary Episcopal Church, 435–36, 444; Church of the Incarnation, 435; St. James Episcopal Church, 435–36; St. Thomas Episcopal Church, 436

Religion, growth in, **437–40**

"Report on Economic Conditions of the South," National Emergency Council and, 486

Republican Party: Eisenhower, Dwight D., and, 155–56; Equal Rights Amendment and, 164

Resettlement Administration, 35, 215, 268, 527–29

Reuther, Walter, 7, 296, 298, 436, **440–42**

Rishel, Virginia, 126

Rivington Street Settlement. See College Settlement

Robeson, Paul, 510–11

Robins, Margaret Dreier, 25, 144, 580–81

Robinson, Corinne Roosevelt (aunt), 168–69, **442–43**

Robinson, Douglas, 442, 448
Roche, Josephine, 365, 572
Rogers, Edith Nourse, 549. *See also* Wagner-Rogers Bill
Roosevelt, Alice Lee, 318
Roosevelt, Anna Eleanor (daughter). *See* Halsted, Anna Eleanor Roosevelt
Roosevelt, Anna Eleanor (ER), Activities and Positions (arranged chronologically): College Settlement volunteer (1903–1904), 1, 452, 469, 483–84; National Consumers' League volunteer (1903–1904), 228, 363–65, 420, 594; American Red Cross volunteer (1917–1918), 10–14, 228, 396, 421, 453; New York State League of Women Voters legislative committee chair (1921–1924), 301, 314–15, 546–47; Bok Peace Prize policy committee member (1923–1924), 66–67, 298, 301–2, 547, 585; Women's City Club, board of directors and legislative committee, (1924–1928), 61, 295, 575–576; *Women's Democratic News* editor (1925–1928), 45, 135, 254, 384, 577; Val-Kill Industries co-owner (1927–1936), 107–8, 136, 263–64, 542–43; Todhunter School teacher (1927–1932), 107, 135–36, 232, 515–18, 520; Democratic presidential campaign of Alfred E. Smith, head of women's work in (1928), 129, 349, 455, 479–80, 493; *As First Lady of New York State (1929–1932)*: contributor to national magazines, 181; unofficial inspector of state institutions for FDR, 212, 254, 326, 455, 520; *Babies-Just Babies* editor (1932–1933), 44–45, 61, 224, 234, 578; radio broadcaster, commercial (1932–1951), 310–11, 331–33, 425–29, 521, 526, 580; *As First Lady of the United States (1933–1945)*: ceremonial role, 190–94, 559–60; Democratic National Convention (1940), address to, 130, 449, 496, 553; New Deal,

advocate for, 295, 375–79, 406, 414, 518, 520–21, 571, 576, 583–85; press conferences, 9, 64–65, 88, 153–55, 201–3, 255, 411–17, 533; ranking among First Ladies, 189–90; travel, 64, 203, 515, 518, 520–21; trips during World War II: United States, 587, England, 12, 26–27, 515, 521, 587, Latin America, 13, 312, 515, 521, 587, South Pacific, 12–13, 521, 587; White House Conferences on women, host for, 557–58; lecturer for W. Colston Leigh Bureau (1935–1941) and (1946–1962), 494–497, 520, 523; magazine columnist: *Woman's Home Companion*, 1933–35; *Democratic Digest*, 1937–1941; *Ladies' Home Journal*, 1941–49; *McCall's*, 1949–62, 61, 70, 125, 299–301, 333–35, 569–70; newspaper columnist (1935–1962), "My Day," 354–59; Office of Civilian Defense, Assistant Director (1941–1942), 104, 130, 251, 347, 387–90, 494, 587; United Nations, U.S. Delegate (1945–1953), 146, 147, 197, 275–76, 284, 312, 433–34, 491, 505, 522, 525–26, 533, 535–39, 539–41, 597; Human Rights Commission, chair (1947–1953), 146, 147, 256–60, 309, 398, 533, 536–37, 540–41; television broadcaster (1949–1962), 509–512, 524; American Association for the United Nations volunteer (1953–1962), 5–8, 398, 497, 523, 532, 539. (*See also* specific subjects)
Roosevelt, Anna Eleanor (ER), personal life: anti-Semitism, 240, 275, 281–84, 344; awards, 41–43, 522; birth control, views on, 60–62, 576; childhood, 83–87; clothing, 96–100; death, 124–25, 231–32, 290, 292, 298, 505, 539; education, 160, 488–90; finances, 180–84, 430, 475, 580; genealogy, 205–9; Gurewitsch, A. David, relationship with, 219–21, 309, 477, 522–24; health, 230–32; Hickok, Lorena, relationship with, 232–37, 439;

homes of, 75–76, 107–8, 135–36, 159, 169, 180–81, 183, 221, 263–65, 303, 325, 381–82, 466, 543, 566; Lash, Joseph P., relationship with, 12–13, 14–16, 18, 57–59, 65, 174–75, 305–8, 594; marriage and family, 167–70, 323–27, 453–56, 470–72, 519–20, 586–87 (*See also individual family members*); memorials, 337–39; Miller, Earl, relationship with, 234, 318, 339–43, 405, 439, 462, 476–78; religion, 435–440; Rutherfurd, Lucy Mercer, and, 405, 439, 470–72, 476–77, 566; sexuality, 5, 234, 476–78

Roosevelt, Anna Hall (mother), 83–86, 208, 405; **443–46**; ER, relationship with, 85, 438, 444–46, 477; religion and, 435, 446

Roosevelt, Curtis Dall (grandson), 224, 436

Roosevelt, Edith Kermit Carow, 170, 184, 318–19, 467–68, 494

Roosevelt, Eleanor (niece), 192

Roosevelt, Elliott (father), 83–86, 319, 435, 439, **446–48**; alcoholism of, 421, 442; marriage, 443–46; ER, relationship with, 84–86, 447–48, 477; Roosevelt, Theodore, and, 85–86, 442, 445, 448, 467

Roosevelt, Elliott (son), 350, **448–51**, 461, 477, 522, 586; agent for ER, 300, 428, 449–50, 510; farming venture with ER, 263, 449–50, 462. Works: *As He Saw It*, 88, 449; *Mother R* (with James Brough), 450; *A Rendezvous with Destiny* (with James Brough), 450; *An Untold Story* (with James Brough), 450

Roosevelt, Elliott, Jr. (brother), 85–86, 105, 444, 447

Roosevelt, Franklin Delano (FDR), 430, **451–56**; American Youth Congress and, 18–19; antilynching movement and, 28–30, 561–63; Arthurdale and, 31–32, 34; Assistant Secretary of the Navy, 396, 420, 453, 466, 471, 520, 555, 565; awards, 41; "brains trust," and, 527; Campo-

bello Island and, 75, 107, 454; Catholics and, 498–99; Churchill and, 87–89, 248; death, 328–29, 456, 472, 508; Fair Employment Practices Committee and, 296, 360–61, 562; family (*See individual family members*); finances of, 180–82; gubernatorial campaigns and elections: (1928), 129, 455, 576; (1930), 133; Holocaust and, 239–40, 282–83; Hoover, Herbert, and, 242–44; Hopkins, Harry L., and, 246–48; Howe, Louis, and, 253–56, 454, 471; Hyde Park and, 262–64, 449, 451, 499, 542, 581; labor and, 294–96, 581; LeHand, Marguerite "Missy," and, 316–18, 454, 508; marriage to ER, 323–327, 453–56, 470–72, 519–20, 586–87; New Deal and, 375–79; Perkins, Frances, and 400–2; polio illness of, 75, 129, 326, 454, 466; presidential campaigns and elections, 306, 455, 460, 466, 527; press conferences of, 153–54, 413; religion and, 438; 460; Roosevelt, Theodore, and, 452–53, 468; Rutherfurd, Lucy Mercer, relationship with, 5, 224–25, 319, 325, 453–54, 456, 471–73, 476–77; Schneiderman, Rose, and, 475, 580; Smith, Alfred, and 479–80; Suckley, Margaret, and, 507–8; Tammany Hall and, 420; Top Cottage and, 449, 508; USSR and, 303; United Nations and, 6, 556; vice-presidential campaign (1920), 128, 454; Wagner-Rogers Bill and, 239, 432, 549–41; Warm Springs, Ga., and, 454, 456, 472, 508; Wilson, Woodrow, and, 396, 417, 420, 453; Wiltwyck School and, 568; Women's National Press Club and, 579; Women's Trade Union League and, 475, 580–81; World Court and, 303, 586; World War I, 2, 195, 396, 420–1; World War II, 87, 248, 328, 586–87; Works Progress Administration and, 583–85

Roosevelt, Franklin D., Jr. (son, who died in infancy), funeral of, 435

Roosevelt, Franklin D., Jr. (son) 20, 57, 105, 229, 234, 381, **456–58**, 462, 520, 586; Du Pont, Ethel, marriage to, 457–58

Roosevelt, Gracie Hall (brother), 85, 152, 229, 388, 421, 444, 447–48, **458–59**, 554, 586. Works: *Odyssey of an American Family* (with Samuel D. McCoy), 459

Roosevelt, James (FDR's father), 447, 451, 465

Roosevelt, James (son), 105, 360, **459–62**, 476, 586; Kennedy, John F., and, 461; Truman, Harry S, and, 461, 526. Works: *Affectionately, F.D.R.* (with Sidney Shalett), 461; *My Parents: A Differing View* (with Bill Libby), 461; *A Family Matter* (with Sam Toperoff), 461

Roosevelt, John (son), 264, 450, **462–63**, 520, 544, 586; Citizens for Eisenhower and, 463

Roosevelt, Martha Bulloch "Mittie" (grandmother), 206, 447

Roosevelt, Minnewa (daughter-in-law), 451, 523

Roosevelt, Sara Delano (mother-in-law), 145, 281–82, 344, 447, **463–467**, 508, 586; church affiliation, 435; ER and 324–25; 401, 439, 465–67, 594; FDR and, 451, 453–54, 463–66, 471; as grandmother, 222–23, 324–25, 466

Roosevelt, Theodore (uncle), 3, 85–86, 137, 318–19, 412, **467–69**, 545; Cowles, Anna Roosevelt, and, 115; ER and, 323, 453, 467–69; FDR and, 452–53, 468; Progressive (Bull Moose) Party and, 1–2, 417, 420; Roosevelt, Elliott (ER's father), and, 85–86, 442, 445, 448, 467; World I, 2, 195, 396

Roosevelt, Theodore, Jr., 319–20, 479, 509

Roosevelt, Theodore, Sr. (grandfather), 168, 206, 447, 465, 467

Rumsey, Mary Harriman, 160, 363, **469–70**

Russell, Bertrand, 512

Rutherfurd, Lucy Mercer, **470–73**; ER and, 405, 439, 470–72, 476–77; FDR and, 5, 222, 224–25, 319, 325, 453–54, 456, 471–73, 476–77; Miller, Earl, and, 341

Rutherfurd, Winthrop, 454, 472

St. Elizabeth's Hospital, 566

Sanger, Margaret, 61–62

Scharf, Lois, 54, 58–59

Scheider, Frank, 513–14

Scheider, Malvina Thompson. *See* Thompson, Malvina

Schneiderman, Rose, 144–45, 161, 294, **474–76**, 580–81; FDR and, 475, 580

Schumann-Heink, Ernestine, 233

Sexuality, ER's, 5, 234, **476–78**

"She-she-she" camps, 213, 481, 574, 592

Shoumatoff, Elizabeth, Madam, 472

Simkhovitch, Mary, 2, 211

Slade, Madeleine, 552

Smith, Alfred, 107, 126, 129, 346, 401, 420, **478–80**; gubernatorial campaign (1924), 509, 520, 577; Moskowitz, Belle, and, 348–49; New Deal and, 479–80; presidential campaign (1928), 132, 349, 455, 470, 478–80, 493, 576

Smith, Ed, 29

Smith, Hilda Worthington, 213, **480–82**, 558, 572, 574

Smith, Lillian, **482–83**, 487. Works: *Killers of the Dream; Strange Fruit*

Social Security Act (1935): ER's views on, 213, 295; national health insurance and, 365–66; Perkins, Frances, and 401, 573; women and, 574–75

Social Security Board: Dewson, Molly, and, 133, 213; Woodward, Ellen, and, 213, 583

Social settlements, 1, 419, **483–85**, 594

Socialists, 14, 16–17, 146

Sojourner Truth housing project (Detroit), 93
Southern Christian Leadership Council, 289
Southern Conference Movement: The Southern Conference for Human Welfare (SCHW) and The Southern Conference Educational Fund (SCEF), 51, 91, 94–95, 149, 482, **485–88**; "Southern Patriot" and, 487
Southern Tenant Farmers Union, 213
Souvestre, Marie, 4, 67–68, 96, 115, 301, **488–90**, 516, 519, 594
Spain, Civil War, and, 11, 14–15, 18, 88, 205, 397, 432, 490, 506
Spain, relations with, **490–92**, 499
Spanish Children, Joint Committee for, 404, 432
Speeches, ER's, 254, **492–98**, 514; ER's speaking tours, 492–497, 520, 523
Spellman, Francis Joseph, Cardinal, 269, 492, **498–502**, 526, 550–51
Springwood, 263–65; FDR and, 451; Roosevelt, Sara Delano, and, 263, 475
Stalin, Joseph, 248, 449
Stevenson, Adlai E. II, 7, 21–22, 102, 131, 155–57, 289, **502–5**, 512; civil rights and, 31–22, 362, 504; eulogies of ER, 122–23, 337, 505, 539; presidential campaigns: (1952) 155–56, 442, 463, 504, 527; (1956), 131, 156, 288, 362, 381, 442, 504
Stimson, Henry, L., 563
Stix, Thomas, L., 510–11
Stone Cottage, 264, 450, 462–63, 542
Strayer, Martha, 412, 414
Streitmatter, Rodger, 59, 477
Strong, Anna Louise, 211, 404, **505–7**, 552
Student Nonviolent Coordinating Committee, 292
Subsistence homestead program, 31–32, 34, 255, 404. *See also* Arthurdale
Suckley, Margaret, 166, 456, **507–8**, 514

Sun Yat-sen, 81
Swartz, Maud, 144, 475

Taft, Helen, 186
Taft, William Howard, 420
Taft-Hartley Act, 297
Talmadge, Eugene, 91
Tammany Hall, 380–81, 420, 457, 478
Taylor, Glen H., 418
"Teapot Tour," 320, 479, **509**
Television, **509–12**; margarine commercial, ER's, 511–12; "Meet the Press," ER and, 510–11; "Mrs. Roosevelt Meets the Public," 510–11; "Prospects for Mankind," ER and, 512, 524
Temple, Shirley, 593
Theta Sigma Phi, 62, 65
This I Remember (Roosevelt, Eleanor), 37, 39, 55, 69, 244, 300, 333, 450
This Is My Story (Roosevelt, Eleanor), 37–38, 55, 69, 298–99
This Troubled World (Roosevelt, Eleanor), 69, 80
Thomas, J. Parnell, 251, 402
Thompson, Malvina, 99, 108–9, 303, 413–15, **512–15**; travels with ER, 341–42, 430, 520–21, 515; Val-Kill and, 515, 543
Time, 45
Tito, Josip, of Yugoslavia, 523, 543
Todhunter, Winifred, 516
Todhunter School, 107, 135–36, 232, **515–18**, 520, 594
Tomorrow Is Now (Roosevelt, Eleanor), 70
Top Cottage, 449–50, 462, 508
Travels, ER's, 495, 515, **518–25**; in childhood and youth (1887–1905), 518–19; with FDR and family (1905–1929), 519–520; as First Lady of New York State (1929–1932), 520; as First Lady of the United States (1933–1945): domestic trips, 515, 518, 520–21, 587; Puerto Rico, 64, 203; overseas during World War II: England, 12, 26–27, 515, 521, 587; Latin America, 13, 312, 515, 521,

587; South Pacific, 12–13, 521, 587; in post-White House period (1945–1962), 8, 522–524, 536

Triangle Shirtwaist Company fire, 401, 479

Trip to Washington with Bobby and Betty, A (Roosevelt, Eleanor), 68

Truman, Bess, 186–87, 373, 416, 560

Truman, Harry S, 20, 284, 296–97, 491, **525–27**; ER appointed U.S. Delegate to United Nations by, 131, 147, 525–26, 535; ER's advice to, 88, 131, 275–76, 284, 296–97, 525–26, 597; NAACP and, 361; national health insurance and, 366; Perkins, Frances, and, 402, 526; presidential campaign and election (1948), 526; Roosevelt, James, and, 461, 526; vice--presidential nomination (1944), 553

Truman Doctrine, 525

Tugwell, Rexford G., 215, 418, 455, **527–30**

Union of Soviet Socialist Republics (USSR), 20, 256, 303, 525–26, 597; ER's **Trips to**, 198, 511, 524, **531–32**; ER's **Views on**, 19, 197–98, 505–7, **532–34**; Cold War and, 101–2, 491–92; Finland, invasion of, 19, 507, 533; Germany, invasion by, 19, 533; Germany, nonaggression pact with, 15, 18, 505–6

United Auto Workers (UAW), 440–41

United Nations, 5–8, 147, 440, 491, 497, 505, 522, 525–26, **534–39**, 556; Du Bois, W.E.B., and, 146, 361; Human Rights Commission, 146, 147, 256–60, 309, 398, 533, 536–37, 540; Korean conflict and, 6; International Court of Justice, 585–86; Israel and, 275–76, 284, 597; FDR and, 6, 556; refugees and, 197, 312, 433–34, 538, 597; Spain and, 491–92, 499; Stevenson, Adlai, and, 502–3, 505, 539; USSR and, 147, 197, 533, 536–38; Vandenberg, Arthur, and, 545–46. *See also* American Association for the United Nations; Human Rights,

internationalization of; Universal Declaration of Human Rights

United Nations Relief and Rehabilitation Administration, 583

United Negro College Fund, 51

Universal Declaration of Human Rights, 8, 146, 147, 258–59, 398, 533, **539–41**. *See also* United Nations

Val-Kill, 107–8; 135–36, **542–44**; ER's cottage at, 263–65, 385, 409, 454, 457, 462–63, 515, 567–68. *See also* Eleanor Roosevelt Center at Val-Kill

Val-Kill Industries, 31, 107–8, 136, 263–64, 385, 542–43

Vandenberg, Arthur, **544–46**

Vanderlip, Frank Arthur, 546

Vanderlip, Narcissa, 314–15, 430, **546–47**; Bok Peace Prize and, 66, 302, 397, 547

Velde, Harold, 336

Video Material, **547–48**

Vishinsky, Andrei, 147, 538

Von Hesse, Elizabeth, 494

Wagner, Robert F., 29, 360, 420, 479, 493, 549–51

Wagner-Rogers Bill, 239, 282, 407, 432, 433, **549–51**

Wald, Lillian, 2, 160, 196, 226, 364, 483, 505, **551–553**

Wallace, Henry A., 20, 46–47, 251, 525, **553–54**; Progressive Party of 1948, 417–18, 553; vice-presidential nomination (1940), 130, 449, 496, 553

War Refugee Board, 240

Ware, Caroline, 58–59, 573

Ware, Susan, 477

Warm Springs, Ga., 454, 456, 472, 508

Weaver, Robert, 48, 267, 561

Welles, Sumner, 6, 199, 407, 433, **554–57**

West, J.D., 191

White House, food in, 5, 191–92, 372–73

White House Conferences, 377, **557–559**; on Camps for Unemployed

Women, 377, 481, 558; on Emergency Needs of Women, 557–58, 574, 582, 584; on How Women May Share in Post-War Policy Making, 558; on Participation of Negro Women and Children in Federal Welfare Programs, 558, 584
White House Social Office, 559–61
White, Walter F., 23, 48, 50–51, 82, 89, 91, 93, 482, 487, 561–64; antilynching movement and, 29–30; NAACP and, 359–62
Wilhelmina, Queen of the Netherlands, 373–74
Wilkie, Wendell, 218
Wilkins, Roy, 360–62, 504
Williams, Aubrey, 90, 141, 561, 564–65; National Youth Administration and, 47, 367–69, 584
Wilson, Edith, 184–85
Wilson, Ellen Axon, 137, 184
Wilson, Paul, 401
Wilson, Woodrow, 46, 137, 256, 453, 469, 545; presidential campaign and election (1912), 226, 417
Wilson ERA Sunday Evening Suppers, 565–67
Wiltwyck School, 68, 225, 264–65, 407, 543, 567–69
Winant, John G., 229
Wisdom of Eleanor Roosevelt, The (Roosevelt, Eleanor), 70
Wise, Stephen, Rabbi, 282, 406, 551
Woman suffrage, 2, 79, 420, 576
Woman's Christian Temperance Union, 422
Woman's Day, 299
Woman's Home Companion, 299, 569–70
Woman's National Democratic Club, 120, 125–26, 228, 570–72
Woman's Peace Party, 2, 80
Women and the New Deal, 211–13, 290–91, 377, 557–58, 571–75, 582–83, 584; camps for unemployed, 213, 377, 414, 481, 558. See also Great Depression; New Deal
Women's Bureau, U.S. Department of

Labor, 24–25, 401, 403, 558; Equal Rights Amendment and, 162
Women's City Club, 61, 132, 145, 295, 349, 425, 546, 552, 575–76
Women's Democratic News, 45, 135, 254, 346, 384, 577–78; ER's contributions to, 577
Women's Division of the Democratic National Committee, 149; Dewson, Molly, and, 126, 133, 171, 572–73; ER and, 129, 133, 171, 349, 493, 571; Hickok, Lorena, and, 236
Women's Division of the New York State Democratic Committee, 135, 149, 343–44, 345–46, 349, 384, 518, 577; ER and, 129, 315, 319, 493, 509, 520
Women's International League for Peace and Freedom, 2, 226–27, 250, 384, 397
Women's Joint Legislative Conference (WJLC), 144–45
Women's National Press Club, 45, 64, 416, 578–79
Women's Trade Union League (WTUL), 1, 25, 80, 144–45, 376, 406, 552, 579–82; ER and, 135, 161, 163, 212, 294–95, 474–75, 579–81, 594; FDR and 475; Schneiderman, Rose, and, 294, 474–75, 580–81
Woodward, Ellen, 211–12, 290, 557–58, 572, 582–83, 584
Works Progress Administration (WPA), 558, 583–85; African-Americans and, 584; arts projects and, 194, 378, 582, 584–85; Hopkins, Harry, and, 247, 583–84; National Youth Administration, and, 367–68, 584; women's programs in, 247, 290–91, 574, 582, 584; Woodward, Ellen, and, 582, 584; Workers' Education Program, 481
World Court, 67, 80, 196, 302–3, 315, 396, 534, 547, 585–86
World Federation of United Nations Associations, 37, 523–24, 532
World War I, 2, 195, 396, 420–21, 422, 453, 545, 587, 593

World War II, 256, 560, **586–90**, 596;
  Anglo-American relations, 26–27;
  ER and, 196–97, 533, 535, 586–90;
  Vandenberg, Arthur, and 545;
  women and, 587–88
World Youth Congress, 18, 591
Wotkyns, Eleanor Roosevelt (niece),
  436
Wyman, David, 433, 551

You Learn by Living (Roosevelt,
  Eleanor), 70,

Your Teens and Mine (Roosevelt,
  Eleanor, and Helen Ferris), 68
Youth, 14–19, 542, 584, **591–95**. *See
  also* American Student Union;
  American Youth Congress; Interna-
  tional Student Service; National
  Youth Administration; Youth Ali-
  yah
Youth Aliyah, 284, 596, 598
Yugoslavia, 523

Zionism, 241, 275, 283–84, **596–98**. *See
  also* Israel; Jews

EDITORS

MAURINE H. BEASLEY is Professor of Journalism at the University of Maryland, where she specializes in women and media. She has published seven books, including *Eleanor Roosevelt and the Media: A Public Quest for Self-Fulfillment* (1987) and *The White House Press Conferences of Eleanor Roosevelt* (1983).

HOLLY C. SHULMAN is Research Associate Professor at the University of Virginia. She focused initially on media history and is the author of *The Voice of America: Propaganda and Democracy, 1941-1945* (1990).

HENRY R. BEASLEY has been Director of International Affairs for the National Marine Fisheries Service, an agency of the U.S. Department of Commerce.

CONTRIBUTORS

MARY JANE ALEXANDER is former assistant professor of journalism at Saint Michael's College, Colchester, Vermont.

CARL SFERRAZZA ANTHONY, Washington, D.C., historian and writer, is the author of books on First Ladies.

JEAN HARVEY BAKER is professor of history at Goucher College, Towson, Maryland.

VIRGINIA W. BEAUCHAMP is associate professor emeritus of English at the University of Maryland, College Park.

PAUL S. BELGRADE is a professor in the English Department at Millersville University, Millersville, Pennsylvania.

PATRICIA BELL-SCOTT is professor of child and family development and women's studies, University of Georgia, Athens.

MICHAEL BERENBAUM is a writer, lecturer, and teacher consulting in the conceptual development of museums and the historical development of films. He is also an adjunct professor of theology at the University of Judaism in Los Angeles. He is the former president of the Survivors of the Shoah Visual History Foundation and former director of the United States Holocaust Research Institute.

JASON BERGER is assistant professor of communications studies at the University of Missouri–Kansas City and has written a book on Eleanor Roosevelt.

ROGER BILES is professor and chair of the History Department at East Carolina University, Greenville, North Carolina.

ALLIDA M. BLACK, assistant professor and history coordinator for the Women and Power program, George Washington University, Washington, D.C., is the author/editor of books on Eleanor Roosevelt and editor of the Eleanor Roosevelt and Human Rights Project, first phase of publication of the Eleanor Roosevelt Papers.

DIANE M. BLAIR is assistant professor of communication at California State University, Fresno.

RANDOLPH BOEHM is senior editor of University Publications of America, Bethesda, Maryland.

CARL JOSEPH BON TEMPO is a graduate student in American history at the University of Virginia, Charlottesville.

EILEEN BORIS is professor of studies in women and gender at the University of Virginia, Charlottesville.

BONNIE BRENNEN is associate professor of journalism at the University of Missouri, Columbia.

JANE BRISSETT, Duluth, Minnesota, is a freelance medical writer.

JAMES MACGREGOR BURNS is senior scholar at the James MacGregor Burns Academy of Leadership at the University of Maryland, College Park, and professor emeritus of political science at Williams College, Williamstown, Massachusetts.

BETTY BOYD CAROLI is former professor of women's history at the City University of New York and author of books on First Ladies.

GINGER RUDESEAL CARTER is assistant professor at Georgia College and State University, Milledgeville, Georgia.

WILLIAM H. CHAFE is dean of the faculty of arts and sciences at Duke University, Durham, North Carolina.

CLAUDIA CLARK is visiting assistant professor of history at Miami University of Ohio.

MIRIAM J. COHEN is professor of history at Vassar College, Poughkeepsie, New York.

ROBERT COHEN is director of the social studies program of the School of Education at New York University.

ANN MAUGER COLBERT is coordinator of the journalism program at Indiana-Purdue universities at Fort Wayne, Indiana.

ANNE CONSTANTINOPLE is professor of psychology and director of the American culture program at Vassar College, Poughkeepsie, New York.

BLANCHE WIESEN COOK is Distinguished professor of history at John Jay College and the Graduate Center, City University of New York, and author of a multivolume biography of Eleanor Roosevelt.

STACY A. CORDERY is associate professor of history and coordinator of women's studies at Monmouth College, Monmouth, Illinois.

JOHN M. CRAIG is professor of history, Slippery Rock University, Slippery Rock, Pennsylania.

JANET M. CRAMER is assistant professor of communication and journalism at the University of New Mexico, Albuquerque.

ED CRAY is professor of journalism at the University of Southern California, Los Angeles.

NICHOLAS J. CULL is professor of American studies, University of Leicester, England.

JAMES CHOWNING DAVIES is professor emeritus of political science, University of Oregon, Eugene.

KENNETH S. DAVIS, Manhattan, Kansas, is a biographer of Franklin D. Roosevelt and author of books on the Roosevelt era.

ANELIA K. DIMITROVA is assistant professor of communication at the University of Northern Iowa, Cedar Falls.

HASIA R. DINER is the Paul S. and Sylvia Steinberg professor in American Jewish history at New York University.

EILEEN EAGAN is associate professor of history at the University of Southern Maine, Gorham.

WILLIAM J. EATON, curator, Humphrey Fellowship Program, University of Maryland, College Park, is a Pulitzer Prize–winning journalist and former *Los Angeles Times* correspondent.

JOHN A. EDENS is director of central technical services at the University Libraries of the State University of New York at Buffalo.

JILL EDWARDS is professor and chair of the Department of History at the American University in Cairo.

KATHLEEN L. ENDRES is professor of communication and interim director of women's studies at the University of Akron.

DORIS FABER, Ancram, New York, is a writer and the biographer of Lorena Hickok.

JEWELL FENZI is the chair of the oral history program of the Woman's National Democratic Club, Washington, D.C.

J. KIRKPATRICK FLACK is associate professor of history at the University of Maryland, College Park.

GERALD P. FOGARTY, S.J., is the William R. Kenan Jr. professor of religious studies and history at the University of Virginia, Charlottesville.

ANN COTTRELL FREE, Bethesda, Maryland, is a journalist and writer who was chair of Eleanor Roosevelt's Press Conference Association.

RUSSELL FREEDMAN, New York City, winner of a Newbery medal for biography for young people, received a Newbery honor award in 1993 for his book on Eleanor Roosevelt.

RICHARD M. FRIED is professor of history at the University of Illinois at Chicago.

FELICE D. GAER, director of the Jacob Blaustein Institute for the Advancement of Human Rights, New York City, chaired the steering committee of the national coalition for the fiftieth anniversary of the Universal Declaration of Human Rights.

JOYCE C. GHEE, Hyde Park, New York, former Dutchess County historian, served on the Visual Environmental Committee that led efforts to preserve Eleanor Roosevelt's home at Val-Kill.

STEVEN M. GILLON is Carol E. Young professor and dean of the Honors College at the University of Oklahoma.

MARGARET ROSE GLADNEY is associate professor of American studies at the University of Alabama, Tuscaloosa.

DOUGLAS GOMERY is professor of journalism at the University of Maryland, College Park.

DORIS KEARNS GOODWIN, historian and biographer, won a Pulitzer Prize for her history of Franklin Roosevelt and Eleanor Roosevelt during World War II.

AGNES HOOPER GOTTLIEB is associate professor of communication and director of women's studies at Seton Hall University, South Orange, New Jersey.

LISA M. GRING-PEMBLE is an assistant professor at New Century College of George Mason University, Fairfax, Virginia.

BETH HALLER is assistant professor of journalism at Towson State University, Towson, Maryland.

MARY A. HAMILTON is associate professor of journalism and mass communication at St. Bonaventure University, St. Bonaventure, New York.

MARGOT HARDENBERGH is former assistant professor of communication at Marist College, Poughkeepsie, New York.

JOAN HOFF is professor and director of the Contemporary History Institute, Ohio University, Athens, and coeditor of a book on Eleanor Roosevelt.

JOYCE HOFFMANN is associate professor in the English Department at Old Dominion University, Norfolk, Virginia.

JUNE HOPKINS is assistant professor of history at Armstrong Atlantic State University, Savannah, Georgia.

SUSAN IKENBERRY teaches American history and government at Georgetown Day School, Washington, D.C.

M. GLEN JOHNSON, former acting president of Vassar College, Poughkeepsie, New York, where he holds the Shirley Ecker Boskey Chair in International Relations, has been president of the board of ERVK (the Eleanor Roosevelt Center at Val-Kill).

SIPRA B. JOHNSON is emeritus associate professor of anthropology at the State University of New York, College at New Paltz.

TRACEY A. JOHNSTONE, a Ph.D. candidate at the University of Toronto, is employed by the polling firm Voter/Consumer Research, Washington, D.C.

JOHN B. KIRBY is professor of history at Denison University, Grandville, Ohio.

RICHARD S. KIRKENDALL is the Scott and Dorothy Bullitt professor emeritus of American history at the University of Washington.

JAAP KOOIJMAN teaches in the American Studies Department of the University of Amsterdam.

BROOKE KROEGER, biographer, is visiting associate professor of journalism at New York University.

JAMES C. LANDERS, Ph.D. candidate in journalism history at the University of Wisconsin-Madison, is assistant professor at Emporia State University, Kansas.

DONALD R. LARRABEE, former owner of the Griffin-Larrabee News Bureau in Washington, D.C., is former president of the National Press Club and director emeritus of the National Press Foundation.

ANDERS G. LEWIS, is a Ph.D. candidate in history at the University of Florida, Gainesville.

RANDOLPH LEWIS is assistant professor and director, interdisciplinary studies, University of Science and Arts of Oklahoma.

LOUIS LIEBOVICH is a professor of journalism and media studies and director of journalism graduate studies at the University of Illinois, Urbana.

JOAN LONDON is a Ph.D. student in mass communication at the University of Maryland, College Park.

RICHARD LOWITT is professor emeritus of history at Iowa State University and a retired professor of history at the University of Oklahoma.

THERESE L. LUECK is professor of communication at the University of Akron.

DIANNE LYNCH is associate professor of journalism at St. Michael's College, Colchester, Vermont.

MICHELLE A. MART is assistant professor of history at Pennyslvania State University, Berks Campus, Reading, Pennsylvania.

EDITH P. MAYO is curator emeritus in political history of the National Museum of American History, Smithsonian Institution, Washington, D.C., and author/editor of books on First Ladies.

JUDITH N. MCARTHUR is a lecturer in history at the University of Houston–Victoria.

ABIGAIL MCCARTHY, Washington author, columnist, and lecturer, was associated with Eleanor Roosevelt in Americans for Democratic Action and in the Stevenson for President campaigns.

JAMES B. MCPHERSON is visiting professor of communication at Whitworth College, Spokane, Washington.

BEVERLY G. MERRICK is assistant professor of journalism at New Mexico State University, Las Cruces.

ROBERT W. MERRY is president and publisher of *Congressional Quarterly*, Washington, D.C., and the biographer of Joseph and Stewart Alsop.

LINDA E. MILANO is assistant director of the Theodore Roosevelt Association, Oyster Bay, New York.

FRANCESCA MILLER, who is affiliated with the Department of History, University of California, Davis, is a faculty fellow of the university's center in Washington, D.C.

KRISTIE MILLER is a historian and Washington correspondent for the *NewsTribune*, LaSalle, Illinois.

DAVID T. Z. MINDICH is associate professor and Chair of the Department of Journalism at Saint Michael's College, Colchester, Vermont.

BETTY C. MONKMAN is curator of the White House and author of articles on White House history.

HENRY MORGENTHAU III, Cambridge, Massachusetts, author and broadcast producer, is the son of Elinor F. and Henry Morgenthau Jr. and produced Eleanor Roosevelt's *Prospects of Mankind* television series.

ROBERT W. MORROW is a Ph.D. candidate in American history at the University of Maryland, College Park.

ROBYN MUNCY is associate professor of history at the University of Maryland, College Park.

CATHERINE GILBERT MURDOCK is a lecturer in American studies at Bryn Mawr College, Bryn Mawr, Pennsylvania.

ANNA KASTEN NELSON is distinguished adjunct historian in residence at American University, Washington, D.C.

CARYN NEUMANN is a Ph.D. candidate in history at the Ohio State University, Columbus.

KEITH W. OLSON is professor of history at the University of Maryland, College Park.

JUDY OPPENHEIMER, a Washington journalist, is the biographer of the writer Shirley Jackson.

ANNA R. PADDON, former assistant professor of journalism at Southern Illinois University at Carbondale, has been a Fulbright lecturer in Taiwan.

JUDITH PATERSON is associate professor of journalism at the University of Maryland, College Park.

WILLIAM D. PEDERSON is professor of political science and the director of American studies at Louisiana State University in Shreveport.

THEDA PERDUE is professor of history at the University of North Carolina, Chapel Hill.

ELISABETH ISRAELS PERRY is coholder of the John Francis Bannon Chair in U.S. History and American Studies at St. Louis University.

MARILYN ELIZABETH PERRY is an independent scholar in the Chicago area.

JULIEANNE PHILLIPS is lecturer in history at Baldwin-Wallace College, Berea, Ohio.

KELLY A. J. POWERS, Baltimore, is a contributing writer for *Baltimore* magazine and a freelance writer for national magazines.

RICHARD GID POWERS is professor of history and American studies at the College of Staten Island and at the City University of New York Graduate Center.

ALF PRATTE is professor of communication at Brigham Young University, Provo, Utah.

BARBARA STRAUS REED is associate professor of journalism at Rutgers University, New Brunswick, New Jersey.

LINDA REED is associate professor of African American studies at the University of Houston.

DONALD A. RITCHIE is the associate historian of the U.S. Senate.

KAREN E. ROBBINS is director of women's studies and lecturer in history at Saint Bonaventure University, New York.

NANCY MARIE ROBERTSON is assistant professor of history at Indiana University/Purdue University in Indianapolis.

ELEANOR ROOSEVELT, the niece of Eleanor Roosevelt, lives in Davis, California, and writes about her aunt for an Internet magazine, *Sodamail*.

JOHN A. SALMOND is professor of American history and pro vice-chancellor at La Trobe University, Bundoora, Victoria, Australia.

SCOTT A. SANDAGE is assistant professor of American cultural history at Carnegie Mellon University, Pittsburgh.

LOIS SCHARF, a biographer of Eleanor Roosevelt, is affiliated with Case Western Reserve University, Cleveland, Ohio.

LEONARD SCHLUP holds a Ph.D. in history from the University of Illinois and has contributed to many encyclopedias.

MYRON I. SCHOLNICK is professor of history at Towson University, Towson, Maryland.

INGRID WINTHER SCOBIE is professor of history and government at Texas Woman's University, Denton, Texas.

FRANCES M. SEEBER, Poughkeepsie, New York, chief archivist (retired) at the Franklin D. Roosevelt Library, Hyde Park, New York, has specialized in the papers of Eleanor Roosevelt.

DAVID SILVER is a Ph.D. candidate in American studies at the University of Maryland, College Park.

BRYANT SIMON is associate professor of history at the University of Georgia, Athens.

KATHRYN KISH SKLAR is distinguished professor of history at the State University of New York at Binghamton.

ROBERT A. SLAYTON is associate professor of history at Chapman University, Orange, California.

HAROLD L. SMITH is professor of history at the University of Houston-Victoria, Texas.

SHARON L. SMITH is a Ph.D. student in American history at the University of Delaware, Newark.

MOLLIE SOMERVILLE, Washington, D.C., was a White House aide to Eleanor Roosevelt and her daughter, Anna, during the New Deal years, and is the author of a memoir about Eleanor Roosevelt.

PATRICIA MEYER SPACKS is the Edgar F. Shannon professor of eighteenth-century literature at the University of Virginia, Charlottesville.

JOAN SPENCE, Hyde Park, New York, served on the Visual Environmental Committee that led efforts to preserve Eleanor Roosevelt's home at Val-Kill.

DANIEL A. STRASSER is the executive director of the Eleanor Roosevelt Center at Val-Kill (ERVK), Hyde Park, New York.

RODGER STREITMATTER is professor of journalism at American University, Washington, D.C., and editor of a book of letters between Lorena Hickok and Eleanor Roosevelt.

PATRICIA SULLIVAN is a fellow at the W. E. B Du Bois Institute for Afro-American Research, Harvard University, Cambridge, Massachusetts.

MARTHA H. SWAIN is Cornaro Professor Emerita at Texas Woman's University and now teaches at Mississippi State University, Mississippi.

LEONARD RAY TEEL is associate professor and director of the International Center for Media Education at Georgia State University, Atlanta, Georgia.

MIEKE VAN THOOR has been associated with the Roosevelt Study Center in Middelburg, the Netherlands.

MELISSA WALKER is assistant professor of history and politics at Converse College, Spartanburg, South Carolina.

BRYAN WARD, Westover, West Virginia, is the former historian at the Arthurdale New Deal Homestead museum.

GEOFFREY C. WARD, a biographer of Franklin D. Roosevelt, is former editor of *American Heritage*, a documentary film writer, and winner of the Parkman Prize and a National Book Critics Circle Award.

SUSAN WARE, an independent scholar affiliated with Radcliffe College, Cambridge, Massachusetts, is a historian of American women and the author of books on women in the New Deal era.

HILDA R. WATROUS, Asheville, North Carolina, is an independent historian who has written on Eleanor Roosevelt and the League of Women Voters.

MARTHA S. WATSON is professor and dean of the Greenspun College of Communication at the University of Nevada, Las Vegas.

LIZ WATTS is associate professor of journalism and graduate coordinator of the School of Mass Communication, Texas Tech University, Lubbock, Texas.

SCOTT W. WEBSTER is program director for the Center for the Advanced Study of Leadership at the James MacGregor Burns Academy of Leadership at the University of Maryland, College Park.

LYNN Y. WEINER is professor of history and acting dean of the College of Arts and Sciences at Roosevelt University, Chicago.

SARA E. WILSON is a student academic adviser, College of Arts and Sciences, American University.

VERONICA A. WILSON is a Ph.D. candidate in American history at Rutgers University, New Brunswick, New Jersey.

BETTY HOUCHIN WINFIELD, professor of journalism at the University of Missouri, Columbia, is the author of a book on Franklin D. Roosevelt and the news media.

ALLAN M. WINKLER is professor of history at Miami University of Ohio.

KELLY A. WOESTMAN is associate professor of history and history education coordinator at Pittsburg State University, Pittsburg, Kansas.

NANCY BECK YOUNG is assistant professor of history at McKendree College, Lebanon, Illinois.

J. WILLIAM T. YOUNGS is professor of history at Eastern Washington University, Cheney, Washington, and the author of a biography of Eleanor Roosevelt.

ROBERT H. ZIEGER is professor of history at the University of Florida, Gainesville.